THE RUSSIAN GRAPHOSPHERE, 1450–1850

SIMON FRANKLIN
University of Cambridge

CAMBRIDGE
UNIVERSITY PRESS

CAMBRIDGE
UNIVERSITY PRESS

University Printing House, Cambridge CB2 8BS, United Kingdom

One Liberty Plaza, 20th Floor, New York, NY 10006, USA

477 Williamstown Road, Port Melbourne, VIC 3207, Australia

314–321, 3rd Floor, Plot 3, Splendor Forum, Jasola District Centre,
New Delhi – 110025, India

79 Anson Road, #06–04/06, Singapore 079906

Cambridge University Press is part of the University of Cambridge.

It furthers the University's mission by disseminating knowledge in the pursuit of education, learning, and research at the highest international levels of excellence.

www.cambridge.org
Information on this title: www.cambridge.org/9781108492577
DOI: 10.1017/9781108592307

First published 2019

Printed in the United Kingdom by TJ International Ltd, Padstow Cornwall

A catalogue record for this publication is available from the British Library.

Library of Congress Cataloging-in-Publication Data
Names: Franklin, Simon, author.
Title: The Russian graphosphere, 1450–1850 / Simon Franklin.
Description: Cambridge ; New York, NY : Cambridge University Press, 2019. | Includes bibliographical references and index.
Identifiers: LCCN 2018044398 | ISBN 9781108492577
Subjects: LCSH: Russian language – Writing – History
Classification: LCC PG2096 .F73 2019 | DDC 491.71/1–dc23
LC record available at https://lccn.loc.gov/2018044398

ISBN 978-1-108-49257-7 Hardback

Contents

Figures

Acknowledgements

The conventional attribution of sole authorship masks multiple collaborations and contributions.

The University of Cambridge supported the project by funding a Research Associate during a period when I had substantial administrative responsibilities. When I was able to step away from those responsibilities, a Major Research Fellowship from the Philip Leverhulme Trust gave me time to immerse myself again in research. The Dame Professor Elizabeth Hill Fund has been helpful in facilitating research trips and acquiring some of the illustrations. Clare College, Cambridge has continued to provide my principal workplace, a delightful environment and stimulating conversation. I am particularly grateful to the European University at St Petersburg. Without the twice-yearly visits for meetings of the university's Board of Trustees, I would certainly not have been able to spend such productive time in Russian libraries and archives.

Many colleagues in Russia have been generous with advice, feedback, bibliographical references, archival information and transcription, and access to archives and special collections in libraries and museums. They include: Aleksei Alekseev of the Russian National Library in St Petersburg, who first put me on the trail of the N. P. Likhachev ephemera collections in the archive of the Institute of History; in Moscow, Iuliia Shustova of the Russian State University of the Humanities, Dzhamilia Ramazanova, of the Rare Books Department of the Russian State Library, Kirill Khudin, Elena Korchmina, Olga Kosheleva, Tatiana Lapteva, Abram Reitblat and Anatolii Turilov, as well as Sergei Ivanov, who has been a constant source of ideas, suggestions and lively discussion; in St Petersburg Iuliia Khodko of the Russian Museum, Irina Voznesenskaia of the Library of the Academy of Sciences, Aleksandra Chirkova of the archive of the Institute of History, and Roman Grigorev and Iuliia Plotnikova of, respectively, the departments of prints and of textiles at the Hermitage Museum.

Katherine Bowers was a valued Research Associate in Cambridge for three years. Stephen Lovell and Emma Widdis provided thoughtful comments on a draft of the first chapter. Mel Bach, of the Cambridge University Library, has been wonderfully helpful in locating and ordering some of the rather offbeat books that I made a habit of requesting. I am grateful also for the insights of the anonymous readers for Cambridge University Press, and for the meticulous scrutiny of the final text by its copy-editor, Karen Anderson.

Through the generosity – whether of resource, or of time, or of spirit – of all these institutions and individuals, the present book became far better than it would otherwise have been. If, despite their support, it is still short of what it could or should be, the fault is mine.

A Note on Transliteration and Dates

Complete consistency in transliteration is barely possible, and not necessarily desirable.

Transliteration of Cyrillic in quotations of words, or in bibliographic references, uses the 'modified Library of Congress' system that is more or less standard in online library catalogues. Where such words or names appear in the main text, simply as words rather than expressly as transliterations, I omit the apostrophe that would indicate the 'softness' (palatalisation) of the preceding consonant.

Geographic names are a problem. Many of the places changed jurisdiction, and their official names, several times during the four centuries covered by this survey. There are places for which any choice of form may be contentious. For the purposes of this book I apply a sequence of choices.

Where a place-name has become a standard, established English word, I use it in preference to any variety of transliteration: hence Moscow and St Petersburg, not Moskva and Sankt-Peterburg. Where a place has had fundamentally different names, I tend to give first the 'historic' name followed by its modern equivalent in brackets: hence Reval (Tallinn). Where there is a choice of spellings for what is essentially the same place-name I tend to use the forms that are preferred in the relevant modern state: hence Vilnius, Lviv, Pochaiv, Chernihiv and Ostroh, rather than Vilna, Lvov (or Lwów, or Lemberg), Pochaev, Chernigov and Ostrog. The choice between Kiev and Kyiv is borderline: Kyiv is the preferred form in modern Ukraine, Kiev is a long-established English word.

Mutatis mutandis similar principles apply to personal names. The names of Russia's imperial rulers are by convention anglicised: hence the tsars Peter, Alexander, Nicholas, Paul, not Petr, Aleksandr, Nikolai, Pavel. Quite illogically, however, the names of the earlier rulers of Muscovy are, by convention, transliterated rather than anglicised (hence Ivan, Mikhail, not John, Michael), as are all other personal names. Names of non-

Russians culturally active in Russia are normally given in russified form. Hence, for example, Maksim Grek, or the Likhud brothers, rather than Maximos, or the Leichoudes brothers. Some anomalies inevitably remain.

All dates derived from Russian sources are given in the 'old style' – that is, according to the Julian calendar, which was in use in Russia until 1918. Most Russian sources before the start of the eighteenth century date events on a scale starting from the creation of the world rather than from the birth of Christ. To convert *anno mundi* dates to the Common Era, one should subtract 5508 – bearing in mind, however, that the *anno mundi* year in Muscovite documents normally ran from September to August, not from January to December. Dating according to the Common Era was officially introduced by Peter I on 1 January 1700.

Abbreviations

AN	Akademiia nauk
AN SSSR	Akademiia nauk Soiuza sovetskikh sotsialisticheskikh respublik
BAN	Biblioteka Akademii nauk
BLDR	*Biblioteka literatury Drevnei Rusi*
Bykova and Gurevich, *Dopoln.*	T. A. Bykova and M. M. Gurevich, *Opisanie izdanii, napechatannykh pri Petre Pervom. Svodnyi katalog. Dopolneniia i prilozheniia*
Bykova and Gurevich, *Grazhd.*	T. A. Bykova and M. M. Gurevich, *Opisanie izdanii, napechatannykh pri Petre Pervom. Svodnyi katalog. I. Opisanie izdanii grazhdanskoi pechati, 1708–ianvar' 1725 g.*
Bykova and Gurevich, *Kirill.*	T. A. Bykova and M. M. Gurevich, *Opisanie izdanii, napechatannykh pri Petre Pervom. Svodnyi katalog. II. Opisanie izdanii, napechatannykh kirillitsei. 1689–ianvar' 1725 g.*
CASS	*Canadian-American Slavic Studies*
ChOIDR	*Chteniia v Imperatorskom obshchestve istorii i drevnostei rossiiskikh*
Cracraft, *Culture*	James Cracraft, *The Petrine Revolution in Russian Culture*
Cracraft, *Imagery*	James Cracraft, *The Petrine Revolution in Russian Imagery*
FOG	*Forschungen zur osteuropäischen Geschichte*
GBL	Gosudarstvennaia Biblioteka imeni V. I. Lenina (subsequently RGB)
GPB	Gosudarstvennaia publichnaia biblioteka (subsequently RNB)

Guseva, *Izd. kirill. XVI v.*	A. A. Guseva, *Izdaniia kirillovskogo shrifta vtoroi poloviny XVI veka: svodnyi katalog*
Guseva, *Svod XVIII v.*	A. A. Guseva, *Svod russkikh knig kirillovskoi pechati XVIII veka tipografii Moskvy i Sankt-Peterburga*
HUS	*Harvard Ukrainian Studies*
JGO	*Jahrbücher für Geschichte Osteuropas*
Marker, *Publishing*	Gary Marker, *Publishing, Printing and the Origins of Intellectual Life in Russia, 1700–1800*
MGU	Moskovskii gosudarstvennyi universitet
Mosk. kirill. izd. RGADA	*Moskovskie kirillovskie izdaniia v sobraniiakh RGADA Katalog. Vyp. 1–3*
MPD – fakt i faktor	*Moskovskii pechatnyi dvor – fakt i faktor russkoi kul'tury*, ed. I. V. Pozdeeva et al.
Nemirovskii, *Slavianskie izdaniia*	E. L. Nemirovskii, *Slavianskie izdaniia kirillovskogo (tserkovnoslavianskogo) shrifta 1491–2000. Tom II, kn. 1 (1551–1592); kn. 2 (1593–1600)*
PSTGU	Pravoslavnyi Sviato-Tikhonovskii gumanitarnyi universitet
PSZ	*Polnoe sobranie zakonov Rossiiskoi imperii*
PSZ.2	*Polnoe sobranie zakonov Rossiiskoi imperii. Sobranie vtoroe*
RAN	Rossiiskaia akademiia nauk
RGADA	Rossiiskii Gosudarstvennyi arkhiv drevnikh aktov
RGB	Rossiiskaia gosudarstvennaia biblioteka
RGGU	Rossiiskii gosudarstvennyi gumanitarnyi universitet
RNB	Rossiiskaia natsional'naia biblioteka
SEER	*Slavonic and East European Review*
SK 1801–1825	*Svodnyi katalog russkoi knigi 1801–1825*
SK Inostr.	*Svodnyi katalog knig na inostrannykh iazykakh, izdannykh v Rossii v XVIII veke*
SK XVIII v.	*Svodnyi katalog russkoi knigi grazhdanskoi pechati XVIII veka, 1725–1800*
SKKDR	*Slovar' knizhnikov i knizhnosti Drevnei Rusi*
SPb II RAN	Sankt-Peterburgskii institut istorii Rossiiskoi akademii nauk

SPbGU	Sankt-Peterburgskii gosudarstvennyi universitet
SPF ARAN	Sankt-Peterburgskii filial arkhiva Rossiiskoi akademii nauk
TODRL	*Trudy Otdela drevnerusskoi literatury*
Zernova, *KKP XVI–XVII veka*	A. S. Zernova, *Knigi kirillovskoi pechati, izdannye v Moskve v XVI–XVII vekakh*
Zernova and Kameneva, *SK kirill. pech. XVIII v.*	A. S. Zernova and T. N. Kameneva, *Svodnyi katalog russkoi knigi kirillovskoi pechati XVIII veka*

CHAPTER 1

Concepts and Contexts

The Graphosphere

To begin with the jargon: the word 'graphosphere' in the title of this book is a near-neologism.[1] It needs explaining. For present purposes the graphosphere is the space of the visible word. The graphosphere, or *a* graphosphere, is formed wherever words are encoded, recorded, stored, disseminated and displayed through visible signs. The study of the graphosphere represents a holistic, non-hierarchical approach to the production, functions and dynamics of visible words in their environments. The decision to limit the graphosphere to words, rather than to include all forms of graphic representation, is pragmatic rather than principled. One can imagine a legitimately wider notion of the graphosphere that encompasses all graphic depiction, of which words are a subset. Not that the study of words excludes pictures or design. On the contrary, they will figure prominently; but only when they also relate to the space of visible words.

The purpose of using a near-neologism is not to promote an esoteric term for its own sake, or to expound a general theory of the visible word, or to stake a claim to a putatively nascent academic discipline. The justification lies in the extent to which the notion of the graphosphere can be useful in informing an approach to some practical questions of cultural history.[2] The validity derives from demonstration, not from assertion. Nevertheless some introductory framing is necessary, both with regard to the meanings, boundaries and implications of the study of the graphosphere as here understood, and with regard to how the 'graphospheric' approach relates to other disciplines and conventions applied to cultures of visible words.

Among the many ways of conceptualising the graphosphere, four should be highlighted in particular. In the first place, the graphosphere can be imagined as a whole, as a physical entity or system with properties such as shape, borders, degrees of density and the like. Secondly, the graphosphere has to be analysed in terms of its specific components, the modes and materials and technologies of the visible words from which a graphosphere derives its existence. A third set of questions shifts attention from the formal to the functional: what are the social or political or cultural roles and implications of the particular components in the graphosphere and their configurations? Fourth come the subjective and even individual questions: what do graphospheric phenomena mean not just for those who produce them but for those who experience them or engage with them? And then there is time. Graphospheres emerge, graphospheres change, as do their components and their functions, as do perceptions and experiences of them. These four distinct but complementary aspects of the graphosphere – in themselves, in combination, and over time – help bring into focus its character in a given society and its variables in comparisons across societies. Some prefatory remarks should be made about each of them.

With regard to their overall physical shapes and textures, graphospheres can be mapped. They have external boundaries and internal zones, contours and landmarks. The external boundaries divide spaces with visible words from spaces with no visible words. Internal boundaries, and the zones that they delineate, can be marked by a variety of criteria. One can differentiate, for example, according to the types of space, such as the public and the private, or the interior and the exterior, or the urban and the rural, or spaces of routine work as opposed to spaces of periodic ritual or ceremony, and so on. Alternatively, zones on the graphospheric map may be distinguished from one another according to the density of verbal presence, shaded to indicate how they compare on a scale of relative saturation or sparseness. Or the map could be coloured according to the predominance or proportions of particular technologies or functions of verbal production, display or consumption. Or, applying a different set of criteria, one could map graphospheres primarily in relation to social or cultural landscapes, rather than primarily in relation to physical geography.

Whatever the cartographic principles, the maps will be dynamic. Over time the boundaries shift and the zones mutate. In general one would probably expect graphospheres to grow, and in general they do; but not always, and not consistently. Apart from macro-historical shifts in the locus and focus of civilisations, states or cycles of prosperity, there are more nuanced variables in, for example, taste, etiquette, custom or regulation, or in local social structures or market conditions.

As in cartography, so in graphospheric conceptualisation, one can choose the level of magnification, and hence the degree of amalgamation or separation, or of singularity or plurality: that is, the extent to which zones and fluctuations are represented as elements of a larger system or as their own local or temporary systems. Graphospheres emerge and develop independently of one another, and within each of them local graphospheres may form.

The larger the scale of the map, the more clearly it brings into view the second set of features: no longer the general shapes but the constituent elements, the physical objects and types of object with visible words, whose presence creates a graphosphere. For introductory purposes it makes sense to start with the larger picture, but the real study of the graphosphere begins with real objects. Before the age of electronic storage the most capacious repositories and potential displays of words tended to be sheets of absorbent materials that can retain signs traced in ink: papyrus, palm leaf, parchment, paper. However, the range of materials and techniques is huge. Visible words have been created in stone, in wood or bark, in ceramics from clay tablets to porcelain, in metals, glass, textiles, plaster, wax, even on the living body. They have been painted and drawn, scratched, chiselled and carved, moulded and cast, stamped and embossed, sewn, seared with heat or acid. The range and distribution of materials and techniques varies from time to time, from place to place, from society to society. Some modes of forming visible words occupy their own discrete zones of the graphosphere, others come into contact with each other, compete, advance, retreat, mingle, interact, form hybrids. Their existence and coexistence may be to varying degrees stable or unstable. Such shifts and drifts and swirls are part of the graphospheric ecology. Clearly the individual components have to be studied in themselves, but in a graphospheric perspective they are also viewed in their systemic connections. The graphospheric approach – holistic and non-hierarchical – must therefore be as inclusive as the evidence permits. For historians of the ancient world, this is obvious, normal, habitual. When written sources are comparatively scarce, all that survive are reckoned valuable. As the graphosphere diversifies and thickens, or as conditions for survival improve, so historians tend to become more selective. Some forms of visible words are privileged because they are regarded as especially significant as cultural artefacts or as historical sources, while objects reckoned routine or ephemeral can tend to be ignored. For exploration of the graphosphere as such, selectivity is in principle unacceptable, despite the fact that it is in practice unavoidable.

Inclusiveness, in a survey of a graphosphere's components, extends to their origins (i.e. whether locally made or imported), to the signs by which words are represented (i.e. the range of alphabetic or ideogrammatic conventions), and to the sounds which those signs are supposed to encode (i.e. the languages). With regard to origins: on the one hand, the objects in the graphosphere are products, and their modes and conditions of production are relevant; on the other hand, they are constituents of a graphosphere by virtue of their presence, not by virtue of their provenance. Thus the history of the formation of a local graphosphere is not just the history of the local production and distribution of the types of object found within it. In the formation of a graphosphere, import is a form of production. Variations in the origins of objects with visible words, and of their scripts and languages, may or may not have semantic resonance in a given graphospheric context.

The third aspect is function: social, political, cultural, economic, aesthetic. The first two sets of questions are still rooted in the physical. They involve synchronic and diachronic mapping of the graphosphere's overall shape and of the components, features, contours and variations in its internal terrain. Introduce the question of functions, and the focus switches from observation to explanation and hence (to a greater extent) to speculation. What accounts for the particular way in which a graphosphere emerges and mutates in a given society? What affects or determines the changing balances and imbalances in the production and uses of its components? What accounts for the particular patterns of ecological success and failure, the patterns of adaptation and accommodation? And how do we explain differences, both small and large, *between* graphospheric ecologies?

Still further along the path from the observable to the speculative, the fourth set of questions relates to meaning: to perceptions of the graphosphere by those who encounter it, move within it, experience it, engage with it. In a broad sense this could be reduced to a question of how graphospheres are read; but only in a very broad sense. Reading in its narrow and most habitual sense, which suggests the application of literate skills to re-encode graphic signs as words, is merely one among many forms of engagement with the graphosphere. Clearly there must be *some* correlation between the emergence and growth of graphospheres and the acquisition and spread of literacy, but visible words are not just signs to be deciphered verbally by the literate. In the first place, universal or near-universal personal literacy, whether as a fact or as an aspiration, is a feature of modernity, when illiteracy can be economically disabling and socially stigmatised. In many pre-modern societies the idea of mass personal literacy would have seemed odd and unnecessary. The visual encoding and decoding of words was a job for the specialists. For the rest, access to the uses of the sign was available orally, through dictation and listening. Secondly, the semantics of objects with visible words are not purely verbal. They can mean more than they say, or more than they mean to say. Or, to invoke another of the lexical extensions favoured in cultural history, graphospheres are – and are constituted from – cultural texts, not just verbal texts.

Such, in skeletal outline, are some of the basic aspects of what is here implied by the word 'graphosphere'. A graphosphere is a thing, not a theory. However, to identify and focus on the graphosphere does imply a particular kind of approach to the study of visible words. What makes a graphospheric approach particular? How does it relate to other ways of looking at equivalent objects and their implications? I do not claim that the graphospheric approach is a radical innovation. No element of it is in itself new. It draws on many traditional disciplines and overlaps with several existing conceptual frameworks.

At the granular level, with regard to its components, the study of the graphosphere is the study of what are sometimes designated *material texts*. The 'material text' approach grew out of, or outgrew, what used to be (and often still is) called book history.[3] Book history is likewise concerned with real objects rather than with sets of words irrespective of their forms of embodiment. Moreover, book history as a field of study has come to include more than just books.[4] The label 'material texts' does away with the restrictive connotations of linkage to a particular form of object. The notion of the material text is appropriate to the study of the graphosphere since it is similarly inclusive and non-hierarchical. However, the notion of material texts is more open than the notion of the graphosphere. It is about things, not necessarily about spaces or systems or interconnections. It opens paths to the unrestricted study of all manner of objects. Naturally, material texts can be, should be and often are analysed contextually, but the label does not in itself imply an approach which is either spatial or holistic. Graphospheres are formed from material texts, but the study of material texts does not have to involve consideration of graphospheres. One could therefore say that a graphospheric approach is merely one way of thinking about material texts.

In its more systemic and dynamic aspects the study of the graphosphere has obvious affinities with the study of *information technologies*: their functions, their interrelations, the social and cultural implications of innovation and change. Here, too, there is a choice of narrower or broader definitions. In modern popular lexicographical sources the phrase 'information technology' tends to be defined specifically, and often exclusively, with reference to computers: 'the study or use of systems (especially computers and telecommunications) for storing, retrieving and sending information'; 'the technology involving the development, maintenance and use of computer systems, software and networks for the processing and distribution of data'; 'the application of computers and telecommunications equipment to store, retrieve, transmit and manipulate data'.[5] The modern age is indeed distinctive in the rapidity with which information technologies develop and mutate, in the global range of their availability and accessibility, in the extent to which they put production and dissemination into the hands (literally) of every user and, partly in consequence, in the extent to which such transformations have stimulated reflection on their own implications, theories of the ways in which changes in information technologies may relate to changes in society and culture, in the political and economic order. For some influential commentators, such features of the contemporary leap in technologies justify the labelling of the present as *the* 'information age'.[6]

Despite the narrowness of the dictionaries, less 'presentist' understandings of information technology are well established. Technologies for the encoding, storage and communication of information can be traced back several millennia. All ages are, in their own ways, information ages, and the heightened contemporary awareness of links between technological and socio-cultural change has prompted fresh reflection upon analogous issues in relation to the past. One way of doing this is simply to project current concepts onto past practices, such as the idea that graffiti and other kinds of inscription can be seen as kinds of 'social media'.[7] More common are macro-historical schemata based on the identification of key, epoch-defining changes in dominant technologies of information.[8] Within this, by far the most attention has been paid to three moments, or three clusters of inventions and the ages that they are perceived to have facilitated: the invention and spread of writing, the invention and spread of printing, and the invention and spread of electrical and electronic media. In each case the modern experience throws up questions that can productively be posed of the past, while past analogies can usefully nuance and modify assumptions about the present and future.

As it happens, one such macro-historical scheme already uses the word 'graphosphere'. For the French philosopher and journalist Régis Debray the graphosphere is the age of print, which is preceded by the 'logosphere' (the age of manuscript, of handwriting) and followed by the 'videosphere'.[9] This is not compatible with the holistic and inclusive notion of the graphosphere in the present study. Aside from the obvious etymological quibble (it might seem more natural to assume that the 'logosphere' should refer to the spoken word while the 'graphosphere' should refer to the written word), the main difference lies in the fact that Debray's graphosphere is one phase in a sequence of dominant technologies, whereas here it represents a general phenomenon of human history and culture. It may accommodate changes in dominant technologies, but at every stage it also encompasses their coexistence and interactions. It is a general framework, not a label for a particular period.

Writing is the application of a principle, not a technology as such. The principle is that sounds or words or thoughts can be represented through systems of visual signs. Writing turns words into objects, or renders them as parts of objects, as material texts. Writing separates message from messenger, speech from speaker. It allows the word to be contemplated, preserved over time, transported across distances, copied, corrected, distributed, bought and sold, independently owned. Interest in the social, cultural, political, economic and even psychological implications of writing has generated an enormous range of scholarly literature[10] exploring the ways in which the potential properties of writing have or have not been realised in a wide variety of media and through a range of technologies over more than five millennia.

Printing introduced a new technology, not a new principle. It was a particular way of making visible words: a type of writing, writing by type. Such, at any rate, is the shorthand generalisation. In fact, print can also be taken as a generic designation that covers several different and widely contrasting technologies. 'Impressions' can be and have been made from materials as disparate as stone and potatoes, linoleum and human skin (the finger-print). The Phaestos disk, with a spiral of symbols impressed in clay, possibly from the second millennium BCE, has been claimed as a specimen of the 'typographic principle'.[11] The particular technology of 'impression' that is associated with significant social and cultural change is the printing press with movable type. However, even this is perhaps too general. In the first place, the history of movable type can be traced, if not from the Phaestos disk, at least from medieval China and Korea. Studies of print as a technology associated with major socio-cultural change focus more specifically on the introduction of movable type using alphabetic script, as a phenomenon in Western and Central Europe from the mid fifteenth century.[12] Secondly, there is a major divide, from the mid nineteenth century, between the dominance of the flat-bed hand press (where each impression had to be 'pulled' individually) and steam-driven rotary presses capable of producing many thousands of impressions per hour. Hand presses and industrial presses are forms of printing in the broad sense, but as methods of creating and replicating the visible word they are barely comparable. They are closer lexically than technologically.

Changes in technologies of the word have been linked to a range of societal and cultural processes: the emergence of bureaucratic administration and hence the emergence first of early states, then of complex centralised states; the emergence of analytical and critical thought, of textual fixity and canonicity; the Reformation; the rise of capitalism and/or absolutism; the paradoxes which mean that devices for the dispersal of knowledge are also devices for the centralisation of knowledge, and that technologies which extend the possibilities for self-expression and the individual construction of identity are likewise technologies of social control, of surveillance and regulation. Allowing for temporal and regional specificity, variations on such themes permeate discussion across the ages. A particular contribution of the historical and comparative study of information technologies is to modify the temptation to embrace, both in interpretation and in prediction, the ostensible 'logic' of technologies in relation to change. To what extent can new technologies (new in the present, new in the past) be reckoned as causes of socio-cultural change, or as catalysts or enablers or facilitators of change, or, in the most passive variant, simply as instruments whose innovative or transformative potential may or may not be activated depending on other circumstances? Do developments in information technology make things happen, do they help to shape the way things happen, or do they extend the range of things that *may* happen? Straightforward techno-determinism, while still common in popular futurology, has gone out of historiographical fashion.

If definitions and implications of technologies themselves are a distraction, they can be removed so as to leave just the study of information. Graphospheres are spaces of information: a graphospheric approach is necessarily concerned with the production, presence, uses, perceptions and history of visible information, and hence can draw on studies of information in history, whether or not these amount to a coherent field of *Information History*.[13] Again prompted in part by modern sensibilities, historians have begun to explore patterns and implications of the creation, gathering, storage, retrieval, use and dissemination of information. This tends to switch the focus (or, in a different perspective, to expand the definition) beyond technology as material artifice so as to include human activities, strategies and institutions: from archival methods to intelligence organisations, from postal services to newspapers, from central ministries to informal networks. With regard to the early modern period, for example, aspects of the history of information have been invoked in accounts of the rise of (again) bureaucratic government, centralised states and early capitalism.[14]

The graphosphere is a space, not just an agglomeration of objects. In its spatial emphasis the graphospheric approach is partially analogous to a branch of sociolinguistics concerned with the *linguistic landscape*.[15] In principle linguistic landscapes must exist wherever there are visible signs that represent language: inside, outside, public, private, monolingual and monoscriptal, multilingual and multi-scriptal, in a single room, across the megalopolis. To this extent a linguistic landscape *is* a graphosphere, or a graphosphere must be a linguistic landscape. In practice, however, research on linguistic landscapes tends to focus on contemporary multilingual display in public spaces. Other words are available. 'Textscape' is sometimes used and could be an adequate equivalent, except that it has already been adopted for a wide range of quite different purposes: in advertising and PR, as a brand name in software or as an art concept.[16] 'Scriptural economy' is a phrase coined by Michel de Certeau while ruminating on the relations of writing and orality,[17] and the phrase is adopted by Lisa Gitelman referring to a 'totality of writers, writings and writing techniques',[18] but without the spatial or physical specificity of 'graphosphere'. Still more broadly, the graphosphere has affinities with, and owes an obvious lexicographical and conceptual debt to, what the semiotician Iurii Lotman termed the semiosphere.[19]

Thus, while the graphosphere is perhaps an unfamiliar word, it does not represent an entirely new set of concepts and concerns. It draws on a range of traditional and contemporary disciplines and approaches. Translated out of academese, it is simply a way of looking at words, at cultures of writing, at how and why words come to be where they are in the world around us. Indeed, just as a summary of the graphospheric concept can sound excessively and impracticably inclusive, so a summary of its disciplinary sources and affinities can sound excessively and impracticably eclectic. The graphospheric approach is capacious. This may be a virtue or a defect. The proof, one way or the other, lies not in the tightness or looseness of prefatory abstractions but in the usefulness or redundancy of the explorations prompted by them. However, before outlining the particular ways in which the concept is applied in the present study, it is appropriate to consider features of its context.

Russia, 1450–1850

By comparison with the abstractions of the graphospheric approach, the phrase 'Russia, 1450–1850' looks reassuringly safe: a place, a set of dates, clear boundaries in space and time; step inside and look around. In fact the phrase is slippery, elusive in a different way, and perhaps no easier to grasp. Some crude facts can illustrate the problem. In the mid fifteenth century the population of the principality of Moscow ('Muscovy') was around five million; in the mid nineteenth century the population of the Russian Empire was more than seventy million. In 1450 the principality of Moscow occupied an area of just over 400,000 square kilometres; by the second half of the nineteenth century the area of the Russian Empire was approximately fifty times larger, extending from the Baltic to the southern Caucasus, from Ukraine to Alaska. A visitor to Muscovy in 1450 would have seen and heard few traces of any language other than Slavonic: the East Slavonic vernacular and the Church Slavonic of the liturgy. By the mid nineteenth century the visitor could have seen dozens of written languages and could have heard hundreds of spoken languages and dialects. In 1450 training in the skills of reading and writing was largely (though by no means exclusively) for churchmen; by 1850 Russia had academies and universities, and the apartment blocks of St Petersburg and Moscow were packed with quill-pushing bureaucrats, while salons thronged with journalists, poets and ladies of letters. 'Russia, 1450–1850' is, so to speak, a moving target. The transformations are so striking, so radical, so fundamental, that one could legitimately wonder whether the phrase makes coherent sense, whether the Muscovy of 1450 and the empire of 1850 can properly be labelled with the same word, as if they were the same place. Graphospheres emerged and mutated within spaces that were themselves mutating.

This is not so unusual. Russia's geopolitical and demographic transformations were perhaps at the extreme ends of a spectrum, but there is barely a country where one would not expect to find major changes, and sometimes radical disruptions, in the course of four centuries. Nevertheless, the designation 'Russia, 1450–1850' looks peculiar even in the context of the historiography of Russia. Neither date coincides with the common chapter breaks in traditional narratives of Russian history. It ignores the grand divide that for well over two hundred years has not only structured a great deal of academic writing but has become embedded in popular imagination, even in language. The emblem and the perceived prime cause of the break between epochs is Peter I, Peter the Great. Russia divides into the pre-Petrine and post-Petrine. The pre-Petrine is Muscovy, the post-Petrine is the Russian Empire. In this binary scheme the pre-Petrine has been associated with traditional, inward-looking, church-dominated medievalism, while the post-Petrine has been associated with modernisation, westernisation, Europeanisation. Symbols of the change are many: the replacement of Moscow with the new capital, St Petersburg, as a 'window onto Europe'; Peter's insistence on West European dress and his tax on beards; the official switch, on 1 January 1700, from the old Orthodox calendar counting the years from the Creation, to the western Christian calendar counting from the birth of Christ. From Aleksandr Pushkin's metaphor of Peter – prompted by Étienne Falconet's equine monument – as the horseman raising Russia onto its hind legs,[20] to modern accounts of the 'Petrine revolution',[21] whether he is represented as the man who set Russia upon its true path or its false path, as the architect of Russia's modernity or as the betrayer of its distinctive heritage, as a force for civilisation or as an agent of the Antichrist, Peter's place as *the* pivotal figure continues to dominate the historical imagination.[22] In terms of periods rather than moments, the age of Russia's modernisation tends to be conceived as stretching from the late seventeenth century (starting slightly before Peter's reign) until the second quarter of the nineteenth century.[23]

Periodisation is a puzzle with no correct solution. Periodisations are necessary artifices, retrospective framings. They represent and misrepresent. They are always over-neat, hence dangerous when they become over-habitual. They are formed and unformed and deformed depending on the criteria that historians choose to regard as significant or definitive. Or so historians might perhaps prefer to suppose. In practice periodisations can easily escape and outflank professional control. They become culturally entrenched assumptions, as if axioms rather than convenient hypotheses or useful artifices. To dislodge Peter in the popular imagination would be hard, perhaps impossible (whether or not one regards it as desirable), but historians rightly seek to stress deficiencies in the conventional scheme. On the one hand, several of the ostensibly Petrine innovations have earlier roots, so that aspects of Russia's 'modernisation' should be tracked across the seventeenth century and perhaps earlier.[24] And, conversely, many of Peter's initiatives failed to take root in his own time, so that focus on Petrine change can obscure underlying continuities of practice and structure. Break the spell of personality and a case can be made for a 'long early modernity' in Russia stretching from the sixteenth century to the early nineteenth century. Certainly there are signs that a historiographical pendulum has been swinging in that direction. The appropriateness of the Petrine divide is debated in academic journals.[25] Major synthetic and thematic histories span the gap.[26] Different criteria produce different types and shapes of narrative. What, then, is the justification for a graphospheric survey labelled 'Russia, 1450–1850'?

A case made on the basis of political events may be superficially plausible, but is rather tenuous. The second half of the fifteenth century marks the fading of Muscovy's subordination to the Mongols, as well as the start of Muscovy's rapid territorial expansion and dominance. Some have also seen a culturally or even providentially resonant divide in the mid fifteenth century, as heralded by Moscow's rejection of the Union of Florence in 1439 and the subsequent fall of Constantinople to the Ottoman Turks in 1453. An events-based justification for a mid-nineteenth-century division is likewise possible but strained. One would have to make much of dates such as 1855 or 1861, with the death of Nicholas I or the emancipation of the serfs. However, for present purposes such external markers are fortuitous, not definitive. The principal reasons for choosing here to explore the period 1450–1850 are graphospheric.

The 'graphospheric' excuse for beginning from the second half of the fifteenth century is derived from a cluster of disparate phenomena, few (or none) of which may be regarded as particularly dramatic or decisive in themselves, but which together reflect initial stages in the emergence of the early modern graphosphere. A continuous practice of public inscription in Muscovy can be traced to the late fifteenth century. In the second half of the fifteenth century, after decades of coexistence, paper replaced parchment as the almost exclusive material for the production of manuscripts. The same period also saw the end of the continuous or regular tradition of using birch bark as a material for inscription.[27] Wax replaced metal as the normal material for seals. With regard to the linguistic landscape, in the late fifteenth century regular coinage ceased to be bi-scriptal in Cyrillic and Arabic, becoming monolingually Slavonic. Towards the end of the century Muscovites could also see the first prominent public lapidary inscriptions in Latin. With regard to technologies of the visible word: the craft of casting cannons in bronze was brought to Moscow in the late 1480s, and cannons (and bronze-cast bells) became regular bearers of monumental inscriptions. Or, with respect to a more familiar technology: although Muscovite printing did not start until the middle of the sixteenth century, active engagement with products of the printing press (via imported books) can also be dated to the final decade of the fifteenth century. Finally, with regard to institutions of production: the emergence of regular specialised administrative personnel is normally traced to the second half of the fifteenth century, an initial phase in the emergence of a state bureaucracy.

These fragmentary graphospheric stirrings extend across categories: material, technological, linguistic, socio-cultural. They are not reducible to a single initiative or cause or moment, but together they constitute movement, or the beginnings of movement, in the emergence of the Russian graphosphere.

The later chronological boundary of the present survey, in the mid nineteenth century, is also imprecise. Again it corresponds to no 'killer' event of epochal significance, nothing that suggests a clean break. Nevertheless it makes a kind of sense, for two reasons: one is a kind of ending, the other is a kind of beginning.

On the one hand, by the mid nineteenth century the modern Russian graphosphere had taken shape. Not that it was in any way finalised, since graphospheres are always changing; but key features were recognisable and established. In public spaces, in private spaces, in commercial and administrative spaces, a graphospheric ecology had emerged. Cities teemed with clerks, collectively a machine for producing massive quantities of handwritten documents. Print, if not entirely unrestricted, had made the transition from quasi-monopoly ownership to market commodity, diffused in its production, diverse in its products. The public graphosphere had taken on its principal forms and genres and had seeped into its principal locations. Shop signs and posters, trade notices, street signs, house signs, mileposts, inscribed statuary, all had become familiar. Indeed, by the mid nineteenth century such phenomena had come to be perceived not only as environmental facts but also as cultural themes prompting reflection, analysis, interpretation. These general processes are reducible to more granular microprocesses, which will be explored in the following chapters. As in the case of incipient features in the late fifteenth century, so in the case of completed transitions by the mid nineteenth century, the overall picture emerges from details that are often unrelated. In 1851, after nearly a hundred years of handwritten verification (albeit to a diminishing extent) all signatures on Russian banknotes were printed; towards the mid nineteenth century plaques of private fire insurance companies proliferated on houses in major cities; branding as a form of punishment (and identification) was formally abolished in 1863. In the middle decades of the nineteenth century steel-nib pens came to replace quill pens.[28] And so on.

On the other hand, alongside this partial completion there were new departures. One such innovation was the introduction of the industrial-scale, steam-driven rotary press. The rotary press, which enabled a huge increase in the capacity to reproduce words quickly and in very large quantities, represents (arguably) a technical leap potentially as transformative as the introduction of hand presses and movable type. However, the rotary press still counts as print. A more radical new beginning was the introduction and early use of the electrical telegraph. The electrical telegraph represents the most fundamental change in the technology of the word since the invention of script. It reversed all previous practices of encoding, distribution and retrieval of words. It made words *in*visible. The text was de-materialised. The telegraph separated speech from speaker without the need to turn words into things. It was, in a sense, the first 'anti-graphospheric' technology of information. In its invisibility it differed not only from script-based technologies but also from sign-based communication such as smoke signals, flag semaphore or indeed the optical telegraph. Electrical telegraphy's trick of dematerialisation, of turning words into invisible, intangible and inaudible signals, was an initial but crucial departure. Its functions were limited to encoding and distribution. It did not yet provide a means of storage. Nevertheless, it was the first in the accelerating sequence of non-manual, non-mechanical technologies of information. The first public telegraph office in Russia opened in 1852. The telegraph and the rotary press added fresh elements to the graphospheric ecology, prompted fresh shifts in its shape and contours. They did not, of course, instantly create a new epoch, but in the history of the Russian graphosphere the mid nineteenth century provides a reasonable moment if not for an entirely new narrative, at least for an intonational pause.

Aims and Limits

Such is the general approach and the general context. What, more specifically, does this book try to do, and not to do? There are three main aims: description, interpretation, and to a lesser extent comparison. The movement of chapters is from the descriptive to the interpretative. Comparison is episodic throughout.

The descriptive sections address the first two of the four aspects of the graphosphere as outlined above: its components and its shape. They are intended to serve as a kind of provisional introductory reference guide to the types and configurations of material texts in Russia over the period. What kinds of objects did it consist of? How did they come to be there? What institutional, political, commercial, technological or cultural structures brought them into being? What kinds of signs (scripts, languages) did they display? What here counts as a visible word? The focus is predominantly on alphabetic script, but this can lead to anomalies. In some contexts the alphabetic and the non-alphabetic serve more or less identical functions. For example, if a manufacturer puts a unique mark on a product, does it really make sense to include it here if it is formed from letters but not if it is an identifying design, to draw a line between alphabetic and ideogrammatic representation, between *logos* and logos? If a patron orders a personalised dinner service, or if a bibliophile commissions a bookplate, should it make a difference whether it is marked with monogrammed initials or with a crest? Or, conversely, a common iconographical label for the Mother of God is derived from a form of abbreviation in Greek (ΜΡ ΘΥ). It serves as a recognisable ideogrammatic identifier, but in what sense should it be regarded as an alphabetic inscription in a Russian context? Dividing lines are fuzzy. For the most part the present study sticks to the alphabetic, venturing occasionally into the greyer areas in order to test the extent or the quality of their greyness. Sometimes it turns out that the choice of visual code is not entirely neutral.

Still there are gaps. As a reference guide to the Russian graphosphere(s) over four centuries, the descriptive sections are a long way from being comprehensive. The guide is introductory and provisional. First, there are gaps related to the paradoxical problems of evidence at both ends of the chronological scale: at the beginning a scarcity, at the end a superabundance. For the late fifteenth century one is dependent on scraps which may or may not be fully representative and whose surviving quantities and proportions are certainly skewed by the contingencies of survival. By the mid nineteenth century the graphosphere was being flooded with many millions of objects every year, so the problem is not survival but partial knowledge and even more partial selectivity. In the late fifteenth century a picture of the graphosphere can only be lightly sketched, whereas for the mid nineteenth century it is daubed with the broadest and roughest of brushes. The survey is also geographically lopsided. Much of the evidence relates to Russia's main urban centres, Moscow and St Petersburg. Provincial graphospheres need further research, especially in the empire's zones of cross-linguistic contacts.

A second category of gap is a consequence of fashions in scholarship, in librarianship and in archival convention. A holistic interest in cultures and functions of writing has been normal for periods where written sources are scarce. For more recent periods, attention to written remains has tended to be more selective and hierarchical. Books, manuscripts and luxury objects are noted, catalogued and analysed, while a lot of conventionally lower-status material seems to lie below the scholarly radar. In the Russian context, alongside copious studies of books, manuscripts and museum treasures, there has been very little investigation, or even bibliographical or archival awareness, of the mass of objects that are lumped together under the deprecating and often inaccurate label of 'ephemera': printed matter other than books, manuscript materials not accorded the status of historical or cultural sources, plus the huge variety of non-luxury types of objects with secondary writing. 'Ephemera' are as important and integral to the graphosphere as are illuminated manuscripts or works of great literature. Academic neglect of ephemera has been common. For their preservation and description we are often indebted to the obsessions of private collectors. A degree of scholarly recognition has followed, ephemera have become academically more respectable and bibliographically more visible,[29] the emergence of the non-hierarchical notion of 'material texts' has helped to rectify the imbalance; but very little of this has yet been reflected in research in and into Russia. Beyond assembling diverse bits of information on conventionally unglamorous categories of material text, part of the research for the present book has involved identifying, and creating taxonomies and chronologies for, categories of material that have been almost wholly overlooked.[30] Surfaces have begun to be scratched, but, pending quite a lot of exploration of unknown unknowns (to borrow the phrase made popular by Donald Rumsfeld), significant aspects of the complexion and topography of the Russian graphosphere will remain distorted or obscure. And, while on the subject of scratched surfaces, a particularly regrettable gap is created by the absence of almost any detailed research on tertiary writing of the period – above all, of graffiti.[31]

A third kind of gap is a consequence of choice. At the start of the relevant period, by far the most dense area of the late medieval graphosphere was the interior of a church.[32] Across all four centuries the Orthodox Church specialised in the production of images great and small, and its images normally bore signs of writing: the icons and the frescoes, the liturgical silver, the pendants and reliquaries, the vestments. For the most part I take this as an initial and fairly stable given, and devote relatively little attention to the ecclesiastical graphosphere, except in areas of notable change or where ecclesiastical fashion overflowed into other areas. With regard to the eighteenth and nineteenth centuries, the history of Russian written culture is most commonly represented on the basis of literature and thought. Here the literary and intellectual heritage occupies limited space. Maybe this amounts to under-emphasis in over-compensation for traditional over-emphasis, but in the graphospheric approach the balance needs to be shifted. Finally, for present purposes the geographical limits of the graphosphere are largely restricted to the Russian heartlands, not to the wider empire. The rise of empire has implications for the linguistic landscape of

Moscow and St Petersburg, but no attempt is made to look closely at local graphospheres in, for example, Tiflis (Tbilisi), Erevan, Warsaw or even Vilnius. For this I offer no justification other than the limits of competence and time.

After description – though also unavoidably implicit in description – comes interpretation. The third and fourth of the listed aspects of the graphosphere are functions and meanings. Here to speak of gaps would be misleading. To admit to leaving gaps is also to assume that, were the gaps to be filled, some kind of completeness would be attainable. This cannot be said about interpretation. There are no gaps because there is no notional whole. I should again stress that the graphosphere is an object of study to which many different approaches may be applied. The study of the graphosphere does not imply or require the application of a specific theory. The lines of interpretation here are simply examples of those which have seemed initially promising. In particular, three clusters of questions recur. One set of questions relates to production: the graphospheric implications of shifts in institutions of production, in techniques of production and (to use a somewhat unfashionable phrase) in ownership of the means of production. A second set of questions focuses on functional differentiation and adaptation, on the dynamics of shifting boundaries and mixed zones and hybrids in the graphospheric ecology: what were the various technologies of the word used for? How were they distinguished from or combined with each other? A third set of questions relates to status and authority, whether in intention, in function or in perception: to what extent did various graphospheric phenomena emerge as instruments of authority? To what extent does graphospheric change reflect or respond to changes in the authority of, respectively, civil or ecclesiastical structures, economic pressures or simply taste and fashion? In what senses were various graphospheric elements themselves perceived as authoritative?

Functions can be inferred; meanings are elusive. The overwhelming majority of producers and viewers of the graphosphere were unreflexive, or left no articulated reflection about their intentions or about their experience. Of the two, intended meaning is occasionally more accessible. The graphosphere contains enclaves of explanatory zeal. Intended meaning also has the advantage of being singular, reflecting the moment, the individual or the institution. Perceived meanings mutate and multiply. They are plural, unstable and most often unattested. With the transition to meanings, the idea of a reference guide dissolves. In the present study, attention is devoted more to what the graphosphere was than to what it meant, more to the broad processes of its formation and fluctuation than to its myriad semantic nuances. Some aspects of subjectivity in the graphosphere are explored in places, but this is an obvious area for further detailed work.

Many other lines of thought could productively be pursued. The graphosphere offers an enabling approach, not a prescription, and the questions explored here are indicative, not definitive.

Finally, comparison. The principal aim here is to outline, account for and begin to explore the graphospheres of Russia. A subsidiary aim is comparative, to consider similarities and differences, to identify what was or may have been distinctive to Russia, and what was shared more widely. To be consistently or thoroughly comparative is impossible. In the first place the requisite breadth and depth of granular knowledge across centuries and societies would tax the capacity of even a large-scale collective project, let alone an individual exploratory monograph. Secondly, the current scope for comparison is in any case skewed both by the gaps in research and by the lack of comparably graphospheric surveys of other societies.

That said, in one area research is abundant and comparisons are already traditional: the emergence, dissemination and implications of print. For non-Russianists the reasons given for the chronological scope of this book may seem like laboured special pleading in support of a structure which is, for Western Europe, conventional. The period 1450–1850 is not a habitually proposed span in accounts of the history of Russia, but it *is* familiar, predictable and unproblematic as a shorthand for the age of the rise of print cultures and their interactions with manuscript cultures in Western and Central Europe: from the beginnings of movable type to the beginnings of long-distance telegraphic communication.[33] For those accustomed to regarding West European developments as a kind of norm, Russia can be a challenge. Despite some contact with West European print and printers, there was no print revolution in Russia in the fifteenth century. Despite the native adoption of printing, there was no print revolution in Russia in the sixteenth or seventeenth centuries, or even (I will argue) through most of the eighteenth century. Although this survey starts in the age of Gutenberg, the fortuitous chronological coincidence serves to emphasise Russia's non-Gutenbergian developments, and hence the perils of generalising about the 'agency' of print.

Beyond print, in the wider graphosphere, comparisons will be non-systematic, opportunistic, serendipitous. Sometimes they suggest analogies and equivalence, sometimes contrasts. Here, too, there is a lot more to be done.

CHAPTER 2

Production in the Graphosphere, I: Primary Writing

The writing on objects can be described as primary, secondary or tertiary.[1] When the principal purpose of the production of an object is that it should bear a written text, then it is classified as an object with primary writing. The typical technologies of primary writing, in the relevant period, are handwriting and printing, and the most common material is paper. Secondary writing can be integral to an object's production and function, but is not its principal purpose: the object is created *with* writing, but not *for* writing. The technologies and materials of secondary writing are more diverse than those of primary writing. For example, secondary writing may be cast, incised, moulded or applied. Objects with secondary writing be formed from almost any material, including metal, wood, glass, textiles, plaster, ceramics and also paper. Secondary writing covers much of the diversity of what are more commonly labelled 'inscriptions'. Tertiary writing is that which is applied to an object which already exists for other purposes. Much tertiary writing would broadly be described as graffiti. The boundaries between categories are not always clear. Some objects could arguably be placed in more than one category. For example, a shop sign might be regarded as displaying primary writing, insofar as the signboard is manufactured in order to be written upon; or it may be regarded as secondary, insofar as it is a piece of writing affixed to something else (the shop). For practical purposes the lack of an absolutely precise taxonomy of objects is not a hindrance.

In very general outline the history of primary writing tends to be imagined first in relation to the invention and spread of handwriting, then in relation to the invention and spread of print. There was not a straightforward transition from the dominance of one technology to the dominance of the other. An important variable concerns the nature of their coexistence and interactions. A feature of the dynamics of primary writing in the Russian graphosphere was the continual expansion (quantitative, geographical, social, generic, thematic) in the production of handwriting, while print was, for most of the period, a 'niche' technology.

A prerequisite for the extensive production of objects with primary writing was the production of their principal material: paper. In early medieval Rus there were two main kinds of writing materials: an expensive kind and a cheap kind. The expensive material was parchment, animal skins. The cheap kind was birch bark. We know a great deal more about parchment manuscripts, since, by the nature both of the material and of the texts, they have been much better preserved and conserved in institutions and collections. Birch-bark documents were discarded and lay undiscovered and largely unsuspected in the ground until they began to be identified by archaeologists in the mid twentieth century. However, by the mid to late fifteenth century the material basis for primary writing had changed. Birch bark seems to have stopped being regularly used, and parchment had in most contexts given way to paper. Nearly seven decades of excavation have revealed well over a thousand birch-bark documents dating from the early eleventh century to the mid fifteenth century, but none subsequently.[2] If there was a regularly used, cheap and disposable writing material in sixteenth-century Muscovy, we do not have any strong evidence for what it may have been. Paper was used sporadically in the late fourteenth century, but became the dominant material for primary writing only during the fifteenth century.[3]

It is tempting to suppose that the two phenomena – the apparent abandonment of birch bark and the spread of the use of paper – were connected: that birch bark was rendered redundant by the availability of paper as a better cheap alternative to parchment. The flaw is in the assumption that, because paper was cheaper than parchment, it was a cheap material. It was not; certainly not by comparison with birch bark, which was free. Muscovy did not produce its own paper. There is some evidence of projects for paper mills from the 1560s, and some short-lived ventures in the third quarter of the seventeenth century, but the continuous history of Russian paper-making begins only from the start of the eighteenth century.[4] So, for the first three hundred years of its regular use in Russia, all paper, whether for writing or for printing, was imported, mainly from Western Europe. The supply of the basic material for handwriting and printing was dependent on trade. If paper replaced birch bark, it was not because it rivalled the latter on price. More likely the change can be linked to the fact that many of the quasi-formal uses of birch bark, such as recording debts and tax dues and payments, describing property for assessment or testament, etc., were being institutionalised, absorbed into the emerging bureaucratic structures, which did use paper. When, in a series of measures initiated in January 1699, Peter I introduced the obligatory use of officially stamped paper (*gerbovaia bumaga*) for certain transactions, it was partly in the interests of security but partly also as a revenue-raising device replacing a tax on the transaction. In any case all such stamped paper was imported. Local production of watermarked (rather than stamped) *gerbovaia bumaga* began in 1724.[5]

There were many stages in the transition to truly cheap paper: from the establishment of local production, through the arrival of machine-made paper as a cheaper alternative to traditional hand-milling, to the introduction of the processes for making wood-pulp paper instead of rag paper. Some eighty paper mills were founded in Russia during the eighteenth century: a few by the government, some on estates, but mostly by merchants as commercial ventures. Over the first three decades of the nineteenth century there are records of around 180 producers of writing paper.[6] The first factory for producing machine-made paper, several times more efficient than hand mills, opened in Peterhof in 1818. From the early nineteenth century Russia even became a net exporter of paper, especially to Central Asia and the east. The first Russian factories producing cellulose (wood-pulp) paper date from the 1880s.

From Monastery to Ministry: The Rise and Rise of Handwriting

The volume of handwriting expanded massively throughout the four centuries covered by the present study. This section surveys the institutions which, in overlapping sequence, played the most dynamic roles in that expansion: the great manuscript-producing institutions of the church, and the burgeoning document-producing institutions of the state. There were others: schools, universities, academies, businesses, clergy and non-monastic religious communities, quasi-private institutions such as salons and literary societies, eventually personal correspondence. Their graphospheric roles and relations will figure in later chapters, but the framework for the expansion of handwriting from the fifteenth century to the nineteenth was formed from monasteries and (by various names) ministries.

Monastic Writing

In the mid fifteenth century monasteries were the principal institutional producers and consumers of manuscript books. In absolute terms monastic production continued to expand until at least the first half of the eighteenth century. In comparative terms, however, by the late seventeenth century monasteries had lost their dominant institutional position both in the production of handwritten materials and as contributors to the graphosphere more widely.

The age of monastic expansion in Muscovy, and then in the Russian Empire, lasted from the late fourteenth century to the early eighteenth century. Statistics for the numbers of monasteries over the period cannot be entirely reliable, but a recent calculation produces the following summary table of the chronology of monastic foundation.[7]

14th century	152
15th century	257
16th century	536
17th century	708
18th century, first half	208
18th century, second half	32

The very sharp fall in the number of new foundations in the later eighteenth century can be attributed directly to legislation following Catherine II's manifesto of 1764 on the secularisation of monastic landholdings. Authority over monastic lands was devolved to a department constituted for the purpose (the *Kollegiia ekonomii*), which would allocate to selected monasteries the resources deemed sufficient for their needs, while those not included in the list for state support had to depend on their local communities.[8] Hundreds of monasteries became instantly unsustainable and had to close. Although many monasteries, large and small, continued to exist and thrive right through the nineteenth century, the economic, social and culture-producing power of monasteries was irrevocably diminished.

The foundation figures in the table mask a considerable diversity in size and nature. Monasteries could range from just a few individuals to substantial economic and social institutions. The largest, the Trinity-St Sergii monastery at Sergiev Posad to the north-east of Moscow, in 1700 held land which included some 20,000 homesteads – that is, not far short of 150,000 people.[9]

The best-known tend to be the largest, the major cenobitic (communal) monasteries which have survived or have left the most abundant traces of themselves. Many of the most prestigious houses founded during the fourteenth and fifteenth centuries trace their origins according to the classic pattern of monastery-formation derived from early Christianity and emulated in Byzantium and in early Rus. A holy man (almost always a man) leaves the 'world' in order to live a contemplative life in some remote place (typically a desert, cave, mountain or forest). He attracts admirers and disciples, who form a community around him. He then either consolidates and leads the community, or leaves in order to renew his isolation – upon which the pattern may repeat itself. The result is that sparsely populated areas may become dotted with substantial monastic communities, which in turn stimulate economic activity and further population influx. The monastic movements from the late fourteenth to the sixteenth centuries are often termed monastic 'colonisation', especially of areas of the north, as typified by such major houses as the Trinity-St Sergii monastery, the monastery of St Kirill on the White Lake (the Kirillo-Belozerskii monastery), or the nearby Ferapontov monastery; or, from the fifteenth century, the monastery on Solovetskii Island in the White Sea, two of whose founders were themselves from the Kirillo-Belozerskii community. However, one should not overestimate remoteness. Suburban or urban monasteries also mushroomed, to the extent that, in the absence of a massive fortress such as the Moscow Kremlin (whose monumental masonry walls date from the late fifteenth century), the physically dominant presence of large walled monasteries came to be a defining and characteristic feature of the late medieval Russian cityscape.

Monasteries made and required books. They had to maintain daily devotional practices as stipulated by their Rule (*ustav*), and they often encouraged or required substantial further non-liturgical reading (e.g. communally, in the refectory at mealtimes).[10] However, monastic book culture was not fully self-contained. Books could flow in and out. Apart from in-house copying, monasteries accumulated books by donation or by purchase. They could also produce books for outsiders on commission. Moreover, not all copying *in* monasteries was necessarily conducted *by* monks. They could employ outside professionals as scribes, even providing work-space within the monastery. For example, one of the best-known scribes of the early sixteenth century is Mikhail Medovartsev. Mikhail began his career in Novgorod, but for his final three decades (he died in the early 1530s) he was based in the Nikolskii monastery (Nikolo-Grecheskii; Nikoly Starogo) on what is now Nikolskaia Street in central Moscow, just a couple of hundred metres from the Kremlin walls. More than twenty extant manuscripts have been linked to him. Indeed, his cell in the monastery has been described as a manuscript workshop, where he oversaw the work of at least four other scribes. Perhaps owing in part to the location of the monastery, Mikhail Medovartsev was well placed to fulfil commissions, producing books not just for the monastery but for outside clients, including the grand prince. Yet through all this – it has been argued – he remained a layman, not a monk.[11]

We cannot know, or even guess to within any sensible order of magnitude, the total number of manuscript books produced by, in or for monasteries at any given time. The only firm evidence consists of books which have survived,[12] plus in some instances books which are described in early inventories. Even here we have to be careful when translating the figures to a modern readership. What is a book? A modern default assumption might be that a book generally contains a particular work. Anthologies and compendia exist but are unlikely to be reckoned the norm. The book is the novel, or the biography, or the scholarly monograph, not just the physical object. With regard to medieval manuscripts, this assumption is not valid. There is no regular one-to-one relationship between the book-as-object and the book-as-work. Nor, indeed, was there a consistent relationship between the contents of a book and its title.[13] The contents of the book-as-object were generally determined by the function of the text for its intended users, not by considerations of authorial identity or integrity. Some compilations were geared to the calendar, to prescribed services and associated readings linked either to the fixed cycle of months and saints' days or to the movable cycles dependent on the date of Easter. Others were for broader edificatory reading. In both cases a manuscript book was likely to include many works by many authors (sometimes known, often anonymous). The repertoire of works should not be confused with the repertoire of books.

A good example is provided by the activities of the scribe Efrosin of the Kirillo-Belozerskii monastery in the late fifteenth century. Efrosin's annotations have been identified in more than thirty manuscripts,[14] but his most substantial output consists of six large volumes for which he was the principal scribe. Efrosin's manuscripts are bulky, ranging from 421 to 638 leaves (that is, in modern terms, between 842 and 1276 pages). Two of them, including the longest (which Efrosin tells us he wrote out over the course of four years), consist of readings for monastic services. The other four, in smaller format, were probably for 'cell' reading. Together they include an enormous range of 'works', often described as encyclopedic. These are anthologies, florilegia. The full list of the titles of the works and extracts which they contain runs to more than 700 items, and the detailed scholarly description of their contents fills nearly 300 pages of a large-format, late twentieth-century small-print journal.[15] Many of these works are very brief, taking up no more than a leaf or three: individual prayers, homilies, extracts from canon law, accounts of miracles, advice. Some are substantial: thirteen leaves of the *Tale of Drakula*; fifty-eight leaves of the pilgrimage of the abbot Daniil to the Holy Land; 174 leaves of the novel of Alexander the Great.[16]

Equivalent compilations are typical of monastic book production. Somewhat earlier, Kirill Belozerskii himself (1337–1427), founder of Efrosin's monastery, had a notable collection of manuscripts, to some of which he also contributed as a scribe. One of them is a compendium which includes such diverse material as extracts from canon law and on the differences between the Latin and Greek churches, practical advice on medical blood-letting, tables of the phases of the moon, commentaries on psalms, a list of monastic names, a Life of Saints Boris and Gleb.[17] While embodying broad monastic principles, many of the compendia reflect the choices of their compilers.[18]

With such compendia the line between scribe and compiler or editor, or even scholar, becomes somewhat blurred.[19] While copying mainly the works of others, scribes could adapt received texts and create their own combinations. Although most scribal production consisted of copying, few texts and compilations, especially in non-liturgical, non-scriptural functions, were fully stable. It is hard to define when a manuscript copy becomes a new 'book' in the compositional as well as the physical sense.

If book-counting is hard in theory, it is not much easier in practice. We can to some extent measure the expansion of the monastic graphosphere by counting the numbers of real manuscript books that have survived. Not all surviving manuscript books are known and described, but the rough provisional figures, based on manuscripts in the libraries of Russia and the countries of the former Soviet Union, suggest there may be around 4,000 from the fifteenth century and perhaps 12,000–14,000 from the sixteenth century.[20] I am not aware of estimates of the number of surviving manuscript books from the seventeenth century, but they would certainly be very much greater. However, there is no reliable way to assess to what extent the increases in numbers are attributable to increases in production or to the higher rates of survival among more recent manuscripts.

The organisational structure of monastic book production was also subject to wide variation. Monastic writing could be a solitary pursuit, or a highly co-ordinated collective process. At the solitary end of the spectrum, Abbot Dosifei of the Solovetskii monastery explains how, in his efforts to record the lives of two of the monastery's founders, Zosima and Savvatii, he secluded himself in his cell (*sedokh v kelii uediniaias'*) and focussed on writing down all that he could remember of them. Subsequently, in 1503, he gave these notes to Spiridon, a monk of the Ferapontov monastery and formerly metropolitan of Kiev, requesting that the latter reshape them in the appropriate hagiographic manner.[21]

Dosifei and Spiridon were working as individuals, albeit with varying degrees of support from outside and inside the monastery. Sometimes it is possible to conjecture that manuscript copying was an organised collective process in a particular monastery: for example, when parts of a source manuscript have been distributed for copying among several scribes working in parallel rather than in sequence; or when a significant cluster of manuscripts can be traced to the same monastery at roughly the same period, whether on the basis of scribal colophons, or by inference through the identification of a 'house style' of decoration, or even because the paper can be traced to the same batch. Making a manuscript book was in any case a collaborative project. The skills of the scribe, the miniaturist and the binder were distinct. There is no doubt that, at least in some monasteries, book production was not devolved to individuals but was regulated, regularised, organised. However, the details, including the arrangement or allocation of physical space, are rarely clear. Scholars often refer to monastic workshops (*masterskie*), or scriptoria: that is, to rooms set aside for the specific purpose of book production.[22] The provision of scriptoria is what one might expect by analogy with West European monastic book culture. However, explicit contemporary documentary evidence for the existence of scriptoria in Russian monasteries before the seventeenth century is hard to find, especially for the earlier period. Indeed, one distinguished historian of monastic book culture states plainly that 'in sixteenth-century monasteries there were *no* regular workshops analogous to scriptoria', since copying was conducted in individuals' cells.[23]

In a sense, the physical arrangements are a detail. The main point is that monastic book production was an institutional function, not (or not only) a personal activity. Indeed, monasteries were increasingly *required* to exercise institutional oversight. The *Stoglav* Council of 1551 insisted, rather optimistically, that all manuscript copies must be made from correct originals, and should themselves be checked for correctness; that uncorrected manuscripts may not be sold, or were liable to confiscation post-sale, for which both the vendor and the purchaser would be held responsible.[24]

The more recent the period, the better the evidence for the organisation of monastic copying. Perhaps the most extreme example is from the early eighteenth century, from the Old Believer community on the Vyg, in

Karelia. Already by the turn of the eighteenth century the Vyg community was substantial, numbering around 2,000 settlers. In 1706 a sister house was founded for women, some 20 km away on the river Leksa. This provided the basis for what is surely a unique scriptorium, staffed by women from the Leksa monastery. The second abbot of the Vyg community, Semen Denisov (younger brother of its principal founder Andrei Denisov) laid down rules for the female scribes (*pisitsy, gramotnitsy*) in the scriptorium (*gramotnaia kel'ia*), and also wrote instructions to one of their overseers, a certain Naumovna, on the proper conduct of her charges.[25] In the instructions to Naumovna Semen stresses that the scribes must behave in a seemly fashion: no whispering, gossiping or laughing in the scriptorium, no idleness, no shirking the communal monastic life except in case of illness. In his formal rules Semen's main concern was to stress that the women must write only what they were told, and were strictly forbidden to write anything that had not been explicitly approved. It has been estimated that in the early nineteenth century the Vyg female scriptorium employed up to two hundred women.[26]

Distribution and sales were important stimuli to monastic book production. Monastic manuscripts were not just confined to the monastery, but entered the wider graphosphere, particularly in churches and in the houses of the wealthy. The Nikolskii monastery, in the shadow of the Kremlin, was well placed to take commissions from prestigious clients, and to keep Mikhail Medovartsev in the monastery for the purpose. A mid-seventeenth-century annotation in one of the manuscripts from the Solovetskii monastery says that, while the book itself remained in the monastery, saints' lives could be copied from it and sold for profit (*v denezhnuiu kaznu na prodazhu*).[27]

Monasteries were the major institutions of preservation. From the earliest surviving inventory, which catalogues objects in the Solovetskii monastery in 1514, we learn that the abbot and scribe Dosifei had donated 46 of the monastery's 107 manuscript books, which were stored mostly in the treasury, while a few altar Gospels were kept for regular use in the monastery's churches.[28] A series of sixteenth-century inventories illustrates the growth of the collection: 211 manuscripts in 1582; 481 in 1597. The inventory of the Kirillo-Belozerskii monastery for 1601 lists approximately a thousand manuscripts, and around fifty printed books.[29] By the end of the seventeenth century both monasteries had close to a couple of thousand books. This scale of acquisition was unusual. A more normal monastic collection in the mid seventeenth century might include between 100 and 350 books.[30] Some monastic collections also functioned as lending libraries. The Kirillo-Belozerskii monastery, for example, loaned books both within its own properties and beyond. Its register of internal loans (*knigi rozdatochnye*) to monks has been preserved.[31]

In addition to the manuscripts, monastic inventories reflect the incursions of printed books. The first mention of a printed book in a monastic library is the single *Apostol* (the Acts and Epistles from the New Testament) in the Solovetskii monastery in the inventory of 1582. In 1597 the collection had increased to thirty-eight, while the Kirillo-Belozerskii monastery in 1601 had around fifty printed books. By the end of the seventeenth century, a clear majority of monastic books for liturgical use were printed.[32]

Thus far we have focussed on books, as the typical product of monastic handwriting over the centuries. However, the larger monasteries also developed institutional habits of paperwork in their administration. Monastic record keeping in early Rus may well have been more regular than secular equivalents. In the early modern era monasteries shared the state's growing predilection for cumulative administrative records. Monastic document production grew significantly in the sixteenth and seventeenth centuries,[33] partly because monasteries needed to define and protect their material interests in the context of the expanding documentary requirements of the state.

Handwriting and Bureaucracy

On 7 November 1458 Ilia, son of Stefan (or Stepan) Borodatyi, died. His father Stefan ordered a stone cross to be carved and inscribed in his memory.[34] The grieving father went to some expense. There are deep relief carvings of the Crucifixion, and of his and his son's heavenly protectors – the prophet Elijah (Ilia) and St Stephen. Medieval inscribed East Slav memorial stone crosses are very rare.[35] Rarer still is the fact that Stefan's cross served not only as a pious memorial but also as a formal document. After recording Ilia's death, the inscription sets out the details of a donation. Stefan gave the monastery two villages, together with income, and stipulated that Ilia and all Stefan's family should be commemorated every Saturday by two priests and a deacon. This is more than a commemorative inscription, more even than a deed of donation. It is a kind of contract. As it happens, contracts and documents were Stefan's business. The inscription states his profession: he was a *d'iak*, a state secretary. The *d'iak* Stefan Borodatyi from Rostov is known from other sources from the 1450s onwards. He was a trusted figure in the administration in the latter years of Grand Prince Vasilii II (1425–62) and the early years of Ivan III (1462–1505). He appears as signatory to documents relating to monastic land, and as an envoy to Poland.[36] The cross of the *d'iak* Stefan can serve as an emblem of the beginning of the age of the *d'iak* and more generally of the rise of a dedicated document-producing administration.

The growth of bureaucratic administration, while ancient in origin, is a particular feature of the development of the pre-modern, and then the modern, state. Russia is no exception.[37] From the mid fifteenth century to the mid nineteenth century the institutional history of Russian bureaucracy can be broken down into several phases: the early emergence of specialised administrative personnel over the second half of the fifteenth century; the formal institutionalisation and proliferation of chanceries (*prikazy*) from the mid sixteenth century; their replacement by colleges (*kollegii*) under Peter I; the creation of ministries (modelled on Napoleonic France) in 1802 under Alexander I. However, across four centuries, through successive structural reforms, and regardless of the institutional packaging, two underlying processes remained constant: an increase in the numbers of bureaucrats both in absolute terms and as a proportion of the population; and an increase in the quantity and variety of documents which they produced and required.

Until approximately the mid fifteenth century, princely administration was largely 'seigniorial'. The prince deliberated (or not) with his boiars, who, in turn, could be delegated to act on his behalf. For most purposes memory still served as the principal information repository. Formal documentation and record keeping were sparse. Scribes, when used, were technical assistants under princely or boiar supervision. Around the mid fifteenth century, gradually but perceptibly, this began to change.[38] One indicator of transition is the fact that some non-boiar scribes (*d'iaki*) begin to be identifiable in positions of administrative responsibility, as secretaries in the higher rather than the lower sense, as an identifiable set of specialised administrators. The new *d'iaki* were often landowners, but not among the boiar elite; and they were scribes, but not mere copyists. They could validate documents on behalf of the Grand Prince.[39] The names and careers of several of the early *d'iaki* are known not just from documents which they authenticated but from chronicle narratives. Over the sixteenth and seventeenth centuries these new-style *d'iaki*, in the role of state secretaries, supported by an ever growing cohort of clerks (*pod'iachie*) would become the core personnel of the chancery system.[40] Before the mid sixteenth century little is known either about what the structures were called or about physical arrangements. The term *izba* ('chamber') occurs from the 1540s and 1550s. Regular use of the term *prikaz* ('chancery') dates from the 1560s and came to dominate, such that the late Muscovite administrative structure is known as the *prikaz* system.[41]

In the *prikaz* system chanceries proliferated. Between the mid sixteenth century and the early eighteenth century, some 150 *prikazy* were founded. In the seventeenth century there were in any given year approximately sixty to seventy active chanceries. They varied hugely both in size and in longevity. Some were stable, long-term institutions, others had a more fleeting presence. Some had substantial staffs and internal subsections (usually *stoly*, 'desks'), others could make do with minimal personnel. Thus, for example, the Ambassadorial Chancery (*Posol'skii prikaz* – in effect, the department for foreign relations) existed from 1549 right through to 1718,[42] while the Chancery for Cathedral Affairs (*Prikaz sobornogo dela*, set up to oversee restoration of Kremlin churches) seems to be attested only for 1653. In 1627/8 the largest *prikaz* was the Chancery of the Grand Court (*Prikaz Bol'shogo Dvortsa*), with fifty-four clerks, while the Musketeers' Granary Chancery (*Prikaz Sbora streletskogo khleba*) had just two. Sixty years later the balance had shifted. Although the Chancery of the Grand Court had increased its staff by nearly 500 per cent to 261 clerks, now it was a distant second in size, dwarfed by the 446 clerks of the Service Land Chancery (up from 36 in 1627/8), while in 1668/9 the Apothecary Chancery (*Aptekarskii prikaz*) had 2 clerks.[43] As for the overall size of the administration: in the 1640s it is estimated that the central chanceries employed 837 secretaries and clerks (55 of the former, 782 of the latter), with a further 774 in local institutions, making a total of 1,611. Half a century later the numbers had almost trebled to 4,657, with 2,739 in the central chanceries and 1,918 locally.[44]

In the seventeenth century Muscovy's chancery system was regarded as a noteworthy feature of its governance, highlighted in descriptions for foreigners. Adam Olearius (1599–1671) served as secretary to an embassy from Frederick II, Duke of Holstein-Gottorp, to Muscovy and Persia in 1633–5. Olearius's subsequent description of Muscovy and Persia became an international bestseller. First published in German in 1647, it went through several revisions, and appeared in French, Italian, Dutch and English editions in the 1650s and 1660s. In his section on governance, Olearius lists the names, functions and heads of thirty-two 'prikazi'.[45] More limited in contemporary reach (it was first published nearly 200 years after the author's death), but more detailed in content, was the description of thirty-seven *prikazy* by a Russian who knew them well from experience: the former *pod'iachii* of the Ambassadorial Chancery, Grigorii Kotoshikhin, whose account of Muscovy was written at the request of the Swedish government after his defection in 1664. Kotoshikhin's chapter on the *prikazy* is by far the longest in his work.[46]

Growth in the production of documents does not in itself thicken the graphosphere anywhere other than in the places where the documents were produced. Bureaucratic expansion brought vastly more people into the production process, in more places, but what were the implications for a wider graphosphere in this early period? We can, in crude outline, trace stages of broadening engagement, from passive inclusion to active participation.

Tax registers were among the earliest types of regularly compiled central administrative documents in Muscovy. A census official (*pisets* – originally 'scribe', 'clerk', but developing this specialised meaning) travelled with his team of assistants to inspect a given district and listed all persons and/or properties and/or objects relevant to the assessment of tax liability. The results were preserved as *pistsovye knigi*, census books. The earliest *pistsovye knigi* date from the second half of the fifteenth century.[47] A useful example is the sequence of surviving *pistsovye knigi* for the town of Staraia Russa near Novgorod.[48] The first in the sequence, dating from 1497/8, is the earliest surviving such document for any substantial urban settlement in Rus. It lists 1,133 homesteads (*dvory*), including those on land belonging to monasteries and churches, and their 3,763 named adult inhabitants, and assesses their individual and collective dues.[49] Those adults may well have been aware, through the visits of the census officials, that their existence was being recorded in writing, and that the written document had practical conquences for them, but their role in its production was passive. As a physical object the census record may or may not have been visible to them.

A more active kind of involvement is implied in a subsequent form of census document in the Staraia Russa sequence: the variant known as a *dozornaia kniga*, a record of a supplementary inspection. Such supplementary inspections were normally carried out at the request of the inhabitants. An extensive specimen from 1611 is structured around a collation of the observable facts with those recorded in a previous description. Often it is noted that a given homestead, listed in the earlier survey, was now empty, on several occasions with the explanation that it had been 'burned by Lithuanians'.[50] In other words, the town had been badly affected by war, and the inhabitants requested that their tax assessments be updated accordingly. Each section of the document concludes with a summary of the amount by which the previous liabilities have been reduced.[51] A further updated survey for 1624 lists extensive resettlement on empty plots, but also includes a long catalogue of deaths leading to the abandonment of previously worked land.[52] This census is also far more detailed. It includes exact measurements of plots of land, as well as inventories of valuables in the churches (icons, silver, books).[53]

Census records were compiled locally but held centrally. The next degree of participation was the copying of central records on behalf of, and to be retained by, those who were affected by them. For examples of this we move up the social scale, and from general surveys to the records of military service. In Muscovy the principal means of support for elite troops was through grants of properties which were meant to enable them to maintain and equip themselves. However, for much of the period military preferment was claimed on the basis of lineage and status rather than merit alone (the practice known as *mestnichestvo*, place-holding, formally abolished in 1682). The state therefore had to keep track of the families, their lands and their service records. The documents that were retained and renewed for the purpose were the *razriadnye knigi* (deployment books).[54] The official state versions of the deployment books, which survive in a sequence starting from the mid sixteenth century, include administrative records going back to 1475, and there is some evidence that notes on deployment were maintained from the 1460s.

The service records were supplemented by a cluster of related lists: genealogies (*rodoslovnye knigi*), temporary service lists (*boiarskie knigi, boiarskie spiski, zhiletskie spiski*), campaign and regimental lists (*pokhodnye* and *polkovye spiski*), payment lists (*okladnye knigi*), muster lists (*smotrennye spiski*), even – since genealogy and precedence mattered so much – wedding lists (*svadebnye rospisi*). These and other subsidiary lists, along with the record of individual rulings, went into the compilation and periodic revisions of the definitive *razriadnye knigi*. With the use of *razriadnye knigi* and related documents, Muscovite servitors – the emerging service gentry – found that their careeers depended on the information in the registers and archives. Several of them evidently reckoned that passive reliance on central documentation was not enough. They commissioned their own copies of (or extracts from, or supplemented versions of) the deployment, genealogical and matrimonial records. Many of the surviving manuscripts are from the archives of elite families.

Beyond the compilative records – far more numerous, far more broadly accessed and circulated in the wider graphosphere – was the incessantly multiplying mass of contingent documents, the diverse and ever diversifying bits of paperwork needed during the course of a transaction, petition, negotiation, dispute, court case, report etc. For any period these are almost impossible to track with precision, but an impression of patterns of growth in the early period can be formed from an inventory of the tsar's archive from the 1570s. The inventory lists large amounts of materials that have not survived.[55] It describes the contents of some 230 numbered boxes of various sizes.[56] Apparently the archive contained rather few documents from the fifteenth century. For the first half of the sixteenth century there was a preponderance of materials linked to foreign relations, while from the mid sixteenth century onwards domestic documents began to dominate. Eighty-nine boxes contained only domestic documents, in a kaleidoscope of forms, serving a wide variety of functions, including, as the list's modern editor puts it, 'all kinds of books, registers, extracts, releases, permits, decrees, memos, missives, transcripts, testimonies, cases etc.'[57] Beyond a general sense of quantity and variety, the inventory is hard to decode, since there was no consistent terminology of chancery documents, nor is there now a comprehensive modern scholarly taxonomy.[58] Even the standard handbooks are of rather little help for the most productive period of the *prikaz* system in the seventeenth century.[59]

One aid to survival was the way in which Muscovite record-keeping practice turned contingent documents into cumulative records. Some types of cumulative document in Muscovite administration were copied out as codices: that is to say, as what we would reckon normal books, on double-sided sheets joined at the inner margins. However, common practice before the late seventeenth century created a different format. First a document was produced in a rough, preliminary version. Then the fair copy was written on one side of one or more half-width sheets of paper. The sheets were then glued together end to end. Large numbers of such documents relevant to a particular process or case were similarly joined to form scrolls (*stolbtsy*; literally 'columns'). The authenticity of the *stolbtsy* was verified by the signature of scribes across each glued join on the reverse (i.e. blank) side.[60] The general switch from *stolbtsy* to books (codices) for the cumulative record of documents was decreed in a series of measures between 1700 and 1702.[61] To some extent, therefore, modern historians can reconstitute the more granular production of paperwork from surviving *stolbtsy*. For example, records of court cases typically consist of heterogeneous documents glued end to end: from initial complaints, through transcriptions of witness statements and other testimony (including testimony under torture), correspondence, reports and rulings.[62] The growth of documentary practices and requirements in court cases was a further catalyst for the growth of document-producing judicial personnel, whose presence, in turn, accelerated the growth of the paperwork.[63]

By the late seventeenth century the *prikaz* system had become too successful. It had become a vehicle not just for meeting demand but for generating fresh demand that overstrained its own capacity. Or, to view it in a different way, the *prikaz* system became overstrained because it was not really a system. Chanceries had formed, disappeared, expanded, contracted, multiplied and diversified with the growth of the state, but there was no overall design. Structural and procedural reforms in the early eighteenth century, and then again in the early nineteenth century, were systemic. However, they streamlined the bureaucracy only insofar as they were means for coping with the continuing growth. They were the organisational technologies for a thickening graphosphere of administrative writing. Peter I initially added to the numbers of *prikazy*, but in a series of measures beginning in 1717 and culminating in his General Regulation (*General'nyi reglament*) of 1720 he redesigned the administration around a much smaller (initially nine, then twelve) number of institutions, the 'colleges'.[64] This was followed in 1722 by his reform of the administrative career structure based on the Table of Ranks, which introduced the principle of advancement determined by qualification and merit rather than seniority and precedence.[65] Alexander I's manifesto of 8 September 1802 announced the establishment of ministries (eight, initially) rather than colleges.[66]

Administrative growth accelerated. Here the numbers are more eloquent than the structures. It has been estimated that in the mid eighteenth century the imperial bureaucracy consisted of some 10,000 officials. By 1800 the total was closer to 40,000, and by the mid nineteenth century the number had risen to around 112,000, including some 30,000 chancery copyists too junior to be graded in the fourteen ranks. This is not just an absolute increase in numbers. It represents a very signifiant increase in the proportion of bureaucrats in the population. Between 1750 and 1850 the empire's population approximately trebled, from about twenty-three million to some seventy million. Over the same period the number of civil servants increased tenfold.[67] As for the quantities of administrative documents: calculations of notional requirements for the mid nineteenth century reach figures that sound too grotesquely large to be routinely realistic. Provincial governors are said to have been supposed to sign more than 100,000 documents per year.[68] Some kinds of complex transaction are reckoned to have generated more than 1,300 documents each. The annual production rate of a single large ministry (the ministry of the interior) is calculated to have been in excess of thirty million documents, the overwhelming majority of which were handwritten.[69] It is hard to know how much credence to give to the figures, but even allowing for a wide margin of error the point remains essentially the same.

Bureaucracies produced bureaucrats who wrote. Bureaucrats who wrote did not necessarily only write bureaucratic things. The institutions of production were not the only contexts for the uses of the product. The expansion of writing in state service (or in church or monastic service) helped to generate what might be called 'spin-off' cultures of handwriting, a kind of graphospheric overspill. From as early as the first half of the sixteenth century we find *d'iaki*, and then a wider range of chancery staff, writing beyond their professional brief. Some took commissions to produce copies of devotional books. Others composed: from the *d'iak* Fedor Kuritsyn, in charge of diplomatic affairs under Ivan III in the late fifteenth century and associated with at least two literary and polemical works (including the *Tale of Drakula*),[70] to the 'chancery poets' or the 'printing office poets' of the seventeenth century.[71] One scholar has even described the chancery employees (or some of them, at any rate) as the 'intellectual elite' of Russia before the influx of foreigners in the late seventeenth and early eighteenth centuries.[72]

Most scribes were copyists. Deep into the nineteenth century, scribal copies could provide an effective alternative to printed publication. A dramatic illustration of scribal copying on an organised quasi-industrial scale relates to the dissemination of the play *Woe from Wit* (*Gore ot uma*) by Aleksandr Griboedov. Griboedov's play was finished in 1824. Short extracts were printed in a theatrical almanac in 1825. However, already in the second half of 1824 manuscript copies were being made, partly through individual initiatives, but partly through the efforts of Griboedov's friend Andrei Zhandr, who organised 'a whole chancery' of scribes to churn out multiple copies. The numbers are striking. By February 1831, when the censorship committee discussed the possibility of a printed edition, it was estimated that over 40,000 manuscript copies were already in circulation – more than for any printed book of the time.[73]

As bureaucracy spawned writers, so, eventually, writers spawned images of bureaucrats. Towards the mid nineteenth century the intellectual elites began to take note of scribes and copyists. If the *d'iak* Stefan Borodatyi can stand as a figure emblematic of the beginning of the processes outlined in this section, then some of the emblematic figures of its maturity are found in fiction. The government clerk, the minor civil servant, began to feature in Russian literature from approximately the mid 1830s: for example, in the Petersburg tales of Nikolai Gogol, or in Aleksandr Pushkin's narrative poem *The Bronze Horseman*. However, the most focussed and forensic fictional explorations of urban scribedom itself (rather than of city-dwellers who happened to be scribes) appeared a decade or so later, in early stories by Fedor Dostoevskii. Two contrasting tales, in particular, can exemplify Dostoevskii's reflections on the life of handwriting: his first published work, *Poor Folk* (*Bednye liudi*), from 1846, and *A Weak Heart* (*Slaboe serdtse*), published two years later. Both works are, in a sense, studies in the psychology of scribedom. In both works, the central characters reveal and discover themselves through the act of writing, but with very different implications. In one case, writing is an escape into self-expression; in the other case, writing is a catalyst for self-destruction. In one case it is a mode of psychological liberation, in the other it it becomes a burden too great to bear.

Poor Folk is an epistolary novella, a sentimental correspondence between Makar Devushkin and Varvara Dobroselova. Both live impecuniously in somewhat squalid conditions. Devushkin inhabits a partitioned-off area of a kitchen, from where he can see the window of Varvara's flat. What Devushkin does is write. Copying is his work, but writing is also his preoccupation. His vicarious delights are derived partly in his participation on the fringes of the literary circle of his 'friend' Rataziaev, partly through his relationship with Varvara. For Rataziaev he undertakes additional copying, and with Varvara he corresponds. The novel consists of his and Varvara's letters to each other over a six-month period from April to September. The letters are tender, sensitive, often effusive. He writes to her about his affection for her, about the small presents that he chooses for her. She writes to him about the tribulations of her life, of her affection for him and about ways out of her hopeless poverty. He writes to her about literature, about style, about his admired friend Rataziaev, although the examples that he quotes enthusiastically to Varvara strike her as somewhat tawdry. Varvara prefers to stick to Pushkin. Eventually she accepts an advantageous proposal from a Mr Bychkov, whom she barely even pretends to like. Devushkin is devastated. For Makar Devushkin, writing is an emotional necessity. Through the act of writing, and copying others' writings, and writing about writing, he finds meanings and purposes, feelings and aspirations that transcend the squalid day-to-day of his immediate surroundings. He writes because he needs to write, not because he is obliged to write. Writing gives him not just a link to people he loves and admires, but an inner life. Physically he inhabits his corner of the kitchen, but his mind is not contained. Writing is his means of immersion in a life which he never quite manages to lead.

The central figure in *A Weak Heart*, Vasia Shumkov, is like Makar Devushkin only in that he is sensitive and a scribe. In almost all else this is a story of a quite different pathology of writing. At the start of the story Vasia is happy, as he explains to his good friend Arkadii. He is engaged to Lizanka; and he is thrilled and grateful that the head of his office, Iulian Mastakovich, has generously given him some extra copying which will bring him money so that he can afford to marry. But he constantly puts off the copying. He prepares his quills, makes plans, falls asleep, finds distractions. His non-writing becomes obsessional. He is always about to finish. Naturally he loses Lizanka, but still he cannot let Iulian Mastakovich down. More and more frenzied, more and more nervous, he sits and scribbles and scribbles and scribbles; but the paper, as Arkadii discovers, is blank. His mind is gone. The doctors take him away. Such a pity, such a waste, reflects Iulian Mastakovich, since the copying was not particularly important anyway. Arkadii gazes over the Neva at twilight, and suddenly understands what has driven his friend to insanity.

A Weak Heart is in a tradition of tales of how the city first oppresses, then distorts and eventually destroys the minds of the poor and powerless trapped inside its seemingly unyielding physical and social structures. Vasia Shumkov, however, is the first for whom the catalyst for insanity was writing itself; or, rather, the catastrophic gulf between the perceived obligation to write and his incapacity to do so. He is the opposite of Makar Devushkin. Devushkin lives in order to write, Vasia believes he is obliged to write in order to live; but he cannot write so he loses his grip on his life. His mind is destroyed by an obsession with writing that turns out to be empty in all ways: empty because he actually writes nothing, empty because there had been nothing significant to write. For Makar Devushkin writing was an escape into deeper feelings and meanings; for Vasia Shumkov writing was an abyss of non-meaning, the ultimate obstacle to engagement with his own life. Makar Devushkin wants to write and finds a kind of freedom. Vasia Shumkov believes he is obliged to write, and is crushed. Either way, in the literary imagination towards the middle of the nineteenth century the government clerk – the quintessential handwriter – becomes a symbol of the distorting implications of urban modernity.

Printing: Russia's Non-Gutenberg Moments?

'Printing', in the present section, means printing with movable type, the technology whose introduction into Europe is associated with Johannes Gutenberg and his press in Mainz in the mid fifteenth century.

The European 'printing revolution' of the late fifteenth and early sixteenth centuries did not extend to Russia. This is either a puzzle, or not a puzzle. It is a puzzle if one takes literally the notion of technology as an agent or driver of change, or if one sees Western Europe as a norm. It need not be such a puzzle if one abandons a 'techno-determinist' assumption, or if one chooses not to hold up Western Europe as the model. Here the account of print in Russia is framed in terms of 'non-Gutenberg moments', but this should not be taken to imply that Russia *should have been* more Gutenbergian, more like Western Europe. The purpose of the ostensibly negative comparison is to help locate and interpret difference.

We do not need to define precisely the 'printing revolution'. On the one hand, nobody would seriously argue that in Western and Central Europe the introduction and spread of printing in the second half of the fifteenth century and the first half of the sixteenth century put an end to the culture of manuscripts, caused the development of entrepreneurial capitalism, and was the sole or principal reason for the flourishing of humanist culture, the Reformation, the rise of science and the emergence of the early modern state. On the other hand, few would deny some role for printing in facilitating or contributing to at least some of these phenomena. We can choose to regard the printing revolution as rapid, or slow, or to reconceptualise revolution as evolution. Pendulums swing, scholars rightly dispute the adequacy of any paradigm that looks like turning into a dogma. In the comparison with Russia a basic contrast is nevertheless plain. Johannes Gutenberg began printing in the early 1450s. By the end of the fifteenth century one could travel the length and breadth of Western and Central Europe – from Leiden to Capua, from Nantes to Brno – and never be very far from a printing press.[74] In Russia in 1500 there were no printing presses at all, and by 1650 there was just one, or perhaps two. How should we explain such a stark difference in the dynamics of engagement with the new technology?

Many kinds of explanation have been offered. Some relate to the individual circumstances of particular episodes. Others look at recurrent patterns. Some see political hostility, or popular suspicion, or government repression, or cultural indifference. Others stress the positive aims and values of Muscovite culture that were served by such printing as there was and that rendered wider use of print redundant. Others point to a likely lack of demand for the product given the high costs of early production.[75] One problem with much of the literature on the subject is that it tends to assume that the issue relates specifically to engagement with print in the sixteenth and seventeenth centuries, before Peter I. Here, however, the argument is that Russian printing was in certain fundamental respects 'non-Gutenbergian' almost to the end of the eighteenth century. Therefore, without necessarily rejecting local explanations, I focus on structural features that are relevant to the entire period.[76]

The present study will highlight two factors, above all, that help to provide an explanatory framework for the reception and production of print in Russia. The first of the two factors relates to ownership: specifically, to ownership of the means of production. In Russia, almost continuously from the origins of native printing through to the final years of the eighteenth century, printing was a monopoly or near-monopoly. Almost all presses, for almost all of the period, were either owned directly by the state, as departments of the administration, or were allocated and licensed to state institutions (which included, from the early eighteenth century, the church). Printing was an instrument of policy. The scale and scope of printing were as robust as the priorities of its monopoly owner. In Western Europe, too, patrons played a role, but the most striking feature is their diversity. Elizabeth Eisenstein makes the point that the proliferation of presses in Western Europe does not correlate well with the rise of major centres of political power. More important was 'the presence in late medieval Europe of numerous small political units: bishoprics, communes, free cities, and other assorted quasi-independent states'.[77]

The second factor is, in part, a corollary of the first, although it relates to structures of economic activity rather than to ownership as such. In Russia, before the late eighteenth century, printing was not a commercial, market-based activity. That is to say, the products of the printing press were available to be bought and sold, but the technology itself was not. There was a market in books, but not in the skills of the printer. The archives of the Moscow Print Yard in the seventeenth century show that printers were well aware of budgets and costings, that they were subject to financial constraints. But this was a market limited by the choices and purposes of the suppliers. Sales might affect what was *re*printed, but were of little consequence in shaping or extending the range of what was printed. Nor is it adequate to object that there was simply no demand for greater quantity or variety.[78] In open markets, supply does not just meet demand, it can create demand. In much of Western Europe printing shops were businesses. Some, to be sure, had patrons prepared to subsidise production in the interests of prestige or piety or power, but in general printers survived or failed or thrived by their success in offering their skills and their technology for sale. The market in the technology of printing was a powerful driver both of the proliferation of competing printers and in the diversification of their products; and, conversely, the presence of a printing press could boost local urban economies well beyond the market for its own productions.[79] To put it crudely, in Russia the monopoly printers hoped that demand would meet supply, while in the more commercial west printers competed to stimulate and then meet demand.[80]

To reduce several centuries of cultural phenomena to two major causes is of course an oversimplification. Nor is the argument fully demonstrable, since we cannot re-enact the scenario or rerun the experiment. Nor would it be remotely reasonable to reduce the printing revolution in Western Europe to the operations of a particular kind of market. Nor is Western Europe necessarily the only or the most appropriate point of comparison: there are other places (Turkey, for example, or China) where printing also did not spread in the same way as in Western Europe or with the same social and cultural implications. Nevertheless the usefulness and validity of the approach do not depend on (or amount to a claim to) completeness.

Monopoly ownership, and the absence of competitive, market-driven production, will be *leitmotifs* of the discussions in several of the following chapters. However, print in the Russian graphosphere was not limited to print produced in Russia (or in Russian). The history of printing in Russia is only one aspect of the history of the Russian engagement with print. The place of production could be, but was not necessarily, a relevant determinant of graphospheric function. Most histories of print in Russia begin with the first Moscow-printed books. Here the sequence of 'non-Gutenberg moments' begins more than half a century earlier.

Russia's first non-Gutenberg moment occurred at the end of the fifteenth century. In the 1490s Archbishop Gennadii of Novgorod commissioned a Church Slavonic version of the Bible. The 'Gennadian Bible', finished in 1498/9, was innovative in at least three respects. In the first place, despite more than half a millennium of Slavonic Christianity, this was the earliest complete and continuous text of the Bible in Church Slavonic. Until the Gennadian version, Slavonic Christianity had known books of the Bible, but not the Bible as a book. Liturgical and 'reading' versions of the New Testament were common enough, as were the readings from the Old Testament necessary to ecclesiastical and monastic devotion. Chunks of the Old Testament also appear in chronographic or prophetological compilations.[81] When added together, these collectively would amount to almost a complete Bible, but they were *not* added together before Gennadii. Secondly, the revisions and fresh translations commissioned by Gennadii were not based on the Greek Septuagint, which was the traditionally authoritative text in eastern Christianity. In the 1490s there were in any case no printed versions of the Septuagint, the earliest being the Aldine version of 1518 and the Greek text in the 'Complutensian' polyglot Bible of 1520. Instead, Gennadii's translators turned to the Latin Vulgate, and in places even to German and Czech. Thirdly, the sources for these revisions and fresh translations were not manuscript texts, but printed books. Several of the printed sources have been identified: editions of the Latin Vulgate printed by Koberger (Nuremberg, 1487) and Kessler (Basel, 1487 or 1491); the Low German Bibles of Heinrich Quentel (Cologne, c. 1478); the Czech Vulgate (Prague, 1488 or 1489).[82] New translations filled gaps in the received texts of, especially, Jeremiah and Ezekiel, while the books of 1–2 Chronicles, Ezra, Nehemiah, 1–2 Esdras, Tobit, Judith, the Wisdom of Solomon and 1–2 Maccabees were translated from scratch.[83]

Besides providing source texts for individual sections, the West European printed Bibles probably contributed to the very notion of producing a Bible as a single book. The first use, in Russia, of the Latinism *Bibliia*, as a feminine singular noun uniting in one object all the 'books' of its Greek neuter plural prototype (*ta biblia*), seems to be its appearance on the verso of the first leaf of the manuscript of the Gennadii Bible, in a roundel containing the title and production details of the book: 'In 7007 [1499] this book was written, called *Bibliia*, that is [the book of] both Testaments, the Old and the New'.[84] Anybody with the most fleeting acquaintance with West European printing of the second half of the fifteenth century could hardly have been unaware of the prominence of the Bible. The *Incunabula Short Title Catalogue* (*ISTC*) lists some fifty editions of the Latin Bible before 1500, plus further printings in German, French, Italian and Czech.[85]

Between them the translators in Novgorod were quite adequately aware of print. Archbishop Gennadii put together an international team: Gerasim Popovka (apparently the supervisor), Dmitri Gerasimov, Vlasii Ignatov and Timofei Veniaminov, a Catholic monk called Benjamin (Veniamin), possibly from Croatia, Nicolaus Bulow from Lübeck and, most intriguingly in the present context, another Lübecker, Bartholomaeus Ghotan. Bartholomaeus Ghotan was himself a jobbing printer. He had worked in Lübeck, Magdeburg and Stockholm, printing in Latin and in vernacular languages, anything from a lavish missal to ephemeral broadsides and almanacs. He even brought with him several of the products of his own press. Maybe he hoped to ply his craft in Novgorod itself. But Bartholomaeus Ghotan did *not* introduce the practice of printing to Russia.[86] As for the notion of actually replicating Gennadii's manuscript project in printed form: a further eighty-two years would pass before the first East Slav printed Bible, produced in 1581 in Ostroh (in Ruthenia) by Ivan Fedorov; and, in a pleasing but doubtless spurious chronological symmetry, a further eighty-two years passed before the publication, in 1663, of the first complete Bible to be printed in Moscow. Even this turned out to be an isolated episode. The next complete printed Bible in Russia appeared eighty-eight years later, in 1751. Only then did the printing of Bibles become relatively regular. The lack of use for the Bible as such was noted by visitors. The Englishman Giles Fletcher, who led an embassy to Moscow in 1588, found it striking that even the higher clergy knew the Scriptures only insofar as they recited and sang them in the perfomance of the liturgy.[87]

Besides the Bible, there were other engagements with imported printed books in the early decades of the sixteenth century, in many cases involving members of the same team of translators.[88] Nor was Bartholomaeus Ghotan the only immigrant with direct experience of printing. A still more influential figure in Muscovite letters, in the second quarter of the sixteenth century, was a Greek monk, born Michael Trivolis around 1470 but known in Moscow by his monastic name of Maximos, and given the sobriquet 'the Greek': hence 'Maksim Grek'. As a young man Michael had lived and worked in northern Italy – Florence, Padua, Milan, Venice. He knew several of the distinguished humanists of the day, was impressed by the preaching of Girolamo Savonarola, and in Venice was associated with (and perhaps employed by) the printer Aldus Manutius. In 1502 he became a novice in the monastery of San Marco in Florence, and in 1506 (after a couple more years with Aldus) left Italy to settle in the Vatopedi monastery on Mt Athos. In 1516 he was invited to Moscow to assist in a translation of commentaries on the Acts and Epistles and on the Psalms. This turned out to be his final major journey and by far his longest sojourn. Once in Muscovy, Maksim was never allowed to leave. He died at the Trinity monastery of St Sergii, probably in December 1555.[89]

Maksim Grek produced a substantial corpus of translations from Greek,[90] although most of them were probably derived from manuscript originals. He was also involved in polemics against the translation work of Nicolaus Bulow.[91] He attacked the 'German deceiver'[92] as a proponent of 'Latin' theology and ecclesiology and as an advocate of astrology. Specifically with regard to material translated from printed Latin sources: Maksim derided Bulow's dissemination of Johannes Stöffler's *Almanac*, with its talk of planetary signs and of propitious and unpropitious days, and its prediction of a deluge in 1524.[93] Again, therefore, the products of the printing press had some cultural resonance in Russia; but again engagement with the products was divorced from any engagement with the technology.

About printed books themselves, as physical objects, there was almost total silence. The colophon to one of the translations by Nicolaus Bulow states that the original was a printed book.[94] Apart from this, the only source that indicates any local curiosity is a letter from Maksim Grek to the man who commissioned several of his translations, Vasilii Mikhailovich Tuchkov. Maksim possessed Aldine printed books. Tuchkov noticed the Aldine device of an anchor with a fish twisting round its shaft, and asked Maksim to explain. Maksim begins: 'you have bid me explain the meaning of the emblem which you saw in a printed book'.[95] After referring to his own past links with Aldus Manutius in Venice, Maksim explains that the anchor represents firm faith and the fish represents the soul. That is to say, the first recorded inquiry about an imported printed book, as an object, relates to ornament, not to text. This is consistent with the broader Muscovite receptivity to West European printed ornament.[96]

Besides Latin and German and Greek, another potential source for imported printed books was Slavonic. Slavonic printing is much older than Russian printing. The earliest printing in Slavonic languages, in Latin script, dates from 1468. I have already noted that Gennadii's translators may have used a Czech source printed in 1488 or 1489. Slavonic printing in Cyrillic characters began in 1491, when Schweipolt Fiol produced an *Oktoechos* at his press in Krakow.[97] Over the following decades Cyrillic printing presses operated (more or less sporadically) in Cetinje, Targovishte, Prague, Venice, Vilnius and Gorazde and at the Milesheva, Grachanitsa and Rujno monasteries in Serbia. Several of these early Cyrillic printed books may have found their way to Muscovy,[98] although evidence is sparse. For example, among the nearly 150 copies of pre-1550 Cyrillic printed books in the collections of the Russian State Library, only one includes marginal inscriptions which might place it in sixteenth-century Muscovy.[99] A mid-sixteenth-century manuscript of the Gennadian Bible adds prefaces from Francis Skaryna's editions of several books of the Bible, and a monastic inventory of books from 1545 has a couple of entries which probably also allude to Skaryna's editions.[100] Maksim Grek almost certainly used parts of Skaryna's Cyrillic Bible.[101] So: there is limited but tangible evidence of the presence and use of some Slavonic and Cyrillic printed books in Muscovy before Muscovite Cyrillic printing.

Thus, from the 1490s and through the first half of the sixteenth century, a range of printed books began to feature in the Russian graphosphere. However, contact with the products of print did not at this stage prompt

Muscovites to adopt the technology of printing. How is this non-influence to be explained? Should it be attributed to hostility or to indifference? Some have argued that there was strong resistance.[102] The most dramatic reported incident of hostility to imported printed books is referred to in a tantalisingly brief note sent c. 1552 by the Polish king Sigismund Augustus, about an episode which had occurred during the reign of his father, Sigismund I (d. 1548). It seems that printed copies of the Scriptures 'in the Russian language' (*lingua russica imprimi*, most likely a reference to books printed by Skaryna) were brought to Moscow, where the prince ordered them to be burnt, on the grounds that they had been produced under the authority of the Roman church.[103] Nowhere, however, is it stated that printing itself was suspect. The polemics and the reported polemics relate to provenance ('Roman', 'Latin', 'German'), not to technology.[104] There is no statement of technophobia as such. Printing is neither attacked nor lauded.

Russia's second non-Gutenberg moment was the episode which, at first glance, ought to have been the most closely analogous to the Gutenbergian: the introduction of the printing press to Moscow, the beginning of native printing. However, the episode lasted only about fifteen years, from approximately 1553 to 1568. The published output during this period amounts to just eleven known titles. Printing then disappeared from Moscow for a further two decades, until 1589, although in the late 1570s a further two titles were printed outside Moscow, at Ivan IV's residence at Aleksandrovskaia Sloboda. Somewhat later in the century there was a further brief episode of provincial printing: two editions of a short liturgical text relating to a local icon, produced in Kazan.[105]

The earliest Moscow-printed books were produced anonymously. Seven such imprints survive from the mid sixteenth century: three editions of the Gospels (in three different typefaces), two editions of the Psalter (which share typefaces with two of the Gospels), a Lenten Triodion and a Festal Triodion (again, in different typefaces). They were probably produced over the course of about a decade, starting around 1553.[106] Although these anonymous publications were not particularly rare (most survive in several dozen copies), and although – according to inscriptions from the 1550s and 1560s in surviving copies – they appear to have been quite widely distributed,[107] the circumstances of their production remain obscure. The first known, named printer was Ivan Fedorov. In 1564, in collaboration with Petr Timofeevich Mstislavets, he produced his *Acts and Epistles* (*Apostol*), Moscow's earliest dated imprint. In the following year Fedorov published two further books; or, rather, two printings of the same book, a Breviary (*Chasovnik*), issued within a month of each other in September and October 1565.[108] Then he left Moscow. The final publication in this episode was another Psalter, printed by Nikifor Tarasiev and Nevezha Timofeev in 1568.[109]

Why were the Moscow presses founded, and why did they so quickly founder? The evidence is very limited. There are statements in four near-contemporary Muscovite colophons: in all three of Fedorov's publications of 1564–5, and in Tarasiev and Timofeev's 1568 Psalter. Fedorov also provides a retrospective narrative some years later, in his next *Apostol* printed in Lviv in 1574. Otherwise we have only later anecdotes and speculations. Regarding the institutional structures, all four Muscovite colophons make it clear that the presses were founded on the authority of Tsar Ivan IV and of respective metropolitans (Makarii, then Afanasii).[110] The colophons to the *Apostol* and the Psalter both suggest that among the reasons was a desire to avoid scribal inconsistency and error and hence to obtain reliable correct texts.[111] Others have suggested that print was adopted in order to solve a problem of dissemination, to meet a need for more liturgical books than could be produced quickly by scribes. But what was the need? Some take up a hint in Fedorov's colophon that Ivan IV turned to print in order to provide books for new parishes after the conquest of Kazan in 1552. However, the chronological indicators in the 1564 colophon allow various interpretations.[112] Others have pointed out that initial interest in print seems to have pre-dated the conquest of Kazan, and may have been prompted by a catastrophic loss of books in a fire in Moscow in 1547.[113] The uncomfortable fact is that this first stage in the adoption of print, this apparently momentous event in Muscovite cultural history, passed unexplained and virtually unrecorded at the time except – briefly – by some of the printers themselves.

Nor do we know why the episode ended. Two decades later Giles Fletcher reports on the burning of a printing press 'some yeres past in the other Emperor's time', and there was a suspicion that the arson had been 'by the procurement of the Clergy men.'[114] However, if this story has any basis, it probably refers to a later incident, since Fedorov's type and plates survived to be re-used.[115] Fedorov himself, in an autobiographical section of his 1574 Lviv colophon, claims that he was driven out of Moscow by the jealousy and malevolence of 'many officials and hierarchs and teachers', ignorant both of letters and of spiritual wisdom,[116] and some scholars support the view that the introduction of printing was halted, at least in part, because of a technophobic reaction.[117] Perhaps Fedorov found that support had evaporated because of a change of personnel and political priorities: the onset of Ivan's *oprichnina* in 1565, and/or the resignation of Metropolitan Afanasii in May of the following year.[118] There is no independent evidence, no visible controversy. Printing started, and fizzled out. And then it started again, and fizzled out again. A curious feature of the colophon to the 1568 Psalter of Nikifor Tarasiev and Nevezha Timofeev is that it tells of how Ivan IV, along with Metropolitan Afanasii, decided to establish a printing press, and of how this book – that is, the Psalter of 1568 – was the press's first publication.[119] This contemporary version of the origin of Muscovite printing contains not a word about Fedorov (who also claimed the patronage of Ivan IV) or of Afanasii's predecessor, Metropolitan Makarii. It is as if this was a new beginning. The initiative survived no longer than its first book: another false start.

Ivan Fedorov has acquired a spurious modern reputation as the emblematic Muscovite 'first printer' (*pervopechatnik*). His significance for the history of Muscovite printing and, *a fortiori*, for the history of Muscovite culture, was marginal. However, in the wider history of East Slav Cyrillic printing, Ivan Fedorov must indeed be reckoned a major figure. Although he always represented himself as a Muscovite, by far the longest and most productive part of his career was spent outside Muscovy. In Zabludov, on the estate of the Lithuanian noble Grigorii Khodkevich (Grzegorz Chodkiewicz), in 1569 he produced a Gospel Homiliary (*Evangelie uchitel'noe*) and in 1570 a Psalter. In 1574, having moved to Lviv, he produced a second *Apostol* and a primer. A second edition of the primer came out in 1578, now under the patronage of Prince Konstantin Konstantinovich Ostrozhskii. Also in Ostroh Fedorov printed a Gospel and Psalter (1580), plus a concordance to the New Testament (1580), as well as his complete Bible (1580–1).

Ivan Fedorov can be credited with a remarkable list of 'firsts': not only the first dated Moscow-printed book, but the first book printed in Ukraine (the 1574 *Apostol*), the first printed East Slav primer, the first systematic East Slav alphabetic printed index, the first East Slav printing of Greek (in the primers), and – the culmination of his *oeuvre* – the first complete printed Cyrillic Bible. Along the way, he was also responsible for the first printed editions of any work by an author from early Rus (a sermon of Kirill of Turov, included in the *Gospel Homiliary*), the first printing of any work of an early Bulgarian author (the treatise on the origins of Slav letters, attributed to the monk Khrabr, included in the 1578 version of the primer) and the first East Slav printed calendar, which is also the earliest surviving specimen of East Slav printed ephemera (a verse calendar by Andrei Rymsha).[120] The contrast between the two phases and contexts of Ivan

Fedorov's career is indicative. After he left Moscow, he became a craftsman for hire, moving from patron to patron, selling his skills wherever he found a market for them. That is, his employments fit a pattern for the career of a jobbing printer in early modern Europe: market-driven (where market variants include serial patronage) and peripatetic. The non-Muscovite dynamic of production gave him the scope for a non-Muscovite type of career, as a participant in a non-Muscovite mode of diffusion for the technology of print.

The continuous history of institutionalised printing in Moscow began in the late 1580s. In 1587 Tsar Fedor Ivanovich again decided to found a press. The first book to be completed, in November 1589, was a Lenten Triodion. Fedor's printer was Andronik Timofeev Nevezha. A decade earlier Nevezha had been the printer under Ivan IV's patronage at Aleksandrovskaia Sloboda. He may also have been the Nevezha Timofeev who worked with Nikifor Tarasiev on the 1568 Moscow Psalter.[121] He had therefore been closely involved in the spasmodic earlier initiatives of Fedor's father. On this occasion, however, the foundation became permanent. After the 1589 Triodion Nevezha produced a further nine titles until his death in late 1602 or early 1603.[122] From 1603 his son, Ivan Andronikov Nevezhin, was responsible for another seven titles. In 1606 and 1610 two volumes were printed at the same press by Anisim Mikhailov Radishevskii, and in 1609 Nikita Fedorov Fofanov worked on a menaion.[123] Rather than being a periodic royal initiative, printing had become an activity embedded in the administrative structure of the state.[124] The Moscow Print Yard (*Pechatnyi dvor*) on Nikolskaia Street just east of the Kremlin had occasional precursors, but as a continuous institution it can plausibly be traced to the press set up under the patronage of Tsar Fedor Ivanovich in the late 1580s.

Production was interrupted in 1611 after a fire at the press, during the troubled period of Polish occupation, when conditions for restoring and reviving it were not favourable. On this occasion the hiatus lasted four years, and again it was ended by royal foundation or refoundation. In 1613 the new tsar, Mikhail Romanov, tried briefly to set up a press at Nizhnii Novgorod, under Nikita Fofanov, but in mid 1614, after the incomplete printing of just one book, Fofanov returned to Moscow and work resumed at the Print Yard. The first book at the restored press, a Psalter, was completed on 6 January 1615. If we choose to regard the break in 1611 as yet another in the sequence of significant interruptions to a tradition that was still fragile, then the start of the continuous institutionalised history of printing in Russia dates from January 1615.

However we choose to resolve question of origins, seventeenth-century Muscovite printing quickly became established on a different level. The first sixty years of Muscovite printing resulted in fewer than forty editions. This constituted not much more than about 10 per cent of Cyrillic printed book production over the period. Almost as many titles were produced in Venice, let alone at the press of the Mamonichi in Vilnius.[125] From 1615 to 1700 the Moscow Print Yard issued well over four hundred known editions, with print runs totalling more than a million copies.[126] Production came to resemble a small factory rather than a craft workshop. Records of the Print Chancery survive from 1619 onwards, and allow a fairly detailed reconstruction of many aspects of the Print Yard's operations. By the late 1620s the Print Yard was operating ten presses,[127] and the norm for the rest of the century was between eight and a dozen. Each press was run by a team of at least eleven, supervised by two compositors. At peak periods the Print Yard had more than 150 employees.[128]

Although it can be defined institutionally as being subject to the palace administration through the Print Chancery, the principal function of the Moscow Print Yard was to serve the practical needs of the church. Almost all its books were devotional in a broad sense, supporting ecclesiastical practice, education and edification.[129] The balance of production can be presented in various ways. If we were to judge by what might appear in catalogue entries or bibliographies – that is, by named titles and editions – then the two largest categories of output were liturgical, and exegetic or edificatory. Each of these would account for around 40 per cent of catalogue entries. If, however, we judge by the numbers of copies printed, then these are outnumbered by alphabet books (*azbuki*) and primers (*bukvari*). In statements of the output of the Print Yard, the discrepancy between titles and print runs can be illustrated at its widest point, in a comparison between the production of *azbuki* and the production of Bibles. The Moscow Print Yard published just one edition of a complete Bible, in 1663. The 1663 Bible was the first and only Moscow-printed Bible before the mid eighteenth century. A standard unit of production at the Print Yard was 1,200 copies. The 1663 Bible was issued in a double print run: that is, 2,400 copies. *Azbuki* were printed in, for example, double runs in 1651 and 1654, then further double runs in March and June 1655, single runs in June and August 1657, a quadruple run (4,800 copies) in August 1658, further double runs in March 1659 and February 1660, and so on. Demand grew. By 1670 the minor multiples of the 'normal' print run of 1,200 copies were clearly not enough: 6,000 were printed in August 1667, 9,600 (split between two issues) in July and November 1668, and eventually 12,000 in November 1670 (i.e. ten times the early norm), and this huge print run was repeated in mid 1673, and again in September 1674.[130] It has been calculated that, in the second half of the seventeenth century, the Moscow Print Yard produced more than fifty issues of the *azbuka*, with a combined print run of well over a quarter of a million copies.[131]

From these figures it would seem that *azbuki* kept the presses far busier than Bibles, and in a sense this was the case. Certainly *azbuki* were a more regular and important part of the press's business. However, if we look instead at the actual outlay of resources, the gap narrows again. Each *azbuka* could be printed on a single sheet of paper, folded three times to make eight leaves or a maximum of sixteen sides or pages. Thus, for example, for the double print run of 1652 the press bought only four reams and sixteen quires of print-quality paper: that is, 4 x 500 plus 16 x 25 sheets = 2,400 sheets.[132] A quarter of a million *azbuki* require a quarter of a million sheets of paper across half a century. This is significantly less than the nearly 400,000 sheets required for the 2,400 copies of the sole edition of the Bible in 1663.

How does this relate to markets? I have asserted that a characteristic feature of Russian printing was that it was not driven by a market in the technology. However, this does not mean that market forces were irrelevant to production. The archives of the Print Chancery include detailed records of costs and of sales. At first, sales were, in effect, subsidised. The job of the press was to supply churches with the necessary books. It was not required to generate profits, but it was normally expected to cover its costs. Initially this was interpreted as covering only the direct costs of production, but, following a fire in 1634, the sale price of books included a mark-up to cover overheads and depreciation.[133] For example, the unit cost for the production of the press's most expensive book, the 1663 Bible, was about three and a half roubles (after allowing for approximately 100 free copies for proof-readers, the Palace Chancery and others), and the sale price was five roubles – enough to buy fifteen bullocks or more than a year's supply of bread.[134] By contrast, the unit cost of the 1652 *azbuka* was one *polushka* (½ denga or ¼ kopek) per copy. It was put on sale at 2 dengas (1 kopek): a handy mark-up of 300 per cent, but still 500 times cheaper than the Bible.

Two other imprints operated in Moscow during the period. Both were relatively short-lived. From 1633 to 1642 Vasilii Burtsov ran a parallel operation on two presses in a room in the same building as the Print Yard. He acquired equipment with the aid of a subsidy from the patriarch, but otherwise seems to have been a licensed independent printer, hiring his own workers. Burtsov produced approximately twenty titles, similar in repertoire to those of the main Print Yard, though with some distinctive features of design. He is particularly noted for his influential primers (*bukvari*) of 1634 and 1637.[135] Some forty years later another Moscow-based press was set up independently of the Print Yard. Again the initiative can hardly be said to signal a move away from the dominance of the state, since the patron was Tsar Fedor Alekseevich, and the location of the new press was the Kremlin itself. Fedor founded the press in 1679 as a vehicle for his own mentor, Simeon Polotskii. Although Polotskii died in August 1680, his Upper Printing House (Verkhniaia tipografiia) survived until 1683. Among its publications were four books by Polotskii himself, as well as a number of official documents.[136]

Outside Moscow the Muscovite print landscape was beginning to become more complicated. Between 1658 and 1661 three books were printed at a press set up by Patriarch Nikon at the Iverskii monastery which he had founded at Valdai to the south-east of Novgorod. Nikon imported both the equipment and its operators from the monastery of the Epiphany at Kutein (Orsha, in Belarus).[137] The first book was conventional, a Horologion (1658), but the second was his own work, *Paradise of the Spirit* (*Rai myslennyi*, 1658–9), followed by *Spiritual Nourishment* (*Brashno dukhovnoe*, 1661). In July 1658, in dispute with Aleksei Mikhailovich about the balance of authority between church and tsar, Nikon unilaterally absented himself from his patriarchal duties. The press at the Iverskii monastery could thus be regarded as Russia's first unofficial – even 'dissident' – press.

The source of Nikon's equipment – Kutein – indicates the main additional dimension of printing in Muscovy in the late seventeenth century. Ruthenia had long been a source of Cyrillic books printed in far greater abundance than in Muscovy. Sometimes the import of such books was unimpeded, sometimes it was resisted. We have seen reference to an alleged episode of such resistance in the first half of the sixteenth century. In 1627–32 there was an attempt to ban the import and distribution of 'Lithuanian' printed books and manuscripts, ostensibly on the grounds that they may be doctrinally contaminated. Measures included expulsions of 'Lithuanian' book traders, confiscation of books and burning of books.[138] With the annexation of 'left-bank' Ukraine in mid century, parts of a previously non-Muscovite printing tradition found themselves within Muscovy's political orbit. In Kiev, in particular, the press at the Caves monastery had been producing books regularly since its foundation in 1615.[139] From mid century, therefore, Muscovy incorporated a flourishing kindred but distinct tradition of print culture. This was an important component of the broader contact with and reception of Ukrainian learning and cultural practices, which had significant repercussions for Muscovite culture itself in the latter part of the century.

The next candidate for a Russian 'Gutenberg moment' is the early eighteenth century and the innovations associated with Peter. One scholar has put the claim bluntly: the Petrine reforms 'entailed the full implantation in Russia of the European print revolution.'[140] The claim is misleading. Peter I did make radical changes to the culture of print in Russia. He introduced a new mission for print, which involved expanding the repertoire and changing the appearance. However, Peter did nothing to change the essential features of the structures within which the technology of print functioned in Russia. The new mission was developed, as before, in the context of print's service to the state.[141] Previously print had, in effect, served the state through supporting the church. Peter turned print into an instrument of state administration and information: both as a practical tool of governance, facilitating what might be called 'hard' power, and as a medium for projecting an approved image of the state and its culture (that is, as a medium for what might now be called 'soft' power). In adding this functionality, he also introduced a graphic device by which to distinguish it from the products of print's traditional (and by no means defunct) mission. This was his 'civil' typeface.[142]

Under Peter, print looked different, and it conveyed new messages in non-traditional contexts. But this was not a printing revolution. On the contrary, in one fundamental respect Peter's strategy for print was deeply conventional. The contents and functions and appearance of print continued to be determined in an entirely 'top-down' process and structure. Petrine Russia did not become a country of market-orientated jobbing printers. There was no move to dismantle or relax or circumvent the monopoly of ownership of the means of production. As before, print served power. What changed was simply that those in power adjusted and expanded the definitions and parameters of such service.

On the surface there were adjustments in governance, and even a degree of institutional diversification. The Moscow Print Yard was retained, though under a succession of different supervisory arrangements. Oversight had traditionally been exercised by the patriarch, but on the death of Patriarch Adrian in 1700 Peter forbade the election of a successor. In 1701 the Print Yard was placed under the supervision of the Monastery Chancery (*Monastyrskii prikaz*). In 1719 oversight was transferred briefly to the Exchequer, or Office of Expenditure (the *Shtats-kontora kollegiia*), whence in 1721 it was passed on to the College of Church Affairs (*Dukhovnaia kollegiia*), or (as it was renamed almost immediately) the Holy Synod. Meanwhile four new printing houses were authorised in St Petersburg: the 'St Petersburg press' in 1711; two contrasting presses in 1719, one attached to the Senate, one to the Aleksandr Nevskii monastery; and in 1721 a press at the Naval Academy.

Fringe developments contribute to an impression of diversity. In 1705 Peter gave permission to Vasilii Kiprianov to establish a 'Civil press' (*Grazhdanskaia tipografiia*) in Moscow, with quite an ambitious stated programme of book-publishing. In fact Kiprianov printed just two 'proper' books in nearly twenty years (1716 and 1723, on mathematics and on geometry), while his main occupation was as a maker and publisher of engravings.[143] In 1703 the exiled King Archil of Georgia was allowed to set up a press at the village of Vsekhsviatskoe, or Vsesviatskoe, just outside Moscow (now absorbed into the city, in the Sokol region), to print books in the Georgian language. The first, a Psalter, appeared in 1705.[144] In 1722 a 'campaign press' was set up temporarily in Astrakhan, after the equipment and type was floated down the Volga in a flat-bottomed boat in order to print Peter's manifesto reassuring the local population, in Turkish.[145] In the meantime, the empire gained further presses by default. After the annexation of Livonia and Estonia in 1710, much of the local infrastructure was left unchanged, including printing presses in Riga and Reval (modern Tallinn).

In hindsight the most prescient of the Petrine organisational initiatives (if the measure of prescience is the extent of future development) was the founding of the Naval Academy press in 1721. The major distinctive development in Russian print production in the second and third quarters of the eighteenth century was the expansion of presses licensed to educational and scholarly institutions. By imperial decree of 4 October 1727 the Petersburg press and the Aleksandr Nevskii monastic press were to be closed, and their equipment was to be transferred to the Synod press in Moscow, leaving just the Senate press to print official publications. However, the same decree also confirmed the status of a new and highly significant venture: the Academy of Sciences press. Over the next three decades the Academy of Sciences press was responsible for about half of all new titles printed in Russia.[146] In the 1750s and 1760s a cluster of St Petersburg military schools were authorised to run presses: the Naval Cadet Corps from 1753, the Infantry Cadet Corps from 1757, the Artillery and Engineering Corps in 1765. And, perhaps most momentously of all, the practice spread to Moscow, where the virtual monopoly of the church (through the Synod press) was finally broken by the establishment of Moscow University Press, which has operated continuously from 1756, the year after the University's foundation.[147]

Whether directly run by departments of the administration, or licensed to the institutions, almost all printing houses were ultimately owned or controlled by the state. The next shift was indeed towards the growth of private participation in, and eventually ownership of, printing houses. The process was rapid, but can be broken down into a series of overlapping phases.

In the first phase, the institutional publishing houses began regularly to take private commissions, in effect to sell their services. This could take place subtly or blatantly. The subtle way was to require a contribution towards the cost of publication, a financial subsidy even when a given book was formally issued (published) by the press. Thus, for example, the Society for the Printing of Books, whose leading lights were Nikolai Novikov and Karl Müller, reached a part-funding agreement with the Academy of Sciences press for the publication of translations.[148] In a variant version of this practice, institutional presses could simply agree to print for a fee, without acknowledgement of their own involvement. Such was the case with, for example, the rise of what tend, somewhat misleadingly, to be called 'private journals', which began to appear between 1759 and 1764, and then again from 1769 onwards. One consequence, for the first time in Russia, was a clear division between the function of printer and the function of publisher. All the 'private' journals were printed at the established institutional presses, although often the press was not mentioned. Thus, for example, the 1769 journals *Adskaia pochta, I to i sio, Ni to ni sio, Poden'shchina, Smes'*, and *Truten'* all included references to the place of publication, but not to a printing house, though in fact all of them were printed either at the Academy of Sciences press or at the Naval Cadet Corps press. *Adskaia pochta* (*The Infernal Post*) even satirised the situation on its title page, which proclaims: 'Published by me. Printed here' (*Izdal v svet ia. Napechatano zdes'*).[149]

This was, indeed, straightforward commercial printing, even if still only at the institutional presses. The printing house controlled the machinery, not the publication. A journal could switch from press to press without noticeable change in identity. Thus *Zhivopisets* (*The Painter*) began with the Academy of Sciences press in 1772–3, but reprints and revised editions were produced at the Artillery and Engineering Corps press (1775) and Moscow University Press (1781). Nor was the practice limited to journals.

Institutional presses also printed privately subsidised books, although this was not always transparent. For example, in 1772 the Academy of Sciences press published a Russian translation by Stefan Pisarev, from Greek, of the *Life of Peter the Great*, originally written in Italian by Antonio Catiforo. Only from the translator's preface does one learn that Pisarev had been commissioned to make the translation some thirty years previously, and had become so frustrated at the lack of official publication that he had at last decided to publish it himself (*izdat' ee v pechat' ot sebia*).[150]

The next logical step in the transition was the private leasing of institutional presses themselves. From 1773 the Artillery and Engineering Corps press was leased to a succession of German printers: Johann Schnoor (1773–6), then Christian Klein (1777–84; with Bernhard Hecke until mid 1777). The Moscow Senate press was leased continuously from 1778 (to Otto Meier, then Fridrikh Gippius (Friedrich Hippius), then Vasilii Okorokov), and Moscow University Press from 1779 (to Nikolai Novikov until 1789, then for a few months to Aleksandr Svetushkin; to Okorokov from August 1789 to 1793, and to Christian Rüdiger and Christopher Claudia until the end of the century).

Leasing, in turn, paved the way to outright private ownership. The first printer to be allowed to set up his own press in this period was Johann Mihael Hartung. Originally from Austria, Hartung had twenty years of experience as a printer, and from 1767 he had been working at the Senate press.[151] In 1771 he received permission to publish non-Russian books, which in practice meant mainly Latin and German. In the long view it was not a precedent. There had been licensed 'niche' publishers before – most recently the Georgian press at Vsesviatskoe, which was revived by permission of the Synod at the request of Prince Bakar, son of Vakhtang VI of Georgia, and which produced a series of religious books in the Georgian language between 1737 and 1744.[152] However, by the 1770s foreign-language books, both imported and locally printed, had become as 'mainstream' as Russian-language books in the Russian graphosphere.[153] In 1776 Johann Weitbrecht and Johann Schnoor were allowed to set up a press to publish Russian books.[154]

Finally, on 15 January 1783, the transition was completed. Catherine II decreed that printing presses were to be treated in the same way as any other manufacture, and that therefore 'both in our two capitals and in all the towns of our empire we permit anybody to establish a printing house, should he so desire, without requiring permission from anybody, but simply informing the police board [the *uprava blagochiniia* – literally the directorate of good order] in the town where he intends to operate the press.' This was not quite freedom. Or, rather, freedom to set up a press did not imply freedom to print whatever one liked. The decree had a potential sting in the tail: the police board was to check all books prior to publication, and to forbid those which were either contrary to the laws of church or state, or which might tend to corrupt.[155] The state ceded oversight of ownership of the means of production, but not oversight of the product. Nevertheless it was a momentous change, and the opportunities were at the time far more significant than the potential restrictions. In a way the decree of January 1783 implied a recognition of what was already happening, as several of the cumbersome institutional presses were increasingly being either sustained through private commissions or actually run by private individuals.[156]

Discussion of Catherine's decree of 1783 tends to have focussed on questions of cultural liberalism. In the context of the present survey its more significant aspect is its economic liberalism. Catherine redefined the use of the technology of print as a form of manufacture like any other: an industry, a commercial activity. Here, at last, was the key component that had been missing in all of Russia's previous printing non-revolutions. No longer was the market in print restricted to whether the presses could sell that which patrons and the institutions required them to produce. Printers could sell their services to produce that which people were prepared to buy.

The consequences for the proliferation of presses, and for the expansion and diversification of print as a component of the Russian graphosphere, were dramatic. In 1700 there were just three printing houses in the lands controlled by Russia: one in Moscow, one in Kiev, one in Chernihiv. In the 1770s there were perhaps a dozen. By the mid 1790s there were approximately fifty. Around half of them were clustered in St Petersburg and Moscow, but others were in Astrakhan, Bendery, Berdichev, Ekaterinoslav, Iaroslavl, Kaluga, Kharkiv, Kiev, Klintsy, Kostroma, Kursk, Nizhnii Novgorod, Perm, Reval (Tallinn), Riga, Ruzaevka, Smolensk, Tambov and Tobolsk.[157] Gary Marker calculates that nearly 80 per cent of Russian books produced in Russia in the dozen years following the decree of 1783 were printed at private presses.[158] And that is before one begins to consider 'non-books' (Russia's first provincial newspaper was produced weekly in Tambov in 1788),[159] or indeed non-Russian books.

Not all the new presses were viable, let alone successful. Nor had they been in Western Europe in the post-Gutenberg century. Markets needed testing, many businesses were short-lived, many books lay unsold. The statement that printers could choose to produce for the market does not mean that there was a market for everything that printers chose to produce. But the fundamental dynamic of printing had changed. Printing became unrecognisably diffused and diffuse.

The dissolution of the official monopolies should not be taken to imply that all subsequent, market-driven printing was unofficial. 'Top-down' commissions remained very important. Indeed, the relaxation of central limits on the licensing of presses could in some contexts, especially in the provinces, lead to a sharp increase in administrative printing. Paradoxically, in the early 1800s the governor of the Olonets region insisted that he needed a printing press because he lacked the scribal resources to keep pace with the demand for the copying of documents.[160]

Until the 1780s it is quite simple to keep track of the institutional structures of Russian printing and publishing, and of its output of books and journals. Bibliographies for the eighteenth century, while never perfect, are impressively close to being comprehensive. Updates and adjustments are always needed, but the century is well covered by a handful of reference works.[161] All are landmarks of bibliographical research, but all are achievable. For the first half of the nineteenth century the task is immeasurably more difficult. Imprints appear and disappear, relocate, re-form with slightly different names, merge. It is no accident that, despite some ambitious initiatives, no comprehensive bibliographical guide to Russian printing and publishing of the period, or even of the first half of the period, has yet come close to completion.[162] The relationship between the role of publisher and the role of printer became subject to multiple permutations. A partial, preliminary checklist quickly reaches more than 200 publishers, but that calculation (or whatever the eventual total might be) hides an indeterminate number of presses.[163]

If one seeks a Russian analogy for the 'Gutenberg moment', as a complex phenomenon in the social, economic and cultural history of the technology of printing with movable type, then the clearest parallels are in the late eighteenth and early nineteenth centuries. The catalyst was the commercialisation of the technology: the shift, in several overlapping stages beginning c. 1760, from a market in the *products* of the presses to a market in the *services* of presses and the dispersal of *ownership* of presses. The culmination was the decree of 1783 recognising and legitimising print as a commercial activity like any other. A consequence, over the ensuing decades, was an unprecedentedly rapid (in Russia) proliferation and diversification of printing presses and print production.

It is no coincidence that the dissolution of institutionalised ownership of the means of production was closely followed by the institutionalisation of means of control over the product. Institutions of control gave way to institutions of oversight. The decline of ownership coincided with the rise of censorship, or of a particular structure of censorship. Censorship is a very broad concept. To say that the institutional history of Russian censorship dates from the turn of the nineteenth century is not to imply that all earlier publication had been free and unrestricted. On the contrary, practical censorship was embedded in the institutional structures of publication. Rulers of church and state had always assumed, since well before the age of print, that it was their prerogative, their duty, to prevent the circulation of materials deemed harmful. Occasionally the need for vigilance was articulated, but for the most part it had been implicit. Such, at any rate, was the case with respect to books printed in Russia. Oversight of imported books was trickier. Publishers were inaccessible, so booksellers had to be held accountable for what they sold. As we have seen, episodic attempts to ban or limit the import of printed books are recorded at least from the first half of the sixteenth century. Over the eighteenth century, as the trade in foreign books became more lively and diverse, so the obligations imposed on importers and booksellers came to be more regularly asserted, though in rather general terms.[164] The new component, at the turn of the nineteenth century, was rise of censorship as a formally constituted institution.[165]

In October 1796 Catherine II rescinded her 1783 decree on private presses, and at the same time stipulated that censorship offices should be set up in several cities. Her successor, Paul, consolidated the ban on private presses and the restrictions both on Russian publications and on the import of books. In a succinctly worded decree of 18 April 1800 he took the latter to its logical extreme: 'Since various books imported from abroad lead to the corruption of faith and civil law and morals, we order that henceforth and until further instruction the import into our state of all kinds of books, in whatever language, without exception, is to be forbidden; and the same applies to music.'[166] In a sense, therefore, one could argue that Catherine's decree of 1783 marked another not-quite-Gutenbergian episode, another initiative not quite carried through. However, the hiatus was brief and the process could not be reversed. In March 1801, Alexander I revoked the ban on private presses; and in 1804, after a prolonged period of consultation, he issued the first comprehensive decree on censorship. Censorship was established as a state institution with the function of pre-screening all locally printed books prior to publication and all imported books prior to distribution.[167]

To some extent the institutionalisation of censorship might be regarded as a counterbalance to the relinquishing of ownership of the means of production, but it is not merely a different means to the same ends. Censorship did not nullify the consequences of the marketisation of the technology of print. Fashion in censorship fluctuated, but the sphere of the non-state was far greater than the sphere of the anti-state, and hence the new opportunities for print as a marketable technology were far greater than the restrictions imposed on it as a means of expression, as is clearly shown by the very rapid expansion of printing and publishing over the first half of the nineteenth century.

On Books and Non-Books

Histories of primary writing tend to privilege the history of books. Books are repositories of and monuments to culture, non-books are sources. Books are in libraries, non-books are in archives. Besides implied differential evaluation, it would be easy to form the impression of a simple set of functional contrasts between the uses of handwriting and print with respect to books and non-books: monastic handwriting produces books, bureaucratic handwriting produces non-books; the rise of the handwritten non-book coincides with the rise of printing, whose typical product is the book; and so on. Such general contrasts are not wholly groundless, but nor are they satisfactory. When is a book not a book? Is 'bookness' affected by length, so that a non-book must be short? Is 'bookness' a quality of the physical object, such that a book is a certain kind of *thing*, regardless of the nature or extent of the text inside it (hence the possibility of making a 'blank book' with no words at all)? Or, if physical definitions founder with the appearance of the electronic book, is bookness generated by qualities of text, such that the book is the work, not the object? And, if a book is a kind of work, how can we distinguish it from a non-book? By its length, or its contents, or its functions? Is there a relationship between non-bookness of form and non-bookness of function? And so on. We sort-of intuit answers to such questions without needing to define the terms too closely, without having to pursue each attempt at a definition to its illogical conclusion.

Below books in the hierarchy, there is a marked mismatch in visibility and status between handwritten non-books and printed non-books. Few historians of pre- or early modernity can expect to manage without the close study of handwritten non-books. Non-books are the prime or primary sources. Time spent poring over handwritten documents is a more or less obligatory phase on the journey to professional esteem. Even apart from their contents, handwritten documents retain a kind of aura as manuscripts. By contrast, in histories and bibliographies of Russian printing, printed non-books barely exist. There are objective and subjective reasons for this lack of attention. For much of the period in question the production of printed non-books was indeed minimal by comparison with the production of handwritten non-books, so to that extent the contrast might be reckoned fair. But it is also a distortion. Printed non-books are almost invisible in some measure because they have not been sought, or because they have barely been noted even when seen. Printed non-books consist of the wide diversity of forms and genres and styles and functions that have tended to be lumped together under the revealingly disparaging and often misleading label of 'ephemera': decrees and proclamations, permits, travel passes, entry passes, coach tickets, theatre tickets, diplomas and certificates, receipts, membership cards, insurance policies, advertisements, separately issued poems and song-sheets, bookplates and other labels, and so on. Often such objects are in broadsheet format (printed on one side of a single sheet).[168]

The conditions of Russian printing before the late eighteenth century were genuinely less conducive to the proliferation of non-books than were the conditions for printing in Western Europe.[169] Often in Western Europe, it was non-books, far more than books, that made printing a viable business, as early modern print shops churned out indulgences, prayers, passes, receipts, announcements, edicts, invitations, news-sheets, verses, songs and other 'ephemera' in their tens of thousands.[170] In Muscovy, with a limited number of official patrons, few presses, 'top-down' decisions on their repertoire, and no opportunities for jobbing printers to offer their skills for hire in a customer-led market, several of the principal drivers of non-book production were lacking. It is predictable that the more voluminous and diverse production of printed non-books should have accelerated from the late eighteenth century, as the technology was opened to the opportunities of the market.[171] Nevertheless, printed non-books in the earlier period were not as negligible as seems to be implied by their virtual invisibility in the historiography. There is a scarcity of direct evidence. Few types of early Russian printed non-book survive, none earlier than the mid seventeenth century. Only recently have scholars begun to look at the relevant information in the records of the Print Chancery archive, where there are multiple references to the production of non-books which have not survived. But the scarcity of direct evidence has been compounded by the traditional lack of interest, or perhaps the lack of prioritisation. Librarians and archivists have rarely catalogued printed non-books, scholars have rarely pursued them, and the otherwise impressively thorough bibliographies even of eighteenth-century printing have generally ignored them. The lack of attention to printed non-books leads to a distortion of the history of printing in Russia, and to misrepresentation of the dynamics of the visible word in the graphosphere.

The rare exceptions have been collectors, or scholar-collectors.[172] Russia is far from unique in this. In Western Europe, too, though somewhat earlier, the path of 'ephemera' from neglect to scholarship has led via the collectors' market. However, in the history of printing in Western Europe the importance of 'ephemera' is by now widely acknowledged. There is nothing, now, controversial in the assertion that 'it seems increasingly realistic to consider the products of the press as stretched along a spectrum of print, within which the book has (in physical terms at least) a modest place.'[173] In Russia the printed non-book has remained almost entirely below the bibliographical and scholarly radar. The explorations of printed non-books in the present work emerge from some preliminary archival study, but much more remains to be discovered, analysed and assimilated into histories of print in Russia.

Collecting non-books in Russia is not new. Pavel Ivanovich Chichikov, the (anti-)hero of Gogol's novel *Dead Souls* (1842) travels around with his box of personal possessions, including compartments 'filled with visiting cards, funeral invitations, theatre tickets and the like, collected as mementos.'[174] Chichikov's attachment to such serendipitous scraps of paper is presented as essentially trivial, vacuous, analogous almost to his spurious attribution of personal qualities to the 'dead souls' whose registrations he is selling. Perhaps he was a man ahead of his time. Now his collection of non-books would be more interesting than his collection of non-people.

CHAPTER 3

Production in the Graphosphere, II: Secondary Writing

Some Features of Secondary Writing

Secondary writing is that which is produced as part of an object, but is not its prime purpose. An object with secondary writing is created *with* writing, or is supplemented or modified by writing consistent with its function (by contrast with tertiary writing – graffiti), but is not created *for* writing. Most examples of secondary writing would fall within the traditional category of 'inscription'.

It is not possible to construct a compact narrative of secondary writing arranged according to the principal technologies and materials of production, analogous to the stories of primary writing in manuscript and print. In the first place, there are too many materials, too many techniques, too many types of object. Since almost any kind of more or less solid object *may* bear an inscription, a history of objects with secondary writing would amount almost to a general history of objects. The objects are too varied and too disparate for coherent summary. They range from a brick to a bronze cannon, from a wax seal to a glass goblet, from a liturgical embroidery to an insurance company's plaque, from a snuff box to a triumphal arch, from a gravestone to a satirical print. All of them have their own histories. One could write a very thick book only on objects with secondary writing, and still it would be far from comprehensive.

A second major difference between secondary writing and primary writing, which again militates against a comparable narrative based on modes of production, is that there is often no consistent link between material and function. Consider, for example, a genre as esoteric (though necessary in context) as the inscriptions on roadside mileposts. Legislation in the mid to late eighteenth century specified, at various times, that such signs should be branded with hot irons, daubed in oil paint or affixed on metallic plates. It would not be helpful to distribute the treatment of such signs among separate narratives of branding, painting and metalworking respectively. They belong together in an account of signage.[1] Similarly, an ownership mark for a book may be handwritten, or stamped or tooled in the binding, or affixed as a label (that is, a bookplate). Or, if mileposts and bookplates are too obscure to justify the generalisation, there is the utterly mainstream example of devotional imagery. Orthodox devotional imagery almost always included inscription as part of the composition. The images, and the lettering, may be painted on wood, cast in metal, poured in enamel, embroidered in textiles, drawn or printed on paper, carved, moulded, stamped. Iconographic conventions of secondary writing span the material and technological boundaries.

In some ways, therefore, secondary writing is *less* coherent than primary writing. Secondary writing is more diffuse in its materials, and in the techniques of its production, and in the functions of the objects of which it is part. In other ways, however, secondary writing is *more* coherent, more compact than primary writing. Despite the very wide diversity of types and functions of objects, the functions of the writing itself tend to be more consistent. Secondary writing almost always relates to the object itself, or to what is depicted on the object. Whether the 'object' is a coin, or a statue, or a shop, the functions of secondary writing tend to stay within an equivalent range of possibilities. Most commonly, secondary writing serves as a form of identification. Secondary writing may identify, for example, aspects of the life-cycle of the object: where or by whom the object was made, who caused it to be made, who owned it, who donated it, who received it. Other secondary writing identifies qualities of the object such as its weight or value. Secondary writing can identify a depiction of which it is part, the characters or scenes, the name of a sculpted figure. It may name that to which it is attached, such as a shop or a street. The hallmark on a silver goblet, an artist's signature or the potter's scratched initial, the issuer's name or device on a seal or coin, the watermark in paper, the donation inscription embroidered on a silk purse, the saint's name on the icon, the goddess's name on the plinth of a statue, the calibrations on a scientific instrument or clock face: all are identifiers. In such cases secondary writing works as a kind of caption or label.

Beyond identification, and overlapping with it, are the words beginning with 'auth-': authority and authorisation, authenticity and authentication. Secondary writing often serves as an additional mode of assurance, if not quite a guarantor, that an object is what it purports to be. In the economic sphere this relates especially to coins and eventually banknotes, in the administrative sphere the obvious examples are seals and stamps, in the religious sphere the inscriptions help to authenticate the image, in commerce the manufacturer's mark certifies the product. Authentication was increasingly a matter of regulation.[2] For example, in February 1744 the Senate forbade the sale of imported goods from China unless they had been properly stamped.[3] Russian paper manufacturers did not merely watermark the paper but also stamped the packaging.[4] In April 1785 Catherine II decreed that all towns must have officially stamped (*kleimennye*) weights and measures, and in April 1797 Paul specified the precise lettering for each side of the scales: the letters 'T' (for *tovar*, 'goods') on one side, and 'G' (for *giri*, 'weights') on the other side.[5] And so on. In these capacities a history of secondary writing is closely linked to histories of regulation and control.

In addition to identification, authorisation and authentication, secondary writing could serve as a kind of cultural marker. All writing can convey messages beyond the verbal, meanings beyond meaning: through its visual qualities, through its very presence. However, secondary writing is perhaps especially liable to non-verbal readings because it is more generally outward-facing, on display as part of the design of an object. One kind of cultural message is simply a matter of taste and fashion. Thus, for example, in the sixteenth century and especially the seventeenth several kinds of high-value, high-status objects tended to be decorated with thick bands of lettering that was often so ornate as to be barely legible. In the eighteenth century this style of decoration went out of fashion, leading to a thinning of the graphosphere around luxury non-devotional objects.[6]

A more complex example relates to pictures. In the Orthodox tradition of devotional imagery, secondary writing was and is almost invariably reckoned an essential component of the composition. Iconographic inscriptions were not merely labels or captions, they were emblematic. The correct representation of writing helped to assure the correctness of the image. The place of inscription in devotional imagery was more secure than style or fashion. Through the eighteenth and nineteenth centuries, when it was common for Russian icon-painters to follow compositional and stylistic models from West European religious painting and printing,[7] the practice of inscription was, for the most part, retained, a sign of the status of the picture as an Orthodox devotional image. By contrast, the western-style *non*-devotional painting that developed in Russia from the early eighteenth century was easily distinguishable by its *lack* of inscription in the composition (aside from the artist's signature). Thus, in a painted picture the presence or absence of secondary writing was a marker of cultural difference. Printed pictures followed separate conventions. The western-style elite engravings of the early eighteenth century could be ostentatiously verbose, although the texts were frequently displayed in quasi-separate spaces such as cartouches or scrolls or on architectural features, rather than in the 'free' space of the picture. Russian 'popular' prints (*lubki*; singular: *lubok*), whether iconographic or secular, likewise tended to feature secondary writing, often copiously.[8]

Secondary writing expanded. Since it is part of an object, the increase in and diversification of secondary writing is linked, on the one hand, to the increase and diversification of the import and production of objects – that is, to trade and manufacture. And it is linked, on the other hand, to regulatory requirements for the use of writing on such objects and on transactions more generally – that is, to the expansion of the state. Fluctuations in taste and fashion ensured that the graph of expansion was not everywhere smooth, but the general direction was consistent.

In terms of the quantity of words, a comparison between secondary writing and primary writing is no comparison. A single thick volume may contain more words than the combined total on tens of thousands of objects with secondary writing. As a presence in the graphosphere, however, secondary writing is much more prominent and significant than might be implied by a mere word-count. Most manuscript and printed books are closed most of the time. They are, in a sense, potential presences in the graphosphere of visible words, reminders of the words within them. Secondary writing is worn on the outside, is displayed in public places, passes from hand to hand. Like manuscript and printed 'non-books', its graphospheric significance is greater than its conventional cultural status.

Some Materials and Types of Secondary Writing

The following survey is highly selective. Not only is it very far from a comprehensive account of all types of object with secondary writing, but it also leaves out many types of object that figure in subsequent chapters of the present book. What does it not include, and why does it include what it does? In the first place, it focusses on histories of production. It therefore does not contain sections on materials which, for various reasons, are not usefully summarised in this way. Thus there is no separate section about secondary writing in or on wood, although later chapters consider several examples ranging from a carved pew to shop signs, not to mention panel icons. Nor is there a section about secondary writing on the plaster of church walls, since this is simply a constant. Paper, too, is absent, although there is subsequent discussion of secondary writing in paper production (watermarks) and on printed pictures, and on banknotes.

Several of the objects discussed below were made from metals, but the discussion falls a long way short of full coverage of metallic objects with secondary writing. Manufacturers' marks span all materials, but manufacturers' marks and makers' names figure here only in genres where they are visually highlighted (e.g. on clocks and cannons), not when they are discreetly positioned out of normal eyesight (e.g. silver hallmarks). Nor is there any attempt in this chapter to cover every genre: the 'superexlibris' on a leather binding;[9] postmarks on letters;[10] bricks;[11] weapons;[12] samovars;[13] gingerbread moulds;[14] playing cards;[15] and much more. In addition, although some of the following remarks reflect archival research, coverage is unavoidably restricted by the extent of previous publication by scholars, curators and collectors.

With so many caveats and exclusions, what is left? A more or less representative sample, a kind of metonymic set of specimens to convey an approximate impression of the whole, from the self-evidently important to the apparently trivial, from the constant to the ephemeral. The focus is on particular materials, and on types of objects which have what might be described as a production history.

Small Metal Objects: Coins, Medals, Jetons, Beard Tokens

Coins

Several of the principalities of Rus started minting their own coins in the second half of the fourteenth century,[16] and until the late fifteenth century the majority of inscriptions were bilingual, or at any rate had the appearance of being so. Arabic inscriptions indicated the Mongol ruler, in many cases accompanied by a Cyrillic reference to the local prince on the reverse. Coins with purely Cyrillic inscriptions were, in the early period, rare.[17] Over the first half of the fifteenth century, as Mongol oversight of Rus slackened, so the Arabic inscriptions on Rus coins changed. Increasingly the inscriptions became Arabic in appearance but not in substance. They became visual simulacra of Arabic, decorative pseudo-Arabic, ideograms emblematic of Arabic, rather than graphic representations of specific verbal messages in real Arabic.[18] By the late fifteenth century both Arabic and pseudo-Arabic inscriptions had disappeared from regular coinage. The emergence first of sporadic monolingual, Cyrillic-only coinage and then of a continuous tradition (probably after 1480) reflected changes in political claims and status.[19]

As Moscow absorbed the local principalities, so the diversity of coinage was subsumed into a single Muscovite system, usually associated with the currency reforms of Elena Glinskaia (mother of the infant Ivan IV) between 1535 and 1538.[20] The reign of Ivan IV saw the beginning of the large-scale influx of West European thalers into Muscovy. Thalers – silver coins weighing around 27–29 grams – became the standard denomination in the Holy Roman Empire from the mid 1520s, and were produced at numerous mints throughout Europe. Thalers circulated as currency in the western areas of the Rus lands, and in Moscow were used as raw material for the production of local silver coins.

Thalers, in Russian *efimki* (singular: *efimok*), were a key component of the near-catastrophic monetary reforms of Tsar Aleksei Mikhailovich between 1654 and 1663. Partly in response to the financial strains of war, Aleksei attempted to weaken links with the traditional silver standards and to introduce coins with nominal values different from the exchange value of the equivalent weight of metal. He introduced copper coinage for smaller denominations, and he devised a Russian silver rouble (the first such coin) which was made through restamping imported thalers: that is, in effect it was a thaler with its images and inscriptions defaced or replaced. The problem was that a rouble consisted of 100 silver kopeks, or around 45–47 g of silver, whereas the converted thaler weighed barely 60 per cent of that. Market rates for the thaler in mid century, based on the value of the metal, had been around 50–60 kopeks.[21] The government was quickly forced to realise the impracticability of such a mismatch. The silver rouble was withdrawn and replaced with a different adaptation of the thaler which retained its West European markings and inscriptions (that is, there was no attempt to disguise the fact that it was a thaler), but was over-stamped with a small roundel of the equestrian figure representing the Muscovite tsar, and a stamp with the date '1655' (Fig. 3.1). The value of these over-stamped thalers (*efimki s priznakom*) was set at a more realistic 64 kopeks. They were produced in huge quantities, estimated at up to a million,[22] and were used to pay the army.

Coins were probably the most widely distributed forms of object with visible writing. Through the distribution of the over-stamped thalers, the Muscovite state officially issued its troops with coins bearing Latin inscriptions. Moreover, the date-stamp '1655' was deceptively innovative. It represents an early use, in an official Muscovite text, both of Arabic numerals and of a date calculated from the birth of Christ rather than from the creation of the world.

The mid-seventeenth-century reforms were nevertheless a failure. Loss of confidence, not in the over-stamped thalers but in the subsequent lower-

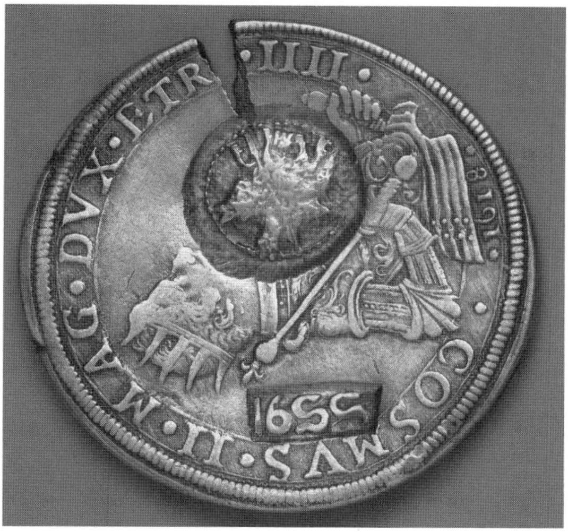

Fig. 3.1: A *tallero* of Cosimo II de' Medici, 1618, over-stamped '1655' in Moscow. The State Hermitage Museum, St Petersburg; photo: Vladimir Terebenin

denomination copper coinage,[23] fuelled inflation and famine, which eventually sparked the so-called copper riot of July 1662.[24]

Elements of Aleksei Mikhailovich's ideas on currency were picked up in the far more effective reforms of Peter I at the start of the eighteenth century. Influenced partly by what he had seen at the Tower mint in London (then under the direction of Isaac Newton), Peter determined that his new coins should be machine-minted. Over the course of his reign he phased out the practice of hand-pressing coins from silver wire. More substantively, Peter reduced the weight of a silver kopek to one-hundredth of the weight of a silver thaler (which could therefore become the basis of a new rouble), and he successfully introduced regular copper coinage.[25] Peter's coins bore inscriptions which stated, often as their most prominent component, the denomination of the coin. This, too, was innovative. Russian coin inscriptions had traditionally been concerned almost exclusively with attributes of authority, not with practical information about the exchange value of the object. A very brief exception had been Aleksei Mikhailovich's rapidly withdrawn silver rouble of 1654. After Peter it remained the norm for coins to bear inscriptions indicating their value.[26]

Foreign inscriptions did not entirely disappear. They were used occasionally on standard Russian coins, but principally on coins produced for non-Russian parts of the empire: the Baltic provinces, Poland, Georgia.[27]

Over the course of the eighteenth century Russian coins also acquired an additional function as collectors' items. Restrikes from the original dies, or official replicas from new dies, were produced for the collectors' market. They are not forgeries, and they are to be distinguished from modern unofficial copies.[28] Such practice is not unique to Russia, but its frequency and prominence in Russia appear to be distinctive to the extent that the word 'novodel' has made its way into English numismatic terminology. In the nineteenth century collectors sometimes went beyond restrikes and replicas and commissioned their own fantasy historical coinage.[29]

Medals

Novodels are symptomatic of the zone of overlap between coins and medals. In the eighteenth century coins and medals were often designated by the same word (*moneta, maneta*), and they intermingled in collectors' cabinets.[30]

The earliest Muscovite medals appear to date from the second half of the fifteenth century, from the reign of Ivan III. Gold tokens modelled on Hungarian ducats, but with Cyrillic inscriptions, were initially produced for use in diplomacy.[31] Although the first such *ugorskie* were probably issued in tiny quantities, they set a precedent. Over the sixteenth and seventeenth centuries they, along with the larger *korobel'shchiki* (based on English 'nobles' and their continental equivalents), and the even larger *portugaly* with Cyrillic inscriptions, were produced to mark events as diverse as coronations and ceremonial visits to shrines. Such medals were most frequently produced as rewards for troops: gold medals (*zolotye*) for senior ranks, and silver gilt kopeks (*moskovki*) for lower ranks. Here the definitions of and distinctions between coins and medals can be slippery. Commemorative campaign medals had an exchange value based on the weight of metal, and some scholars regard them as coins,[32] though they were not issued *as* coins for general circulation.[33] The basis for regular Russian coinage was silver. Foreign gold coins could circulate as currency, but native gold issues were for special occasions. Many of the early gold medals have holes near the top, suggesting that they were used as pendants. An anonymous portrait of Prince Vasilii Vasilevich Golitsyn (1643–1714), head of the Ambassadorial Chancery under the regency of Sofia, depicts him holding a text of the 1686 'eternal peace' with Poland and wearing a chain with his campaign medal for service as commander of the Muscovite armies on the Crimean campaign of 1687.[34]

Peter I took the production and use of commemorative medals to new levels, in three ways: technological, practical and semantic. Technologically the production of medals changed along with Peter's innovations in the minting of coins. He also vastly expanded the use of medals. Precise numbers are hard to calculate, partly because of different conventions of counting variants, and partly because some 'Petrine' commemorative medals were in fact issued by successors, but it is reasonably safe to say that more than a hundred separate issues of medals are associated with the period of his sole reign.[35] Peter's uses of text and illustration reflect his wider interests in symbols and emblems, adopting the visual and verbal vocabulary of emblem books.[36] Versions of the same medal were often issued in different metals – gold, silver or cheaper alloys – to be awarded depending on the relative rank or distinction of the respective recipients.

The intensive production of medals under Peter I was followed by a less active period until the renewal of interest under Catherine II.[37] Petrine and post-Petrine medal production and design were in dialogue with medal-making in Western Europe. Indeed, the boundaries of the native and the foreign were permeable. Russian medals were generally made at Russian mints. The Moscow mint in Kadashevskaia sloboda was founded in 1701, the St Petersburg mint in 1724, though it was not in operation continuously for its first couple of decades. However, the production of Russian medals was not straightforwardly a matter of setting up mints and telling them to get on with it. Different stages of the process could be conducted in different places. Moreover, for at least the first half-century, the development of fully native medal production was hampered by a continual shortage of locally trained medallists.

A example of split production is a series of twenty-eight medals issued in 1713 and 1714, to commemorate key events of the Northern Wars, from the capture of Schlüsselberg in 1702 to the battle of Hangö and the taking of Neuschlot in 1714.[38] The series, originally conceived as consisting of twenty-five medals, was commissioned in Augsburg from the German medallist Philipp Heinrich Müller (1654–1719). However, this did not mean that Müller actually made the medals. He designed and manufactured the dies. These were then sent to Russia, and the medals were struck from them at the Moscow mint. Müller's series was instantly prestigious both in Russia and beyond. In 1716 several medals from the series were reproduced in a German book on historical medals. In Russia the series was re-issued, copied and imitated many times, both for commemoration and for collectors, for at least the next two centuries, during which it stimulated yet more grandiose projects for medals on the Petrine theme, not to mention the comparably ambitious series of twenty medals, produced over almost two decades between 1813 and 1830, marking key events in the war against Napoleon.[39] Müller's Russian-commissioned series of medals is saturated with Latin inscriptions, including not just the forms of imperial titles or place-names, but descriptions and literary aphorisms and citations, sometimes extending to several lines of verse.[40] The use of Latin could subsequently become an issue of occasional controversy,[41] and the lack of locally trained medallists capable of producing dies to the highest level was a *leitmotif* throughout the eighteenth century.[42] The situation was not fully remedied even by the introduction of training courses at the Academy of Arts. However, to commission dies from abroad was relatively rare. The more common solution was to recruit the medallists to work in Russia.

There was huge variation in the quantities issued and distributed. At one extreme, the state honoured individuals or small groups with personal medals, each of which bore a unique inscription.[43] At the other extreme, between 1774 and 1778 Catherine issued almost 150,000 silver medals to troops who had served in the Russo-Turkish war. Limited-issue medals for diligence or excellence were also awarded by educational institutions and learned societies, including Moscow University, the various cadet corps schools, the Academy of Arts, the Academy of Medicine and Surgery, the Moscow Agricultural Society and the lycées at Tsarskoe Selo and elsewhere.[44]

Similar to, though institutionally distinct from, the commemorative and campaign medals were the formally instituted Orders.[45] The first Russian Order, the Order of St Andrew 'the First-Called', was established by Peter I in 1698 or 1699. In 1713 Peter established Russia's only Order for women, the Order of St Catherine.[46] The Order of St Aleksandr Nevskii was first awarded in 1725. The Order of St George, the first Order specifically for military distinction, was founded in 1769, followed by the Order of St Vladimir in 1782. The Order of St Anne was adopted as a dynastic Order when the future Peter III came to Russia as designated heir to the throne in 1742, and was formally instituted as a state Order in 1797.

The inscriptions on commemorative, campaign and Order medals were of many types and designs: textual inscriptions around the border of the obverse and/or reverse; monograms; sequences of abbreviations; textual inscriptions in lines filling the obverse. The inscriptions were generally in

Russian, though there were exceptions, such as the Latin inscription around the medallion at the centre of the star of the Order of St Anne (*amantibus justitiam, pietatem et fidem*).[47] Many of the craftsmen employed to design and make the medals were foreigners, whose signatures or monograms sometimes appear in Latin script.[48]

Medals and their designs and inscriptions migrated. From the late eighteenth century they were being imitated in other decorative media (ivory, silver, even fabrics). Already in the eighteenth century, substantial collections of Russian medals were being formed abroad.[49] Moreover, perhaps more than coins, the words on medals were likely to be read, or at least gazed upon at leisure. Coins were far more numerous, yet their designs and messages were subordinate to their practical functions. Medals were made and distributed to be looked at. According to a minute of a committee on medals in the early 1770s, 'a medal without an inscription is mute'.[50]

Jetons

Jetons can be regarded as a subcategory either of medals or of coins. The term designates several types of small commemorative tokens or badges. The name reflects the practice of throwing them to crowds on the relevant occasions. Jetons were issued fairly regularly by the imperial mints, mostly to mark coronations or deaths, but also for miscellaneous occasions including the celebration of peace treaties, the foundation of the Academy of Arts in 1765 and of the Russian Academy in 1783, as well as the fiftieth anniversary of the foundation of the Academy of Sciences, and the inauguration of Catherine II's monument to Peter I in 1782. The earliest catalogued jetons appear to have been struck to mark Peter's formal adoption of the imperial title in 1721.[51] Jetons could be produced in very large quantities. For example, at the coronation of Elizabeth in 1742, 1,200 gold and nearly 17,000 silver jetons were apparently thrown to the populace. Inscriptions, specifying the occasion of issue, were almost always in Russian.

Beard Tokens

Beard tokens were an unusual form of tax receipt, which owed their existence to the anti-beard policy of Peter I.[52] The first tokens were struck in 1698, though only one undisputed example exists, so the extent of distribution is unclear. Explicit legislation was linked to the batches of tokens issued in 1705, and these are the most common.[53] Nine varieties are known, and restrikes and replicas began to be issued for the collectors' market as early as the mid eighteenth century. The 1705 beard tokens (Fig. 3.2(a)–(b)) were circular, double-sided and about 24 mm in diameter, with the date on one side (in old Cyrillic letter-numerals), and on the other side a relief depiction of a nose, moustache and beard underneath the legend 'the money has been received' (*dengi vziaty*). The token had to be shown on demand, carried on the person or (in the case of the 1724–5 versions which had holes for the purpose) sewn into the outer garment. These later tokens were therefore single-sided. They were also rhomboid rather than circular, and bore two inscriptions: on the flat surface, 'the tax for the beard has been received' (*s borody poshlina vziata*) followed by the date in Arabic numerals; and around the edge, in raised lettering, the motto 'a beard is a superfluous burden' (*boroda izlishna tiagost'*). The ban or tax on beards for all except peasants, clergy and schismatics was sporadically restated until the early 1750s.

Wax: Seals

Until the late fifteenth century most East Slav seals were metallic discs, most commonly of lead, stamped on both sides between a pair of matrices. From the sixteenth century onwards most were made of wax: not beeswax but various composites designed to be malleable when heated and hard when cooled.[54] Double-sided pendant seals, appended with a cord, become relatively rare, mainly limited to important state documents. The norm

Fig. 3.2(a), (b): Beard token, dated 1705. The State Hermitage Museum, St Petersburg; photo: Vladimir Terebenin

was for single-sided seals that were pressed directly onto the document. The metallic component of the sealing process was therefore no longer the seal itself but the object which was pressed into the wax to form the impression, such as a signet ring.[55] A less common variant was the almost flat, paper-covered 'wafer seal'.[56] The use of seals was integral to the conduct of international, state, church and eventually institutional and private business and administration. Few instruments are as resilient. Inevitably, they were also targets for forgery.[57]

The prime function of a seal's inscription and representation is to identify distinctively and reliably the source of authority. At the grander end of the political and ceremonial scale, the seal was also designed to be impressive. Centrally issued seals generally bore one or both of the two symbols of power: a horseman with a lance slaying a dragon (derived from the symbol of Moscow's rulers) and a double-headed eagle. Sometimes the equestrian image was depicted in a medallion on the eagle's breast. On the 'Great Seals' of the tsars, the eagle and horseman were surrounded by inscriptions with their ceremonial titles.[58] The 'great' and 'lesser' state seals were usually double-sided pendants. Seals of city and regional authorities displayed their local emblems. Several were already in use by the mid to late seventeenth century: the bear of Iaroslavl, the winged dragon of Kazan, the deer of Nizhnii Novgorod, various fur-bearing animals for Siberian towns. Local seals with local coats of arms proliferated during the course of the eighteenth century, as did the personal seals of members of aristocratic families.[59] Hence the study of Russian seals is often allied to the broader study of heraldic emblems. However, away from grand display, seals in daily use were often purely textual. For example, the customs seals required as certification of payment, especially after legislation of the 1650s and 1660s, ignored symbols and conveyed plain verbal information: the location of the relevant customs office (e.g. 'Seal of the Smolensk customs'),[60] sometimes the year and even occasionally the month. The verbal messages on seals were almost always in Russian. A rare exception was the seal authorised for use by the Academy of Sciences between 1735 and 1799, which depicted the goddess Athene and the Academy's Latin motto (*hic tuta perennat*).[61]

Silver and Gold Vessels

The most consistent functions and contexts for fine silverware in early Rus were devotional: liturgical vessels, silver and jewelled and enamelled book covers, and the like. The early modern period is marked by an increase in the demand for non-liturgical silverware, and by the gradual expansion of such demand outwards from the court and through the layers of the elites. Silverware was produced and traded throughout the principalities of Rus, both before and after their incorporation into the Muscovite state.[62] Centres of production included: Moscow, especially the workshops of the Moscow Kremlin;[63] Novgorod, where documents suggest that around eighty to a hundred silversmiths were active at any given time from the late sixteenth to the early eighteenth centuries;[64] Pskov;[65] several of the towns on the middle Volga, especially Iaroslavl.[66] As one might expect, gold was less widespread. However, with allowances for a difference in value and quantity, most of the remarks to be made about silver objects are equally applicable to gilt or gold equivalents.

Hallmarks and manufacturers' marks on decorative silver or gold were normally designed to be inconspicuous. Textual inscriptions were optional extras which moved in and out of fashion. A distinguishing feature of Russian gold and silverware in the sixteenth and seventeenth centuries was its demonstrative verbosity. Russian silver, gilt and gold goblets, plates, bowls, mugs and ladles of the period are instantly identifiable by their inscriptions. The characteristic feature is in the design. These are not restrained, thin-lined messages artfully subordinate to the shape and decoration of the object. Muscovite inscriptions come in thick bands of chunky lettering in the most prominent locations. Wrapped around the outer rim of goblets, sometimes also in medallions on the bulging sides, circling the upper borders of plates, they drew attention to themselves. In many cases they were not just prominent elements of the decoration: they *were* the decoration. This was not writing *in* design, it was writing *as* design.[67] As if to emphasise the point, despite being in plain view, they were not always plainly legible. Often they were not formed from large, square, separate letters for ease of decipherment. Instead they were crafted in the ostentatiously quasi-cryptic form known as *viaz'*, woven script, where the letters interlock and overlap in what could be viewed as a continuous band of vaguely letter-like design.[68] It is as if such inscriptions were more eloquent as representations of text than as bearers of verbal messages.

As features of design such thick ribbons of inscription were not invented in Muscovy. They were rooted in Orthodox tradition, in the production of silver and gold vessels for the church. For a thousand years prominent bands of inscriptions – some commemorative, others Eucharistic – had been crafted around the rims of silver liturgical cups and plates. They survive on Byzantine silver at least from the sixth century,[69] on Rus vessels at least from the twelfth century.[70] They were an inherited norm, which became yet more pronounced in Muscovy with the proliferation of luxury silver objects both for liturgical and for non-liturgical use. Characteristic of Muscovy are various types of drinking vessel: the *bratina* ('fraternal cup', 'loving cup'), a bulbous communal drinking-cup (Fig. 3.3); and the *kovsh,* the shallow flat-bottomed drinking scoop or ladle (Fig. 3.4). The *kovsh,* in particular, came to be regarded as a quintessentially Russian form. Based on a traditional wooden vessel thought to have been used for drinking mead, *kovshi* were apparently first translated into silver in the sixteenth century. *Kovshi* survived the transformations of fashion into the imperial age, and jewelled and enamelled *kovshi* enjoyed a revival as luxury 'Russian-style' trinkets by Fabergé and others at the turn of the twentieth century.

Inscribed *bratiny, kovshi* and other goblets, beakers and plates were commissioned by tsars and patriarchs, monasteries and bishops, noblemen

Fig. 3.3: Coconut goblet (*bratina*), inscribed 'The coconut of Izot Ivanov, [may he] drink from it for good health', c. 1650–1680.
© The Trustees of the British Museum

Fig. 3.4: Wine scoop (*kovsh*), 1691, showing *viaz'* inscription.
© Victoria and Albert Museum, London

and noblewomen. They were brought as gifts to rulers of state and church, and they were distributed as gifts to faithful and meritorious servitors. In the mid seventeenth century an inscribed *bratina* was a habitual reward. Around the end of the century an inscribed silver *kovsh* became a standard token of recognition and recompense for administrative service such as tax collecting.[71] Thus, through the growth in the practice of giving inscribed silver vessels as rewards, these eloquent objects found their way into the homes of the service gentry, contributing to the creation of a domestic graphosphere.

Inscriptions on ecclesiastical vessels displayed liturgical quotations. The inscriptions on primarily secular vessels commonly proclaimed ownership or donation or commemoration. *Bratiny* and other cups wished their users good drinking (e.g. 'the cup of a good man: drink from it for good cheer, praying to God and praising the sovereign'),[72] or extolled the virtue of the vessel: 'a wise man is like a gold vessel: that which flows forth from him makes men healthy'; 'perfect love is like a gold vessel for them that drink from it; having drunk, we may become joyous with love'.[73] Presentation *kovshi* and *bratiny* recorded the name and service of their recipients: the inscription on a *bratina* from c. 1628–30 states that it was a gift to Mikhail Danilovich 'for his service to the tsar', while in 1654 a courtier received a *kovsh* 'for service in Crimea';[74] an inscription on a silver *kovsh* records that it was presented to the *d'iak* Makarii

Artemevich Polianskii on 23 October 1689 'for his service and for the construction of New Bogoroditskii fortress on the river Samara'.[75]

Such inscriptions could be open to abuse. In a letter to Prince Andrei Kurbskii, Ivan IV (or his ghost writer) complained that some boiars had appropriated items of gold and silver treasure that were rightfully his, and had turned them into new gold and silver vessels on which they had inscribed the names of their own parents so as to give a spurious appearance of legitimacy through inheritance.[76]

The circulation and production of silverware were international. The Moscow Kremlin museums house some of the world's finest collections of North and West European silverware of the sixteenth to eighteenth centuries, the fruits of diplomatic gift exchange, of royal patronage, acquisitiveness and largesse. The treasuries of the tsars and emperors and patriarchs and monasteries gleamed with fine silver from Tudor and early Stuart England, from Germany, from Holland.[77] Silversmiths, too, were itinerant. Craftsmen from Western Europe were prominent in the workshops of Russia. Imported objects were by no means treated as untouchable. On one level it was common to add discreet inscriptions recording the source ('a gift from the English king') and, almost invariably, the weight.[78] On another level of intervention, imported plates and goblets could be adapted to local taste, treated as blanks available for embellishment with iconographic or other decoration, plus, around the rims, thick Cyrillic inscription in the familiar manner.[79] Some West European silversmiths recognised the market opportunity and themselves produced vessels with thick-banded Cyrillic inscriptions for the Russian market.[80]

In the first half of the eighteenth century a shift of taste in Russian elite culture affected the graphospheric properties of silverware, as it also affected secondary writing in other media. Russian non-liturgical gold and silverware from the eighteenth century either lost its inscriptions, or else displayed them differently, no longer in thick bands, but more discreetly engraved, often subordinate to other decorative features such as enamelled bands or medallions.[81] The only more or less regular exceptions were deliberately traditionalist genres such as presentation *kovshi*.[82]

Enamelled vessels constitute a distinctive subset. Many inscribed silver and (especially) gold chalices, goblets etc. were further embellished with enamel, in some cases extending to the inscriptions.[83] Alternatively, victims of the mid-eighteenth-century fashion for snuff boxes could order an enamelled version which, from across a room, would look not so terribly different from its more expensive porcelain equivalent.[84] A distinctive style of painted enamelled silverware is associated both with the Stroganov workshops at Solvychegodsk (sometimes known as Usolsk enamels, after the previous name for the settlement) in the late seventeenth and early eighteenth centuries, and with the Kremlin workshops in Moscow.[85] One characteristic genre was notably wordy: a type of silver drinking bowl covered with painted enamel pictures. The illustrations were identified by prominent captions. Sometimes they were also accompanied by running texts with fragments of narrative or citation. Some of the bowls show scenes from the Old Testament (Fig. 3.5), others are allegorical.[86] Some compositions seem frivolous by conventional Muscovite criteria. Thus a representation of the five senses consists of a series of scenes featuring a young man and a voluptuous young woman, both in West European

Fig. 3.5: Enamelled silver drinking bowl, Moscow or Solvychegodsk, c. 1690. The Walters Art Museum, Baltimore

dress and with West European hairstyles. In the central medallion, labelled 'touch' (*osiazanie*) the man has his hand on the woman's breast.[87]

Heavy Metal: Cannons, Bells

The technology of casting cannons in bronze was brought to Moscow by Italian craftsmen in the late 1480s. Chronicles record the casting of a 'great cannon' by the *friazin* ('Frankish', here 'Italian') Pavlin (Paolo), an event considered memorable enough to be recorded pictorially in the prestigious and elephantine *Illustrated Chronicle* of the late sixteenth century.[88] The earliest surviving local cannon, by the master Iakov, dates from 1491. The mid sixteenth century saw the casting of a series of enormous cannons which became, in effect, public monuments: in the 1550s by Kaspar Ganusov (more than 19,000 kg) and Stepan Petrov (nearly 17,000 kg). These giants served on military campaign in the early 1560s, but were later put on public display in Red Square, near the Frolov gate. Here they were joined by the most monstrous gun of all, Andrei Chokhov's 'Tsar Cannon' (as it has come to be known) of 1586, weighing more than 38,000 kg.[89] Chokhov's cannon was not even made to be fired. Its internal workings were never completed. Its function was to impress, and part of its impressive display was the eloquent cast decoration on its barrel, which included an equestrian representation of the Muscovite ruler, and two inscriptions (in Russian) declaring the patronage of the tsar and his wife, and the date of the cannon's manufacture by Chokhov.

Although bells had been cast in Rus in earlier centuries, inscriptions had been rare. The proliferation of inscribed Muscovite bronze-cast bells dates from the sixteenth and seventeenth centuries. Bells ranged in size from a few dozen kilograms to several thousand kilograms, but the principles of design were broadly stable.[90] The inscriptions were in thick bands of Cyrillic *ustav* or – more or less standard by the seventeenth century – *viaz'* lettering around the shoulder and/or the rim (Fig. 3.6), and in exceptional cases could extend also around the main body (waist, skirt) of the bell. The inscriptions on substantial bells for specified patrons were normally made as part of the manufacturing process: that is, they were cast in bronze, not added later.[91] However, the bell-makers at the foundry (the *Pushechnyi dvor*) also produced smaller bells for general sale on the market, and these could be inscribed subsequently to order.[92]

The principal elements of the inscriptions were: the name of the patron or patrons (sometimes a very long list of titles and family members); the date; the church or monastery for which the bell was destined;

Fig. 3.6: The 'Rostov' bell, 1687.
© Moscow Kremlin Museums; photo: V. E. Overchenko

and the maker. The maker's name was a common but not absolutely standard feature: no bell commissioned by Boris Godunov names its maker, nor do the very largest bells commissioned by Aleksei Mikhailovich.

Once a bell was in place, its inscriptions may have been visible as decorative bands, but hardly as texts, except perhaps to the monks who rang the chimes. Nevertheless, the inscriptions were reckoned important textually as well as aesthetically. We know of at least two major bells whose inscriptions followed the instructions of Tsar Aleksei Mikhailovich himself. The most remarkable is the monstrous 2,125-pood (approximately 35-tonne) bell cast for the monastery of St Savva Storozhevskii (Sabbas of Storozhi) at Zvenigorod. Aleksei Mikhailovich's inscription covered virtually the whole enormous outer surface and included three bands not even cast in standard *viaz'* but in a kind of cryptographic script – to no obvious purpose, since in content it is a conventional donor inscription.[93]

At the opposite end of the scale of size and monumentality were the little bells (*kolokol'chiki*) attached to the yokes of horses. For many a traveller the constant, relentless clanging of the bell *was* the sound of the road.[94] Generally about 7–10 cm in height and 10–15 cm in diameter at the base, these bells were often inscribed. A catalogue of 800 such bells, from over a dozen centres of production, includes some 650 inscribed examples, starting from the 1800s. Elements of the inscriptions, cast around the skirt of the bell, could include the date, the craftsman's name, and sometimes a brief phrase or folkloric tag (e.g. *dar Valdaia*, or *kogo liubliu, togo dariu*: 'a gift from Valdai'; 'the one I love, to him I give'). The genre is light, and so is the appearance. These bell inscriptions are not in solemn bands of *viaz'*, but mostly in imitation of informal cursive script.[95]

Stone

Lapidary inscription was rare in early Rus. A continuous tradition of lapidary inscription begins from the second half of the fifteenth century. Eventually stone became a material for a broad range of genres and styles of secondary writing, but three were particularly prominent: commemorative and funerary inscriptions, foundation inscriptions and sculptural inscriptions.

The cross commissioned by Stefan Borodaty in memory of his son in 1458 is a very rare specimen of early commemorative lapidary inscription.[96] The genre that, starting sporadically from the late fifteenth century, developed into a regular tradition was the inscribed gravestone.[97] Starting with minimal inscription on plain flat slabs, gravestone inscriptions became gradually more elaborate, culminating in the visually and verbally ornate sculpted funerary monuments of the late eighteenth century.[98]

The custom of fixing stone plaques on the walls of buildings, with information about their foundation, construction, dedication or renovation, also dates from the end of the fifteenth century. The earliest known examples are the two plaques, in Latin and in Russian, recording the construction of the Frolov tower of the Moscow Kremlin in 1491. Over the sixteenth century equivalent inscriptions appeared on the walls of other monumental buildings, including churches.[99] In the latter half of the eighteenth century such lapidary labels also migrated beyond buildings, marking additions to the fabric of the city: dates recording the completion of several of the granite embankments (1764, 1767), marble signs on the completion of parts of the Peter and Paul Fortress (1780–5), the date of a bridge (1788), flood marks (1777, 1788) and so on.[100] This flurry of urban lapidary signage was also the context for the introduction of St Petersburg street signs (1768), which were initially carved on marble.

Sculpted imagery plays a notably muted role in the medieval tradition of Orthodox representation. The fashion for statues was given its principal stimulus at the start of the eighteenth century, when Peter I began to order sculptures from abroad, mainly from Italy. Inscribed sculptures – or rather, sculpted or cast bronze figures or busts with inscribed plinths – populated the Summer Gardens, then the parks around the royal palaces, then the estates of the aristocracy, especially from the latter half of the century.[101] The practice of setting up inscribed monuments in public squares as well as parks and gardens began with the inauguration of Catherine II's monument to Peter I (the 'Bronze Horseman', by Étienne Falconet) in St Petersburg on 7 August 1782. Over the following decades, albeit gradually, inscribed public monuments increased in number and variety.[102] The earliest such monument in Moscow was a memorial to Minin and Pozharskii, completed in 1818.[103]

Textiles

Devotional Embroidery

The fifteenth to seventeenth centuries were a Golden Age for Muscovite iconographic luxury textiles.[104] Luxury iconographic textile production was distinctive in that the workshops were largely organised by women, in the *svetlitsy* (light chambers) of noble and princely houses, including the Moscow Kremlin.[105] Women of the Stroganov family patronised embroidery workshops at Solvychegodsk over several generations, from the late sixteenth century through to the end of the seventeenth.[106] The materials were expensive and often imported: silk or satin, velvet, gold and silver thread, pearls and precious stones. The principal purposes of the iconographic embroideries were devotional, to be donated to churches and monasteries. There were cloths for covering liturgical vessels (the *sudar'*, typically around 50 x 50 cm, or the somewhat larger *vozdukh*),[107] or cloths for covering the whole altar table.[108] A tomb cover (*pokrov*), bearing the image of the saint, could be more than two metres in length. Icon covers or hanging veils (*peleny*) were suspended from wooden panel icons, replicating their images.[109] There were processional icons and banners, and ecclesiastical vestments ranging from hats and cowls through to the large, richly illustrated and ornamented *sakkoi*, the robes that were the prerogative of the patriarch and selected senior bishops.[110] A common and distinctive feature of the luxury iconographic embroideries is the prominence, quantity, length and types of their inscriptions. Even among other, related iconographic forms they were ostentatious in their displays of lettering.

There were two principal locations for the inscriptions on the luxury textiles: in the central pictorial panel and around the borders. The essential components of the central panel inscriptions were the labels identifying the figures depicted, as was standard in Orthodox devotional imagery. The texts around the borders allowed more scope for variation, though here, too, conventions developed. For example, the border inscriptions on *peleny* often consisted of quotations from liturgical hymns related to the saint represented in the central panel. Sometimes the text around the border was the donor inscription. The border lettering tended to be large, often in elaborately formal *viaz*, in the manner of manuscript or printed headpieces. The style and execution of the central 'label' inscriptions were more varied.

Unlike the vast majority of panel icons, the luxury iconographic textiles were generally neither anonymous nor timeless. We do not know who created the preparatory designs, but very often we know when, where or by whom or under whose patronage the embroideries themselves were made, and by whom they were donated to which churches. Sometimes the donor inscription was placed discreetly on the reverse, such as that which records the completion, in 1657, of a *pokrov* of Metropolitan Iona of Moscow, commissioned by Grigorii Dmitrievich Stroganov, presumably from the workshop of his mother, Anna Ivanovna.[111] However, such reticence was by no means universal. On a *pelena* of the Mother of God and Child, made in 1630 at the workshop of Domnika Mikhailovna, wife of Prince Fedor Ivanovich Mstislavskii, the donor inscription proclaims itself in large lettering across the full width of the central panel itself (Fig. 3.7).[112] In some instances the selection and combination of conventional elements have been interpreted as implying statements about the circumstances or aspirations of the women who made or commissioned them.[113] One of the most specific texts is found on an embroidery from a series of depictions of the tsarevich Dmitrii made at the Stroganov workshop. This large *pelena* (140 x 89 cm) bears two inscriptions on the reverse. The first provides fairly full, but standard, information: the date (1654), the makers (Anna Ivanovna Stroganova and the nun Marfa Veselka), the donor (Dmitrii Andreevich Stroganov) and the recipient (the church of the Annunciation). The second inscription is unexpected: we learn the

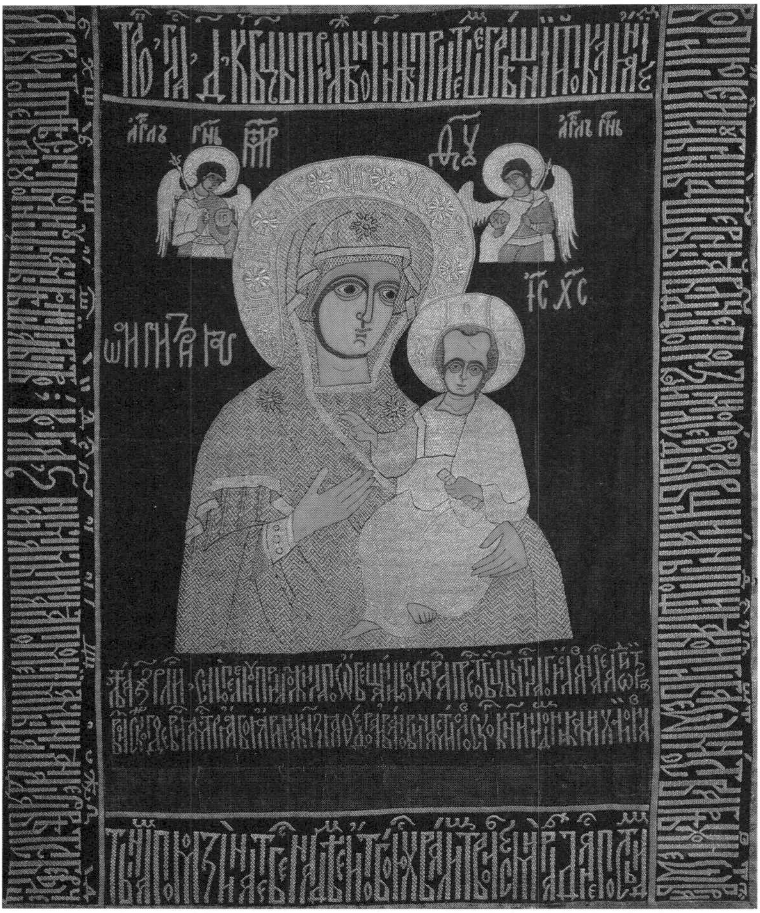

Fig. 3.7: Devotional embroidery of Mother of God and Child 'Hodegetria', 1630; workshop of Princess Domnika Mikhailovna Mstislavskaia. © Moscow Kremlin Musems; photo: V. N. Seregin

quantity and cost of the materials, how much gold, silver, pearls and silk, amounting to a total of 364 roubles and 60 kopeks – lest the monks underestimate the generosity of their patron.[114]

Devotional Printed Textiles: Antimensia

Antimensia could appear in a history of textiles, or of printing, or of administrative documents, or of liturgy. The antimension, or *antimins* in

Slavonic, combined three functions. It was a rectangular cloth placed under the liturgical vessels on the altar table. In this function it was equivalent to the 'corporal' in the western Christian rite. However, while corporals were, typically, white and unadorned, an antimension had a second function as an icon, a bearer of a sacred image connected with Christ's Passion. The third function of the antimension was as a formal administrative document. An antimension was issued to each church by a bishop or metropolitan as proof of consecration and hence of permission to celebrate the liturgy.[115] Early hand-painted antimensia generally depicted a Cross, plus a textual inscription around the border. From the mid seventeenth century onwards the most common images on antimensia were the Lamentation or the Entombment.[116]

Uniquely among liturgical textiles, in the seventeenth century antimensia came to be printed. Throughout the century antimensia were being printed in Ukraine.[117] Evidence for Muscovite printed antimensia from the

Fig. 3.8: Antimension (*antimins*), 12 December 1655; printed on cloth, with details filled in by hand.
© Moscow Kremlin Museums; photo: V. N. Seregin

first half of the century is sporadic and uncertain, but from the 1650s block-printed antimensia were among the most regular products of the Moscow Print Yard (Fig. 3.8).[118] Indeed, in Muscovy the printing of antimensia became not merely a convenience or an option, but a requirement. The mass introduction of printed pictorial antimensia in Moscow dates from c. 1652, and is associated with Patriarch Nikon. Sometimes the print runs were substantial – several thousand copies – presumably for diverse distribution or for the general use of the patriarch. Other print runs were smaller, for allocation to particular bishops, who, in turn, would consecrate them for churches under their authority: 50 for the Archbishop of Tver and Kashin on 14 March 1674; 103 in February 1675 for Iona, Bishop of Viatka, who supplied the cloth himself; 69 on 9 December of the same year, for Filaret, Bishop of Nizhnii Novgorod.

Antimensia occupy a particular niche in the history of Muscovite block-printing. The earliest were woodcuts, in technique and manner very close to printed book illustrations. The plates for some antimensia from the 1670s onwards were made of tin. Copper-engraved antimensia date from the 1690s, slightly anticipating the intensive use of this technique in secular engravings of the Petrine period. However, in practice the successive techniques did not replace one another, but coexisted, since early plates could remain in use for a century or more.

Antimensia were produced in various sizes and at varying levels of expense. A standard antimension was a rectangle measuring approximately 28 x 35 cm, but in the 1690s Patriarch Adrian ordered large engraved antimensia on coloured satin cloths measuring 48 x 53 cm. The basic iconography remained stable, as did the essential verbal components. The figures in the central image, and sometimes in additional iconographic roundels on the four corners, were labelled in the usual way. However, the more substantial, non-iconographic texts appeared in border panels above and below the central image and, in early examples, on either side of it. Typically, these texts labelled the main image, named the ruler and sometimes the patriarch or bishop, and indicated part of the rudiments of the date, leaving gaps in which the year and month and day of consecration were to be written by hand. In other words, these antimensia were designed to be technological hybrids: block-printed, but fully activated only when the handwritten components were added. They can be counted among the earliest printed blank forms.[119]

In the early history of Muscovite printing antimensia are notable in several respects. They are the only known objects which were regularly printed on cloth. They appear to be unique in the use of tin for block-printing. They were the earliest regularly printed works of iconography not intended as book illustrations. They represent a unique generic hybrid of the liturgical and the bureaucratic, while being among the earliest types of Muscovite printed administrative documents in general, and of printed blank forms in particular.

Banners

The history of Russian military banners can be divided into three overlapping phases: the iconographic; the non-Christian representational; and the emblematic or heraldic.

The Golden Age of the iconographic banner in Muscovy ran from the mid sixteenth century to the late seventeenth century. The most prestigious banners of this period were monumental in scale. The largest of them, such as Ivan IV's 'Great Banner' of 1560, or the cluster of banners ordered by Aleksei Mikhailovich in 1653–4, measured between 4 m and 5.5 m along the top edge, and could be up to 2.3 m high.[120] They were formed of a rectangular section closest to the shaft (the 'hoist') and an outer section (the 'fly') in the form of a triangle tapering down to the lower horizontal, which was therefore shorter than the upper edge. These banners were profusely illustrated with iconographic scenes. The decoration was created in mixed media: partly painted, partly embroidered. Paul of Aleppo, who saw the banners of Tsar Aleksei Mikhailovich on parade in Moscow in 1654, when they were new, was hugely impressed. In his account of his visit he wrote that the banners were 'large and much to be admired, astonishing the beholder with their beauty, the execution of the figures painted on them, and the richness of their gilding'. He was also struck by their iconography, and listed some of the images: the Mother of God, military saints such as St George and St Demetrius, the Archangel Michael, scenes from the Apocalypse.[121]

Perhaps understandably, as a foreigner, while marvelling at the scale and the images, Paul of Aleppo said nothing about the inscriptions. In fact the large Muscovite military banners were verbose far beyond the traditional requirements of their iconography. They were almost as saturated with text as with image. For example, on Ivan IV's Great Banner a section of the hoist depicted a mounted figure of Christ in a roundel encircled by cherubim and seraphim, while in the lower section multiple mounted figures in white garments formed the Heavenly Host. In the fly was another mounted figure, this time with wings: the Archangel Michael, on a golden steed, holding aloft a cross in his left hand. The background was strewn with golden stars. Next to the pictures, and along all sides of the banner except for that closest to the shaft, ran elaborate inscriptions. Some of them identified the figures, others were extensive quotations from the Book of Revelations.[122] Prince Dmitrii Pozharskii, who led the Russian troops to victory over the Polish invaders in 1612, had a large crimson battle standard depicting Christ Pantocrator on one side and the Archangel Michael on the other. The Archangel Michael was flanked, on his left, by the Old Testament figure of Joshua, and on his right by the city of Jericho, which Joshua captured. The identifying inscriptions were almost as prominent as the figures themselves, and 'textual' inscriptions ran right round all four sides of each scene: part of the Old Testament narrative of Joshua, and a prayer addressed to Christ.[123] The banner of one of the regiments of Aleksei Mikhailovich, the Bolshoi polk, dated 10 November 1653 (i.e. one of the banners seen by Paul of Aleppo), included a narrative text of more than 230 words concerning a miracle of St Demetrius, as well as several substantial prayers, a 60-word inscription recording Aleksei Mikhailovich's commissioning of the banner and, along the lower edge of the diagonal, another 60-word inscription asserting that the banner was for the exclusive use of the regiment.[124]

Non-Christian representation, usually from classical mythology, began to appear on Muscovite banners during the seventeenth century, perhaps prompted by the influence of large numbers of foreigners who served in the tsar's armies.[125] It reached its peak in the early part of the reign of Peter I. For example, a banner of the Preobrazhenskii regiment, from 1700, shows, against a black ground with blue floral decoration, in the centre, under a crown, a curtain being drawn back by Mars and Neptune, revealing a view of the sea and of a ship in which Saturn teaches a youth to row; in the background, flanking a sword which descends from the sky, on one shore a city burns, while on the opposite shore ships are being built; in front of the curtain is a large bronze cannon and a ribbon with the Latin inscription *Anno Domini 1700*.[126] The Preobrazhenskii banner is traditional in the prominence of narrative illustration, but a harbinger of future fashion in the significantly reduced role of verbal text.

From the early eighteenth century Russian campaign banners largely abandoned biblical or even neoclassical representation, and almost completely abandoned verbal text, adopting instead the language of heraldic emblems. This, the third phase in their history, was deliberate policy, reflecting Peter I's particular interest in heraldry and emblems. In his military reforms of 1708 he assigned each regiment to a territorial base, and from 1712 he linked their standards to their respective towns and regions. This does not mean that the designs on banners were thenceforth fixed. On the contrary, regimental colours became a recurrent topic of interest for Peter's successors, and instructions about new colours were issued from time to time.[127] Border inscriptions became slightly more frequent in the first half of the nineteenth century, but there was no return either to the pictorial focus or to the visual verbosity of the pre-Petrine era.

Gentry Needlework

The production of Russian 'golden' embroidery (the luxury iconographic textiles) declined in the early eighteenth century. Changes in the lives of aristocratic women, and in fashions in clothing, upholstery and decoration, affected the organisation, the methods and the styles of production.[128] In place of the *svetlitsa* professional and serf seamstresses applied their skills in a different, non-devotional context. By comparison with peasant embroidery of the same period,[129] Russian gentry embroidery has not been extensively studied, exhibited or published. The following remarks are therefore to some extent provisional. They are based on published and unpublished materials.[130] The high period of gentry decorative embroidery ran from the second half of the eighteenth century through approximately to the mid nineteenth century, when organised production began to switch to factories.

Decorative fashion among the gentry tended to follow Western Europe. A gentlewoman's library might well include needlework journals from France, Britain, Germany, Austria, Spain.[131] In addition to clothes and upholstery, decorative embroideries could adorn everyday objects such as purses and pocket-books, beakers and notebooks, inkstands and pencils, even pouches for toothbrushes, as well as panels on screens and tables, and framed pictures. Ladies created images in silk, or wool, or cotton, though a particular favourite was beadwork.[132] Common pictorial motifs included flowers and animals, scenes from classical mythology and from rural life in its more idyllically picturesque forms.

Russian decorative needlework of the late eighteenth and early nineteenth centuries was not, for the most part, textual. Inscriptions were occasional, optional extras. Often we have no more than a monogram, occasionally with a date.[133] Sometimes the embroideries state who made them, and when, or, very occasionally, what is depicted: 'Katerina Derzhavina sewed [this]. 1782', beneath a Chinese rustic landscape in coloured silk; 'Elizaveta I. Dengina embroidered [this]. 30 September 1830', beneath a beadwork pastoral idyll; 'May 1803 in the village of Popovka. A.R.' across the lower border of an agricultural scene.[134] Sometimes there are snatches of verse: a corrupted quatrain from an 1821 poem by Pushkin; a dedicatory quatrain (also with mistakes) represented in mirror-writing; a pastoral scene on a pocket-book cover with a verse line welcoming the advent of spring.[135] The most verbose needle-pictures were those which, rather than classical mythology or 'sentimentalist' idylls, reproduce *lubok* prints and include their often substantial texts.[136] Among the wordiest inscriptions are also dedications, on embroideries made as gifts, such as a silk wallet produced for a wedding, dated 30 March 1796, with the monograms of the happy couple and a congratulatory inscription ending with the hope that their hearts may be entwined as closely as the letters in the monograms (Fig. 3.9);[137] or another silk purse whose maker assures the dedicatee that 'neither distance nor time can separate me from you'.[138]

Appropriately for the social milieu, embroidered gifts were often inscribed in French: '*à l'amitié* ' on the pedestal of an urn in a rustic scene;[139] '*L'amitié vous offre*' on the flap of a purse.[140]

The arrangement of a majority of these inscriptions in the overall composition is noteworthy. They were normally displayed along the rim, outside the frame of the picture itself; or on the flap of a wallet, or on its reverse side partly covered by the flap rather than on its fuller outer surface; or within a medallion

Fig. 3.9: Embroidered silk wallet with inscriptions congratulating a couple on their marriage on 30 March 1796. The State Hermitage Museum, St Petersburg

or cartouche. They were, for the most part, captions or accompanying inscriptions, not part of the central image. Lettering by itself was rarely a component of the main composition. Moreover, the textual segments of embroideries seem often to have been rather crudely executed. Elegance was in the picture, perhaps in the monogram, but the words were presented as if in a different aesthetic frame, marginalised in all senses.

This suggests a distinction between the conventions of such pictures in Russia and some of their equivalents in much of Western Europe and in North America. In particular, it seems that Russia did not assimilate the most 'textual' of western traditions of embroidery: the making of samplers. In many countries of Europe and North America sampler-making was part of a girl's education, whether in the schoolroom or in home tuition.[141] Textual compositions are typical of samplers in virtually every age and country in which they were produced. To demonstrate the skill of embroidering an alphabet, or variant alphabets, or a calligraphically precise poem, or the multiple place-names on a map embroidered in silk with print-like precision – these were among the staples of the sampler genre, as girls developed and displayed their accomplishments. The nature and frequency of texts reflect the extent to which sampler-making was not just a practical skill but part of moral education. Indications that words in textiles might have an edificatory function appear in Western Europe as early as the fifteenth century, even before the age of emblems, as in illustrated manuscripts of Henri Baude's *Ditz moraulx pour faire tapisserie*.[142] As one commentator puts it, with the rapid development of textual samplers from the late seventeenth century 'it is as though sampler-making had suddenly become an extension of the writing lesson. Here is the Creed and the Ten Commandments and a patchwork of quotations of variable length from the Old and New Testaments, hymnals, Psalters and catechisms, all muddled up with trite, stilted little poems [...] All are grave, some are sad, and nearly all forecast rewards for the good child and punishments for the bad.'[143]

In Russia, so far as can be surmised on the basis of present state of research, this does not seem to have been the case. Needlework was, of course, a traditional pursuit, and was on school curricula for girls from the age of six, at least from the second half of the eighteenth century,[144] but the cultural imports in Russia's enlightenment did not, apparently, extend deeply into the culture of moral education through embroidered words. The idea of needlework as a moral activity perhaps lies behind the sharp remarks of one observer of attitudes among Russian gentlewomen in the mid nineteenth century: 'Many of the ladies never do any work, and are almost ignorant of the use of the needle. "Why should I sew, when I have others to do it for me?" is a common question.'[145]

Ceramics, Porcelain

Architectural Ceramic Tiles

Glazed ceramic tiles begin to adorn buildings in Muscovy from the sixteenth century. A spectacular and relatively early example is the church of the Intercession on the Moat, otherwise known as St Basil's Cathedral, on Red Square. Decorative ceramics became particularly widespread in the mid to late seventeenth century, both on churches and on secular buildings. Sometimes the decoration was limited to individual tiles, sometimes to bands and friezes, and sometimes substantial sections of facades were coated with multi-coloured tiles with abstract, floral and sometimes figurative motifs.[146] Inscription was by no means standard, but it became quite widespread. The simplest inscriptions were limited to individual tiles with verbal captions labelling iconographic scenes or figures.[147] Occasionally the scenes were narrative, secular or mythological, such as the remarkable series of tiles from the church of the Trinity in Kostroma, dating from around 1650. The series includes an inscribed depiction of a siege complete with cannon and scaling ladders, as well as inscribed tiles of a gryphon, a unicorn and an eagle.[148] At the most verbose end of the spectrum are continuous texts composed entirely of ceramic tiles put together in friezes, such as the verse text, dated June 1683, around the drum of the cupola of the church of the Resurrection at Patriarch Nikon's New Jerusalem monastery,[149] or the detailed ceramic foundation inscription on the belfry of the church of St Adrian and St Natalia in Moscow, dated 1686–8.[150]

'Dutch' Stoves

There are two types of Russian stove. The traditional Russian stove, used both for baking and as a source of heat, was a more or less standard fixture of any dwelling including the peasant hut. If a traditional stove was faced with tiles, they were either plain, or decorated in relief. Large houses, especially from the turn of the eighteenth century onwards, began to install what became known as 'Dutch' stoves. These were for heating only and were usually tiled. From the 1700s to approximately the 1760s 'Dutch' stoves tended to be faced with flat painted tiles. Initially such tiles were decorated in blue and white, following the example of the Delftware popular in Europe. Subsequently the Russians also experimented in polychrome painting. The tile decorations were sometimes geometric or floral, but sometimes they were figurative and inscribed. A large stove with painted inscribed tiles might be more than two metres in height and consist of several hundreds of individually labelled figures or scenes. In the houses in which they were installed, such stoves may well have been the most prominent feature of the domestic graphosphere. Popular subjects included exotic animals or peoples ('a wild beast', under a picture of a camel; 'a Chinese merchant'; 'a Japanese lady'), or illustrations and mottoes drawn from emblem books.[151] A curious feature of the inscriptions is that, despite the expense of the object which they adorned, they were almost invariably executed crudely (Fig. 3.10). The lettering was uneven, almost careless, in no sense elegant. Words were often misspelt. Occasionally the inscriptions were entirely symbolic: cartouches with a few squiggles of pretend-writing, the mere idea of an inscription, signs of a potential verbal presence with no verbal content.[152]

The fashion for inscribed stove tiles gradually declined in the latter decades of the eighteenth century. By the turn of the nineteenth century Russian 'Dutch' stoves were being faced predominantly with plain tiles, with neither picture nor inscription. The aesthetic focus was now directed

(a) (b)

Fig. 3.10(a), (b): Tiles for 'Dutch' stove, mid eighteenth century, inscribed 'I grieve sorely for him' and 'I ride on my journey'. Velsk Regional Museum

more towards elegant architectural integration of stove and domestic interior, rather than towards the decoration of the stove as a separate object.[153]

Porcelain

The European discovery of how to manufacture porcelain, rather than having to import it from China, coincided with the European turn in Russian elite taste in the first half of the eighteenth century. With Russian aristocratic appetites whetted by imported Meissen, in 1744 the empress Elizabeth approved the opening of the Nevskaia Porcelain Factory, which from 1765 was known as the Imperial Porcelain Factory. This is the name which, with an eighty-year interlude when the Soviet authorities renamed it the Lomonosov Porcelain Factory, it retains to this day.[154] Such was the demand that Elizabeth's successor, Catherine II, was prepared to accept and even to patronise what might have seemed like competition for a lucrative market. In 1766 the first Russian private porcelain factory was founded, by the Englishman Francis Gardner.[155] Until the end of the eighteenth century the Imperial Porcelain Factory and the Gardner Factory were the only local manufacturers. Private factories increased in number over the first half of the nineteenth century.[156]

Porcelain was a new medium. It had no Orthodox past, no earlier tradition to develop, adapt or overcome. It was the first purely secular medium for the production of ostentatiously luxurious decorative objects for domestic and ceremonial use. Whereas in several other media secular artworks in the eighteenth century became verbally more reticent than their Orthodox predecessors, Russian porcelain of the mid to late eighteenth century was often a medium typified by the display of writing. Those who commissioned, owned or donated fine porcelain were keen that their patronage, ownership or donation should be declared by the objects themselves. This was the age of the monogram and the motto, not as discrete elements within or beside a larger patterned or pictorial design but often a principal component of the design.

The market potential for vanity inscriptions was recognised from the earliest years of manufacture. Thus on 19 March 1753 a curious announcement appeared in the St Petersburg Gazette. Dmitrii Vinogradov, director of the Nevskaia Porcelain Factory, requested that 'all persons of noble birth, courtiers in particular, of both sexes, who would like to have porcelain snuff boxes in the shape of a packet with inscriptions' should send 'forms, specifying the inscription and the language desired'. Mr

Fig. 3.11: Packet snuff box inscribed to Savva Ivanovich Krenitsyn; St Petersburg, 1764. The State Hermitage Museum, St Petersburg; photo: Vladimir Terebenin

Vinogradov further declared that he would be pleased to satisfy all such requests, at a price of twenty roubles per inscribed snuff box.[157] Clearly Vinogradov struck a chord (Fig. 3.11). Examples of these early personalised snuff boxes indeed demonstrate the range of languages and hands.[158] Both factories did a brisk business in monogrammed cups and saucers, jugs and the like.[159] However, the grandest inscribed commissions were the huge ceremonial dinner services, sometimes running to several hundred pieces. Some simply bore the owner's monogram. Among the earliest was a monogrammed service presented by Catherine II to Grigorii Orlov in or around 1765 (Fig. 3.12).[160] Others were historical and bore appropriately explanatory inscriptions: a small service commissioned in 1775 to celebrate victory in the Russo-Turkish war of 1768–74 included an allegorical monument with the inscription 'Le 10 Juillet 1774';[161] in the dinner service commissioned in 1784 to mark the annexation of Georgia, a sculptural piece included allegorical figures of Russia and Georgia on either side of a pedestal with a roundel bearing the words 'Georgia, participant in the Glory and Prosperity of Russia'.[162] Others were quasi-heraldic. Perhaps the

Fig. 3.12: Teapot, coffee pot and tea caddy from the 'Orlov' porcelain service; St Petersburg, 1762–1765. Hillwood Estate, Museum and Gardens; photo: Edward Owen

most ambitious was the series of four large dinner services commissioned by Catherine II from the Gardner Factory between 1777 and 1785 for use at the annual gatherings of the members of the principal state Orders. The standard device, repeated on hundreds of pieces in each set, depicted the arms or emblem of the relevant Order, surrounded by its motto, 'for Service and Valour', around a monogram for the Order of St George; 'for Faith and Faithfulness' for the Order of St Andrew; 'for Labour and the Fatherland' for the Order of St Aleksandr Nevskii; and 'Usefulness, Honour and Glory' for the Order of St Vladimir.[163]

From the turn of the nineteenth century Russian porcelain became less verbal. Inscription, where it occurred, was more frequently outside the 'frame' rather than an integral part of the main decorative design, as caption for the picture rather than as ownership identification. Thus a Gardner Factory series of scenes of European peasant women merely labels them as it would label a book illustration or an engraving (from which the scenes were derived): 'Paysanne des environs de Vienne', 'Femmes Croates de Iluin et d'Ogulin', 'Une jeune paysanne de la haute

Carniole en habit de fête', 'Iuive polonoise'.[164] There was, however, still a market for occasional customised inscriptions, especially when marking the item as a gift.[165]

Glass

The first glassworks in Muscovy was founded in 1639. After a slow start, due both to a lack of craftsmen and to a lack of initial demand, it survived until 1769, making mainly window glass and pharmaceutical vessels. The first state glass factory, intended to produce tableware for the court, was founded on the initiative of Tsar Aleksei Mikhailovich in 1668. In the second decade of the eighteenth century the focus of luxury glassmaking switched to St Petersburg, especially to the Iamburg and Zhabino factories, then in the late 1730s to the St Petersburg Glassworks. Small private factories had begun to appear from the late seventeenth century, and proliferated across the country, including Siberia, over the course of the eighteenth century. A list of known Russian manufacturers up to the first half of the nineteenth century contains information on nearly 250 glassworks.[166]

Engraved inscriptions were an additional luxury. From the mid eighteenth century they tended to be limited to monogrammed initials. Fuller textual inscription, though not unknown in later glass, is a particular feature of the earliest period of Russian luxury glassware from the St Petersburg factories, often on commission for, or as gifts to, Peter I himself. Textual inscriptions included mottoes to accompany images copied from emblem books, as well as toasts and other phrases associated with the culture of drinking (Fig. 3.13).[167] The formulae could be engraved in Cyrillic or in Latin, occasionally in French. Some latinate phrases were engraved in Cyrillic lettering.[168] Imported glass, too, could be inscribed to local taste, such as the Saxon lidded goblet of the late seventeenth or early eighteenth century which was engraved, probably after its importation, with a long laudatory Cyrillic formula to Peter.[169]

Clocks, Sundials and Other Instruments

Instruments for measuring need calibrations. To be read is integral to their purpose, whether by means of numbers or notches or words or pictures or other symbols. Those who create implements for measuring or marking time, or distance, or temperature, or location, need also to create the display of signs that enable their devices to convey the relevant

Fig. 3.13: Glass goblet engraved with Latin monogram (AP) and Cyrillic drinking inscription ('Health to His Honour Anton Ivanovich Petrov'), mid eighteenth century. Hillwood Estate, Museum and Gardens; photo: Edward Owen

information. The signs are necessary to the design. And design mattered. The elegance of some eighteenth-century scientific instruments is not an accidental byproduct of their functionality. Whether the taste of the day or the style of the maker valued intricacy, or preferred simplicity, the aesthetics of practical knowledge contributed to its pleasures and status. Scientific instruments could delight as well as inform, and the attentiveness to design also extended to their qualities as elements in the graphosphere. As in other areas of specialised manufacture, Russia acquired scientific instruments by three means: the import of the objects; the import of people who could make the objects; and the training of local craftsmen.

The instruments with the longest history were clocks, both mechanical and solar. The earliest depicted tower clockface in Moscow, showing the twelve hours in Cyrillic letters, was purportedly made in 1404, although the illustration is in a mid-sixteenth-century manuscript which probably reflects its own time.[170] The first in a sequence of clocks to adorn the Frolov (later Spasskii) tower of the Kremlin was installed in 1585. By the second half of the seventeenth century tower clocks had become a relatively common sight not only in Moscow but also in provincial towns such as Kolomna, Velikii Ustiug, Arkhangelsk, Tver, Krasnoiarsk and Eniseisk, and in several monasteries.[171] Portable clocks and automata were being imported into Muscovy at least from the mid sixteenth century, often as diplomatic gifts,[172] and clocks and sundials were being made in Muscovy at least from the early seventeenth century. By the early eighteenth century the repertoire ran from carriage clocks and mantel clocks through to pocket watches. Apart from the essential calibrations, it was common for clockmakers to advertise their craft with inscriptions on the face itself. The script or language varied depending on the maker or taste. Thus a compass and sundial by the Englishman Benjamin Scott, who spent several years in St Petersburg working first for the Admiralty, then for the Academy of Sciences, before his death in 1751, is inscribed in Latin letters (including *B. Scott Fecit* on the main dial),[173] while a 24-hour clock combined with an equatorial sundial by Nikolai Chizhov (1731–67) is elaborately inscribed in Russian.[174] In the most uncluttered space on the dial Chizhov declared that he was both the designer and the maker (*Vymyshlial i delal Nikolai Chizhov 1761 goda*). Sometimes, rather in the manner of the makers' inscriptions on some engravings, credit for design and for manufacture is split, as on a 24-hour clock from the mid nineteenth century showing global time zones. The inscriptions here are almost ludic in their quantity, arrangement and density, including more than seventy place-names from around the world, to which the hands point in turn as they complete their daily cycle. An inscription in one of the few areas of free space announces that this ostentatiously ingenious device was designed by Petr Khavskii and executed by Dmitrii Gavrilov.[175]

Apart from clocks and sundials, the age of the rise of the scientific instrument in Russia was the eighteenth century. With the creation of a navy came the need for compasses and other navigational aids. With attempts to map the empire came the need for surveying equipment such as geodesic astrolabes (or circumferentors).[176] In 1751, when the Academy of Sciences organised an expedition to Arkhangelsk to observe a solar eclipse, its requirements included quadrants, a clock, a micrometer, telescopes, an astrolabe, a thermometer.[177] Just as the Kremlin Armoury had its icon workshop and its silversmiths and jewellers, so several of the newer institutions had their instrument workshops, including the Admiralty and, above all, the Academy of Sciences.[178] The importance of draughtsmanship and design is underlined by the fact that the Academy of Arts, too, had classes on instruments and on clocks.[179]

The Human Body

Writing can be visible on the clothed body and on the unclothed body. Several types of object with secondary writing could be displayed on the clothed body, fixed to it in non-intrusive ways: medals suspended from the neck, beard tokens sewn into outer garments, or the cloth registration tags of St Petersburg cab drivers, sewn onto the back of the collar, as required from the eighteenth century,[180] and as depicted in prints from the early nineteenth century.[181]

Secondary writing directly on the unclothed body, as part of its 'production' (so to speak), is found in the popular myth of 'royal marks', by which pretenders from the seventeenth century to the nineteenth supported their claims to legitimacy. Such marks included various images and symbols (crosses, stars, state regalia) but were seldom textual. Very occasionally they included a name.[182]

And there was branding. Strictly speaking, branding was a form of tertiary writing, not secondary writing, since it was created on an object (here, a human body) which already existed for other purposes. Nevertheless, it should be mentioned here. Direct marking of the body through mutilation and/or branding was embedded in Muscovite and then imperial judicial practice.[183] It was both a punishment and a form of identification, so that convicted criminals would be recognised as such. From time to time decrees stipulated how the culprit should be marked. Sporadic legislation in the seventeenth century required the marking of the face with initial letters signifying the category of offence: 'B' for *buntovshchik* (rebel), 'V' for *vor* (thief) and so on. A decree of 1746 laid down that a thief should be branded not with the initial letter but with all the letters of the complete word (*VOR*, with or without the final hard sign) distributed across the forehead and cheeks. This genre of writing was by no means unique to Russia. The branding of miscreants with initial letters was practised in late medieval and early modern England: 'R' for rogue, 'T' for thief, 'V' for vagabond and the like.[184] Punishment by branding was formally abolished in Russia in 1863.

A more trivial instance of bodily marking, retold in modern mythology but with dubious grounding in fact, concerns the story of Petr Telushkin, who in 1830 heroically scaled the church spire in the Peter and Paul Fortress to repair the angel at the top. As part of his reward Telushkin is said to have been given a permit entitling him to free drinks in any tavern. He lost the permit, so the entitlement was certified with a stamped mark under his chin, to which he could point. This is said (without great conviction) to be the origin of a modern drinking gesture. Three years later, in 1833, in his late twenties, Petr Telushkin died, allegedly of alcohol abuse.

CHAPTER 4

Scripts and Languages of the Graphosphere

Graphospheres are formed by the presence of visible words. What kinds of words were present in the Russian graphosphere, and by means of what signs were they made visible? That is to say: what were the languages and the scripts? This chapter introduces the principal features of the Russian linguistic landscape and tracks their changes across the four centuries. The most notable changes were in the appearance of Russian and in the patterns of proliferation of non-Russian; or, more properly, in the appearance of Cyrillic and in the patterns of the proliferation of non-Cyrillic. In a sense the messages of script are separable from, and sometimes as important as, the messages of language. Script is visible, language is not; script is accessible to all who look, language only to those who can decipher or who can have others decipher for them. Moreover, if the question is put initially in terms of script, it avoids the danger of implying that there was a straightforwardly binary linguistic contrast between the Russian and the foreign. On the one hand, Cyrillic covered more than Russian: as a notionally standard language, Russian emerged only in the latter part of our period, over the eighteenth and early nineteenth centuries. On the other hand, some varieties of non-Russian and non-Cyrillic became, at times, so well embedded in Russia's cultural practices and graphospheric habits that they can be reckoned foreign only in their origins.

Cyrillic: Slavonic, Russian

Cyrillic

Broadly speaking, an alphabet is subject to change in one or both of two ways: with respect to its repertoire of signs (i.e. the number and range of letters) and with respect to their appearance (design, typeface etc.). There have been many varieties of the Cyrillic alphabet. Sometimes the variations have been semantically significant, where changes in the visible code imply changes in cultural message and orientation.

The modern Russian version of the Cyrillic alphabet has a repertoire of thirty-three letters, if one includes two vowels with diacritics (the obligatory й and the often optional ё). Before the reforms of 1918 the standard version had thirty-six letters. Handbooks of Church Slavonic and of early East Slavonic paleography tend to list between thirty-eight and forty-three signs, depending on whether they treat digraphs and iotated vowels as variants or as separate items.[1] Muscovite printed primers in the seventeenth and eighteenth centuries regularly listed forty-five letters, and sometimes as many as forty-seven, while the alphabetic exercises (syllabic exercises, acrostics) in the same books often focus on a somewhat smaller repertoire.[2] As a set of graphemes, therefore, over the past half-millennium or so, the Cyrillic alphabet has been far more variable in its repertoire than, for example, the Latin or Greek alphabets. Early panegyrics of Slavonic letters had praised them in terms of an assumed special relationship between signs and sounds.[3] Late reforms reduced the repertoire in the interests of phonological rationalisation. In the intervening centuries, convention, fashion, aesthetics, theology and inertia held sway in various configurations. Towards the latter part of our period, the advocacy of a reduced repertoire was represented as a mark of rational modernity.

Cyrillic lettering in Muscovite and Russian manuscripts has tended to be divided into four categories of shape and manner. These categories are also used with regard to Cyrillic secondary writing, and to print, although the history of printed letter-forms is complicated by an additional factor whose significance will be considered below. The four main categories are:

ustav: large, distinct, evenly spaced square letters of regular shape and height, with very few elements extending either above or below the line, and (in early medieval manuscripts) no division between words. The closest designation in West European paleography would be 'uncial'. In effect, *ustav* was a script consisting only of what would now be called capital letters. It was the near-universal script of manuscript culture in early Rus. By mid-fifteenth-century Muscovy it was almost obsolete in manuscripts, though not in lapidary and other monumental inscriptions.

poluustav, 'semi-*ustav*', often rendered as 'semi-uncial': smaller, less regularly spaced and shaped letters, with more elements above and below the line, with more frequent superscript letters, abbreviations and ligatures.[4]

Poluustav represents a fairly broad spectrum, from quite formal, square lettering close to *ustav*, to smaller, more rounded lettering, with more frequent flourishes. From the mid fifteenth century *poluustav* was the dominant style of writing in devotional books, and in the sixteenth century it became the basis for the typefaces in Muscovite printed books. The influence was mutual, each mimicking the other. Seventeenth-century manuscript *poluustav* was influenced by printed lettering.[5] Even in the nineteenth century the *poluustav* of devotional manuscripts often imitated printed books.[6]

skoropis': literally 'speed-writing', cursive.[7] Chronologically, Muscovite cursive expanded roughly in parallel with *poluustav*, and with the switch from parchment to paper as the standard material of manuscript books and documents. Cursive became the normal script for routine administrative documentation, and then for virtually all informal and private writing. Early cursive was quite similar to *poluustav*. However, while *poluustav* remained comparatively conservative, cursive hands developed an ever widening range of local, temporal and individual characteristics. Unfortunately, the more recent the range of cursives, the less thoroughly they are described in the handbooks of handwriting, very few of which extend into systematic 'neography' of the nineteenth century.[8]

viaz', or woven lettering. *Viaz'* was not used for ordinary or extensive texts. It was a formal style of decorative lettering, used, for example, for the headings of works in manuscripts and printed books,[9] and, especially in the sixteenth and seventeenth centuries, for formal secondary writing on icons, textiles, metalware etc.[10] In a band of *viaz'* the letters are made to interlock and overlap: for example, through variation in size and height, or by sharing vertical lines. In *viaz'* the decorative function can dominate over the verbally communicative function to such an extent that the most elaborate bands of *viaz'* become quasi-cryptographic, although one should stress that *viaz'* retains spelling conventions, while alphabetic cryptography works by disrupting them.[11]

Manuscripts have styles of handwriting, printing has typefaces and fonts. The typefaces of early Muscovite printing were based on *poluustav*. Thus, the printed books of the church (that is, almost all Muscovite printed books before the eighteenth century) were designed to look roughly like their manuscript equivalents. In countries where Cyrillic printing was somewhat less restricted in its repertoire, it was also somewhat less restricted in its typography. From the late 1580s Ruthenian printers, notably in Vilnius, began to produce some secular administrative texts in Cyrillic typefaces reminiscent of cursive hand, or at any rate at the extreme cursive-like end of the *poluustav* spectrum.[12] Ruthenian printing thus articulated a functional division in the appearance of lettering – and hence of the look of the printed page – equivalent to the visual distinction which existed in handwriting. In early Muscovite printing even the relatively few administrative printed documents in the seventeenth century were presented in the familiar *poluustav* of church books.

This changed under Peter I. Peter I is often said to have reformed the Cyrillic alphabet. This is not quite the case. There was no change to the existing Cyrillic alphabet in its traditional spheres of use. Instead, Peter introduced a modified version for a specific context, for non-ecclesiastical printing. His proposed modifications were twofold: a slight reduction in the repertoire of letters (that is, of the alphabet as such), and – the most striking element – a change in their appearance through the introduction of a new typeface. Peter was personally involved in overseeing the design of his 'civil typeface' (*grazhdanskii shrift*). The civil typeface has affinities with several other forms of lettering. The contrast between a page of the old printed *poluustav* and a page of civil type is rather like the contrast between 'black-letter' (or 'Gothic') type and 'antiqua' type in printed versions of the Latin alphabet, as can be seen in the contrast between two administrative documents falling either side of the transition: a request for safe passage (*oboronitel'nyi list*) of 1706 in the traditional type (Fig. 4.1), and decree of 1715 in the civil type (Fig. 4.2). However, Petrine civil type also has visual affinities with some variants of early-eighteenth-century Cyrillic cursive, with the letter-forms of the Amsterdam Cyrillic printing that Peter had sponsored around the turn of the century, and with the Cyrillic lettering of early-eighteenth-century engravers. It is not easy to say which should be regarded as the principal source or sources.[13] Perhaps there was no single model. The aesthetics of letter-form were being explored and illustrated well before the new typeface was introduced. In 1692 the royal children were presented with a manuscript primer by Karion Istomin which, two years later, was engraved as a block-book by Leontii Bunin, a draftsman and engraver at the Kremlin Armoury workshops. In the primer each of the thirty-eight letters is depicted in multiple versions. Sometimes there are more than twenty variants, followed by several articulations of the Latin and Greek equivalents (where such existed).[14]

Equivalent in some respects to the introduction of the civil typeface was a change in the conventions of representing numbers. Traditionally, letters of the Cyrillic alphabet also served as numerals. Arabic numerals appear

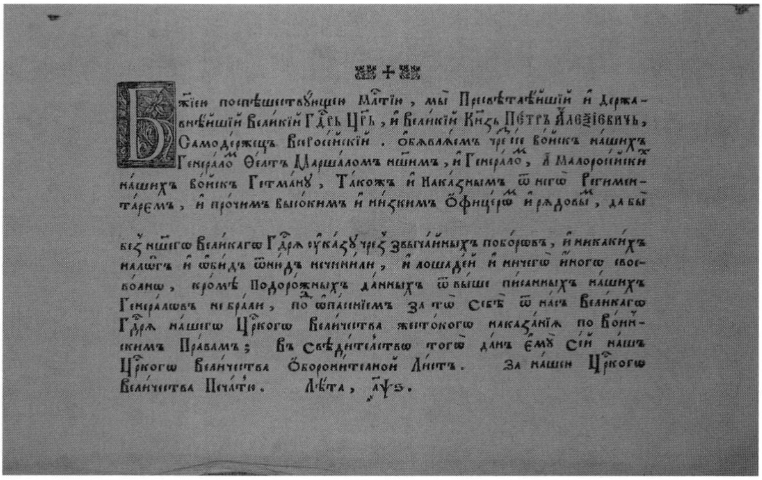

Fig. 4.1: Military pass requesting safe passage (*oboronitel'nyi list*), 1706, in traditional Cyrillic typeface. St Petersburg Institute of History of the Russian Academy of Sciences

sporadically in Muscovy over the second half of the seventeenth century,[15] but became standard with the civil typeface.

The first book in the new typeface, a work on geometry, was printed in March 1708. Thenceforth civil type was to be the medium for print in government and administration, in scholarship and learning, eventually in literature and more widely in non-devotional culture. It was not intended to replace all other letter-forms. On the contrary, its visual semantics depended on the church retaining its habitual manner of printing. Civil type was designed to distinguish the traditional from the new, the ecclesiastical from the secular. The strictly alphabetic element of the Petrine civil typeface (that is, the slight reduction in the repertoire of letters) was trivial by comparison with the significance of the design. This was a momentous shift in the visual semantics of the printed word.[16]

Virtually all modern Russian Cyrillic typefaces are descendants, albeit with modifications,[17] of Peter's civil version, as is the modern alphabet with its reduced repertoire of signs. By mid century it was widely referred to as the 'Russian alphabet', and contrasted with the 'church alphabet'. Vasilii Trediakovskii, in his *Conversation Between a Foreigner and a Russian on the Old and New Orthography*, written in 1747, called it the 'new' as opposed to the 'old', while stating succinctly that Peter's intention was that it should

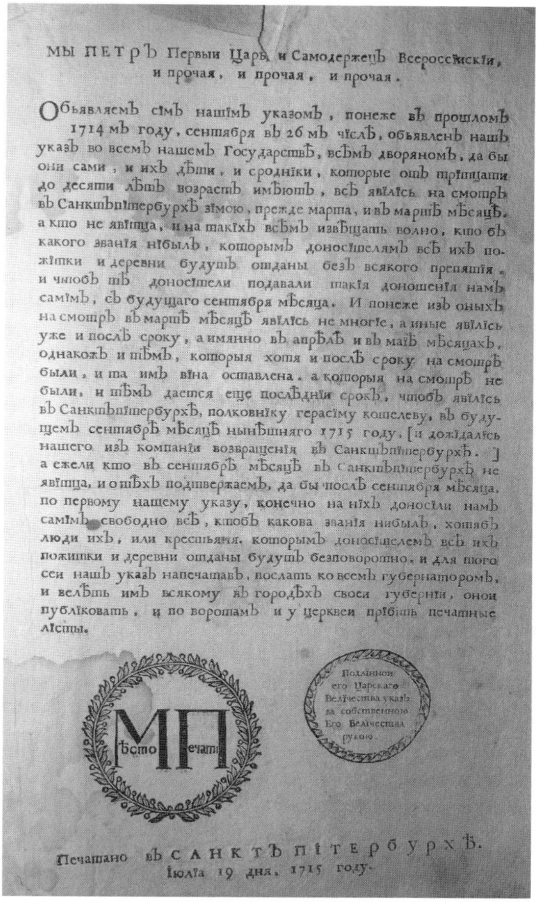
МЫ ПЕТРЪ Первыи Царь и Самодержецъ Всероссійскіи, и прочая, и прочая, и прочая.

Обьявляемъ сімъ нашімъ указомъ, понеже въ прошломъ 1714 мъ году, сентября въ 26 мъ числѣ, обьявленъ нашъ указъ во всемъ нашемъ Государствѣ, всѣмъ дворяномъ, да бы они сами, и ихъ дѣти, и сродніки, которые отъ тріццати до десяти лѣтъ возрастъ имѣютъ, всѣ явілісь на смотръ въ Санктъпітербурхѣ зімою, прежде марта, и въ мартѣ мѣсяцѣ. а кто не явітца, и на такіхъ всѣмъ извѣщать волно, кто бъ какого званія нібылъ, которымъ доносітелямъ всѣ ихъ пожітки и деревни будутъ отданы безъ всякого препятія. и чтобъ тѣ доносітели подавали такія доношенія намъ самімъ, съ будущаго сентября мѣсяца. И понеже изъ оныхъ на смотръ въ мартѣ мѣсяцѣ явілісь не многіе, а иные явілісь уже и послѣ сроку, а имянно въ апрѣлѣ и въ маіѣ мѣсяцахъ, однакожъ и тѣмъ, которыя хотя и послѣ сроку на смотрѣ были, и та имъ віна оставлена. а которыя на смотрѣ не были, и тѣмъ дается еще послѣдніи срокъ, чтобъ явілісь въ Санктъпітербурхѣ, полковніку герасіму кошелеву, въ будущемъ сентябрѣ мѣсяцѣ нынѣшняго 1715 году, [и дожідалісь нашего изъ компаніи возвращенія въ Санктъпітербурхѣ.] а ежели кто въ сентябрѣ мѣсяцѣ въ Санктъпітербурхѣ не явітца, и о тѣхъ подтверждаемъ, да бы послѣ сентября мѣсяца, по первому нашему указу, конечно на ніхъ доносіли намъ самімъ свободно всѣ, ктобъ какова званія нибылъ, хотябъ люди ихъ, или крестьяня. которымъ доносітелемъ всѣ ихъ пожитки и деревни отданы будутъ безповоротно. и для того сеи нашъ указъ напечатавъ, послать ко всемъ губернаторомъ, и велѣть имъ всякому въ городѣхъ своеи губерніи, онои публіковать, и по воротамъ и у церквеи прібіть печатные лісты.

Печатано въ САНКТЪПІТЕРБУРХѢ. Іюлія 19 дня, 1715 году.

Fig. 4.2: Decree of Peter I, 9 July 1715, printed in the new 'civil' typeface

look like 'modern – not Gothic – Latin type', while thereby 'distancing itself as far as possible from Greek, which was the basis of our old alphabet, which is now used in printing only by the church'.[18]

It would be easy to form the impression that the new had quickly marginalised the old, that the church alphabet was restricted to a small, traditionalist monocultural enclave, while all the exciting developments in education, learning and administration were represented – at any rate in print – through the civil typeface. However, caution is needed. The 'church alphabet', which in modern Russian bibliographical scholarship tends, somewhat confusingly, to be called the *kirillitsa*, maintained a presence in diverse areas of print culture throughout the eighteenth century. In the first place, a comparison of the numbers of titles in each typeface can mislead. The fullest modern catalogues of eighteenth-century printed books list substantially more titles in the civil typeface (nearly nine thousand between 1725 and 1800) than in the *kirillitsa* (around two thousand over the century from presses in Moscow and St Petersburg), but print runs for the latter were often far larger than for the former.[19] Secondly, the typographic distinction between the religious and the secular was not fully consistent. Although *kirillitsa* was quite quickly perceived to be the preserve of the church, in practice secular texts continued to be produced in the traditional type throughout the century. In the first half of the century only three presses actually possessed civil type.[20] In addition to some non-devotional books, significant quantities of 'non-books' are likely to have been printed in *kirillitsa.*[21] The standard bibliographies, though acknowledging that such texts exist, do not systematically list them,[22] but there was certainly a great deal more than has been catalogued. For example, in mid century the press in provincial Chernihiv, which lacked the civil typeface, regularly issued *kirillitsa* copies of central decrees.[23] Thirdly, through the eighteenth century almost all elementary education still began, and usually ended, with the church alphabet.[24] Systematic grammars for advanced study or for foreigners were based on civil typeface and on the reduced 'Russian' repertoire of letters, but the mass-printed primers, which presented little more than syllabic exercises, a catechism and a few prayers for recitation, were based on the church alphabet. For foreigners and an educated Russian elite, civil type was presented as the norm. Not so at the base of the pyramid of learning. Primers based on civil types were produced in tiny print runs by comparison with the church versions. For example, between 1737 and 1763 the Synod press issued primers every year, usually with a print run of 24,000 copies, sometimes 48,000. According to one calculation, nearly half a million church primers were printed at the Synod press during the peak period of the 1750s and 1760s.[25] Only towards the end of the century were there stronger attempts to produce and disseminate primers which presented civil type as the norm, although even these still included the 'church alphabet' and associated exercises.[26]

Because most basic education continued to use the medium of the 'church alphabet', it has been argued that the civil typeface, although ostensibly a simplification, in fact served as a barrier for the poorly educated, who would have found it hard to decipher.[27] The suggestion seems strained. The difference in letter-forms may well have been emblematic of an educational divide, but I am not aware of evidence that letter-forms contributed to maintaining that divide. Vasilii Trediakovskii noted that, confronted with texts in Peter's first version of the typeface, hesitant readers might initially have had some difficulty with three of the characters which were transferred directly from the Latin alphabet, but he saw no difficulty in recognising letter-forms which were merely modifications of existing Cyrillic.[28] If someone with a basic church education had wished to read publications of the Academy of Sciences, the typeface was surely the least of the potential barriers.

Over the nineteenth century the 'church alphabet' became more thoroughly marginalised, partly as a consequence of the very significant expansion in printing in what was by now the standard version of the alphabet, partly because the church began to lose its domination of primary education just in the period when the growth of literacy was at its fastest, and partly because the repertoire of *kirillitsa* texts became ever narrower, reduced largely to reprints. At the same time, however, the 'church alphabet' also began to acquire a new function, which was subsequently to prove productive: as a design option, an archaising set of letter-forms no longer necessarily associated with the ecclesiastical.[29]

Slavonic, Russian

The idea (and the reality) of a standard Russian language is relatively recent. In Muscovy there was no set of agreed rules and conventions that defined 'correct' writing and educated speech. The essential features of Contemporary Standard Russian (CSR) emerged over the eighteenth century and the first few decades of the nineteenth century. CSR was derived from twin bases: Church Slavonic and East Slavonic. The linguistic history of Muscovy and the Russian Empire is the story of how these two strands developed in four respects: in themselves, in relation to one another, in response to additional linguistic contacts, and in reaction to new cultural stimuli and challenges. These developments and interactions involved changes not only in written and spoken expression, but also in ideas about what cultural or cultured expression ought to be.

Church Slavonic was the language of ecclesiastical and devotional writing, and hence of most written culture for most of the Middle Ages. East Slavonic is a generalised label for the Slav vernacular dialects in the Rus lands, which were also the linguistic bases for some less voluminous forms of early writing, notably law codes, informal correspondence, and varieties of inscription. Church Slavonic and East Slavonic were most likely seen as functionally distinct registers, mutually comprehensible in principle if not always in practice, rather than as separate languages.[30] Church Slavonic differed from East Slavonic in some of its sound structures (phonology) and inflections (morphology). These reflect its regional origins among the South Slavs. Since it had been created as a language of translation, Church Slavonic was also distinctive in its sentence structures and in a lot of its vocabulary. One of its principal early functions was as a vehicle for the translation of devotional texts from Greek. Often it mirrored Greek syntax, for example in the use of participial and other subordinate clauses. The lexical range of Church Slavonic included large quantities of words specific to the Christian culture and devotional practices which it served.

Through the Middle Ages the relations between Church Slavonic and East Slavonic changed in apparently contradictory ways. On the one hand, the two grew further apart: structural changes in the vernacular rendered it ever more remote from the comparatively stable forms of Church Slavonic. On the other hand, the two grew closer together, as centuries of coexistence and familiarity, of interaction and of the broadening of written cultures, led to mutual contamination. Vernacular elements became assimilated into some modes of writing whose core was Church Slavonic, and, conversely, elements of Church Slavonic became assimilated in some modes of writing closer to the vernacular. The markers of difference likewise changed. Twelfth-century notions of what constituted a Church Slavonic or a vernacular feature were not the same as their counterparts in the seventeenth century or the eighteenth century.[31] The system may appear to have been enclosed, but it was not static.

In pre-Muscovite Rus the written language of administration had occupied a minor niche in the linguistic landscape. In Muscovy 'chancery language' (*prikaznyi iazyk*), based largely on vernacular forms, became a major feature, counterbalancing the devotional register both in bulk and in visibility.[32] New demands on written culture set new choices in written language. From the mid seventeenth century until the early nineteenth century, successive waves of cultural, technical, educational, scholarly, social and aesthetic reorientation posed more acute challenges to Muscovite conventions of written (and to some extent spoken) communication. The challenges included: serial and unprecedented engagement with aspects of the scholarly, scientific and literary pursuits of Western Europe; the expansion of printing in the non-devotional sphere; the establishment of non-ecclesiastical elite institutions of education and learning (the Academy of Sciences, Moscow University, cadet schools, eventually lycées); a significant influx of foreigners into both cultural and technical employment; and, in consequence, shifting fashions in public and private expression. Such changes and challenges elicited new linguistic responses as written culture was expected to 'say' new things, to accommodate new terms and concepts, to reflect and express new moods and modes of thought and feeling. At the same time they prompted new reflections on written language itself, on norms and variations, on grammar and style, on what, in Russia, written language was, or could be, or should be.

In retrospect, from within modern assumptions and sensibilities, such concerns can seem odd. We are used to standard (which is not to say static) languages, and we tend to reserve our occasional indignation for fringe issues of style and usage. It is easy to forget that diglossic, bilingual or multilingual cultures of writing have been common. Among East Slavs, a more complex situation than the Muscovite was that of Ruthenia. Here from the late fourteenth century a quasi-vernacular written language was in use for a broad range of purposes, from administration to biblical translation. This language has been labelled with a wide variety of names. The currently favoured versions tend to be either 'Ruthenian' or the self-definitions *prosta mova* ('simple' or 'common' language) or *rus'ka mova* (Rus language).[33] *Prosta mova* also became a language of printing. Its relationship to Church Slavonic was somewhat equivalent to that between the Polish vernacular and Latin. Printing presses produced books and documents in all four languages. In Muscovy before the seventeenth century, despite the expansion of chancery language, there was no equivalent to *prosta mova*. Indeed, Ruthenian texts in *prosta mova*, when copied by Muscovites, tended to become 'slavonised', as if scribes regarded the language merely as poor Church Slavonic which needed correcting.[34] Nevertheless, as we shall see, in the latter part of the seventeenth century multilingual Ruthenian bookmen familiar with Latin, Polish, Ruthenian, Church Slavonic and in some cases Greek played important roles as stimuli for new developments in Muscovite linguistic thinking and practice.[35]

Muscovite sensibilities with respect to linguistic norms and registers had traditionally been honed through habit and practice, not through systematic analysis and description in the form of grammars. In early Muscovite print culture practical primers were common, but formal grammars were virtually non-existent. Moreover, grammatical description of Russian was preceded by formal description of Church Slavonic. The first (and only) grammar issued by the Moscow Print Yard, in 1648, was a revised version of the Church Slavonic grammar of the Ruthenian scholar Meletii Smotrytskyi.[36] Smotrytskyi (c. 1578–1633) was educated at the Jesuit college in Vilnius, and in Leipzig and Wittenberg. His grammar was first published in what is now Vievis (in Lithuania) in 1619. Vernaculars are often taken for granted by native speakers, and it is not uncommon for grammars of vernaculars to be produced first by foreigners. In the case of Russian, the earliest printed grammar was written by a German, Wilhelm Ludolf, and was published in Oxford in 1696.[37] Systematic description of Russian in Russia – initially also for the benefit of foreigners – began in the eighteenth century. The earliest known grammars of Russian by a Russian were written by Vasilii Evdokimovich Adodurov (1709–80). Adodurov published a brief grammar in German in 1731, and wrote a more substantial grammar in 1738–40.[38] However, the Russian version of the latter remained in manuscript. A Swedish version, translated (without acknowledgement) from students' notes on Adodurov's lectures, was printed in Stockholm in 1750.[39] Finally, in this somewhat convoluted sequence, the first grammar of Russian by a Russian, printed in Russian and in Russia, was that of Mikhail Lomonosov, the polymath founder of Moscow University, issued in St Petersburg in 1757.[40] Lomonosov's grammar became the foundation for subsequent Russian formal descriptions of Russian. However, it is worth noting that in its own time it, too, was taken up just as readily by foreigners. An expanded German version was produced in 1764.[41] A French version of 1768, produced after Lomonosov's death and not explicitly attributed to him, became a standard textbook not just for foreigners resident in Russia, but also in France and even in Britain.[42]

Alongside the emergence of structural description came stylistic prescription, or attempts at prescription, regarding how Russian should actually be written. Over the eighteenth century the main debates revolved around the roles of, and relations between, Church Slavonic and vernacular Russian; or, more properly, between Slavon*isms* and Russ*isms*. Nobody argued for pristine Church Slavonic or for some notionally pristine vernacular as an exclusive written norm to meet eighteenth-century cultural demands. In practice the discussions focussed on words and forms derived from or associated with the respective languages or registers. There was in any case no simple line to be drawn between the two. For example, where a Slavonism and a Russism were derived from the same root, sometimes the difference was felt as stylistic (the Slavonism sounding more solemn), but sometimes the original differences in enunciation had become lexicalised so as to produce words with distinct meanings, such as *golova* ('head' in East Slavonic and Russian) as opposed to *glava* ('head' in Church Slavonic, but lexicalised in the sense of 'chief' or 'chapter' in Russian). Church Slavonic morphology had also become productive even in the emergence of neologisms, as, for example, in scientific terminology. Thus, although the debates referred to language, in detail they were more about the aesthetics of culture and identity than about fundamentals of language as such.[43]

Peter I had declared that new knowledge (the kind of knowledge that was to be conveyed in the civil typeface) should be translated 'not in high Slavonic words, but in the simple Russian language'.[44] 'Simplicity' was more simply stated than achieved, given the sheer scale of technical and conceptual innovation. Much of the post-Petrine discussion focussed on *belles lettres* rather than on science and technology. The poet and scholar Vasilii Trediakovskii (1703–69) first echoed Peter in advocating a vernacular free of grandiloquent Slavonisms, but later switched to the opposite extreme, arguing that the dignity of letters was best served through the Church Slavonic forms.[45] Mikhail Lomonosov, besides writing his grammar, also formulated a theory of literary usage. He conceived the available vocabulary as being arranged on a kind of five-point scale: at one extreme obsolete Slavonisms, and at the other extreme vernacular vulgarisms, both of which he would exclude from the language of literature. The remaining three points of the scale consisted of acceptably comprehensible Slavonisms, acceptably decent vernacular words and, in between, the words common both to Church Slavonic and to Russian. On this scale of language he superimposed a hierarchy of literary genres. For example, it was appropriate for odes and epics to be written in 'high' style, using the top two registers of vocabulary, while satires were properly written in the 'low' style.

Lomonosov's proposal was not a description of literary practice in the mid eighteenth century. It was an attempt to suggest a rational framework in a period of linguistic innovation, experimentation and disorientation that can seem chaotic. Its virtue was that it allowed for flexibility around a common core. Its principal defect, as a lasting solution, is that it was tied to the assumptions of a particular moment, a hierarchical notion of styles to fit a hierarchical system of literary genres in a hierarchical socio-cultural setting, with the court and its attendant panegyric genres at the apex of prestige and of linguistic dignity. As the demands of culture changed, so the Lomonosovian hierarchy became obsolete even as a theory. Towards the end of the century significant areas of elite culture became, in a sense, privatised. As the gentry were freed from obligatory service, as private presses proliferated after the ending of the virtual state monopoly, as the court and the learned institutions began to be supplemented, as loci and arbiters of cultural value, by the emergence of 'society' or 'polite society', as the rational order of neoclassicism was challenged – even undermined – by the more subdued modulations of pre-romantic sensibility, so cultivated discourse came to be judged by different standards: more reflective than declamatory, more sensitive than celebratory, more intimate than public. This was 'sentimentalism', the Russian version of the cult of true feeling, where the aesthetics of expression were to be determined not by etymology or genre but by 'taste'. And the 'taste' that mattered was that of sensitive gentlewomen immersed in francophone cultural fashion. The most prominent proponent and perhaps the most felicitous exponent of the new style was the writer and historian Nikolai Karamzin (1766–1826).

If the discussions of the eighteenth century revolved around Slavonisms, in the early nineteenth century the 'Slavonism–Russism' dichotomy was complicated by a third element, no less contentious: Gallicisms. The new style not only owed a lot to French taste, it also took a lot from the French language. In part this meant the import of words, but Gallicisms went deeper. They could permeate expression in ways that are now not obvious but which then, to their opponents, could sound just as barbaric. There was a proliferation of calques – compound words formed from Russian elements to render a French compound (e.g. *in+fluence* becomes *v+liianie; dé+veloppement* becomes *raz+vitie*). Still more insidious were the semantic Gallicisms, familiar Russian words used in non-traditional abstract meanings appropriated from their French equivalents: *trogat'* – 'to touch', in the sense of *toucher*, 'to stir the heart', 'to move to pity'; *utonchennyi* – 'refined', with regard to taste or manners (*raffiné*).[46] Then there were phraseological Gallicisms, syntactic Gallicisms, all underpinned by a wider cultural and aesthetic Gallicism of manner, mood and genre. Gallicism was therefore far more than just a few intrusive words which grated on the ears of purists. Lexical barbarism was merely the surface, beneath which the cultural cross-currents flowed deep.

As in the case of Lomonosov's hierarchy of styles, so in the case of Karamzin, the virtues of the system were also its weaknesses. A virtue was that, in appealing to the taste of polite society, the Karamzinians insisted that norms of a standard language of culture should be rooted in socio-cultural practice rather than in linguistic history. And, since good taste was not contingent on genre, they promoted a single set of linguistic practices, an integrated standard language of culture rather than a scale of options. The defects lay in the fact that, in its own way, the Karamzinian approach was as restrictive as that of Lomonosov. In place of stylistic variation according to genre, one now had stylistic homogeneity according to a particular notion of taste. Both systems were essentially static, both could be rendered redundant at the next turn of the wheel of fashion.

The final step, obvious in retrospect, was to emancipate the writer from the tyranny either of genre or of taste. In terms of the crude succession of cultural and literary movements and trends, this elevation of the writer can be associated with the rise of romanticism in Russia. The position was succinctly stated in a polemical exchange in 1821. Aleksandr Shishkov (1754–1841), a retired admiral, long-term literary conservative and future minister of education, argued succinctly for the primacy of language over the writer: 'writers are the creators of their compositions, not of the language'. The response, just as succinct, came from the writer Aleksandr Bestuzhev (1797–1837): 'writers are the creators of the language'.[47] With allowances for rhetorical overstatement this is a fair encapsulation of the romantic reversal of power. *All* the resources of language – high and low, solemn and vulgar, conventional and innovative, indigenous or imported – were at the disposal of the writer, to be manipulated, varied, combined or modified as he or she judged fit. In practice the early-nineteenth-century notion of the primacy of the writer was rather moderate. Nobody was arguing either for linguistic anarchy or for the proliferation of literary idiolects. Such extensions of the doctrine could wait another hundred years until the experiments of the twentieth-century avant-garde. The romantic assertion of individuality was again about style and expression rather than about language as such. Language was a tool for expression: flexible, adaptable, variable, integral.

Assertion has little traction without example, without felicitous and persuasive demonstration. Many writers and essayists, teachers and scholars, printers and craftsmen, even bureaucrats and officials, contributed to the formation of Russian.[48] Yet the polemics within, around and through literature are widely held to encapsulate the process. Among the many quasi-hagiographical formulae that have become attached to the figure of Aleksandr Pushkin is that he was the 'founder of the Russian literary language'.[49] The claim derives from an assessment of Pushkin's writing as a whole, and of its influence. However, although Pushkin was not a theorist, he did produce a kind of manifesto on language and style. Pushkin's verse novel, *Evgenii Onegin*, was his masterpiece in all senses: his most brilliant sustained work, and his demonstration of formal virtuosity, switching from linguistic register to linguistic register, from convention to supposedly incompatible convention, flaunting Gallicisms and Slavonisms alike, taking sideswipes at purist critics real and imagined.

And all this led not to the creation of a mere potpourri of whimsically macaronic verse, not to a game of glittering appearances, but to a novel which, in a sense, released his successors from such constrictions and from the need for such play.

Although the debates about language tended to revolve around literature, and although even in modern Russian the common expression for the standard language is the 'literary' language, and although the emergence of a standard language depended on a great deal more than just the masterworks of a few poets, nevertheless the path travelled by literature can legitimately represent the main stages in the emergence of what is now regarded simply as the Russian language, of Contemporary Standard Russian, of the norms and conventions of educated writing and speech which, *mutatis mutandis*, continue to exist today.

Non-Cyrillic: Greek, Latin, German, French and Others

Mid-fifteenth-century Muscovy was a largely monoglot, largely monoscriptal principality. Mid-nineteenth-century Russia was a multi-ethnic, multilingual, multi-scriptal empire. The presence and the diversity of non-Slavonic languages grew mainly through territorial expansion, partly through immigration, partly through fashions in education, scholarship and polite discourse. Through its eastwards expansion in the sixteenth and seventeenth centuries Muscovy incorporated, alongside the many unwritten languages of Siberia, a sizeable Muslim population with texts in Arabic. Through the westward expansion from the mid seventeenth century Russia annexed substantial territories populated by Ruthenians – whose vernaculars were East Slav, but whose manuscript and print cultures included Latin, Polish and sometimes Greek (as well as Church Slavonic and *prosta mova*) – Poles and Baltic Germans. Through the expansion south of the Caucasus in the late eighteenth and early nineteenth centuries Russia added to its population Christian Georgians and Armenians with long traditions of writing in their own languages, as well as Turkic-speaking Azeris with a tradition of writing in Arabic script. Immigration was demographically less significant, but had cultural consequences disproportionate to its scale.[50] From the Italian architects engaged by the grand prince in the late fifteenth century through to governesses for the children of the gentry in the nineteenth century, and taking in merchants, diplomats, translators and interpreters, soldiers, doctors, cannon makers, silversmiths and goldsmiths, engineers, teachers and scholars, sculptors and artists, not to mention occasional would-be conquerors, foreigners brought linguistic diversity into areas of life beyond the reach or concerns of imperial conquest.

What were the implications of such changes for the graphosphere? Clearly, the presence of and contacts with non-Slav-speakers were hugely important, but the links between ethno-linguistic change and graphospheric change are not straightforward. One cannot predict or explain shifting patterns in the graphosphere by simple extrapolation from the patterns of conquest and immigration. The ethno-linguistic map and the graphospheric map are related, but far from identical. Changes in the latter depended also on different specific types of contact and interaction, on aspects of the state's linguistic and cultural policies and on changes in linguistic and cultural fashion. One can distinguish between, on the one hand, non-Russian languages of the Russian Empire and, on the other hand, non-Russian languages in Russian culture. With regard to their impact on the Russian graphosphere, or indeed with regard to their influence on the Russian language itself, there was an almost inverse relationship between the two: the most prominent non-Russian languages in Russian culture – whether interacting with the Russian language or visible in the Russian graphosphere – were *not* native to non-Russian peoples of the empire. The interactions were consequences of cultural choice, not of mere proximity. The non-Russian languages of the Russian Empire barely overlap with the non-Russian languages of Russian culture. Almost by definition they lacked the prestige, and influence flowed in the opposite direction. Indeed, if we focus on the dominant culture of the empire's ruling elites rather than on the wider human geography of the empire itself, then it can appear that linguistic shifts were due entirely to policy rather than to demography.

Here, as so often, Peter I has conventionally been regarded as a pivotal figure in a scheme that emphasises a stark contrast between an isolated, introverted, monoglot pre-Petrine culture and the outward-facing, receptive, polyglot culture of the Petrine age and beyond. The origins of this perception can be traced to the Petrine era itself. It is succinctly stated, for example, by the diplomat Petr Pavlovich Shafirov, who, in the dedication (to the tsarevich) of his treatise on the Russo-Swedish war, announced that:

> Hitherto nobody from among the Russian people was able to read books or writing except in the Russian language. It was considered a blemish rather than an accomplishment. Now, however, we see His Majesty himself speaking in German, and several thousands of his subjects from among the Russian people, men and women, skilled in various European languages, such as Latin, Greek, French, German, Italian, English and Dutch, such

> that in this, as in many other behaviours, it is not invidious to compare [Russians] with all other European peoples.[51]

Such panegyric is rarely concerned with nuance. The genre demands dramatic contrast, and in any case Shafirov had a vested interest. He was himself a noted linguist, who accompanied Peter on his European journeys, and who had served as a translator at (and for a while *de facto* director of) the Ambassadorial Chancery, where his father had also worked as a translator. Shafirov's contrast between the Petrine and the pre-Petrine is not entirely unfounded, but nor is it adequate. Non-Slavonic languages and scripts were not absent from Muscovy before Peter, but Petrine policy did bring about a significant change in their status, visibility, diversity and density. Before the turn of the eighteenth century a visitor to Muscovy would have seen few open signs of non-Cyrillic writing. This is not because they did not exist, but because the import and production of non-Cyrillic writing were generally enclosed activities. If the visitor had had access to some of the chanceries – in particular the Apothecary Chancery and the Ambassadorial Chancery – or to the Moscow Print Yard, or to some of the monasteries, or to the courts of the tsar or the patriarch, then he would have found pockets of the quite regular presence of non-Cyrillic materials, of bi-scriptal or even multi-scriptal micro-graphospheres. But they were inward-facing, private, in some cases even secret. An equivalent visitor after the start of the eighteenth century would have encountered a very different linguistic landscape. Partly the change was quantitative: a very great deal more foreign-script material was indeed in use after 1700. However, underpinning the quantitative change was a change in cultural self-projection and, for some, self-perception. The presence of non-Cyrillic scripts was no longer a private matter for institutions and occasional scholars. Foreign scripts were no longer kept out of the general gaze, within the institution or the schoolroom. They proliferated on open display: in parks and public squares, on widely distributed official documents, in (and eventually on) shops and market stalls. The presence of non-Cyrillic script became part of the public persona of official culture. That which had been closely guarded as a source of potential contamination came to be injected, in ever larger doses, into the bloodstream.

Here, too, we should differentiate as Shafirov does not. Just as the pre-Petrine linguistic landscape was not barren of all but Slavonic and Cyrillic, so the post-Petrine graphospheric landscape was not a garden in which all flowers bloomed equally. Several languages which were widely spoken by resident non-Russians, or which were widely studied by educated Russians, or which even served as rich sources of new vocabulary that was absorbed into the Russian language itself,[52] nevertheless played only minor roles in the graphosphere. In order for a language and/or script to become prominent in the graphosphere, it was not sufficient merely that there should be a resident population using that language and/or script, nor was it sufficient that people speaking and writing the relevant language(s) may have contributed prominently to Russian commercial, political or cultural life. Not all cultural and linguistic appropriations take place at the graphospheric level. This survey of the non-Slavonic, non-Cyrillic components of the graphosphere is concerned only with one aspect of the wider linguistic interactions. It focusses on what might be called the major graphospheric languages, those that were most prominent in cultures of writing, those whose words were most visible. Over the first half of the nineteenth century major non-Russian graphospheric languages declined, yet 'minor' non-Russian languages proliferated. This proliferation was partly due to the increased production of written and printed materials for and within non-Russian populations of the empire, but it was partly also linked to the rise of academic scholarship in the humanities, as reflected in publications by universities and learned societies. Missionary activity also had a role, as led by the Bible Societies. In 1450 it would have been impossible to find a complete Bible in Muscovy in any language. In 1818 the Bible Society bookshop in Moscow was selling scriptural texts in more than twenty languages.[53]

Greek

Strictly speaking, Greek should be reckoned graphospherically minor. Nevertheless it merits its own subsection because of its importance for the pre-history and the early stages of multilingual culture in Russia. Greek appears in the Russian graphosphere in four main contexts: as a component of conventional iconography; as a source-language (mostly in manuscript, but occasionally printed) for the translation or emendation of Slavonic devotional texts; as a diplomatic language, especially in ecclesiastical diplomacy; and as a language of scholarship. Apart from iconography, secondary writing in Greek was rare.[54] Here we focus mainly on primary writing.

Apart from the residual Greek formulae in iconography, very few Muscovites before the seventeenth century would have had occasion to see any significant amount of written or printed or inscribed Greek. The Greek roots of the Faith were known but churchmen in Rus were not routinely educated in the language that would have equipped them to study the sources. There were exceptions, but they are notable as such. Timofei Veniaminov, one of the translators in the circle of Archbishop Gennadii in Novgorod in the late 1480s and early 1490s, was apparently trying to learn Greek, in the course of which he wrote out sections of Gospel readings in Greek, transcribed into Cyrillic characters, leaving spaces for interlinear translation into Slavonic,[55] but otherwise the extant Greek manuscripts traceable to fifteenth- and sixteenth-century Muscovy are very scarce, were written by visiting 'Greeks', and usually remained in Muscovy only briefly, until their creators departed with them.[56] Their association with Muscovy is an accident of their creators' peregrinations, not a fact of local culture.

An exception, as a long-term resident Greek bookman in Muscovy through the second quarter of the sixteenth century, was Maksim Grek.[57] Maksim produced copious translations from Greek, based both on manuscripts and on printed books in his possession. His isolation as a scholar of Greek is highlighted by his distinctive mode of translation. One of his collaborators, Dmitrii Gerasimov, reveals in a letter that Maksim would render the Greek into Latin, which Dmitrii and another associate, Vlas, converted into a Slavonic version, which they dictated to scribes.[58] Maksim does seem to have tried to train some locals to read Greek. Indeed, one surviving Greek manuscript of a Psalter, in his own hand, was perhaps commissioned by a pupil; but in no meaningful sense can one talk of a 'school' of Greek around Maksim.[59]

Schooling in Greek was available abroad, but in the sixteenth century attempts to acquire the language were patchy. In 1551 Ivan IV wrote to Patriarch Dionysios of Constantinople asking him to receive a certain Fedor Obriuta, that the latter might learn Greek for diplomatic purposes. Obriuta returned only after seven years. In 1583 another letter from Ivan IV to a patriarch of Constantinople (Jeremiah) names two other laymen sent to study 'Greek language and letters': Griaznusha Ushakov and Fedka Vnukov. The sum of our information about them is that the patriarch complained that they were too old to learn the language properly.[60]

The transformation in the status and presence of Greek in Muscovite elite culture dates from the mid seventeenth century. One scholar has even characterised this as 'Moscow's Greek century'.[61] The diplomatic, ideological, ecclesiastical and educational projects of the tsar and the patriarch led to the import of ecclesiastical and other ceremonial objects inscribed in Greek,[62] to the import of Greek manuscripts on an unprecedented scale, to the local production of Greek manuscript books and documents, and to an influx of people trained in the use of Greek. The influx of people included East Christian hierarchs and their envoys on diplomatic missions seeking to gain Muscovite material and political support, and scholars (some native Greek-speakers, but mainly from Ruthenia) invited to drive the process of reform and to help train native Muscovites to do likewise.[63] In 1653–5 Patriarch Nikon sent the monk and diplomat Arsenii Sukhanov to acquire Greek books from the monasteries on Mt Athos. Arsenii's negotiations with the monasteries were spectacularly productive. Some five hundred manuscripts were dispatched to Moscow, to form the core of the collections at the patriarchate and the Print Yard.[64] Greek-speaking monks and churchmen bought and copied manuscripts for their own collections,[65] or for their work as teachers or translators.

How was a knowledge of Greek transmitted? In many cases doubtless informally, from master to pupil or circle of pupils.[66] In the mid seventeenth century there were several attempts to embed the teaching of Greek through the establishment of schools, but in practice they were on a small scale and tended to be short-lived.[67] The continuous institutional history of schooling in Greek is most plausibly traced to 1681, when a school was opened on the territory of the Moscow Print Yard by a certain Timofei, a monk of the Chudov monastery who had spent nearly fifteen years in Constantinople. Timofei's school was perhaps first conceived as a Greek school to serve the needs of the Print Yard itself, but it expanded the curriculum to include Slavonic and received grants to support the education of poor children. The Print Yard school has been described as Russia's first public primary educational institution.[68] At its peak in 1684–5 it is estimated to have had 200–250 pupils. Annual records of its book acquisitions are preserved: a total of nearly five hundred books, mainly in Greek, although there were also multiple copies of Slavonic primers.[69] In 1685 the Greek brothers Ioannikii and Sofronii Likhud (or Ioannikios and Sophronios Leichoudes) arrived in Moscow and organised classes in more advanced Greek, to which the first cohort from Timofei's school could progress. Two years later, in 1687, the Likhud brothers opened their 'Slavo-Graeco-Latin Academy' in purpose-built premises.[70] The brothers devised their own courses in manuscript, but also relied on imported printed books.[71]

The Print Yard was at the intellectual core. Many of the major cultural figures of the day worked for greater or lesser periods either for or in the Print Yard. Arsenii 'the Greek', born in Salonica and educated in Venice, Rome and Padua, was a 'corrector' (*spravshchik*) at the Print Yard from 1654 to 1662.[72] Epifanii Slavinetskii had oversight of many of the key publications over the same period (although he held no official position). Evfimii Chudovskii is documented as having been an employee of the Print Yard between 1653 and 1659, and then again from 1670 to 1678. Dionisii 'the Greek', archimandrite of the Iviron monastery on Athos, came to Moscow in 1655 on the invitation of Arsenii Sukhanov to work as a *spravshchik* at the Print Yard. He stayed in Moscow until 1669. From 1661 to 1664 Arsenii Sukhanov himself was director of the Print Yard. Even the Likhud brothers spent some time as *spravshchiki* in the mid 1690s. The Print Yard and the Print Chancery also accumulated one of the major libraries.

Among the stimuli for the attention to Greek at the Moscow Print Yard were the reforms of liturgical books instigated in the early 1650s by Patriarch Nikon. Nikon and his successors were not interested in printing Greek books, but they needed Greek books as authoritative sources for revisions in Slavonic printed books. In theory, they needed manuscripts – the older, the better, preferably ancient and on parchment. In practice, they often used Greek printed books.[73] This provided ammunition for opponents of reform: ancient manuscripts may well be of pure provenance, but Greek printed books were issued in the lands of the Latins, who had insidiously insinuated their own heretical and blasphemous practices. Even before Nikon's reforms, Greek texts printed in centres of Latin Christianity had been regarded as dubious, among Greek churchmen as well as in Moscow.[74] Hence a request, in 1645, to set up a Greek printing press in Moscow, free both from Turkish prohibition and from 'Latin' contamination.[75] And hence the strident objections not only of Russian 'Old Believers', but also of some who were in any case less infatuated by all things Greek. Thus, for example, Silvestr Medvedev, notable scholar and virulent critic of the Likhud brothers, on several occasions lambasted Nikon's bookmen for betraying Nikon's own declared principles, and for using 'recent Greek books printed in the cities of the Latin faith and of the Lutheran and Calvinist heresies, and which are not in agreement with ancient manuscripts.'[76]

A century earlier, Maksim Grek had viewed such matters quite differently. The distinguished or notorious defector Prince Andrei Kurbskii, in the preface to his compilation of translations from the works of John Chrysostom (his *Novyi Margarit*), recalls the inspiration he had received from Maksim, about the value of learning. In particular, he remembers Maksim telling him how, after the fall of Constantinople in 1453, the treasures of Greek theology were sent for preservation to Venice, where the grateful and knowledge-hungry Italians translated them into Latin, printed them (*daiut v druk*) in large quantities, distributed them throughout the western lands, and made them available for purchase at accessible prices (*lekhkoiu tsenoiu*).[77] For Maksim Grek – as befitted a former associate or pupil of Aldus Manutius – Latin printings of Greek books were signs of virtue. In the seventeenth century the same story was recycled as a warning against heresy.

Despite the impressive numbers of imports, and despite the enthusiasm of the reformers and the vehemence of their opponents, and despite even the occasional treatise extolling the virtues of the Greek language and its forms and its letters,[78] Greek books and manuscripts remained somewhat esoteric objects circulating among a small group of scholars. The establishment of the Print Yard school and then of the Academy point forwards to an age of the more regular inclusion of Greek in elite education, but the visible impact was small. In the second half of the seventeenth century the Greek of printed books and manuscripts, for all the significance legitimately ascribed to it by cultural historians, barely figured in the wider graphosphere. Greek lay behind significant parts of late Muscovite book culture, but was not a prominently visible part of that culture.

There was practically no local Greek printing in Moscow before the eighteenth century. This is in eloquent contrast with the traditions in Ruthenia.[79] Ivan Fedorov's Ostroh Primer of 1578 began with exercises in the Greek alphabet, followed by a section of parallel texts in Greek and Slavonic.[80] The preface and afterwords to Fedorov's 1581 Ostroh Bible were printed in parallel columns of Greek and Slavonic.[81] The first Greek–Slav grammar had been printed in Lviv as early as 1591,[82] one of a small cluster of books (and one broadside) issued with Greek typefaces at the Lviv Brotherhood press in 1591–3.[83] The Print Yard school imported multiple copies of the 1591 grammar, but no Muscovite equivalent was printed, nor did Muscovite seventeenth-century primers repeat Fedorov's bilingual preliminary section. Karion Istomin's 1694 engraved blockbook primer included the names of Greek letters, but this was only a faint prelude to the first Muscovite printed primer with any significant Greek content, the trilingual textbook printed in 1701 by perhaps the most distinguished alumnus of the Print Yard school and the Likhuds' Academy, Fedor Polikarpov.[84] As with grammars and primers, so with lexicography. Bilingual and polyglot glossaries and thesauri (almost always using Cyrillic transliteration) had existed for centuries.[85] Epifanii Slavinetskii compiled a monumental Greek-Slavonic-Latin dictionary, but (despite a plan to publish it, backed by the patriarch of Moscow, in 1697) it remained in manuscript.[86] The first major Moscow-printed trilingual lexicon was produced in 1704 by Fedor Polikarpov (though its sales were weak).[87] The Academy was also involved in the development of multi-scriptal printing with Greek alongside the new civil typeface, as in their detailed account of the inscriptions on the triumphal arch erected outside the Academy in 1709 to mark Peter's victory at Poltava.[88]

Perhaps paradoxically, rather than signal a Grecophile victory in finally establishing Greek as a language of Muscovite printing, Polikarpov's grammar and lexicon herald the start of the more diverse polyglot print culture of the eighteenth century, in which Greek held an honourable but more peripheral position, outflanked and hugely outnumbered by the massed ranks of printings in the Latin-script languages of Western Europe.[89] On the one hand, for better or worse, Greek retained its association with the church.[90] On the other hand, it acquired, and retained for a long time, a certain *cachet* as part of an enlightened education.

Latin

If the 'short' seventeenth century can be called Russia's age of Greek, then the 'long' eighteenth century was Russia's age of Latin in two senses: with regard to the rapid rise to visibility of languages written in the Latin alphabet, and with regard to the unprecedentedly extensive uses of the Latin language itself. We start with Latin in the narrower sense, with regard only to the Latin language. Latin primary writing in Russia appears in an overlapping succession of three principal contexts and functions: first, from the late fifteenth century, as a language of imported source material for translations and adaptations into Slavonic; secondly, as a working language in areas of the central administration; and, thirdly, from the early eighteenth century, as an openly cultivated and disseminated language of education, of science and scholarship, and even of literature. Latin secondary writing (that is, mainly inscriptions) was a language of display, sporadically from the late fifteenth century, more intensively from the early eighteenth century.[91]

In the early phase, when restricted mostly to the role of a source-language for translation into Slavonic, Latin primary writing would barely have figured in the graphic environment of anybody but translators, of whom there were few. Nevertheless there were notable flurries of activity. Archbishop Gennadii's group of translators, who in Novgorod in the 1490s worked on the first Slavonic version of a complete Bible[92] plus some biblical commentary and exegesis,[93] is also linked to other translations from Latin. Among them are, for example: a work on the Latin language itself, the

Ars minor of Donatus, on the eight parts of speech, which was probably the most widely disseminated work of its type in the late Middle Ages;[94] a treatise on the calendar by the thirteenth-century writer Guillaume Durand (William Durandus the Elder); perhaps a compilation based on works by Lactantius.[95] However, the activities of Gennadii's bookmen were not the start of a crescendo of interest in Latin. Latin learning among East Slavs developed in the areas which were part of the Grand Duchy of Lithuania, and then of the Polish–Lithuanian Commonwealth, whence some translations migrated eastwards, but simply as texts in Slavonic, with no implications for the place of Latin itself in the Muscovite graphosphere.

The more persistent presence of Latin primary writing was in a less bookish context: diplomacy. Latin was a language of diplomatic exchange: Moscow's rulers received, and occasionally sent, diplomatic documents in Latin. The Ambassadorial Chancery was an enclave of necessarily multilingual activity. It needed a permanent staff of interpreters and translators, often recruited from among long-term foreign residents and their descendants, since the relevant expertise was rarely to be acquired through a Muscovite education.[96]

Another area of the regular presence and use of Latin in the *prikaz* system was medicine. In Muscovy the more or less regular presence of foreign medical experts seems to date from the late fifteenth century. Their institutionalisation may be traced from the second half of the sixteenth century, though the records of the Apothecary Chancery survive only from the late 1620s onwards.[97] From the mid seventeenth century we know quite a lot about these foreign experts: their origins, the requirements for their qualifications, and many episodes of their practice in Muscovy.[98] Their authoritative knowledge was derived from printed books, and their working language was Latin. The practitioners of the Apothecary Chancery were trained at West European institutions using common printed textbooks of the age. The Chancery required that they be properly qualified. In the eyes of the Muscovite officials, the print-based training of the West European medical practitioners was a guarantor of their expertise. Imported books formed the basis of a reference library, which consisted mainly of medical textbooks but which also included, for example, Bibles in Latin and Italian, a copy of the Nuremberg Chronicle of 1493, Tycho Brahe's *Epistolarum astronomicarum libri* and the collected works of Cicero.[99]

Uses of Latin began to pick up in the second half of the seventeenth century. The late-seventeenth-century Latinists were at first clustered around the Kremlin, often with the patronage of the tsar. Although their main output was devotional, their translations extended to secular works.[100] As in previous generations, many of them were educated outside Muscovy, but unlike their predecessors they took steps to create a succession not just through passing knowledge to an informal circle of disciples, but through introducing Latin into the classroom. Thus, although Latin primary writing still barely figured on the linguistic landscape beyond the specialist institutions, the foundations were laid for its establishment and growth.

A central figure in, and symbolic representative of, the import, pursuit and institutionalisation of Latin learning was the polyglot theologian, sermonist, printer, poet, dramatist and tutor to the tsar's children, Samuil Petrovskii-Sitnianovich, better known as Simeon Polotskii (1629–80). Educated at the Mohyla College in Kiev, and then probably at one of the Jesuit colleges (or the Academy) at Vilnius, Samuil took the name Simeon on becoming a monk. He had already built a reputation as a bookman before he emigrated to Moscow (from Polotsk) in 1664.[101] Among his rhetorical accomplishments was Latin verse composition. No Latin verses are known from the Moscow period of his life, but Latin hexameters were included in his trilingual (Ruthenian, Polish, Latin) panegyric on the occasion of Tsar Aleksei Mikhailovich's visit to Polotsk in 1656.[102] In Moscow Simeon's voluminous works included an enormous encyclopedic compilation of aphorisms adapted into Slavonic verse from Latin prose originals, which he called the *Garden of Many Flowers* (*Vertograd mnogotsvetnyi*),[103] and a set of verse captions based on original Latin captions to the suite of biblical engravings by Matthaeus Merian.[104] His verse adaptation of the Psalms (*Psaltir' rifmotvornaia*) was controversial in its day both for its departures from the received versions and for its reflection of a 'Latin' practice (although it was not rendered specifically from the Latin language).[105] As head of the monastery of the Saviour, built just a couple of hundred metres from the Kremlin, on a street where stallholders sold icons and thence known as the 'monastery of the Saviour Behind the Icons' (Zaikonospasskii monastyr'), Simeon set up a school. After Simeon's death, the same monastery housed part of what came to be known as the Slavo-Graeco-Latin Academy. For the last two years of his life Simeon also ran a printing press in the Kremlin, in the 'Upper Printing House' (Verkhniaia tipografiia).

In the eighteenth century Latin primary writing became more visible. Having been a source-language from which erudite men rendered and disseminated texts in Slavonic, it became a primary language of education, of science and scholarship, and of public ceremonial declamation and display. The first Moscow-printed books with substantial elements of Latin were, as in the case of Greek, Fedor Polikarpov's trilingual grammar of 1701 and his lexicon of 1704. In the eighteenth century it became widely assumed – and sometimes prescribed – that Latin should be part of the curriculum of post-primary education. At seminaries from the 1740s Latin even spread to the primary curriculum.[106] In institutions of higher education and scholarship such as the Academy of Sciences (founded in 1724) and Moscow University (founded in 1755) Latin became a – often the – major language of instruction and learned communication, especially in the natural and mathematical sciences.[107] Far more was at stake than merely the import and distribution of Latin textbooks. Latin became a language of original writing, and speaking: of lectures and of public disputations, of dissertations, of laboratory and experimental records and annotations, of reviews and monographs.[108] Russian bookmen flaunted their rhetorical virtuosity in Latin odes, epigrams, epitaphs and occasional verses.[109] Latin books not only filled the shelves of the institutions charged with stocking and teaching them, but adorned the private libraries of men of means and culture.[110] Nor, now, did the Latin books have to be imported (though many were): in the eighteenth century Latin became one of the major languages of printing in the Russian Empire. In terms of the number of titles, Latin was the third language of printing, some way behind Russian and German. However, if we consider only St Petersburg imprints, and exclude printing in the German-speaking towns of Riga and Reval, then the gap between German and Latin closes dramatically: just over one-third of St Petersburg foreign-language imprints were in German, and just under one-third in Latin.[111]

Latin secondary writing followed a similar pattern: sporadic and unsystematic from the late fifteenth century, widespread and multi-generic from the early eighteenth century. Latin epigraphy's first false dawn was in 1491, when Antonio Solari's inscription was mounted in the wall of the Kremlin above the Frolov gate.[112] This did not start a trend. Latin public or quasi-public monumental inscriptions appeared with any semblance of regularity only from Peter's import of Italian statues for his Summer Garden in St Petersburg. Instances of widely visible Latin prior to this are very rare, limited perhaps to the import of West European coins, especially when redistributed as payment to troops, as in the case of very large quantities of the over-stamped thalers (*efimki s priznakom*) issued in the mid 1650s. Apart from this, pre-eighteenth-century Latin secondary writing is occasionally to be found on imported luxury objects. One genre, however, was an exception: engravings. In the seventeenth century imported engravings, some with Latin captions and inscriptions, were widely distributed. They were available on public sale, and found their way into many ecclesiastical and state institutions, as well as private collections.

In the eighteenth century the genres of Latin secondary writing proliferated, especially in ritual, commemorative or ceremonial contexts.[113] Latin captions and mottoes on commemorative medals, on institutional, military and familial crests, funerary inscriptions, Latin on public monuments[114] – all contributed to the broader, outward-facing visibility of Latin beyond the schoolroom, the university, the academy, the ministry, the library. For much of the century Latin was a script of prestigious formal inscription, even in contexts where many viewers would not have been able to decipher, let alone translate, the words that it signified.

In some of these functions Latin persisted into the nineteenth century, although from the latter part of the eighteenth century its hegemony was increasingly subject to challenge. For example, until the 1770s Latin was a common language of inscription on commemorative medals, whether recording events of Russian history, or awarded to individuals as signs of recognition.[115] However, minutes of the committee set up in 1772, to determine the subjects, designs and inscriptions for a new set of medals commemorating events since the time of Peter, reveal sharp disagreement over the question of language. Against the suggestion that, following European and Russian precedent, the inscriptions should be in Latin, it was objected that Russians should be able to read about the virtuous deeds of their monarchs without first having to learn Latin.[116] A more public linguistic polemic is implied in the inscriptions to the two most celebrated equestrian monuments to Peter the Great: Falconet's dramatic 'Bronze Horseman', commissioned by Catherine II and unveiled in 1782, and the more conventionally classical statue by Carlo Rastrelli, commissioned by Peter himself in 1716, cast in 1747, but set up on a public pedestal only in 1800, by Catherine's son Paul. Catherine's reads 'Catherine the Second to Peter the First' in two languages, Latin and Russian. Paul's inscription, 'A Great-Grandson to a Great-Grandfather' is in Russian only. The implied statement of linguistic difference is all the more eloquent because of the obvious formal similarity.

German

For the first half-dozen decades of the eighteenth century German was by some distance the dominant foreign language in Russia.[117] If we were to move beyond the graphosphere into a notional 'audiosphere' so as to include spoken German, then no other language comes close. However, if we stick to visible German in the Russian graphosphere, then its history is in some respects comparable to, parallel to and linked to that of Latin. The prominence of German in the 'audiosphere' was due to the presence of German-speaking residents and visitors. There had been German-speaking residents in towns of northern Rus since the Middle Ages. Novgorod was fully integrated into the Baltic trade routes, with a stable community of German merchants who for centuries even had their own written laws.[118] In Moscow and its suburbs a succession of districts were at various times set aside for foreigners and thus deemed to be the *nemetskaia sloboda* – usually rendered 'German quarter', more properly 'foreign quarter', since almost any westerners could be labelled *nemtsy*. The earliest formally designated *nemetskaia sloboda* dated from the 1570s, to house prisoners of war and others who entered the tsar's service after the Livonian War. For much of the first half of the seventeenth century there was no official *nemetskaia sloboda*, although most foreigners did live in clusters, until a new *sloboda* was allocated in 1652.[119] Resident Germans included blacksmiths, silversmiths and goldsmiths, painters and engravers, tailors and carpenters. German translators and interpreters were recruited into the Ambassadorial Chancery.[120] German doctors were prominent in the Apothecary Chancery. Germans even played a role in court culture, through introducing theatrical entertainment: performances on 16 February 1672 and again in May of the same year were catalysts for the establishment of Russia's first court theatre, and for attempts to recruit German actors.[121]

Until the end of the seventeenth century, signs of written German were, like Latin, restricted. Spoken by many, German was seen by few. For the most part it, too, was restricted to being an occasional source-language for translations into Slavonic. German printed books were among those used by the translators who worked on Gennadii's Bible in the 1490s, but noted translations from German books over the sixteenth and even seventeenth centuries are sparse: an illustrated herbal ('Garden of Health') in 1534, important as a medical textbook;[122] somewhat incongruously, a handbook of military tactics, printed in Moscow in 1647 – the first, and by some definitions the only, secular book to be printed in Russia before the eighteenth century.[123] In the seventeenth century German printed books were even to be found among the possessions of some nobles and senior churchmen, though not in the institutional collections of churches or monasteries.[124]

However, in the seventeenth century one type of German source was translated assiduously and regularly: not books, but newspapers. The first newspaper is reckoned to have been the *Relation aller Fürnemmen und gedenckwürdigen Historien*, published in Strasburg in 1605 by the printer Johan Carolus.[125] Over the next couple of decades newspapers began to appear in several other German-speaking cities (Wolfenbüttel, Basel, Frankfurt-am-Main, Berlin, Hamburg). Newspapers were founded in Amsterdam in 1618 and 1619, in England from 1621. The first attempt at a daily newspaper was undertaken by Theodor Ritsch in Leipzig in 1650, though success in this more ambitious type of venture was more sporadic.[126] West European newspapers were brought to Moscow by Russian and foreign merchants and envoys at least from 1621, and possibly earlier. Most were German, but they also included newspapers printed in Holland.[127] The first imports were occasional, but they became more frequent. From the late 1650s the import of West European newspapers was an official policy, and in 1665 the establishment of a postal service to the west (via Riga) enabled the tsar to place a regular order for the supply of newspapers every two weeks. In the late 1660s there were more or less regular deliveries of nine German and six Dutch papers.[128]

However, although the newspapers were imported to Muscovy, they were not for distribution. They were intelligence sources, to be translated and summarised for government use only.[129] Thus, despite their regular import over many decades, German newspapers did not figure in the Muscovite graphosphere outside the Kremlin. Occasionally the discrepancy was noted. In 1647 the anonymous author of a Russian story of a polemic with Lutherans remarks: 'In foreign [*nemetskikh*] lands tales of military deeds are written and printed in books and on broadsides [*na listakh*]. Why are we slow, or afraid, or ashamed, to write and print about what happens in the Slavonic land?'[130]

The end of German's graphospheric obscurity was due, above all, to policy decisions by Peter I. Peter's innovation lay not only in the fact that he recruited German and Dutch experts to help him take forward his programmes of reforms in government, science, technology and education. Foreign recruitment in itself was a traditional practice, although Peter's initiatives were far more ambitious in scale and diversity than those of his predecessors. Germans came as scholars and teachers, as accountants and actuaries, as archivists and bookbinders, as architects and landscape gardeners, as mining engineers, as musicians, actors and artists.[131] The earliest printed German issued by a Russian ruler was Peter's manifesto of April 1702 welcoming foreigners to Russia and guaranteeing them unhampered entry, freedom of worship, access to justice according to their own laws, and freedom to depart.[132] The decisive aspect, however, was a shift of attitude and values with regard to what was seen and unseen, public and private, isolated or integrated. Rather than form ever more enclaves so as to protect the local population against contamination by sight or contact, the foreign experts were to be integrated with native elites, their skills were to be acquired, their languages were to be taught and heard and seen. Most of the professors of the Academy in St Petersburg were Germans. German, along with Latin, became a medium for display, an outward-facing sign, emblematic of a shift in identity no less than the switch from Moscow to St Petersburg, from domes to spires, from beards to smooth chins, from kaftans to West European dress. The first German schools were founded in Moscow in the 1700s, in St Petersburg in 1709, even in distant Tobolsk in 1711. German alphabetic primers were printed from the 1710s.[133] The first bilingual Russian–German grammar, by Martin Schwanwitz, rector of the Academy *gymnasium*, was published in St Petersburg in 1730.[134] Educated Russians conducted correspondence in German. Russia's rulers (some of whom, in the eighteenth century, were native speakers of German) received verse panegyrics in German.[135] Nor was the study of German limited to those with a technical or secular education: German was taught in Orthodox seminaries, not only in Moscow and St Petersburg but also, by the later eighteenth century, in the provinces.[136] The base for German was boosted in 1710 by the annexation of Riga, whereby the empire acquired a Germanic city with its own traditions of writing and printing.

The most thoroughly studied evidence of German primary writing in the Russian graphosphere is the production and influx of books. The major catalogue of eighteenth-century foreign-language printing in Russia lists well over three thousand titles. More than two thousand of them are in German. Of the German titles, around two-thirds were printed in Riga and Reval. Of the remainder, almost all – more than six hundred titles – were printed in St Petersburg, and around seventy in Moscow.[137] By the early nineteenth century there was also some capacity for the printing of German in non-Germanic provincial towns, although a decree of 20 March 1817 suggests that the central authorities considered that the quality of print was not up to the standard required for official publications.[138] However, books printed in Russia, culturally significant though they may be, constituted a minority of the German books in the graphosphere. From the early eighteenth century books were imported in large quantities. They were imported partly to serve the needs of the new institutions, but they were also available for wider sale in bookshops, where they were acquired by Russians and resident Germans alike. The Academy of Sciences bookshop in St Petersburg opened in 1728, and issued regular catalogues. Its catalogue of 1731 listed 517 titles in German, 280 in French, 219 in Latin, 28 in Dutch and 1 in Italian.[139] From the shops, German books flowed onto the shelves of institutional and private libraries. In the mid 1730s the Academy of Sciences already possessed some 16,000 volumes. The language represented in the largest number of volumes was Latin, but the collections included 2,486 titles in German (and, by comparison, 1,367 titles in French).[140] German books were prominent in the private libraries of scholars and writers.[141]

While German books have been quite exhaustively catalogued, at any rate for the eighteenth century, most of the non-books, the administrative documents and ephemera, have not been systematically studied or described. Russia's first German newspaper, the *St Peterburgische Zeitung*, was published from 1727. It survived until 1915.[142] However, the fullest catalogue of German books printed in eighteenth-century Russia explicitly excludes any publication that does not have its own title or title page.[143] Newspapers do therefore figure, but most other non-books do not. The catalogue of Russian books in the civil typeface from the latter's introduction in 1708 until the death of Peter in 1725 adds an appendix listing foreign-language publications over the same period, including a smattering of administrative documents.[144] This is almost certainly just the tip of the iceberg, about whose overall mass we can only speculate on the basis of occasional random annotations, references and discoveries. For example, for the Petrine period the catalogue of books in the civil typeface, together with its supplementary volume, lists just three such documents, or perhaps four, over a period of ten years: a decree issued in St Petersburg on 1 January 1716 laying down strict controls over correspondence with Sweden; a decree on the conditions under which prisoners of war may be allowed to become Russian subjects, printed in St Petersburg in April 1721; a decree on the succession to the throne, enacted at Preobrazhenskoe on 5 February 1722 and printed in St Petersburg and in Moscow on 4 May.[145] The fourth document is the Senate's announcement of Peter's death and of the accession of Catherine I, issued on 28 January 1728 and ostensibly printed in German in Riga on 3 February, but possibly in fact printed abroad.[146] These must represent only a small part of what once existed.

German printings of administrative documents were mostly directed at the German-speaking populations of the Baltic provinces. They include translations of central decrees, as well as regular documents issued by the local administration. Thus, for example, one small group of uncatalogued documents[147] includes a German version of the first substantive printed decree, issued on 17 March 1714, the day after Peter's stipulation of 16 March that all decrees of general applicability must be printed. The document concerns the duties of government inspectors (*fiskaly*). The bibliographies record the Russian versions printed in St Petersburg on 20 March and in Moscow on 12 April.[148] The German version claims to have been printed in Moscow on 20 March.[149] Moving into the 1720s, this group of documents includes: Peter's decree of 17 April 1722 on measures to avoid tampering with the texts of decrees (German text printed in Riga on 20 August); an announcement on the coronation of the future Catherine I, first printed in St Petersburg on 15 November 1723, and then in Riga on 5 December; a ban on the unauthorised wearing of regimental colours (St Petersburg, 7 December 1724; Riga, 17 January 1725); an order issued in Riga on 20 February 1725, from Anikita Repnin, governor-general of Livonia, which includes a translation of the Senate's decree of 3 February concerning the approved formulae for the new empress's (i.e. Catherine I's) titles on various types of document; Catherine's decree of 1 February 1726 stipulating that peasant passports would be regarded as valid only if printed, not if handwritten (translation published in Riga on 9 February 1727).[150]

Even these few specimens suggest a fairly regular practice of translating decrees into German, starting as early as printed decrees began to be produced routinely in Russian. Initially the German versions were printed mainly in St Petersburg and/or Moscow, but from the early 1720s the more regular pattern was for them to be printed in Riga. The February 1725 order from Anikita Repnin made the procedure explicit. The Russian preamble to the original decree of the Senate refers back to a previous decree on approved titles that had been issued by Peter on 11 November 1721. Repnin's order added the information that Peter's decree had been 'translated into German, printed and published *sub dato* 9 December 1721'.[151] Repnin's order also reflects a shift from the straightforward translation of imperial edicts to their repackaging as instructions from the governor-general, whence it was a short step to the routine printing of local administrative instructions in German.

By the middle of the eighteenth century German printing seems to have been common in a wider range of 'ephemeral' contexts. In 1755 the oath to be sworn on the appointment of a certain Christopher Richter to the civil service rank of college counsellor (*kollezhskii sovetnik*) was printed in German.[152] Nor were German residents the only addressees and users of German non-books. The earliest known printed passport for foreign travel, issued on 15 April 1719 to the mining engineer Georg Wilhelm de Hennin (or Henning), has a handwritten German translation of its Russian text on the verso. The continuous record of such documents is under-researched, but at any rate by the 1760s the German translation on the verso had become a regular, printed component, the norm.[153] Indeed, German eventually became a common feature of many types of document dealing with transactions which may (but may not) involve foreigners. For example, although passes for official travel using post-horses (*podorozhnye*) were printed in Russian alone, tickets for the stagecoach between St Petersburg and Moscow (founded in 1820) printed the rules for passengers in parallel columns of Russian and German.[154]

For still more outwardly directed German in the graphosphere, we can turn to gravestones and shop signs, and indeed street signs. Initially these were limited to designated 'foreign' space. German was among the many languages inscribed on tombs in Moscow's mainly sixteenth-century cemetery for non-Orthodox Christians (inscribed slabs from the abandoned cemetery were then used as construction material for the Danilov monastery, which thus, somewhat incongruously, had multilingual writing embedded in its very fabric).[155] An engraving of the German Quarter in 1705, by Adriaan Schoonebeek, shows a large sign in Dutch on the side of one of the buildings.[156] By the early nineteenth century German names were among those displayed above shops on the main commercial streets of both capital cities.[157] As for the streets themselves: in the late 1760s, when Catherine II required that the streets of St Petersburg be labelled with their names, she stipulated that the signs were to be carved in marble and that the names were to be written both in Russian and in German.

German continued to be a significant presence in parts of the Russian graphosphere well into the nineteenth century, both within and beyond the resident German-speaking communities.[158] In some Russian institutions German remained not merely a *subject* of instruction but a *language* of instruction through to the end of the eighteenth century.[159] However, from the second half of the eighteenth century the relative prominence of German in the linguistic landscape declined. It was squeezed partly by the spread of Russian itself as a language of writing in ever more areas of knowledge, culture and display, and partly by the adoption of French as the prestige language of polite society.[160]

French

The age of French as the most prominently privileged foreign language in Russia runs from the second half of the eighteenth century almost to the middle of the nineteenth century. In plain chronological terms, therefore, it looks as if French was the successor-language to German. In cultural, functional and graphospheric terms, however, this was far from being the case. In the first place, there was no sharp break, no demonstrative abandonment of German in favour of French, but a long period of overlap and nuanced differentiation. Secondly, French did not simply replace German in the same cultural spaces, nor did it directly replicate the functions of German. Indeed, the rise of French is a reflection and indication not merely of a shift in preference from one foreign language to another, but of a shift in the societal and cultural functions that the foreign languages served. As had been the case with regard to German, the fashion for French was reinforced from the very top. From the 1750s the empress Elizabeth encouraged the use of French at court. Elizabeth was following the broader European fashion for French as the prestige language of polite discourse.[161] From the court, the fashion for French spread to the higher nobility, and thence, over time, to broader sections of the gentry.

The rise of German had been enabled, and its position had been maintained, through two forms of infrastructural support: formal institutions of education and learning; and the incorporation into the empire of a substantial population of native speakers of German. Neither type of infrastructural support was available to French to an equivalent extent. One could even say that, in the case of the spread of French, causation was reversed. Rather than becoming fashionable because it was widely studied, French became widely studied because it became fashionable. Rather than serving, to an appreciable degree, a subject population for whom it was a native language, French writing and printing served principally native Russians for whom it was a second language of choice. German was a spoken language of teaching partly because it was the first language of many of the teachers, and also because it was a written language of learning. French became not merely a medium of instruction, but its subject and object. To read and speak German (probably in that order) was a path to knowledge and advancement; to speak and read French (probably in that order) became a sign of social and cultural identity.

If we were to choose an institutional context emblematic of the functions of German in the age of its dominance, it would most likely be the Academy of Sciences. If one were to pick an institutional context emblematic of the functions of French, it may be the court, or the Academy of Arts[162] or, increasingly, the salon or the soirée. The fashion for French was encouraged at court, but the subsequent spread of French coincided with the emergence of elite cultural practices beyond the court and the church and the official institutions, with the privatisation and domestication of parts of elite culture. A culture of *francophonie* became embedded in the home life of the gentry, in their exchanges with each other, in their accomplishments and entertainments. As part of this process the culture and cultivation of French, far more than of other languages here surveyed, involved the participation of women.[163]

Among the foreign-language books printed in the Russian Empire in the eighteenth century, the number of French titles (526) is roughly equal to the number of Latin titles (555). There were four times as many titles in German (2,218) – although the gap is significantly narrowed if we discount what one might call the 'Riga effect' and consider only books published in St Petersburg and, to a far lesser extent, Moscow.[164] As in the case of German, these figures are merely indicative. If we are concerned not with production but with availability and circulation, then we must include the very large quantities of French books that were imported from abroad, and began to be acquired and collected in the first half of the century, well before French became foregrounded as the preferred language of high society.[165] Moreover, the numbers themselves are not the only, and perhaps not the most important, indicative feature. The differences were qualitative as well as quantitative. French books were distinctive in their balance of subjects and genres. In the first place, a very high proportion of French books in mid-eighteenth-century collections contained works of literature and history.[166] Of the French books available in the 1750s from the Academy bookstall in Moscow, and at the bookstall of Moscow University, over half contained works of literature and history, while fewer than 10 per cent dealt with natural sciences or mathematics.[167] Secondly, although the books were in the French language, they were not necessarily printed in France; nor were they necessarily originally written in French. The Academy bookstall stocked large numbers of translations from other languages into French, and a substantial part of its inventory consisted of French books printed in the Netherlands. Among the items listed for sale were, for example, forty-two works translated from English, and forty-five translated from Greek or Latin. Among the translations from English were the three large epistolary novels of Samuel Richardson (*The History of Sir Charles Grandison; Clarissa: Or the History of a Young Lady*; and *Pamela: Or Virtue Rewarded*) in twenty-three volumes, and Milton's *Paradise Lost*, as well as multi-volume sets of essays by Joseph Addison and David Hume.[168] French printed books thus reflect the wider role of French as an international intermediary language of culture.

French books retained this function into the early part of the nineteenth century. The French book could become an emblematic object. When Pushkin writes, in his verse novel *Evgenii Onegin*, that his heroine, Tatiana, saw in Onegin a fusion of the heroes of her favourite novels, including 'the incomparable Grandison',[169] he is not implying that Tatiana read English literature in English, or even in Russian. The natural assumption is that her reading of fiction – charming, and by the 1820s somewhat *passé* by the standards of the capital (the more sophisticated poet-narrator finds Grandison merely soporific) – was in French; like an emanation of the poet's Muse, who, he claims, appeared to him in the guise of a young lady from the provinces, with sadly pensive eyes, and in her hand a petite French tome.[170] We do not need to see inside the decorously doleful Muse's little book. It is, so to speak, graphospherically metonymic, evocative of a particular kind of cultural aura – not of France, but of polite Russian *francophonie*.

No less eloquent than the printed book, as expressions of francophone sensibility, was a subset of handwritten non-books: not, in this instance, official documents, but genres of – to put it oxymoronically – private display. Typical modes of Russian francophone composition are occasional verses, affectionate correspondence, memoirs and diaries, aphorisms and reflections.[171] Some Russians published novels in French, though as often as not they were printed in France rather than in Russia, and hence, although they may count as specimens of Russian francophone literature, they barely feature in the Russian graphosphere itself.[172] By contrast, the manuscript album, or *liber amicorum*, a centrepiece of the salon, is a composite genre of selectively shared intimacies.

This is not to say that *all* French primary writing in Russia was squeezed into such a cultivated straitjacket. French was also a language of diplomacy, and it was a language of learning and of social thought. Indeed, one of the best-known and most resonant radical critiques of the Russian social order, Petr Chaadaev's *Lettres philosophiques* (1829–31), was written in French. French could also be used for utterly official purposes, whether alongside German and/or Latin, or superseding them in the latter part of the century. The minutes of the Academy of Sciences were kept in Latin between 1725 and 1734, in German from 1734 to 1742, then again in Latin until 1766, before reverting to German again from 1766 to 1773 – whereupon they switched to French, until 1803.[173] From time to time the government supported the publication of francophone newspapers as vehicles of official, outwardly directed messages: a French version of the *St Petersburg Gazette* in the late 1760s, during the Seven Years War; *Le Journal du Nord* from 1807, to counter Napoleonic propaganda. Between 1825 and 1828 *Le Journal de St.-Pétersbourg* was even the first place of publication for government decrees.[174] But in general francophone newspapers in Russia tended to be sporadic, poorly subscribed and short-lived.

The more outwardly visible French of secondary writing reflected fashion over the same period, from the boudoir to the streets, for example in the inscriptions on personalised gifts and keepsakes, but above all (in several senses) in the proliferation of French shop signs along the central thoroughfares of Moscow and St Petersburg from the early nineteenth century. In 1812, with Napoleon's troops advancing, in a fit of linguistic patriotism the governor of Moscow, Count Fedor Rostopchin, instructed that French signs be removed. In more peaceful times they sprouted again, to the delight of the cosmopolitan consumers and to the indignation of linguistic purists.[175]

Others

Several foreign languages whose written forms used the Latin alphabet enjoyed, at various times, high cultural presence, which was not translated into high graphospheric impact. The most prominent examples are Polish, Italian, Dutch and English. The political, cultural and linguistic impact of Poland and Polish is a major and recurrent theme in Russian history, but a minor footnote to the Russian graphosphere. Polish was at various times the language of the oppressor and of the oppressed, of the occupier and of the occupied, of a culture to be admired and of a culture to be rejected. In Ruthenia Polish was one of the several languages of manuscript and print cultures. The Polish language, and aspects of Polish literary culture, enjoyed high status among Russian bookmen in the late seventeenth and early eighteenth centuries.[176] The bibliography of foreign-language books printed in Russia in the eighteenth century lists forty-seven titles in Polish: far more than in Dutch and English combined, but a very long way behind Latin, German or French, and even Italian. In the first half of the nineteenth century (1815–41) coins were minted with Polish inscriptions, though these were intended for local use.[177]

Italians were conspicuous contributors to the shaping and adornment of urban spaces in Russia,[178] but not to the adornment of its graphosphere. Italian architects were commissioned to work on Moscow's Kremlin walls and on its main cathedral in the late fifteenth century, and to create some of St Petersburg's grandest palaces in the eighteenth century. In 1697 the Likhud brothers set up an Italian school.[179] Peter I ordered sculptures from

Italy for his Summer Garden. Italian artists trained and inspired Russian painters, Italian opera dominated the musical stage from the 1730s, when the empress Anna Ioannovna 'solidly initiated the Italianating of Russian court music, which was continued by all the following eighteenth-century Russian rulers.'[180] Much to the irritation of the Russian musical elite, Italian opera also enjoyed a popular revival from the 1820s.[181] From its foundation at the end of the eighteenth century, the Black Sea town of Odessa was in some respects an outpost of Italian culture,[182] whence, indeed, the nineteenth-century revival of Italian opera was re-exported back to Moscow and St Petersburg. At the other end of the spectrum of artistic prestige, towards the mid nineteenth century Italians were apparently prominent among St Petersburg's street entertainers.[183] In the eighteenth century Italian ranked fourth in the list of foreign languages of printing in Russia, with more than a hundred titles.

The period of the special prominence of Dutch-speakers, books, prints and manuals in Russian commercial, political, technological, cultural and even linguistic affairs was relatively brief and intense, spanning the late seventeenth and early eighteenth centuries.[184] Nevertheless, Dutch, too, remained graphospherically peripheral. Dutch was one of the languages of newspapers imported as sources for the *kuranty*, but, as we have seen, this brought very restricted visibility. Peter I encouraged the learning of Dutch, imported books in Dutch and commissioned Cyrillic books from printers in Holland.[185] The first specimen of Dutch-language printing in Moscow dates from as early as 1708, as part of a propagandistic 'non-book' commissioned by Peter: a bilingual (Russian and Dutch) single-sheet description proclaiming victory in the battle against the Swedes at Lesnaia.[186] But, despite such an auspicious start, Dutch did not become a language of significant local book production or document production or inscription. The bibliographies of printed books record only five Dutch titles issued in Russia in the eighteenth century.

Despite four centuries of active and varied commercial, diplomatic, military, practical and eventually cultural contacts, English, too, barely figured in the Russian graphosphere. Some of the early signs might appear to have been favourable. The British were a regular, growing and periodically influential presence in Russia, starting with the expedition of Richard Chancellor in 1553–4 and the foundation of the Muscovy Company in 1555. Over the following centuries the British in Moscow, then in St Petersburg and across the country, included merchants, soldiers and engineers, doctors and artists, valets and governesses.[187] Ivan IV considered taking an English wife. Peter I lived in London for more than three months in 1698.

In the late eighteenth and early nineteenth centuries Russian court and gentry culture was in some respects avowedly anglophile,[188] and there was periodic Russian interest in studying the language. Nevertheless, spoken English and, even more emphatically, written English never became integral to Russian court or aristocratic or intelligentsia culture. The multi-faceted interest in Britain did not spill over into a fashion for the acquisition and display of its language.[189] Some of the early signs might have appeared promising. English words in transcription figure in Russian manuscript glossaries of the seventeenth century.[190] The earliest Russian translation of an English printed text seems to have been one of the editions of Charles I's 'Declaration to his Subjects' of 1648.[191] The earliest Russian-printed text in English dates from 1721: 'Regulations and Instructions' addressed to foreign seamen in Russian ports, so that they should 'know how they ought to behave themselves and what they are to observe.'[192] But subsequently – almost nothing. The catalogue of foreign-language books printed in Russia in the eighteenth century records just six titles in English. In the age of anglophilia or 'anglomania' the presence not only of expatriates but also of some enthusiastically anglophone Russians ensured that there was a market for English-language books, but French continued to serve as a regular intermediary between the two cultures and languages.

A crude but eloquent indicator of movements in linguistic fashion is provided by publications of multilingual dictionaries. In 1704 Fedor Polikarpov published his trilingual lexicon of Russian, Latin and Greek. In 1731 the Imperial Academy of Sciences issued a translation of a late-seventeenth-century German–Latin lexicon (supplemented by Adodurov's brief grammar), and Sergei Volchkov's translation of a German-Latin-French dictionary was published in two parts in 1755 and 1764.[193] The first native multilingual lexicon with an emphasis on modern languages was produced in 1763 by Grigorii Poletika, although this was actually a rather limited set of thematic word-lists, in six languages: Polikarpov's three, plus French, German and – perhaps incongruously – English.[194] The new standard polyglot dictionaries of the 1780s dropped English and (finally) both Greek and Latin, but added Italian, as in Matvei Gavrilov's 1781 lexicon with headwords in German, and Ivan Sots's bulky two-volume version of 1784–7, with headwords in French.[195]

A very slight shift, at any rate in the official perception of the importance of English as a written language, can perhaps be sensed around the start of the second quarter of the nineteenth century. We can compare, for example, the languages in which two major, outward-facing official publications were issued: Catherine II's multilingual edition of her instructions to the commission charged with drafting a new code of laws, issued in 1770 (two years after the monolingual Russian edition); and the 1826 report of the Commission of Inquiry into the attempted coup of 26 December the previous year (the 'Decembrist' revolt). Catherine's high-minded, luxuriously printed (and unrealised) project was issued in four languages: Russian, Latin, German and French, with four separate title pages, and the subsequent text in four parallel columns across each double-page spread.[196] The multilingual publications of the investigation of the Decembrists are more surprising. Subsequent mythologies of Nicholas I's reign have highlighted the execution of the ringleaders as a shameful episode in the history of Russian despotism, an episode which one might think the authorities would be keen to conceal, yet for Nicholas it was nothing of the kind. The punishment was a demonstration of justice and mercy after due process, and the new tsar was keen that justice should be known to have been done. The detailed report of the Commission of Inquiry was issued both in Russian and in translation into three foreign languages: German, French and now not Latin but English.[197] Revealingly, however, the English version was translated from the French. By coincidence, the first grammar of Russian written in English was printed in St Petersburg only in the following year, 1827.[198] Previously, anglophone would-be russophones had had to rely on the textbooks in French or German.

Also sporadic are the graphospheric traces, mainly in secondary writing, of non-Latin, non-Cyrillic scripts and languages. In the late fifteenth century, there were still some residual reminders of Mongol overlordship in the Arabic or pseudo-Arabic inscriptions on coins. A late-fifteenth-century manuscript apparently includes some annotations in Permian characters (an adaptation of Cyrillic, devised as a missionary alphabet in the late fourteenth century).[199] Some scribal monograms and brief annotations in late-fifteenth-century documents were written in Uighur script, perhaps as a relic of its usage in Mongol administration before it was replaced by Arabic, or perhaps as a form of cryptography.[200] An early-sixteenth-century helmet, traditionally but not unanimously linked with Ivan IV, bears a pseudo-Arabic inscription.[201] A sixteenth-century imported ceremonial sabre belonging to Prince Fedor Mikhailovich Mstislavskii bears the Arabic inscription of its maker as well as the Slavonic inscription of its owner.[202] From 1804 to 1833 the imperial government minted coins for Georgia, with the dates inscribed using letters of the Georgian alphabet.[203]

Recourse to print in non-Latin, non-Cyrillic scripts was similarly episodic. A Psalter in Georgian was printed in Moscow in 1705, and a Georgian primer was printed in St Petersburg in 1737.[204] On 15 July 1722 Peter I, while on campaign in Astrakhan, issued a proclamation for the local populace, in Turkish. This was a carefully planned propaganda effort. The typeface had been ordered in April, and the press was dispatched by boat down the Volga.[205] In the mid eighteenth century the Academy of Sciences press produced occasional 'non-books' in Arabic script, in the form of ceremonial addresses for distinguished visitors, but very little is known about their frequency.[206] Between 1785 and 1798 Johann Karl Schnoor printed at least five editions of the Koran for Kazan Tatar readers.[207] In Kazan itself, Arabic-script printing became established over the first half of the nineteenth century, first at the Kazan *gymnasium*, then at the university and eventually, in the 1840s, at a few private presses.[208] In 1793 the Imperial press (at the time leased by Schnoor's one-time colleague Johann Weitbrecht) printed an ode to Catherine II by the Persian ambassador, with parallel texts in Russian and Persian.[209] In the first half of the nineteenth century the production and/or dissemination of works in or incorporating non-Cyrillic, non-Latin scripts was more regularly established both in the capitals and in the non-russophone regions for three purposes: missionary work through the efforts of the Bible Societies, orientalist scholarship, and the education of colonised peoples.[210]

CHAPTER 5

Places and Times of the Graphosphere

The graphosphere is a spatial concept. In this chapter we consider two kinds of graphospheric space: the public and the domestic. The designations are not precise. Here they refer to location, not to function. 'Public' means out of doors, and will extend to enclosed outdoor spaces such as parks and cemeteries. 'Domestic' means indoors in buildings intended, at least in part, for accommodation. 'Domestic' therefore includes grand houses and palaces, despite their sometimes public functions. This leaves major gaps. It must be stressed in advance that, whether within or beyond such definitions, this chapter is not an attempt to delineate all the spaces of the graphosphere over four centuries. In particular, we are not here concerned with the principal spaces of production: the monasteries and the ministries, the printers, the workshops and the factories, the schools, universities and academies. Nor, indeed, is the focus on some of the interior spaces most commonly associated with the dense presence and display of words: the interiors of churches or of libraries. The presence of words in such places is obvious and is treated elsewhere. Here the questions are more limited and less thoroughly investigated. What kinds of words would one encounter in the streets or in the home? When, how and why did visible words spread, or not spread, into such spaces? And what can be inferred about modes of response to them, about how they were read and perceived?

The Public Graphosphere

A culture of publicly visible writing is characteristic both of the city in classical antiquity and of urban modernity. By contrast, the medieval city, across Europe, was outwardly mute. This was a difference in the very idea of the city. In the ancient city, visible writing was part of the fabric of the urban experience. The main streets and squares were lined with inscriptions: formal and informal, funerary, commemorative, legislative, commercial, triumphal or devotional. The medieval city was more inward-facing. In medieval Rus, Byzantium or early Muscovy, the principal space for the display of words was inside a church.[1] Byzantium still had pieces of inscribed antique statuary, but in Muscovy, apart from a few signs of writing on exterior wall paintings,[2] or on the devotional images paraded on feast-day processions or on military banners, public open spaces were free of visible words. In parts of Western Europe an aesthetic of urban inscription returned to the Renaissance city.[3] In Russia the formation of a public graphosphere was a slow and uneven process. Sporadic beginnings can also be traced to the late fifteenth century, but there was little systematic or programmatic display before the turn of the eighteenth century, and a continuous practice of habitual, prominent and diverse public inscription became established only in the early decades of the nineteenth century.

Phases in the emergence of a Russian public graphosphere can be identified according to a range of criteria: according to straightforward chronology; or with regard to location, or the institutional base, or form and genre of verbal message, or type of object, and so on. Here we focus on the development of an overlapping sequence of functions. For the first couple of centuries the sparse inscriptions consisted mainly of commemorative labels. From the late seventeenth century urban sites began to be used more programmatically for the display of public announcements, for the projection of official political and cultural messages, for the purposes of public information and education. Somewhat later, and into the early nineteenth century, inscriptions began to serve as administrative labels, as devices for, so to speak, the indexation of space both in the city and across the empire. Finally, and decisively, came the spread of urban writing that was no longer driven 'top down' by institutions of church and state but 'bottom up' by the activities of trade and commerce: the proliferation of shop signs and trade signs.[4]

Beyond description and categorisation is the problem of meaning. What did public writing signify for those who encountered it? How was it read? How did who engage with it? To trace meanings in the public graphosphere is both much simpler and much more complex than to trace meanings of, say, books. It is incomparably simpler because of the nature of the texts. Most of them are very brief, and the intended verbal messages tend to be concisely informative. Some forms of public inscription may be literary or allusive, but in general the inscriptional genres tend to favour clarity of message above nuance of exposition. Nevertheless, in the semantics of the public graphosphere there is also a particular form of complexity. The writing in a book is, by and large, perused by someone who chooses to open it. Engagement with the words in a book is an action dictated by choice, so that readers, though diverse, form a self-selecting subgroup. By contrast, the words on the streets are thrust before the gaze of anybody and everybody who happens to encounter them, whether literate or illiterate, active or passive, curious or impervious. Viewers may barely register their existence, or may experience a mainly aesthetic awareness of, for example, shape and colour, or may skim the words perfunctorily for information, or may choose to peruse them closely. In what follows, the remarks on reading the graphosphere represent only a tentative and somewhat serendipitous beginning. The scope of the survey is also almost entirely limited to Moscow and St Petersburg. To some extent, provincial developments can be extrapolated from patterns of development in the capitals, but more research is needed.

Beginnings: Commemoration and Patronage

Public inscription began to appear in Muscovy from the late fifteenth century. For almost two hundred years the growth of inscription was slow and density was low. The objects were disparate and limited: gravestones, stone plaques marking the foundation or completion of buildings (including churches), bronze cannons, bells, military banners, tower clocks. Almost all the inscriptions were types of commemorative label, marking the name of the deceased, the builder, the cannon maker, the patron. The exceptions were tower clocks and military banners. The major banners of this period were iconographic, and in a sense their display on parade was equivalent to the temporary mobile displays of icons in church processions on feast-days. The basic display on a tower clock was not verbal, but used Cyrillic letters in their numerical sense. Every incipient tradition is significant, but, even when taken together, the sum of public inscription was so meagre as to be almost negligible, almost irrelevant to the experience of public spaces. Most people in most places for most of the time could have lived most of their lives without being aware of it.

The pre-history of a Russian public graphosphere continued for a long time, and can appear so fragmented as to be virtually random, but was not entirely without shape. The signs of pattern relate both to chronology and to location. The chronological regularity lies in the fact that, despite the heterogeneity of the objects, the origins of several of these early types of public writing can be traced to approximately the same period. A continuous tradition of inscribed grave-slabs in Russia begins from the 1490s. The earliest foundation inscriptions on a public building date from

1491, and the custom spread during the sixteenth century. The earliest surviving local cannon likewise dates from 1491, and the major monumental inscribed cannons date from the mid to late sixteenth century. Bell-casting began earlier, but the continuous tradition of large inscribed bells is also traceable from the sixteenth century. According to the chronicle narrative, Muscovy's earliest tower clock was installed at the start of the fifteenth century, but this appears to have been an isolated case, and the more habitual use of tower clocks was rather later, from the end of the sixteenth century and subsequently. So, not all the chronologies coincide, and one can certainly not speak of any co-ordinated programme of public inscription, but some kind of momentum did begin to emerge from the end of the fifteenth century in the case of lapidary inscriptions, and from the mid sixteenth century in the case of several other genres.

The spaces of the early public graphosphere are equally sparse, but also not entirely without pattern. The most clearly defined area of graphospheric growth was the cemetery. Over the course of a couple of centuries, from its origins in the 1490s, the practice of inscribing gravestones became fairly widespread in major monastic cemeteries.[5] From the initial bare record of names, the inscriptions, on horizontal slabs, went through phases of increasingly informative formulae, adding the date according to the calendar of church festivals, the year, sometimes even the hour, the lifespan, the social standing of the deceased. Eighteenth-century cemeteries adopted the whole range of rhetorical funerary genres that befitted an enlightened empire, including a rich variety of inscriptional forms and, from the latter part of the century, sculpted figurative monuments.[6] Yet the cemetery is only a semi-public space. It is separate, enclosed even when open. Nobody was going to stumble across an inscribed gravestone merely in the course of a walk through the town. Although funerary inscription, both authentic and imaginary, eventually acquired a cultural profile as a genre of writing, it was not fully part of a fully public graphosphere. Something similar could be said about inscribed bells. Although they were often visible in Russia's open-sided belfries, the writing itself would be barely discernible, let alone decipherable, from ground level: another graphospheric element that might in theory be reckoned public while in practice barely impinging on the daily experience of space.

If we are looking for a particular place in which public writing, even in these early centuries, seems to have acquired sufficient density to be counted as a characteristic feature, it would be at the very heart of Muscovy, on and outside the entrance to the Moscow Kremlin facing onto Red Square: the Frolov gate and tower (renamed the Spasskaia tower in 1658). It began with just two inscriptions carved on stone tablets, one on the inner façade, the other on the outer façade. Both recorded the construction of the tower in 1491 by the Italian architect Pietro Antonio Solari on the orders of the grand prince Ivan III. The inscription on the inner wall was in Slavonic, but the entrance inscription, visible from Red Square, was (and is) in Latin.[7] For Solari this was normal, in the manner of equivalent inscriptions in contemporary Italy.[8] In Muscovy it was wholly exceptional. To a limited extent, the practice became naturalised. Several other inscriptions recording construction, in Slavonic, date from the early sixteenth century, both in Moscow and in smaller towns.[9] But it was on Red Square that, gradually, a graphospheric cluster emerged. In the mid sixteenth century the monumental inscribed cannons, when not on campaign (and the biggest of them all was never on campaign) stood on display outside the Kremlin. In 1585 the first of a series of clocks was installed in the Frolov tower. At least from the early seventeenth century, prints and books were on sale at stalls on the 'vegetable row' (*ovoshchnoi riad*) in a market just off Red Square, and by the early eighteenth century bookstalls and print-stalls were clustered in front of the Spasskaia tower itself; but that was already at the start of a different phase in the growth of a public graphosphere.[10] Otherwise, outside the cemetery, public writing before the end of the seventeenth century consisted mostly of occasional scraps. The first signs of a regular, planned, programmatic approach to writing in public spaces are features of the next phase, at the turn of the eighteenth century.

Proclamation and Edification

From the late seventeenth century the state began to use public spaces systematically for the display of authoritative and approved writing. The state's visible words served, in particular, two functions. The first function was regulation: public posting became one of the standard devices for disseminating decrees. The second function was educative, or propagandistic: the projection, into public space, of the cultural images and messages promoted by and conducive to the dignity of the state. In sum these initiatives amounted to a radical shift in the use of the city as a space of visible words, as a place onto which the state could inscribe messages from and about itself. At the same time, the change in practice reflected a change in ideas. It was part of a broader 'inscriptional' aesthetic in

Russian elite culture. A catalyst (or at any rate a context) for new graphospheric facts was a new graphospheric imagination.

In May 1682 an uprising of the Moscow musketeers (the *strel'tsy*) installed Sofiia Alekseevna, elder half-sister of the nine-year-old future tsar Peter I, as regent. As part of the settlement, Sofiia issued a decree, one of whose stipulations was that the actions of the *strel'tsy* were to be, in effect, retrospectively legitimised, and that they were not to be deemed rebels. The text of this decree was embossed onto two large brass plates, which were then fixed to what was described as a 'pillar' – actually a kind of four-sided plinth or pedestal – on Red Square.[11] The structure survived for only a few months, but the precedent was revived in the late 1690s. In March 1697 Peter I set up another pedestal on Red Square, on which to display the heads of a group of failed conspirators: an eloquent but non-verbal text. Two years later, in 1699, after suppressing the catastrophically unsuccessful revolt of the *strel'tsy*, Peter placed such plinths not only in Red Square, but also in ten other locations around the city. Each column was four-sided, and to each side was fixed a cast-iron plate displaying lists of the names of the traitors. In the absence of any other free-standing public monuments, this was major incursion into the Muscovite cityscape. Moreover, Peter's metallic decree-stands proved more durable than their predecessor from 1682. They stood throughout his reign before being removed in 1727 before the coronation of Peter II. One of the cast iron plates survives to this day.[12]

These late-seventeenth-century structures were, in effect, public noticeboards. The monumental display of legislation was not unusual in the antique city.[13] In Russia the monumentality turned out to be transient, but the function was robust. In the second half of the seventeenth century, government decrees quite often specified the means by which they were to be promulgated. Traditional devices included public proclamation, and the distribution of handwritten copies to the relevant offices and regions. From the 1690s, the texts of some decrees begin to stipulate that copies should also be made for public display, to be affixed to gateposts, walls, and church doors.[14] From March 1714 Peter decreed that all decrees of general applicability must be printed, not handwritten, and it became common for broadside versions to be produced for public posting. Thus, for the purposes of legislation, paper, rather than metal or stone, became the favoured material both of record and of display. From March 1714, print – specifically, the printed non-book – became a regular component of the public graphosphere.

The public posting of decrees raises questions of readership. How effective was such display really expected to be in a largely illiterate population? Clearly the texts themselves still had to be read aloud if they were to reach a wider audience. Visual display was only one among several devices for dissemination. One may conjecture, nevertheless, that the presence of the material text was a message in itself, a visible and tangible reminder and attribute of authority, even if most 'readers' had to rely on others for its decipherment. For Peter the purpose was to make the texts of decrees available, and to stress repeatedly in the texts themselves the principle that ignorance of the law would not be counted as an excuse. Those who could not read should have access to the text via those who could. And all could (or should) understand that through words posted in public – especially printed words, since the technology of print was a state-controlled monopoly – the voice of the tsar was made manifest to his people.

Peter's more dramatic transformation of the urban graphosphere was created not by the posting of sheets of paper, but by monumental construction in the form of triumphal arches. The regular practice of constructing triumphal arches to celebrate victories began in 1696 after Peter's Azov campaign. The most magnificent and elaborate were set up in Moscow in 1709 to mark the victory over the Swedes at Poltava. These were not permanent additions to the city. They were stage props constructed for 'one-off' performances, for the triumphal entries of the ruler and his troops. They were made of wood, painted to resemble marble, and copiously decorated. They served imperial ceremonial, not urban, design. They can be classed as ephemeral monuments, or monumental ephemera.[15] Deliberately reminiscent of equivalent public display in ancient Rome and, more pertinently, in contemporary Western Europe, over the course of the eighteenth century such spectacles became naturalised in Russia, not only to mark military victories but also to celebrate more peaceable occasions such as coronations. In the early years, however, they were deeply unfamiliar. They were alien types of cultural text that needed to be read; or, rather, the Russian spectator needed to be educated in how they were meant to be read. At the most general level they might simply be seen as projections and emblems of imperial magnificence, but this was merely a beginning. The monuments in themselves were architectural texts, but they also displayed pictorial and verbal texts. They were copiously inscribed. Specifically, they were covered in narrative, symbolic and emblematic compositions: classical, mythological, biblical, historical and allegorical scenes, together with captions or mottoes. The inscriptions were multilingual: in Russian, in Latin and occasionally in Greek. The level of graphospheric saturation was unprecedented in the Russian cityscape. So were the representational, linguistic and semantic conventions. How were viewers to know what to make of them?

The solution, or an attempt at a solution, was to publish leaflets and even substantial books describing the monuments and explaining what the images and inscriptions were meant to mean. At least seven such works were produced in the Petrine period.[16] There was precedent in the late seventeenth century. In 1672, in the context of earlier royal ceremonial, Tsar Aleksei Mikhailovich instructed the icon-painter Simon Ushakov, together with the court clerk Nikita Klementev, to write an inventory of the depictions and inscriptions (more than one hundred of them) in the Golden Hall in the Moscow Kremlin.[17] A more immediately pertinent model was the Russian translation, from Dutch, of the account of the triumphal entry of William of Orange into The Hague on 5 February 1691 after the battle of the Boyne.[18] The Russian guides to the early triumphal arches are authoritative statements of how the monuments and their pictures and texts were intended to be read. We know this because in several cases the authors of the guides were also the authors of the decorative and inscriptional programmes. For example, at least three accounts of arches constructed outside the Slavo-Graeco-Latin Academy were written in the first person by their designers, teachers at the Academy, especially the 'prefect' Iosif Turoboiskii. An extract from the first such account, from 1703, gives a flavour of his exposition:

> On the cornice[19] are the following: first, Mars, with the inscription *ferro metuendus*, which is to say 'fearsome on account of his weapon'. Next Jason, who with the other Argonauts sailed to Colchis for the Golden Fleece; with the inscription *tulit pretium non vile laborum*, which is to say 'he received no mean recompense for his labours'. For this signifies our most majestic monarch, who in this age, first among his ancestors, the tsars of Russia, conquered the enemy by sea – indeed, the Finnic sea – for which he received as his desired recompense two Swedish ships.[20]

Turoboiskii makes no concessions to the wider culture. He had been recruited from Kiev, where he had taught at the Mohyla Academy. He was steeped in neoclassical learning, and his works are rhetorical compositions for his fellow initiates. Even though most of the print run of the 1703 pamphlet was unsold, he maintained the elevated polyglot presentation, especially in the expansive *Politikolepnaia apotheosis* describing the decorative programme of 1709, replete with literary commentaries in Latin and

Greek.[21] Nevertheless, even the uncompromising Turoboiskii was aware that the intended reading was not the only reading. Put strange structures with strange signs on the street, and people will make strange sense of them. His occasional polemical asides, particularly in his account of the arch constructed in 1704, provide a rare glimpse of how this graphospheric disruption might have been perceived by less friendly eyes:

> You, my honourable reader ... do not emulate the ignorant, those who know nothing, who have been nowhere and have seen nothing, but who like the tortoise stay under their shell and never emerge, and who, when they see anything new, are startled and spew forth all kinds of profanities.[22]

The 'ignorant', in Turoboiskii's brief paraphrase, commit two errors. First, they do not understand allegory, the deeper meaning of symbols and emblems. And, secondly, they utterly misconstrue the category of cultural space created by such monuments:

> This [arch] is not a temple, or a church built in the name of some saint. It is a political, which is to say a civil, tribute [*politicheskaia, siest' grazhdanskaia pokhvala*] to those who have laboured for the integrity of their fatherland and who by their labours have, with God's help, conquered their enemies. [Such arches] have been set up from ancient times (as in Rome when the emperor Constantine defeated Maxentius) among all civilised rather than barbarian peoples [*vo vsekh politichnykh, a ne varvarskikh narodakh*], in order that virtue, thus praised and honoured, may grow.[23]

The inscribed triumphal arch was not a pagan affront to Christianity. It was a civil homage to a Christian ruler. It embodied and represented the creation of a new, civil space for prestigious culture. The inscribed arches were, in the most literal sense, part of a process of making civil: that is, a process of civil-isation.

The triumphal arches did not have to bear the civilising burden alone. They were temporary emanations of an aesthetic of urban inscription that existed before and after and without them. In Russian elite culture of the late seventeenth and early eighteenth centuries actual inscription was but one manifestation of the inscriptional imagination, of the graphospheres of the mind. In the first place, the structures themselves were more permanently preserved on paper than in the streets, perpetuated both in the printed and manuscript descriptions and in the many engravings commissioned for the purpose (Fig. 5.1).[24] But the inscriptional imagination was broader. Again following West European habit, inscriptions in engravings of the period were routinely presented architecturally, as if carved on plinths, panels and pediments.[25] Even abstract concepts could be framed

Fig. 5.1: Engraving of triumphal arch at the court of Aleksandr Menshikov; Pieter Pickaert, 1710.
© State Russian Museum, St Petersburg

architecturally. Thus, for example, an engraved headpiece in the *Arifmetika* of Leontii Magnitskii, published in 1703 (the year of the first of the printed accounts of the triumphal arches) represents learning as an eight-columned temple, with components of arithmetic (addition, subtraction, multiplication, division) inscribed on steps leading up to a central throne, and with branches of learning (optics, architecture, geometry and so on) inscribed on the pillars (Fig. 5.2).[26] And the graphospheric imagination extended beyond the visual. 'Inscriptional' verse constituted a significant strand in

Fig. 5.2: Arithmetic Enthroned in the Temple of the Sciences; from Leontii Magnitskii, *Arifmetika* (Moscow, 1703)

Russian baroque poetry, as a literary conceit, whether or not the verses were actually destined to become part of any object other than the paper on which they were written.[27]

For a section of the elite, therefore, the Petrine arches were entirely compatible with the contemporary graphospheres of the mind, with the new culture of emblem and symbol, with representational and verbal panegyric, with the rhetoric of imperial prestige. Other readers were doubtless in need of education and cultivation.

In less bombastic but also more permanent mode, inscriptional cultivation was developed through antique statuary. The locations were parks and gardens. Like cemeteries, these were on the margins of the public and the private, open-air enclosures with variable rules of access. Peter I worked on plans for his Summer Gardens from 1704. Antique statuary, ordered from abroad, was integral to the concept and remained a characteristic feature of the gardens throughout many subsequent redesigns and remodellings.[28] The sovereign's guests, or a somewhat wider public from the mid 1750s when restrictions on access were loosened by the empress Elizabeth,[29] could admire the landscaping, promenade along the avenues, socialise with and display themselves to one another.[30] And, should they be curious, they could pause to read the labels incised into the bases and pedestals of the sculptures.

Mostly the inscriptions were simply labels identifying the figures represented in the sculptures, sometimes also the maker. Some, however, were more elaborate. Jacob von Stählin tells the story of a conversation between Peter and his Swedish garden designer. Peter said that he wished the garden to be educative, to 'convert this place of mere amusement into a kind of school'. The Swede assumed he meant that books – suitably protected – were to be left on the benches. Peter laughed and explained his idea. One area was to consist of four fountains joined by avenues, and the fountains and the avenues were to be ornamented with figures from Aesop's fables. Moreover, 'as the Czar knew that few people would be able to find out the meaning of these figures, and that a still smaller number would comprehend the instruction conveyed in the fables, he ordered a post to be placed near each of them: on these posts a sheet of tin was fastened, on which the fables and their morals were written in the Russian language'.[31]

This account may or may not reflect an actual conversation. However, it does catch one aspect of Peter's purported intentions: that his parks and gardens should be places of education and edification as well as pleasure and contemplation, and that inscriptions were integral to this vision.[32] The explanatory tablets with the texts of the fables and morals were graphospherically prominent equivalents to the printed guides to the triumphal arches.

There was precedent in Russia for the use of inscriptions not just as parts of and labels for monuments but as more detailed explanatory guides. In the later Muscovite period ecclesiastical inscriptions had already been getting longer, and included more factual and narrative components. On the walls of seventeenth-century churches, chronicle-style inscriptions could run to several hundred words, detailing the names of patrons and patriarchs, the dates of the commencement and completion of the structure and/or its decoration, the names of all members of the teams of painters.[33] An extraordinary specimen of the inscriptional aesthetic in late-seventeenth-century Muscovy was the New Jerusalem monastery at Istra, some forty miles north-west of Moscow, founded by Patriarch Nikon in 1656. Inscriptions in the New Jerusalem monastery are remarkable for their sheer quantity, for the range of their locations, for the variety of materials and techniques, for the diversity of their forms and subjects.[34] Beginning in

Nikon's time, they were developed by his successors over the latter part of the century. They are on interior and exterior walls, and around the base of cupolas and 'tent' towers, and on bells. They are painted on plaster, wood or copper, moulded in tiles, cut into brick or stone or metal, cast in bronze.[35] Besides traditional genres such as biblical and patristic and devotional citations, and captions to the iconography, the New Jerusalem inscriptions include: indications of the symbolic spatial equivalences between the monastery and its prototype in the Holy Land; a lapidary guidebook to the main church, presumably for pilgrims and visitors, consisting of a series of forty-eight inscribed stone tablets mounted at eye level in various locations; several verse descriptions of frescoes; some verse epitaphs; a prayer in five couplets of syllabic verse displayed in ceramic tiles around the exterior of the base of the cupola; and a 'chronicle' of the monastery, inscribed on stone tablets, again in syllabic verse including acrostics.[36]

Russian public educational inscription thus began in a quasi-devotional setting, but, following the example of Peter's Summer Garden, the practice was developed further in the grand parks that proliferated through the eighteenth century. For example, on Aleksandr Borisovich Kurakin's estate at Nadezhdino in Saratov province, the park itself, laid out in the 1790s, became the subject of an elaborate set of signs and captions. Kurakin explained that 'on each path one will find several posts with placards of its name, so that visitors will be overwhelmed by ideas and corresponding sensations'.[37] The texts on Kurakin's signs were not limited to the display of evocative names. They included four-line iambic hexameter verses explaining how he wished each temple and path to be interpreted and experienced.[38]

The late seventeenth and early eighteenth centuries were an age of what might be called the 'inscriptional turn' in Russian elite culture, and this may appear to have had profound consequences for the emergence of a public graphosphere. In practice, however, the look of public urban space was not immediately transformed. Each of the major initiatives was in its own way restricted in its impact. The display of decrees was an important practice and signal, but, after the initial experiments with embossed metal on solid structures, it reverted to pieces of paper with small print, which can hardly be counted as permanent and prominent features of the cityscape. The magnificence of the triumphal arches was avowedly temporary, a ceremonial graphospheric creation whose afterlife was assured only by – again – its recording on paper. Park statuary, like cemeteries, was part of separate, enclosed space. The tradition of fully public inscribed statuary began only towards the end of the eighteenth century, with the monument to Peter the Great, Falconet's 'Bronze Horseman', unveiled in 1782. Further such monuments appeared through the first half of the nineteenth century both in the capitals and in some provincial cities, but they remained rather rare.[39] In the Petrine age itself, despite the creative flowering of the inscriptional imagination, most of the time most of the city was still devoid of visible lettering.

Administrative Labels: The Indexation of Public Space

In the third phase the state's interventions in the public graphosphere were of a very different type. Instead of communicating information *from* the ruler *to* those who frequented the relevant spaces, they focussed on communicating information *on and about* the spaces, partly as aids to orientation for the users of those spaces, but mainly (in the first instance) also for the practical administrative purposes of the state itself. This was the phase of the spread of official signage: mileposts, street signs, house signs. Only with the spread of official signage did visible writing become permanently, regularly, indeed compulsorily embedded in the fabric of the city.

The first official signage was not urban. It marked the routes and distances *between* settlements. 'Mileposts' here renders the Russian *verstovye stolby*, which mark not miles but versts. A verst (Russian *versta*) is 500 sazhens, which, in the system in place from the early eighteenth century, comes to almost exactly a kilometre (1.067 km). Some kind of route marking was essential and ancient, especially in winter when snow obliterates so many features of the landscape. However, with specific regard to their inscriptions the trail of legislation begins in the 1720s. The initiatives, therefore, are again Petrine, though some of the tasks identified by Peter continued to be worked out subsequently for at least a hundred years.

On 7 August 1722 Peter instructed the Senate to arrange measurement of the distance of the direct route from Moscow to Tsaritsyn (now Volgograd), and to set up 'posts with inscriptions' (*stolby s nadpisiami*) along the way, 'as has been done on the Novgorod and other roads'. In addition, at the onset of winter, they were to arrange to measure the Moskva, Oka, and Volga rivers along the ice, and set up posts showing the distance between towns on the banks.[40] Route measurements and their markings were to become a recurrent theme in imperial legislation. Successive rulers accepted that mileposts were necessary for the efficient administration of the empire, for the movement of people and goods on official business. However, mileposts were also a cause of administrative headaches. Stone posts were expensive to install, but wooden posts, in Russia's climate, could also be expensive because of the need for regular maintenance and repair. In the inscriptions it was hard to sustain accuracy and consistency.

Such concerns and frustrations were reflected in successive decrees. On 23 August 1739 the Senate complained that many of the mileposts around St Petersburg were rotted and their inscriptions had become illegible. New posts were to be set up in co-ordination with the *Iamskaia kontora* – the Office of Posts (in a different sense).[41] Here, and again in a series of decrees of the mid 1740s, we also find reference to the problem of inaccuracy as roads changed their courses, so that surveyors needed to be sent to remeasure the routes, reposition the posts and recalibrate the inscriptions.[42] This was about money as well as time. On 16 August 1744 the empress Elizabeth complained to the Senate that the posts along the road from Moscow to Kiev indicated a total distance of 856 versts, but the charge for transport assumed a distance of 969 versts. On 27 November the Senate reported that their delegated surveyor had measured the route at 890 versts and had repositioned the posts accordingly.[43]

The inscriptions, too, were a recurrent theme: the techniques used to make them, their forms, information, shape and location. Paint was the obvious medium, but in 1740 the Senate decided that in the long term it would be more economical to burn the lettering into the posts with specially made branding irons. In 1744 the inscriptions were to be painted again. In 1746 the Senate even specified the colours of the oil paints – scarlet and ochre. In 1760 it was decreed that inscriptions should be written on a triangular metal plate to be affixed to each post.[44] In the early nineteenth century Alexander I expressed periodic irritation with the state of the mileposts. In detailed legislation of 1803, 1817 and 1819 he specified their height, their design according to official drawings, and the exact wording and arrangement of the inscriptions: when they should state the distance from Moscow or St Petersburg, and when they should only give the distance between post stations. He complained not just of inconsistency, but also of excess verbiage. His 1817 decree on roads is particularly informative both about mileposts and about other genres of roadside signage: labelled pointers at crossroads; border signs at administrative boundaries stating which *guberniia* or *uezd* one was entering or leaving; signs stating the tariff at toll bridges or ferries; and, at the entrance to every settlement, a post with a signboard stating the name of the settlement, who it belonged to, and the number of 'souls' in its population, 'as is the custom in Little Russia'.[45] Alexander's 'striped mileposts' (*versty polosatye*) became embedded in the Russian cultural imagination through their appearance in one of Pushkin's best-known poems, 'The Winter Road'.[46]

Mileposts extend the graphosphere into the countryside, in long ribbons they inscribe the empire: in real space for the efficient operations of the post roads, in imagined and reconstructed space for accurate reduction onto paper by cartographers.

Labelling of the city itself began later. On 8 May 1768 Catherine II instructed the St Petersburg police chief, Nikolai Chicherin, to 'order that, at the end of every street and alley, signs [here *doski* – 'boards' or 'tablets'] are to be attached bearing the name of that street or alley in the Russian and German languages; if any streets and alleys are as yet unnamed – please name them' (Fig. 5.3).[47] This, the mid to late 1760s, was also the period when stone plaques, such as those which had previously marked the construction of buildings, also began to appear on other parts of the city's structures: inscribed dates on the embankments and a bridge, flood-marks and so on.[48] After the streets and the embankments – the houses themselves. According to Catherine's *Charter for the Rights and Privileges of the Towns of the Russian Empire* (*Gramota na prava i vygody gorodam Rossiiskoi imperii*), published on 21 April 1785, each building was to be allocated a street number, in order to simplify the task of drawing up lists of inhabitants,[49] though nothing is said here about the public display of such numbers. Finally, in 1804, in order to facilitate the administration of a new property tax, the authorities in St Petersburg required that the identifying information be made visible. Metal plaques were henceforth to be fixed above the entrances to all non-governmental buildings, stating not only the

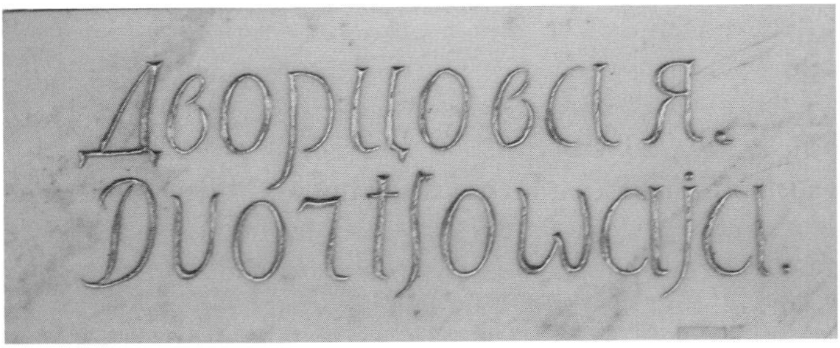

Fig. 5.3: Early St Petersburg street sign inscribed 'in the Russian and German languages', late 1760s; marble (restored)

number and the district but also the owner's name.[50] This sequence of measures on the systematic numbering of houses is roughly consistent with the chronology of equivalent legislation in parts of Western Europe. In France, for example, a requirement for universal house numbering was introduced in 1791, also for tax purposes.[51]

As in the case of mileposts, this process of inscribing the city with indications of its own physical and human geography, though undertaken for administrative reasons, also facilitated wider interactions and benefits. The city was now visibly indexed in the public graphosphere, and this 'real space' index, too, could be transferred to paper, through the compilation of printed directories. St Petersburg's first address book was published in 1809 and was issued more or less simultaneously (by different publishers) in German, French and Russian. Its author, Heinrich Christoph von Reimers, acknowledged in his introduction the importance of the recent fact that, over the course of 1804, signs had been fixed on every house.[52] Not that the indexing worked to everybody's satisfaction, either *in situ* or on paper. An Englishman, Edward Thompson, who published his *Life in Russia; or, the Discipline of Despotism* in 1848, complained that, when he tried to deliver a letter to a resident of a building just off Nevskii Prospekt, he was unable to do so, for there was no visible directory of residents of the 170 flats (even though there may well have been names on the individual doors).[53] The government recognised the problem, and around the same time devised a bureaucratic solution. In 1851, in the second, expanded edition of *All Petersburg in Your Pocket* by Aleksei Grech, readers were informed that now, if they wanted to find out where anybody lived, they had only to go to the Bureau of Addresses (*Adresnyi stol*): 'a new and highly useful institution, which can be used by private individuals who wish to find out anybody's place of residence'.[54]

Though installed for practical reasons, towards the mid nineteenth century street signs and house signs made their way into literature as objects of cultural reflection, markers of the human geography and character of the city.

Most such official indexation was fixed, but some was mobile. The beard tokens issued in 1724–5 were made to be sewn onto outer garments, so that a bearded man's certificate of exemption might be visible as he walked the streets.[55] The city cab services were regulated, and each cab driver (*izvozchik*) was issued with a licence number, which had to be visible. Legislation on such licence tags dates from at least the mid eighteenth century. Usually the drivers were required to have the numbers sewn to the back of their outer garment. This distinctive feature of the graphosphere was a curiosity recorded by foreigners in ethnographic engravings from the early nineteenth century.[56]

The Commercial Graphosphere

Outside the cemetery, despite the many initiatives of state and church, the urban public graphosphere remained rather thin. Walking through the city one could find writing if one looked for it, but rarely was it thrust before one's gaze. The decisive changes were generated not by an institution but by an activity, not 'top down' but 'bottom up'. The activity was trade. Its graphospheric contribution was in the spread of shop signs. The role of the state was not to drive the transformation, but simply, and for a while unwillingly, to remove the barriers to it.

The spread of trade signs and shop signs cannot be mapped precisely in either time or space. The process can be approximately imagined through a succession of three types of evidence: legislation, illustration and description. The trail of legislation starts towards the middle of the eighteenth century. Illustrations become informative from approximately the second and third decades of the nineteenth century, while in the 1830s and 1840s such signs became objects of documentary description, literary evocation and even quasi-philosophical contemplation.

Around the mid eighteenth century imperial decrees began to express concern both about the location of signs and about what they displayed. On 8 November 1746 the Senate ordered that hostelries (*kabaki*) in Moscow and St Petersburg must not display boards with the words 'official drinking house' (*kazennyi piteinyi dom*). There was no objection to the designation 'drinking house'; it was the word 'official' that was to be deleted.[57] In 1749 the *Kamer-kollegiia* issued an order banning all excess graphic elements from signs advertising hostelries and tobacco shops. Henceforth they were to use only the prescribed wording: 'In this house drinks are sold', 'in this house tobacco is sold'.[58] In a decree of 14 October 1752 the empress Elizabeth declared that along the main embankments 'there should be no signs [*vyveski*]; many such signs, of various trades, are now visible even opposite the court of Her Imperial Majesty; signs are permitted on the street along the Moika'.[59]

Catherine II also took an interest in signs and their appearance. She accepted that a zonal restriction, with a blanket ban in specified areas, was damaging to trade, so in March 1770 she rescinded Elizabeth's decree of 1752. Instead of a general ban, she regulated the form. In a decree which was to be generally applicable both to St Petersburg and to Moscow, she stipulated that trade signs made of wood or canvas were permissible either when fixed flat to walls, or when suspended from a protruding arm not exceeding one *arshin* in length.[60] Decency required that there should be no signs advertising men's underwear, or funeral services, and there were to be no paper or leather signs attached to fences or shutters (that is, 'proper' fixed signs were acceptable, random posters were not).[61] This is consistent with Catherine's broadly facilitative legislation on urban trade. For example, in successive decrees of 28 June and 8 July 1782 she overturned previous restrictions and permitted merchants throughout the empire to trade from shops in their houses rather than just in designated markets and trading rows. In principle these decrees all but abandoned a restrictive principle of urban zoning for retail trade in favour of facilitating the autonomous spread of private shops.[62]

The implication of this sequence of decrees is that on-street painted trade signs became increasingly familiar features of the urban landscape during the third quarter of the eighteenth century. For this early period, however, we have little direct evidence regarding what was actually displayed on such signs. The likelihood is that they were principally pictorial rather than verbal.[63] The regular presence of verbal inscriptions is attested only for institutions selling alcohol and tobacco.

Paintings, drawings and engravings of the cityscape, by both Russians and foreigners, are a feature of the first half of the nineteenth century. Their coverage is neither consistent nor systematic, but in some cases there are revealing contrasts between consecutive depictions of the same or equivalent spaces. With regard to the principal shopping streets of St Petersburg, illustrations suggest that the decisive proliferation of shop signs took place over the first couple of decades of the century. We can compare, for example, the views of Nevskii Prospekt around 1800, by the Swedish artist Benjamin Patersen, with scenes from the panorama of the same street in the mid 1820s by Vasilii Sadovnikov, which in the early 1830s was turned into a widely admired series of lithographs. Patersen's St Petersburg was not completely sign-free. His view of Palace Square from the bottom end of Nevskii Prospekt shows a red sign in French in the right foreground. However, his long perspective view down the central part of Nevskii Prospekt, from Gostinyi Dvor on the left, is wordless (Fig. 5.4). This is in stark contrast with the equivalent scenes in Sadovnikov's panorama, which shows that by the 1820s Petersburg's most fashionable street had become saturated with signs (Fig. 5.5).[64] Reviewers at the time were especially impressed by the fullness and accuracy of their representation.[65]

Fig. 5.4: Benjamin Patersen, Nevskii Prospekt. Watercolour, 1799

Fig. 5.5: Segment of *Panorama of Nevskii Prospekt*. Lithograph by Petr Ivanov, 1835, after watercolour by Vasilii Sadovnikov, late 1820s. © State Russian Museum, St Petersburg

Illustrations of Moscow imply a slightly slower proliferation of commercial signs. Although on some streets they had undoubtedly existed previously, in views of Moscow they seem not to have become regular features until the late 1830s.[66]

In the middle decades of the nineteenth century shop signs and trade signs spread not just along the main commercial thoroughfares but more widely.[67] The evidence comes from written descriptions, both documentary and fictional. The documentary evidence consists partly of correspondence, partly of dedicated essays on urban signage. The evidence of fiction must, of course, be used with caution. Particularly useful, however, is the genre of 'physiological sketch' (*fiziologicheskii ocherk*) that became fashionable in the mid 1840s. 'Physiological' writings sought to reveal the anatomy of the city, especially the unglamorous, unromanticised faces, habits and habitations of its ordinary occupants, to map its social geography, perhaps as a prelude to diagnosing its ills. Like the authors of openly documentary sources, the authors of this type of fiction sought both to inform and to interpret.

The earliest detailed description of shop signs in Russia was published in Moscow in 1836. It was written by Fedor Distribuendi – presumably a pseudonym – about whom nothing appears to be known apart from his authorship of a 68-page booklet entitled *A View of Moscow's Shop Signs*.[68] The archives of the Moscow Censorship Committee reveal that the manuscript was submitted in September 1835 by a certain Ensign Brazhnikov, which possibly gives us a name if not a biography.[69] Distribuendi (or 'Distribuendi') was aware of being the pioneer of a new subgenre in the literature about Moscow. Much had been written about the beauties of Moscow's buildings, streets and parks, but for some reason nobody had hitherto paid due attention to the signs, which were so abundant and varied. This was what had prompted him to produce his survey. Distribuendi makes it clear that, by the mid 1830s, shop signs in Moscow were no longer just occasional exotic features. They had become widespread on all the main streets of the capital; so widespread and so diverse, indeed, that they could be confusing.[70] Distribuendi sets himself the task of providing a classification, a systematic guide, since 'system is the soul of any scholarly work'.[71] His purpose was to impose order on variety, to reveal the regularities behind the motley surface impressions. Variegation or motliness – *pestrota*, a kind of disorderly profusion – is a notion which crops up regularly in descriptions of the signs both of Moscow and of St Petersburg.[72] In the face of such motliness, Fedor Distribuendi attempted to create a taxonomy, which consisted of twenty-five types of 'normal' sign, arranged according to the type of establishment that they adorned (tailor, cobbler, barber, milliner, jeweller, bookshop etc.). In addition to 'normal' signs, Fedor devised two other categories: the 'elegant' and the 'curious'. A normal sign was of regular shape, gave the name of the business in correct Russian, and in most cases displayed a pictorial symbol appropriate to the establishment (e.g. scissors for a tailor, boots for a cobbler). His 'curious' signs were characterised either by tasteless design or by semi-literate inscription, and 'elegant' signs either showed particular graphic inventiveness or flaunted their French. Although Distribuendi welcomed the profusion of signs, he found the motliness troubling: it 'disfigures the Moscow streets, turns them into a kind of caricature gallery that is wearisome to the eye'. The 'normal' should be the norm. He even favoured regulation, in the service of regularity.[73]

Others were drawn more towards the 'curious' or the 'elegant'. The prominence of French, or, to a lesser extent, of other foreign languages, was a *leitmotif* of responses to urban signage. This could be regarded as a delight or an abomination. As early as 1811 or 1812 Konstantin Batiushkov noted the combination of French and unsightly disorderliness in the shop signs plastered over the buildings of Moscow's fashionable streets such as Kuznetskii Most and Tverskaia.[74] Shortly afterwards, in the face of Napoleon's invasion, French shop signs were banned on the orders of the military governor of Moscow, Fedor Rostopchin. Twenty-one years later, in a letter to his wife, written from Moscow on her twenty-first birthday (27 August 1833), Aleksandr Pushkin cheerfully conveyed the 'important news' that French shop signs were reappearing on Kuznetskii Most.[75] Pushkin's wife, Natalia Goncharova, would surely have agreed with the 'physiological' essayist Petr Vistengof, who, in his *Sketches of Moscow*, published in 1842, argued that foreign shop design and service raised the overall standards, and that there was a correlation between the quality of the sign and the quality of the goods.[76]

However, not everybody read the prominence or dominance of French on shop signs in some areas as a mark of sophistication and taste. On the contrary, it was satirised, even reviled, as a symptom of cultural subservience, a national affront. The spectrum of readings runs from mild irony to biting polemic. At the gentler end of the spectrum was the young essayist Ivan Kokorev, whose collection of sketches of Moscow in the 1840s included a section on signs: 'the inscription, the inscriptions! That's what quickens the heartbeat. Such progress!, Such development! [. . .] And no trace whatever of the spirit of Russia! Paris, a veritable Paris.'[77] A harder-edged attack on the French street-texts of central St Petersburg was launched in a near-contemporary essay by Egor Rastorguev, whose *Strolls Along Nevskii Prospekt* was published in 1846.[78] For Rastorguev the predominance of French suggested neither elegance nor sophistication. It was humiliating. He was indignant at the asymmetry of attitudes: Russians went abroad in the spirit of appreciation and took pains to learn the relevant languages; these foreign traders came to Russia in order to make profits and were quite shameless in their ignorance of the Russian tongue. Worse still, even Russian traders had become infected by the fashion for the foreign: everything and everybody was advertised as being 'de Paris'.[79]

In central Moscow in the mid 1830s Fedor Distribuendi had focussed almost exclusively on Russian signs, although we know that French signs were there to be described if he had chosen to do so. In central St Petersburg in the mid 1840s Egor Rastorguev noticed (or wished to draw attention to) exclusively French signs, although we know that the linguistic landscape was not in fact so monoglot, or so mono-scriptal, as he asserts. Each read and responded to the urban text of his choice: in the one case according to his desires, in the other case according to his fears.

In stark contrast to the francophone sophistication of the 'elegant' signs were what Distribuendi had termed the 'curious' signs. Although he acknowledged that they were numerous and ubiquitous, Distribuendi preferred not to peruse them in detail. 'Physiological' authors showed greater curiosity. One vivid account of what one might call 'off-street' signs is given in a sketch called 'Nooks and Crannies of Petersburg' (*Peterburgskie ugly*), by Nikolai Nekrasov. In search of accommodation, Nekrasov's narrator turns into the inner courtyard of a large building, where 'my eyes encountered a patchwork of signs, which had been attached to the building just as carefully on the inside [i.e. in the courtyard] as on the outside [i.e. facing the street]'. The signs advertised anything from coffins to tin plates to the services of a certified midwife.[80] In quoting some of the signs, Nekrasov's narrator highlights their non-standard Russian: misspellings, incorrect word division, sub-literary use of words. There is a similar air of slightly amused intellectual condescension in other accounts of the wider culture of urban signage towards the middle of the century. Odd locutions are also highlighted in another essay in the same 'physiological' collection, Evgenii Grebenka's evocation of the unfashionable district known as the 'Petersburg Side' (*Peterburgskaia storona*),[81] and in a brief article on St Petersburg signs, by an author designated merely as 'T', which appeared in 1848 in the weekly magazine *Illiustratsiia*.[82]

In the 'curious' locutions cited by these observers, many of the types of linguistic deviation turn out to be recurrent, rather than individual aberrations. This impression is confirmed by 'T', who, in a footnote, points out that some non-standard inscriptional usages had themselves become conventional through habit. In other words, the 'curious' signs were curious to the intellectuals but normal in their own contexts. Fedor Distribuendi and some of his successors present an image of a neutral (and preferable) Russian standard, marred on the one side by francophone affectation and on the other side by semi-literate aberration. Instead, one should perhaps imagine a linguistic landscape where different conventions predominated in their respective graphospheric zones.

The 'motliness' of the urban public graphosphere became ever more pronounced over the first half of the nineteenth century. Inscribed statuary became more common not just in parks but also in public squares. More public buildings displayed inscriptions marking their purpose and/or foundation.[83] Theatres commissioned posters. From the second quarter of the century fire insurance companies fixed their own inscribed metal plaques to buildings which were insured through them.[84] The government made increasing use of newspapers for the publication of current official notices, but there were also occasional intensive poster campaigns, such as the frequent broadside bulletins and exhortations distributed by Moscow's military governor, Fedor Rostopchin, in the early summer of 1812 as Napoleon's army approached.[85] An ever more diverse assemblage of smaller objects with primary or secondary writing formed a kind of shifting background presence, coming in and out of the field of vision through trade and exchange in public places: books and prints, both through street stalls and through the independent bookshops that began to proliferate from the end of the eighteenth century;[86] coins and banknotes; manufacturer's tags.

A dense and varied public graphosphere was recognised as a mark of urban modernity. Nevertheless, in some of the responses to the phenomenon of public writing, there was a tendency to make a symbolic distinction between Moscow and St Petersburg. Moscow was represented as traditionally chaotic, St Petersburg was represented as rationally labelled. Thus in 1836 Gogol wrote: 'Moscow says "if the buyer needs something, he'll find it". Petersburg thrusts its signs in one's face [. . .] Moscow is one big market; Petersburg is a well-lit shop.'[87] Vissarion Belinskii picked up the contrast in his essay 'Petersburg and Moscow', which served as a preface to the 1845 collection *The Physiology of Petersburg*: Moscow looks inwards on itself; St Petersburg faces outward. Moscow is uninterested in helping you find your way around. To find a flat in Moscow is 'pure torment', whereas in Petersburg the doors will often display 'not only the number but also a bronze or iron plaque with the name of the occupant'.[88] Graphospheric difference had become part of the perceived individuality and character of the respective cities.

Aspects of the Graphospheric Imagination

The public graphosphere not only generates imaginative reflection; it is generated *by* the imagination; and sometimes it may exist primarily *in* the imagination. Any graphospheric fact is preceded by an imagined fact. The idea of an inscription precedes its realisation. However, beyond this rather obvious sequence, the relationship between imagined public writing and actual public writing fluctuated. A real inscription may first have to be imagined, but an imagined inscription does not have to become real. Or rather: products of the epigraphic imagination may often be more densely realised on paper than in the spaces for which they are notionally imagined.

In the mid fifteenth century there was no public graphosphere to speak of, and no sign of a sense that there might be such a thing. From around the turn of the sixteenth century inscriptions began to be displayed sporadically in various contexts, but there was no fundamental shift in the appearance or notion of public space. In the late seventeenth century and early eighteenth century the *idea* of an inscribed, graphospherically dense city gained cultural currency among the Russian elite. This is partly reflected in the top-down initiatives for the placing of inscribed objects in public places, but hardly less significant, and arguably more numerous and diverse, are the expressions of the inscriptional imagination: the 'epigraphic' poetry that existed almost entirely in manuscript, the inscriptional motifs in illustrations and engravings, the rhetorical descriptions, the emblem books. Indeed, even the most monumental of actual public inscriptions were, in a sense, partly imaginary, in that they were merely the temporary realisations of an urban graphosphere whose permanent record was on paper rather than in the streets.

From the second half of the eighteenth century the inscriptional imagination was reinforced by the literary conventions that became fashionable among devotees of the cult of true feeling. The settings were rustic rather than urban, and the genres were bucolic and elegaic. A topos of bucolic verse was the carving of lovers' names or initials on trees.[89] Borrowed from classical and neoclassical translations, the motif appears in Russian verse and prose from the 1750s onwards. In the 1790s the literary device enjoyed a curiously intense reification in the cult of 'Poor Liza', the eponymous heroine of the story by Nikolai Karamzin. After her doomed romance with a young nobleman, Liza, a sensitive flower girl (since 'even peasant girls are capable of love'), drowned herself in a pond near Moscow's Simonov monastery, where she and her temporary lover, Erast, used to walk. 'Liza's pond' became a focus of pilgrimage for tender souls paying homage to her memory, and inscribing the memory of themselves on the trees around the pond.[90] Epitaphs, too, proliferated in the poetry of Russian sentimentalism, both as self-contained genres and as motifs embedded in the 'graveyard poetry' that became especially influential after the appearance, in 1802, of Vasilii Zhukovskii's translation of Thomas Gray's 'Elegy Written in a Country Churchyard'. This age of literary epitaph coincided with the period when actual verse epitaphs became more common. Often it is hard to be sure when a surviving text lived only on the page or in stone, or both.[91]

From the mid eighteenth century through to the mid nineteenth century the urban graphosphere became notably – decisively – thicker, not as a result of the imposition of an urban aesthetic, but as a consequence of practical developments in patterns of commerce, and in the state's administrative requirements that the city and its inhabitants be indexed. Despite the ostensibly prosaic causes and contexts, here, too, there was scope for the inscriptional imagination, whether in artful and inventive design, or in imaginative interpretation, or in verse. At the start of each major phase of its development and growth, public graphospheric innovation was to varying degrees marked by the presence of the non-native, the non-Cyrillic: from Solari's Latin plaque over the new grand entrance to the Moscow Kremlin, through the Latin inscriptions on several of the eighteenth-century triumphal arches, to the French shop signs that so enchanted or irritated viewers on fashionable streets such as Kuznetskii Most and Nevskii Prospekt. By the second quarter of the nineteenth century the sheer abundance and variety of signage became a literary *leitmotif.* At the same time, writers and illustrators came to describe and to explore the meaning of the phenomenon of writing on their streets, probing the ways in which this denser public graphosphere reflected and created their sense of urban space.

Domestic Graphospheres

For present purposes a 'domestic' space is the interior of a structure, one of whose principal purposes is residential. So, domestic graphospheres may be found in palaces or country houses or monastic cells or urban apartment blocks or peasant huts, but the working definition excludes the interiors of, for example, shops or factories or clubs or theatres, or even institutions of writing such as libraries. Thus the adjective 'domestic' does not always imply 'private', since residences at any social level may include spaces that, whether regularly or occasionally, are assumed to be open to the gaze of outsiders. Finally, we are here mainly concerned with visibility, with display, not with dissemination or production. This is not a survey of domestic reading and writing as such.

Certain very broad patterns of change in domestic graphospheres are obvious from the start. It is barely worth stressing that the diversity and volume of writing to be found in homes in the mid nineteenth century bear little meaningful comparison with the situation in the mid fifteenth century. In the mid fifteenth century with the exception of inscriptions on devotional images, specimens of writing would have been almost entirely absent from the dwellings of the overwhelming mass of the populations of the principalities of Rus, and rare even among elites, at any rate outside the monastery. By the mid nineteenth century the situation was unrecognisably different. Writing was produced in huge quantities both for homes and in homes. Depending on taste and inclination, the studies and salons and boudoirs of the lettered might be littered with books and manuscripts, notes and papers, newspapers and journals, visiting cards, invitations, diplomas and certificates and all manner of jottings and inscribed paraphernalia, while even the unlettered might festoon their walls with inscribed woodcuts or lithographs.

Beyond such generalities, the history of domestic graphospheres becomes more elusive. In the first place the social, geographic, cultural, functional and architectural range of spaces is too broad to permit an integrated history across four centuries. Secondly, the emphasis on display must involve a wider exploration of domestic fixtures and furnishings, of the history of shelving and cupboards and cabinets, of open or glass-fronted cases, of *étagères* and whatnots. Very little is known or knowable about early domestic display. As far as I am aware, the first illustration of 'built-in' shelving is to be found in Fedor Polikarpov's trilingual grammar of 1701.[92] Designated display furniture – shelving and open-fronted cupboards, glass display cases etc. – spread in Russia from the eighteenth century: first in the reception rooms and studies of the grand palaces, then into the homes of the gentry, and eventually into urban apartments. Glass-fronted display shelving, for objects in his collections, was one of Peter I's innovations in his study in his Summer Palace.[93] By the mid nineteenth century the miscellaneous clutter of small objects was as characteristic of a Russian drawing room as of its equivalent across much of Europe.

Thirdly, there is an acute problem of inadequate sources, or of inadequate identification and publication of sources, in all but a very few areas. In principle the best sources are systematic documents in the form of formal inventories and descriptions.[94] Apart from that, a reconstruction or re-imagining of domestic graphospheres has to rely on such scraps as are provided by three types of source: the implications of surviving objects such as those surveyed earlier in this study;[95] the visual evidence of illustrations of interiors;[96] and such gleanings as can be picked from a mass of allusions in non-systematic written materials such as literature, memoirs, letters. In all of this there is the problem of under-research. Some types of domestic display are quite well known, but many questions remain unasked and huge numbers of potential sources of evidence remain untapped. I have merely scratched some surfaces, and the following remarks are offered as no more than a provisional framework for further exploration.

Primary Writing

In pre-eighteenth-century Russia, books were not generally kept in open domestic storage. Or so it seems. Most research on pre-Petrine book ownership has focussed on acquisition, distribution and donation rather than on storage and display, so one must be wary of premature generalisation. The fragments of evidence are not entirely consistent – nor, indeed, would one expect them to be so. In some monasteries monks could keep books in their cells or borrow them from the monastic store.[97] Throughout the period there were monk-scholars who had collections to hand. Designated store rooms (*knigokhranitel'nitsa, knigokhranil'nitsa, knigokhranil'naia palata* etc.)[98] are attested from the mid sixteenth century. Some were separately constructed, most were in rooms allocated within existing monastic buildings,[99] while in the Kirillo-Belozerskii monastery (according to the extensive inventory of 1601) two rooms for books were created in the bell tower.[100] However, book collections tended to be kept in trunks, not on shelves or in open-fronted cupboards. Upright cupboards are attested for some non-monastic (royal, aristocratic, patriarchal) collections from the second half of the seventeenth century, but these were probably closed-fronted.[101] Great monastic or other institutional libraries with purpose-built cases for rows of chained folios were not part of the Russian medieval legacy. Books stored in trunks might be reckoned parts of a potential graphosphere, or perhaps parts of a mental graphosphere associated with a given space, but the shift to the visibility of open storage on shelves and desks was largely a phenomenon of the eighteenth century.

Over the eighteenth century not only did domestic book collection gather pace,[102] but the *image* of domestically visible books and documents became more fashionable as part of the projection of their owner's cultural persona. In art, where books or scrolls had previously been part of the iconography of bishops and evangelists and occasionally of Christ, books and documents migrated into portraits of the gentry. Portraits of aristocratic men in the mid to late eighteenth century might, typically, emphasise attributes in the arts both of war and of peace. A man might choose to be depicted in military uniform, or festooned with badges of his distinction, or leaning on a table strewn with books and papers, or sitting informally at his desk.[103] A pair of portraits of Prince Platon Aleksandrovich Zubov, painted in the early 1790s by Johann Baptist Lampi, nicely catches the range. One of the two shows only the head and shoulders and focuses on the prince's formal dress and honours: a chain with the insignia of the Order of St Andrew, a diamond-encrusted miniature of the empress Catherine II. In the other portrait the prince is seated at his desk, on which are a globe, an unfolded map, three leather-bound books (one propped up to face him, though it is closed), and implements for writing (quill, inkwell, blotter). The blotter holds down some paper on which the prince has been writing. His left arm rests on the back of the chair, and in his right hand he holds a part-folded manuscript document.[104] Women, too, were occasionally depicted with documents and implements of writing or drawing.[105] Sometimes an assemblage of documents and scraps of writing in a domestic setting became the main subject of the picture, a form of still life. A cluster of such *trompe l'oeil* canvasses dating from 1737, by different hands – two by Grigorii Teplov, one each by Trofim Ulianov and Petr Bogomolov – suggests a particular moment of fashion.[106]

From at least the 1780s grand houses were quite often designed with built-in library shelving. Moreover, in some properties, such as the Moscow house of Rostislav Evgrafovich Tatishchev, the built-in bookshelves were not confined to a designated 'library' room, but formed part of the main ballroom.[107] Sometimes in interior design the symbolism of domestic books could take precedence over functionality: part of the shelving in Tatishchev's ballroom concealed a *trompe l'oeil* door to the adjacent dining room. Not that Tatishchev's library was an illusion: the fineness of his books was noted even by an officer in Napoleon's occupying army, Marie-Henri Beyle – better known by his later *nom de plume*, Stendhal. The point here is not that all grand houses had grand libraries with grand collections of books. Tatishchev's house is at one extreme on the spectrum – as, in a different milieu a generation later, was the picture of the enormous, bookcase-dominated study of the writer Vasilii Zhukovskii (1783–1852).[108] In the late eighteenth and early nineteenth centuries book-strewn tables, shelves, and whatnots became somewhat more frequent objects of depiction not just in the quasi-private space of the study or boudoir, but in more explicitly public reception rooms, whether in grand residences, in normal urban apartments or in country houses.[109] However, there are also plenty of illustrations of studies or boudoirs[110] with writing tables, occasionally with the odd book or two, but no shelving.[111] In other words, changes in domestic interior design and furnishings[112] presuppose only a *potential* presence of visible books and papers, but it is hard to gauge how frequently such potential was realised.

Variations in the presence of primary writing are reflected in literature, as an aspect of characterisation, most famously in Pushkin's verse novel *Evgenii Onegin*. When Onegin settles in his uncle's house on the country estate, he finds in the study 'not the faintest smudge of ink', but just a ledger of expenses plus an old calendar from 1808: 'the old man had much to do, and didn't look at other books'. This is the same study that Tatiana later visits after Onegin's departure, and where she finds the 'pile of books' whose contents, along with Onegin's marginalia, seem to her so strange and revealing. Later, when established in high society, Tatiana sighs that she would happily give up all the trappings of success 'for a shelf of books', and for the rustic garden and the places where she and Onegin had met – at which point the reader recalls the narrator's encounter with his Muse, in a garden, in the guise of a provincial young lady, with melancholy in her eyes and a French book in her hands.[113] None of this compares with Pushkin's own library of more than 4,500 volumes.

To trace the presence of books is not quite the same as to trace the visibility of writing. Most books are closed most of the time, and even when they are open they conceal most of their contents. A closed book on open storage is a visible reminder of the presence of writing, a powerful stimulant to the graphospheric imagination but not a significant item of graphospheric display. The visible part is the binding. The primary purpose of a binding is to protect and preserve the pages contained by it. A secondary purpose may be to convey information either about the contents of those pages (e.g. their title or author) or about the status of the object (e.g. a library mark or ownership stamp). Changes in fashions of storage may also bring about changes in the messages inscribed on the bindings. In the period when books were generally stored in trunks, their bindings tended to be solid (leather over wooden boards) but plain. They seldom gave specific indications of the contents of the volume. Blind-stamped *viaz'* lettering in the centre of the upper board might indicate the name of the book,[114] although sometimes a stamp with the generic phrase 'this book is called' (*kniga glagolemaia*) was used without the addition of a specific title, so that tooling functioned as a formulaic decorative component more than as a source of verbal information. The stamps on the central panel of the upper board could be quite varied in their decoration, sometimes extending to representation: birds, dragons, lions and unicorns, iconographic scenes.[115] In rare instances the boards might also be decorated with a gilt device indicating the owner (a *supralibros*, or *superexlibris*). The earliest Muscovite 'superexlibris' is found on a copy of Ivan Fedorov's 1564 *Apostol* belonging to Ivan IV.[116] Some collectors continued to commission bindings with gold-stamped 'superexlibris' through the eighteenth century,[117] but in general such marks of bibliophilic extravagance tended to give way to the printed paper bookplate.[118]

With the appearance of shelving, and especially with the appearance of shelving as display rather than simply as storage, the spine acquired greater graphospheric potential. The juxtaposed spines of books on shelves can speak eloquently, though succinctly. They label the objects and they project aspects of their owner's cultural persona. Spine lettering could be tooled directly onto one or more of the panels or could be created separately and glued on. Gilt-lettered leather bindings were an optional extra, according to means and taste. The cheaper version was the publisher's printed paper wrapper, which might include lettering both on the spine and on the upper and lower covers. Printed wrappers first appeared in Russia in the late eighteenth century and became common from the early nineteenth century.[119]

Non-books probably penetrated domestic spaces earlier and more widely than books. Whether for the purposes of estate management, polite correspondence or village litigation, papers of all kinds became part of domestic life. For example, the 1689 inventory of the residence of Vasilii Golitsyn describes his archive of unbound documents in his lower *stolovaia palata*: the tsar's decrees relating to his service, military administrative records for 1676–81 and 1687, and the like.[120] Visibility is, again, another matter, hard to assess. The late-eighteenth-century trend in aristocratic portraiture shows that some of the elite chose to be represented alongside miscellaneous papers artfully strewn beside them; but these are portraits of individuals putting themselves into a particular kind of frame, while the more general depictions of interiors very rarely show papers left on tables except in designated spaces such as studies. One might surmise that a greater density of visible paperwork was likely to be found where accommodation was too cramped to allow much functional subdivision: in the apartments of those who wrote non-books for their living, the low-grade scribes whose abodes hugely outnumbered both those of the gentry and those of the intellectuals in the demography of the early-nineteenth-century city.

Secondary Writing

Apart from what happened to be left open on a desk, primary writing in a domestic setting was largely stored, not displayed: books in bindings, documents in boxes or drawers. Most types of visible word, including the inscriptions on bindings, fall into the category of secondary writing.

We start with the walls. Across the centuries, across social divides, pictures provided both graphospheric continuity and differentiation. The continuity was in the domestic presence of icons. The differentiation derives from changes both in their relative prominence and in the sharp graphospheric contrasts between the types of pictures which came to supplement them. The presence of icons, which almost always included inscriptions, is perhaps the only feature that links domestic graphospheres of the Rus principalities of the mid fifteenth century with those of the Russian Empire of the mid nineteenth century. At both ends of the chronological scale, in a majority of homes in which words were visible, the most prominent texts on display (often the only texts on display) were the inscriptions on devotional images.

Less constant, however, was their social distribution, and their density and relative prominence in different settings over time. Two developments, in particular, may be reckoned somewhat counterintuitive, especially by contrast with changes in the public graphosphere. First, in certain types of setting the wall-based components of the domestic graphosphere grew significantly *less* dense rather than more dense. And, secondly, there is no consistent correlation between the density of the wall-based domestic graphosphere and the levels of literacy; indeed, sometimes there was a reverse correlation, whereby a higher density of visible writing was present in settings where there was a relatively lower level of literacy.

At one end of the spectrum, the extreme example of graphospheric saturation was the Golden Hall, one of the throne rooms in the Moscow Kremlin. This was a place of quasi-public ceremony, but within a royal residence. Decorated for the young Ivan IV in the late 1540s or early 1550s, the Golden Hall and its anteroom were covered ceiling to floor in paintings. In the upper registers of the Golden Hall was a large composition representing Divine Wisdom. On the lower registers were depictions of past rulers of Rus and Muscovy. On the walls surrounding those present in the room were narrative scenes illustrating, first, the baptism of Ivan's ancestor Prince Vladimir Sviatoslavich of Kiev, and then the transfer of fragments of the True Cross and of Byzantine imperial regalia to Rus, as narrated in the *Tale of the Princes of Vladimir*.[121] This was a central narrative – perhaps *the* central narrative – of mid-sixteenth-century Muscovite political ideology. It told of how the ruling family was descended from the kin of the Roman emperor Augustus, and of how the Byzantine emperor arranged that the prince of Kiev should be crowned as a tsar.[122] The Golden Hall paintings were copiously supplemented with narrative and explanatory inscriptions. The structure was demolished in 1752, but we know of its iconography and inscriptions from the very full description by Simon Ushakov and Nikita Klementev commissioned by Tsar Aleksei Mikhailovich in 1672.[123] The composition included a great deal more than the standard iconographic labels. There were non-traditional inscriptions, perhaps derived from West European engravings, on representations of books, banners and scrolls.[124] And there were extensive narrative texts: for example, the four scenes from the story of Vladimir's baptism were accompanied by some 250 words of text, and a further 150 words are fitted into the depictions of the Byzantine gifts to Vladimir Monomakh.

The Golden Hall was the place for some of the state's formally choreographed ceremonies, such as receptions of foreign envoys. Courtiers and foreigners alike were presented with the spectacle of the tsar flanked by visual and verbal depictions of the stories central to his own legitimation and quasi-sacralisation. Regardless of whether the individuals present could actually read the texts (or the pictures),[125] the ruler in ceremonial mode was as if inscribed into his surroundings, enveloped by the words and images that contained and justified him. This was an obvious extension of visual language from church to palace, not only because the decoration was broadly iconographic and hence brought a general aura of the sacral, but because of the particular presentation of Ivan IV as ruler in a specific narrative wrapping. At approximately the same time as the Golden Hall was being painted, an ornately carved wooden pew was set in the Cathedral of the Assumption in the Moscow Kremlin, for the personal use of the tsar. In remarkable detail, on twelve panels of carved relief, it, too, presented a series of narrative scenes illustrating the *Tale of the Princes of Vladimir*.

Moreover, like the Golden Hall, the royal pew was also unprecedentedly verbose. Each of the twelve relief pictures included a carved caption or description of what was depicted. In addition, the door panels at the front of the pew display roundels with four relief carvings that consist only of words: a version, again, of the text of the *Tale of the Princes of Vladimir*.[126] There had been pictorial relief carvings on other royal seats in Russia,[127] but none with scenes from Russian history, and none with extensive inscription. In the royal pew, as in the Golden Hall, the graphospheric surround was integral to the representation of the ruler. Such dense association of ruler with iconographic text did not survive the transition from tsardom to empire. In a way, Peter I's triumphal parades were equivalent acts of ceremonial self-framing, but in a demonstratively different wrapping of images and visible words.

These were extremes. Without the ideology of rulership a grand but non-royal residence of the late seventeenth century might also include some rooms thickly painted or hung with iconographic scenes appropriately inscribed.[128] At the other end of the spectrum were icons in the peasant home. We do not know how early the practice of keeping domestic icons became widespread. Direct evidence is minimal. The mid-sixteenth-century *Domostroi* (*Book of Household Management*) dictates that 'every Christian' should hang the holy images of icons on the walls of every room in his house,[129] but, notwithstanding the generalisation ('every Christian'), the *Domostroi* was addressed to the elite. In the mid seventeenth century the archdeacon Paul of Aleppo, who accompanied his father, Patriarch Makarios of Antioch, on extensive travels through Orthodox Eastern Europe, stressed that icons adorned the houses not only of the wealthy, but also of 'peasants also in the villages, for the love of all the Russians for images and their faith in them are exceeding great.'[130] By the eighteenth century, at any rate, devotional images were being painted in large quantities for domestic devotion and were peddled throughout the towns and villages of Russia.[131]

The wide circulation of religious images was enhanced by their availability as prints. Printed pictures on religious themes became increasingly popular from the late seventeenth century onwards. Not everybody welcomed the innovation. In the 1680s Patriarch Ioakim expressed his concern about the trade in cheap woodcuts. First, they were made without regard for the proper skills of the icon-painter, hence they were not true likenesses, hence they could be reckoned blasphemous rather than pious. And, secondly, people were buying them in order to adorn their rooms, not in order to venerate the images.[132] In other words, Ioakim was worried that an effect of the spread of cheap woodcuts was to turn icons into mere pictures, to turn devotional images into elements of interior decoration. He was struggling against an unstoppable tide. By the late 1680s the houses of the wealthy were also hung with painted and printed icons alike.[133]

As domestic icons became more and more accessible to the masses (whether viewed as objects of formal veneration or as pious adornment), so they became less and less central to the décor of the homes of the elites. In a peasant's wooden house in the nineteenth century, where the single main room had many functions, the icons were likely to be prominent in the place of honour (the *krasnyi ugolok*). In palaces and mansions of the eighteenth and nineteenth centuries, whose many rooms could be differentiated by function, icons tended to recede to the private quarters.

Apart from the contrast in the relative prominence of icons, domestic graphospheres differed in the inscriptional content of the pictures which replaced or supplemented them. Icons may have been a constant, but they were by no means always dominant even in the pre-imperial age. With respect to the visibility of writing on non-devotional pictures in domestic spaces, the emerging social differentiation was paradoxical: the place of inscription remained fairly constant in the cheaper and lower-status types of picture for popular distribution, yet became quite sharply diminished in the post-medieval elite genres. Here we should distinguish between prints and paintings. West European engravings (*friazhskie listy*) were modish elements of interior decoration in the palaces of the Muscovite elite at least by the 1680s, as were portraits (*parsuna, persony*) and maps. Some were hung as individually framed compositions, but in places large numbers of *friazhskie listy* were glued in place like wallpaper.[134] We know very little about the contents of these early *friazhskie listy*, but one might assume that, like Russian high-status engravings of the eighteenth century, they *could be* quite verbose but were not necessarily so. In Russian 'popular' prints (a genre often termed *lubok*), many of which were also derived from West European compositions, a strong verbal component was more or less standard. Some limited their texts to labels and captions, but others added verses, explanations, biblical quotations and paraphrases, literary fragments, even extensive narratives.[135] Writing was at least as prominent as in the iconographic tradition, often more so. Indeed, one could argue that the texts in popular prints were stronger graphospheric presences since they were not such formulaic elements of formulaic images. The early chronology of the distribution of non-devotional *lubok* prints is hard to establish, but there is abundant evidence – literary, archival, artistic, ethnographic – of their ubiquity by the late eighteenth or early nineteenth century (Fig. 5.6).[136]

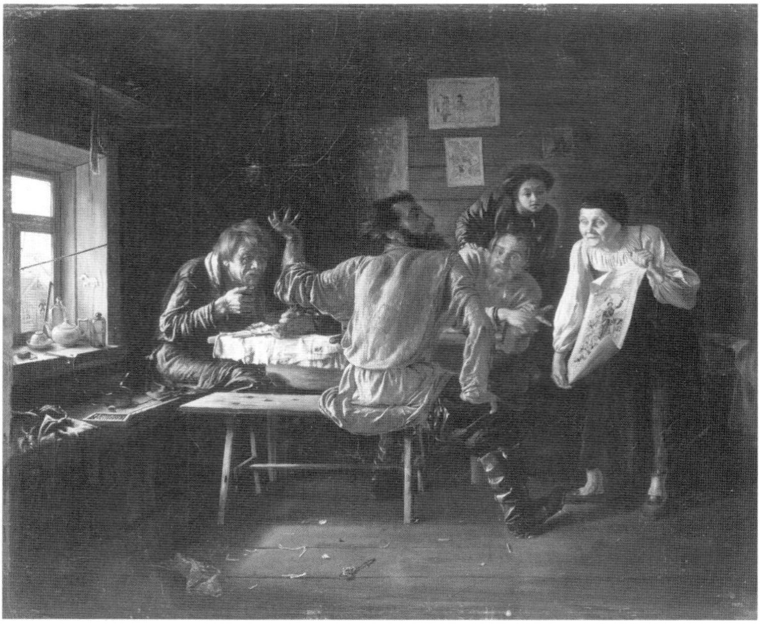

Fig. 5.6: Popular prints in a peasant hut: Pavel Chistiakov, *Three Peasants*, 1858.

The contrast is even stronger in paintings than in prints. To adorn one's residence with original non-devotional paintings has always been a sign of affluence. In icons the representation of words was an essential component of the image. In the non-devotional painting that became fashionable from the eighteenth century, inscription (aside from an artist's signature) was almost wholly absent. Because of the ubiquity of inscription on devotional painting, its absence on 'art' painting or 'academic' painting was in itself a distinguishing cultural marker. Graphospheric absences can be as eloquent as presences. As the walls of the wealthy filled with mute images, the walls of comparatively modest dwellings continued to be places of verbal display, whether painted or printed, devotional or non-devotional: through printed or painted icons, through popular non-devotional prints, even in some places (particularly in Old Believer communities in the late eighteenth and early nineteenth centuries) through painted copies of popular prints.[137] There is no reason to suppose that such word-rich pictures were displayed only in the houses of the literate. Words were part of a picture, whether or not one could read them. There is no necessary symmetry between changing fashions in the display of words and changing patterns in the acquisition of literacy skills.

From paintings and prints on walls, we turn to the miscellaneous other types of domestically displayed objects: the gifts, souvenirs, mementoes, decorations, luxury acquisitions and bric-a-brac for which there is no generic name. They are the objects – whether expensive or cheap, unique or generic – whose presence people choose to make meaningful for themselves: goblets and vases, glasses and teacups, silver spoons and porcelain figurines, clocks and automata, cushion covers and silk purses, medallions, snuff boxes, tea caddies, samovars, biscuit moulds. A loose, non-technical but felicitous phrase for such goods is 'treasured possessions'.[138]

In 1720 a Muscovite craftsman, Marko Petrovich Popov, engraved a folding gilt reliquary. On the front he fashioned representations of St Peter and St Paul. On the reverse – the Annunciation, a host of saints and the inscription, which stated that the work was commissioned by a resident of Ustiug, Afanasii Mikhailovich Ponomarev, 'for his house'.[139] The reliquary is remarkable partly for its quality, partly because it gives us the names of a Moscow metal-engraver and of a provincial patron, but mainly (in the present context) because it reminds us of how rare it is to find an inscription which specifies that an object is intended for the home. Information about patrons, donors, makers and recipients is relatively common, but in the early part of our period the domestic destination of objects is almost never made explicit.

Until the end of the seventeenth century there was little distinction between the writing on devotional and non-devotional domestic objects. As we have seen, such items as goblets, scoops and beakers were inscribed in somewhat similar ways to their liturgical equivalents, with thick bands of *viaz'* lettering in the ornamental ecclesiastical manner. Even imported, non-inscribed objects were sometimes 'nativised' through the addition of inscriptional ornamentation in the Muscovite mode.[140] Here also, however, across the eighteenth century the complexion of the elite domestic graphosphere changed radically. As the quantity and diversity of acquired decorative objects increased, so the prominence of inscription sharply decreased, as did its aesthetic association with devotional precedent. In the sixteenth and seventeenth centuries not only was inscription obligatory on devotional images, but heavily inscriptional ornament was very common even on objects which lacked representational imagery. In the eighteenth and nineteenth centuries decorative inscription was optional. In very few types of object can it be reckoned the norm. Where it occurred, the letter-forms generally avoided the *viaz'* style reminiscent of medieval manuscripts and liturgical books, and adopted either more modern cursive forms or the appearance of the Petrine 'civil' type.

The change was not instantaneous or total. One could posit a kind of intermediate phase in the late seventeenth and early eighteenth centuries, characterised by the fashion for a new (to Russia) type of edificatory combination of word and image: the emblem.

Depending on how broadly it is defined, the culture of emblems can be said to have flourished in Western Europe, to varying degrees, almost from the Renaissance to the nineteenth century. In domestic inscription one of the functions of emblem culture – by no means ubiquitous or consistent, but frequent enough to be noted by scholars of different media and disciplines and areas – was edification, moral instruction. In this tradition, moral reminders might be displayed on any interior surface, or on a broad range of objects with secondary writing.[141] The morally instructive function of domestic inscription has also been stressed with regard to the role of textual samplers – needlework compositions – in girls' education.[142]

In Russia the fashion for emblems was particularly pronounced in the early eighteenth century, encouraged by Peter I. A book of emblems, *Symbola et emblemata*, printed in Amsterdam in 1705, was among the publications that Peter commissioned from Holland, with engravings of 840 pictorial devices, their descriptions in Dutch, and the relevant mottoes in Russian, Latin, French, Italian, Spanish, Dutch, German and English.[143] The multiple inscriptions on the triumphal arches and other structures erected for festive ceremonial spectacle were heavily emblematic. Where domestic inscription was prominent in the first half of the eighteenth century, it, too, was often linked to motifs from emblem books. The fashion spanned technologies of depiction: the dozens of captioned pictures adorning the painted tiles of a 'Dutch' stove;[144] captioned roundels copying the title page of *Symbola et emblemata* on an engraved glass goblet;[145] inscribed roundels on a pewter tray and accompanying mug;[146] a *chinoiserie* lacquer box for writing implements, with an 'oriental' scene on the lid and with visual and verbal quotations from *Symbola et emblemata* across the front;[147] even the painted ceiling of a palatial hall.[148] However, pervasive though emblems were for a while, the fashion faded. Emblems did not disappear completely, but they lost, and never regained, the multimedia prominence that they enjoyed in the first three or four decades of the eighteenth century.

After the age of emblems, the emphasis in domestic inscription shifted from the edificatory to the 'occasional', in various senses: commissioned for use on particular occasions, issued in commemoration of specific events in public life, acquired or donated to mark a meaningful moment in private life and so on. Occasional pieces can be very grand indeed, such as the dinner services made for the annual gatherings of members of the Orders of St George, St Andrew, St Vladimir and St Aleksandr Nevskii.[149] More common, however, are the comparatively modest, 'one-off' mementoes, the inscriptional reminders of the gift, the wedding or the name-day, the token of appreciation on retirement from service. Such forms of secondary writing span media and social groups: from the gift of a gold dish from Ivan IV to his wife in 1561,[150] or the presentation *kovshi* of the late seventeenth century and later, or the personalised snuff boxes advertised by Nevskaia porcelain factory in the 1750s, or the wallet embroidered with the newlyweds' entwined initials, a congratulatory inscription and the date of the wedding (30 March 1796),[151] through to the fictitious (in the 1840s) name-day gift of a teacup whose gilt inscription ('as a token of affection') was much admired by the guests of its recipient, the kindly old bachelor Dmitrii Ivanovich, who displayed it on a cupboard in his reception room (until it was accidentally broken).[152] As the market for small display objects expanded over the eighteenth century, so also did the production of purpose-made souvenirs, and what might now be called 'collectibles', more generalised commemorations of people or occasions rather than individually personalised gifts: the issues and re-issues of the series of medals commemorating the Northern War and other Petrine achievements, as well as the restruck coins and other medals ('novodels'); a gold and tortoiseshell snuff box depicting the Peter and Paul fortress and ships on the Neva and inscribed 'S.PETERSBURG' (in Latin letters), probably dated c. 1719;[153] a painted and enamelled *bonbonnière*, now in the Victoria and Albert Museum, depicting Falconet's statue of Peter I and inscribed (in Cyrillic) '6 August 1782', the date of the monument's official unveiling;[154] the monogrammed bust of the current tsar in the halls of the loyal aristocrat.[155]

If we stretch somewhat the definition of 'occasional', then a fair proportion of secondary domestic inscription accompanies the occasions of eating and drinking. In the early eighteenth century Russian glass goblets might be expensively engraved with drinking formulae. From mid century guests at a grand house might dine off their host's monogrammed plates and drink from monogrammed cups. Alternatively, one could carry the words out of the house on portable objects, such as a copper travelling bottle with a drinking inscription and the date 1736.[156] Sometimes words themselves were for eating: gingerbread moulds with textual inscriptions date from at least the second quarter of the nineteenth century, possibly the late eighteenth century.[157] Perhaps surprisingly, however, the practice of inscribing samovars with medals and other signs of distinction seems to have been a phenomenon of the late nineteenth and earlier twentieth centuries. Lettering on earlier samovars was generally limited to very discreet makers' marks on or under the base.[158]

The visual properties of inscription varied widely, from the ostentatiously elegant to the casually informal. In the absence of *viaz'*, all are both symptoms and signals of the desacralisation of the domestic graphosphere. Nowhere is this more marked than in a curious style that can be characterised, somewhat oxymoronically, as 'ostentatiously informal'. Quite commonly, in disparate genres and objects, one finds letter-forms that, if they had been encountered in isolated cases, might be dismissed as semi-literate, semi-educated. But their occurrence is too regular to be coincidental. Moreover, the assumption of ignorance or incompetence will not stand scrutiny, since the 'ostentatiously informal' lettering is often juxtaposed, on a single object, with evidence of a perfectly professional level of competence. Some diverse examples: on the captions on the tiles on 'Dutch' stoves, mis-shapenness and mis-spelling are almost obligatory, far beyond random errors of copying; on an engraved glass goblet the owner's monogram is a model of elegance, yet the drinking inscription looks casually irregular, with crooked lines and uneven letter forms; similarly an embroidered silk purse displays the decorously intertwined monograms of the newlyweds to whom it is presented, yet the congratulatory inscription – also embroidered – looks almost as if it has been roughly scrawled in ink, disrupting the otherwise careful composition; even the cursive on a presentational snuff box is a long way short of what one would call 'copperplate' hand.[159] And so on. These are luxury objects, treasured possessions. Such studied informality in the domestic graphosphere, as if a kind of extreme anti-*viaz'*, is unlikely to be semantically neutral.

These remarks on the nature and development of Russian domestic graphospheres are preliminary, tentative, exploratory. Nevertheless, some relevant features and factors emerge. The configuration of domestic graphospheres varied according to material means, social position, cultural values, taste and fashion, trends in social interaction and commemoration. An eventually decisive shift in direction picked up momentum from the late seventeenth century and into the eighteenth century. Among the signs and catalysts of change were: the intensification of the spread and influence of engravings, both 'popular' and imported; the new fashion for a non-devotional language of edificatory inscribed imagery in the form of emblems; the desacralisation of script in expanding parts of the domestic graphosphere; an elevation (from the second quarter of the eighteenth century) in the status of the document – both written and printed – in the representation of interiors; and the rise of cultures of collecting.

* * *

The present chapter is headed 'places and times'. For the most part, the two have been considered together. In its respective places, the graphosphere changes over time. Each type of graphosphere has been surveyed diachronically. However, it would be remiss to end without mentioning the importance, for the graphosphere, of non-linear time: time as moments, or time as repeated cycles. Many aspects of the graphospheric dynamic can be reckoned 'occasional' in one or both of two ways. On the one hand, a graphospheric phenomenon may be by nature and purpose temporary, formed or created for an occasion and then dismantled or dissolved. On the other hand, even if the writing itself remains permanently or quasi-permanently *in situ*, it may be *experienced* on particular occasions, in particular phases of life or of the year or of the day. Graphospheres are not constants, which merely exist or merely grow. They, or parts of them, can appear and disappear and reappear, or expand and contract. We can construct them around ourselves, or walk in and out of them or through them as we choose. Sometimes we merely, if vividly, imagine them.

Ritual and ceremony are particularly propitious occasions for temporary thickening of the graphosphere: the medals and badges of the military parade; the inscribed images held aloft at the Easter procession around the church; the inscribed plates for the annual dinner of members of the Orders. Some of the most densely inscribed spaces are most likely to be experienced on ritual occasions: the interior of the church during the services; in late Muscovy the Golden Hall of the Kremlin during formal diplomatic receptions; the visit to the cemetery in an act of remembrance. In more mundane mode, the experience of graphospherically denser or thinner zones fluctuates with the rhythms of ordinary life: a stroll in the park adorned with inscribed statues; or just a trip to the shops.

In its multiple 'occasionalities' the graphosphere eludes static depiction. One cannot capture the dynamic qualities of the graphosphere by describing only the production and locations of the objects from which it is constituted. It forms and dissolves, re-forms and mutates, as a kind of ecosystem, of which we ourselves are part, and to aspects of which we turn in the following chapter.

CHAPTER 6

Aspects of the Ecology of the Graphosphere

This chapter explores aspects of the graphospheric 'ecology', mainly with regard to relations between the primary technologies of handwriting and print. The focus is on considering some of the ways in which handwriting and print coexisted with, interacted with, competed with, complemented or supplemented each other. Their respective zones of usage mutated, separated, overlapped, merged. The 'ecological' metaphor here refers to these patterns of interrelationships both in themselves and in changing contexts and environments.[1] The relations of script and print have been quite widely studied (with or without the ecological metaphor) with regard to early modern Western Europe and beyond,[2] but sporadically with regard to Russia. When viewed separately, each of the two technologies has its own zones of usage, with its own mutating shape and boundaries. The first section of the present chapter is about these respective zones of usage: their areas of specificity and/or overlap, their adaptations to each other. The second section explores movements across the technological boundaries: transfers from manuscript to print, or – more particularly, because less predictably – in the reverse direction, from print to manuscript and beyond. The third section is about combinations of the two, about contexts in which print and manuscript shared the same spaces: that is, about forms of technological hybrid.

Zones and Boundaries

The shifting boundaries of print and manuscript will here be surveyed in five contexts, with respect to five kinds of text, or five cultural zones: the ecclesiastical and devotional, the administrative, the educational and scholarly, the literary, and the personal.[3] Any such division into cultural zones is problematic if one seeks consistency and stability. In the first place the categories are not tightly defined. They overlap, they bleed into each other. Secondly, they are not comprehensive. Between them, even when broadly defined, they do not cover all of primary writing. Some kinds of materials do not easily fit the scheme – newspapers, for example, or trade catalogues and other commercial ephemera, or travel writing. Thirdly, the categories are unstable in themselves and in relation to one another. As cultural values and assumptions change, so an identical text might be allocated to different cultural zones at different times. For example, manuscripts of a medieval world chronicle, or of an account of the fall of Jerusalem to the Romans, or even an account of the conquests of Alexander the Great, could be reckoned explications of sacred history, of the interventions of God in the world, and hence as broadly religious if not narrowly devotional. The same texts, in post-medieval printed editions, might instead be associated with historical scholarship, or antiquarian curiosity, or literary narrative. A similar category change might be envisaged with regard to, say, grammars and primers. A seventeenth-century or eighteenth-century primer for reading Church Slavonic could arguably be classed as ecclesiastical, while later grammars might be reckoned either as pedagogical tools or as non-devotional scholarship.[4] The ecology of the technologies of primary writing did not function within a fixed system of cultural categories, but has to be superimposed onto a cultural ecology that was itself changing in quite fundamental ways.

Until the end of the seventeenth century Russian printing was almost entirely ecclesiastical and devotional.[5] If our definition of 'ecclesiastical and devotional' is fairly broad, then the only exceptions are perhaps two books and a small number of non-books: a translated manual of infantry tactics, published in 1647, the code of laws promulgated in 1649, a customs statute of 1654 in large broadside format; and land grants, which began to be printed from 1668. Imported print was not so restricted. For example, in the seventeenth century the government received regular deliveries of West European newspapers, while the foreign doctors at the Apothecary Chancery possessed not only their Latin medical textbooks, but also miscellaneous non-medical works including the Nuremburg Chronicle, Tycho Brahe on astronomy, and the orations of Cicero.[6] However, none of these was for circulation or on open library shelves. The greater diversity within a small number of specialist institutions was not such as to undermine the general picture.

To say that print culture of the period was overwhelmingly ecclesiastical and devotional is not the same as saying that the ecclesiastical and devotional culture of the period was overwhelmingly printed. It was not. Print seeped slowly even into what might be regarded as its own core territory. We can track its progression partly through surviving inventories of monastic and other holdings. The earliest mention of a printed book in a Russian monastic inventory dates from 1582: a Gospel, in the Solovetskii monastery.[7] On the basis of surviving inventories one scholar has calculated that, in the first half of the seventeenth century, around 17 per cent of all the books described were printed, while for the second half of the seventeenth century the proportion had increased to just over 42 per cent.[8] However, the global figures are in some respects misleading. There is significant variation between types of institution. For example, by the end of the seventeenth century the proportion of printed books in some of the smaller monasteries appears to be higher than in some of the larger monasteries.[9] And it is yet higher in churches. According to property censuses of the town of Ustiug for the period 1676–83, of the approximately seven hundred books in the local churches, around 85 per cent were printed.[10] The reason for the apparent inconsistency is that most of the printed books were not just religious but liturgical. Everybody needed liturgical books. The differences in the proportion of printed books reflects not the absolute quantity of such books, but the extent to which a given institution also possessed non-liturgical books. The smaller monasteries had less extensive and diverse collections; hence a greater proportion of their holdings consisted of liturgical books, which therefore account for the greater proportion of printed books. Parish churches needed almost nothing but liturgical books, so the proportion was limited only by accessibility. These were the books that were in most regular ritual use. Thus, from an almost negligible presence towards the end of the sixteenth century, by the late seventeenth century the most prominent books in liturgical use in monastic and other churches were printed.

This is not a huge claim for the spread of ecclesiastical and devotional printing in Muscovy some two hundred years after the first Russian engagements with the technology, or more than a hundred years after the start of Muscovite printing itself. The broader explanations and implications are treated elsewhere. However, there was a particular additional stimulus for the strengthening of the position of print in the distribution of liturgical books in the second half of the seventeenth century. It happened to be compulsory. In the 1650s Patriarch Nikon had used the Moscow Print Yard specifically for the purpose of issuing 'corrected' liturgical books. The printed versions were deemed definitive. Orthodox worship, as defined by the patriarchate and endorsed by the council, was embodied in the Nikonian printed texts. Although one may assume a degree of voluntary compliance among those who accepted the reforms, the authorities from time to time adopted more proactive measures. Thus, for example, in December 1677 Patriarch Ioakim (1674–90) instructed the bishop of Novgorod to confiscate old parchment manuscripts from monasteries and churches, and to replace them with the latest Moscow-printed editions.[11] In December 1697 Patriarch Adrian (1690–1700) decreed that all churches should be equipped with the correct printed liturgical books.[12]

However, for the same reason, just as print seemed to be coming close to fully occupying the zone which had been marked as its initial and continuing priority, so a new niche was created for manuscript among those who did *not* accept the Nikonian reforms. Old Believer devotional culture was manuscript-based. This was mainly out of necessity rather than principle. When Old Believers had the opportunity to gain access to printing presses, they were not slow to take advantage.[13] However, the culture of manuscripts remained robust among Old Believer communities until the twentieth century.[14]

In the early centuries the zone of print was marked out *within* the zone of handwriting. Print was not called upon to do anything different, anything new. It was, in a sense, a more controllable form of handwriting. Its tasks were traditional. It was a device to facilitate standardisation and dissemination, but not innovation. Its place *within* the traditional cultural zone of handwriting was maintained by its visual properties. The typefaces of early Muscovite printed books followed the forms of manuscript *poluustav*, just as their woodcut ornamentation – the headpieces and initials – generally picked up on manuscript equivalents. Within the borders of their shared zone, manuscript and print were presented so as to seem virtually interchangeable.

The second context is administration. In a game of 'fantasy statistics' it might be curious to try to imagine the total production of all forms of visible writing from the mid fifteenth century to the mid nineteenth century. On the basis of the very roughest of impressions, I would hazard two guesses: first, that by most criteria, at least until the first quarter of the nineteenth century, handwritten words remained in the majority throughout; and, secondly, that this is in large measure due to the dominance of handwriting in administration. Administrative writing was overwhelmingly a manuscript zone, though again with a specific and expanding niche for printing. Administration was by far the biggest growth area of writing, and the most visible and best-documented context for change was the expansion of administrative apparatus of the state and the concomitant proliferation of bureaucratic procedures. The general process was inexorable, irrespective of the particular structures. Whether through the many chanceries (*prikazy*) of the sixteenth and seventeenth centuries, or the

Petrine 'colleges', or the nineteenth-century ministries, or the local offshoots and subsections and equivalents that sprouted across the expanses of the empire, the tendency to produce and require more and more paperwork was consistent.[15] And that is merely at the level of central and local government. To the weight of official bureaucratic verbiage one would have to add – in this fantasy game – the similarly expanding mass of formal and informal documents generated in the administration of non-governmental (though not necessarily non-state) institutions: regulations and accounts and receipts and contracts and memoranda and announcements and instructions and certificates and inventories generated in almost any organisation and institution where writing came to be regarded as the essential medium of internal and external transactions and records, whether in education or in manufacture or in trade, on private estates – or, indeed, in institutions of the church.

Within the administrative sphere, printing came to occupy some limited subzones. One of them relates to the emergence of technological hybrids: blank forms. I will consider blank forms later in the present chapter, in the section on hybrids. Here I should mention the other administrative genre, or set of genres, that was particularly conducive to print: texts that conveyed what one might loosely call monologues of power – decrees and instructions, statutes and codes and all manner of regulation. The use of print in administration started with and was initially dominated by legislation. In most cases the original, definitive, signed and sealed versions were prepared in manuscript. Print was for dissemination, where it served as a guarantor of standardisation and as a technological defence against distortion or forgery.[16]

No Muscovite printed legislative texts are known for almost a hundred years after the introduction of Muscovite printing. In the mid seventeenth century there was a notable – and notably brief – spate of printed rule-making, which consisted of just three texts. Two of them were rather ambitious, summative books, the third was a single decree. The books were a compilation of state laws (the *Ulozhenie*), printed in 1649, and the compilation of ecclesiastical law (the nomocanon, or *Kormchaia*), prepared for publication in the same year but not finally issued until 1653.[17] The single document was a decree on customs duties, printed in 1654. The customs decree (*Ustavnaia gramota; Tamozhennaia ustavnaia gramota*), though a much shorter text, was grandly formatted. It was printed on two large sheets, but on one side only, so that the text could run continuously when the sheets were glued together, forming a long poster or broadside, or scroll.[18]

This initiative in printed legislation began in 1649 and ended in 1654. It was a false start. It did not signal the start of a continuous tradition of the use of print for promulgating and disseminating official pronouncements. The practice was picked up again early in the eighteenth century: with the occasional broadsides giving accounts of Peter's military operations, starting with the *Iurnal* on the siege of Nöteburg issued on 27 December 1702; or with the official news-sheets (*Vedomosti*), which began to appear regularly from January 1703.[19] The continuous printing of legislative texts dates from March 1714, when Peter announced that print was the compulsory medium for all decrees of general relevance.[20] From then onwards, legislative texts were normally in the zone of print, at least at the point of issue in St Petersburg or Moscow. Dissemination was not always perfectly efficient, so local handwritten copies remain common through the eighteenth century. At the turn of the nineteenth century, as provincial printing presses became established, local authorities, too, began regularly issuing their announcements and instructions in print.

The third zone is that of education and learning. Primers for the teaching of basic literacy were among the regular products of East Slav printing at least from the second half of the sixteenth century. Primers were printed by Ivan Fedorov in Lviv (1574) and in Ostroh (1578). Over the next fifty years primers were printed in Vilnius (several editions, starting with that of Lavrentii Zyzanii in 1596), Ostroh, Vievis, Kiev, Kutein and even Venice.[21] Moscow picked up the habit much later. The earliest recorded Moscow-printed primers date from 1634. One, printed by Vasilii Burtsov, is known from surviving copies, while the existence of the other is inferred only from references in the Print Chancery archives.[22] Indeed, archival references are the principal source for Muscovite primers and alphabet books for the rest of the seventeenth century. They note twenty-eight separate printings between 1634 and 1695. Very few copies survive. Mostly they are thin, flimsy volumes intended for heavy use, hence the low survival rate and the lack of extant examples. The archival records plausibly suggest that, at least from the mid seventeenth century, the printing of primers and alphabet books became routine business for the Moscow Print Yard: initially in editions of a few hundred, then of a few thousands, growing by the mid eighteenth century to annual printings of tens of thousands of copies.[23]

In non-devotional higher learning the ecology of media was more complicated. Traditional Muscovite Church Slavonic written cultures included little that would nowadays count as scholarship beyond the collation and explication of devotional texts. From the second half of the seventeenth century and the first half of the eighteenth century, print culture expanded significantly into new kinds of learning, supported by new kinds of institutions – schools, academies, eventually a university. Much of this learning was imported, the media of its import were human (i.e. the import of teachers) or printed. The association of the new learning both with print and with foreignness carried over into the Russian institutions established in the late seventeenth century and through the middle decades of the eighteenth century. In the mid eighteenth century the clearest sign of the association of print with the zone of learning is in the fact that almost all the permitted presses were operated through institutions of learning: the Academy of Sciences, the Infantry Cadet Corps, the Naval Cadet Corps, the Artillery and Engineering Cadet Corps, Moscow University, the Military College. Indeed, alongside the Senate press representing government administration, and the Synod press representing the ecclesiastical and devotional sphere, the scholastic presses constituted one of the three key components of the institutional foundations of Russian printing in the mid eighteenth century.

The most salient feature of learned printed books in Russia, at least until the latter decades of the eighteenth century, is that they were to a considerable extent foreign, either in language or in origin. In the first phase of such print culture, all the books were imported. The few major non-monastic institutional libraries of the late seventeenth century are notable for the dominance of foreign-language books. In the next phase, especially from the second quarter of the eighteenth century, foreign-language books were printed in Russia. In the third phase, starting roughly in parallel with this but continuing longer, foreign learning began to be domesticated through the printing of Russian translations.[24] In the final phase learned works were written and published in Russian. Despite some sporadic exceptions, the continuous history of Russian as a language of scholarly composition and printing begins in the second half of the eighteenth century.

An example of this sequence of phases is provided by medical books. In the seventeenth century the doctors of the Apothecary Chancery worked with imported Latin textbooks. The transition to native print can be traced over the course of the eighteenth century. In Peter I's military hospital school, run from 1707 by Nicholas Bidloo from Leiden, the books were likewise imported (the quality of the library was noted by a Danish visitor in 1710), the instructors were foreign, the pupils were Russian, the mode of instruction was dictation, the language of instruction was Latin. By the middle of the century medical textbooks had begun to be printed in Russia but in Latin, such as the *Syllabus seu index omnium partium corporis humanae figuris illustratus: in usum studiosorum qui in nosocomiis Petropolitanis aluntur*, published by the Academy of Sciences in 1744 and consisting substantially of anatomical illustrations. Next came translations. In 1757 the Academy printed a Russian version of Lorenz Heister's *Compendium anatomicum*.[25] No original Russian anatomical textbook was printed until 1801.[26]

One quasi-exception serves to underscore the rule. On 28 February 1718 Peter I issued a broadside announcement concerning the healing qualities of the waters near Olonets in Karelia. The following year he issued another notice, with 'rules for doctors' for the use of the waters, which, it seems, had been proved to help treat scurvy, bile, hypochondria (i.e. diseases of the stomach), vomiting, kidney stones, diarrhoea, haemorrhages, epilepsy, tapeworms and much more besides. The notice was issued in St Petersburg on 20 March, in two formats, broadside and small folding leaflet, and in Moscow on 6 April (in the smaller format).[27] The Olonets waters at Martsialnye Vody enjoyed a brief period of popularity between 1719 and 1724, after which they were abandoned until a spa resort was opened in 1964. The decrees of 1718 and 1719 have been claimed as the first Russian printed medical texts,[28] but the claim is strained. These were brief decrees, administrative documents, 'non-books' for the occasion, not professional expositions.

The association with print relates specifically to what can loosely be called the 'new' learning, such as technology or the natural sciences as practised in Western Europe: the learning whose establishment in Russia was linked to printing more or less from the start. However, not all activities that might be broadly defined as learned, and non-devotional, were likewise automatically assimilated to the zone of print. As we shall see with regard to 'literature', some types of non-devotional writing, once established locally in manuscript and in the Russian language (or in Church Slavonic) were more resilient to technological change. A particularly stark example is the history of Russia itself. Manuscript chronicles continued to be copied, compiled and composed through the sixteenth and seventeenth centuries, but printed narratives of Muscovite history, and printed editions of chronicle sources, began to appear regularly only from the 1760s. A brief introduction to history, by Ilia Kopievskii, was printed in 1699 at Jan Tessing's press in Amsterdam. A composite chronicle text may have been prepared at the Moscow Print Yard in 1703, but was not published.[29] A precursor was the history of south-western Rus by Innokentii Gizel, archimandrite of the Caves monastery in Kiev, first published at the Caves press in 1674. Gizel's *Sinopsis*, dedicated to

Tsar Aleksei Mikhailovich, was copied in Muscovite historiographical manuscripts in the late seventeenth century, and was re-issued in print several times in Kiev, Moscow and St Petersburg in the late seventeenth and early eighteenth centuries, even making the transition to the civil typeface;[30] but it stood alone.[31] Periodicals occasionally included articles on historical themes.[32] Mikhail Lomonosov's concise chronology was printed in 1760, and his more extensive account of early Rus appeared posthumously in 1766. Vasilii Tatishchev worked on his *Russian History from the Earliest Times* (*Istoriia rossiiskaia s samykh drevneishikh vremen*) for at least twenty years before his death in 1750, but the first volume did not appear in print until 1768.[33] The first printed editions of Russian historiographical source texts – those of the so-called Radziwill Codex of the *Primary Chronicle* and the first part of the so-called *Nikon Chronicle* – had been published in the previous year. One might speculate that the transition from manuscript to print may, at least in part, have been linked to or dependent on a shift in cultural perception, a shift in category whereby chronicle narratives were repackaged as subordinate to historical scholarship.

The fourth zone is literature. If literature is defined in relation to uses of verbal artistry, then there is much that is literary in devotional texts. For present purposes the boundaries of the literary are narrower, defined in relation to functions of pleasure and leisure (with or without edification). Literature, in the sense of *belles lettres,* constituted a negligible proportion of printed books in Russia, in any language, until its fairly rapid growth in the second half of the eighteenth century.[34] To a limited extent it had existed as a zone of manuscript culture before it came to be associated with print. Similarly, long after the printing of literature became commonplace, the handwritten literary text could still have particular status, function and resonance.

Over the seventeenth century, Muscovite writing was beginning to fill out with forms and styles and genres that would be plausibly reckoned literary by fairly diverse criteria: historical and chivalric romances, satirical and parodic tales, drama, fables.[35] Here, as a brief example, we will consider the graphospheric ecology not of a genre but of a form: verse.

Before the seventeenth century early Rus and Muscovite written culture included much that was in a broad sense poetic, but almost nothing that could be formally classified as verse. The poetic lay in the qualities of language: in imagery and metaphor and simile, in the rhythms of rhetoric, in assonantal cadences that approximated to rhyme, whether in liturgical chants or in rhetorical homilies. In a highly inflected language such as Church Slavonic, rhetorically parallel syntactic structures will often end in a similar set of sounds. However, rhythm and assonance do not yet amount to a formal system of versification. Some of the biblical and Byzantine originals of and models for medieval Rus writing had been written in verse. Byzantine writers knew about classical metres, and wrote their own syllabic verse. The Slav translations were in more or less rhetorically marked prose. In Muscovite written culture the rise of verse was a phenomenon of the seventeenth century.

A glance through an anthology of seventeenth-century Russian verse (*virshi* – a word borrowed from Polish) shows a range of forms, themes and styles that is surprising if one is accustomed to the notion of Russian literature as a post-Petrine phenomenon.[36] The building block of seventeenth-century Muscovite verse was the rhyming couplet. In the early part of the century the length of the lines tended to be variable, but by mid century syllabic verse, in which each line of a given poem has the same number of syllables, had become the standard form. This is in contrast to the syllabo-accentual verse of later, classic Russian poetry, constructed from metrical feet. Some seventeenth-century poems were based on lines as short as eight syllables, some as long as sixteen syllables, but the preferred line lengths were eleven or thirteen syllables. These were the norms, the core habits of composition, although within and around the rhyming, isosyllabic framework some variation was possible, such as truncated lines, or non-rhyming supplementary lines.[37] The themes could be devotional, panegyric, satirical, epistolographic, allegorical, gnomic, polemical, edificatory, pedagogical, theological, epigraphical, theatrical.[38] The scale of composition ranged from a single couplet to several thousands. Many of the authors worked in the chancery system, to the extent that it has become common to speak of a 'chancery school' of seventeenth-century Muscovite poetry.[39] Indeed, a good number of them worked in or around the Moscow Print Yard. Yet most of this output has become widely accessible only from the second half of the twentieth century, because in its day almost none of it was printed. With a few exceptions, verse was in the zone of manuscript culture.

The printing of East Slav *virshi* began earlier in Ruthenia (as, probably, did the writing of *virshi*, though this is harder to track), in the late sixteenth century. Two genres predominated: verse prefaces and/or colophons; and so-called heraldic verses – panegyric explications of the heraldic devices of the printers' patrons. In Ruthenia such verses became quite common from the age of Ivan Fedorov onwards. In Muscovy they were rare. Sixty lines of heraldic verse by Andrei Rymsha, arranged in six ten-line stanzas of rhyming couplets, appeared on the verso of the title page of Fedorov's

Ostroh Bible of 1581, on the theme of the device of Fedorov's patron, Prince Konstantin Ostrozhskii, which was printed on the same page. In the late sixteenth century heraldic verses, many of them also by Rymsha, figured in half a dozen books printed in Vilnius and a couple printed in Lviv.[40] By the end of the first third of the seventeenth century, besides Vilnius and Lviv,[41] heraldic and other prefatory verses had been printed in books issued in Derman, Uhortsy and Kiev.[42]

In Moscow the printing of prefatory or heraldic verses was, at best, episodic. There were verse prefaces to Burtsov's primer of 1637, and the *Kirillova kniga* of 1644, but far more verse prefaces were written than made the transition to print.[43] Just two sets of heraldic verses were printed, and both can count as exceptions: in 1659 in a book printed not at the Moscow Print Yard but at the press of Patriarch Nikon at his Iverskii monastery;[44] and in a cluster of prefatory verses in the 1663 Bible.[45] A brief flurry of verse characterised another set of books printed at the Upper Printing House set up by Simeon Polotskii. Five of the books issued by the Upper Printing House between 1679 and 1683 had verse prefaces and/or colophons.[46]

Two further late-seventeenth-century exceptions should be mentioned. The first was a single-leaf 'non-book': an engraving of the Crucifixion with allegorical subsidiary scenes, captioned with verses by Simeon Polotskii's pupil, amanuensis and neighbour in the Zaikonospasskii monastery – and editor at the Moscow Print Yard – Silvestr Medvedev (1641–91). The engraving was produced in 1689 in the Solovetskii monastery. Remarkably, we have a complete sequence of realisations of the verses across media: from Medvedev's manuscript, through the engraving, to a painted icon derived from it.[47] The second exception, better known, also involves engravings. In Karion Istomin's block-printed primer of 1694,[48] each page is devoted to one letter of the alphabet and consists mainly of illustrations showing a range of letter-forms and of objects whose names begin with the relevant letter. At the foot of each page are verses commenting on the illustrations.[49] This link of verse with illustration connects Istomin's primer and Medvedev's engraving both to the earlier tradition of printed heraldic verses and to an emerging fashion for printed verse captions at the start of the eighteenth century. Thus, for example, in 1702 even an infantry manual was prefaced with an emblematic illustration (of the double-headed eagle hovering above a pile of weaponry), elucidated in ten lines of verse.[50] Fedor Polikarpov's trilingual Slavonic-Greek-Latin grammar of 1701 included twelve sets of verses, eleven of which were directly linked to illustrations. Polikarpov adapted themes from previous primer illustrations and added verses where previously there had been none.[51] In Polikarpov's trilingual lexicon of 1704, the verso of the title page also has the combination of image and verse: a picture of a vase of flowers, with verses about flowers of language.[52]

Free-standing verse was another matter. In Ostroh, in 1581, Ivan Fedorov produced a broadside verse calendar by Andrei Rymsha. No other such printed verse non-book is recorded, but, in view of what is known about non-book survival rates, it would be rash to conclude that no others existed. The first and only Muscovite pre-Petrine printed book entirely in verse was Simeon Polotskii's metrical version of the Psalter, issued in 1680 at the Upper Printing House. Polotskii was aware that the book was innovative for Moscow but not for much of Europe. His own immediate prototypes were Polish, but metrical psalms had long been staples of West European printing. For example, the versions by Thomas Sternhold and John Hopkins were routinely appended to editions of the Geneva version of the English Bible in the late sixteenth and early seventeenth centuries. Simeon Polotskii's metrical psalms did not generate a tradition in Muscovite publishing. They were not reprinted. Their productive afterlife was in manuscript copies, just as the overwhelming mass of Polotskii's voluminous poetic output remained in manuscript.

Over the first quarter of the eighteenth century the culture of verse diversified further, but the only addition to the genres that passed through the technological filter into print in notable (though still not substantial) numbers was panegyric addressed to people rather than to their heraldic devices.[53] Moreover, it became gradually more common for laudatory verses to be printed separately, as free-standing broadsides or pamphlets, rather than as prefaces or appendages to books. Initially there was a strong Ruthenian or Polish element. The first two examples are *Triumph of the Polish Muse* (*Tryumf Polskiei Muzy*), Daniil Gurchin's laudatory verses to Peter I and Aleksandr Menshikov, printed in Moscow in 1706 following a victory over the Swedes; and the *Epinikion* of Feofan Prokopovich (1681–1736), part of his *Panegirikos* to Peter, printed at the press of the Caves monastery in Kiev after the battle of Poltava in 1709.[54] By the late 1720s printed panegyric and celebratory verses had spanned the boundaries of typeface and language, appearing both in traditional Cyrillic and in civil type, in Russian and in German and in Latin, printed in Moscow, St Petersburg, Riga, Reval.[55] Odes constituted the largest single category of printed verse for most of the century.[56]

Arguably a key moment in print's expansion into the zone of literature was the publication, in 1730, of Vasilii Trediakovskii's translation of Paul Tallemant's *Voyage de l'isle d'amour*, supplemented with a selection of poems in Russian and French (plus one in Latin).[57] A case could be made for regarding this as the first modern novel to be printed in Russia and in Russian, together with the first selection of lyric love poetry. Nevertheless, through the mid eighteenth century manuscript remained the most common mode of literary reproduction.[58] A major shift occurred during the latter decades of the century. As Gary Marker has shown with respect to his category of 'leisure books' (somewhat broader than 'literature'), by the 1780s the market was 'incomparably' greater than in the 1720s and 1730s.[59] This was the case not only for books in Russian, but also, especially, in French.

The process was not inexorable. We have spoken of the diffusion and privatisation of print as if it led unequivocally to the expansion of print into areas previously dominated by manuscript. However, the broader privatisation of literary culture had paradoxical consequences. On the one hand, no longer were certain types of literature barred from print on institutional, cultural or even economic grounds. On the other hand, in some contexts the prevailing ethos of elite literary production led, for a while, to a renewed status for the older technology. In crude terms: as the high-style declamatory genres of Russian classicism gave way to an aesthetic of intimacy and reflection, as panegyric and epic became sidelined by lyric, as the locus and focus of elite literature shifted from the court to the salon, as the judgement that mattered was not that of the sovereign, or that of the Academy, or indeed that of the markets (which distressingly failed to live up to the expectations of the intellectuals),[60] but that of one's friends – so the incursions of print were countered, if not fully halted, by a renewal of the status of the manuscript and of informal dissemination.

The salons and literary circles of the first half of the nineteenth century – core institutions of literary production and discussion and evaluation – while not necessarily anti-print, could be ambiguous about its status.[61] Some literary societies were clear that part of their purpose was to foster, criticise, improve and prepare members' works for publication. This was explicit from as early as 1805 in the printed rule-book of the St Petersburg Society for Lovers of Sciences, Letters and the Arts.[62] Even the self-consciously flippant Arzamas society (1815–18), whose members included the precociously talented teenager Aleksandr Pushkin,[63] had at one stage plans for a journal. Some of the literary circles of the late 1830s and 1840s had close links with editorial offices. At the same time, however, print was held, as it were, at a distance, on the fringes, a potential outcome but not the main activity. Aspirations for print were balanced by what has been called, in another context, the 'stigma of print'.[64] At the heart of the salon and circle were conversation, ephemerality, oral recitation and critical discussion, often the manuscript entry in the album or *liber amicorum*. The ethos was conducive to the high-minded civilised amateur's affectation of indifference towards vulgar print. Better to disdain pre-emptively the medium of the market than to wait to be disdained by it. And even where print was an outcome, it was not necessarily the end product. Printed poems re-entered the world of discussion and criticism, were recopied by hand into albums, and perhaps in turn reworked when the cycle of media brought them round to print again.

A nice example of the dynamics of media is explored by Katherine Bowers in her study of a single poem, 'Farewell to My Dressing Gown' ('Proshchanie s khalatom') by Petr Viazemskii (1792–1878).[65] The dressing gown stands for the informality of the life of friendship and shared cultural and literary enjoyments that Viazemskii was about to leave in order to take up a government post in Warsaw, to which he was appointed in August 1817. Later in the same autumn Viazemskii's poem was read out (in the author's absence) at a meeting of Arzamas's court of literary judgement. Pushkin copied it into his notebook. It was discussed in correspondence between members of the group, the image figured in a speech by the poet Vasilii Zhukovskii, and it seeped out into literary culture, through allusions in poems by Anton Delvig (1798–1831) and in several poems by Pushkin. By the time it was printed, in 1821, it was already, in a sense, a classic. Though it continued to be cited, the most active, seminal and productive period of its literary existence was over. Publication in print was one phase of the poem's life, but its most vibrantly influential and productive phase was in manuscript, and indeed in speech. The status of the handwritten text in this period was linked to the status and aura of the ostensibly informal in culture. Even though the salon and the literary circle can be regarded as institutions, and some of them adopted institutional trappings such as constitutions, committees, minutes etc., their ethos was self-consciously unofficial.

The fifth cultural zone of primary writing takes a further step along the path to informality: the personal, the private. It includes private correspondence, notes and memos, diaries, casual jottings. Of all the five zones this is perhaps the simplest to circumscribe, but the most difficult to describe. Its principal graphospheric characteristics are plain, since, almost by definition, it is overwhelmingly the preserve of handwriting, a monomedia cultural reserve, a self-contained niche. With little concern for markets, minimal requirement for multiple copies, and a premium on immediacy, personal and private writing was obviously not a prime target for colonisation by print. However, the history of personal writing in early modern Russia is obscure. One would not expect it to have been voluminous by comparison with that of much of Western Europe, or to find such abundance as is becoming available through, for example, the Early Modern Letters Online project based at the Bodleian Library in Oxford,[66] but the history of Russian letter-writing is still under-investigated, even on the basis of such source publications as exist,[67] as are other modes of informal personal writing such as private diaries, memos and notes.

Medieval and early modern Russian pastoral, polemical and political writings from time to time took the form of epistles. There were also manuscript guides to letter-writing.[68] From the late eighteenth century it becomes harder to draw a clear line between the private and the quasi-public, and this, in turn, has some implications for the technological boundaries. Private correspondence was not conducted *in* print but could be influenced *by* print, and could in turn have an effect *on* print. William Mills Todd, for example, distinguishes at least three genres of letter: the personal, the business and the familiar.[69] At the more literary end of the scale, the 'familiar letter' was in constant dialogue with literary (including printed) precedent, it could itself be subsequently printed, and it helped to sustain epistolary styles which also surfaced in printed fiction. Indeed, the 'familiar letter' is a challenge to the categories in this survey, since in any given case the difference between the personal and the 'familiar' might be functional rather than formal. Genuinely private correspondence, no less than semi-public exchanges, could become infused with literary formulations. Even away from the literariness of the *literati*, in the more authentically personal sphere, letter-writing was a taught craft, drawing on manuals and precedent and models as well as on spontaneous expression.[70] Moreover, that which can be said of the dialogic form (the letter) can also be said of the monologic form, the diary, which at the literary end of the spectrum was analogous.

Notwithstanding such interactions, private writing remained overwhelmingly a manuscript activity until technologies of print could be brought into the home, starting with the domestic adoption of that hybrid invention the 'type-writer' in the second half of the nineteenth century.[71] The boundaries were fully erased only with the electronic technologies that have led to such a dramatic shift from pen to keyboard or keypad, from commercial press to desk-top printer to 'smart' device and social media. When the technologies of production and effective distribution of the text are devolved to the level of the individual, there is little space left for a mainstream, robust manuscript culture even of private writing.

There was no single pattern or process according to which print did or did not encroach on or expand into the zones of manuscript. These five rough sketch-maps of zones of print and manuscript – religious and devotional, administrative, educational and scholarly, literary, and personal – highlight just some of the variations in the relationship of the technologies of primary writing across culture and time. Taken together, overlaid upon each other, they begin to suggest some of the nuances which come more sharply into focus as we turn to the more dynamic questions of graphospheric interactions.

Crossing Boundaries: Aspects of 'Reverse Technology Transfer'

The boundaries between the zones of the respective technologies were permeable in both directions. Handwritten words could make the transition to print, printed words could be copied by hand. Broadly speaking, one would probably tend to think of the former as the norm: in the beginning was the manuscript. Here we focus mainly on the latter, on the less predictable type of technological transition: from print *into* manuscript. Even with this restriction the permutations are unmanageably varied, so the samples are taken from a small subset of such transitions. What happened when the crossing of technological boundaries coincided with the crossing of cultural boundaries, when products of imported print culture became products of local manuscript culture? What were the patterns of the phenomenon that might be termed 'reverse technology transfer',[72] when the reception of imported print involved a switch of medium to manuscript?

In late Muscovy, such 'reverse technology transfer' was the norm. Indeed, before the mid sixteenth century it was unavoidable: when there was not yet any printing in Muscovy, any local reproduction and dissemination of the products of imported print culture could only be through conversion to the medium of manuscript. Similarly, because of the specific and restricted zone of Muscovite print, reverse technology transfer remained by far the most common mode of assimilation of imported print at least until the eighteenth century. Nor should this be imagined to be a 'mere' technicality. Reverse technology transfer could be symptomatic of deeper processes of cultural adaptation or resistance. Perhaps the most dramatic example is provided by the fate of imported newspapers.

West European printed newspapers were brought to Moscow by Russian and foreign merchants and envoys at least from the early 1620s.[73] Did this perhaps signify a growing popular interest in current events in Western Europe, fed by the availability of and expanding demand for newspapers? Not at all. The newspapers' points of origin were diverse, but in Muscovy they were narrowly channelled to a single destination for a single purpose. They were ordered by the government as sources of data for use in the compilation of intelligence reports. A government chancery prepared manuscript digests, usually in just two copies. In the case of newspapers, therefore, reverse technology transfer was part of a radical reversal not only of medium but also of status and usage. A print form designed to be widely accessible was translated into a manuscript form so restricted, so exclusive, so inaccessible to any but the narrowest elite, that it seems the very antithesis of the original function of its West European source. The texts were imported, but not the technology, the purpose, the genre or the spirit. A medium for the popularisation of print was contextually filtered so as to become a medium for exclusive government intelligence. This is not simply a reversion of technology, but a complete inversion of function. The origins of internally generated, outward-facing printed newspapers in Russia tend to be traced to 1702–3 with the early issues of the official bulletin, *Vedomosti*, but the continuous history of newspapers should probably start in 1727 with the founding of *St Peterburgische Zeitung*, followed in 1728 by the 'relaunch' of *Vedomosti* as *Sankt-Peterburgskie vedomosti* under the aegis of the Academy of Sciences.[74] By this stage reverse technology transfer had become irrelevant.

A second and more complex example can be explored through the multimedia transformations of West European printed pictures – especially, for present purposes, with respect to the relationship between images and words. West European printed images found paths into Russian culture almost from the start of West European printing itself, long before the dominant 'westernising' turn in the eighteenth century. Initially this, too, involved reverse technology transfer, but eventually it led to a remarkable diversity of adaptations.

The first area of transfer was mostly non-textual. It involved what is broadly termed 'ornament' in manuscripts and printed books: headpieces and tailpieces, and to some extent initial letters. One of the characteristic decorative styles of late-fifteenth-century Russian manuscripts is known as the 'neo-Byzantine'. Typically, a manuscript decorated with neo-Byzantine ornament would have richly coloured headpieces, often on a gold ground, with floral motifs in a geometric frame, and perhaps also initial letters in the form of exotic birds and animals.[75] Sporadically, from the late fifteenth century, new features began to appear in some of the neo-Byzantine headpieces: occasional swirls of acanthus or thistle leaves and flowers, often in more subdued and limited colours. These are identified as the first elements of the 'early printed style' of decoration, derived from West European printed books and engravings.[76] Gradually interactions between the neo-Byzantine and 'early printed' components became more diverse. In some manuscripts the 'early-printed-style' components appeared as minor frills; in others they came to constitute a fully defined frame for a neo-Byzantine headpiece; in others a large and distinct black and white 'early-printed-style' medallion turns into the central element of the polychrome headpiece itself. From the second quarter of the sixteenth century, neo-Byzantine decoration, with embedded or distinct 'early-printed-style' components, characterises several of the most prominent practices of manuscript decoration.[77] Gradually the 'early-printed-style' medallions became larger, eventually dominant. The logical conclusion was the appearance of wholly black and white 'early-printed-style' ornament, free-standing, emancipated from its polychrome neo-Byzantine wrapping.

The chronology and origins of 'early printed style' in Russian ornament cannot be traced precisely. The situation is complicated by the fact that at least some of its decorative elements had analogies in much earlier manuscript ornament, which pre-dates any possible influence of print. However, from the early sixteenth century some printed models can be identified: in particular, a set of six engraved sheets with specimens of decorative initial lettering and ornament, produced by the German engraver Israhel van Meckenem.[78] Israhel van Meckenem died in 1503, and it is not clear when or how a set (or sets) of his engraved specimens reached Muscovy. However, their use as exemplars for Russian bookmen through to the mid sixteenth century is broadly accepted.

Headpieces and initials in 'early printed style' were adopted by the first Muscovite printers.[79] The paradox was that such ornaments, though originally borrowed in Russia from printed sheets and books, reached Russian printed books not directly from their West European printed prototypes, but via the adapted versions which had developed in Russian manuscripts. Thus, in the case of ornament, reverse technology transfer of imported material was followed by a subsequent recrossing of the boundary, in a sequence from print, to manuscript, and thence again into print.

West European sources for elements of Muscovite visual culture of the mid to late sixteenth century represent a growing field of inquiry. There are recent general surveys of the question,[80] as well as detailed analyses of individual images.[81] West European engravings, together with their verbal captions, are posited to have informed some of the images and inscriptions in the Golden Hall of the Moscow Kremlin.[82] However, a huge amount of potentially relevant material is yet to be explored – not least the nearly 18,000 miniatures of the *Illustrated Chronicle* (*Litsevoi letopisnyi svod*), which are now all available online.[83] Russian exposure to and adaptations of printed images from the seventeenth century have been more extensively researched, and provide our main example of reverse technology transfer of West European printed pictures into Muscovite cultures of writing.

Picture Bibles – albums of illustrations, with no text except for brief prose or verse captions – were common throughout Europe. These could be quite substantial objects, often with between two hundred and four hundred plates. The most widely used in Russia were those published in Amsterdam by Claes Visscher (Nicolas Joannes Piscator; 1587–1652) and his descendants – his son and grandson, also called Nicolas Joannes. The principal editions of 'Piscator's Bible' are those of 1639, 1643, 1650 and 1674. Other cycles are associated with the names of Matthaeus Merian, Peter van der Borcht and Pieter Schut. Just to confuse matters, later editions of Merian's and other illustrations were published by the Visschers (or the Piscatores). Piscator and Merian became the best-known names, but the genre was earlier, and some sixteenth-century suites were also known and used in late-seventeenth-century Moscow, such as those by Hieronymus Wierix, published with Hieronymus Natalis's *Evangelicae historiae imagines* in Antwerp in 1593.

The simplest form of reverse technology transfer of biblical illustrations was from printed to painted pictures. It would be hard to overstate the extent to which such engravings permeated diverse areas of Russian visual culture in the late seventeenth and early eighteenth centuries. They have been identified as sources of, for example, frescoes in the churches of Iaroslavl, of icons and frescoes in several Moscow churches, as well as in Rostov, Kostroma, Vologda, and Uglich, even of decorated enamelware.[84] Suites of West European biblical illustrations were used in the school of painting in the Kremlin Armoury, whose director, Ivan Saltanov, ordered a volume to be acquired for the school in 1685. Moreover, the pictorial echoes of the West European engravings are not just found in the copying of whole compositions. Individual figures, even details such as furnishings or drapes, were borrowed out of context, were combined with each other or with different compositions.[85] Imported biblical engravings simply fed into the general pictorial vocabulary.

Beyond their transmission into Russian visual culture, the picture Bibles are significant because of verbal responses to them. They generated local genres of writing in manuscript. The original captions were in Latin. In Russia, they were usually provided with new captions in Russian, written by hand in the lower margin of each page. Sometimes these Russian captions were translations of the Latin texts in the engravings, sometimes they were independently composed. Some were in prose, others – also echoing an equivalent practice in Western Europe[86] – were in verse. Each of the several hundred leaves of a given album was thus a linguistic and technological hybrid, with captions engraved in Latin and handwritten in Russian.

We will consider hybrids later in the present chapter. Here the more noteworthy aspect is the fact that some of the cycles of verse captions migrated beyond the immediate pictorial environment for which they had been created. They were copied separately, as if free-standing compositions. Some of the separately copied caption cycles are anonymous,[87] others are by leading *literati* of the age. A cycle of captions to illustrations of Matthaeus Merian, in nearly a thousand lines, was written by Simeon Polotskii.[88] The most extensive literary response was that of Mardarii Khonykov.[89] Khonykov, like many of the leading bookmen of the late seventeenth century, worked at the Moscow Print Yard. His enormous cycle of verses on the pictures in Piscator's Bible runs to well over three thousand lines. Despite its origin as a set of captions, it was shaped and framed as an independent literary work, complete with its own prefatory address to the reader, in two sections: first, a 28-line acrostic which revealed his own name as author; then fourteen lines on the source, 'Nikolai, son of Ioann, Piskator'. Khonykov even gives the respective dates: he 'published' (*izdavyi*) his own verses in the year 7187 (according to the traditional Orthodox calendar calculating from the Creation, which here converts to a year running from September 1678 to August 1679 CE), using the 1674 edition of Piscator.[90] Mardarii Khonykov's verses are known in at least ten manuscript copies. In one manuscript compilation of world history, put together around 1703, much of biblical history is related via the medium of Mardarii Khonykov's verses.[91]

That was not the end of the journey across media. Parts of the verse cycles both by Simeon Polotskii and by Mardarii Khonykov migrated beyond the relatively enclosed world of literary manuscript culture and into the wider graphosphere, as captions accompanying monumental painting. In the church of the Resurrection in the town of Tutaev (formerly Romanov-Borisoglebsk), to the north-east of Iaroslavl, a set of frescoes on themes from the Song of Songs is inscribed with the relevant verses from the cycle by Simeon Polotskii. The frescoes most likely date from the mid to late 1670s, notably close to the time of composition of the verses themselves.[92] Somewhat later, in the mid 1730s, in the church of St John the Theologian in Kostroma, an equivalent set of frescoes based on the Song of Songs was captioned with verses from the cycle by Mardarii Khonykov.[93]

The biblical albums were thus subject to at least three kinds of reverse technology transfer: from printed picture to painted picture (whether on wood or on walls or on enamels), from printed caption to manuscript composition, and from manuscript composition to painted caption. Indeed, their adaptation into Russian cultures of hand-painting and handwriting were far more diverse, immediate and profound than their adaptation by 'direct' technology transfer, that is, into the culture of Russian engraving. Biblical engravings were, of course, produced in Muscovy, but there were very few sustained attempts to produce a direct generic equivalent of the West European albums on a comparable scale.[94] The most plausible explanation lies in the difference between the status and functions of the Bible itself in western and eastern Christianity. Russians used Piscator and others in the illustration of biblical scenes, but had little reason to require or create or print full sets of illustrations to the complete Bible as such, since the Bible as such – as a complete book from Genesis to Revelations – played a minimal role in Russian devotional culture. By the mid sixteenth century the Bible was already the most widely printed single book in Western Europe, even before its production and dissemination were strongly boosted by the Reformation and the proliferation of vernacular Bibles. By extreme contrast, as we have seen, only one edition of a complete Bible was printed in Russia before the mid eighteenth century.[95] Thus, as in the case of West European newspapers (though in more diverse and creative and nuanced ways), reverse technology transfer of biblical engravings involved not only a shift of medium but also adaptation to a different configuration of cultural functions.

The suites of biblical illustrations constitute only one set of examples of a broader phenomenon. Imported devotional engravings seeped deep into the Russian graphosphere, and their traces can turn up in the most remote and unexpected places. For example, in May 1778 Savva Matveevich Chasovnikov, a priest in the village of Grediakino in the Userd district (near Belgorod, to the south-west of Voronezh), completed a manuscript *sinodik*. The term *sinodik* is applied to various types of text.[96] In Savva's case it denotes a version of a popular compilation of brief biblical, hagiographic and apocryphal texts and illustrations broadly connected with death and commemoration.[97] Block-printed *sinodiki* had existed in Muscovy since the late seventeenth century.[98] Manuscript *sinodiki* of this type often drew on printed versions. Savva's *sinodik* includes twenty-three miniatures, most of them full-page. In addition to the Church Slavonic edificatory texts, the versos and margins are packed with the names of families from Grediakino and surrounding settlements who are to be commemorated. The illustrations are in typical 'folk iconographic' mode. Several of them echo the Muscovite printed cycles, some are personal, such as the portraits of the patron saints of Savva and his wife Stefanida. But there are twists in the presentation. The picture of the creation of Adam has bilingual, bi-scriptal captions: *Bog" Otets"* in Slavonic, *Deus Pater* in Latin, *Adam"* and *Adamus* (Fig. 6.1). The miniature of the Creation itself is more elaborate in its verbal display: again both *Bog" Otets"* and *Deus Pater*, but also representations of the sun and the moon labelled *sol* and *mensis*, above a quotation from Psalm 74:16, in Latin alone: *tuus est dies et tua est nox*. There is no consistency, no policy of bilingual captioning, just residual signs of the seepage of verbal elements from imported engravings deep into the manuscript culture of the Russian village.

Hybrids

Print and handwriting coexist in the same spaces, as parts of the same physical objects, which become technological hybrids. Types of hybridity are widespread and diverse.[99] The most common are probably the handwritten interventions in printed books: the ownership and donation inscriptions, the marginalia and comments which, when old, so delight the bibliophile or scholar, yet, when new, so vex the librarian. In many such cases the fact that the object becomes a technological hybrid is merely incidental, since the manuscript interventions in the margins or endpapers or flysheets of a printed book are essentially the same as the manuscript interventions in the margins of an equivalent handwritten book. They individualise the generic, turn a text into a possession or a gift, express aspects of the reader through personal interventions and responses, contribute to the biography of the object and to an understanding of its meanings. Any historian of books will recognise the sense of discovery, even revelation, experienced by Pushkin's Tatiana as she immerses herself first in the books that had been owned by Evgenii Onegin, then in the marks that he had made in their margins; although any historian of books will also appreciate the caution of Pushkin's otherwise indulgent narrator,

Fig. 6.1: The Creation of Adam, from a manuscript *sinodik* of the priest Savva Chasovnikov of Grediakino village, 1778

who suggests that such evidence – a reading of Onegin's implied reading of his reading – while it has helped to improve Tatiana's understanding, is unlikely to have perfected it.[100]

Marginalia in early manuscript and printed books have become standard components of bibliographical description,[101] and in many areas the cultural aspects of marginalia attract scholarly attention,[102] but I am not aware of any substantial or systematic study of handwritten annotations in Russian books of the eighteenth or early nineteenth centuries.[103] The hybridity created by such interventions is optional, occasional, casual. Here I will briefly indicate just a few varieties of such hybrids that seem suggestive or significant. However, the main focus of attention will be a different type of hybrid: not those which are the result of individual interventions, but those which form what we will call *structural hybrids*. A structural hybrid is an object which is made specifically to accommodate both print and handwriting, an object whose proper functioning presupposes and depends on the presence of both. The classic genre of structural hybrid is the printed blank form.

Optional/Casual/Occasional Hybrids

By far the most common additions to the 'made' book are indications of ownership and donation. Ownership and donation inscriptions in early East Slav printed books can appear in virtually any blank space, but the most characteristic mode is the record of acquisition, ownership or donation divided into individual words or short phrases distributed across the lower margins of several consecutive rectos (i.e. the right-hand page of an opening) at or near the start of a book. In the eighteenth century, especially in non-devotional books, these became less common, replaced by ownership and donation inscriptions on the front endpaper or flyleaf. Unless, that is, manuscript was replaced in this function by print in the form of a bookplate. The bookplate has a curious technological evolution. Its precursor is the hand-drawn ornamental ownership mark or monogram. Examples of such individualised devices have been traced in Russia from the late fifteenth century.[104] As we have seen, the Russian 'superexlibris' – an ownership device stamped on the binding – dates at least from the mid sixteenth century. However, the history of 'proper' bookplates, as separate non-book objects pasted into books by their owners, begins towards the end of the seventeenth century. The earliest thus far identified, still hand-drawn, is that of Stepan Gerasimovich Dokhturov, dated 1671.[105] Scholars give different dates for the earliest engraved bookplates. An engraved bookplate from 1691 was pasted by hierodeacon Stefan Sakharov into several books that he donated to his former monastery.[106] The first engraved bookplates indicating ownership rather than donation are perhaps those of the Scottish doctor Robert Erskine ('Areskin' in Russia), from the start of the eighteenth century.[107]

Beyond ownership and donation, there is no limit to the extent to which a book *could* be annotated or supplemented or defaced. A representative study of marginalia in Russia would not be limited to marginalia in Russian.[108] And, beyond marginalia as such, there are print-plus-manuscript optional hybrids that are created through interleaving, through binding or pasting additional pages. Examples can be found throughout the period: a copy of Ivan Fedorov's Ostroh Bible of 1581 was hybridised in Muscovy with additional leaves of manuscript miniatures in the 1630s.[109] Aleksandr Pushkin had his copy of a printed edition of the *Tale of the Campaign of Igor* (*Slovo o polku Igoreve*) bound for him with additional blank pages interleaved for his handwritten annotations.[110]

Rarely does one find extensive annotations which reflect on the process of annotation itself. Remarkable exceptions are the sets of marginalia found in two books that belonged to Iosif, archimandrite of the monastery of John the Baptist at Krasnaia Sloboda in Penza province. Iosif's approach to marginalia was idiosyncratic. Rather than record his purchase, ownership or donation in a brief inscription distributed across the first few leaves, his habit was to write a continuous inscription across the lower margins of every leaf in the book; indeed, on every side of every leaf. Two of his books survive thus inscribed. Both sets of inscriptions date from 1706. One of the books was a *khronograf*, a compilation of world history: 634 leaves, or 1,268 pages, with Iosif's inscriptions throughout.[111] The other is Iosif's copy of Piscator's Bible.[112] To call these 'marginal inscriptions' is barely adequate to the scale. They are substantial compositions. Generically they are hard to characterise. They are somewhat improvised, often repetitive, occasionally formal, linguistically in places almost chatty. Iosif includes, for example, an inventory of the monastery's valuable possessions, a record of his own donations and an account of a theft in 1702. One of their express functions was security. Taking a common habit of individuals and institutions to grotesquely obsessive extremes, Iosif made sure that every page bore the marks of the books' rightful ownership and location. He repeatedly stated that he had given the books not just to the monastery but specifically to its library, and that the books were on no account to be removed from there. He directed his strongest invective against the practice of lending books to laymen, who mistreat them to the point of destruction[113] and then fail to return them. The most dire divine vengeance would be inflicted upon anyone who removed the books from the monastery.

More distinctive as a process, and more limited in its scope, is the reverse kind of hybrid, created through the addition of printed material to a handwritten object. To paste printed textual material into manuscript books would be unusual in most circumstances except, perhaps, the specific genre of the scrapbook. More common, in Muscovy as elsewhere, are hybrids created through the addition of printed ornament or illustration.[114] In Muscovy the earliest specimens, though still very rare, date from approximately the age of the first Moscow-printed books. Four manuscripts from the mid sixteenth century include pasted-in engraved headpieces and marginal decorations associated with a certain 'Feodosii', whose name appears as a signature in one of the headpieces. This Feodosii has been hypothetically (though by no means indisputably) identified with a known painter, son of the artist Dionisii.[115] Feodosii's ornamental paste-ins are additionally unusual because they are copper engravings. In early Muscovite printed ornament and illustration, the standard method was woodcut. If we accept the dates and attributions, Feodosii would be the earliest-known Muscovite copper engraver, predating others by about a century.

In later devotional manuscript books, from the last quarter of the seventeenth century right through to the nineteenth century, illustrative and ornamental paste-ins are not such great rarities.[116] Where a scribe or owner wanted to embellish a text, it was convenient to be able to take from the supply of ready-made (printed) materials. Sometimes all that was wanted was a decorative headpiece, or an illustrative frontispiece; but printed paste-ins could be combined with manuscript text in large numbers – just as suites of engravings could be bound in with printed books so as to form deluxe 'extra-illustrated' copies. The sources of such illustrations could be imported or local. For example, in the 1650s or 1660s the relevant sections of a large manuscript narrative of world history were interleaved with more than 350 engravings from the 1643 edition of – once more – Piscator's Bible.[117]

Among the most common Russian block-printed books from the late seventeenth to the early nineteenth century was the *sinodik*. As we have seen, illustrated *sinodiki* were also widely produced in manuscript. It is not surprising, therefore, that we also find mixtures of the two: a *sinodik* with handwritten texts decorated with woodcut headpieces and bound in with around fifty woodcut illustrations.[118] Or, in a different mode, a manuscript account of the 133 iconographic types of the Mother of God, probably written around 1716, includes more than ninety engravings of the various iconographic types, seventy-eight of which were cut from compilative plates (each with twelve images) by Grigorii Tepchegorskii.[119] The compilers of such hybrids were eclectic in their plundering of illustrations from printed books. Thus, for example, besides rather obvious borrowings such as woodcuts of King David stuck into manuscripts of the Psalter, one can find more incongruous migrating images such as printed illustrations from Fedor Polikarpov's trilingual Slavonic-Greek-Latin grammar of 1701: Moses receiving the tablets of the Law, used anachronistically as the frontispiece to a manuscript of Josephus's *History of the Jewish War*; a portrait of Patriarch Gennadios of Constantinople, used as an entirely inappropriate frontispiece to a manuscript tract by a different author, Nektarios of Jerusalem; or, a little more plausibly, a portrait of Gregory the Theologian inserted into a manuscript handbook of rhetoric.[120]

Structural Hybrids, I: In Book Culture

The casual hybrid can be contrasted with a phenomenon which has broader and deeper implications for the history of the graphosphere: the structural hybrid. The structural hybrid is not an optional mixture of print and manuscript. It is a mode of production in which both technologies are necessary, in which the lack of one or the other leaves an object functionally incomplete. Typically, the structural hybrid consists of – or at any rate includes – a printed template with blank spaces to be filled in by hand. The printed template defines the genre, the handwritten additions specify its particular contents. Structural hybrids span books and non-books, although the uses and consequences of hybrid non-books were far more diverse and important. In Russia, both have their origins in the second half of the seventeenth century.

In the manuscript book culture of late-seventeenth-century Muscovy, structurally hybrid headpieces and title pages became quite fashionable. Several of the known engravers of the day, including Leontii Bunin, Vasilii Andreev and Afanasii Trukhmenskii, produced ornamental frames which left space for the relevant titles to be written in by hand (Fig. 6.2).[121] The styles of ornament reflect elements of design picked up from West European printed books, although in Muscovy they were introduced as adornments mainly to traditional devotional manuscripts, which thus became, in a sense, aesthetic as well as technological hybrids.[122]

The most elaborate structural hybrid in the book culture of this early period was a form of calendar. It was produced not in Moscow or in any other major centre of population and commerce, but in the remote northern monastery of St Antonii on the Siia river (the 'Antonievo-Siiskii' monastery). The monastery had no tradition of printing, but in the early 1670s someone among the brethren was an accomplished maker of woodcuts. Around 1670 the monastery produced, seemingly for its own use rather than for sale or distribution, a set of blocks which could be used either together or in combination with additional texts to form a calendar book.[123] The woodcuts include a blank frame for a title page, a composite portrait of the monastery's founder (printed from three blocks for separate parts of the portrait and background, plus further blocks for the

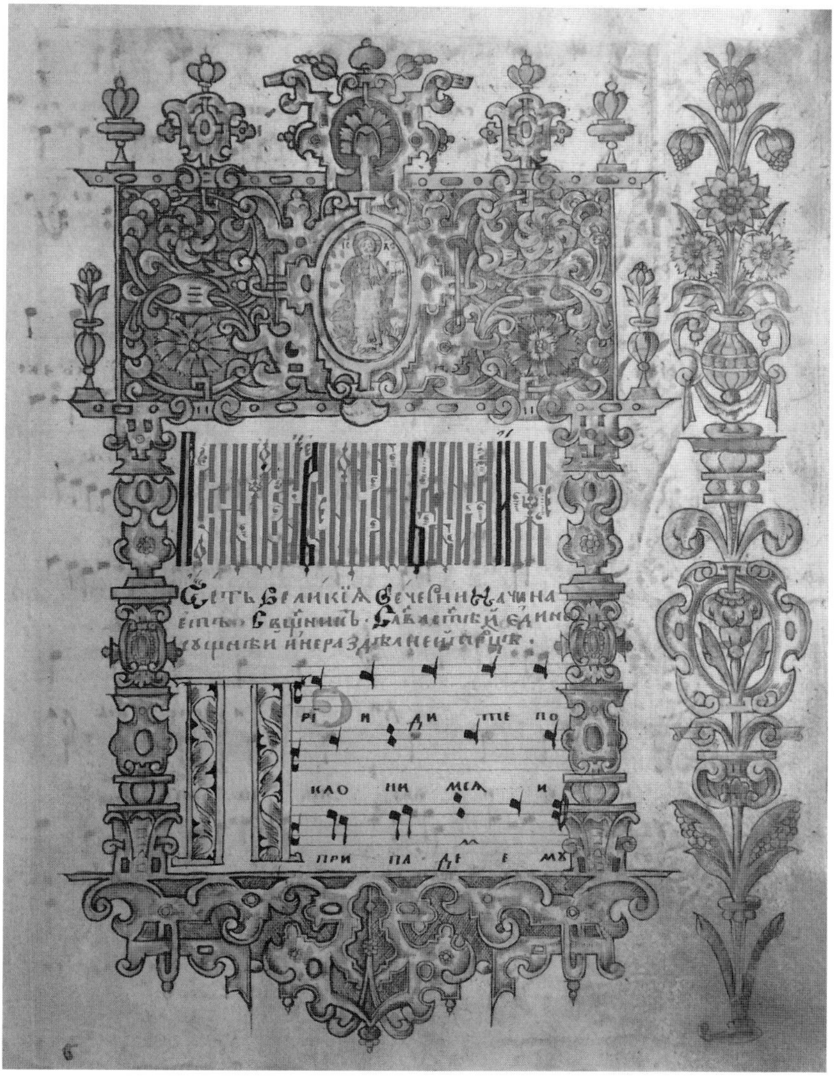

Fig. 6.2: Title page of an early-eighteenth-century music manuscript; engraved frame, hand-coloured, from a plate attributed to the circle of Leontii Bunin, late 1690s

surrounding captions), and a curiously abstract design indicating hymns for matins and vespers. However, the distinctive components are not these single-sheet compositions, but several different forms of elaborate woodcut grids that form cells to be filled in by hand: a seven-day grid – duplicated in as many copies as required for a given calendar – with blank columns for the names of saints; a set of 56-cell grids of hymnographic cycles.

Six sets of these calendars survive.[124] No two are identical. The fullest copy consists of ninety-eight leaves, of which some forty-six are woodcuts, while the remainder contain manuscript texts.[125] At the other end of the spectrum, one copy consists of a partial set of the woodcut grids and ornament.[126] This latter is sometimes described as 'defective', but perhaps is merely provisional: its blank title page remains not merely unfilled but untrimmed, uncut – not a remnant of a once-complete copy but a printer's sheet not yet turned into part of a book (Fig. 6.3). These calendars are structurally hybrid books composed in whole or in part of structurally hybrid plates. They are hybrids of hybrids.

Calendrical cycles, with their individualised contents framed in repetitive forms, are particularly suitable material for structural hybrids. As it happens, the ecclesiastical versions pioneered at St Antonii's monastery on the Siia river are unique in their time. Although occasional hybrid elements can be found in subsequent manuscript calendars,[127] they did not serve directly as catalysts for a continuous tradition, but the practice of producing hybrid calendars was revived after a break. Almanacs and calendars were among the most regularly and prolifically printed books of the eighteenth century, issued in large quantities by the Academy of Sciences press in St Petersburg.[128] However, printed calendrical blanks do not seem to have been regular components. The first issue mentioned as having an integral set of a dozen such pages seems to be a version of the calendar for 1780.[129] Thereafter, at any rate on the basis of serendipitous observation (in the absence of any systematic survey) it appears that such hybrid components became rather more frequent, sometimes as optional supplements. Thus a copy of the standard calendar for 1782 includes a dozen blanks for notes.[130] The French version of the court almanac for 1786 begins with a 48-page calendar with 4 pages allocated to each month. One page prints lists of saints for each day according to the calendars of the Latin and Greek churches respectively, one prints times for the rising and setting of sun and moon, while two pages serve as miniature diaries, each printing the dates only and leaving spaces for manuscript annotation.[131] A copy of the equivalent almanac for 1790 drops the initial hybrid calendar but adds, as a supplement, a hybrid accounting calendar (introduced as a *secrétaire*), with blank columns for income and expenditure for each day of the week, then for each day of the month.[132] Over the early decades of the nineteenth century printed blank account books and ledgers proliferated as standard equipment rather than as curious novelty items.

Fig. 6.3: Unused engraved frame for title page of calendar, early 1670s; monastery of St Antonii on the Siia River. Russian State Library, Moscow

Structural Hybrids, II: Non-Books – the Printed Blank Form

In the culture of books, structural hybrids are products of occasional whim or fashion. The true destiny of the structural hybrid was in the culture of non-books. The essential component of a structural hybrid is a printed blank form. In itself the printed blank has no function until hybridised, until 'filled in', until activated by the addition of the handwritten particulars. The blank form is the classic, almost quintessential bureaucratic, non-bookish application of print. It is also a generally under-appreciated product of human civilisation. Forms can, of course, be created and copied by hand,[133] but their scope is massively expanded by print and by the post-print technologies. Printed blanks appeared in the age of Gutenberg.[134] Their successors, the myriad varieties of interactive template, lie behind virtually every online transaction. The history of printed blanks in Russia is not well known. Indeed, it is barely known at all. Most types of the relevant documents are very rarely described or catalogued. The problem is not unique to Russia. With reference to their survival and study in Western Europe, too, blank forms have been called 'among the most elusive products of the print industry'[135] which 'are usually treated as a sort of stationery and thus are frequently excluded altogether from catalogues.'[136] My provisional attempt at a systematic arrangement of the evidence is based partly on published sources but mainly on documents from several archives and libraries in St Petersburg and Moscow, with additional material from institutions and collections in London, Edinburgh, Oxford and Cambridge. However, a great deal of evidence surely remains untouched, undiscovered, unidentified, and the present summary will need modification.

The history of printed 'non-book' blanks in Russia begins just after the mid point of the seventeenth century and can be divided into six phases.[137] The first phase was dominated by the church, which was the institutional pioneer of printed blanks in Russia. Three types of ecclesiastical printed blank, utterly different from one another in function, appear in the second half of the seventeenth century. The earliest recorded Muscovite printed blanks for ecclesiastical appointments (*stavlennye gramoty*) date from February 1652, when, over a period of four weeks, Patriarch Nikon put in orders for a total of seven thousand blanks, in five batches, for the appointment of priests, archpriests and deacons.[138] Thereafter there is evidence for approximately forty subsequent issues over the second half of the century, with print runs ranging from a few dozen to a few thousand. These *stavlennye gramoty* represent the Muscovite church's first regular use of printing for administrative purposes. Unless, that is, one also counts printed pictures – in which case, alongside the *stavlennye gramoty* for priests, we should include the woodcut and engraved liturgical cloths known as antimensia, which were produced regularly from the 1650s onwards.[139] Possession of a validated antimension was an administrative requirement, proof of consecration and of permission to celebrate the liturgy. Antimensia were printed with gaps in the side panels or lower panels for details to be filled in by hand. Thus antimensia, too, were blank forms, templates that became fully functional only when hybridised through the handwritten additions.

The third type of ecclesiastical blank form whose origins in Muscovy likewise date from the 1650s consists of certificates of absolution (in the sources: *razreshal'nye, razreshatel'nye* or *razreshennye gramoty*; in modern convention: *razreshitel'nye gramoty*). The term covers two kinds of document: indulgences issued to the living, and a form of posthumous indulgence placed in the hands of the deceased.[140] Despite a tradition of Orthodox polemics against the sale of indulgences as one of the defining abominations of the 'Latin' church, the sale of *razreshitel'nye gramoty* to living beneficiaries was not unknown. The peculiar feature of certificates of absolution is that they were not a local administrative requirement; indeed, they were not even issued for internal use by the Muscovite church. To issue or sell certificates of absolution was a privilege of the patriarchs of the eastern church. The printing of Slavonic *razreshitel'nye gramoty* can be traced at least to the first decade of the seventeenth century. The earliest evidence is for an issue printed in Lviv in 1608.[141] At the Moscow Print Yard the archival record points to their production from the mid 1650s.[142] The first record of blank *razreshitel'nye gramoty* – referring to an order, also issued by Nikon, for one thousand to be printed for the Serbian patriarch – dates from 28 May 1655.

In the second phase in the history of printed 'non-book' blanks in Russia, the church was joined by the state. In December 1667 a carpenter named Elizar was paid the sum of thirteen altyn and two dengas by the Moscow Print Yard for the materials needed to make a large tympanum for the printing of land grants (*zhalovannye gramoty*).[143] The first batch was produced at the Moscow Print Yard the following year. The innovation turned out to be very successful, at least for a while. Almost overnight print replaced manuscript as the preferred medium for the production of grants of land in the name of the tsar. At one level they were typical blanks, consisting of a printed text of the generic components, with gaps for the name of the recipient, the details of the land to be given and the date of issue. Nevertheless, significant though they are in the history of the administrative uses of print in Russia, these *zhalovannye gramoty* mark only a temporary phase in the emergence of the genre of blank form. They were very grand documents: grand in size, grand in their eloquence and rhetoric, grand in their ornament and presentation. As far as possible they mimicked their handwritten predecessors. Their dense texts, with more than forty lines of print plus more than half a dozen lines in manuscript, filled one side of a full-sized printer's sheet. There were large ornamental woodcut headpieces including a double-headed eagle, and an enormous decorative woodcut initial letter stretching down half the length of the page. A large seal was attached on a cord, and the whole was often protected by a silk cloth. The seventeenth-century printed blank *zhalovannye gramoty* were solemn, memorable, permanent; and a passing fad. In the eighteenth century such luxurious productions tended to revert again to manuscript. The future of the blank form as a genre lay in its flimsier variants. It acquired permanence in the turn towards ephemerality.

The start of the third phase can again be dated fairly precisely. In the early months of 1714 Peter I put into effect two new and far-reaching initiatives in administrative printing. The first and best-known concerned the printing of decrees: henceforth all decrees of general significance were to be issued in print. The second initiative, barely known at all, concerned the printing of blank forms. The continuous tradition of the normal, ordinary, routine administrative blank form, consisting of just a few lines of civil type on small (roughly quarto- or octavo-sized) paper, is a phenomenon of approximately the final decade of Peter's reign (c. 1714–25). In particular, Peter sanctioned the spread of printed blanks for various types of pass and permit: permission to leave the country, certificates of exemption or release from military service, internal travel passes, permission for ships to dock or depart, certificates of the release of prisoners, licence to operate a ship as a privateer, authorisation to use the resources of the postal relays on official business.[144] There were also blank forms certifying the conferral of military rank; and in 1718 Peter sanctioned the mass distribution of blank forms for the purpose of swearing oaths of allegiance.[145]

The innovative or experimental nature of these blanks is evident partly in fluctuations of form, partly in uneven patterns of usage or longevity. Form was a problem both explicitly and implicitly. In June 1714, while on campaign against Sweden, Peter wrote a letter to his Grand Chancellor, Gavriil Golovkin, with two requests: to send blank certificates of rank (*patenty*), and 'a specimen letter, in Russian and German, showing in what manner passes [i.e. here documents of safe passage] are issued to those who are at war with each other, for the Swedes are requesting passes and we do not know how to write them'.[146] Uncertainty or instability of form is particularly evident in, for example, successive issues of certificates of exemption from military service between 1718 and 1722, when variations in shape, wording and modes of authentication, in blanks with essentially identical functions, suggest that there was as yet little sense of an established generic norm.[147] Of the early types of printed blank, only one seems to have instantly achieved a form that remained constant right through to the nineteenth century: the peasant passports for internal travel (*pokormezhnye*, also known as *plakatnye pasporta*), whose issue was specified by Petrine decree of 26 June 1724, and whose printed form was declared obligatory by decree of Catherine I on 1 February 1726 (Fig. 6.4).[148]

Not all the early initiatives in the issue of printed blanks turned out to be long-lasting. Printed travel permits quickly became an established genre, even if their functioning could be problematic. Printed blank authorisations to use the official postal transport services (*podorozhnye*) were probably also quite stable, from their likely introduction in the early period of Petrine blanks, possibly c. 1716–18,[149] though it is hard to locate surviving specimens before the latter part of the century. A certificate of conferral of rank was not so ephemeral as a travel permit, and the genre tended towards pomposity. Even the early versions were normally printed on parchment rather than on paper. However, after just two or three decades of the production of blanks, patents became fully printed documents, including the name of the recipient and the relevant rank.[150] Or rather, production reverted to a functional differentiation between handwritten and printed versions. The official original was a signed and sealed handwritten document. The printed version was a certified copy. In view of the huge numbers of patents issued (eventually for all military ranks and their civil equivalents, from Peter I to Alexander II)[151] a fully printed, individualised text was probably preferable to a blank for security purposes. However, the personalised printed patent also became, in effect, a kind of 'vanity' option that could be customised according to taste and price, in large format and with the addition of decorative engraved borders if desired. The shift seems to have occurred in the late 1730s. By the mid eighteenth century several presses were competing for the lucrative business of printing patents, while the ornamental engraved borders were a speciality of the Academy of Sciences press.[152]

Certificates of appointment were in constant demand. They survive in fairly large quantities, so their evolution can in principle be tracked. In contrast, printed oaths of allegiance were by nature

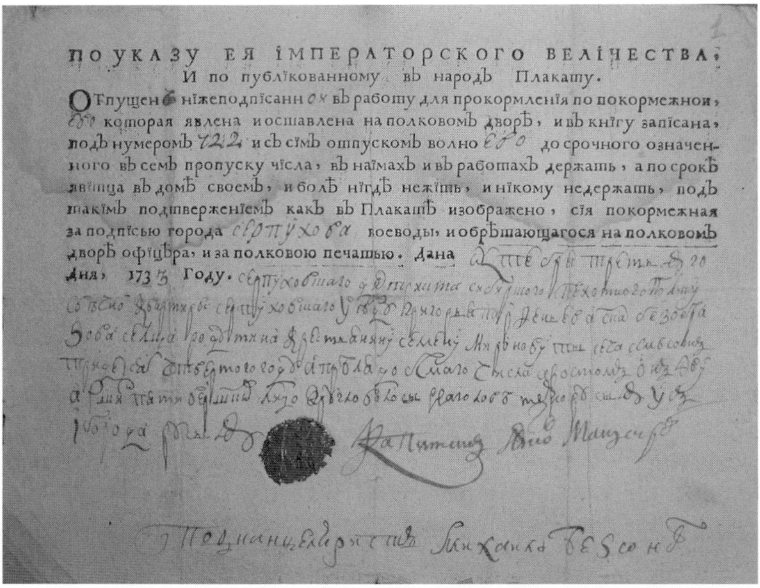

ПО УКАЗУ ЕЯ ІМПЕРАТОРСКОГО ВЕЛІЧЕСТВА;
И по публікованному въ народъ Плакату.
Отпущенъ ніжеподпісанн оу въ работу для прокормленія по покормежной, его которая явлена иоставлена на полковомъ дворѣ, и въ кнігу запісана, подъ нумеромъ 722 и съ сімъ отпускомъ волно его до срочного означенного въ семъ пропуску чісла, въ наімахъ и въ работахъ держать, а по срокѣ явітца въ домѣ своемъ, и болѣ нігдѣ нежіть, и нікому недержать, подъ такімъ подтверженіемъ какъ въ Плакатѣ изображено, сія покормежная за подпісью города серпухова воеводы, и обрѣтающагося на полковомъ дворѣ офіцѣра, и за полковою печатью. Дана
дня, 1733 Году.

Fig. 6.4: Passport issued to the peasant Semen Mironov on 3 October 1733 by the military governor of Serpukhov. St Petersburg Institute of History, Russian Academy of Sciences

occasional products, so have no continuous history, even though they were issued in large quantities. After the initial Petrine issue of oaths as printed blanks, they subsequently reverted to simple continuous texts, specifying that they were either to be signed at the bottom, or recited and affirmed by kissing the Bible and the Cross, but without the need for the name of the signatory to be inserted into a space left blank in the running text.[153] However, the logistics of their mass distribution led to a curious byproduct: special blanks that certified the dispatch and delivery of batches of the oaths, with spaces for writing in by hand the quantity of forms sent, and the names of the courier and of the intended recipient of each batch.[154] As far as I am aware these documents, apparently recorded at least from February 1725, are the earliest specimens of printed blanks for use in the internal regulation of an administrative process. Nor was this a 'one-off'. On 30 July of the same year Catherine issued a decree listing the appropriate use of her various titles in different types of official document.[155] Again, the decree was for wide distribution, and again it was accompanied by a printed blank recording the details of each batch.[156] The implication seems to be that the issue of such blanks had become part of regular procedure in the imperial bureaucracy.[157]

The fourth phase began towards the middle of the eighteenth century and involved the introduction of printed blanks into a new area of transactions: monetary exchange and circulation – first through promissory notes or bills of exchange, then through the issue of banknotes themselves. The first substantial Russian legislation on the uses of paper in monetary transactions was the *Statute on Promissory Notes* (*Ustav veksel'nyi*), approved on 16 May 1729 and published in Russian and German on 5 July.[158] The preamble states that, 'In European countries, instead of transporting money from place to place, money is transferred by the use of papers, called promissory notes [*veksel'*; from the German *Wechsel*]'.[159] Chapter 3 of the legislation presents fourteen templates and exemplars for different types of promissory note.[160] However, the wording of the statute implies an assumption that at this stage all documents were handwritten. The earliest Petersburg issue of a printed blank promissory note or bill of exchange that I have thus far seen is an engraved form dated February 1751, for the sum of 2,000 roubles, or 47.5 stuivers, payable in Amsterdam. However, this blank is in English, and its format is unlike that of any Russian printed or engraved blank of the period.[161] It reflects a certain ambient practice, but not local Russian usage. Evidence for the issue of Russian printed blanks for promissory notes accumulates towards the end of the 1750s. Like some of the earlier travel blanks, they tend to be explicitly named as, or linked to, decrees, rather than issued as self-standing documents. A decree of 6 November 1757 specified the use of promissory notes by the Salt Office (*Solianaia kontora*) in exchange for coinage in a long list of towns throughout the country.[162] A surviving specimen of such a blank, dated 10 October 1759, declares that 'according to the decree of Her Imperial Majesty this first promissory note is issued in St Petersburg from the Salt Office' to one Fedor Fisher, acknowledging receipt of 10,500 roubles in silver coin, the said sum to be paid out at the Salt Office in Moscow.[163] This is a relatively large document, 330 x 205 mm, in 'portrait' format like a decree. Legislation of 18 December 1759 stipulated that 'printed decrees' (*pechatnye ukazy*) were to be issued instead of cash to various categories of state contract supplier, and that such 'decrees' were to be treated as *vekselia*: valid for a specified period, with a specified percentage return, and freely transferrable for the period of their validity, instead of money or goods, until redeemed.[164] Later blanks for promissory notes tended to be engraved rather than typeset, as well as being somewhat smaller (typically c. 115 x 250 mm) on special paper issued for the purpose (*veksel'naia bumaga*).[165]

Banknotes followed at the end of the 1760s. Unlike all other blanks in this survey, the formal history of banknote issues has been mapped in meticulous detail, with information on every watermark, every denomination, every variant of printed or engraved design, even every signatory. As can also be the case with respect to West European and American printed ephemera, the extensive catalogues have often been produced for collectors as much as for historians.[166] The decree on the introduction of paper money was issued on 29 December 1768 (i.e. already in early January 1769 if we were to convert to the Gregorian calendar) and was printed for distribution on 1 February 1769.[167] The decree established two banks, in St Petersburg and Moscow, both of which were subordinate to the Directorate of Banks. They were to be responsible for the operations of the scheme, and would back the notes (*assignatsii*) with cash if required. The banknotes were printed at the Senate press, and had three textual components. First, the paper was watermarked with a text along all four sides: along the top and bottom 'Love for the fatherland/brings benefit to it', and down the sides 'state treasury'. Secondly, there was the printed text stating the exchange value and the serial number.[168] And, thirdly, there were the signatures: four of them, in sequence, at three different institutions. Before being dispatched to the Directorate of Banks, each note had to be signed by two senators. On receipt, the notes were signed again by the Head of the Directorate, and were then sent on to the respective branches in St Petersburg and Moscow, where they were to be certified with yet another signature, that of the branch director. Thus the printed banknote became valid currency only once it had been verified with the full sequence of four signatures.[169] This is why the banknotes can properly be classified as printed blanks, which become fully functional only when 'hybridised' with the handwritten additions.

The balance of security measures was adjusted from time to time. From 1785 the number of required signatures was reduced to three (two on the recto, one on the blank verso). From 1818 one of the two signatures on the recto was no longer handwritten but was added in facsimile as part of the engraved design. From 1851 – neatly at the upper boundary of the period covered by the present survey – all signatures on Russian paper money were engraved in facsimile.[170] With this change banknotes ceased to be hybridised blanks.

The fifth phase is marked by the extension of the use of blank forms into the cultural practices of elite institutions. The relevant documents are, in particular, attestations and invitations. This phase began around the mid eighteenth century, so that in a strict chronological sense it could be seen as a parallel rather than a subsequent development in relation to the fourth phase. However, it was distinct not just in its social space but in the fact that it was less systematic, slower to gather momentum and more limited in its impact. Certificates of institutional membership, graduation or honours are well suited to the issue of blanks. Although generally lumped together with 'ephemera', such documents are often expensively and elegantly produced: issued for an occasion but designed to be kept, to be 'treasured possessions'. They tended to be engraved rather than typeset.

On 1 January 1749 the Chancellery of the Academy of Sciences received a report on work carried out the previous year in the Academy's engraving workshop (*graviroval'naia palata*). Along with royal portraits, pictures of fireworks displays, book illustrations, maps and calibrations for barometers, thermometers and compasses, the list included the cutting of a plate with the text of large certificates for honorary members.[171] The report specifies that this was a single plate, but also refers to the documents' issue to 'members' in the plural, which implies that the purpose was to produce engraved blanks. Since I have not seen any examples printed from the plate that had reportedly been cut in 1748, this remains a supposition. Certainly there was no wholesale switch to engraved blanks for all such documents issued by the Academy. The parchment certificate (in Latin) presented to Mikhail Lomonosov in March 1751, attesting to his appointment as Professor of Chemistry (a post that he had in fact held since 1745), was handwritten, though in a manner easily replicable as an engraved blank.[172] Nevertheless, there can be little doubt that the practice of issuing elegantly engraved blanks for such purposes did become established among various elite institutions over the second half of the eighteenth century. For example, at least by January 1769 the Free Economic Society – founded in 1765 – was recognising the election of new members by issuing them with calligraphically engraved blanks printed on parchment.[173] By the early 1790s the Society's certificate saved on materials (it was printed on paper) but compensated with more elaborate design, including a floral border adorned with the double-headed eagle and the Society's own emblems of a beehive and a ploughman.[174] From the late eighteenth century masonic lodges produced printed blanks – usually in French, sometimes in German – for attestations of membership or rank.[175]

At a more junior level, though still at an illustrious institution: on completing the twelve years of their studies, graduates of the Imperial Society for Young Noblewomen (the Smolnyi Institute) received a bow with the monogram of the institute's foundress, Catherine II, and a handsomely engraved certificate. The certificate was typical of its genre: a large (48 x 39 cm) blank form with handwritten additions of the name of the recipient, the date of graduation and the signatures of the issuing authorities. Thus, for example, the certificate awarded to Praskovia Ivanovna Odintsova on 16 February 1794 attests the fact that she had been deemed worthy of public commendation on account of her assiduous devotion to her studies, her deportment and her acquisition of the knowledge, learning and accomplishments in handicrafts proper to her sex.[176] The certificate is signed (in Latin letters) by the venerable Sophie Delafon, who had been involved in the direction of the Institute since its foundation thirty years earlier, and (in Cyrillic) by three council members, and countersigned by the director and secretary of the chancellery.

Alongside elite attestations were elite invitations, passes and tickets. Archives of the Academy's engraving workshop include references to the production of invitations to theatrical performances in 1759 ('Alexander in India' at Oranienbaum) and to a puppet comedy in 1763, though it is not known whether these were blanks.[177] An annual entry pass for the imperial gardens, produced by the Academy's engraving workshop in May 1765 on commission from the Office of Buildings and Gardens, shows a tree in an urn standing at the entrance to a formal avenue. The pass leaves gaps for filling in the serial number and the final digit of the year for which the pass was valid.[178] An invitation from the Naval College to a celebratory dinner to mark the launch of two ships is engraved in a border that includes a representation of a ship being built.[179] A blank generic invitation to public meetings of the Academy of Sciences, produced in 1776 (with spaces for the date, the time and the name of the invitee) is engraved with a kind of still life of scientific instruments. The archive of the Academy preserves three successive states of this invitation: first, the frame and the pictorial elements; secondly, with the addition of the engraved wording with blank spaces; and finally a copy filled in by hand for a particular meeting and a particular person.[180]

The sixth phase in the history of printed blanks in Russia is most simply characterised as being the age of proliferation and diffusion: the age of the expansion of production beyond the capitals into the provinces; the age of the multiplication of forms and genres and styles and functions; the age when blanks were no longer issued solely by or on behalf of institutions of church and state, but when they came to be routinely commissioned by autonomous organisations, and by private individuals, in trade and commerce, in cultural and social interactions. Signs of this final phase can be glimpsed over the last couple of decades of the eighteenth century, and its growth accelerated rapidly in the first half of the nineteenth century. It is therefore roughly contemporary with, and should probably be linked to, the development – finally – of a diffuse market in the technology of printing: first, with the increase in commercial operations of the institutional presses, then with the appearance of private printers and publishers, and of the spread of printing to the provinces. It is surely no coincidence that the production of 'non-books' in general, and for present purposes of printed blanks in particular, flourished and diversified along with the development of a genuine market for print as such.

The commercial opportunities thereby created could be uncomfortable for those in control of the existing monopolies. When the setting up of private printing presses was permitted by Catherine II's decree of 1783, the engravers of the Academy of Sciences suddenly found that their labour was more widely marketable. They had skills and experience for which there was now increased demand, and some of them took the chance to supplement their earnings with a bit of moonlighting. Their principal employer, the Academy, was not happy. On 8 June 1786 the director of the Academy, Princess Elizaveta Dashkova, issued an order declaring that the Academy's engravers were not permitted to take on extra work at unauthorised presses that engaged, for example, in the printing of visiting cards.[181]

For present purposes the significant feature of blanks in this final phase is simply their range and diversity. In administration the issue of forms extended further into internal documentation, and from state institutions to local institutions. Thus already in the late 1790s the Moscow regional court was sending printed instructions to its district courts in the form of blanks with the addressee and the date to be filled in by hand.[182] At the start of the nineteenth century the government of Tambov issued blanks (crudely printed) in connection with the transport of prisoners.[183] Russian local governors and representatives abroad issued their own increasingly florid printed blank passports.[184] After the relatively brief interlude of printed land grants, the most prestigious imperial documents had already reverted to luxuriously decorative parchment manuscript, but for provincial authorities finely engraved blanks opened new vistas for visual pomposity. For example, an enormous blank (c. 76 x 58 cm, with a plate size of c. 49 x 42 cm), issued in 1803 by the Marshal of Nobility (*predvoditel' dvorianstva*) of the Kiev province (*guberniia*), and countersigned by eight district governors, affirmed its recipient's right to be included in the official books of noble genealogies.[185] In commerce, business and financial administration there are blank receipts and blank account books. The Russian Fire Insurance Company, founded in 1827, issued blanks for its policy documents.[186] Social and cultural institutions issued their own blank passes, such as the engraved blank annual pass for the English Club in Moscow for 1829;[187] or the season ticket at the Bolshoi theatre, for twenty performances in 1845, printed with gaps for the row and seat numbers, and with an additional blank on the reverse with spaces for the date, the name of the owner, the number of performances covered and the sum paid.[188] Society hosts and hostesses had a wide choice of styles from competing suppliers when ordering printed invitations to balls.[189] Libraries and bibliophiles ordered blank bookplates with spaces for shelfmarks or inventory numbers.[190] As for travel documents: eighteenth-century printed blank travel passes or *podorozhnye* were rather plain, unembellished, minimally informative and functional. By contrast the commercial stagecoach company that from 1820 operated a service between Moscow and St Petersburg differentiated itself with the issue of decorative tickets. In an upper panel they included a blank to be filled with the essential factual information: ticket number, number of passengers, departure time, cost etc.; but the lower half of the ticket consisted of the rules of travel, in Russian and German, and the whole document was set in a floridly engraved border somewhat in the style of manuscript headpieces.[191]

It would be hard to overestimate the diffusion of printed structural hybrids – blank forms – through the graphosphere in the first half of the nineteenth century: the range of institutional and private contexts, the geographical and social distribution, the diversity of functions from the truly ephemeral to the permanent possession. Indeed, towards the mid nineteenth century we begin to see signs of the phenomenon through which even the most ephemeral scraps may achieve a kind of secondary permanence as a cultural object, through hoarding, through collecting.[192]

How typical or distinctive is the pattern of development of blank forms that we have reconstructed for Russia? On the one hand, at the broadest level of generalisation, the printed blank is a much later phenomenon in Russia than in Western Europe, not only in terms of absolute chronology (the earliest known Muscovite blanks are some two hundred years later than the earliest known Latin blanks) but relative to the introduction of printing. In Western Europe blanks appear in the age of Gutenberg, in Moscow no printed blanks – and certainly no continuous practices of printing blanks – are known for approximately a century after the first locally printed books. One relevant factor in this, I have suggested, is the absence, in Russia, of a market in the technology of print, the absence of the phenomenon of the jobbing printer until the turn of the nineteenth century.[193] On the other hand, within this overall comparison, at the level of particular types of document, the contrasts are not so straightforward and can even be contradictory. In some areas the emergence of blanks can be seen as typologically analogous in Russia and in Western Europe, even if chronologically disparate. Sometimes the Russian introduction of varieties of form expressly followed West European precedent. And, as we will see in the next chapter, in the issue and use of some types of form Russia did not merely keep pace with developments elsewhere, but even anticipated them.

CHAPTER 7

Aspects of Authority and Status in the Graphosphere

The types of questions that prompted the previous chapters have been, by and large, real. That is to say, even when the surveys have been framed in metaphor (ecological, cartographic), they have been concerned mainly with identifying patterns in the world of things: traceable, verifiable, disputable, correctable. The type of questions in this penultimate chapter are more speculative, to do with attitudes and perspectives. A graphosphere is a complex system of signs that are intended or perceived to imply types of authority and status. Such implied or perceived authority and status may derive from, for example, the verbal message or subject, the producer or other source, the materials, the technology, the size and prominence, the design, the location, the language, the cost – or any combination of these and other qualities. Here we consider just a few indicative aspects. The choice is linked to two of the recurrent concerns of the present book: the dynamics of the relationship between printing and handwriting; and changes in the aesthetics of verbal display.

Technologies of Authority

Technologies of information have always been linked to the exercise of power, to the projection of authority, to mechanisms of control. To borrow imprecisely from the modern jargon of international relations, some of the uses of information technologies serve 'soft' power (prestige, cultural status, reputation etc.), others are implements of 'hard' power (regulation, administration, enforcement etc.). In this section the emphasis is on the latter.

The principal information technology of authority across the four centuries of the present survey was handwriting, especially through the rise of the bureaucratic institutions within which and from which it proliferated. We take this as a given. Beyond handwriting, one might argue that the earliest information technology of 'hard' power was the bodily mutilation of criminals and, in particular, its later and lettered substitute, branding.[1] Besides the punitive value of pain and humiliation, these were means of enabling the malefactor to be identified by 'reading' the markings on the body. Mutilation and branding should not be downplayed as information technologies merely on the grounds that they now seem barbaric and outmoded. They were prescribed, compulsory legislative actions that were also the permanent visible record of those actions, hence forms of administrative documentation. Branding was in its time a humane replacement for mutilation. As Nancy Kollmann comments with reference also to such practices in France, Germany and the Netherlands, 'early modern states marked bodies as communication and control'.[2] Furthermore, branding continued to be practised throughout the period covered by the present survey. It was not finally abolished until 1863.[3]

These were traditional means. Here we focus mainly on the newer technology, print. When, how and to what effect did print intrude upon, supplement or supplant handwriting as an instrument of authority and control? As we have seen, because of the particular conditions of print production in Russia, for the first two and a half centuries it was by default a medium of the authorities (and, by implication, of authority), whether in the projection of soft power or in the exercise of hard power. Handwriting *could be*, and very often was, used as an instrument of authority and control, but it was more diffuse in its production and more varied in its applications and functions. Print (or, rather, locally produced print rather than imported print) had no other context. In the absence of a genuine market in the technology, its link with authority was undiluted. We have mapped the administrative zones of Russian printing in the graphospheric ecology, and have traced the emergence of some of its genres, especially blank forms. However, such mapping and generic description do not in themselves determine or explain how print was applied as a practical instrument.

The systematic recourse to print as an instrument of active governance, both ecclesiastical and political, dates only from the mid seventeenth century, when a cluster of texts suggests a deliberate policy of asserting control not merely of print but through print. No definitive compilations of laws, whether of the church or of the state, were printed in Moscow until the state code (the *Ulozhenie*) of 1649, followed by the church's compilation of canon law (the *Kormchaia kniga*) in 1653. In the 1650s Patriarch Nikon used the presses as his instrument in what was, in effect, an equivalent programme of legislation in the sphere of liturgy and ritual, publishing the definitive series of revised liturgical texts that were intended to be, and were subsequently regarded as, definitive and obligatory for official Orthodoxy, and which became the principal embodiments of official error in the eyes of the schismatics. The 'correction' of texts is mentioned in early colophons as a reason for the use of print even in the mid sixteenth century,[4] but this is not the same as asserting a programmatic or systematic reform. The 'reformist' motif was stressed in a much later account of the origins of Muscovite printing, dating – again – from the mid seventeenth century.[5] At roughly the same time, in less monumental genres, the church also began to use print as a medium of legitimation in its internal practices, through 'non-books' such as certificates of ecclesiastical appointment, printed antimensia and certificates of absolution.

These mid-seventeenth-century initiatives in the exercise of control through print are notable both for the fact that they took place and for the fact that their success was uneven. Although the codes of law retained their formal authority, they were neither reprinted nor updated. In the codification and dissemination of laws, after the *Ulozhenie*, the *Kormchaia kniga* and the revised liturgical books, print ceased to be a medium of ecclesiastical or state legislation until the eighteenth century. The printed versions of Nikon's revised liturgical books remained definitive, but the formal acts of the legislative body – the Council of 1666–7 – that confirmed the reforms (while also condemning Nikon himself) were recorded only in manuscript. The sole printed output was a rhetorical refutation of the schismatics by Simeon Polotskii, commissioned by the tsar and the Council and published at the Moscow Print Yard in 1667 under the title *The Staff of Governance* (*Zhezl pravleniia*). Simeon's *Staff of Governance* consists mainly of point-by-point rebuttals of one hundred criticisms of the Nikonian reforms. In each case Simeon first cites the schismatics' objections, and then explains the Council's refutation. Many of the articles follow a formula. First the schismatics, as cited by Simeon, frame their complaints in terms of a reference to or citation from the Nikonian books. Sometimes they allude to particular texts, sometimes they refer to Nikon's editions in general with a phrase such as: 'in the new books it is printed that . . . ' (*V novykh knigakh napechatano* . . .).[6] In this representation of the polemic, Nikon's imposition through printing was an intrinsic, inseparable part of the reforms which the schismatics found so objectionable. This representation of the role of the Nikonian printed books remained in the tradition of Old Believer polemic against the official church. For example, in the classic Old Believer text, the *Responses of the Hermits to the Questions of the Hieromonk Neofit*, more commonly known as the *Responses of the Shore-Dwellers* (*Pomorskie otvety*),[7] compiled under the leadership of Andrei Denisov in 1723, a substantial section is devoted to a critique of the Nikonian reforms as represented by the 'new printed books' (*novopechatnye knigi*) as contrasted with the venerable 'old printed books' (*staropechatnye knigi*) and parchment manuscripts.

After the flurry of print in the mid seventeenth century, state prescription, as church legislation, reverted to manuscript. Even the preamble to the *Ulozhenie* implies that handwriting took precedence hierarchically, not just chronologically in the production process. It states that the tsar ordered many copies to be printed in order to ensure wide distribution throughout his realm, yet this is a brief note at the end of a fuller account of the solemnity with which the manuscript master copy was compiled and ceremonially ratified.[8] The colophon to the text of the 1654 decree on customs duties likewise focuses on the ceremonial of signing and sealing two copies for permanent preservation and record, rather than on the fact of printing for distribution.[9] The smaller-scale printed administrative documents of the late seventeenth century reflect similarly episodic choices. Arguably, in the seventeenth century only Nikon's liturgical books used print as a technology integral and necessary to establishing and maintaining of their own status.

Where print was merely useful, it could be adopted or discarded at will. In the exploitation of print as a tool of authority, the fundamental transition was from print as a choice to print as an obligation, from the optional to the compulsory. In this, too, the church anticipated the state. Apart from the Nikonian reforms, the other examples of a hard-power role for print are also linked to the performance of the liturgy. In 1675 Patriarch Ioakim instructed that all churches must use only antimensia that had been printed at the Moscow Print Yard.[10] This was not a 'one-off', individual, whimsical decree. In December 1697 Patriarch Adrian issued an extensive set of instructions about church life and worship. The first three of the seventy-two articles all declare the authority of print. Articles 1 and 3 prescribe that in all churches liturgical practice must be in accord with the correct printed service books (*knigi ispravny pechatnye*). Article 2 bans 'old' antimensia: all churches must acquire the new printed versions, duly consecrated.[11] With regard to the specific antimensia, Adrian's instruction superseded that of his predecessor Ioakim, but at the same time it affirmed and reinforced Ioakim's assertion of the status and authority of print in this context. The version was subject to alteration, but the technology was compulsory.

The state's next step towards broadening the repertoire of information technologies as tools of hard power was roughly contemporary with Patriarch Adrian's edict on antimensia. After bodily mutilation and branding, the first non-handwritten instrument was the beard token.[12] Indeed, there is a kind of inverse relationship between the two, since, for traditionalists, the shaving of beards was itself a kind of mutilation (physical, moral, even theological), against which a beard token provided protection (at a price). Peter I initiated his campaign against beards in August 1698, immediately after he returned from his eighteen-month 'Grand Embassy' to Western Europe. It would be easy to think of his tax on beards in light, anecdotal terms, but the action was radical, an offence not merely against Muscovite tradition and habit but against Orthodoxy, a diabolical violation of the proper, divinely established image of masculinity. The 1551 'Hundred Chapter' (*Stoglav*) Council had declared shaving to be heretical, iconography depicted demons as beardless, and a brief tract on the theological justification and necessity of beards is even attributed (probably spuriously) to Patriarch Adrian himself.[13] Although the first tokens were struck in 1698, legislation was linked to the batches issued in 1705.[14] Administratively the beard token was a permit which also functioned as a tax receipt: proof that the beard tax had been paid, and hence proof of permission to be bearded. In their specific form and purpose, beard tokens represent merely a curious episode. As an early phase and symptom of the emergence of information technologies functioning as mandatory tools of hard power, they deserve some prominence.

The obligatory use of print for state purposes began somewhat later. The crucial symbolic date is 16 March 1714, when Peter I announced that henceforth all of his own and the Senate's decrees on matters of general significance were to be disseminated in printed form.[15] This was the first Russian decree on the printing of decrees. The text suggests that it was initially intended as a device to aid distribution. However, it was quickly treated as a criterion of legitimation: not as a subsidiary convenience but as a necessary attribute of validity. After 16 March 1714 the printing of decrees did indeed become the norm. Indeed, it was more than the norm: it became the sole technology of official record for decrees. When Peter subsequently issued compilations of his decrees, nothing was included prior to March 1714.[16] The technological boundary marked, for him, a real turning point in the legislative history of his reign, as if the turn to print inaugurated the age of his authentic, permanently valid law-making.

Procedurally the printed versions continued to reflect a handwritten master copy, duly authenticated with seal and signature. The format and presentation of the printed versions highlighted their procedural provenance. Thus, following the West European practices that served as Peter's models, Petrine and all subsequent printed decrees included a graphic reminder of the presence of the seal in the manuscript original, usually through a roundel with the abbreviation *MP* (*mesto pechati*, 'the place of the seal'; cf. *L.S.* – *locus sigilli* – in Latin decrees of the time). However, although all kinds of instructions continued to be issued by various state institutions in manuscript, there was no retreat from the decision of March 1714, either by Peter or by any of his successors. Peter's decree on the printing of the decrees was a pivotal point in the institutionalisation of print as an instrument of authority.

Apart from decrees, as we have seen, the *practice* of printing a range of administrative documents also accelerated notably from the middle of the second decade of the eighteenth century. However, apart from a stipulation by the Senate regarding *podorozhnye*, there is no specific reference to printing as a *requirement* for the remainder of Peter's reign. In the legislative record it was Peter's successor, Catherine I, who extended the obligatory use of print from central regulation into administrative documentation. By a decree of 1 February 1726 she declared that henceforth peasants travelling within their own region (*uezd*), or up to thirty versts from their villages, may continue to do so with handwritten permits from the landowner. However, peasants travelling outside their own region, or beyond thirty versts from their village, must be in possession of a valid *printed* passport. The blanks for the relevant documents were to be printed by the Senate's press, distributed to the regions by the department of expenditure (the *Kamer-kollegiia*), and issued through the local governors. This two-tier system of permissions had already been laid down by Peter in what is known as his *plakat* of 26 June 1724. The document for long-distance travel thus came to be known as a *plakatnyi pasport*. In view of his broader initiatives in the printing of passes, it is possible that Peter intended that these, too, would be printed, but the explicit requirement was first articulated by Catherine.[17]

What were the contexts and justifications for these measures? Efforts to restrict, control, authorise and otherwise oversee the movement of people were virtually as old as travel. In Muscovy the restrictions had become particularly tight. The assumed norm was immobility. The problem was how to cope with, oversee, track and regulate mobility that was deemed permissible or even necessary. The *Ulozhenie* of 1649 affirmed that peasants were to remain on the land, townspeople in their towns, soldiers with their units. It also included a brief article specifically about the issue of documents (*proezzhie gramoty*) for foreign travel, as well as several other references to passes for domestic travel.[18] Petrine anti-vagrancy legislation claimed two main justifications, one military, the other fiscal. Decrees of 19 March and 30 October 1719 stressed that military desertion was a very serious offence, as was failure to report deserters, and that proof of legitimate travel had to be provided in the form of written documents: nobody may travel from town to town or from village to village without the appropriate travel permit or passport (here, for the first time in legislation, designated by the word *pashport*).[19] However, the reason for the more detailed ruling of 1724 on peasant passports was ostensibly fiscal, related to the imposition and collection of the poll tax.[20] Unmonitored internal travel was a threat to the state's income, since it might enable unspecified numbers of people to evade the census and hence to avoid taxation. A detailed memorandum setting forth the principles for an obligatory internal passport (here termed a *erlyk*) probably dates from the early stages of planning for the poll tax.[21] A decree dated 6 April 1722, on the return of fugitive peasants and their families, stipulated – as a new requirement – that henceforth any peasant who was allowed to travel in order to take paid work must be provided with a letter of release, signed by the lord or overseer (*prikazchik*) or priest.[22] Peter's *plakat* of 26 June 1724 dealt mainly with those local officials who were responsible for the administration for the poll tax. This was the context in which the system of internal peasant passports came to be articulated.

Peter was not the only European ruler concerned to restrict internal travel, nor was Catherine I the only European ruler to stipulate the use of print. Printed blanks for passes were issued in several jurisdictions from time to time in the sixteenth and seventeenth centuries, sometimes in large quantities, but such initiatives rarely solidified into continuous obligatory traditions.[23] During the period when the Petrine project was being devised and enacted, both Germany and, in particular, France introduced passport legislation with the express aim of tackling the problem of vagrants and military deserters.[24] In France suggestions for printed soldiers' passes appear in memos as early as 1701 and 1712, and a royal ordinance made such passes mandatory in 1716. In 1724 it was declared that vagrants should have printed passes.[25] The approximate synchronicity with the equivalent measures in Russia is striking. However, imitation was not a sufficient explanation either for the adoption of the relevant laws in Russia or for the fact that, as we shall see, there were significant differences between Russia and Western Europe in subsequent practice.

The perceived advantages of mandatory print, in the production of decrees and of peasant internal passes, were both general and particular. The general advantages were those that might be expected of the technology. For documents requiring large-scale replication and widespread distribution, print was more reliable and convenient than handwriting, and also cheaper. It was more effective than handwriting as a guarantor of standardisation. Peter's measure in administrative print should be seen partly in the context of his complaints about the detrimental effects of distorted or selective transmission of texts in manuscript. Manuscript transmission meant that responsibility for textual integrity was devolved, and scribes or local officials could take short-cuts. Peter accepted that some local handwritten copying was necessary and inevitable, but that does not mean that he was comfortable with it. In one of his more bad-tempered decrees, issued in April 1722, he railed against sloppy copying, and insisted that no handwritten copy of a decree may be accepted as valid until it had itself been verified, signed and sealed as correct. And this instruction was itself to be printed and distributed and displayed as a permanent reminder in the offices of all judicial personnel.[26] Indeed, Peter's assiduous recourse to administrative print in the final decade of his reign can be set against his periodic expressions of frustration not just at the unreliability of handwriting but at its uncontrollability. On 10 August 1718 he issued a decree forbidding anyone except 'church teachers' to write behind closed doors (*zapershis' pisat'*). The decree went on to state that if anyone knew that writing was taking place in private, and failed to report it, and if the writing was discovered, and was found to be seditious, then the person who failed to report it would be subject to the same punishment as the person who wrote it.[27] This was extreme, and unenforceable even in Peter's time. But he was consistent. As early as January 1701 he had extended his disapproval of private handwriting even into the monasteries: no monk was to be permitted paper and ink in his cell; any writing was to be done only with permission, in the refectory, 'openly and not secretively'.[28] Despite the state's reliance on handwriting for the overwhelming majority of its business, Peter – as other rulers before and after him – abhorred, in the diffuseness of handwritten production, its potential as a medium of subversion.

The decree of April 1722 implies that, besides standardisation, Peter saw print as an important aid to dissemination. From the late seventeenth century the texts of decrees often specified the means of their own dissemination: most commonly public reading, plus display in public places. The texts of Peter's decrees became ever more insistent. The most regularly stated reason, derived from the well-known formula in Roman law, was that ignorance of the law should be no excuse for non-compliance with the law.[29] If one expects laws to be obeyed, people must know about them; and, if one expects to impose sanctions for law-breaking, people must be given at least a reasonable opportunity to know what the law is. If they then fail to take such opportunity, the fault is theirs. This was the reason given in Peter's decree of 16 March 1714 insisting on the use of print. It was 'in order that all may be informed'. For this purpose, print was an addition to the range of devices, not their full replacement. It was necessary but not sufficient. Peter's multimedia instructions for dissemination could include: distribution to all offices of central, local and ecclesiastical administration; internal display in such offices; declamation in public places; posting on gates and on the entrances to churches; reading aloud by priests on major feast-days when one would expect churches to be at their most crowded.

Apart from its reliability, the use of print was more economical. Print was by no means always a cheaper alternative to handwriting, but in these contexts, with respect to the relatively large-scale replication of relatively simple, standard documents, the use of print led to clear and acknowledged savings. Catherine's decree on printed passports is explicit on this point. The peasant passports were not issued free. Peter's *plakat* had specified a cost of two kopeks. In her decree of 1 February 1726 Catherine halved the charge to one kopek, 'since these passes will be printed, not handwritten, and there will be no labour in the writing'.[30] Catherine changed the price because she was changing the technology.

These were among the general advantages of the technology of print that were cited as reasons for its introduction, whether as an additional device or as the sole permitted device, in the production of some of the key types of document relevant to the exercise of social control. The more fundamental issue, however, was security. Print was a major barrier to forgery. Catherine's decision to impose print was taken in the light of reports that peasants were turning up in Simbirsk, on the Middle Volga (the need for seasonal labour along the Volga was one of the main reasons for legitimate peasant mobility) with all kinds of forged (*vorovskie*) handwritten passes, even fakes that had ostensibly been signed and sealed by the relevant authorities.[31] Henceforth, in order that there be no more forged passes, the permits for long-distance travel were to be printed and distributed centrally.

Forgery of official documents was a traditional and never-ending irritant. Seals and signatures were the old methods. In 1699 Peter I had introduced stamped paper (*gerbovaia bumaga*), then, from 1724 (since stamps, too, were susceptible to forgery), officially watermarked paper.[32] Variations on stamping, sealing, signing, watermarking and engraving continued to be developed and refined. Print was but one weapon in the battle.

The relative security of print, as a defence against forgery, was likewise cited in the near-contemporary French provision for printed passes. However, the differences are as instructive as the similarities. Print was a security device because it was less accessible than handwriting. Both in France and in Russia it was far simpler to find a competent and amenable scribe than to acquire a specially printed document. However, in France the 'added value' of the technology was comparatively weak, because of the diffusion of presses. In Russia, at least until the late eighteenth century, because of the official monopoly of ownership of the means of production, a printed document could *only* be official. Print was not merely an additional protection against forgery, it was close to being an absolute guarantor of authority and authenticity (except in the very rare instances when quasi-official Cyrillic documents were printed abroad).[33] This difference perhaps helps to explain why in France the 1724 measure was an isolated attempt. A standard requirement for printed passes was introduced only after the Revolution of 1789.[34] In the last quarter of the eighteenth century it was common for travellers from various European states to obtain printed passes from their countries' embassies or consuls-general while abroad, but the domestic issue of printed passes was rare.[35] In Russia, by contrast, the legislation on printed passes for internal travel was regularly re-affirmed, indeed expanded, through the century. In 1732 a provision equivalent to the peasant *plakat* passport system was introduced for itinerant monks. From 1744 merchants and postal riders were also required to carry printed passes, likewise produced on the Senate's presses.[36]

We have become used to noting delays in Russia's assimilation and exploitation of the potential of print. In some instances the monopolistic control of the means of production can be cited as a factor in such delays. Here, however, with regard to the expanded use of print as a guarantor of documentary authenticity, the monopoly put the Russian authorities at an advantage. The sporadic use of printed internal travel passes in Western Europe pre-dates their appearance in Russia, but Russia was well in advance of any West European country in establishing print as the required norm for internal travel permits. In respect of foreign travel, too, although it is harder to track developments through legislation, Russia seems to have used print consistently earlier than was usual elsewhere in Europe. Printed passports for foreign travel in Europe did not become common until the late eighteenth century, and were not normally issued in Britain before the mid nineteenth century. In Russia the first known printed passport for foreign travel dates to 1719, and the form remained quite stable thereafter.[37]

The peasant *plakat* passports (or *pokormezhnye*) and their successors were innovative in Russia in another respect. As we saw in Chapter 6, over the final decade of Peter's reign several types of permit and pass came to be produced on printed blanks. All of them stated that the bearer was entitled to travel, but none of them – including permits for foreign travel – gave any information about the person of the bearer, apart from their name and sometimes their rank. The *plakat* passports and their successors were different. The legislation of 1724 required physical details of the bearer: 'height, face and distinguishing features'.[38] Curiously, until the nineteenth century the standard printed form itself did not specify which details were to be provided, but the legal requirement was nevertheless observed and the description of relevant physical features was inserted by hand at the end of the document. So, for example, the passport issued to the peasant Semen Mironov in October 1733 (see Fig. 6.4) notes that he was two arshins and five *vershki* (just under five and a half feet) in height, had a round face, and fair hair, moustache and beard. Thus the *plakat* passports were the first – and for a long time the only – regularly issued Russian documents that served the dual functions that we have come to regard as normal for passports: both as travel permit and as identity document.

Such, at any rate, was the law. This is not to say that the practice of using printed documentation worked perfectly ever after, or even that it was implemented consistently. Far from it. Administrative systems based on a technology are only as robust as the human input and as the logistical support. From their inception and through the eighteenth century one could equally well tell the story of printed documents in terms of their glitches, inefficiencies, unintended consequences. Logistical failures at the centre could make compliance impossible. Problems could arise, for example, as a result of inadequate supplies, or difficulty of access to the supply line. The church complained that there was no point in requiring a printed decree to be read in every parish if the state only supplied a small fraction of the number of copies needed. Quite commonly the printed attestations of service rank state that several years had passed between the appointment and the printed certification.[39]

A flaw in the supply of printed 'official statement' documents, such as decrees, or even in the supply of printed attestations of appointment, had few consequences beyond institutional irritation or personal pique. In the case of decrees, handwritten copies continued to be produced, and if necessary could be verified against a printed exemplar. In the case of certificates of appointment, the printed version was in any case not the obligatory authoritative version. Far more serious were the potential consequences of a defect in the supply of documents intended for daily use across the country, and whose printed form was a prerequisite for substantial areas of economic activity. The logistical networks essential for the reliable supply of such documents were complex and fragile. The inefficient or irregular supply of adequate numbers of blank printed passes from the centre to the provinces could have devastating implications for activities dependent on seasonal migrant labour. As early as July 1726, in the summer immediately following Catherine I's decree on printed peasant passports, there was a severe shortage of labour to work on the boats along the Volga and its tributaries, with the result that the movement and delivery of vital goods, especially salt, had come to a virtual standstill.[40]

Throughout the century the pendulum swung between, on the one hand, legislative insistence on the requirement for printed passports and, on the other hand, local or temporary exemptions which recognised the practical difficulties created by strict adherence to the rule. Rigorous adherence, as demanded, for example, by decrees of Elizabeth in May 1743 and March 1744, could result in serious economic losses, such as the episode, in the early 1740s, when the Stroganov family complained that the passport laws contributed to yet another crisis of salt production.[41] Practical adjustments were introduced from time to time, such as the provision, in July 1746, that printed passports for those working in Astrakhan could be issued for up to two or three years, in view of the distance that would have to be travelled for their more regular renewal.[42] In July 1798 the emperor Paul issued a decree legitimising the practice of renewing passports *in absentia*.[43] The concessions were never enough. In practice, either economic activity was damaged through rigorous application of the rules, or handwritten (stamped and sealed) documents were nevertheless accepted – which further exacerbated the problem of forgery.[44]

If, as in these cases, problems were attributable to defects in the *efficiency* of the supply lines, then a consequence of the requirement for print was that documents became too difficult to acquire legitimately. Alternatively, if there were weaknesses in ensuring the *integrity* of the supply line, then printed blanks became too *easy* to acquire (albeit illicitly) and their security was compromised. Even Catherine's legislation of February 1726 recognised the potential problem, stipulating that, on receipt of the blank passes from the *Kamer-kollegiia*, the local authorities must keep them securely, 'in case anybody should obtain such a printed pass and perpetrate just such a forgery' as those which the legislation was designed to avoid.[45] Similarly, in February 1742 the empress Elizabeth instructed the Senate that the office of postal services was to stop issuing printed blank travel authorisations and revert instead to properly authenticated handwritten documents – on the grounds that all kinds of private individuals were getting hold of the blanks and travelling free, which was leading to the impoverishment of postal workers.[46] Here the problem was over-supply rather than under-supply! And it was endemic wherever one found officials prepared to cut corners for convenience or to do favours for friends. The archives preserve some nice examples, from later in the century, of printed *podorozhnye* signed, but otherwise still blank (Fig. 7.1).[47] Matvei Komarov's version of the story of the notorious Moscow criminal and police informant of the 1740s and early 1750s, Vanka Kain, published in 1779, mentions the capture of a fugitive soldier in possession of 'forged printed passports'. On investigation, it turned out that the soldier had acquired them from a certain *pomeshchik*, who, in turn, confessed to having obtained up to three hundred printed blanks from a guard at the Senate, who had stolen them from the Senate's printing house.[48]

The fluidity of late-eighteenth-century practice is neatly exemplified by three passports from the archive of the merchant of the third guild (that is,

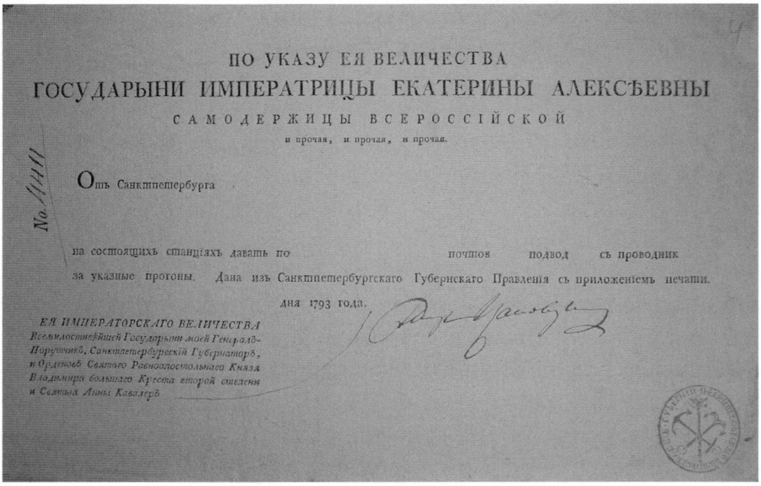

ПО УКАЗУ ЕЯ ВЕЛИЧЕСТВА
ГОСУДАРЫНИ ИМПЕРАТРИЦЫ ЕКАТЕРИНЫ АЛЕКСѢЕВНЫ
САМОДЕРЖИЦЫ ВСЕРОССІЙСКОЙ
и прочая, и прочая, и прочая.

Отъ Санктпетербурга

на состоящихъ станціяхъ давать по почтов подвод съ проводник
за указные прогоны. Дана изъ Санктпетербургскаго Губернскаго Правленія съ приложеніемъ печати.
дня 1793 года.

ЕЯ ИМПЕРАТОРСКАГО ВЕЛИЧЕСТВА
Всемилостивѣйшей Государыни моей Генералъ-Поручикъ, Санктпетербургскій Губернаторъ, и Орденовъ Святаго Равноапостольнаго Князя Владимира большаго Креста второй степени и Святыя Анны Кавалеръ

Fig. 7.1: A breach of security: signed blank permit for the use of official transport (*podorozhnaia*), 1793.
St Petersburg Institute of History, Russian Academy of Sciences

of the lowest category) Nikita Matveevich Khabcheev, from the remote district of Ustiuzhna Zheleznopolskaia, about four hundred miles to the north of Moscow. Three of his travel documents survive, each valid for a year; and all three are different.[49] The first, issued in March 1792, is a handwritten pass, authorised by seal and by local officials (the *burgomistr* and *ratman*). The second, issued in February 1794, begins with the same wording, is likewise authorised with a seal and by the signature of the *ratman*; however, it is not a manuscript but was filled in on a printed blank. The third, from May 1797, is again handwritten, but authorised by stamp rather than by seal, and by the signature of a different official (the *kaznachei*). Moreover, it uses a different set of verbal formulae, following precisely the phrasing, and even the layout, of the printed forms prescribed for peasant *plakatnye* passports, despite the fact that Khabcheev was not a peasant, and that handwritten *plakatnye* passports had repeatedly, for decades, been officially declared invalid. I do not know whether any or all of Nikita Khabcheev's three types of passport were genuine or forged. There is no indication that any was ineffectual.

The *reductio ad absurdum* of the potential efficacy of non-standard, non-printed documents is the anecdote in Aleksandr Pushkin's *Account of a Journey to Arzrum During the Campaign of 1829*, published in 1836. The author is on his way to the front. Arriving in Kars, he requests horses to enable him to reach the Russian army camp. A local officer asks him to show his written authorisation. Judging it unnecessary to search for the right documents ('in view of [the officer's] Asiatic features'), Pushkin hands over the first piece of paper he finds in his pocket. The officer studiously examines it, and orders that 'His Excellency' (i.e. Pushkin) should be given horses, as authorised by the document. Only then, after it is returned to him by the officer, does Pushkin bother to look at the piece of paper. It is the draft of a poem ('To a Kalmyk Girl') that he had written earlier on his journey.[50] Pushkin's trivial story of the draft poem that served as his authorisation for the procurement of horses – with or without the ethnically charged irony at the expense of the illiterate local official with 'Asiatic features' – depends on the recognition of the fact that, in the social life of documents, there is a far from perfect relationship between prescription and perception. The aura of the piece of paper with writing, of the perceived document, could be powerful enough and effective enough, irrespective of the technology that produced the words (and, in this example, irrespective of the words themselves). Equivalent anecdotes are surely widespread wherever elites take delight in mild mockery of the uneducated.[51]

What, then, was or was not the impact of the laws that decreed the obligatory use of print? Or, indeed, of the governmental and institutional monopoly on the ownership of presses? Forgery, which had been a concern under Peter before the introduction of printed passports (as reflected in Pososhkov's project of the early 1720s), was cited as the reason for introducing the requirement for print. And forgery – or, at best, a bending or ignoring of the rules – continued to be a *leitmotif* across the century long after the introduction of mandatory print. Where does this leave the authority of print? Should we conclude that the authority of print was a *desideratum* of successive rulers, but an illusion in practice? That monopoly ownership of the means of production did not in fact enhance the efficacy of print as a tool of social control?

Just because laws are flouted or broken does not mean that they are ineffectual or pointless. We would not argue that laws against homicide are empty *desiderata* merely because murders continue to be committed. The fact that there is tax evasion does not mean that tax regulations have no practical function. When is the rule valid despite exceptions, and at what point do exceptions in fact become the rule? It is not surprising that handwritten documents, especially when made to look official, continued to be treated as authoritative, since the overwhelming majority of authoritative documents – that is, of documents issued by the authorities – were indeed handwritten. Through until the nineteenth century those types of document formally singled out for the *obligatory* use of print were a very small subcategory. So, if that created obstacles, people sometimes found ways of coping or of cheating. However, despite periodic concessions and relaxations, and despite the persistent problem of forgery, a sense of a norm was real. In the 1740s associates of Vanka Kain may have found ways to subvert the system by siphoning off printed blanks before they were even circulated – but this merely underscores the fact that printed forms were acknowledged to be necessary. If the laws on printed forms had had no traction, the Stroganovs would have had no grounds for complaint about the disruptive effect on seasonal labour. Pushkin might have enjoyed duping the credulous officer in distant Kars, but earlier, while still within the empire and still on the imperial post-relay routes, he had cause to be grateful for his official *podorozhnaia*. Arriving in Dusheti late at night, exhausted and with nowhere to stay and nobody to vouch for him, suspicious of a town apparently suspicious of him, he produced his *podorozhnaia*, upon which 'the blessed document had its effect' and he was given a room and some wine.[52]

The two episodes from Pushkin's narrative underscore the malleability of the relationship between intention and perception, between instrumentality and subjectivity. Hence they also undermine somewhat our initial distinction between uses of information technologies in the service of power. The main technology of power – hard and soft – was handwriting. Beyond handwriting, and branding, and beyond the episode involving beard tokens, print had a limited but far from negligible and in some respects distinctive function as a tool of coercion.

Authority of Technologies

One could argue, in circular fashion, that any technology that becomes established in its graphospheric niche probably must have acquired, to a sufficiently functioning extent for a sufficient proportion of its producers and viewers, an aura appropriate to its role. The embroidered inscription on a devotional textile, the lapidary inscription on a gravestone, the legend and abbreviations on a coin or medal, the engraved personalised inscription on the retirement watch, the painted label of the saint on the icon, the ceramic emblem on the stove tile: all become necessary attributes of the objects. Although they may rarely be read, their presence matters both visually and materially: it matters that the funerary text is chiselled rather than painted, that the legend on the medal is struck or cast rather than subsequently scratched. Here, again, we focus on print: mainly in itself, and to some extent in its relations with handwriting. The authoritativeness of print merits particular attention because of the distinctive history of Russian print in relation to the authorities.

The authorities in Russia always regarded printing as their business, whether in a narrow sense of ownership or in a broad sense of oversight and regulation. As I have stressed, from its introduction in the mid sixteenth century through to the relaxation of the rules at the end of the eighteenth century, printing in Russia was an almost complete monopoly of the government and of a small number of licensed religious, educational and scholarly institutions. Where ownership ended, censorship began: first through oversight of imported print, whose production lay outside Russian control; then, after the ending of the monopoly of ownership, through censorship of printing in Russia. Throughout the period, therefore, the authorities either maintained control *of* print or introduced measures to exercise control *over* print. What marked print out was not the fact that it fulfilled official and approved functions (as did handwriting), but the fact that for so long these were virtually its only functions. Print was therefore authoritative almost by definition, and certainly by intended mission.

Apart from its institutional provenance, what were the particular qualities of print that, at various times and in various degrees, contributed to a sense of its authoritativeness? I have already touched on the role of print as a guarantor of authenticity. Here we consider three other qualities that were attributed to print: as a technology of correctness; as a bearer of prestige; and as a means to profit.

When a medieval scribe addresses the reader in his colophon, he begs indulgence for any errors that he has perpetrated in writing out his text. When the mid-sixteenth-century Muscovite printers addressed their readers in colophons, they declared that, by contrast with the work of scribes, their texts were correct. This was a radical and important claim for technological superiority, made in the first printers' colophons in the mid sixteenth century and repeated at key moments for the next hundred years and more. From Ivan Fedorov through to the late seventeenth century, the main explicit claim for print, as articulated by those with a stake in its production, was that print was a guarantor of – or at any rate major aid to – correctness. According to Fedorov in the colophon to his first book, the 1564 Moscow *Apostol*, Ivan IV had instructed that devotional texts be acquired for distribution to churches, but discovered that very few were useful, since their readings had been corrupted by the ignorance and carelessness of scribes. The tsar therefore 'considered how to arrange that books should be printed, as among the Greeks and in Venice and Italy and among other peoples, in order that the sacred books might henceforth be issued correctly'.[53] The printers of the 1568 Moscow Psalter, Nikifor Tarasiev and Nevezha Timofeev, likewise claimed in their colophon that Ivan IV set up a printing press in Moscow 'for the cleansing and correction of [mistakes by] uneducated and unskilled scribes'.[54]

The claim is not that all scribes are always wrong, but that print is more reliably right. The assertion rests partly on an implied affirmation of the printers' own competence: they are neither uneducated nor unskilled. Also implied, however, are features of the production process. A printing house has proof-readers to help ensure the correctness of the text; and print ensures that the same (correct) version is replicated. Every scribal copy risks corruption. Every printed copy is as correct as its prototype.

To what extent, in the mid sixteenth century, were these claims to technological superiority shared or acknowledged? We have the printers' statements, but very little else. We do have evidence that, on the eve of the appearance of the first Moscow-printed books, concern was being expressed in high places about scribal inconsistency and ineptitude, and about how to prevent the circulation and use – even in the Liturgy – of corrupt books. This was among the questions put by the tsar to the 'Hundred Chapter' (*Stoglav*) Council of 1551. It would be tempting to think that the introduction of printing was the response. However, the Council's practical advice refers only to vigilance in monitoring the production and distribution of manuscripts.[55] There is no reference to an alternative technology. The best we can say is that the early colophons do address a current issue, do speak to their patrons' known concerns about the defects of manuscript copying.

The mid-sixteenth-century claim for the correctness of print did not become standard. In Moscow it seems to have been specific to the early exponents in the 1560s. Even Ivan Fedorov backed off somewhat. At the end of his extensive and far from reticent 1574 Lviv colophon he added the conventional scribal plea to the reader to look indulgently on any errors, since 'this was written not by the Holy Spirit, and not by an angel, but by a sinful and corruptible hand'.[56] Since Fedorov here refers to the 'writing' rather than the 'printing', he is perhaps alluding to his composition of the polemical narrative colophon rather than to the text of the *Apostol* (unless the use of the word 'write' can be explained as a mechanical transposition of the conventional formula). However, the 1589 colophon of Andronik Timofeev Nevezha, in the first book printed in Moscow after the twenty-year hiatus, makes no claim to 'correctness' and declares no specific superiority over scribes. According to Nevezha, the press was set up by Tsar Fedor Ivanovich 'so that his realm might be filled with printed divine books'.[57] That is, he refers only to the value of print as an aid to dissemination. Nevezha then signs off with the traditional plea for indulgence for any defects in the book that he, a sinner, has laboured to produce.[58] However, for his next colophon, to his Festal Triodion, completed in November 1591, Nevezha composed a more extensive and grandiloquent peroration: the role of Tsar Fedor Ivanovich in founding a press is likened to that of the Kievan prince Vladimir in bringing Christianity to Rus six centuries earlier. Nevezha echoes Fedorov in the assertion that printed books help bring the word of God to newly colonised areas such as Kazan and Astrakhan, and he repeats the assertion that printed books can be cleansed of the accumulation of scribal errors.[59] Print as correctness, or at any rate as correction, is again mentioned in Nevezha's colophon to his Octoechos of 1594.[60] However, his subsequent colophons and prefaces continue to focus on praise of his royal employers (transferring from Fedor Ivanovich to

Boris Godunov) but make no mention of correctness and correction – either the correction of scribal errors by print, or the readers' indulgent correction of his own errors.[61]

In the sixteenth century, therefore, the printers' claim to the 'correctness' of their medium was, like so many aspects of sixteenth-century Muscovite printing history, episodic. And it is a claim made in rather general terms, without reference to how correctness was to be determined. It seems to imply consistency achieved through a combination of proof-reading and exact duplication. This was not necessarily empty rhetoric. The production of Muscovite printed books was indeed, at times (particularly in the first half of the seventeenth century), linked to attempts to produce corrected texts.[62] However, the systematic application of print as a vehicle for fixing the results of a specific programme of textual correction was a phenomenon of the mid seventeenth century, in connection with the reforms of devotional books carried out under the direction of Patriarch Nikon and embodied in the publications of the Moscow Print Yard.

The Nikonian reforms were introduced with the rhetoric of using print as the technology of textual correction and correctness. Print was in the front line of the attack on, or the defence against, potential heresy. But the debates and polemics around the reforms were more nuanced in their 'philological' assessments. Nobody argued that print was *intrinsically* correct. It could reinforce correctness, but equally it could magnify error. It was as reliable as its provenance, as worthy as those who produced it, as valuable or as dangerous as their piety and skills enabled it to be. The proponents and the opponents of the reforms disagreed about the outcomes, but shared a kind of critical discourse on the comparative merits of different kinds of source materials. They debated the value not just of print and manuscript as such, but about the implications of antiquity, materials and provenance: about correctness in relation to old (parchment) manuscripts, paper manuscripts, 'old printed' books, 'new printed' books, Greek manuscripts, Greek printed books.[63] Provenance trumped technology. Nikon claimed to base his revisions on readings from old Greek and Slavonic manuscripts. In an anti-Nikonian critique, the new printed texts were tainted in part because they used new Greek printed texts, which had been produced by Latins and were hence corrupt.[64] Thus, whereas mid-sixteenth-century colophons had emphasised a contrast between correct print and incorrect (or at best unreliable) manuscript, by the mid seventeenth century there was scope for a contrast between correct print and incorrect print. Print's aura of authoritativeness did not disappear just because it was incorrect. Incorrect print was even more dangerous because of its aura of authoritativeness, amplified by its potential range of duplication and dissemination. And this was all the more reason for print to remain in the correct hands, or to be approved through the correct channels. Controlled print was by definition correct print in the eyes of those who controlled it.

The authority of print was curiously affirmed by those who most vehemently and consistently opposed the print of the authorities. Sometimes cultural and technological inertia (otherwise known as tradition) is weakest where we might expect it to be strongest – as is illustrated in the Old Believer response to the relaxation of the state and institutional stranglehold on the ownership of presses. Since print was the technology of the Nikonian reforms, and since Old Believers were for more than a century excluded from access to presses, it could be (and sometimes is) assumed that Old Believers formed and nurtured a consistent counter-culture based on the authority of handwriting *as opposed to* print.[65] Denied official access to print production for several generations, Old Believers did indeed develop a culture of manuscripts that flourished through to the twentieth century. It was robust and distinctive, and it was kept alive in the diffusion of the relevant skills through local communities. However, the technology of necessity was not necessarily the only technology of choice. In the first place, following the 'philological' debates of the mid seventeenth century, Old Believers retained a distinction between the 'old printed' and the 'new printed' books. Pre-Nikonian printing, as an implied or actual source for handwritten texts, retained an aura of authoritativeness and correctness. Secondly, when Old Believers did manage to find pathways to print, they were not slow in choosing to follow them.

Old Believer printing before the late 1770s was scarce and sporadic. It began with two Horologia and a Psalter commissioned from the press of Maksim Voshchanka in Mogilev (then part of Poland) in 1701 and 1705 respectively, which served as the models for subsequent Mogilev editions in the 1730s, as well as for a Psalter printed in Chernihiv in 1717.[66] This latter is the only known Old Believer book printed within the then borders of the Russian Empire until 1785. The commissioning and import of printed books from abroad became continuous, more intensive and more diverse in the 1770s and 1780s. Between 1776 and 1782 some fifty titles were produced at presses in Mogilev, Vilnius, Pochaiv, Warsaw, Grodno and Suprasl, mostly commissioned by merchants from the Starodub region.[67] This very marked intensification of Old Believer recourse to print is roughly contemporary with the wider expansion and diversification of book-printing in Russia. For the Starodub communities, at any rate (less so for the northerly Pomorie communities), book-printing seems to have been seeping into their normal expectations.

The first legal Old Believer presses in Russia were set up in the Starodub settlement of Klintsy. Their founders, Dmitrii Rukavishnikov (with Iakov Zheleznikov and his son Vasilii), and Fedor Kartashev, were the unintended beneficiaries of Catherine II's decree of January 1783 granting blanket permission for private individuals to set up printing houses. The first books came off the presses at Klintsy in 1785.[68] In 1787 their products were declared illegal (we recall that the 1783 decree had granted the freedom to own a press, but explicitly not the freedom to print whatever one liked). Remarkably, however, the activity continued, thrived, even. The flame from this inadvertently lit candle turned out to be very hard to extinguish. Over the next several decades, active attempts to douse it were sporadic, but not consistent and not particularly effective. Most of the 'foreign' printing houses found themselves within Russia after the Third Partition of Poland in 1795 (Vilnius, Grodno, Pochaiv), but the Uniate monastery of the Holy Trinity at Vilnius continued printing Old Believer books for more than a decade.[69] Rukavishnikov and Zheleznikov ceased printing in 1788 or shortly thereafter,[70] but Fedor Kartashev was resilient, as was his son Akim. From 1786 and through the first two decades of the nineteenth century the Klintsy presses produced more than 180 printed titles. In addition, nearly ninety titles were printed for Old Believers at the press of Pavel (or, in other accounts, Stepan) Seleznev at Makhnivka and Konstantin Kolychev (who acquired it in 1805) at Ianiv.[71] More systematic persecution was initiated in 1817, and Old Believer printing was effectively suppressed from the mid 1820s. Clandestine printing resumed in and around Moscow in the 1860s. Until the post-Soviet era, the only periods of legal Old Believer printing in Russia have been 1785–7 and 1905–18.

The repertoire of Old Believer printed books was, of course, conservative and devotional. A list of titles can make the repertoire sound quite diverse. Emelianova's catalogue of 434 Old Believer editions from the late eighteenth and early nineteenth centuries lists seventy titles.[72] In terms of frequency, however, the balance is very heavily skewed in favour of a very small number of titles which were reprinted far more often than the others. Thus, of the 434 printings in Emelianova's list, 182 – that is, just over 40 per cent – consist of Psalters, horologia and canons. In Voznesenskii's checklist of eighteenth-century editions, the balance is even more heavily weighted towards these three types of book: 129 of his 263 editions, or almost exactly half.[73] The repertoire includes nothing which could persuasively be defined as secular, and almost nothing in civil type.

One feature of Old Believer printed books makes them a particularly intriguing and challenging task for cataloguers and historians (and a dangerous area for collectors and booksellers). Almost all of them falsify the details of their own publication. Some provide neither date nor place, and several give only the date of the text which they purport to be derived from, while the overwhelming majority of those printed in Russia claim to have been printed somewhere else. Thus a book claiming to have been printed at Pochaiv, or Vilnius, or Suprasl, or Lviv, is in fact just as likely to have been printed at Klintsy or Ianiv. Or the printers might bind in an extra leaf with a false colophon, creating the impression that the book itself, and not just the authoritative prototype for its text, was pre-Nikonian. A deliberately ancient appearance is a typical feature of Old Believer printed books. The main reasons for such subterfuge are obvious. In the first place, it deflected the external gaze from an illicit activity; and, secondly, it served as a code for the initiated, a kind of assurance about the authority of the text regardless of the actual printer. This was temporal forgery in the interests of spiritual truth.

The Old Believers' written culture was, by and large, non-printed, but not anti-print. When there was supply, there was demand. When they themselves were in control, Old Believers were happy to subscribe to the correctness and authenticity of print.[74]

The argument for correctness of print, as a defence against the proliferation and compounding of scribal errors, was a very hardy perennial. Exactly the same argument was used, for example, by the censor Osip Senkovskii in 1831, when pressing for an agreement to print Aleksandr Griboedov's play *Woe from Wit*. Senkovskii added that the correct text should be printed in full, without alterations and cuts, since the existence of huge numbers of manuscript copies meant that cuts to the printed edition would only draw attention to themselves.[75] The censorship committee was not persuaded. They did permit a printed edition two years later; but with cuts. For them, correctness meant acceptability, not accuracy. Print, once again, was supposed to counter scribal practice, not to legitimate it.

After 'correctness' we turn to perceptions of another potential property of print: prestige. An early advocate of print-as-prestige was Muscovy's most prolific and versatile versifier, Simeon Polotskii. Arriving in Moscow in 1664, Simeon brought with him the philological skills and baroque literary habits acquired through his education in Kiev and Vilnius.[76] Among Simeon's vast and varied output were several verse cycles that he called 'booklets' (*knizhitsy*), since they were indeed intended as decorative and decorous booklets for royal presentation.

In 1676, at the end of one such 'booklet', *The Sweet-Voiced Lyre* (*Gusl' dobroglasnaia*) Simeon declared that type (*tip*) was a bearer of glory (*slava*), and 'Russia, too, should spread her glory not with the sword alone, but with swift-running type, which becomes everlasting in books; but, *o mores* [. . .] we do not want to shine on the world, with the sun, but we like to abide in the darkness of ignorance.'[77] Simeon Polotskii here articulates with remarkable directness the potential of print to project 'soft' power, while lamenting Russia's failure to exploit it. His point is not that Moscow's rulers and their cultural servitors had been habitually reticent or modest on questions of 'glory'. In ritual, in painting, in manuscript text, in coinage, in the textiles of their banners, a concern to demonstrate status and reputation can hardly be reckoned new. Polotskii's complaint was that a powerful technology for the amplification of 'glory' was being ignored. He was right. Printers sang the praises of their royal patrons,[78] but before the end of the seventeenth century it is hard to see any focussed projection of Muscovite 'glory' prepared for distribution in 'swift-running' (*skorotechnyi*) print, except in dedicatory materials such as the highly propagandistic frontispiece to the Moscow Bible of 1663, and its accompanying heraldic verses about the double-headed eagle and the representation of the tsar.[79]

Simeon Polotskii, too, framed his advocacy of print-as-glory in terms of the prestige of his royal patron. He was a professional writer – for some, Russia's first such – in the sense that he was gainfully employed for the purpose of composing, among other things, works of literature. However, Simeon earned his living through patronage, not through sales. It may not be over-fanciful to imagine a personal plea for himself, to suppose that he may also have had in mind a different 'glory', not of the state or the patron but of the individual; not of the ruler but of the writer. His eulogy to print may have been prompted in part by his desire to run his own press. As we know, the desire was fulfilled, and Simeon Polotskii was given his Upper Printing House in the Kremlin.

The idea of print as an instrument to project the prestige of its patrons was taken up by Peter I and his eighteenth-century successors. It involved not just expanding the subject matter of printed books, but thinking afresh about the look of print, about the printed book as an impressive object, about aspects of form and design that in Russia had hitherto been largely the preserve of manuscript cultures. However – skipping over-lightly across the decades – the cultural space for Polotskii's other implied meaning, the individual dimension of print-as-prestige, opened up to a significant extent only after the diffusion of private printing from the late eighteenth century. And then it was immediately complicated by two factors that might appear to counteract it. On the one hand, there was the 'stigma' of print.[80] In the world of cultivated sensibility print was, to a degree, contaminated by its long association with authority, with glory-seeking patronage, with hierarchy and control. And, on the other hand, there was the dark and dubious lure of its other newly emerging quality, or potential quality: profitability. And profit could be reckoned both demeaning in itself, and dependent on the demeaning acclamation of the 'crowd', the embryonic but rapidly maturing public that might impose its tyrannical tastes as insistently as any patron.

Thus, with the ethos of the new 'post-privatisation' age (both of print and of literary culture) came a new ambivalence about print. Writers were caught between vanity and vulgarity, as the aspiration to print was counterbalanced by the stigma of print. A particularly direct, self-parodic expression of the dilemma of 'glory' and profitability is Aleksandr Pushkin's verse 'Dialogue Between a Bookseller and a Poet', written in 1824.[81] The 'poet' wistfully recalls the time when writing had been a matter of private inspiration, of communion with feelings and with nature, when he had not 'demeaned the gifts of the Muse in shameful trade', but had guarded them as a lover preserves the gifts of his beloved from the 'duplicitous crowd': 'blessed is he who could be a poet in silence'. But the bookseller tries to tempt him with the prospect of the women he would conquer: 'women's hearts crave glory [*slava* – the same word as had been used by Simeon Polotskii]; write for them'. No, says the poet, those were the vain dreams of youth, when I shamefully degraded my talent. Now I choose freedom. 'Fine', says the bookseller, but just remember: 'Our age is commerce; in this iron age there is no freedom without money. What is "glory", but a bright-coloured patch on a poet's tattered shirt [. . .] Let me tell you plainly: you cannot sell inspiration, but you can sell a manuscript.' Resistance collapses. The poet breaks into prose: 'You're right. Here is my manuscript. Let's draw up the agreement.'

Some of the terms need translating: the 'bookseller' here is in effect a publisher. The 'manuscript' is what is sold to the publisher, but the money will come from sales of print. This dilemma, or at any rate this affectation of a dilemma, is a familiar stance of the romantic age. Glory, profit and even popularity (because it is bestowed by the *populus*) are all tainted and irresistible, vulgar and aspirational. Print is the temptation that cannot be denied.[82]

Tyrannies of Taste: On Fashion in the Graphosphere

The graphosphere expands and thickens unevenly. Within its overall growth are several kinds of irregularity. It seeps into different social and geographic spaces at varying rates and to varying degrees. It maintains neither constant pace nor constant direction. At times it can even seem to go into reverse: its density can be dissipated, an area once thick with visible writing can become graphospherically barren. Such fluctuations in density have no necessary link to any equivalent movement in the development of literacy. The flow and ebb of fashion for visible lettering in general, or for particular manifestations of it, can be quite pronounced even among the lettered. In this section we consider, as an example, what has emerged as perhaps the most dramatic such cycle of taste: the thickening of the graphosphere over the 'long' seventeenth century, followed by a cultural switch away from the status of visible words towards the mid eighteenth century. The broader label often applied to this period in Russian elite aesthetics is 'baroque'. The term is emblematic of a wider context, for it situates Russia on the cultural map of early modern Europe. Comparisons with other manifestations of the baroque are productive, but here the focus is on the local, specifically on the implications for the graphosphere, for the display of words.

Moscow baroque taste abhorred clean lines, blank spaces and flat colours. Its manifestations extended from densely polychrome patterns of interior wall decoration, through lush and luxurious clothing, to the refashioning of church architecture. The chronology of the baroque in Muscovy is approximate. There was no one moment of initiation. Elements of baroque-like decorative styles can be traced at least to the mid sixteenth century, though the baroque as a dominant elite aesthetic tends to be associated with the second half of the seventeenth century. The end is perhaps plainer than the beginning. Peter I ostentatiously rejected much of the paraphernalia of baroque affectation – although, as we shall see, he was himself not entirely free of baroque habits.

The heightened fashion for visible words can be explored across four contexts: in relation to the design and manufacture of individual objects; in relation to the 'densification' of inscriptional environments; in relation to varieties of contemporary writing for and about inscription; and in relation to visual experiments in the representation of words and texts.

The first context for the intensified representation of words is the individual manufactured object with secondary writing. Over the sixteenth and, in particular, the seventeenth centuries, a common pattern of inscriptional fashion can be observed across many types of object with secondary writing.[83] This was the age of thick bands of *viaz'*, of visible text as part of the structure of embellishment, where the decorative representation of writing often took precedence over verbal decipherability, as if the message was in the materiality of display as much as in the words. This inscriptional mode was common to objects unrelated to each other by function or location or material: military banners and drinking goblets, bronze cannons and liturgical silver, not to mention 'one-off' luxury examples such as Ivan IV's royal pew in the Dormition cathedral, with its panels carved with narrative.[84] It is as if, across a broad spectrum of elite manufacture, the image of writing was integral to the aesthetics of prestigious objects. The reorientation of elite taste from the early eighteenth century brought a fairly abrupt end to many such manifestations of decorative verbiage. It was not, of course, the end of inscription, but contexts for the development of visible secondary writing became more defined and localised, no longer part of a general aesthetic. Arguably, the early-eighteenth-century fashion for emblems and their inscriptions represents a kind of equivalent projection of the baroque taste for verbal decoration, but across the majority of forms and genres the discontinuities are striking. The representation of words was either banished entirely or else was relegated to discreet corners, or frames or, at best, to cartouches. And, where words did remain, thick quasi-cryptographic *viaz'* tended to give way to thin 'copperplate' cursives.

The second context for the thickening graphosphere was the larger-scale inscriptional environment. The most conspicuous examples here, initially, are churches. Churches had traditionally been 'inscription-rich'. Inscriptions were essential to devotional imagery, and churches were filled with inscribed images large and small, fixed and portable: on row upon row of panel icons in the iconostasis, on the paintings that covered the walls, on the objects used in the devotional performances, on vestments. Yet from the second half of the sixteenth century, and especially over the seventeenth century, this traditionally dense graphic environment tended to become even more thickly packed with visible words. Icons often included longer texts, especially in new compositions involving narrative components.[85] Substantial non-iconographic inscriptions, too, proliferated. In early churches, if we are lucky, we can occasionally find some discreet and barely visible mark left by a painter identifying himself, or perhaps some graffiti recording (officially or unofficially) events. In the early 1650s Ivan Neronov, a priest at the Kazan cathedral in Moscow, articulated the desirability of additional inscription, ordering that edificatory texts be painted on the walls, so that worshippers could see and read and focus their minds.[86] By the late seventeenth century extensive narratives of the foundation and decoration of churches, sometimes as long as two hundred or three hundred words, were routinely painted on interior walls at readable height, in decent-sized lettering and in prominent places: most commonly around the perimeter of the central nave, or on the western wall, in continuous friezes and/or in cartouches.[87] Such inscriptions were intended not merely to be present but to be noticed.

This had become the norm. Churches displayed texts beyond their traditional devotional requirements, texts that captioned or explained not just the images within the building, but the building itself. The most extreme specimen of this tendency is the extensive programme of inscriptions at the New Jerusalem monastery at Istra, some forty miles north-west of Moscow, founded by Patriarch Nikon in 1656, including scriptural citations, systematic explanations of the buildings themselves and of some of its paintings, prayers, a history of the monastery.[88] The inscriptional spaces of the New Jerusalem monastery were not created as a single project. The initiative was Nikon's, but its realisation became a tradition that was maintained over half a century, especially by his successors, the archimandrites German and Nikanor. A. G. Avdeev distinguishes four phases in its development between 1657 and 1710, although almost all the major texts had been composed by the mid 1690s.[89] For Nikon and his successors over the latter half of the seventeenth century, New Jerusalem was more than a place of devotion. It was a monument to be visited and a concept to be explained.

The inscriptions at the New Jerusalem monastery are unique: unprecedented and unimitated in their quantity, diversity and ambition. Yet they also typify a phenomenon of their age, whether visually, generically or functionally. Visually they reinforce the fashion for graphospheric densification. Generically the inscriptions are diverse, collectively they have been likened to a *proskynetarion*, a pilgrims' guide to the holy places of the Holy Land.[90] Viewed in a broader chronological perspective, in creating an educative, informative and edificatory complex of inscriptional spaces they were ecclesiastical precursors of the captioning in the Summer Gardens in St Petersburg, even of some of the programmes of triumphal inscriptions that marked Peter's military victories. Indeed, such projects, though seemingly from different epochs, almost overlap in time. If we tour the New Jerusalem inscriptions in the mid 1690s, we will not have to wait long before we can go on an equivalent tour of the inscriptions on the arches erected in honour of the victory at Azov, and in a very few years we would also be able to enhance our moral education by touring the inscriptions in the Summer Gardens.[91]

The third type of emanation of the enhanced interest in and taste for inscription is, in a loose sense, literary. Before the late seventeenth century, Muscovite writing *about* inscriptions was rather rare. In the late seventeenth century, and continuing into the early eighteenth century, it was suddenly prominent, in several unrelated contexts and genres. Inscriptions were not only to be read; they were to be transcribed and described and copied into inventories, pamphlets and books. How do we know about the copious inscriptions from the Golden Hall in the Kremlin? Because in 1672 Tsar Aleksei Mikhailovich instructed Simon Ushakov and Nikita Klementev to make a record of them. How do we know about the earliest 'stone chronicle' of New Jerusalem? Because, although inscriptions had never previously been reckoned worth noting in monastic inventories, at New Jerusalem they were recorded in an inventory of 1685. How can we trace, at least in part, sources of Peter's interest in, and knowledge of, triumphal inscriptions? Through the Russian translation of the account of the inscriptions at William of Orange's entry into The Hague in 1691. Manuscript copies of the New Jerusalem inscriptions proliferated in the late seventeenth and early eighteenth centuries.[92] Manuscript and printed accounts of the eighteenth-century festivities in Moscow and St Petersburg paid special attention to the inscriptions. The fashion continued to span the ecclesiastical and the secular. The church in the Peter and Paul Fortress in St Petersburg contained a lapidary inscription detailing its history from the laying of the foundations in 1714 to its completion in 1733, as well as a donor inscription for the iconostasis, all of which was noted and copied and circulated in manuscript collections in the first half of the eighteenth century.[93] Moving from the monumental to the marginal, one could add to the list the many manuscript compilations, also from the late seventeenth and early eighteenth centuries, of inscriptions to accompany sets of biblical engravings.

All of this relates to actual inscription, but baroque taste extended beyond such documentary and interpretative genres. Some of Muscovy's baroque versifiers were lucky enough to see their compositions on permanent display. But the inscriptional imagination was more prolific on paper than the available opportunities for its more permanent realisation. The fashion for dense displays of lettering in stone or wood or metal found literary amplification that extended it into graphospheres of the mind.[94]

A fourth type of manifestation of the taste for letters combines the literary and the visual. It takes us into a rarefied zone of elite manuscript culture which, by nature and intent, was accessible to very few people.

In the wider graphosphere its presence is therefore almost negligible. Yet it was part of the same phenomenon, a dimension that is important, in this instance, not because of its broad visibility but because it reflects the interests and pursuits of those who, directly and indirectly, influenced the more outward-facing manifestations of baroque taste. Though itself barely visible, it was close to the core. The activity involves quite bold experimentation in the visual properties of letters and their combinations, in the shapes of text on a page. The practices in question go beyond traditional features of manuscript embellishment such as decorative scripts or 'historiated' initials. In the baroque version the writing involves a kind of illusion: at first the viewer/reader sees an abstract or representational design, which on closer inspection turns out to be formed from letters. In modern critical vocabulary all pictures are texts, all texts are pictures, but here the fusion of the two is literal.

Late Muscovite word pictures have two main sets of precursors or sources: calendar manuscripts and Ruthenian word-picture composition, which in turn drew on West European equivalents. The expression 'calendar manuscript' may mislead. These are not the kinds of calendar that simply list days of the month in sequence, such as the hybrid court almanacs that we considered in the previous chapter.[95] Calendar manuscripts may well include such sequences (usually indicating the relevant saints' days), but they consist mainly of an array of graphic aids for various forms of calendrical calculation, principally linked to the date of Easter and its related cycle of festivals and services. Often the calculations are in plain tabular or grid-like form, but more pictorial designs also became conventional: circular patterns of letters and texts; and, in particular, calculations arranged within and around drawings of a hand.[96] Usually such tables are appended to related devotional texts. However, as the fascination with form became still more pronounced in the latter part of the seventeenth century, substantial manuscripts were created entirely from such pictorial tables. As for the Ruthenian precursors: Latin-educated versifiers had been weaving their compositions into squares, circles, crosses, serpentine twists, stars, pyramids and other shapes since at least the late sixteenth century.[97] In this, as in other areas of culture, some of the leading practitioners in Muscovy were immigrants from Ruthenia.

A striking example of the late-seventeenth-century taste for scriptal embellishment is the alphabet book (*bukvar'*) created in manuscript in 1692 by Karion Istomin as a present for the royal children, and then turned into a block-book by the engraver Leontii Bunin.[98] Istomin's primer highlights the multiple possibilities for shaping the letters of the alphabet

(Fig. 7.2). Each letter is shown in multiple forms, from stiff *ustav* through decorous *viaz'* to florid cursive. There are Greek and Latin equivalents (where they existed). And there is a pictorial component; or, rather, a dual

Fig. 7.2: Page devoted to the letter *iu* from primer of Karion Istomin, engraved by Leontii Bunin, 1694.
Russian Academy of Sciences Library, St Petersburg

pictorial component. In the first place, as befits a primer, Istomin includes pictures of things whose names begin with the relevant letter. Secondly, he also includes pictorial versions of the letters themselves, in the tradition of historiated initials.[99] However, although Istomin's primer does reflect the baroque enjoyment of letter play, its scope is limited to the alphabet alone. For a more elaborate specimen we turn, again, to Simeon Polotskii. For diversity and ambition, and for sheer inventiveness and exuberance in exploring ways of fusing verbal and visual display, it would be hard to find a fitter representative than Polotskii's poetic cycle of 1667, *The Russian Eagle* (*Orel rossiiskii*).[100]

Polotskii's *The Russian Eagle* is, so to speak, the New Jerusalem of manuscript culture. Though not on display in the graphosphere of an actual monument, and invisible to all but the few who had access to the manuscript, it was in its own way no less monumental an expression and celebration and exploration and demonstration of the status and potential of the visible word. The occasion was the formal proclamation of the tsar's son as heir. The work was dedicated to the tsar, Aleksei Mikhailovich, and to his son, Aleksei Alekseevich (whose tutor Simeon became at approximately the same time). It is a substantial composition: the text in the presentation manuscript is written on fifty-three folios (i.e. 106 pages),[101] mainly in verse (of which there are some 1,500 lines) but also including prose and pictures. The eagle is the symbol of both the Muscovite state and its tsar. The work was thus an emblematic and heraldic composition, and a sustained panegyric. Generically it is hard to define. In modern Russian convention it can be called a *poema* – broadly, a long poetic composition. Simeon calls it one of his 'booklets', which is what it was as a physical object: a self-contained presentation manuscript of 'occasional' poems on a given theme. Simeon produced several such 'booklets'.[102] No label quite fits. I introduced it as a cycle. *The Russian Eagle* is put together from thematically linked but compositionally distinct elements. Indeed it is a cycle of cycles. Besides two dedications, a prose panegyric and verse address to the eagle, it includes a cycle of ten poems on the Russian eagle as if by Apollo and each of the nine Muses,[103] and – its longest section – a cycle of twelve poems on the qualities of the heir to the throne, each linked to a sign of the zodiac.[104]

The Russian Eagle was a display of erudition, dexterity and verbal virtuosity. This is not a modern judgement, or not only a modern judgement. The work was designed and presented as such. One can represent Simeon's formal display on four levels: vocabulary and cultural reference;

versification; visually enhanced word-play; and word pictures and concrete poetry.

On the level of vocabulary and cultural reference, in this work Simeon flaunts his familiarity with Greek. Besides Apollo and the Muses, each section has a Greek-derived heading: (in the Slavonic transcription) *afierosis* (twice), *enkomion, eulogion, Faethon i Ikho, akrostikhis, programma, anagramma* (five times). Apart from the section headings and the rhetorical tropes that several of them introduce, the work teems with mythological references and unfamiliar (in a Muscovite context) Graecisms.[105] Polotskii's most recondite locution is probably the borrowed noun *ouranoskopii* (with the gloss 'that is, observer of the heavens'), which then leads to the outlandish verb *uranoskopstvovati* in the poem on Pisces (in Greek *ouranoskopos* is a kind of fish).[106]

At the second level Polotskii demonstrated his command of versificatory dexterity through metrical variation. Thus, in the 'Apollo and the Muses' cycle, his Terpomene and Thalia use couplets of eight-syllable verse, the lines of Erato are of ten syllables, Terpsichore, Polyhymnia and Apollo write in an eleven-syllable line, Euterpe prefers twelve syllables, and Calliope's couplets are composed of thirteen-syllable lines, while Urania and Clio compose in a form of quatrain consisting of three eleven-syllable lines followed by a five-syllable overhanging fourth line that rhymes with the third line.

The third level is visually enhanced word-play. Apart from the large cycles, *The Russian Eagle* is sprinkled with verbal showpieces. Simeon runs through the repertoire of baroque rhetorical games in the manipulation of words on a page. Two dedications (*Afierosis 1* and *Afierosis 2*) are presented as four columns of words or phrases or fragments, in which the first three columns form a continuous text, followed by the third and fourth columns. That is, the letters in the third column are shared.[107] After the zodiac cycle, a 45-line poem entitled *Phaethon and Echo* is a dialogue. Most of the lines consist of a question followed by a one- or two-word response which rhymes with (echoes) the last word of the question. The 'echo' at the end of each line is written in red, as are several (irregular) words which create additional echoes within some of the lines.[108] An acrostic of six-syllable lines, with the first letters picked out in red, wishes the tsar a long life.[109] Perhaps most idiosyncratic of all is a series of five anagrammatic poems (*Anagramma 1–5*), each of which plays with a different rearrangement of the letters in the tsar's patronymic (Mikhailovich). Again, the relevant words are made plain by being picked out in red.[110] Finally, Polotskii closes with a cryptographic representation of his own name, Simeon. As it happens, the late seventeenth century and early eighteenth century were also a period of practical experiments in cryptography in Russia.[111] Simeon's code was simple: it was created by shifting the letters of the alphabet three places. This is a peculiarly non-cryptographic cryptogram, since Simeon states exactly how it works, and is even helpful enough to provide all the means for its decipherment: *The Russian Eagle* closes, fittingly, with the explanatory alphabet. If Simeon was working word-magic, he aimed to delight and impress, not to bamboozle or confuse, and at every stage he showed just how the trick was done.

Which takes us to the fourth level of ostentatious verbal virtuosity: the word pictures. Probably the two most widely reproduced images from the presentation manuscript of *The Russian Eagle* are: the illustration of the double-headed eagle itself, and the heart of verse. The eagle is depicted, as normal for the time, with three crowns, a sword and sceptre, and with the emblematic representation of the dragon-slaying equestrian tsar on its breast.[112] However, here the eagle was additionally placed in the centre of a representation of the sun. The sun consists of forty-eight spiked or wavy rays, and in each ray – a word. The words are the names of virtues that shine forth from the eagle-tsar. The whole is presented as an illustration to a phrase from the Psalter: 'In the sun he has set his tabernacle'.[113] It would be hard to find a plainer image of the sun-king. The second image is a heart, again captioned by a phrase from the Bible: 'out of the abundance of his heart his mouth speaketh'.[114] The heart is created entirely from words (Fig. 7.3). Nor is it merely an outline, but a continuous ribbon that starts at the centre and winds back on itself and around itself several times so as to create a picture with volume and amplitude. The ribbon of words, when read as it twists its way to the heart's eventual completion, forms a forty-line poem in eleven-syllable rhyming couplets.[115]

As a product of the most rarefied level of elite book culture, Simeon Polotskii's *The Russian Eagle* was not a prominently visible element of the Muscovite graphosphere. It survives in just three manuscripts: the presentation copy, the author's working copy, and another copy made by Simeon for incorporation into a collection of his verses.[116] Scholarship, and then the internet, have amplified his verses and word pictures into literary monuments and visual images of his age for incomparably more people now than would have heard or seen them in his own time. Here Simeon Polotskii's *The Russian Eagle* stands for the wider fashion, as the tip of its iceberg or as one end of its spectrum. It is not linked directly to the thick inscriptions on bells and banners and textiles and goblets, or to the wordy foundation narratives daubed on church walls, or to the accumulation of

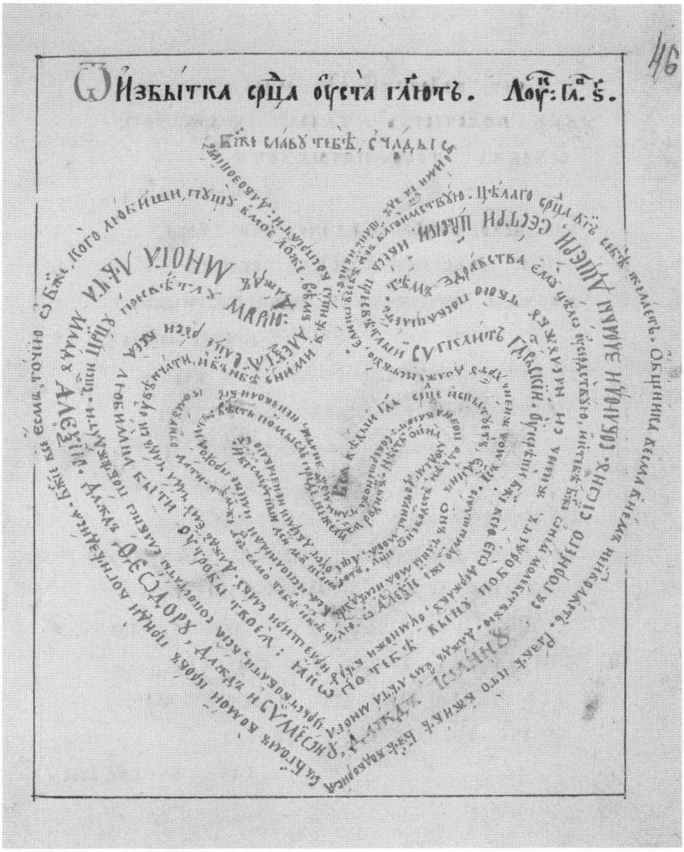

Fig. 7.3: Verses in the shape of a heart, from the presentation manuscript of Simeon Polotskii, *The Russian Eagle*, 1667.
Russian Academy of Sciences Library, St Petersburg

explanatory and historical inscriptions at the New Jerusalem monastery, or to documentary caption-texts or the imaginary inscription-texts, and still less to the captioned emblems on Dutch stoves or on triumphal arches. Taken together, however, these apparently disparate phenomena reflect the taste for verbal display that lies behind the notably dense graphosphere of Russian high culture in the late seventeenth and early eighteenth centuries.

Few of the features of this dense graphosphere were in themselves entirely new, few subsequently disappeared entirely, some were developed and enhanced. Of course people continued to be interested in the visible properties of words, in letter design and type design and page design. Ostentatious panegyric neither began nor ended with Simeon Polotskii. Inscription, epigraph and epigram had bright futures. Word-rich iconography flourished. Yet these were individual developments in their own media and genres. The inner links were broken. The coherent aesthetic which foregrounded the density of words, across the many forms and technologies and contexts of elite culture, was fractured. Clean lines and uncluttered spaces acquired a new status in the post-Muscovite aesthetic. When the spaces began again to be filled, towards the turn of the nineteenth century, mainly in the public gaze rather than in the rarefied productions of the elites, it was for different reasons. As a moment and a movement, there was no equivalent focus on the aesthetics of the visible word in Russia until the avant-garde experiments of the twentieth century.

Authority and Technological Change: The Last Episode

We end almost as we began, with the Bible, with the highest-status text of all, with technologies not just of the word but of the Word. A *leitmotif* of previous chapters has been a recurrent paradox between, on the one hand, the centrality of the devotional in traditional Russian cultures of manuscript and print, but the near-absence of the Bible as such. The earliest documented Russian engagement with print was in the context of the production of a manuscript Bible in the late 1490s under the direction of Gennadii, archbishop of Novgorod. The first complete Cyrillic Bible was produced in 1581 by the first named Muscovite printer, Ivan Fedorov – but in Ostroh, after he had left Muscovy for Ruthenia. No complete Bible was printed in Moscow until the edition of 1663, which was issued in a print run of 2,400 copies and never re-issued. In Russia, especially from the late seventeenth century, extensive imported suites of biblical illustrations were widely disseminated and diversely influential, but without the complete texts that they were designed to accompany. More or less regular printing of Bibles in Russia began only in 1751, at first only in grand folios, eventually in more convenient quarto and octavo formats. And all these Bibles were in Church Slavonic, not in Russian.

Around the mid 1810s, in an episode that lasted just over a decade, all this was to be challenged. The challenge brought sharply into focus conflicting views about language and identity, about the status and value of scriptural reading, about the desirability or danger of making the sacred texts available directly, rather than through the mediation of traditional interpreters. And the issue acquired potency and urgency because those who challenged tradition did so with the aid of a new weapon which gave them a range and a reach hitherto unattainable. The principal actor was the Russian Bible Society, which aimed to further its cause not just with a new mission but with a new and potent technology. The dramatic rise and fall of the Russian Bible Society, from the mid 1810s to the mid 1820s, resonates through discussions of linguistic, religious and educational politics of the period, but it also brings into focus many of the themes that occur and recur in an exploration of authority in the graphosphere.

In 1824 – in the same year that Aleksandr Pushkin wrote his 'Dialogue' satirising his capitulation to commercialism, as a preface to the first part of his verse novel *Evgenii Onegin* – two of Russia's senior church hierarchs, Metropolitan Serafim of Novgorod and Metropolitan Evgenii of Kiev, were taking a firmer stand, in a polemical epistle. The target of their polemic was the Russian Bible Society, which they declared to be both unnecessary and harmful. Among their accusations was the fact that, in distributing the Word of God, the Bible Society used means that were 'entirely mercantile' (*sovershenno torgovye*; cf. Pushkin's *nash vek – torgash*).[117] Why should this high-minded objection to the commercially viable selling of Scriptures have surfaced in the mid 1820s?[118] It would be easy to dismiss the metropolitans' comment as superficial, incidental, a moment of cantankerous conservatism, inconsequential, unworthy of elevation to cultural prominence. This would be a mistake. Peel away the surface polemic, and the charge of commercial viability, or even of commercial motivation, becomes a symptom of a far more substantial unease, of traditional authority over the technology of the Word undermined.

Between 1815 and 1817 the Russian Bible Society instigated the greatest innovation in the technology of printing in Russia since the sixteenth century: printing from stereotype plates, using a cylindrical press.[119] The purpose of both aspects was to facilitate unprecedentedly quick production in very large quantities at low cost. The stereotype process involved turning the typeset page into a single metal plate. It was a form of block-printing, except that movable type was part of the process of making the blocks. The origins of stereotyping are disputable, depending on the definitions of the process.[120] The continuous history of commercial stereotype printing begins in the mid 1800s. The plates were made by pouring a molten alloy into a plaster cast taken from the standing type. Although initially expensive because of the additional processes and materials necessary to create the plates, stereotyping was designed to be significantly more economical than normal printing, especially for large print runs. The stereotype plate was far more resilient to the pressures of multiple usage, and it could be stored for additional print runs, enabling the type itself to be re-used. A potential disadvantage was that, once the plate was cast, its text was immutable. Errors became permanent. With stereotype printing there was no opportunity for the adjustments and corrections within and between print runs that are common in traditional typographic practice. Stereotyping thus dispensed with the multiple variants and 'states' that so exasperate (or delight) bibliophiles and bibliographers. The technique of stereotyping with plaster of Paris matrices had been pioneered in the 1730s by William Ged,[121] but was reinvigorated by the printer Andrew Wilson and his patron, the earl of Stanhope, who patented the process in 1802 and set up a commercial press in 1804. This, as it happens, was the year of the founding of the British and Foreign Bible Society, which immediately saw the potential of the technique in supporting its mission to make the Scriptures available as widely as possible to the peoples of the world in their own languages.[122]

If stereotyping hugely increased the potential for large and multiple print runs, the cylinder press – also a recent invention from Britain – hugely increased the speed of production. With the import (from Britain) of stereotype printing and of a cylinder press, the Russian Bible Society was in the vanguard of printing technology in Europe. In the history of the Russian graphosphere such a situation was unprecedented. For some, it was uncomfortable.

The Russian Bible Society was an offshoot of the British and Foreign Bible Society. During the second decade of the nineteenth century it established a network of branches throughout the country and was active in promoting and distributing Bibles in many languages.[123] However, the most intensely innovative phase of its publishing activities, and one of the catalysts for its own demise, involved the translation of the Bible into Russian. In this the Bible Society was acting on the highest authority. In February 1816 Tsar Alexander I himself decreed that the Society should publish the New Testament in the Russian language. While momentous, the decree was also cautious: the translation was to be vetted by ecclesiastical figures, and was to be printed alongside the traditional Church Slavonic version. Moreover, the tsar stressed that the Russian version was for reading only, while the Church Slavonic version remained inviolable for liturgical use.[124] The tsar also supported in other ways the Bible Society's broader aims in making Scripture accessible. For example, on 6 January 1817 he decreed that those who wished to acquire a Church Slavonic folio edition of the Bible, published the previous year, should be able to do so as cheaply as possible. To this end, following a report from the

Holy Synod, he set the price of unbound copies at twelve roubles fifty kopeks.[125] The tsar's declared aim may have resonated with that of the Bible Society, but the method – price fixing by royal decree – was of another age, another culture.

The Bible Society began cautiously both with respect to the technology and with respect to the text. Initially it used its stereotype process to produce traditional Bibles and New Testaments in Church Slavonic.[126] For the translations into Russian, however, it began by producing books of the New Testament by traditional technology, 'outsourced' (as we might now say) to the publishing house of Nikolai Grech. This allowed for textual correction if necessary, before the fixity of stereotype.[127] In 1822 the first complete New Testament, with parallel Russian and Church Slavonic texts, printed by the Russian Bible Society, was ready for distribution. It was at that point that the Society began to go beyond the original brief as stated in Alexander's authorisation of 1816. It began to issue Russian-only texts, without the accompanying Church Slavonic. Several stereotyped issues of the Psalter were printed in 1822. The first Russian-only text of the complete New Testament was published by the Society in St Petersburg in 1823, with a Moscow edition, printed at the press of Moscow University, following in 1824.[128] Curiously, in view of what was to follow shortly, a supplementary preface, justifying the issue of the Russian-only text, was signed by, among others, Metropolitan Serafim. At the same time the Society translators worked on a far larger project to translate the Old Testament. The first eight books (the Octateuch, from Genesis to Ruth), translated from Hebrew, with indications of divergence from the Septuagint version that lay behind the traditional Slavonic translations, were printed in 1825–6, but were never bound or distributed. When the Society was shut down in 1826, many of the sheets were destroyed. Thirty years later, after the accession of Alexander II, the Holy Synod itself decided to resume the task of producing a Bible in Russian. The first edition of the complete 'Synodal' Bible was issued in 1876.[129] The task of the Russian Bible Society itself took rather longer to complete. The Society was reconstituted in 1991. Its own complete Bible in modern Russian was finally published in 2011.

Translation into Russian was visual as well as verbal. We recall that, following the introduction of civil type by Peter I, the difference between ecclesiastical and non-ecclesiastical texts was generally reflected in the look of the words, not just in their meanings. By and large liturgical texts retained the traditional repertoire and forms of old Muscovite Cyrillic printing, with its roots in earlier manuscript culture, while non-devotional texts were presented in the more 'humanist' forms of the civil type. Before one even started reading what the words said, a simple glance at the page was enough to indicate the cultural context and register. The Bible Society's translations reduced a cultural distinction to a linguistic distinction. Their Church Slavonic versions were, of course, printed in old Cyrillic, but the parallel Russian translations – and eventually the Russian-only editions – were printed in civil typefaces. In consequence, the core devotional texts were made to look non-ecclesiastical, even non-biblical, according to the conventional marks of recognition. The Bible Society versions changed not only the language of the text but the visual semantics of the object.

How were these radically different representations of the Divine Word supposed to be perceived? Who were they aimed at? The obvious and traditional (and in my view correct) answer is that, consistent with the wider mission of the Bible Societies, the purpose was, quite simply, to spread the Word, to make the Scriptures directly available to as many people as possible in their own languages. Linguists have occasionally questioned whether the Russian Bible Society could genuinely have reckoned that their Russian versions would reach a mass readership more effectively than Church Slavonic versions, since until (and including) the early nineteenth century such peasant education as existed began with the 'Cyrillic' (i.e. ecclesiastical) typeface and with exercises in Church Slavonic. However, nice though the academic point may be, it misses the dynamics of missionary translation and distribution. The Russian Bible Society started with Church Slavonic, and shifted to Russian for a reason. Educational practices were changing. More importantly, in missionary practice it was standard – indeed often unavoidable – to disseminate the Word in languages which, initially, few could read, but which most could understand. The point, therefore, was not necessarily an initial mass *direct* readership, but a much wider *indirect* readership of those who could listen, and who might eventually become direct readers as personal literacy spread.

All of this might have had less impact were it not for the numbers. It has been estimated that, in the decade up to 1825, the Russian Bible Society presses produced, in various languages, not far short of a million copies of scriptural texts. Just in 1822–4 its stereotype printings of the Russian-only Psalter amounted to more than 100,000 copies. In Stephen K. Batalden's calculation, 'More than twice as many copies of scripture in the Russian language were published by the RBS Press in just the two-year period, 1821–3, than the Holy Synod had circulated (in Slavonic) from its own presses for the whole period from Peter the Great to 1820.'[130]

The proof of efficacy, or of perceived efficacy, is in the response. In mid 1824 the momentum of the Russian Bible Society was abruptly halted. In May Prince Aleksandr Nikolaevich Golitsyn was dismissed both from his position as minister of education and from the presidency of the Society. In the latter role the tsar replaced him with Metropolitan Serafim, who, though previously on the Society's Council, had come to be one of the most vehement opponents of its publications, while the new appointee as minister of education was an even more voluble critic of the Society, and for the previous two decades a staunch advocate of linguistic traditionalism more broadly, Aleksandr Shishkov. Through 1825 the Society survived in little more than name. In April 1826 its activities were formally brought to a halt by order of the new tsar, Nicholas I, although the sale of its existing publications in Slavonic, Russian and other languages was still permitted.

Among the most vehement critics of the Bible Societies in general, and of the Russian Bible Society in particular, was Shishkov.[131] For him the Russian Bible Society was a fundamental threat to the Orthodox Church and faith. It was tainted by its provenance, by its organisation, by its aims and by its actions. No detail was too small to be dangerous.

Some of Shishkov's objections appear merely philological, variations on a theme familiar to Shishkov-watchers from his critique, two decades earlier, of new styles and foreign influences in literature.[132] For him the very idea of translation from Church Slavonic into Russian was wrong-headed, since these were not two languages but functional variants of the same language. Church Slavonic was the 'high' version appropriate to Scripture. To render the scriptural function into the inappropriate style was dangerous. It undermined the dignity of Scripture and it distorted meaning, since notional equivalents in the two styles were not in fact semantically identical.[133] The risk of error was particularly acute when the Bible Society abandoned the bilingual editions of Russian and Church Slavonic in parallel columns and started printing the Russian text by itself. Mistakes were inevitable.[134]

The dangers of translation were, for Shishkov, symptoms rather than causes. The fundamental threat posed by the Bible Society stemmed not from any particular view of linguistic propriety, but from the Society's fundamental mission. Shishkov was bitterly opposed to the very idea of making Bibles available to all, especially when the Bibles lacked any commentary or explanation. To encourage mass reading of the Bible without textual explanations or institutional intermediaries, without commentaries and without priests, was to invite schism and heresy. He was deeply alarmed by reports that Bible-reading was on the increase among peasants and among soldiers. The express aim of the Bible Societies, however idealistically it was presented, would, if fulfilled, lead not to the strengthening of Orthodoxy but to its weakening.[135]

Nor, in Shishkov's polemics, was the undermining of Orthodoxy an unforeseen consequence of idealism. It was intentional. It was the Bible Societies' darker, unspoken aim. Why did they operate outside the structures of the established church? Why were they so assiduously developing their own universal networks? What was their purpose in 'uniting all faiths by means of the dissemination of Scripture'? The hidden aim of the Bible Societies was to lure the people to their own universal faith, to destroy Orthodoxy and hence – doubtless in the service of their shadowy political masters – to weaken Russia itself.[136]

The Russian Bible Society – perhaps unwittingly, for some of its zealots – was a product and tool of the enemies of Orthodoxy and of Russia, and all its works were tainted. Its Bibles were corrupt and corrupting. Even the physical book, ostensibly revered, was desecrated: 'Dreadful capital will be expended in order that the Gospel book, which in church is borne with such solemnity, should lose its dignity, should be soiled and torn, should lie abandoned under the counter, should even serve as wrapping for domestic objects (as has already occurred), should no longer act upon hearts and minds.'[137] Or, as we might say here: just as the scriptural word became tainted when transferred linguistically from Church Slavonic into the vernacular, and when transferred visibly from old Cyrillic into civil (i.e. secular) type, so the book of the Word – the Gospel – became tainted in an equivalent spatial transfer, a transfer into a different zone of the graphosphere, from the ecclesiastical to the domestic.

In itself the mission of the Bible Society might have been merely an irritant. It was made dangerous by the twin innovations of vernacular Russian translation and potent new technology. Putting a stop to its production was reckoned sufficient protection. Its stock continued to be distributed. And Bible Societies continued to operate in Russia with non-Russian languages. The Protestant Bible Society in St Petersburg, founded in 1827, distributed Bibles in at least ten languages.[138] In 1831 the British and Foreign Bible Society reported on the distribution of some 850,000 books of various parts of the Bible, in a long list of languages that included Armenian, Modern Greek, Ancient Greek, Georgian, Kalmyk, Karelian, Latvian, Moldavian, Mongolian, Mordvinian, German, Persian, Polish, Samogitian, Turkish, Tatar, Cheremisian, Finnish, French, Estonian, Bulgarian, Latin and Serbian.[139] In 1833 the English polyglot George

Borrow was sent to Moscow by the British and Foreign Bible Society to supervise the publication of a translation (by a Russian) of the Bible into Manchu.[140]

As in his earlier campaign against innovation in language, so now in his campaign against unmediated Bible reading, Shishkov was swimming against the tide. The activities of the Bible Society were symptoms of a wider change in mood, fashion, perception and demand. Over the first half of the nineteenth century Bible-reading, mostly in extracts and digests rather than in full texts, became quite widespread.[141]

Several of these motifs are familiar: ownership of, or control over, the means of production; textual authenticity and institutional authority; the vulgarity, even profanity, of a mercantile attitude to spreading the Word of God (as in the charge-sheet prepared by Metropolitans Serafim and Evgenii); the pseudo-authority of the printed book of dubious provenance. It is hard to know whether the reaction of Shishkov and others would have been so virulent if the Russian Bible Society had not been so successful so quickly both in the growth of its regional networks and in the unprecedented scale of its printing. Shishkov does not explicitly refer to stereotyping or to cylinder presses, but they were the technologies which had been introduced by the Russian Bible Society and which had enormously enhanced its capacity to achieve its nefarious aims. For those who were accustomed to (or who aspired to restore) authority over print, the potential reach and implications of the authority of the Bible Society's vastly enhanced printing capacity were profoundly alarming. The closure of the Society meant the removal of its weapons. The technological leap was blocked for a generation. Another false start and another delayed continuation. It seems both incongruous and fitting that the controversy was again provoked by the printing of biblical texts. One thinks of Ivan Fedorov, even of Patriarch Nikon. In the history of Russian printing, the Bible Society episode might be seen as another – perhaps the last – of Russia's non-Gutenberg moments.

CHAPTER 8

(In)conclusion

A History of the Graphosphere?

Where is the grand narrative? The preceding chapters have included many generic surveys, thematic surveys, mini-histories of institutions and objects, languages and scripts, genres and forms, technologies and media, of cultural spaces and of physical spaces. Several of the mini-histories synthesise the work of others: on the story of civil type, for example, or of sixteenth-century printing, or on the emergence of Contemporary Standard Russian. Other mini-histories are new: the focus on non-books, especially the chronology and taxonomy of that under-rated technological hybrid, the printed blank form; the reconstruction of phases in the emergence and mutation of the public graphosphere, and of domestic graphospheres. Each chapter tells stories; and the assemblage as a whole, and the approach that prompts it, is not to be found elsewhere. But, at the end: so what? What about *a* history? Should this not all culminate in an integrated, chronological account of the emergence, development and transformations of the Russian graphosphere across four centuries?

To duck the challenge of narrative summation could be seen as an evasion of historiographical responsibility. In defence, one can always take refuge behind the notion of the premature: the approach is in many respects new, and to tell its quasi-definitive story at this stage would be improperly speculative when so much remains to be explored. However, such a defence, or such an excuse, can be applicable to almost any large-scale study of the past. It may be honest, but that does not necessarily make it adequate. Alternatively, one can turn the absence of synthesis into a matter of principle and intention. The book does not have, and does not have to have, a general conclusion. It is a series of surveys and investigations, not a presentation of a thesis. Its value depends on the extent to which it is felt to be useful as a guide, and on whether it is felt to show, in the accumulation of its mini-narratives, that the approach can produce useful insights.

Nevertheless, even without a master-narrative it is possible to identify some general features, to draw together some threads in trying to account both for the broad development of the graphosphere and for some of its particular manifestations and mutations. Four factors have, to varying degrees, moved in and out of focus in the accounts of graphospheric growth and change: technology; political decisions; institutional requirements; economic activity. What, in summary, was the role of each in the development of the Russian graphosphere?

The first and recurrent observation is that technology alone was not enough. Neither acquaintance with, nor engagement with, nor the acquisition of, a particular technology of writing was sufficient to catalyse the regular use, growth or spread of that technology. There was no inexorable logic which dictated the pace or the extent or even the fact of exploitation of the notional potential of a given technology of the visible word. This negative generalisation about the Russian graphosphere is as applicable to stone carving or to needlework as it is to printing. It also applies to imports, since, for graphospheric purposes, importation is a mode of production. The mere presence of the requisite technology was perhaps the weakest of the four factors.

Political decisions can be crudely divided into the negative and the positive: decisions which prohibit or restrict, and decisions which permit or encourage or impose. *Re*strictive decisions were, in the initial phases of graphospheric growth, fairly effective instruments of containment: restrictions on the ownership of the means of production of print, for example; or, later, restrictions on the placement of signboards. The efficacy of *pre*scription was mixed. Simplest to implement was regulation on routine administrative requirements such as the marking of goods or the calibration of scales or the inscriptions on coinage or the watermarks on official paper. Many of the Petrine initiatives on distribution and display encountered serious logistical obstacles and were not sustainable in their own time. From later in the eighteenth century the reliability, legibility and maintenance of signs on mileposts became a hardy perennial of semi-effective legislation. Top-down decisions that particular types of writing should be displayed or disseminated, or that a particular technology of writing should be employed, were rarely sufficient stimuli in themselves, unless underpinned by an institutional and/or commercial context.

Institution-based writing provided a context for sustainability or expansion. The most solid institutional foundations for writing were those of church and state. Besides the texts from which it derived its teachings, the church required visible writing as a standard component of its core devotional practices. Each church was a complex, multimedia graphic environment. It displayed physical books, inscribed panel icons, perhaps inscribed frescoes, liturgical vessels, embroidered textiles, printed antimensia, perhaps lapidary inscriptions as well. It was conventionally supported by monastic, clerical and in some instances domestic labour. Until the early eighteenth century Muscovite printing, though a department of state, served almost exclusively the institutional needs of the church. As for the state itself: by far the biggest single factor in the expansion of handwriting across the entire period was the growth of bureaucratic institutions: first through the proliferation of chanceries (*prikazy*) over the sixteenth and seventeenth centuries, then in the eighteenth-century 'colleges' and eventually in the nineteenth-century ministries. Handwriting was an essential instrument of the early modern state. The early modern state owed its growth in part to the exploitation of handwriting.

Of the many forms of economic activity, three can be highlighted as particularly significant, and in some instances decisive, in the development of the Russian graphosphere. The first was the development of a monetary economy itself, and hence the production of inscribed objects whose purpose was to bear a specified exchange value: coins from the start of the period; printed (or rather, print-and-manuscript hybrid) paper money and promissory notes from the second half of the eighteenth century. The second significant type of economic activity was the growth and diversification in the production of objects expressly for the market – an activity which is separated, by a blurred but important line, from simply the attempt to sell objects that had been produced. Market-led activity fed and nurtured, in particular, a growing domestic demand, ranging from cheap printed pictures for domestic devotion or adornment, to 'novodel' coins and medals for the nascent collectors' market, or monogrammed dinner services or 'personalised' snuff boxes. The most dramatic implications for the graphosphere followed from the marketisation of the technology of printing from the late eighteenth century. The third type of economic activity was the production of written objects whose purpose was to serve commercial activity: above all, the public signage that transformed the urban graphosphere in the early decades of the nineteenth century. Commercialisation was decisive both in meeting and stimulating private demand, and in the colonisation of public spaces. Control of the means of production was relinquished. In its place came highly selective regulation of what was produced or distributed, but – for all the attention that is sometimes paid to censorship and prohibition in certain sensitive areas – its restraining effect on the total growth of the graphosphere was negligible.

These are some of the broad features of, so to speak, the mechanics of the graphosphere. Not surprisingly, they sound somewhat mechanistic. They can leave a misleading impression in many respects. They focus on conditions for growth or diversification, but can miss the layers of nuance and fluctuation, the cross-currents, the mini-histories. Moreover, behind the general patterns one finds some seemingly paradoxical subpatterns. Thus, on the one hand, in general, Russia was bypassed by the 'print revolution' of Western Europe. Not only was there no print production in Muscovy for a century after Gutenberg, but the age of the jobbing printer selling his skills did not really begin until more than three centuries after Gutenberg. On the other hand, precisely because of these restrictions, in some areas Russia introduced practices that were, in a sense, ahead of their time in the exploitation of print. The official print monopoly was a cause of restrictions which were also opportunities. Control over the means of production hampered the diversification of print cultures, but at the same time rendered print itself a more secure guarantor of authenticity. This enabled the obligatory use of print in some forms of official document – notably, internal passports – to become a standard requirement in Russia long before it became standard in much of Western Europe. The degree of control over the technology affected the degree to which the technology could be used as an instrument of control.

And what of education, of culture, of the processes of the spread of literacy that are often assumed to be central to the history of the written word? The expansion of the graphosphere did to some extent both follow and stimulate the spread of literacy, though in the pre-modern age one did not have to be personally literate in order either to shape or to receive the visual and verbal messages of visible words. The idea of a lettered education as a good in itself, irrespective of institutional or economic or devotional function or career ambition, was rare and mainly late (perhaps best tracked in the rise of education for girls). The presumption that literacy is a prerequisite for social inclusion is a modern phenomenon.

Experiencing the Graphosphere

The graphosphere is a cultural space. An account of process or function is not an account of meaning or perception. How was the graphosphere experienced by those who inhabited it? How was it read, not just as a set of verbal messages but as a visual text, as a locus of implied as well as explicit meanings? What did the graphosphere feel like to those who were in it? How were people affected by graphospheric change? Put in such general terms, the search for graphospheric subjectivity appears to be both essential and impossible. Definitive, comprehensive answers are so remote that even to pose the questions seems somewhat absurd: far more absurd even than the artifice of a grand narrative. And far more premature. Besides the obvious pitfalls of attempting to extrapolate patterns of subjectivity from the almost infinite range of individual perceptions, there is an even greater problem of sources. Sources containing articulate reflection on visible words are very rare in the earlier centuries. In principle one should be able to glean more from the growing quantity and diversity of reflective writings in, especially, the first half of the nineteenth century. But that, too, is a problem, or perhaps a future delight. In search of individual responses, or patterns of responses, to the visible word, one could usefully scour large quantities of personal sources such as diaries and memoirs and correspondence and travelogues, not to mention the imagined-but-telling evidence of fiction.

This is a long way beyond the scope of the present survey. From time to time I have touched on questions of subjectivity in the graphosphere, on how people may have perceived and experienced spaces of visible writing, but such remarks have been episodic, preliminary, unsystematic. There have been occasional glimpses of response and engagement, from Vasilii Tuchkov's curiosity about the anchor device in an Aldine printed book in the library of Maksim Grek, through some nineteenth-century fictional scribes, to the nineteenth-century essays on shop signs. On this basis it is not possible to extrapolate any larger story or cluster of stories. Nevertheless there are a few scraps of thread that, if restored, might be drawn together. Two recurrent subplots, for example, have been the semantics of letters, and the relations between graphospheric fact and what I have called the graphospheric or inscriptional imagination.

Almost wherever lettering exists, it may represent, or be perceived to represent, more than the words that it purports to spell. In Russia, as everywhere, meanings can be conveyed or constructed from the form and design of letters – in themselves, in relation to each other and in relation to the objects of which they are part. The iconographic abbreviations that serve almost as ideograms, the bands of *viaz'* that characterise high-status inscription in the sixteenth and seventeenth centuries, the secretarial scrawl or the careful copperplate undulations, all exude their respective cultural auras, as would the equivalents anywhere. However, a particular feature of

Russian letter-semantics over the latter part of the period, from the early eighteenth century onwards, derived from the interplay of three kinds of script: the ecclesiastical and civil versions of the Cyrillic alphabet; and the Latin alphabet (whether used for Latin itself or for German or French). Not that the Russian graphosphere can be consistently characterised as tri-scriptal: there were many visual articulations of Cyrillic, as well as additional scripts with their own cultural niches (e.g. Greek) or their own bases in the empire (e.g. Georgian, Armenian). Nevertheless, with all appropriate caveats, it was the interplay of traditional Cyrillic, civil type and Latin that produced a characteristic set of cultural resonances. The scripts were rarely neutral alternatives. They marked cultural zones, even cultural values. They could coexist in their more or less separate zones more or less peaceably. They could be juxtaposed with pride. Or, occasionally, they could clash. In Shishkov's critique of the Bible Society publications, the switch to civil type compounded the danger of heresy. For some of the mid-nineteenth-century essayists the density of Latin-script shop signs was a cultural affront, an insult to national dignity.

Where there is culture there is taste, where there is taste there is fashion, where there is fashion there is passion and argument. Diverse responses to aspects of tri-scriptal usage and display reflect not just diverse reactions to what the graphosphere was, but diverse notions of what a graphosphere ought to be. And that, in turn, brings to the fore the role of the graphospheric imagination. In the broadest sense some kind of graphospheric imagination must be a universal both in production and in perception. In a narrower sense fluctuations in the graphospheric imagination could equate to fluctuations in taste. Taste, coupled with accessibility and affordability, is among the factors affecting the shape and texture of the graphosphere: the peasant taste for printed icons, which the patriarch Ioakim found so distasteful; the eighteenth-century taste for text-free canvasses, so distinct from the taste for text-rich imagery in late iconography and in many genres of engraving; the growth in consumer tastes for inscribed 'treasured possessions'. And so on. In a still narrower sense, the graphospheric imagination creates a kind of virtual graphosphere, a graphosphere of the mind, which is contiguous with, or may overlap with, or may have consequences for, but does not necessarily coincide with the graphosphere of real spaces. In the late fifteenth century there is little evidence for a graphospheric imagination extending much beyond the real graphosphere of the church. In the late seventeenth century and early eighteenth century the mind's eye generated inscriptional verse and a density of inscriptional imagery that had little in common with what might have been visible to the physical eye on the streets or even in the graveyards. In the late eighteenth century the graphospheric imagination prompted the creation of a spate of real inscriptions marking the space of the fictional death of a fictional heroine. In Pushkin's narrative of his journey to Arzrum a spurious scrap of paper matched the officer's sense of what a real document might look like, so was as effective as an authentic version. The graphospheric imagination did not develop in straight lines. One can identify some dominant patterns among some social groups during some periods, but closer inspection inevitably blurs the focus as one again confronts the diffuseness and the elusiveness of individual subjectivities.

So we revert to the mini-histories, the explorations of fragments and moments. To sketch some preliminary outlines of the general shapes and features of the Russian graphosphere (or of Russian graphospheres) is in no way to claim that the landscape, its contours and components and ecosystems have thereby been defined and understood. On the contrary: if what is done serves to highlight how much still could usefully be done, then that may count as success of a kind. More broadly, graphospheric specificity is sharpened in graphospheric comparisons. Cross-cultural comparisons in the preceding chapters have been sporadic, and almost entirely limited to Western Europe. Clearly there is more scope for more thorough comparative exploration, and Western Europe does not offer the only or necessarily the most appropriate templates. The particular arguments in this book are about the history of visible words in Russia. The wider proposition is not that graphospheres – Russian or any other – must be encompassed and explained, but that heuristic benefits can and do follow from the identification of the graphosphere as a thing, as an object of study and as a context for studies.

Notes

1 Concepts and Contexts

1. For a trial of its usage as developed here, see my article 'Mapping the Graphosphere: Cultures of Writing in Early Nineteenth-Century Russia (and Before)', *Kritika*, 12.3 (Summer 2011), 531–60. For a different use of the word, see below, pp. 6–7.
2. It emerges, in part, from the notion of the 'graphic environment' explored in an earlier book on an earlier period: Simon Franklin, *Writing, Society and Culture in Early Rus, c. 950–1300* (Cambridge University Press, 2002).
3. See e.g. the workshop on 'Material Texts: Formerly "History of the Book"' at the University of Pennsylvania: www.english.upenn.edu/graduate/working-groups/materialtexts; also, www.english.cam.ac.uk/cmt/. For publications and resources over the broader field, see SHARP, whose remit covers 'communication in material forms': www.sharpweb.org/main/.
4. See e.g. David Finkelstein and Alistair McCleery, *An Introduction to Book History* (New York and London: Routledge, 2005).
5. The websites of Oxford Dictionaries, Merriam-Webster and Wikipedia respectively (all accessed 6 Jan. 2016).
6. See especially the trilogy by Manuel Castells under the general title of *The Information Age: Economy, Society and Culture*, comprising *The Rise of the Network Society, The Power of Identity* and *End of Millennium*, 2nd edn with new preface (Chichester: Wiley-Blackwell, 2010 [1996–8]). Cf. the succinct remarks of E. V. Petrova, *Chelovek v informatsionnom prostranstve: sotsiokul'turnyi aspekt* (Moscow: Institut filosofii RAN, 2014).
7. Tom Standage, *Writing on the Wall: Social Media, the First 2,000 Years* (London, New Delhi, New York and Sydney: Bloomsbury, 2013).
8. E.g. Michael E. Hobart and Zachary S. Schiffman, *Information Ages: Literacy, Numeracy, and the Computer Revolution* (Baltimore and London: Johns Hopkins University Press, 1998); Roger Parry, *The Ascent of Media: From Gilgamesh to Google via Gutenberg* (London and Boston: Nicholas Brealey, 2011).

9. Régis Debray, 'Socialism: A Life-Cycle', *New Left Review*, 46 (Jul.–Aug. 2007), 5–28; cf. Debray, *Cours de médiologie générale* (Paris: Gallimard, 2001), 532–7.
10. Early classics include Jack Goody, *The Domestication of the Savage Mind* (Cambridge University Press, 1977); and Goody, *The Logic of Writing and the Organization of Society* (Cambridge University Press, 1986); for an overview, see David Barton, *Literacy: An Introduction to the Ecology of Written Language*, 2nd edn (Oxford: Blackwell, 2007).
11. Herbert E. Brekle, 'Das typographische Prinzip. Versuch einer Begriffsklärung', *Gutenberg-Jahrbuch*, 72 (1997), 58–63.
12. The starting point for much modern discussion remains Elizabeth L. Eisenstein, *The Printing Press as an Agent of Change*, 2 vols. (Cambridge University Press, 1979). For a flavour of early responses, see e.g. Anthony T. Grafton, 'The Importance of Being Printed', *Journal of Interdisciplinary History*, 11.2 (Autumn 1980), 265–86. For Eisenstein's response to the debates, see her *The Printing Revolution in Early Modern Europe*, 2nd edn (Cambridge University Press, 2005), 313–58.
13. On approaches to the definition of information, see e.g. Toni Weller, *Information History – An Introduction: Exploring an Emergent Field* (Oxford: Chandos Publishing, 2008), 11–22; and Weller (ed.), *Information History in the Modern World: Histories of the Information Age* (Basingstoke: Palgrave Macmillan, 2011).
14. See e.g. Jacob Soll, *The Information Master: Jean-Baptiste Colbert's Secret State Intelligence System* (Ann Arbor: University of Michigan Press, 2009); Edward Higgs, *The Information State in England: The Central Collection of Information on Citizens Since 1500* (Basingstoke: Palgrave Macmillan, 2004); Steven G. Marks, *The Information Nexus: Global Capitalism from the Renaissance to the Present* (Cambridge University Press, 2016). With regard to Russia, see Simon Franklin and Katherine Bowers (eds.), *Information and Empire: Mechanisms of Communication in Russia, 1600–1850* (Cambridge: Open Book Publishers, 2017).
15. Elana Shohamy and Durk Gorter (eds.), *Linguistic Landscape: Expanding the Scenery* (New York and London: Routledge, 2009).
16. See hongtaozhou.com/section/408972_Textscape.html; www.hcsoftware.co.uk/software/textscape/.
17. Michel de Certeau, *The Practice of Everyday Life*, transl. Stephen Rendall (Berkeley: University of California Press, 1984), 131–53.
18. Lisa Gitelman, *Paper Knowledge: Towards a Media History of Documents* (Durham and London: Duke University Press, 2014), x, with regard to developments from the late nineteenth century.
19. Iu. M. Lotman, 'O semiosfere', *Trudy po znakovym sistemam*, 17 (1984), 5–23; transl. Wilma Clark, 'On the Semiosphere', *Sign System Studies*, 33 (2005), 205–29.

20. From Pushkin's poem *The Bronze Horseman*: A. S. Pushkin, *Sobranie sochinenii v desiati tomakh*, ed. D. D. Blagoi et al. (Moscow: Gosudarstvennoe izdatel'stvo khudozhestvennoi literatury, 1959–62), vol. III, 297.
21. Cracraft, *Imagery*, and Cracraft, *Culture*.
22. For a succinct account of these contrasting interpretations, in the form of a dialogue, see Evgenii V. Anisimov, *Petr Pervyi: blago ili zlo dlia Rossii?* (Moscow: Novoe literaturnoe obozrenie, 2017).
23. E.g. Simon Dixon, *The Modernisation of Russia 1676–1825* (Cambridge University Press, 1999); cf. the terms of reference for the online journal *Vivliofika*, 'devoted to the culture and history of the Russian Empire during the "long eighteenth century" (1660–1830)', vivliofika.library.duke.edu/; or John P. LeDonne, *The Grand Strategy of the Russian Empire, 1650–1831* (Oxford University Press, 2004).
24. See, for example, Jarmo Kotilaine and Marshall Poe (eds.), *Modernizing Muscovy: Reform and Social Change in Seventeenth-Century Russia* (London: RoutledgeCurzon, 2004).
25. See the contributions by Russell Martin and Donald Ostrowski to a discussion forum headed 'Divides and Ends: Periodizing the Early Modern in Russian History', *Slavic Review*, 69.2 (Summer 2010), 410–38, and the comments by Nancy S. Kollmann, ibid., 439–47.
26. Gary M. Hamburg, *Russia's Path Toward Enlightenment: Faith, Politics, and Reason, 1500–1801* (New Haven: Yale University Press, 2016); Nancy Shields Kollmann, *The Russian Empire 1450–1801* (Oxford University Press, 2017); cf. L. A. Beliaev and A. V. Iurasov (eds.), *Ot Smuty k Imperii. Novye otkrytiia v oblasti arkheologii i istorii Rossii XVI–XVIII vv.* (Moscow and Vologda: Drevnosti Severa, 2016).
27. See below, pp. 20–1.
28. Slightly later than the spread of steel nibs in Western Europe, from where they were initially imported: see S. A. Reiser, *Russkaia paleografiia novogo vremeni. Neografiia* (Moscow: Vysshaia shkola, 1982), 27–33.
29. E.g. the John Johnson collection in the Bodleian Library: www.bodleian.ox.ac.uk/johnson; also Maurice Rickards, *The Encyclopedia of Ephemera: A Guide to the Fragmentary Documents of Everyday Life for the Collector, Curator, and Historian*, completed and ed. Michael Twyman, with S. du Boscq de Beaumont and A. Tanner (London and New York: Routledge and The British Library, 2000).
30. E.g. below, on 'non-books' in Chapter 2, or on the typology and chronology of blank forms in Chapter 6.
31. For some small glimpses of tertiary writing, see below Chapter 3, on branding and on the literary cult of graffiti on trees.
32. See e.g. Franklin, *Writing, Society and Culture*, 233–41.

33. See e.g. David McKitterick, *Print, Manuscript, and the Search for Order, 1450–1830* (Cambridge University Press, 2003); cf. the different 400-year span, designed to bridge a conventional divide rather than to cover a conventional epoch, in Julia Crick and Alexandra Walsham (eds.), *The Uses of Script and Print, 1300–1700* (Cambridge University Press, 2004).

2 Production in the Graphosphere, I: Primary Writing

1. Franklin, *Writing, Society and Culture*, 15–21.
2. On the chronology, see the chart in Jos Schaeken, *Stemmen op berkenbast. Berichten uit middeleeuws Rusland: dagelijks leven en communikatie* (Leiden University Press, 2012), 25; also the tables in *Novgorodskie gramoty na bereste, tom X (Iz raskopok 1990–1996 gg.)*, ed. V. L. Ianin and A. A. Zalizniak (Moscow: Russkie slovari, 2000), 150–1, and the chronological data on the http://gramoty.ru/ website.
3. On chronology of the use of paper in East Slav documents and codices, see esp. L. V. Stoliarova and S. M. Kashtanov, *Kniga v Drevnei Rusi (XI–XVI vv.)* (Moscow: Universitet Dmitriia Pozharskogo, 2010), 91–126; also the tables in Sergey Lobachev, 'Media and Message in Medieval Russia: Transition from Parchment to Paper', *CASS*, 47 (2013), 307–20 (312–13), although Lobachev's tables imply that all or most of the South Slav manuscripts preserved in Russian collections were imported at the time.
4. See esp. Z. V. Uchastkina, *Razvitie bumazhnogo proizvodstva v Rossii* (Moscow: Lesnaia promyshlennost', 1972); also Z. V. Uchastkina, *The History of Russian Hand Paper-Mills and Their Watermarks*, ed. and adapted J. S. G. Simmons (Hilversum: Paper Publication Society, 1962).
5. See S. A. Klepikov, *Filigrani i shtempeli na bumage russkogo i inostrannogo proizvodstva* (Moscow: Izdatel'stvo vsesoiuznoi knizhnoi palaty, 1959), 28–30.
6. Iu. I. Vishniakova, *Russkie pischebumazhnye fabriki v pervoi treti XIX veka. Spravochnik* (Moscow: Pashkov dom, 2018).
7. Ia. E. Vodarskii and E. G. Istomina, *Pravoslavnye monastyri Rossii i ikh rol' v razvitii kul'tury (XI–nachalo XX v.)* (Moscow: Institut rossiiskoi istorii RAN; Tula: Grif i K., 2009), 535. Note, however, that Vodarskii and Istomina count monasteries in all territories within the Russian Empire's 1917 borders, regardless of the political map at the time of their respective foundations.
8. *PSZ*, no. 12,060. See the summary in Isabel de Madariaga, *Russia in the Age of Catherine the Great* (London: Weidenfeld & Nicolson, 1981), 113–19.
9. Vodarskii and Istomina, *Pravoslavnye monastyri Rossii*, 44.
10. I. M. Gritsevskaia, *Chtenie i chet'i sborniki v drevnerusskikh monastyriakh XV–XVII vv.* (St Petersburg: Dmitrii Bulanin, 2012).

11. N. V. Sinitsyna, 'Knizhnyi master Mikhail Medovartsev', in *Drevnerusskoe iskusstvo. Rukopisnaia kniga*, ed. O. I. Podobedova and G. V. Popov (Moscow: Nauka, 1972), 286–317; R. P. Dmitrieva in *SKKDR. Vyp. 2, Chast' 2*, 109–13; M. V. Kukushkina, *Kniga v Rossii v XVI veke* (Peterburgskoe vostokovedenie, 1999), 108–10. It has been claimed that in the sixteenth century hired clerks constituted a majority of monastic copyists: Vodarskii and Istomina, *Pravoslavnye monastyri Rossii*, 130.
12. On the geographical diversity of manuscript copying, based on the evidence of scribal colophons in extant manuscript books, see A. S. Usachev, 'O geografii napisaniia russkikh rukopisnykh knig v XVI v. (materialy k istorii knigi v Rossii)', *Peterburgskie slavianskie i balkanskie issledovaniia* (*Studia slavica et balcanica petropolitana*), 2015.1, 141–68. A major study of sixteenth-century manuscript production, based on scribal colophons, appeared when the present book was already in production: A. A. Usachev, *Knigopisanie v Rossii XVI veka: po materialam datirovannykh vykhodnykh zapisei* (Moscow: Al'ians-Archeo, 2018), 2 vols.
13. M. S. Krutova, *Kniga glagolemaia. Semantika, struktura i var'irovanie nazvanii russkikh rukopisnykh knig XI–XIX vv.* (Moscow: Pashkov dom, 2010).
14. M. A. Shibaev, 'Predvaritel'nyi spisok avtografov Kirillo-Belozerskogo knizhnika Efrosina', in *Knizhnye tsentry Drevnei Rusi. Knizhniki i rukopisi Kirillo-Belozerskogo monastyria*, ed. N. V. Ponyrko and S. A. Semiachko (St Petersburg: izd. 'Pushkinskii dom', 2014), 81–102.
15. M. D. Kagan, N. V. Ponyrko and M. V. Rozhdestvenskaia, 'Opisanie sbornikov XV v. knigopistsa Efrosina', *TODRL*, 35 (1980), 3–300; see the index of titles, 256–66.
16. Kagan, Ponyrko and Rozhdestvenskaia, 'Opisanie', 175, 121, 174.
17. G. M. Prokhorov (ed.), *Entsiklopediia russkogo igumena XIV–XV vv. Sbornik Prepodobnogo Kirilla Belozerskogo. Rossiiskaia Natsional'naia Biblioteka, Kirillo-Belozerskoe sobranie, no. XII* (St Petersburg: Izdatel'stvo Olega Abyshko, 2003).
18. See also e.g. Gritsevskaia, *Chtenie i chet'i sborniki*, 242–75, on the mid-sixteenth-century compendium of another monk of the Solovetskii monastery, Varlaam Sinitsa.
19. On bookish activity at the Kirillo-Belozersk monastery as pedagogy and scholarship, see Robert Romanchuk, *Byzantine Hermeneutics and Pedagogy in the Russian North: Monks and Masters at the Kirillo-Belozerskii Monastery, 1397–1501* (University of Toronto Press, 2007).
20. Similar estimates are given independently by Kukushkina, *Kniga v Rossii v XVI veke*, 94, and A. S. Usachev, 'O kolichestve sokhranivshikhsia slaviano-russkikh rukopisnykh knig XVI v.', in *Rumiantsevskie chteniia 2010. Ch. 2. Materialy mezhdunarodnoi nauchnoi konferentsii (20–22 aprelia 2010)*

(Moscow: Pashkov dom, 2010), 186–9; see http://opentextnn.ru/history/paleography/?id=4398.

21. From Dosifei's 'Slovo o sotvorenii zhitiia nachal'nik solovetskikh Zosimy i Savatiia', *BLDR*, vol. 13 (2005), 150–2.
22. E.g. N. N. Rozov, 'Solovetskaia biblioteka i ee osnovatel' igumen Dosifei', *TODRL*, 18 (1962), 294–304 (303); A. G. Bobrov, 'Knigopisnaia masterskaia Lisitskogo monastyria (Konets XIV–pervaia polovina XV v.)', in *Knizhnye tsentry Drevnei Rusi XI–XVI vv.: Raznye aspekty issledovaniia* (St Petersburg: Nauka, 1991), 78–98; O. L. Novikova and A. V. Sirenov, 'Sdelano v Chudove', *TODRL*, 55 (2004), 441–50. See also B. M. Kloss, *O proiskhozhdenii nazvaniia 'Rossiia'* (Moscow: Rukopisnye pamiatniki Drevnei Rusi, 2012), 30–46, for a conjectured scriptorium located in one of the Kremlin churches. Also Stoliarova and Kashtanov, *Kniga v Drevnei Rusi*, 207–44.
23. Kukushkina, *Kniga v Rossii v XVI veke*, 127.
24. *Stoglav*, Question 5 and Chapter 28: *Stoglav. Issledovanie i tekst*, ed. E. B. Emchenko (Moscow: Indrik, 2000), 255, 287–8.
25. Instructions to Naumovna in G. V. Markelov, *Pisaniia vygovtsev. Katalog-intsipitarii. Teksty* (St Petersburg: Dmitrii Bulanin, 2004), 374–7; monastic rules for the female scribes are in E. M. Iukhimenko (ed.), *Literaturnoe nasledie Vygovskogo staroobriadcheskogo obshchezhitel'stva*, 2 vols. (Moscow: Iazyki slavianskikh kul'tur, 2008), vol. I, 391–2, 659–60.
26. Vodarskii and Istomina, *Pravoslavnye monastyri Rossii*, 132 (though no source is cited).
27. N. N. Rozov, *Russkaia rukopisnaia kniga. Etiudy i kharakteristiki* (Leningrad: Nauka, 1971), 47, n. 4.
28. Z. V. Dmitrieva, E. V. Krushel'nitskaia and M. I. Mil'chik (eds.), *Opisi Solovetskogo monastyria XVI veka* (St Petersburg: Dmitrii Bulanin, 2003), 33–5, 287.
29. Z. V. Dmitrieva and M. N. Sharomazov, *Opis' stroenii i imushchestva Kirillo-Belozerskogo monastyria 1601 goda: kommentirovannoe izdanie* (St Petersburg: Peterburgskoe vostokovedenie, 1998), 121–36, 276–331. For the full sequence of Kirillo-Belozerskii book lists, see A. P. Balachenkova, 'Knizhnye inventari Kirillo-Belozerskogo monastyria XV–XVII vekov', *Ferapontovskii sbornik*, 5 (1999), 42–59.
30. M. V. Kukushkina, *Monastyrskie biblioteki russkogo severa* (Leningrad: Nauka, 1977), 11.
31. A. A. Romanova, 'K istorii biblioteki Kirillo-Belozerskogo monastyria: "knigi rozdatochnye" 1690–1694 gg.', in *Knizhnye tsentry Drevnei Rusi. Knizhniki i rukopisi Kirillo-Belozerskogo monastyria*, ed. N. V. Ponyrko and S. A. Semiachko (St Petersburg: Pushkinskii dom, 2014), 354–94.

32. See the tables in Kukushkina, *Monastyrskie biblioteki*, 168–76.
33. See, e.g., *Akty Solovetskogo monastyria 1479–1571 gg.*, ed. I. Z. Liberzon (Leningrad: Nauka, 1988); *Akty Solovetskogo monastyria 1572–1584 gg.*, ed. I.Z. Liberzon (Leningrad: Nauka, 1990); Z. V. Dmitrieva, *Vytnye i opisnye knigi Kirillo-Belozerskogo monastyria XVI–XVII vv.* (St Petersburg: Dmitrii Bulanin, 2003); V. I. Ivanov, *Bukhgalterskii uchet v Rossii XVI–XVII vv.: istoriko-istochnikovedcheskoe issledovanie monastyrskikh prikhodo-raskhodnykh knig* (St Petersburg: Dmitrii Bulanin, 2005).
34. T. V. Nikolaeva, *Proizvedeniia russkogo prikladnogo iskusstva s nadpisiami XV–pervoi chetverti XVI v.* (Moscow: Nauka, 1971), no. 100, pp. 92–4, and fig. 66, p. 166; also A. V. Sviatoslavskii and A. A. Troshin, *Krest v russkoi kul'ture. Ocherk russkoi monumental'noi stavrografii* (Moscow: Drevlekhranilishche, 2000), 158–63 (incorrectly dated 1459).
35. On Stefan's cross and commemorative practices and formulae, see A. G. Avdeev, 'O nadpisi na kreste d'iaka Stefana Borodatogo', in G. E. Zakharov and A. Posternak (eds.), *Prikosnovenie k vechnosti. Sbornik statei* (Moscow: PSTGU, 2017), 162–9.
36. Iu. G. Alekseev, *U kormila rossiiskogo gosudarstva. Ocherk razvitiia apparata upravleniia XIV–XV vv.* (Izdatel'stvo Sankt-Peterburgskogo universiteta, 1998), 161–2.
37. The word 'bureaucracy' is here used in its common and somewhat loose sense. For objections to the term, based on a narrower understanding of what it ought to mean, see Hans-Joachim Torke, 'Gab es im Moskauer Reich des 17. Jahrhunderts eine Bürokratie?', *FOG*, 38 (1986), 276–98.
38. Alekseev, *U kormila rossiiskogo gosudarstva*; also A. K. Leont'ev, *Obrazovanie prikaznoi sistemy upravleniia v russkom gosudarstve. Iz istorii sozdaniia tsentralizovannogo gosudarstvennogo apparata v kontse XV–pervoi polovine XVI v.* (Izdatel'stvo MGU, 1961).
39. On their distinctive monograms, some in Uighur script, see below, p. 141.
40. The major prosopographical studies are: S. B. Veselovskii, *D'iaki i podiachie XV–XVII vv.* (Moscow: Nauka, 1975); S. K. Bogoiavlenskii, *Moskovskii prikaznyi apparat i deloproizvodstvo XVI–XVII vekov*, ed. and introd. S. O. Shmidt (Moscow: Iazyki slavianskoi kul'tury, 2006); N. F. Demidova, *Sluzhilaia biurokratiia v Rossii XVII veka (1625–1700). Biograficheskii spravochnik* (Moscow: Pamiatniki istoricheskoi mysli, 2011).
41. Peter B. Brown, 'How Muscovy Governed: Seventeenth-Century Russian Central Administration', *Russian History*, 36 (2009), 459–529; Brown, 'Muscovite Government Bureaus', *Russian History*, 10.3 (1983), 269–330; D. V. Liseitsev, N. M. Rogozhin and Iu. M. Eskin, *Prikazy Moskovskogo gosudarstva XVI–XVII vv. Slovar'-spravochnik* (Moscow and St Petersburg: Tsentr gumanitarnykh initsiativ, 2015). On internal organisation, see Borivoj

Plavsic, 'Seventeenth-Century Chanceries and Their Staffs', in W. M. Pintner and D. K. Rowney (eds.), *Russian Officialdom: The Bureaucratization of Russian Society from the Seventeenth to the Twentieth Century* (Chapel Hill: University of North Carolina Press, 1980), 19–45.

42. Jan Hennings, *Russia and Courtly Europe: Ritual and the Culture of Diplomacy, 1648–1725* (Cambridge University Press, 2016), 69–111.
43. See the tables in Brown, 'How Muscovy Governed', 496–501.
44. See N. F. Demidova, *Sluzhilaia biurokratiia v Rossii XVII v. i ee rol' v formirovanii absoliutizma* (Moscow: Nauka, 1987), 37.
45. *The Travels of Olearius in Seventeenth-Century Russia*, transl. and ed. Samuel H. Baron (Stanford University Press, 1967), 223–6.
46. G. K. Kotoshikhin, *O Rossii v tsarstvovanie Alekseia Mikhailovicha*, ed. G. A. Leont'eva (Moscow: ROSSPEN, 2000), 107–47.
47. Alekseev, *U kormila rossiiskogo gosudarstva*, 126–50.
48. I. Iu. Ankudinov (ed.), *Pistsovye knigi Staroi Russy kontsa XV–XVII vv.* (Moscow: Rukopisnye pamiatniki Drevnei Rusi, 2009).
49. Ankudinov (ed.), *Pistsovye knigi*, 3–34.
50. Ankudinov (ed.), *Pistsovye knigi*, 35–111.
51. Ankudinov (ed.), *Pistsovye knigi*, 84–7, 95, 102, 110.
52. Ankudinov (ed.), *Pistsovye knigi*, 111–275.
53. Ankudinov (ed.), *Pistsovye knigi*, 266–75.
54. V. I. Buganov, *Razriadnye knigi poslednei chetverti XV–nachala XVII v.* (Moscow: AN SSSR, 1962); Marshall Poe, 'Elite Service Registry in Muscovy, 1500–1700', *Russian History*, 21.3 (1994), 251–88; Marshall Poe, 'Muscovite Personnel Records, 1475–1550: New Light on the Early Evolution of Russian Bureaucracy', *Russian History*, 45.3 (1997), 361–77.
55. S. O. Shmidt, *Rossiiskoe gosudarstvo v seredine XVI stoletiia. Tsarskii arkhiv i litsevye letopisi vremeni Ivana Groznogo* (Moscow: Nauka, 1984), 5–186.
56. Shmidt, *Rossiiskoe gosudarstvo*, 44–52.
57. Shmidt, *Rossiiskoe gosudarstvo*, 47–8.
58. S. O. Shmidt and S. E. Kniaz'kov, *Dokumenty deloproizvodstva pravitel'stvennykh uchrezhdenii Rossii XVI–XVII vv. Uchebnoe posobie* (Moskovskii gosudarstvennyi istoriko-arkhivnyi institut, 1985), 27–47, list at least 140 varieties of act, while warning of the problems of inconsistent terminology. See also A. N. Kachalkin, *Zhanry russkogo dokumenta dopetrovskoi epokhi* (Izdatel'stvo MGU, 1988); A. N. Kachalkin, 'Nazvaniia dopetrovskikh delovykh tekstov', *Russkaia rech'*, 2.2 (2002), 73–80.
59. S. M. Kashtanov, *Russkaia diplomatika* (Moscow: Vysshaia shkola, 1970), 146–54; M. N. Tikhomirov, 'Prikaznoe deloproizvodstvo v XVII veke', in Tikhomirov, *Rossiiskoe gosudarstvo XV–XVII vekov* (Moscow: Nauka, 1973), 348–83.

60. Shmidt and Kniaz'kov, *Dokumenty deloproizvodstva*, 14–20.
61. V. N. Avtokratov, 'K istorii zameny stolbovoi formy deloproizvodstva – tetradnoi k nachalu XVIII v.', *Problemy istochnikovedeniia*, 7 (1959), 274–86.
62. Shmidt and Kniaz'kov, *Dokumenty deloproizvodstva*, 47–51; on the accumulation of documents in the course of a case, see e.g. Valerie Kivelson, *Desperate Magic. The Moral Economy of Witchcraft in Seventeenth-Century Russia* (Ithaca and London: Cornell University Press, 2013), 39–41.
63. On the chanceries and judicial personnel, see the summary in Nancy Shields Kollmann, *Crime and Punishment in Early Modern Russia* (Cambridge University Press, 2012), 48–65.
64. Lindsey Hughes, *Russia in the Age of Peter the Great* (New Haven and London: Yale University Press, 2000), 105–11.
65. S. M. Troitskii, *Russkii absoliutizm i dvorianstvo v XVIII v.: formirovanie biurokratii* (Moscow: Nauka, 1974); N. F. Demidova, 'Biurokratizatsiia gosudarstvennogo apparata absoliutizma v XVII–XVIII vv.', in N. M. Druzhinin (ed.), *Absoliutizm v Rossii (XVII–XVIII vv.). Sbornik statei* (Moscow: Nauka, 1964), 206–42.
66. *PSZ*, no. 20,406. On the extension of the process to the regions, see John P. LeDonne, 'Administrative Regionalization in the Russian Empire 1802–1826', *Cahiers du monde russe*, 43.1 (Jan.–Mar. 2002), 5–34.
67. Walter M. Pintner, 'The Evolution of Civic Officialdom, 1755–1855', in Pintner and Rowney, *Russian Officialdom*, 190–226; cf. W. Bruce Lincoln, *In the Vanguard of Reform: Russia's Enlightened Bureaucrats 1825–1861* (DeKalb: Northern Illinois University Press, 1982), 12–13.
68. Lincoln, *In the Vanguard of Reform*, 10. Translated into a modern context of working hours, this would mean that, working eight hours a day, five days per week, for forty-five weeks of the year, one would have to sign a document almost every minute.
69. W. Bruce Lincoln, 'The Daily Life of St Petersburg Officials in the Mid-Nineteenth Century', *Oxford Slavonic Papers. New Series*, 8 (1975), 82–100 (82, 92).
70. Ia. S. Lur'e and A. Iu. Grigorenko, 'Kuritsyn Fedor Vasil'evich', in *SKKDR. Vtoraia polovina XIV–XVI v. Chast' 1*, 504–10; career: Alekseev, *U kormila rossiiskogo gosudarstva*, 203–22.
71. See below, Chapter 6; also Paul Bushkovitch, *Religion and Society in Russia: The Sixteenth and Seventeenth Centuries* (Oxford University Press, 1992), 140–5.
72. Plavsic, 'Seventeenth-Century Chanceries and Their Staffs', 30.
73. N. K. Piksanov, 'Istoriia teksta "Gore ot uma" i printsipy nastoiashchego izdaniia', in A. S. Griboedov, *Gore ot uma*, ed. N. K. Piksanov (Moscow: Nauka, 1969), 331–3.

74. Lucien Febvre and Henri-Jean Martin, *The Coming of the Book*, transl. David Gerard (London: Verso, 1997), 109–27. On sources for the total number of cities with printing presses by 1500 (around 200), see Jeremiah E. Dittmar, 'Information Technology and Economic Change: The Impact of the Printing Press', *Quarterly Journal of Economics*, 126.3 (2011), 1133–72 (1143–4, 1154). On the printing diaspora, see also, e.g., Benito Rial Costas (ed.), *Print Cultures and Peripheries in Early Modern Europe* (Leiden and Boston: Brill, 2013).
75. E.g. see Edward L. Keenan, 'Ivan the Terrible and Book Culture: Fact, Fancy, and Fog. Remarks on Early Muscovite Printing', *Solanus*, 18 (2004), 28–50; Robert Mathiesen, 'Cosmology and the Puzzle of Early Printing in Old Cyrillic', *Solanus*, 18 (2004), 5–27; I. V. Pozdeeva, 'The Activity of the Moscow Printing House in the First Half of the Seventeenth Century', *Solanus*, 6 (1992), 27–55.
76. For a thoughtful overview, see Gary Marker, 'Russia and the "Printing Revolution": Notes and Observations', *Slavic Review*, 41.2 (1982), 266–83.
77. Eisenstein, *The Printing Revolution*, 337.
78. As recently argued by, for example, Alexander Filyushkin, 'Why Did Muscovy Not Participate in the "Communication Revolution" in the Sixteenth Century? Causes and Effects', *CASS*, 51.2–3 (2017), 339–50.
79. Dittmar, 'Information Technology and Economic Change'. On the importance of 'ephemera' in the economy of printing, see also below, pp. 59–60.
80. A. A. Sidorov, 'Rukopisnost' – pechatnost' – knizhnost'', in T. B. Kniazevskaia et al. (eds.), *Rukopisnaia i pechatnaia kniga* (Moscow: Nauka, 1975), 231.
81. See, e.g., A. A. Alekseev, *Tekstologiia slavianskoi Biblii* (St Petersburg: Dmitrii Bulanin, 1999), 13–42.
82. E. Wimmer, 'Zu den katholischen Quellen der Gennadij-Bibel', in *Forschung und Lehre. Abschiedschrift zu Joh. Schröpfers* (Hamburg, 1975), 444–58. On the stages of work, see T. N. Kopreeva, 'Zapadnye istochniki v rabote novgorodskikh knizhnikov kontsa XV–nachala XVI v', *Fedorovskie chteniia 1979* (Moscow: Nauka, 1982), 138–52. See also below, Chapter 4.
83. See Francis J. Thomson, 'The Slavonic Translation of the Old Testament', in Jože Krašovec (ed.), *The Interpretation of the Bible* (Ljubljana and Sheffield: Sheffield University Press, 1998), 655–65; V. A. Romodanovskaia, 'O tseliakh sozdaniia gennadievskoi Biblii kak pervogo polnogo russkogo bibleiskogo kodeksa', in *Knizhnye tsentry Drevnei Rusi. Severnorusskie monastyri*, ed. S. A. Semiachko (St Petersburg: Dmitrii Bulanin, 2001), 278–305.
84. Reproduced in Alekseev, *Tekstologiia*, illustration between pp. 96 and 97; text cited ibid., 196–7.
85. See http://istc.bl.uk/search/search.html.

86. See H. Raab, 'Zu einigen niederdeutschen Quellen des altrussischen Schrifttums', *Zeitschrift für Slawistik*, 3 (1958), 323–35; David B. Miller, 'The Lübeckers Bartholomäus Ghotan and Nicolaus Bulow in Novgorod and Moscow and the Problem of Early Western Influences on Russian Culture', *Viator*, 9 (1978), 395–412.
87. Giles Fletcher, *Of the Russe Common Wealth* (London: T. D. for Thomas Charde, 1591), 86.
88. See below, Chapter 4.
89. I follow the chronology of the biography by Nina Sinitsyna, *Maksim Grek* (Moscow: Molodaia gvardiia, 2008). See also Dimitri Obolensky, *Six Byzantine Portraits* (Oxford: Clarendon Press, 1988), 201–19.
90. See below, p. 120, on his distinctive method of collaborative translation.
91. A. I. Ivanov, *Literaturnoe nasledie Maksima Greka* (Leningrad: Nauka, 1969), 109–14, 120–7 (nos. 132–41, 152–64).
92. Maksim's epistle 'On Fortune' ('Poslanie o fortune'), in *BLDR*, vol. 9 (2000), 306: *bogomerzkoe uchenie prelestnika Nikolaia Germana* (elsewhere in Maksim's works usually *Nikolai Nemchin*).
93. See Sinitsyna, *Maksim Grek*, 148–58.
94. N. Angermann, 'Neues über Nicolaus Bulow und sein Wirken in Moskauer Russland', *JGO*, 17 (1969), 408–19. Note that the colophon gives the date of the source edition according to the western Christian calendar, counting from the birth of Christ (1493), but the date of copying according to the local variant of the traditional Orthodox calendar counting from the Creation (7012 = 1503/4).
95. Text (in two versions) in D. M. Bulanin, *Perevody i poslaniia Maksima Greka* (Leningrad: Nauka, 1984), 198–9.
96. See below, pp. 200–1.
97. E. L. Nemirovskii, *Gesamtkatalog der Frühdrucke in Kyrillischer Schrift, I: Inkunabeln* (Baden-Baden: Verlag Valentin Koerner, 1996), 73–85; E. L. Nemirovskii, *Istoriia slavianskogo kirillicheskogo knigopechataniia XV–nachala XVII veka. I. Vozniknovenie slavianskogo knigopechataniia* (Moscow: Nauka, 2003), 277–373.
98. E. L. Nemirovskii, *Vozniknovenie knigopechataniia v Moskve. Ivan Fedorov* (Moscow: Kniga, 1964), 80–101.
99. E. L. Nemirovskii, *Knigi kirillovskoi pechati 1491–1550. Katalog* (Moscow: Pashkov dom, 2009), 75, no. 2.1, a copy of the 1491 Krakow *Chasoslov*.
100. Nemirovskii, *Vozniknovenie knigopechataniia v Moskve*, 96.
101. Hugh M. Olmsted, 'Maksim Grek's "David and Goliath" and the Skaryna Bible', *HUS*, 19 (1995 [publ. 1997]), 451–75.
102. Miller, 'The Lübeckers Bartholomäus Ghotan and Nicolaus Bulow', 410, posits 'a reaction that was hostile, intolerant, and massive'.

103. A. V. Florovskii, 'Frantsisk Skorina v Moskve', *TODRL*, 24 (1969), 155–8; Olmsted, 'Maksim Grek's "David and Goliath"', 462–5.
104. See also below, pp. 122–3, for Andrei Kurbskii's later report of Maksim Grek's comments on Venetian printing.
105. Dates are disputed: I. V. Pozdeeva and A. A. Turilov, '"TETRATI . . ., PECHATANY V KAZANE" (k istorii i predistorii kazanskoi tipografii XVI v.)', *Drevniaia Rus'. Voprosy medievistiki*, 2001.2(4), 37–49; 2001.4(6), 13–28, proposing 1589–90 and 1595–1600; Guseva, *Izd. kirill. XVI v.*, nos. 97, 130, suggests 1585–90 and 1594–5, while Nemirovskii, *Slavianskie izdaniia*, nos. 159, 220, dates the editions to c. 1579 and c. 1594.
106. M. N. Tikhomirov, 'Nachalo knigopechataniia v Rossii', in M. N. Tikhomirov et al. (eds.), *U istokov russkogo knigopechataniia* (Moscow: AN SSSR, 1959), 13–20; E. L. Nemirovskii, 'Pervaia moskovskaia tipografiia v svete novykh issledovanii. K 450-letiiu so dnia osnovaniia', in *Fedorovskie chteniia. 2003* (Moscow: Nauka, 2003), 11–52.
107. Tikhomirov, 'Nachalo', 25–6. For an inventory of surviving copies see Nemirovskii, *Slavianskie izdaniia*, nos. 83, 85, 86, 90, 92, 115, 119; Guseva, *Izd. kirill. XVI v.*, nos. 3, 5, 9, 10, 30, 33, 34. Current hypothetical dating places the last two anonymous imprints (the 'broad-type' Gospel, and a Psalter) after Fedorov's *Apostol*.
108. Nemirovskii, *Slavianskie izdaniia*, nos. 117, 118; Guseva, *Izd. kirill. XVI v.*, nos. 35, 36.
109. Nemirovskii, *Slavianskie izdaniia*, no. 126; Guseva, *Izd. kirill. XVI v.*, no. 42.
110. Colophons to: 1564 *Apostol* in 'Posleslovіia k izdaniiam Ivana Fedorova', *BLDR*, vol. 12 (2003), 524–6; the two 1565 Breviaries and the 1568 Psalter in Guseva, *Izd. kirill. XVI v.* (nos. 35, 36, 42).
111. See also below, pp. 242–4.
112. Tikhomirov, 'Nachalo', 14–15, for hypotheses. D. M. Bulanin is sceptical in his commentary in *BLDR*, vol. 12 (2004), 619.
113. A. S. Usachev, 'O vozmozhnykh prichinakh nachala knigopechataniia v Rossii. Predvaritel'nye zamechaniia', *CASS*, 51 (2017), 229–47.
114. Fletcher, *Of the Russe Common Wealth*, 85v.
115. See E. L. Nemirovskii, *Ivan Fedorov, okolo 1510–1583* (Moscow: Nauka, 1985), 111–17, for a survey of opinions.
116. Text in Tikhomirov et al. (eds.), *U istokov russkogo knigopechataniia*, 237, fig. 14; *BLDR*, vol. 12 (2004), 528.
117. A. S. Demin, 'Russkie staropechatnye posleslovіia vtoroi poloviny XVI v. (otrazhenie nedoveriia chitatelei k pechatnoi knige)', in Demin et al. (eds.), *Tematika i stilistika predislovii i posleslovii* (Moscow: Nauka, 1981), 45–70.

118. Sergei Bogatyrev, 'The Patronage of Early Printing in Moscow', *CASS*, 51 (2017), 249–88. For a summary of other hypotheses, see Tat'iana Murav'eva, *Ivan Fedorov* (Moscow: Molodaia gvardiia, 2011), 229–35.
119. Guseva, *Izd. kirill. XVI v.*, fig. 42.4–6.
120. See Nemirovskii, *Ivan Fedorov,* esp. the chronological summary, 299–300.
121. A. V. Voznesenskii, *K istorii slavianskoi pechatnoi Psaltiri. Moskovskaia traditsiia XVI–XVII vekov. Prostaia Psaltir'* (Moscow and St Petersburg: Al'ians-Arkheo, 2010), 265–6.
122. Guseva, *Izd. kirill. XVI v.*, nos. 109, 115, 128, 153, 162, 167, 169; Zernova, *KKP XVI–XVII veka*, nos. 17–19.
123. Zernova, *KKP XVI–XVII veka*, nos. 20–9. On a possible further title, see A. A. Guseva, *Rabota s redkimi i tsennymi izdaniiami. Identifikatsiia ekzempliarov moskovskikh izdanii kirillovskogo shrifta 2-i poloviny XVI–XVII vv. Metodicheskie rekomendatsii* (Moscow: GBL, 1990), 89 (no. 162).
124. On the Print Chancery (*Prikaz knig pechatnogo dela*), see Liseitsev, Rogozhin and Eskin, *Prikazy Moskovskogo gosudarstva*, 118–19.
125. For comparative lists up to 1600, see Guseva, *Izd. kirill. XVI v.*, 1290–6.
126. Tables in I. V. Pozdeeva, 'Mezhdu srednevekov'em i novym vremenem: novoe v deiatel'nosti Moskovskogo pechatnogo dvora vtoroi poloviny XVII v.', in *MPD – fakt i faktor, 1652–1700. Kniga 1*, 126–7.
127. For the documents detailing the equipping of the presses, see *MPD – fakt i faktor, 1618–1652*, 187–201.
128. A. V. Dadykin, 'Prikaz knigopechatnogo dela i sotrudniki Moskovskogo pechatnogo dvora vo vtoroi polovine XVII v.', in *MPD – fakt i faktor. 1652–1700. Kniga 1*, 144–5. The overall numbers may have been higher than in the tables, since Dadykin does not include the administration or the affiliated workers (*pribylye* – see pp. 161–5).
129. See below, Chapter 6.
130. *Mosk. kirill. izd. RGADA. Vypusk 3. 1651–1675*, nos. 1, 12, 15, 18, 23, 24, 29, 30, 32, 59, 60, 65, 68, 82, 92, 94. For figures from 1677 and 1693, see S. P. Luppov, *Kniga v Rossii v XVII veke* (Leningrad: Nauka, 1970), 67.
131. See Gary Marker, 'Literacy and Literacy Texts in Muscovy', *Slavic Review*, 49.1 (Spring 1990), 74–89 (esp. tables 1, 2, pp. 81, 84); Pozdeeva, 'Mezhdu srednevekov'em i novym vremenem', 64–5.
132. Data from the Printing Department archive on the 1652 *azbuka* are published in *MPD – fakt i faktor. 1652–1700. Kn. 1*, 267–9.
133. Pozdeeva, 'The Activity of the Moscow Printing House', 53; see the tables of cost and price in the same author's 'Istoriko-kul'turnoe znachenie deiatel'nosti Moskovskogo pechatnogo dvora v pervoi polovine XVII veka', in *MPD – fakt i faktor, 1618–1652*, 33–6.

134. Simon Franklin, 'Printing Moscow: Significances of the Frontispiece to the 1663 Bible', *SEER*, 88 (2010), 79–80.
135. L. I. Sazonova and A. A. Guseva, 'Burtsov Vasilii Fedorov', in *SKKDR XVII v. Chast' 1*, 148–53; on *bukvari* see below, p. 189.
136. N. P. Kiselev, 'O moskovskom knigopechatanii XVII veka', *Kniga. Issledovaniia i materialy*, 2 (1960), 164–9; L. A. Chernaia, 'Verkhniaia tipografiia Simeona Polotskogo', in A. N. Robinson (ed.), *Simeon Polotskii i ego knigoizdatel'skaia deiatel'nost'* (Moscow: Nauka, 1982), 46–59.
137. On the press at Kutein, see Iu. M. Lauryk, *Knigi i knigazbory kutseinskaga Bogaiaulenskaga manastyra u siaredzine XVII st.* (Minsk: Tekhnalogiia, 2012).
138. A. A. Bulychev, *Istoriia odnoi politicheskoi kampanii XVII veka* (Moscow: Iazyki slavianskoi kul'tury, 2004). Bulychev argues that the underlying reasons were political.
139. See Iakym Zapas'ko and Iaroslav Isaevych, *Pam'iatky knyzhkovoho mystetstva. Kataloh starodrukiv, vydannykh na Ukraini, kn. 1, 1574–1700* (Lviv: Vysha shkola, 1981); *Ukrainskie knigi kirillovskoi pechati XVI–XVIII vv. Katalog izdanii, khraniashchikhsia v Gosudarstvennoi biblioteke SSSR imeni V. I. Lenina. Vypusk I. 1574 g.–I polovina XVII v.*, ed. T. N. Kameneva and A. A. Guseva (Moscow: GBL, 1976).
140. Cracraft, *Culture*, 260, 297; Cracraft labels a whole section 'The Print Revolution in Russia' (pp. 257–76).
141. On Peter's reforms and their limitations, see Marker, 'Russia and the "Printing Revolution"', 279, and Marker, *Publishing*, 20–4. Marker's magisterial study informs much of what is outlined in the following paragraphs.
142. For more detail, see below, pp. 105–9.
143. See M. A. Alekseeva, *Graviura petrovskogo vremeni* (Leningrad: Iskusstvo, 1990), 102–8.
144. See A. Z. Abramishvili, 'Iz istorii gruzinskogo knigopechataniia za predelami Gruzii (Rim, 1629–1800 gg. Moskva, 1705–1917)', *Kniga. Issledovaniia i materialy*, 3 (1960), 251–99.
145. Bykova and Gurevich, *Grazhd.*, Appendix I, no. 32 (pp. 497–8).
146. Marker, *Publishing*, 44–5.
147. For a list of eighteenth-century presses, noting the dates of foundation, see *SK XVIII v.*, V, 278–90.
148. See Marker, *Publishing*, 93–5.
149. *SK XVIII v.*, V, no. 126 (p. 116, with illustration).
150. [Antonio Catiforo], *Zhitie Petra Velikogo Imperatora i Samoderzhtsa Vserossiiskogo i Ottsa Otechestva ... na dialekte Italianskom, a potom na Grecheskom: s koego na Rossiiskii iazyk perevel statskii sovetnik Stefan Pisarev* (St Petersburg: pri Imp. AN, 1772). The preface is cited in M. N. Kufaev, *Istoriia russkoi knigi v XIX veke* (Moscow: Pashkov dom, 2003 [1927]), 37.

151. A. Iu. Samarin, 'Novye dokumenty o pervom vladel'tse chastnoi tipografii v Rossii I. M. Gartunge', in *Fedorovskie chteniia 2005* (Moscow: Nauka, 2005), 517–28; S. R. Dolgova, 'O pervykh vladel'tsakh chastnykh tipografii v Rossii (I. M. Gartung i I. K. Shnor)', *Kniga. Issledovaniia i materialy*, 32 (1976), 178–80.
152. Abramishvili, 'Iz istorii gruzinskogo knigopechataniia', 275–94.
153. See below, pp. 131–2, 136.
154. On the procedures for, and status of, permissions for private printing presses in the decade from 1771, see M. Iu. Gordeeva, 'Zarozhdenie chastnogo knigopechataniia v Rossii (po materialam senatskikh ukazov)', in V. P. Leonov (ed.), *Kniga v Rossii. Sbornik 1* (Moscow: Nauka, 2006), 147–56.
155. *PSZ*, no. 15,634.
156. Marker, *Publishing*, 108.
157. Checklist in *SK XVIII v.*, IV, 289–90. On the continuity of the press at Klintsy, see E. A. Emel'ianova, *Staroobriadcheskie izdaniia kirillovskogo shrifta kontsa XVIII–nachala XIX veka* (Moscow: Pashkov dom, 2010), 234–486; also below pp. 246–7.
158. Marker, *Publishing*, 105.
159. Facsimile edition of the fifty-two issues: *Tambovskie izvestiia*, ed. and comm. V. V. Kanishchev, Iu. V. Meshcheriakov and Iu. A. Mizis (Tambovskii gosudarstvennyi universitet, 2012).
160. Cited in Kufaev, *Istoriia russkoi knigi*, 61.
161. Bykova and Gurevich, *Grazhd.*, and Bykova and Gurevich *Kirill; SK XVIII v.; SK Inostr.*
162. See, the two volumes so far published of *SK 1801–1825*, covering the letters A–D and E–L respectively. On some of the problems, see V. I. Kharlamov, 'Metodicheskie i istochnikovedcheskie problemy sozdaniia spravochnykh posobii o rossiiskikh izdatel'stvakh XIX–XX vekov', in *Knizhnoe delo v Rossii v XIX–nachale XX veka. Vypusk 14. Sbornik nauchnykh trudov* (St Petersburg: RNB, 2008), 141–9.
163. I am grateful to Katherine Bowers for compiling the list.
164. See Marianna Tax Choldin, *A Fence Around the Empire: Russian Censorship of Western Ideas Under the Tsars* (Durham: Duke University Press, 1985), 18–22.
165. On the late eighteenth century, see Marker, *Publishing*, 212–32. More broadly, see G. V. Zhirkov, *Istoriia tsenzury v Rossii XIX–XX vv.* (Moscow: Aspekt Press, 2001), 7–64.
166. *PSZ*, no. 19,387.
167. *PSZ*, nos. 17,523, 17,811, 19,807. See Marker, *Publishing*, 226–32.
168. In Russian *listovye izdania* or *listovki*. An older designation, *letuchie izdaniia, letuchie listy* echoes the French *feuilles volants* and/or the German *Flugschriften*.

169. On broadsheet publishing in Western Europe before 1700, see Andrew Pettegree (ed.), *Broadsheets: Single-Sheet Publishing in the First Age of Print* (Leiden and Boston: Brill, 2017).
170. Falk Eisermann, 'Fifty Thousand Veronicas: Print Runs of Broadsheets in the Fifteenth and Early Sixteenth Centuries', in Pettegree (ed.), *Broadsheets*, 76–113. The quantities could be enormous even in provincial print shops: see e.g. Alexander Wilkinson, 'The Printed Book on the Iberian Peninsula, 1500–1540', in Malcolm Walsby and Graeme Kemp (eds.), *The Book Triumphant: Print in Transition in the Sixteenth and Seventeenth Centuries* (Leiden and Boston: Brill, 2011), 78–96 (esp. 87–8).
171. See below, pp. 222–4.
172. N. P. Likhachev, *Katalog letuchikh izdanii i ikh perepechatok* (St Petersburg: Tip. V. S. Balasheva & Ko., 1895). Likhachev's collections are now distributed across several institutions: see the exhibition catalogue *'Zvuchat lish' pis'mena . . . ' k 150-letiiu so dnia rozhdeniia akademika Nikolaia Petrovicha Likhacheva. Katalog vystavki*, ed. A. O. Bol'shakov and E. V. Stepanova (St Petersburg: Izdatel'stvo Gosudarstvennogo Ermitazha, 2012).
173. Michael Harris, 'Printed Ephemera', in Michael F. Suarez and H. R. Woodhuysen (eds.), *The Book: A Global History* (Oxford University Press, 2013), 204–19.
174. N. V. Gogol, *Polnoe sobranie sochinenii v 14 tomakh*, vol. VI (Moscow: AN SSSR, 1951), 54–5.

3 Production in the Graphosphere, II: Secondary Writing

1. See below, pp. 156–8.
2. A. G. Nebolsin, *Zakonodatel'stvo o fabrichnykh i torgovykh kleimakh v Rossii i zagranitseiu* (St Petersburg: Tipografiia V. F. Kirshbauma, 1886), 4–6.
3. *PSZ*, no. 8,876.
4. E. A. Mishina, 'Gravirovannye marki russkikh bumazhnykh fabrik v XVIII veke', in *Russkaia grafika XVIII–pervoi poloviny XIX veka. Novye materialy* (Leningrad: Iskusstvo, 1984), 12–25.
5. *PSZ*, nos. 16,188, 17,938, 18,795; cf. also no. 18,318.
6. See also below, pp. 179–80, 250–1.
7. See e.g. Mikhail Krasilin, 'Russkaia ikona XVIII–nachala XX vekov', in Liliia Evseeva et al., *Istoriia ikonopisi. Istoki, traditsii, sovremennost'* (Moscow: ART-BMB, 2002), 209–30.
8. See below, pp. 177–9.
9. See below, Chapter 5.

10. From the mid eighteenth century: Manfred A. Dobin, *Pochtovye shtempelia Rossiiskoi Imperii: domarochnyi period* (St Petersburg: Standart Kollektsiia, 2009).
11. I. A. Kiselev, *Datirovka kirpichnykh kladok XVI–XIX vv. Po vizual'nym kharakteristikam* (Moscow: Ministerstvo kul'tury RSFSR, 'Rosrestavratsiia', 1990); available as a Word document from www.allbeton.ru/.
12. See e.g. below, p. 141.
13. S. P. Kalinichev, *Samovarnoe delo v Rossii. Katalog-spravochnik* (Moscow: Khobbi Press, 2015), including a catalogue of nearly a thousand manufacturers' marks of more than seven hundred makers (pp. 327–440), starting from the second half of the eighteenth century.
14. I. Z. Zubets, 'Ob odnoi gruppe prianikov i prianichnykh dosok iz kollektsii Gosudarstvennogo muzeiia-zapovednika "Rostovskii kreml"', in *Problemy atributsii pamiatnikov dekorativno-prikladnogo iskusstva XVI–XX vekov* (Moscow: Istoricheskii muzei, 2015), 300–11.
15. There is some evidence for the presence of playing cards in Russia from the sixteenth century. They became fashionable towards the mid eighteenth century: Vyacheslav V. Shevtsov, 'The Introduction of Playing Cards in Russia', *CASS*, 50 (2016), 355–76.
16. A. S. Mel'nikova, V. V. Uzdenikov and I. S. Shikanova, *Den'gi v Rossii. Istoriia russkogo denezhnogo khoziaistva s drevneishikh vremen do 1917 g.* (Moscow: Strelets, 2000), 38; G. A. Fedorov-Davydov, *Monety Moskovskoi Rusi (Moskva v bor'be za nezavisimoe i tsentralizovannoe gosudarstvo)* (Izd. Moskovskogo universiteta, 1981); P. G. Gaidukov and I. V. Grishin, 'Imennye den'gi velikogo kniazia Dmitriia Ivanovicha Donskogo (tipologiia i khronologiia)', in *Velikii Novgorod i srednevekovaia Rus'. Sbornik statei k 80-letiiu akademika V. L. Ianina* (Moscow: Pamiatniki istoricheskoi mysli, 2009), 323–64.
17. Mel'nikova, Uzdenikov and Shikanova, *Den'gi v Rossii*, 39.
18. Fedorov-Davydov, *Monety Moskovskoi Rusi*, 84–7, argues that there was a distinction between major and minor principalities in this respect, with the 'illegible' inscriptions more characteristic of the latter.
19. Gustav Alef, 'The Political Significance of the Inscriptions on Muscovite Coinage in the Reign of Vasili II', *Speculum*, 34 (1950), 1–19; Jacob Emery, 'Species of Legitimacy: The Rhetoric of Succession Around Russian Coins', *Slavic Review*, 75.1 (Spring 2016), 1–21.
20. See A. S. Mel'nikova, *Russkie monety ot Ivana Groznogo do Petra Pervogo. Istoriia russkoi denezhnoi sistemy s 1533 po 1682 god* (Moscow: 'Finansy i statistika', 1989), 14–46.
21. Mel'nikova, *Russkie monety*, 197.
22. I. G. Spasskii, *Russkie efimki. Issledovanie i katalog* (Novosibirsk: Nauka, Sibirskoe otdelenie, 1988), 21; Spasskii, *Talery v russkom denezhnom*

obrashchenii 1654–1659 godov. Svodnyi katalog efimkov (Leningrad: Izdatel'stvo Gosudarstvennogo Ermitazha, 1960). On the over-stamped coins: Evgenii Pukhov, *Moneta 'efimok s priznakom'* (St Petersburg: PremiumPress, 2014).

23. Mel'nikova, *Russkie monety*, 212–26.
24. Philip Longworth, *Alexis, Tsar of All the Russias* (London: Secker & Warburg, 1984), 150–3; K. V. Bazilevich, *Denezhnaia reforma Alekseia Mikhailovicha i vosstanie v Moskve v 1662 g.* (Moscow: AN SSSR, 1936).
25. See A. I. Iukht, *Russkie den'gi ot Petra Velikogo do Aleksandra I* (Moscow: Finansy i statistika, 1994), 9–36; V. E. Semenov, *Monetnoe delo Rossiiskoi imperii* (St Petersburg: Konros-Inform, 2010).
26. Robert P. Harris, *A Guidebook of Russian Coins 1725 to* 1972, 2nd edn (Amsterdam: Mevius & Hirschhorn Int., 1974); G. M. Severin, *Monety Rossiiskoi imperii. Platinovye, zolotye, serebrianye. 1682–1917* (Moscow: Profizdat, 2006); also Mel'nikova, Uzdenikov and Shikanova, *Den'gi v Rossii*, 105–77.
27. V. V. Uzdenikov, *Monety Rossii 1700–1917*, 4th edn (Moscow: IP Media, 2011), 332–64, 428–32.
28. V. E. Semenov, *Poddelki rossiiskikh monet* (St Petersburg: Konros-Inform, 2012).
29. Bernhard F. Brekke, *The Copper Coins of Imperial Russia 1700–1917* (Malmö: Förlagshuset Norden AB, 1977), esp. 14–17. Also Bernhard F. Brekke and Tom Willy Bakken, *The Copper Coinage of Imperial Russia 1700–1917. Supplement 1997. Includes: Errors, Overdates, Overstrikes and Fakes* (Oslo: Norsk Numismatik Vorlag A/S, 1997).
30. E. S. Shchukina, *Dva veka russkoi medali. Medal'ernoe iskusstvo v Rossii 1700–1917 gg.* (Moscow: TERRA, 2000), 7.
31. I. G. Spasskii, 'Monetnoe i monetovidnoe zoloto v Moskovskom gosudarstve i pervye zolotye Ivana III', *Vspomogatel'nye istoricheskie distsipliny*, 8 (1976), 110–31.
32. N. I. Chepurnov, *Nagradnye medali Gosudarstva Rossiiskogo. Entsiklopedicheskoe illiustrirovannoe izdanie* (Moscow: Russkii mir, 2000), 7.
33. I. G. Spasskii, '"Zolotye" – voinskie nagrady dopetrovskoi Rusi', *Trudy Gosudarstvennogo Ermitazha IV. Numizmatika 2* (Leningrad: Izd. Gosudarstvennogo Ermitazha, 1961), 92–134. For the early gold medals, see S. P. Sokolov, *Svodnyi katalog russkikh medalei. 1462–1762* (Kiev: Kupola, 2005), 6–28 (nos. 001–026).
34. On the relationship of this portrait to other portraits of Golitsyn, see Lindsey Hughes, *Russia and the West: The Life of a Seventeenth-Century Westernizer, Prince Vasily Vasil'evich Golitsyn (1643–1714)* (Newtonville, MA: Oriental Research Partners, 1984), 102.

35. Sokolov, *Svodnyi katalog*, 50–355, nos. 041–166; Cracraft, *Imagery*, 268–71, writes of fifty-eight Petrine medals. This figure reflects the manuscript catalogue of Ivan Shlatter, compiled in the 1740s: Shchukina, *Dva veka Russkoi medali*, 38.
36. Shchukina, *Dva veka russkoi medali*, 10–14. See A. E. Makhov, *Emblematika. Makrokosm* (Moscow: Intrada, 2014); on emblems in the culture of the Petrine age, see e.g. A. A. Morozov, 'Emblematika barokko v literature i iskusstve petrovskogo vremeni', *XVIII vek*, 9 (1974), 184–226.
37. M. E. D'iakov, *Medali rossiiskoi imperii*, 2 vols. (Moscow: ZAO Dukhovnaia niva, 2004, 2005). However, D'iakov dates medals according to the events commemorated, which are not always the dates of issue.
38. Shchukina, *Dva veka russkoi medali*, 26–34.
39. Shchukina, *Dva veka russkoi medali*, 126–32.
40. See the index of Latin medal inscriptions in D'iakov, *Medali rossiiskoi imperii*, I, 212–5; II, 250–5.
41. On a controversy in the early 1770s, see Shchukina, *Dva veka russkoi medali*, 65–9.
42. Shchukina, *Dva veka russkoi medali*, 41–2, 74–5.
43. D. I. Peters, *Nagradnye medali Rossii vtoroi poloviny XVIII stoletiia* (Moscow: Arkheograficheskii tsentr, 1999), 35–6 (no. 2); Chepurnov, *Nagradnye medali Gosudarstva Rossiiskogo*, 127–8.
44. See Chepurnov, *Nagradnye medali Gosudarstva Rossiiskogo*, 82–3, 96–8, 112–13; Shchukina, *Dva veka russkoi medali*, 108, 112, 115, 127; E. S. Shchukina, *Monogrammy i podpisi na russkikh medaliakh XVIII–nachala XX vekov* (Kiev: Iunona-moneta, 2002), 34, 73, 75, 128.
45. See V. A. Durov, *Ordena Rossii. Orders of Russia* (Moscow: Voskresen'e, 1993); also G. V. Vilinbakhov, *Simvoly Rossii. Ocherki po istorii russkoi geral'diki* (St Petersburg: Fakul'tet filologii i iskusstv Sankt-Peterburgskogo gosudarstvennogo universiteta, 2009), 365–415, and the illustrations on 416–87.
46. Originally the Order of Liberation, in honour of St Catherine's alleged role in delivering Russian troops from the Turks in 1711. See Durov, *Ordena*, 146–7.
47. Durov, *Ordena Rossii*, 106–7.
48. Shchukina, *Monogrammy i podpisi*, 63–78.
49. Shchukina, *Dva veka russkoi medali*, 62, 102–3.
50. Shchukina, *Dva veka russkoi medali*, 67.
51. I. V. Rudenko, *Pamiatnye zhetony Imperatorskoi Rossii (1721–1917 gg.)* (Rostov-on-Don: Omega Publisher, 2007).
52. Lindsey Hughes, '"A Beard Is an Unnecessary Burden": Peter I's Laws on Shaving and Their Roots in Early Russia', in Roger Bartlett and Hughes (eds.), *Russian Society and Culture and the Long Eighteenth Century: Essays in Honour of Anthony G. Cross* (Münster: LIT Verlag, 2004), 21–34; Evgeny

Akelev, 'When Did Peter the Great Order Beards Shaved?', *Quaestio Rossica*, 5.4 (2017), 1107–30.

53. I. V. Rudenko, *Borodovye znaki 1698, 1705, 1724, 1725. Katalog* (Rostov-on-Don: Omega Publisher, 2013).
54. E. I. Kamentseva and N. V. Ustiugov, *Russkaia sfragistika i geral'dika* (Moscow: Vysshaia shkola, 1974).
55. Sergei Neliubov, 'Ratniki na srednevekovykh russkikh perstniakh', *Tseikhgaus*, 15 (2001), 2–5; Neliubov, 'Simvolika srednevekovykh russkikh perstnei', *Tseikhgaus*, 17 (2002), 4–8.
56. Elissa O'Loughlin, 'Wafers and Wafer Seals: History, Manufacture, and Conservation', *Paper Conservator*, 20 (1996), 8–15.
57. See below, p. 234.
58. Vilinbakhov, *Simvoly Rossii*, 30–62; N. A. Soboleva, *Rossiiskaia gosudarstvennaia simvolika. Istoriia i sovremennost'* (Moscow: Gumanitarnyi izdatel'skii tsentr VLADOS, 2003), 11–79.
59. I. A. Voznesenskaia, 'Lichnye pechati v Rossiiskoi imperii XVIII–XIX vv. (ottiski na deloproizvodstvennykh dokumentakh)', *Vestnik RGGU*, 12(74)/11 (2011), 234–44. On the 'pre-heraldic' period of personal seals, see Iu. M. Eskin, 'Pechati chlenov Boiarskoi Dumy v 1633 godu. K istorii russkoi "predgeral'diki"', *Russia mediaevalis*, 10.1 (2001), 205–23.
60. Kamentseva and Ustiugov, *Russkaia sfragistika i geral'dika*, 162.
61. Kamentseva and Ustiugov, *Russkaia sfragistika i geral'dika*, 189. See also www.ranar.spb.ru/rus/vystavki/id/457/.
62. T. G. Gol'dberg, F. Ia. Mishukov, N. G. Platonova and M. M. Postnikova-Loseva, *Russkoe zolotoe i serebrianoe delo XV–XX vekov* (Moscow: Nauka, 1967); Alexander von Solodkoff, *Russian Gold and Silverwork: Seventeenth–Nineteenth Century* (New York: Rizzoli, 1981).
63. M. M. Postnikova-Loseva, 'Zolotye i serebrianye izdeliia masterov Oruzheinoi palaty XVI–XVII vekov', in S. K. Bogoiavlenskii and G. A. Novitskii (eds.), *Gosudarstvennaia Oruzheinaia palata Moskovskogo Kremlia. Sbornik nauchnykh trudov po materialam Gosudarstvennoi Oruzheinoi palaty* (Moscow: Iskusstvo, 1954), 137–216.
64. M. M. Postnikova-Loseva, 'Serebrianoe delo v Novgorode XVI i XVII vekov', in *Drevnerusskoe iskusstvo. Khudozhestvennaia kul'tura Novgoroda*, ed. V. N. Lazarev, O. I. Podobedova and V. V. Kostochkin (Moscow: Nauka, 1968), 307–34; on the numbers of silversmiths, see pp. 310–11. Also V. V. Igoshev, *Dragotsennaia tserkovnaia utvar' XVI–XVII vv. Velikii Novgorod. Iaroslavl'. Sol'vychegodsk* (Moscow: Indrik, 2009).
65. M. M. Postnikova-Loseva, 'Serebrianoe delo Pskova XVI–XVII vekov', in *Drevnerusskoe iskusstvo. Khudozhestvennaia kul'tura Pskova*, ed. V. N. Lazarev, O. I. Podobedova and V. V. Kostochkin (Moscow: Nauka, 1968), 157–73.

66. V. V. Igoshev, *Iaroslavskoe serebro XVI–XVIII vv.* (Moscow: Modus graffiti, 1997); also M. M. Postnikova-Loseva, 'Mastera-serebrianiki gorodov Povolzh'ia XVII veka. Iaroslavl', Nizhnii Novgorod, Kostroma', in *Drevnerusskoe iskusstvo. XVII vek*, ed. V. N. Lazarev, O. I. Podobedova and V. V. Kostochkin (Moscow: Nauka, 1964), 272–315.
67. Postnikova-Loseva, 'Zolotye i serebrianye izdeliia', 148, 152.
68. N. G. Troepol'skaia, 'Paleograficheskii analiz nadpisei na serebrianoi zhalovannoi posude XVII–XVIII vv.', in *Voprosy slaviano-russkoi paleografii, kodikologii, epigrafiki. Trudy Gosudarstvennogo ordena Lenina Istoricheskogo muzeia. Vypusk 63* (Moscow: Gosudarstvennyi istoricheskii muzei, 1987), 62–70. On viaz' and other styles of lettering, see below, pp. 103–4.
69. See e.g. the sixth-century patens and chalices in the Dumbarton Oaks collections: BZ.1963.36.1–3; BZ.1924.5; BZ.1955.18, online at http://museum.doaks.org/PRT2611?sid=18576&x=452747&x=452748.
70. A. A. Medyntseva, *Gramotnost' v Drevnei Rusi. Po pamiatnikam epigrafiki X–pervoi poloviny XIII veka* (Moscow: Nauka, 2000), 155–68.
71. Postnikova-Loseva, 'Zolotye i serebrianye izdeliia', 178–81.
72. British Museum, 1878, 1230.636; the almost identical inscription on a wine cup, Victoria and Albert Museum M.169:1, 2–1923; cf. the coconut cup mounted in silver, British Museum AF.3173, inscribed 'the nut of Izot Ivanovich. Drink from it for good health' (Fig. 3.3.).
73. Postnikova-Loseva, 'Serebrianoe delo v Novgorode', 315, 329.
74. Postnikova-Loseva, 'Zolotye i serebrianye izdeliia', 180.
75. Ibid., and plate 27; not the town of Samara on the Volga, but a fortress near what is now Dnipro, in Ukraine.
76. *Perepiska Ivana Groznogo s Andreem Kurbskim*, ed. Ia. S. Lur'e and Iu. D. Rykov (Leningrad: Nauka, 1979), 28.
77. See T. G. Gol'dberg, 'Iz posol'skikh darov XVI–XVII vekov. Angliiskoe serebro', in Bogoiavlenskii and Novitskii (eds.), *Gosudarstvennaia Oruzheinaia palata*, 435–506; Charles Oman, *The English Silver at the Kremlin 1557–1663* (London: Methuen, 1961); Olga Dmitrieva and Natalya Abramova (eds.), *Britannia and Muscovy: English Silver at the Court of the Tsars* (New Haven and London: Yale University Press, 2006); N. E. Abramova, *Serebro Anglii XVI–XX vekov* (Moscow: Gosudarstvennyi istoriko-kul'turnyi muzei-zapovednik 'Moskovskii Kreml'', 2014); G. A. Markova, *Nemetskoe khudozhestvennoe serebro XVI–XVIII vekov v sobranii Gosudarstvennoi Oruzheinoi palaty* (Moscow: Iskusstvo, 1975).
78. E.g. Dmitrieva and Abramova (eds.), *Britannia and Muscovy*, nos. 3–5, 7, 9, 11, 12, 14–16, 18–27, 31–2; cf. Abramova, *Serebro Anglii*, nos. 1–115.
79. E.g. Postnikova-Loseva, 'Serebrianoe delo v Novgorode', 328–9; Igoshev, *Iaroslavskoe serebro*, 90–2 (nos. 87–9, pp. 169–71).

80. E.g. Victoria and Albert Museum M.98–1926, a Cyrillic-inscribed mid-seventeenth-century parcel-gilt beaker made in Hamburg.
81. I. D. Kostina, *Proizvedeniia moskovskikh serebrianikov pervoi poloviny XVIII veka. Katalog* (Moscow: Gosudarstvennyi istoriko-kul'turnyi muzei-zapovednik 'Moskovskii Kreml'', 2003), nos. 118–23, 168, 182–6, 208, 245–7 etc.; Anne Odom, *Russian Enamels: Kievan Rus to Fabergé* (London: Philip Wilson Publishers, 1996), nos. 39–41; N. V. Kaliazina, G. N. Komelova, N. D. Kostochkina, O. G. Kostiuk and K. A. Orlova (eds.), *Russkaia emal' XII–nachala XX veka iz sobraniia Gosudarstvennogo Ermitazha* (Leningrad: Khudozhnik RSFSR, 1987), nos. 95, 100, 119.
82. Kostina, *Proizvedeniia moskovskikh serebrianikov*, nos. 55–6, 60, 62, 74, 85, 95, 96, 108, 114, 125, 145, 153, 162–7, 192, 249, 318, 351–2, 360.
83. See e.g. M. V. Martynova, *Moskovskaia emal' XV–XVII vv. Katalog* (Moscow: Gosudarstvennyi istoriko-kul'turnyi muzei-zapovednik 'Moskovskii Kreml'', 2002), nos. 32, 72–5.
84. Kaliazina et al. (eds.), *Russkaia emal' XII–nachala XX veka*, nos. 105, 113; cf. also nos. 82–4, 86–90, 96–8.
85. I. A. Bobrovnitskaia, *Russkaia raspisnaia emal' kontsa XVII–nachala XVIII veka. Katalog* (Moscow: Gosudarstvennyi istoriko-kul'turnyi muzei-zapovednik 'Moskovskii Kreml'', 2001). Further on Stroganov silver, mainly ecclesiastical and often heavily inscribed, see V. V. Igoshev, *Stroganovskoe khudozhestvennoe serebro XVI–XVII vekov* (Moscow: BuksMArt, 2018).
86. Bobrovnitskaia, *Russkaia raspisnaia emal'*, 23–9; Odom, *Russian Enamels*, nos. 12, 13; images and descriptions on the Walters Art Museum website.
87. Bobrovnitskaia, *Russkaia raspisnaia emal'*, no. 15.
88. E.g. *Ioasafovskaia letopis'* (Moscow: AN SSSR, 1957), 126 (fol. 134v of the manuscript); *Litsevoi letopisnyi svod XVI veka. Russkaia letopisnaia istoriia. Kniga 17. 1483–1502 gg.* (facsimile edition; Moscow: AKTEON, 2010), 73 (fol. 410 of the 'Shumilov' manuscript of the original).
89. E. L. Nemirovskii, *Andrei Chokhov (okolo 1545–1629)* (Moscow: Nauka, 1982); Sergei Bogatyrev, 'Bronze Tsars: Ivan the Terrible and Fedor Ivanovich in the Décor of Early Modern Guns', *SEER*, 88.1–2 (Jan./Apr. 2010), 48–72.
90. A. F. Bondarenko, *Istoriia kolokolov Rossii XI–XVII vv.* (Moscow: Russkaia panorama, 2012); Bondarenko, *Iz istorii kolokolov Rossii. Izbrannye trudy po otechestvennoi kampanologii* (Moscow: Russkaia panorama, 2014); A. A. Glushetskii, *Kolokol'no-liteinoe delo v Rossii vo vtoroi polovine XVII–nachale XX veka. Entsiklopediia liteishchikov* ([Moscow]: Ekonomicheskaia gazeta, 2010). On Russian bells and West European bells in the Kremlin collections, see I. D. Kostina, *Kolokola XIV–XIX vekov* (Moscow: Gosudarstvennyi istoriko-kul'turnyi muzei-zapovednik 'Moskovskii Kreml'', 2015).

91. For an exception, see Bondarenko, *Iz istorii*, 374–5, the engraved inscription on a 200-pood (3,276 kg) bell made in 1636 for the monastery of the Nativity in Vladimir by the recently arrived German master Ivan (Hans) Falk. Bondarenko surmises that Falk was not yet competent to cast directly in Cyrillic.
92. Bondarenko, *Iz istorii*, 310.
93. Bondarenko, *Iz istorii*, 308–10. On habits of verbose inscription through to the nineteenth century, see Glushetskii, *Kolokol'no-liteinoe delo*, 242–52.
94. E.g. Pushkin's poem 'The Winter Road', or the popular romance *Monotonously Tinkles the Bell* (*Odnozvuchno gremit kolokol'chik*).
95. P. N. Iakovleva, *Podduzhnye, podsheinye kolokol'chiki, bubentsy i botala v sobranii Novgorodskogo muzeiia-zapovednika* (Novgorodskii muzei-zapovednik, 2010); A. A. Glushetskii, *Rossii bronzovoe slovo: o chem govorit duzhnyi kolokol'chik* (Moscow: Tsentr delovoi informatsii ezhenedel'nika 'Ekonomika i zhizn'', 2007). The *kolokol'chiki* were open-based, like cowbells. The enclosed jingles (*bubentsy*) attached to bridles were generally not inscribed.
96. On Stefan's cross, see above, pp. 28–9. On another such early inscribed cross, see S. A. Gavrilov, 'Borisoglebskii krest 1467 g.', *Sovetskaia arkheologiia*, 1985.2, 213–22; G. V. Popov, 'Belokamennyi krest 1462/1467 goda iz Borisoglebskogo monastyria v Dmitrove', in *ΣΟΦΙΑ. Sbornik statei po iskusstvu Vizantii i Drevnei Rusi v chest' A. I. Komecha* (Moscow: Severnyi palomnik, 2006), 325–46.
97. L. A. Beliaev, *Russkoe srednevekovoe nadgrobie. Belokamennye plity Moskvy i Severo-Vostochnoi Rusi XIII–XVII vv.* (Moscow: MODUS – GRAFFITI, 1996); L. A. Beliaev (ed.), *Russkoe srednevekovoe nadgrobie, XIII–XVII veka: materialy k svodu. Vypusk 1* (Moscow: Nauka, 2006); V. A. Berkovich and K. A. Egorov, *Moskovskoe belokamennoe nadgrobie. Katalog* (Moscow: TM Prodakshn, 2017). See also the emerging online corpus, http://cir.rssda.su/.
98. See below, p. 146.
99. See below, p. 147.
100. V. N. Timofeev, E. N. Poretskina and N. N. Efremova, *Memorial'nye doski Sankt-Peterburga. Spravochnik* (St Petersburg: Art-biuro, 1999), 382, 390–1, 404, 407, 515.
101. S. O. Androsov, *Ital'ianskaia skul'ptura v sobranii Petra Velikogo* (St Petersburg: Dmitrii Bulanin, 1999); Androsov, *Ot Petra I k Ekaterine II. Liudi, statui, kartiny* (St Petersburg: Dmitrii Bulanin, 2013); I. V. Riazantsev, *Skul'ptura v Rossii XVIII–nachala XIX veka* (Moscow: Zhiraf, 2003); S. O. Androsov, A. V. Bertash and M. G. Talalai, *Antichnye i bibleiskie siuzhety v kamne i bronze. Peterburgskoe gorodskoe ubranstvo* (St Petersburg:

Informatsionno-izdatel'skoe agentstvo 'LIK', 2006); also Cracraft, *Imagery*, 220–31.

102. See Riazantsev, *Skul'ptura v Rossii*, 366–79, on the main public monuments of St Petersburg as a 'thematic zone'.
103. E. M. Kukina and R. F. Kozhevnikov, *Rukotvornaia pamiat' Moskvy* (Moscow: Moskovskii rabochii, 1997), 246.
104. N. A. Maiasova, *Drevnerusskoe shit'e. La broderie russe ancienne* (Moscow: Iskusstvo, 1971); Maiasova, *Drevnerusskoe litsevoe shit'e. Katalog* (Moscow: Krasnaia ploshchad', 2004). On textiles in the Russian Museum, see L. D. Likhacheva, *Drevnerusskoe shit'e XV–XVIII vekov v sobranii Gosudarstvennogo Russkogo muzeiia. Katalog vystavki* (Leningrad: Gosudarstvennyi Russkii muzei, 1980). Also Eugenia Tolmachoff, *Ancient Russian Ecclesiastical Embroideries* (The Bulletin of the Needle and Bobbin Club, 31, 1947).
105. A. R. Kruglova, *Zolotoshveinoe rukodelie velikokniazheskikh i tsarskikh masterskikh XV–XVI vekov* (St Petersburg: Kolo, 2011).
106. A. V. Silkin, *Stroganovskoe litsevoe shit'e* (Moscow: Progress-Traditsiia, 2002); also Tolmachoff, *Ancient Russian Ecclesiastical Embroideries*, 38–54.
107. For a glossary of terms, see Maiasova, *Drevnerusskoe litsevoe shit'e*, 465–6.
108. A. S. Petrov, 'Drevnerusskoe shit'e: podvesnye naprestol'nye peleny. Opyt atributsii', in *Lazarevskie chteniia. Iskusstvo Vizantii, Drevnei Rusi, Zapadnoi Evropy. Materialy nauchnoi konferentsii 2009* (Izdatel'stvo MGU, 2009), 212–30.
109. A. S. Petrov, 'Shityi obraz pod ikonoi. Izobrazheniia na podvesnykh pelenakh', in E. S. Smirnova (ed.), *Tserkovnoe shit'e v Drevnei Rusi: sbornik statei* (Moscow: Galart, 2010), 69–81.
110. E.g. Maiasova, *Drevnerusskoe litsevoe shit'e*, nos. 107, 108, 123, 124; Silkin, *Stroganovskoe litsevoe shit'e*, nos. 86, 95.
111. Maiasova, *Drevnerusskoe litsevoe shit'e*, 330–1 (no. 113).
112. Description in Maiasova, *Drevnerusskoe litsevoe shit'e*, 270–1 (no. 88).
113. Isolde Thyrêt, *Between God and Tsar: Religious Symbolism and the Royal Women of Muscovite Russia* (DeKalb: Northern Illinois University Press, 2001), 22–7, 48–9, 107–8.
114. Silkin, *Stroganovskoe litsevoe shit'e*, 192–5 (no. 21).
115. M. A. Alekseeva, 'Maloizvestnye proizvedeniia russkogo iskusstva XVII–pervoi poloviny XVIII veka – gravirovannye antiminsy', in *Pamiatniki kul'tury. Novye otkrytiia. Ezhegodnik 1982* (Leningrad: Nauka, 1984), 430–51; repr. in Alekseeva, *Iz istorii russkoi graviury XVII–nachala XIX v.* (Moscow and St Petersburg: Al'ians-Arkheo, 2013), 9–34; S. G. Nikolaeva, *Kollektsiia gravirovannykh antiminsov v sobranii Gosudarstvennogo muzeiia istorii religii* (St Petersburg: Aktsioner i Ko., 2003).

116. On the painted images, see Konstantin Nikol'skii, *Ob antiminsakh pravoslavnoi russkoi tserkvi* (St Petersburg: Tipografiia Iakova Greia, 1872), 128–228; Oksana Yurchyshyn-Smith, 'Development of Byzantine Iconographic Tradition in Ukrainian Antimensia of the XVIIth Century', *Byzantinoslavica*, 59 (1998), 320–4; Yurchyshyn-Smith, 'The Antimension (1620) of Theophanes, Patriarch of Jerusalem', *Oriens christianus*, 88 (2004), 93–110.
117. L. A. Oshurkevich, 'Ukrainskie antiminsnye graviury XVII–pervoi poloviny XVIII veka', in M. A. Alekseeva and E. A. Mishina (eds.), *Narodnaia kartinka XVII–XIX vekov* (St Petersburg: Dmitrii Bulanin, 1996), 53–70; also Oksana Iurchyshyn, 'Antyminsy Gravera Illi', *Rodovid*, 3.12 (1995), 20–8.
118. Alekseeva, *Iz istorii russkoi graviury*, 12, identifies seven variants. On at least eight separate issues recorded in the archives of the Print Yard between 1657 and 1675, see *Mosk. kirill. izd. RGADA. Vyp. 3*, 201, 210, 213, 222–6. For extracts from the archival documents on the materials, processes and costs, see *MPD – fakt i faktor. 1652–1700 gody. Kniga 2*, 497–501.
119. See below, pp. 214–15.
120. The dimensions vary in different descriptions. These are taken (in conversion from measurements in *arshiny* and *vershki*) from what is still the most detailed work on Russian banners, Lukian Iakovlev, *Russkie starinnye znamena* (Moscow: Sinodal'naia tipografiia, 1865), nos. 3572–80.
121. Paul of Aleppo, *The Travels of Macarius, Patriarch of Antioch*, transl. F. C. Balfour, vol. I (London: Oriental Translation Fund of Great Britain and Ireland, 1836), 367 (Book VIII, section 1).
122. Soboleva, *Rossiiskaia gosudarstvennaia simvolika*, 130–1; Sergei Bogatyrev, 'The Heavenly Host and the Sword of Truth: Apocalyptic Imagery in Ivan IV's Moscow', in Valerie Kivelson, Karen Petrone, Nancy Shields Kollmann and Michael S. Flier (eds.), *The New Muscovite Cultural History: A Collection in Honor of Daniel B. Rowland* (Bloomington, IN: Slavica, 2009), 77–90. See the high-resolution drawing at www.vexillographia.ru/russia/images/gr oz1.jpg.
123. Soboleva, *Rossiiskaia gosudarstvennaia simvolika*, 132; Iakovlev, *Russkie starinnye znamena*, no. 3586; D. Strukov and I. Popov, *Risunki k izdaniiu 'Russkie starinnye znamena' Lukiana Iakovleva* (Moscow: Khromolitografiia V. Bakhman, 1865). Note Arsenii Petrov, '"Znamia Ermaka" iz sobraniia Oruzheinoi palaty: legenda i fakty', *Quaestio Rossica*, 4.1 (2016), 157–69, who re-dates to the late seventeenth century a banner conventionally associated with Ermak in the 1580s.
124. Iakovlev, *Russkie starinnye znamena*, no. 3575 (pp. 10–14).
125. Soboleva, *Rossiiskaia gosudarstvennaia simvolika*, 134–6.

126. Vilinbakhov, *Simvoly Rossii*, 190–1, and illustration, 326.
127. Vilinbakhov, *Simvoly Rossii*, 151–285, along with the illustrations on pp. 325–63. For an example of the level of detail in legislation, see 194–6, the text of the instructions on banners in the *Tabel' ob oruzheinykh i amunichnykh veshchakh* of 28 October 1731.
128. E. Iu. Moiseenko, *Russkaia vyshivka XVII–nachala XX veka. Iz sobraniia Gosudarstvennogo Ermitazha* (Leningrad: Khudozhnik RSFSR, 1978).
129. On 'folk' ornament see, for example, G. S. Maslova, *Ornament russkoi narodnoi vyshivki* (Moscow: Nauka, 1978).
130. I am grateful to Nina Tarasova and Iuliia Plotnikova for enabling me to look at parts of the collections in the Hermitage museum.
131. S. I. Liakisheva, 'Kul'tura russkogo usadebnogo rukodeliia', *Kul'tura: teoriia i praktika. Elektronnyi nauchnyi zhurnal*, 2015.1 (4) (Moskovskii gosudarstvennyi universitet, 15 Feb. 2015), http://theoryofculture.ru/issues/36/753/.
132. E. Iu. Moiseenko and V. A. Faleeva, *Biser i stekliarus v Rossii. XVIII–nachalo XX veka* (Leningrad: Khudozhnik RSFSR, 1990); Iu. V. Plotnikova, 'Miniatiurnye vyshivki kontsa XVIII–pervoi chetverti XIX veka iz sobraniia Otdela istorii russkoi kul'tury', *Soobshcheniia Gosudarstvennogo Ermitazha*, 60 (2003), 40–5.
133. E.g. Hermitage Museum, ERT-6797: a wallet with the monogram initials 'KM' and the date 1821.
134. L. Yefimova and R. Belgorodskaya [L. V. Efimova and R. M. Belgorodskaia], *Russian Embroidery and Lace*, transl. Alexandra Ilf (London: Thames & Hudson, 1987), no. 8; Moiseenko, *Russkaia vyshivka*, nos. 92, 163; cf. also ibid., no. 155 (a topographic pocket-book cover labelled 'Tobol'sk'); Elena Iurova, 'Vyshivka v inter'ere russkogo bidermeier', *Pinakoteka*, 4 (1998), 90–6, nos. 9, 10 (two signed rustic scenes from 1840); Moiseenko and Faleeva, *Biser i stekliarus*, no. 28 (a cushion cover depicting Eros in a goat-drawn chariot, signed 'Korsakowa 1822'). Note that Elizaveta Dengina's 1830 beadwork scene is identical to that embroidered in cross-stitch by A. Menshutkina in 1819 (ERT-17559): both were copied from the same engraving.
135. Iurova, 'Vyshivka v inter'ere', no. 1; Moiseenko and Faleeva, *Biser i stekliarus*, 82 and no. 29.
136. E.g. Moiseenko, *Russkaia vyshivka*, nos. 108, 109.
137. Hermitage Museum ERT-8878.
138. Hermitage Museum, ERT-17989.
139. Hermitage Museum, ERT-17990; cf. ERT-5279.
140. Hermitage Museum, ERT-6796.
141. Mary Jaene Edmonds, *Samplers and Sampler Makers: An American Schoolgirl Art 1700–1850* (Los Angeles and London: Charles Letts, 1991). On Britain,

Germany, France, Italy, Spain, the Netherlands, even the Ottoman Empire, see Carol Humphrey, *Samplers* (Cambridge University Press, 1997).

142. Laurence Grove, '"Pour faire tapisserie"?/ Moveable Woodcuts: Print/ Manuscript,Text/Image at the Birth of the Emblem', in David Graham (ed.), *The Emblematic Age in France: Essays in Honour of Daniel* S.*Russell* (Glasgow Emblem Studies, 2001), 95–119.
143. Joan Edwards, *Sampler Making 1540–1940: The Fifth of Joan Edwards' Small Books on the History of Embroidery* (Dorking: Bayford Books, 1983), 12.
144. E. Likhacheva, *Materialy dlia istorii zhenskogo obrazovaniia v Rossii*, 4 vols. (St Petersburg: Tipografiia M. M. Stasulevicha, 1890–1901), vol. I, 152; vol. II, 24, with respect to the Novodevichii monastery school curriculum as decreed in 1765 (*PSZ*, no. 12,323), and the curriculum prescribed for girls at orphanages in 1797. In the foundation charter of the Smolnyi Institute needlework was prescribed for girls aged six to nine: [I. I. Betskoi], *Ustav vospitaniia dvukhsot blagorodnykh devits* (St Petersburg: [Senate press], 1764), section 2.
145. *The Englishwoman in Russia; Impressions of the Society and Manners of the Russians at Home. By a Lady Ten Years Resident in that Country* (New York: Charles Scribner, 1855), 44.
146. S. A. Maslikh, *Russkoe izraztsovoe iskusstvo XV–XIX vekov*, 2nd edn (Moscow: Izobrazitel'noe iskusstvo, 1983); S. I. Baranova, *Moskovskii arkhitekturnyi izrazets XVII veka v sobranii Moskovskogo gosudarstvennogo ob"edinennogo muzeia-zapovednika Kolomenskoe-Izmailovo-Lefortovo-Liublino* (Moscow: MGOMZ, 2013).
147. E.g. Baranova, *Moskovskii arkhitekturnyi izrazets*, nos. 38–42 (polychrome tiles with cherubim), 72 (the Cross), 79 (panels with the Evangelists) etc.
148. Baranova, *Moskovskii arkhitekturnyi izrazets*, nos. 3–10.
149. A. G. Avdeev, *Starorusskaia epigrafika i knizhnost'. Novo-Ierusalimskaia shkola epigraficheskoi poezii* (Moscow: PSTGU, 2006), 197–8. See also below, pp. 154–5.
150. Baranova, *Moskovskii arkhitekturnyi izrazets*, nos. 63–6; also p. 77; I. I. Pleshanova, 'Pskovskie arkhitekturnye keramicheskie poiasa', *Sovetskaia arkheologiia*, 1963.2, 212–16.
151. See esp. Maslikh, *Russkoe izraztsovoe iskusstvo*, 21–6, and the copious illustrations of stove tiles: esp. figs. 213, 215, 216–25, 240–4, 264–6, 273.
152. Maslikh, *Russkoe izraztsovoe iskusstvo*, fig. 244.
153. L. V. Tydman, 'Pechi v inter'ere domov-dvortsov Moskvy XVIII v.', in V. P. Vygolov (ed.), *Pamiatniki russkoi arkhitektury i monumental'nogo iskusstva. Stolitsa i provintsiia* (Moscow: Nauka, 1994), 69–93.
154. See Tamara V. Kudriavtseva, *Russian Imperial Porcelain* (St Petersburg: Slavia, 2003).

155. Elena Ivanova, *Farfor v Rossii XVIII–XIX vekov. Zavod Gardnera* (St Petersburg: Palace Editions, 2003). On the Gardners in Russia, see Anthony Cross, *By the Banks of the Neva: Chapters from the Lives and Careers of the British in Eighteenth-Century Russia* (Cambridge University Press, 2007), 73–4.
156. A. L. Badurova, 'Razvitie chastnoi farforovoi promyshlennosti Peterburgskoi gubernii v kontsa XVIII–pervoi polovine XIX vv.', in N. A. Asharina (ed.), *Iz istorii russkoi keramiki i stekla XVII–XIX vekov. Sbornik trudov* (Moscow: Gosudarstvennyi ordena Lenina Istoricheskii muzei, 1986), 21–32.
157. Cited in Kudriavtseva, *Russian Imperial Porcelain*, 17. See S. N. Kaznakov, *Paketovye tabakerki Imperatorskogo farforovogo zavoda* (St Petersburg: [n.p.], 1913), 17.
158. E.g. illustrations in Kudriavtseva, *Russian Imperial Porcelain*, 12.
159. E.g. from the Gardner Factory: Ivanova, *Farfor v Rossii*, catalogue nos. 69–75, 107–26 (figs. 31, 41–3); from the Imperial Factory: Kudriavtseva, *Russian Imperial Porcelain*, illustrations on pp. 36, 44.
160. Anne Odom, *Russian Imperial Porcelain at Hillwood* (Washington, DC: Hillwood Museum and Gardens, 1999), 24–7.
161. Ivanova, *Farfor v Rossii*, catalogue no. 5, fig. 2.
162. G. D. Agarkova, T. L. Astrakhantseva and N. S. Petrova, *Russkii farfor* (Moscow: Planeta, 1993), 17; also *Imperatorskii farforovyi zavod 1744–1904* (St Petersburg: Sankt-Peterburg orkestr, 2003), 81–2.
163. Ivanova, *Farfor v Rossii*, catalogue nos. 6–19, 20–66; figs. 282–303; also Nataliia Sipovskaia, 'Ordenskie servizy', *Pinakoteka*, 5 (1998), 16–23. On heraldic marking on Russian porcelain, see G. V. Vilinbakhov, *Geral'dika na russkom farfore: katalog vystavki* (St Petersburg: Gosudarstvennyi Ermitazh, 2008).
164. Ivanova, *Farfor v Rossii*, catalogue nos. 294–6, figs. 195–8.
165. Elena Ivanova and Irina Popova, *Farfor chastnykh zavodov Peterburga* (St Petersburg: Palace Editions, 2008), catalogue nos. 122, 141, figs. 89, 92, from the 1830s.
166. N. A. Asharina, 'Russkie zavody khudozhestvennogo stekla XVII–XVIII vv.', in Asharina (ed.), *Iz istorii russkoi keramiki i stekla XVII–XIX vekov. Sbornik trudov*, 3–16, and Appendix, 45–61; Nina Asharina, Tamara Malinina and Liudmila Kazakova, *Russian Glass of the Seventeenth–Twentieth Centuries* (Corning, NY: Corning Museum of Glass, 1990); also Karen L. Kettering, *Russian Glass at Hillwood* (Washington, DC: Hillwood Museum and Gardens, 2001).
167. Asharina, Malinina and Kazakova, *Russian Glass*, figs. 2–9, 15–17, 21–6; cf. N. N. Kachalov, *Steklo* (Moscow: Izdatel'stvo AN SSSR, 1959), 217–76 (on

the St Petersburg Glassworks); I. V. Gorbatova, *Khudozhestvennoe steklo XVI–XVIII vekov* (Moscow: Trilistnik, 2006).

168. Gorbatova, *Khudozhestvennoe steklo*, nos. 80, 81.
169. Gorbatova, *Khudozhestvennoe steklo*, no. 24; cf. no. 26 with a formula in Latin; also no. 40; also I. V. Gorbatova, 'K voprosu o tak nazyvaemoi "aptekarskoi posude Petra Velikogo"', in A. K. Levykin (ed.), *Dekorativno-prikladnoe iskusstvo Zapadnoi Evropy* (Moscow: Moskovskii Kreml', 2006), 264–71.
170. Reproduced in A. F. Bondarenko, *Kolokola v miniatiurakh Litsevogo letopisogo svoda XVI v.* (Moscow: Russkaia panorama, 2014), fig. 46.
171. O. N. Mel'nikova, *Iz istorii chasov v Rossii XVII–nachalo XX veka* (Moscow: Istoricheskii muzei, 2016), 5–8.
172. Ivan Zabelin, *Domashnii byt russkikh tsarei v XVI i XVII stoletiiakh. Chast' I*, 4th edn (Moscow, 1918; repr. Moscow: Iazyki russkoi kul'tury, 2000), 234–7.
173. Mel'nikova, *Iz istorii chasov*, 19; on Scott and other British instrument makers in Russia, see Cross, *By the Banks of the Neva*, 224–39.
174. Mel'nikova, *Iz istorii chasov*, 22–5; for varieties of inscription, see the abundant illustrations in the same book, and also T. A. Fokina, *Chasy masterov i predpriiatii Rossii XVIII–nachala XX vekov iz sobraniia Politekhnicheskogo muzeiia. Katalog* (Moscow: RQPF 'NIK', 2007), 38–53 (nos. 1–11).
175. Mel'nikova, *Iz istorii chasov*, 57.
176. Aleksei Golubinskii, 'New Technology and the Mapping of Empire: The Adoption of the Astrolabe', in Franklin and Bowers (eds.), *Information and Empire*, 59–74.
177. Mel'nikova, *Iz istorii chasov*, 26.
178. I. V. Beneva, *Istoriia Instrumental'noi palaty Peterburgskoi Akademii nauk (1724–1766)* (St Petersburg: Nauka, 1999).
179. V. Iu. Matveev, *Mekhanicheskie iskusstva i Imperatorskaia Akademiia khudozhestv* (St Petersburg: Ruda i metally, 2010).
180. *PSZ*, nos. 10,200 (24 Mar. 1754), 17,562 (18 Nov. 1796).
181. E.g. the series of aquatints by Philibert-Louis Debucour, after paintings by Michel François Damame de Martrait (c. 1806): British Museum, no. 1895,1015.89; Ashmolean Museum, Talbot Collection, E-1002.
182. Maureen Perrie, '"Royal Marks": Reading the Bodies of Russian Pretenders, Seventeenth–Nineteenth Centuries', *Kritika*, 11.3 (Summer 2010), 535–61. On the relationship of 'royal marks' and symbols on coinage, see Emery, 'Species of Legitimacy'.
183. Nancy Shields Kollmann, 'Marking the Body in Early Modern Judicial Punishment', *HUS*, 28 (2006), 557–65.
184. Edward Higgs, 'Personal Identification as Information Flows in England, 1500–2000', in Weller (ed.), *Information History in the Modern World*, 13–30.

4 Scripts and Languages of the Graphosphere

1. L. V. Cherepnin, *Russkaia paleografiia* (Moscow: Gosudarstvennoe izdatel'stvo politicheskoi literatury, 1956), 96–8; I. V. Levochkin, *Osnovy russkoi paleografii* (Moscow: Krug, 2003), 36–7; A. E. Chekunova, *Russkoe kirillicheskoe pis'mo XI–XVIII vv. Uchebnoe posobie* (Moscow: RGGU, 2010), 14.
2. Iu. E. Shustova, 'Azbuka v pechatnykh kirillicheskikh bukvariakh iuzhnoslavianskoi i vostochnoslavianskoi traditsii v XVI–nachale XVIIIv.', *Ocherki feodal'noi Rossii*, 14 (2010), 402–94 (esp. 473–94).
3. Franklin, *Writing, Society and Culture*, 190–5.
4. L. M. Kostiukhina, *Paleografiia russkikh rukopisnykh knig XV–XVII vv. Russkii poluustav* (Moscow: Gosudarstvennyi istoricheskii muzei, 1999).
5. L. M. Kostiukhina, *Knizhnoe pis'mo v Rossii XVII v.* (Moscow: Gosudarstvennyi istoricheskii muzei, 1974), 63.
6. E.g. N. V. Savel'eva, *Ocherki istorii formirovaniia pinezhskoi knizhno-rukopisnoi traditsii: opisanie rukopisnykh istochnikov* (St Petersburg: Dmitrii Bulanin, 2003), 27, 40 and nos. 421, 422, 625, 658, 659, 660 etc.
7. The word 'cursive' can be interlingually confusing: modern Russian *kursiv* means 'italic' in a printed text.
8. Cherepnin, *Russkaia paleografiia*, 543–53.
9. On early *viaz'*, see *Zaglavnoe pis'mo drevnerusskikh rukopisnykh knig XIV–XV vv. Al'bom zarisovok M. G. Gal'chenko* (Moscow: Tsentral'nyi muzei drevnerusskoi kul'tury i iskusstva imeni Andreiia Rubleva, 2004).
10. See above, pp. 74, 79, 83. For examples of *viaz'* in various media, see Figs. 3.4, 3.6, 3.7, 3.8 and 6.2.
11. On alphabetic cryptography, see M. N. Speranskii, *Tainopis' v iugoslavianskikh i russkikh pamiatnikakh pis'ma* (Leningrad: AN SSSR, 1929; repr. Moscow: LIBROKOM, 2011).
12. E.g. Guseva, *Izd. kirill. XVI v*, nos. 110, 121, 131.
13. Ivan L. Kaldor, 'The Genesis of the Russian "Grazhdanskii shrift" or Civil Type', *Journal of Typographic Research*, 3.4 (Oct. 1969), 315–44, and 4.2 (Spring 1970), 111–38; A. G. Shitsgal, *Grazhdanskii shrift 1708–1958* (Moscow: Iskusstvo, 1959), 21–114; also Shitsgal, *Russkii tipografskii shrift. Voprosy istorii i praktika primeneniia* (Moscow: Kniga, 1985), 38–40.
14. Facsimile edition: [Karion Istomin], *Bukvar' sostavlen Karionom Istominym, gravirovan Leontiem Buninym, otpechatan v 1694 v Moskve* (Leningrad: Avrora, 1981). Further on Istomin's primer, see below, pp. 254–6.
15. Among early examples, the date '1655' on over-stamped thalers: above, pp. 66–7.
16. See e.g. V. M. Zhivov, 'Azbuchnaia reforma Petra I kak semioticheskoe preobrazovanie', *Trudy po znakovym sistemam*, 19 (1986), 54–67.

17. Shitsgal, *Russkii tipografskii shrift*, 51–98.
18. V. K. Trediakovskii, 'Razgovor mezhdu chuzhestrannym chelovekom i rossiiskim ob ortografii starinnoi i novoi i o vsem, chto prinadlezhit k sei materii', in Trediakovskii, *Sochineniia*, vol. III (St Petersburg: A. Smirdin, v tipografii AN, 1849), 76, 77. However, German, the most widespread foreign language of printing in Russia in the first half of the eighteenth century, continued to be produced in Gothic typefaces.
19. *SK XVIII v.*; Guseva. *Svod XVIII v.*
20. E. L. Nemirovskii, 'Sosushchestvovanie kirillovskogo tserkovnoslavianskogo i grazhdanskogo shriftov v XVIII v.', in *Tri stoletiia russkogo grazhdanskogo shrifta (1708–2008)* (Moscow: Pashkov dom, 2008), 156–9.
21. T. A. Afanas'eva, 'Izdaniia kirillicheskoi pechati XVIII veka svetskogo soderzhaniia', in *Problemy istochnikovedcheskogo izucheniia rukopisnykh i staropechatnykh fondov* (Leningrad: GPB, 1979), 183–99; Afanas'eva, 'Izdaniia zakonodatel'nogo kharaktera kirillicheskoi pechati v XVIII v.', in *Istochniki po istorii otechestvennoi kul'tury v sobraniiakh i arkhivakh Otdela rukopisei i redkikh knig* (Leningrad: GPB, 1983), 96–114.
22. Zernova and Kameneva, *SK kirill. pech. XVIII v.*, includes only items of five pages or more, printed in Moscow and St Petersburg, although the editors admit (p. ii) that *kirillitsa* non-books were numerous. Guseva, *Svod XVIII v.*, 15, promises a catalogue of around 600 such items printed in St Petersburg and Moscow.
23. T. N. Kameneva, 'Knigopechatanie v Chernigove (1646–1818)', *Problemy istochnikovedeniia*, 8 (1959), 267–313.
24. Gary Marker, 'Faith and Secularity in Eighteenth-Century Russian Literacy, 1700–1775', in Robert P. Hughes and Irina Paperno (eds.), *Christianity and the Eastern Slavs. Volume II. Russian Culture in Modern Times* (Berkeley, Los Angeles and London: University of California Press, 1994), 3–24; Max Okenfuss, *The Discovery of Childhood in Russia: The Evidence of the Slavic Primer* (Newtonville, MA: Oriental Research Partners, 1980).
25. Guseva, *Svod XVIII v.*, nos. 7–31; T. A. Afanas'eva, 'Izdaniia azbuk i bukvarei kirillovskoi pechati v XVIII veke', in *Iz istorii rukopisnykh i staropechatnykh sobranii* (Leningrad: GPB, 1979), 33–60.
26. V. P. Bogdanov and G. V. Karpiuk, *Ot azbuki Ivana Fedorova do sovremennogo bukvaria* (Moscow: Prosveshchenie, 1974), 17–64; E. L. Nemirovskii and Iu. E. Shustova, 'Kirillicheskie azbuki i bukvari XVI–XVIII vv.: bibliograficheskii svod izdanii', in M. V. Tendriakova and V. G. Bezrogova (eds.), *'V Rossii nado zhit' po knige'. Nachal'noe obuchenie chteniiu i pis'ma. Stanovlenie uchebnoi knigi v XVI–XIX vv.* (Moscow: Pamiatniki istoricheskoi mysli, 2015), 185–338; cf. N. A. Zemtsova and A. B. Shitskova, 'Azbuki, bukvari, propisi grazhdanskoi pechati, izdannye v XVIII v.

(bibliograficheskii ukazatel')', ibid., 339–50. For the contents of late-eighteenth-century primers with both alphabets, see D. N. Ramazanova and Iu. E. Shustova, *Kirillicheskie bukvari iz sobraniia Nauchno-issledovatel'skogo otdela redkikh knig Rossiiskoi gosudarstvennoi biblioteki: opisanie izdanii i ekzempliarov* (Moscow: Pashkov dom, 2018), 201–10 (nos. 43–6).

27. Marker, 'Faith and Secularity', supported by Zhivov, *Iazyk i kul'tura*, 491–3.
28. Trediakovskii, 'Razgovor', 245.
29. E.g. in the tendency, towards the mid nineteenth century, to use 'Cyrillic' rather than cursive lettering on secular *lubok* prints: see Iuliia Khod'ko, *Svetskii lubok. Konets XVIII–nachala XX veka* (St Petersburg: Palace Editions, 2015), 12.
30. For a summary of discussion, see Franklin, *Writing, Society and Culture*, 83–9. See also B. A. Uspenskii, *Istoriia russkogo literaturnogo iazyka (XI–XVII vv.)*, 3rd edn (Moscow: Aspekt Press, 2002). For an extensive history based on the notion of 'registers', see V. M. Zhivov, *Istoriia iazyka russkoi pis'mennosti*, 2 vols. (Moscow: Russkii fond sodeistviia obrazovaniiu i nauke, 2017), esp. vol. I.
31. V. A. Chernov, *Russkii iazyk v XVII veke. Morfologiia* (Izdatel'stvo Krasnoiarskogo universiteta, 1984), 20–1.
32. On Muscovite hybrids, see M. E. Remneva, *Puti razvitiia russkogo literaturnogo iazyka XI–XVII vv.* (Izdatel'stvo MGU, 2003), 165–303. For a more polarised account of linguistic registers, see A. N. Kozhin, *Literaturnyi iazyk Moskovskoi Rusi* (Moscow: Russkii iazyk, 1984).
33. B. A. Uspenskii, *Kratkii ocherk istorii russkogo literaturnogo iazyka (XI–XIX vv.)* (Moscow: Gnosis, 1994), 86–101; Julia Verkholantsev, *Ruthenica Bohemica. Ruthenian Translations from Czech in the Grand Duchy of Lithuania and Poland* (Berlin, Münster, Vienna, Zurich and London: Lit Verlag, 2008), 1–17.
34. A. A. Gippius, 'Russkoe "neknizhnoe" zhitie Nikolaia Chudotvortsa v iazykovoi situatsii Litovskoi i Moskovskoi Rusi XV–XVII vv.', in Vyacheslav V. Ivanov and Julia Verkholantsev (eds.), *Speculum Slaviae orientalis: Muscovy, Ruthenia and Lithuania in the Late Middle Ages* (Moscow: Novoe izdatel'stvo, 2005), 68–83. The result was not 'pure' Church Slavonic, but a typical Muscovite bookish hybrid.
35. For a case study in what one might now call 'code switching', see Giovanna Brogi Bercoff, 'Plurilingualism in Russia and in the Ruthenian Lands in the Seventeenth and Eighteenth Centuries: The Case of Stefan Javors'kyj', in Ivanov and Verkholantsev (eds.), *Speculum Slaviae orientalis*, 9–20.
36. *Grammatiki slavenskiia pravilnoe sintagma . . .* : see V. G. Korotkii in *SKKDR. XVII v., Chast' 2*, 346–50; *Mosk. kirill. izd. RGADA. Vyp. 2*, 258–63 (no. 113).

On earlier works on grammar in the Ruthenian lands, see V. V. Nimchuk, *Movoznavstvo na Ukraini v XIV–XVII st.* (Kiev: Naukova dumka, 1985).

37. Heinrich Wilhelm Ludolf, *Grammatica russica* (Oxford: e theatro Sheldoniano, 1696).
38. [V. E. Adodurov] B. A. Uspenskii, *Pervaia russkaia grammatika na rodnom iazyke* (Moscow: Nauka, 1975); Helmut Keipert with Andrea Huterer, *Compendium grammaticae Russicae (1731). Die erste Akademie-Grammatik der russischen Sprache* (Munich: Verlag der Bayerischen Akademie der Wissenschaften, 2002); K. A. Filippov and S. S. Volkov (eds.), *Vasilii Evdokimovich Adodurov. 'Afangs-Gründe der Rußischen Sprache' ili 'Pervye osnovaniia rossiiskogo iazyka'* (St Petersburg: Nauka and Nestor-Istoriia, 2014). For critical comments on the latter edition, see Andrei A. Kostin, 'Acribiia i ameleiia, ili Gde *byt' dobroi zemle?* (grammatika Adodurova v kontekste i bez)', *Slověne*, 2006.1, 263–99.
39. Michael Groening, *Rossiiskaia grammatika. Thet är Grammatica russica, eller Grundelig handledning til ryska språket* (Stockholm: Pet. Momma, 1750). Groening's section on useful phrases is from a different source: C. L. Drage, 'Russian Model Conversations, c. 1630–1773', in Bartlett and Hughes (eds.), *Russian Society and Culture and the Long Eighteenth Century*, 149–66 (esp. 162–5).
40. Despite '1755' on the title page: M. V. Lomonosov, *Rossiiskaia grammatika* (St Petersburg: Imp. AN, 1755 [1757]). On the various states of the first edition, see *SK XVIII v.*, no. 3,774.
41. [M. V. Lomonosov], *Russische Grammatik. Verfaßet von herrn Michael Lomonoßow ... aus dem Rußischen übersetzt von Johann Lorenz Stavenhagen* (St Petersburg: Imp. AN, 1764).
42. [Jean-Baptiste Charpentier], *Élémens de la langue russe ou Méthode courte et facile pour apprendre cette langue conformement à l'usage ...* (St Petersburg: Imp. AN, 1768).
43. See e.g. V. M. Zhivov, *Iazyk i kul'tura v Rossii XVIII veka* (Moscow: Shkola 'Iazyki russkoi kul'tury', 1996).
44. Cited in Uspenskii, *Kratkii ocherk*, 119.
45. B. A. Uspenskii, *Iz istorii russkogo literaturnogo iazyka. XVIII–nachala XIX veka* (Izdatel'stvo MGU, 1985); Uspenskii, *Vokrug Trediakovskogo. Trudy po istorii russkogo iazyka i russkoi kul'tury* (Moscow: Indrik, 2008).
46. N. A. Meshcherskii, *Istoriia russkogo literaturnogo iazyka* (Izdatel'stvo Leningradskogo universiteta, 1981), 169–72. On calques, see May Smith, *The Influence of French on Eighteenth-Century Literary Russian: Semantic and Phraseological Calques* (Oxford and New York: Peter Lang, 2006).
47. Cited in Rudolf Neuhäuser, *The Romantic Age in Russian Literature: Poetic and Aesthetic Norms (An Anthology of Original Texts 1800–1850)* (Munich: Otto Sagner, 1975), 30.

48. V. D. Levin, *Ocherki stilistiki russkogo literaturnogo iazyka kontsa XVIII–nachala XIX v.: leksika* (Moscow: Nauka, 1964).
49. E.g. Meshcherskii, *Istoriia russkogo literaturnogo iazyka*, 193–207; Uspenskii, *Kratkii ocherk*, 167–83.
50. T. A. Oparina, *Inozemtsy v Rossii XVI–XVII vv.* (Moscow: Progress-Traditsiia, 2007); S. P. Orlenko, *Vykhodtsy iz Zapadnoi Evropy v Rossii XVII veka: pravovoi status i real'noe polozhenie* (Moscow: Drevlekhranilishche, 2004); Roger P. Bartlett, *Human Capital: The Settlement of Foreigners in Russia 1762–1804* (Cambridge University Press, 1979).
51. Facsimile of 1717 edition in P. P. Shafirov, *A Discourse Concerning the Just Causes of the War Between the Swedes and Russia: 1700–1721*, introd. William E. Butler (Dobbs Ferry, NY: Oceana Publications, 1973). The relevant passage is on p. 5 of the facsimile.
52. On lexical imports, see Cracraft, *Culture*, 377–485, listing foreign words first attested in writings of the Petrine period; also E. E. Birzhakova, L. A. Voinova and L. L. Kutina, *Ocherki po leksikologii russkogo iazyka XVIII veka. Iazykovye kontakty i zaimstvovaniia* (Leningrad: Nauka, 1972).
53. *O piatom general'nom sobranii Moskovskogo otdeleniia Rossiiskogo Bibleiskogo obshchestva v 1818 godu* (Moscow: Universitetskaia tipografiia, 1818), 33–5; also below, p. 266.
54. See below, n. 62; also A. G. Avdeev and A. Iu. Vinogradov, 'Rekonstruktsiia grecheskoi stroitel'noi nadpisi 1634/35 g. iz Moskvy', *Voprosy epigrafiki*, 6 (2012), 43–9; or, on eighteenth-century luxury objects: *Pod tsarskim venzelem: proizvedeniia Imperatorskogo farforovogo zavoda iz sobraniia Gosudarstvennogo Ermitazha; katalog vystavki v gosudarstvennom komplekse muzeev Moskovskogo Kremlia, 17 oktiabria 2007–13 ianvaria 2008* (St Petersburg: Izdatel'stvo Gosudarstvennogo Ermitazha, 2007), 78, no. 20.
55. B. L. Fonkich, *Grecheskie rukopisi i dokumenty v Rossii v XIV–nachale XVIII v.* (Moscow: Indrik, 2003), 35–44.
56. Fonkich, *Grecheskie rukopisi*, 45–56.
57. See above, pp. 42–3.
58. A. I. Ivanov, *Literaturnoe nasledie Maksima Greka*, 41; Bulanin, *Perevody i poslaniia Maksima Greka*.
59. Fonkich, *Grecheskie rukopisi*, 45. Cf. Kukushkina, *Kniga v Rossii v XVI veke*, 107–8.
60. S. M. Kashtanov, 'K istorii russko-grecheskikh kul'turnykh sviazei v XVI v.', in *Moskhovia I. Problemy vizantiiskoi i novogrecheskoi filologii. K 60-letiiu B. L. Fonkicha* (Moscow: Indrik, 2001), 209–17.
61. Ekkehard Kraft, *Moskaus griechisches Jahrhundert: russisch-griechische Beziehungen und metabyzantinischer Einfluss 1619–1694* (Stuttgart: Franz Steiner Verlag, 1995).

62. N. P. Chesnokova, 'Relikvii khristianskogo Vostoka v Rossii v seredine XVII veka (po materialam Posol'skogo prikaza)', *Vestnik tserkovnoi istorii*, 2(6) (2007), 91–128; on a ceremonial quiver and bow-case, inscribed in Greek syllabic verse to Tsar Aleksei Mikhailovich, see V. G. Chentsova, 'Tsarskie sabli, saadak i pastyrskii posokh: k istorii veshchei iz Muzeev Moskovskogo Kremlia, privezennykh s Khristianskogo Vostoka v seredine XVII v.', *Kapterevskie chteniia*, 7 (2009), 234–49.
63. Olga B. Strakhov, *The Byzantine Culture in Muscovite Rus': The Case of Evfimii Chudovskii (1620–1725)* (Cologne, Weimar and Vienna: Böhlau Verlag, 1998), 15–55: V. G. Chentsova, *Ikona Iverskoi Bogomateri (ocherki istorii otnoshenii grecheskoi tserkvi s Rossiei s serediny XVII v. po dokumentam RGADA)* (Moscow: Indrik, 2010).
64. Fonkich, *Grecheskie rukopisi*, 115–218.
65. Fonkich, *Grecheskie rukopisi*, 230–74.
66. E.g. as in the case of Epifanii Slavinetskii and his pupil, Evfimii Chudovskii: Strakhov, *The Byzantine Culture in Muscovite Rus'*, 101–250.
67. B. L. Fonkich, *Greko-slavianskie shkoly v Moskve v XVII veke* (Moscow: Iazyki slavianskikh kul'tur, 2009); cf. the polemical review by L. A. Timoshina, '"Greko-slavianskie shkoly" i russkaia zhizn' XVII v.', *Ocherki feodal'noi Rossii*, 14 (2010), 558–699.
68. D. M. Volodikhin, *Knizhnost' i prosveshchenie v Moskovskom gosudarstve XVII v.* (Izdatel'stvo Moskovskogo gorodskogo ob"edineniia arkhivov, 1993), 9–79; Fonkich, *Greko-slavianskie shkoly*, 101–87.
69. D. N. Ramazanova, 'Grecheskie pechatnye knigi iz biblioteki Tipografskoi shkoly (novye materialy)', *Kniga. Issledovaniia i materialy*, 86 (2007), 104–17.
70. Nikolaos A. Chrissidis, *An Academy at the Court of the Tsars: Greek Scholars and Jesuit Education in Early Modern Russia* (DeKalb: Northern Illinois University Press, 2016).
71. D. N. Ramazanova, 'Rukopisnaia i pechatnaia kniga v uchebnoi praktike Slaviano-greko-latinskoi akademii v kontse XVII veka', in Tendriakova and Bezrogova (eds.), *'V Rossii nado zhit' po knige'*, 42–52.
72. There were normally between four and six *spravshchiki*: see Dadykin, 'Prikaz knigopechatnogo dela i sotrudniki Moskovskogo pechatnogo dvora', 144–5.
73. A. A. Dmitrievskii, 'Novye dannye po ispravleniiu bogosluzhebnykh knig v Moskve v XVII i XVIII vv.', *Palaeoslavica*, 12.2 (2004), 71–197; written in the early 1900s but unpublished for more than a century: see Olga B. Strakhov, '"Russkii Goar" A. A. Dmitrievskii i ego stat'ia ob ispravlenii Sluzhebnika v Moskve v XVII i XVIII vv.', *Palaeoslavica*, 12.2 (2004), 47–70. Cf. the less accurate edition by A. G. Kravetskii: A. A. Dmitrievskii, *Ispravlenie knig pri Patriarkhe Nikone i posleduiushchikh patriarkhakh* (Moscow: Iazyki slavianskoi kul'tury, 2004), and also Strakhov's critique of the study by

Paul Meyendorff, *Russia, Ritual and Reform: The Liturgical Reforms of Nikon in the Seventeenth Century* (Crestwood, NY: St Vladimir's Seminary Press, 1991).

74. Olga B. Strakhov, 'Attitudes to Greek Language and Culture in Seventeenth-Century Muscovy', *Modern Greek Studies Yearbook*, 6 (1990), 123–55; also Strakhov, *The Byzantine Culture in Muscovite Rus'*, 21–5.
75. Fonkich, *Greko-slavianskie shkoly*, 16–27.
76. Sil'vestr Medvedev, *Izvestie istinnoe pravoslavnym i pokazanie svetloe o novopravlenii knizhnom i o prochem*, ed. and introd. Sergei Belokurov, *ChOIDR*, 1885.4, 3rd pagination, 4, 6–7, 10–12; also Medvedev, 'Kniga o Manne khleba zhivotnogo': extracts in Aleksandr Prozorovskii, 'Sil'vestr Medvedev (Ego zhizn' i deiatel'nost'). Opyt tserkovno-istoricheskogo issledovaniia. Prilozheniia', *ChOIDR*, 1896.4, 500. See David A. Frick, 'Sailing to Byzantium: Greek Texts and the Establishment of Authority in Early Modern Muscovy', *HUS*, 19 (1995; publ. 1997), 138–57.
77. Andrei Kurbskii, 'Predislovie k Novomu Margaritu', *BLDR*, vol. 9 (2001), 564.
78. Fonkich, *Greko-slavianskie shkoly*, 232–67.
79. Iaroslav Isaievych, 'Greek Culture in the Ukraine: 1550–1650', *Modern Greek Studies Yearbook*, 6 (1990), esp. 108–15.
80. Facsimile: *Azbuka Ivana Fedorova 1578* (Moscow: Kniga, 1983), fols. 2–8. On the alphabets on fol. 2 as a learning exercise, see Iu. E. Shustova, 'Azbuka v rossiiskikh izdaniiakh bukvarei XVII–pervoi chetverti XVIII v.', in *Tri stoletiia russkogo grazhdanskogo shrifta (1708–2008). Materialy nauchnoi konferentsii* (Moscow: Pashkov dom, 2008), 106–28 (esp. 111–12).
81. *Bibliia sirech' knigi vetkhago i novago zaveta po iazyku slovensku. Fototipicheskoe pereizdanie teksta s izdaniia 1581 goda* (Moscow and Leningrad: Slovo – Art, 1988), on the first and last leaf apart from the title page: i.e. fols. [2–2v], and 78–78v of the final (fifth) foliation.
82. Guseva, *Izd. kirill. XVI v.*, no. 16: pp. 813–14 and fig. 116.1–7; see D. N. Ramazanova, 'Bytovanie pervoi Greko-slavianskoi grammatiki (L'vov, 1591) v slavianskikh zemliakh v XVII–XVIII vv.', in *Fedorovskie chteniia 2003* (Moscow: Nauka, 2003), 277–84.
83. N. P. Kiselev, 'Grecheskaia pechat' na Ukraine v XVI veke. Ivan Fedorov i ego posledovateli', *Kniga. Issledovaniia i materialy*, 7 (1962), 171–98.
84. Bykova and Gurevich, *Kirill.*, no. 15. On manuscript Greek grammars for and from the Likhud brothers' schools, see I. A. Voznesenskaia, 'Rukopisnye uchebniki brat'ev Likhudov nachala XVIII v. v peterburgskikh khranilishchakh', *TODRL*, 59 (2008), 369–75.
85. L. S. Kovtun, *Azbukovniki XVI–XVII vv. Starshaia raznovidnost'* (Leningrad: Nauka, 1989), esp. 23–31.

86. Olga B. Strakhov, 'Jepyfanij Slavynec'kyj's *Greek-Slavic-Latin Lexicon*: The History, Contents, and Principles Underlying the Composition of Its Greek Portion (Preliminary Remarks)', *HUS*, 28 (2006 [publ. 2009]), 269–85; also in Igor Ševčenko and Olga B. Strakhov, 'Stikhi Manuila Fila v perevode Evfimiia Chudovskogo: u istokov russkogo vizantinovedeniia', *Palaeoslavica*, 18.1 (2010), 69–92.
87. Bykova and Gurevich, *Kirill.*, no. 35.
88. [Iosif Turoboiskii], *Politikolepnaia apotheosis dostokhvalnyia khrabrosti vserossiiskago Gerkulesa ... Petra Aleksievicha ...*, printed in 1709: Bykova and Gurevich, *Grazhd.*, no. 26; text in E. A. Tiukhmeneva, *Iskusstvo triumfal'nykh vrat v Rossii pervoi poloviny XVIII veka* (Moscow: Progress-Traditsiia, 2005), 157–212.
89. D. N. Ramazanova, 'Knigi grecheskoi pechati tipografii Moskovskogo universiteta vo vtoroi polovine XVIII v.', in D. N. Bakun and A. Iu. Samarin (eds.), *Knizhnaia kul'tura. Opyt proshlogo i problemy sovremennosti. K 250-letiiu vuzovskogo knigoizdaniia v Rossii* (Moscow: Nauka, 2006), 243–8.
90. See above on Trediakovskii's comments on civil type as contrasted with the Greek-linked church alphabet. The association of Greek with Orthodoxy was likewise underscored in foreign accounts: see e.g. John Glen King, *The Rites and Ceremonies of the Greek Church in Russia* (London: W. Owen, J. Dodsley etc., 1772).
91. Iu. K. Vorob'ev, *Latinskii iazyk v russkoi kul'ture XVII–XVIII vekov* (Saransk: Izdatel'stvo Mordovskogo universiteta, 1999); Vorob'ev, *Latinskii iazyk v Rossii XVI–pervoi treti XIX veka (kul'turologicheskii aspekt)* (Saransk: Izdatel'stvo Mordovskogo universiteta, 2015); see the review of the latter by Vladislav Rzheutskii [Rjéoutski], 'O latyni v Rossii, i ne tol'ko', *Vivliofika*, 5 (2017), 143–8.
92. See above, pp. 41–2.
93. Francis J. Thomson, 'The Corpus of Slavonic Translations Available in Muscovy: The Cause of Old Russia's Intellectual Silence and a Contributory Factor to Muscovite Cultural Autarky', in B. Gasparov and O. Rayevsky-Hughes (eds.), *Christianity and the Eastern Slavs I: Slavic Cultures in the Middle Ages* (Berkeley, Los Angeles and Oxford: University of California Press, 1993), 187–8.
94. V. S. Tomelleri (ed.), *Der russische Donat: vom lateinischen Lehrbuch zur russischen Grammatik* (Cologne: Böhlau Verlag, 2002).
95. V. A. Romodanovskaia, 'Sochineniia Laktantiia v perevode russkikh knizhnikov XV–XVI vv.', *TODRL*, 54 (2003), 407–34.
96. Vorob'ev, *Latinskii iazyk*, 14–19; N. M. Rogozhin, *Posol'skii prikaz. Kolybel' rossiiskoi diplomatii* (Moscow: Mezhdunarodnye otnosheniia, 2003); A. V.

Beliakov, *Sluzhashchie Posol'skogo prikaza 1645–1682 gg.* (St Petersburg: Nestor-Istoriia, 2017), 93–166.

97. Clare Griffin, 'The Production and Consumption of Medical Knowledge in Seventeenth-Century Russia: The Apothecary Chancery' (unpublished Ph.D. thesis, University College London, 2012), 6–7; also Cross, *By the Banks of the Neva*, 120–58.
98. Maria V. Unkovskaya, *Brief Lives: A Handbook of Medical Practitioners in Muscovy, 1620–1701* (London: Wellcome Trust, 1999); Sabine Dumschatt, *Ausländische Mediziner im Moskauer Rußland* (Stuttgart: Franz Steiner Verlag, 2006).
99. E. A. Savel'eva, *Katalog knig iz sobraniia Aptekarskogo prikaza* (St Petersburg: Alfaret, 2006).
100. Thomson, 'Slavonic Translations', 193–4.
101. A. M. Panchenko, 'Simeon Polotskii' in *SKKDR. XVII vek. Chast' 3*, 362–79.
102. D. L. Liburkin, *Russkaia novolatinskaia poeziia: materialy k istorii. XVII–pervaia polovina XVIII veka* (Moscow: RGGU, 2000), 26–34.
103. Simeon Polockij [Polotskii], *Vertograd mnogocvetnyj*, 3 vols., ed. Anthony Hippisley and Lydia I. Sazonova (Cologne, Weimar and Vienna: Böhlau Verlag, 1996–2000).
104. Text in Simeon Polockij, *Vertograd mnogocvetnyj*, vol. III, 452–510. See O. A. Belobrova, 'Simeon Polotskii – avtor virsh k graviuram Biblii Mattiasa Meriana', *TODRL*, 49 (1996), 526–8.
105. Printed in 1680. See I. Z. Serman, '*Psaltyr' rifmotvornaia* Simeona Polotskogo i russkaia poeziia XVIII v.', *TODRL*, 18 (1962), 214–32. For Simeon's prefaces to the printed edition, anticipating objections and explaining his methods, see Simeon Polotskii, *Izbrannye sochineniia*, ed. I. P. Eremin (Moscow: Leningrad: AN SSSR, 1953), 210–17. More on Simeon Polotskii's writings, see below, pp. 246–8, 257–9.
106. E. I. Kislova, '"Latin" and "Slavonic" Education in the Primary Classes of Russian Seminaries in the Eighteenth Century', *Slověne*, 4.2 (2015), 72–91.
107. Vorob'ev, *Latinskii iazyk v russkoi kul'ture*, 32–66.
108. Vorob'ev, *Latinskii iazyk v russkoi kul'ture*, 66–88.
109. Liburkin, *Russkaia novolatinskaia poeziia*, esp. 186–209.
110. N. S. Kartashov and I. M. Polonskii (eds.), *Biblioteka A. A. Matveeva (1666–1728). Katalog* (Moscow: GBL, 1986).
111. G. Kratts, 'Nemetskoiazychnye izdaniia v Moskve i Sanktpeterburge XVIII–XX vv.', in L. V. Slavgorodskaia (ed.), *Nemtsy v Rossii. Problemy kul'turnogo vzaimodeistviia* (St Petersburg: Dmitrii Bulanin, 1998), 179–80.
112. See below, p. 147.
113. Vorob'ev, *Latinskii iazyk v russkoi kul'ture*, 185–97.

114. E.g. O. V. Budaragina, *Latinskie nadpisi v Peterburge* (St Petersburg: Kolo, 2016).
115. Vorob'ev, *Latinskii iazyk v russkoi kul'ture*, 204–13.
116. Shchukina, *Dva veka russkoi medali*, 67.
117. Kristine Koch, *Deutsch als Fremdsprache im Russland des 18. Jahrhunderts* (Berlin and New York: Walter de Gruyter, 2002); overview in Kristine Dahmen (formerly Koch), 'The Use, Functions and Spread of German in Eighteenth-Century Russia', *Russian Review*, 74.1 (Jan. 2015), 20–40.
118. See E. A. Rybina, *Inozemnye dvory v Novgorode XII–XVII vv.* (Izdatel'stvo MGU, 1986); Wolfgang Schlüter, *Die Nowgoroder Schra in sieben Fassungen vom 13. bis 17. Jahrhundert* (Dorpat: C. Mattiesen, 1911).
119. V. A. Kovrigina, *Nemetskaia sloboda Moskvy i ee zhiteli v kontse XVII–pervoi chetverti XVIII vv.* (Moscow: Arkheograficheskii tsentr, 1998), 25–6.
120. Norbert Angermann, 'Deutsche Übersetzer und Dolmetscher im vorpetrinischen Russland', in Eckhard Hübner et al. (eds.), *Zwischen Christianisierung und Europäisierung: Beiträge zur Geschichte Osteuropas in Mittelalter und früher Neuzeit. Festschrift für Peter Nitsche zum 65. Geburtstag* (Stuttgart: Franz Steiner Verlag, 1998), 221–49.
121. Claudia Jensen and Ingrid Maier, 'Orpheus and Pickleherring in the Kremlin: The "Ballet" for the Tsar of February 1672', *Scando-Slavica*, 59.2 (2013), 145–84, and the same authors' 'Pickleherring Returns to the Kremlin: More New Sources on the Pre-History of the Russian Court Theatre', *Scando-Slavica*, 61.1 (2015), 7–56.
122. T. A. Isachenko, *Perevodnaia moskovskaia knizhnost' XV–XVII vv.* (Moscow: Pashkov dom, 2009), 128–212.
123. Johann Jacob von Wallhausen's *Kriegskunst zu Fuss*, a manual of infantry formations, printed in translation as *Uchenie i khitrost' ratnago stroia pekhotnykh liudei*.
124. B. V. Sapunov, 'Nemetskie knigi i gazety v Moskve v XVII stoletii', in *Nemtsy v Rossii: russko-nemetskie nauchnye i kul'turnye sviazi* (St Petersburg: Dmitrii Bulanin, 2000), 91–6.
125. Johannes Weber, 'Strassburg, 1605: The Origins of the Newspaper in Europe', *German History*, 24.3 (2006), 387–412.
126. Ingrid Maier (ed. and introd.), *Vesti-kuranty. 1656 g., 1660–1662 gg., 1664–1670 gg. Inostrannye originaly k russkim tekstam*, Pt 2 (Moscow: Iazyki slavianskikh kul'tur, 2008), 26–33. For translations and their originals from the early 1670s, see I. Maier, S. M. Shamin, A. V. Kuznetsova et al., *Vesti-kuranty. 1671–1672 gg.* (Moscow: Azbukovnik, 2017).
127. Maier, *Vesti-kuranty*, 54–7, 74–87.

128. Maier, *Vesti-kuranty*, 57–60; S. M. Shamin, *Kuranty XVII stoletiia. Evropeiskaia pressa v Rossii i vozniknovenie russkoi periodicheskoi pechati* (Moscow and St Petersburg: Al'ians-Arkheo, 2011), 74–92; Daniel C. Waugh and Ingrid Maier, 'Muscovy and the European Information Revolution: Creating the Mechanisms for Obtaining Foreign News', in Franklin and Bowers (eds.), *Information and Empire*, 77–112.
129. See also below, pp. 199–200.
130. From the 'Povest' o konchine tsaria Mikhaila Feodorovicha': cited in Shamin, *Kuranty XVII stoletiia*, 79; also *SKKDR. XVII v. Chast' 3*, 140.
131. P. I. Khoteev, *Nemetskaia kniga i russkii chitatel' v pervoi polovine XVIII veka* (St Petersburg: Biblioteka RAN, 2008), 18–25.
132. *PSZ*, no. 1,910; German text: *Pis'ma i bumagi Petra Velikogo*, vol. II (St Petersburg: Gosudarstvennaia tipografiia, 1889), 39–44; see Khoteev, *Nemetskaia kniga*, 17.
133. Bykova and Gurevich, *Grazhd.*, Appendix. 1, nos. 8, 14, 36 (dated 1714, 1718, 1724).
134. A German grammar for Russians studying in Germany had been published in Berlin in 1713: see Koch, *Deutsch als Fremdsprache*, 216–22.
135. Ulrike Jekutch [Iekush], 'Nemetskoiazychnaia okkazional'naia literatura v Rossii XVIII veka', in P. Bukharkin, Jekutch and N. Kochetkova (eds.), *Okkazional'naia literatura v kontekste prazdnichnoi kul'tury Rossii XVIII veka* (St Petersburg: Filologicheskii fakul'tet SPbGU, 2010), 93–106.
136. E. I. Kislova, 'Nemetskii iazyk v russkikh seminariiakh XVIII veka: iz istorii kul'turnykh kontaktov', *Vestnik PSTGU III: Filologiia*, 2015.1(41), 53–70.
137. These are extrapolations from *SK Inostr.* For statistical calculations and tables, see Gottfried Kratz, *Deutschsprachige Drucke Moskauer und Petersburger Verlage, 1731–1991. Aus den Beständen der Universitäts- und Landesbibliothek Münster: Ausstellungskatalog* (Lüneburg: Institut Nordostdeutsches Kulturwerk, 1995), 7–13, 28–33.
138. *PSZ*, no. 26,740.
139. Khoteev, *Nemetskaia kniga*, 120. On eighteenth-century catalogues of foreign books, see *SK Inostr.*, vol. III, 173–209. On the Academy of Sciences lists, see N. A. Kopanev, 'Rasprostranenie inostrannoi knigi v Peterburge v pervoi polovine XVIII v. (Po materialam akademicheskikh knizhnykh katalogov)', in S. P. Luppov (ed.), *Russkie knigi i biblioteki v XVI–pervoi polovine XIX veka* (Leningrad: BAN, 1983), 38–53.
140. Khoteev, *Nemetskaia kniga*, 297–300.
141. S. P. Luppov, *Kniga v Rossii v poslepetrovskoe vremia 1725–1740* (Leningrad: Nauka, 1976).
142. *SK Inostr.*, vol. IV, 47–128.

143. *SK Inostr.*, vol. I, 6.
144. Bykova and Gurevich, *Grazhd.*, Appendix 1, 483–503, listing thirty-nine items; cf. also Bykova and Gurevich, *Kirill.*, Appendix 2, 307–10. Some wider surveys indicate that administrative and legislative documents were issued in German, but give no details: Koch, *Deutsch als Fremdsprache*, 58; Michael Schippan, *Die Einrichtung der Kollegien in Russland zur Zeit Peters I.* (Wiesbaden: Harrassowitz Verlag, 1996), 276.
145. Bykova and Gurevich, *Grazhd.*, Appendix 1, nos. 9, 19, 29. The respective Russian originals are *PSZ*, nos. 2974, 3778, 3893.
146. Bykova and Gurevich, *Dopoln.*, no. 606; *PSZ*, no. 4,643; included in the list of printings with spurious publication data in *SK Inostr.*, vol. III, appendix III, no. 44 (p. 248).
147. In a private collection; details available from the author.
148. Text in *PSZ*, no. 2,786; references in Bykova and Gurevich, *Grazhd.*, no. 82.
149. *Translat: ORDRE Der Fiscalen Amt und Pflicht betreffend* ... Note, however, that the decorative initial seems to have been printed from the same block as was used in documents printed in Riga in the 1720s. The publication details of the earliest German versions of decrees need further investigation.
150. These are German translations of the Russian decrees to be found in *PSZ*, nos. 3,970, 4,366, 4,610, 4,647, 4,827.
151. Russian original of the earlier decree: *PSZ*, no. 3,850.
152. In RGADA: http://rgada.info/opisi/248-opis_7/0259.jpg. I am grateful to Iu. E. Shustova for drawing this to my attention.
153. On de Hennin's passport, see Simon Franklin, 'Printing and Social Control in Russia 3: Blank Forms', *Russian History*, 42 (2015), 126–7; on German in passports, see Simon Franklin, 'Printing and Social Control in Russia 1: Passports', *Russian History*, 37 (2010), 229–31.
154. E.g. Spb II RAN, coll. 238, op. 2, ed. khr. 211–1, fol. 25 (a ticket for the 16.00 stagecoach on 7 April 1845); cf. a specimen, for a 18 June 1842 (from a private collection).
155. D. A. Drboglav, *Kamni rasskazyvaiut ... Epigraficheskie latinskie pamiatniki XV–pervaia polovina XVI v. (Moskva, Serpukhov, Astrakhan')* (Izdatel'stvo MGU, 1988), 22–66; Beliaev, *Russkoe srednevekovoe nadgrobie*, 270–83. On subsequent foreigners' cemeteries, see A. G. Avdeev and V. Iu. Pirogov, 'Kladbishche inozemtsev v Mar'inoi Roshche', *Voprosy epigrafiki*, 1 (2006), 36–48; V. V. Rytikova, 'Nemetskie familii v stareishem nekropole Sankt-Peterburga', in G. I. Smagina (ed.), *Nemtsy Sankt-Peterburga. Nauka, kul'tura, obrazovanie* (St Petersburg: Rostok, 2005), 521–32.
156. A. V. Sazikov and T. B. Vinogradova, *Naruzhnaia reklama Moskvy. Istoriia, tipologiia, dokumenty* (Moscow: Russkii mir, 2013), 16–17.

157. See below, pp. 160–7.
158. Slavgorodskaia (ed.), *Nemtsy v Rossii*, 69–128; also S. I. Mel'nikova, 'K istorii nemetskogo teatra v Sankt-Peterburge: izdanie podnevnogo repertoira za 1799 g.', in Dittmar Dahlmann and Galina Smagina (eds.), *Nemtsy v Rossii. Nemetskii mir Sankt-Peterburga* (St Petersburg: Rostok, 2013), 182–91.
159. Dahmen, 'The Use, Functions and Spread of German', 33–5.
160. Dahmen, 'The Use, Functions and Spread of German', 37–8.
161. Vladislav Rjéoutski, Gesine Argent and Derek Offord (eds.), *European Francophonie: The Social, Political and Cultural History of an International Prestige Language* (Oxford, Bern, Berlin etc.: Peter Lang, 2014); Derek Offord, Lara Ryazanova-Clarke, Vladislav Rjéoutski and Gesine Argent (eds.), *French and Russian in Imperial Russia*, 2 vols. (Edinburgh University Press, 2015). Unfortunately the major synthesis on this subject was published shortly after the present book had already gone into production: see Derek Offord, Vladislav Rjéoutski and Gesine Argent, *The French Language in Russia: A Social, Political, Cultural, and Literary History* (Amsterdam University Press, 2018).
162. On French domination of professorial positions at the Academy of Arts, see Rosalind P. Blakesley, 'Pride and the Politics of Nationality in Russia's Imperial Academy of Fine Arts, 1757–1807', *Art History*, 35.5 (Dec. 2010), 800–35.
163. Nina Dmitrieva and Gesine Argent, 'The Coexistence of Russian and French in the First Third of the Nineteenth Century: Bilingualism With or Without Diglossia?', in Offord, Ryazanova-Clarke, Rjéoutski and Argent (eds.), *French and Russian in Imperial Russia*, vol. II, 228–42.
164. See above, nn. 111, 137.
165. See e.g. L. A. Marikhbein, 'Istoriia chastnykh kollektsii frantsuzskoi knigi v Rossii XVIII–XIX vekov i ikh rol' v razvitii russko-frantsuzskikh kul'turnykh sviazei' (Diss. na soiskanie uchenoi stepeni kandidata istoricheskikh nauk; Moscow: Rossiiskii gosudarstvennyi sotsial'nyi universitet, 2008).
166. P. I. Khoteev, 'Frantsuzskaia kniga v biblioteke Peterburgskoi Akademii nauk (1714–1742 gg.)', in S. P. Luppov (ed.), *Frantsuzskaia kniga v Rossii v XVIII v.* (Leningrad: Nauka, 1986), 5–58.
167. N. A. Kopanev, 'Rasprostranenie frantsuzskoi knigi v Moskve v seredine XVIII v.', in Luppov (ed.), *Frantsuzskaia kniga v Rossii*, 59–172.
168. Kopanev, 'Rasprostranenie frantsuzskoi knigi', catalogue nos. 6, 327, 491, 614–16. Note that these were French editions printed in Basel, Leiden, The Hague, Dresden, Göttingen and Amsterdam.
169. Pushkin, *Evgenii Onegin*, 3.IX.
170. Pushkin, *Evgenii Onegin*, 8.V.

171. On the range of Russian francophone writing, see E. P. Grechanaia, *Kogda Rossiia govorila po-frantsuzski: russkaia literatura na frantsuzskom iazyke (XVIII–pervaia polovina XIX veka)* (Moscow: IMLI RAN, 2010); also the essays in Offord, Ryazanova-Clarke, Rjéoutski and Argent (eds.), *French and Russian*, vol. I.
172. Grechanaia, *Kogda Rossiia govorila po-frantsuzski*, 271–314.
173. Vorob'ev, *Latinskii iazyk v russkoi kul'ture*, 83.
174. See Vladislav Rjéoutski and Natalia Speranskaia, 'The Francophone Press in Russia: A Cultural Bridge and an Instrument of Propaganda', in Offord, Ryazanova-Clarke, Rjéoutski and Argent (eds.), *French and Russian*, vol. I, 84–102.
175. See below, pp. 164–6.
176. S. I. Nikolaev, 'O kul'turnom statuse pol'skogo iazyka v Rossii vo vtoroi polovine XVII–nachale XVIII veka', *Russkaia literatura*, 2015.2, 132–8; Nikolaev, *Pol'skaia poezia v russkikh perevodakh. Vtoraia polovina XVII–pervaia tret' XVIII veka* (Leningrad: Nauka, 1989); Nikolaev, *Pol'sko-russkie literaturnye sviazi XVI–XVIII vv. Bibliograficheskie materialy* (St Petersburg: Nestor-Istoriia, 2008).
177. Uzdenikov, *Monety Rossii 1700–1917*, 337–9.
178. See L. A. Tsyganova, *Ital'ianskie mastera v Rossii XVIII veka: zhizn' i tvorchestvo* (Moscow: Principium, 2013).
179. N. P. Chesnokova, 'Dokumenty po istorii ital'ianskoi shkoly v Moskve (1697–1700 gg.): opyt sravnitel'nogo analiza', *Kapterevskie chteniia*, 9 (2011), 281–321; D. N. Ramazanova, 'Istochniki dlia izucheniia ital'ianskoi shkoly Ioannikiia i Sofroniia Likhudov (chelobitnye uchenikov i uchitelei)', *Ocherki feodal'noi Rossii*, 13 (2009), 293–313.
180. Marina Ritzarev, *Eighteenth-Century Russian Music* (Aldershot: Ashgate, 2006), 39.
181. Richard Taruskin, *Defining Russia Musically: Historical and Hermeneutical Essays* (Princeton University Press, 1997), 186–234.
182. Anna Makolkin, *A History of Odessa, the Last Italian Black-Sea Colony* (Lewiston, NY: Edwin Mellen Press, 2004); Makolkin, *The Nineteenth Century in Odessa: One Hundred Years of Italian Culture on the Shores of the Black Sea (1794–1894)* (Lewiston, NY: Edwin Mellen Press, 2007).
183. D. V. Grigorovich, 'Peterburgskie sharmanshchiki', in *Fiziologiia Peterburga* (Moscow: Sovetskaia Rossiia, 1984), 84–106. The collection was first published in 1845.
184. J. Braat et al. (eds.), *Russians and Dutchmen* (Groningen: Institute for Northern and Eastern European Studies, 1993); C. Horstmeier et al. (eds.), *Around Peter the Great: Three Centuries of Russian–Dutch Relations* (Groningen: Institute for Northern and Eastern European Studies, 1997);

E. Waegemans (ed.), *Russia and the Low Countries in the Eighteenth Century* (Groningen: Institute for Northern and Eastern European Studies, 1998); B. S. Makarov, *Gollandskie sadovye mastera v Sankt-Peterburge. Pervaia polovina XVIII veka* (St Petersburg and Groningen: NRTs, 2013).

185. M. J. Okenfuss, 'Inauspicious Beginnings: Jan Thessing, Amsterdam, and the Origins of Petrine Printing', in Waegemans (ed.), *Russia and the Low Countries*, 15–24.
186. Bykova and Gurevich, *Grazhd.*, no. 13, and further on p. 484.
187. T. L. Labutina, *Anglichane v dopetrovskoi Rossii* (St Petersburg: Aleteiia, 2011); Cross, *By the Banks of the Neva.*
188. S. V. Litvinov, 'Anglomaniia v Rossii kak sotsio-kul'turnoe iavlenie (posledniaia tret' XVIII – seredina XIX vv.)' (Avtoref. diss. na soiskanie uchenoi stepeni kandidata kul'turologicheskikh nauk; MGU, 1998).
189. Anthony Cross, 'English – A Serious Challenge to French in the Reign of Alexander I?', *Russian Review*, 74.1 (Jan. 2015), 57–68.
190. M. P. Alekseev, *Slovari inostrannykh slov v russkom azbukovnike XVII veka* (Leningrad: Nauka, 1968), 144–8.
191. Ingrid Maier and Nikita Mikhaylov [Mikhailov], '"Korolevskii izvet ko vsem poddannym" (1648 g.) – pervyi russkii perevod angliiskogo pechatnogo teksta?', *Russian Linguistics*, 33.3 (Nov. 2009), 289–317.
192. Bykova and Gurevich, *Grazhd.*, Appendix I, no. 19; also printed in Dutch, German and Italian.
193. *SK XVIII v.*, nos. 881, 4692.
194. [G. A. Poletika], *Slovar' na shesti iazykakh: rossiiskom, grecheskom, latinskom, frantsuzskom, nemetskom i angliiskom, izdannyi v pol'zu uchashchagosia rossiiskogo iunoshestva* (St Petersburg: Imp. AN, 1763).
195. Matvei Gavrilov, *Neues deutsch-französisch-lateinisch-italianisch-russisches Wörterbuch. Novyi Leksikon na nemetskom, frantsuzskom, latinskom, italianskom i russkom iazykakh* (N. Novikov at Moscow University Press, 1781); I. V. Sots, *Nouveau dictionnaire françois, italien, allemand, latin et russe* (Moscow University Press, 1784, 1787).
196. *Nakaz ee Imperatorskago Velichestva Ekateriny Vtoryia samoderzhitsy vserossiiskiia dannyi Kommissii o sochinenii proekta novago Ulozheniia* (St Petersburg: Imp. AN, 1770). On the previous editions in Russian, German and French, see *SK XVIII v.*, nos. 2,149–50, and *SK Inostr.*, nos. 594–6. A Dutch translation had been published in Amsterdam in 1769: Arend H. Hussen Jnr, 'Catherine the Great's Instruction (*Nakaz*) to Her Legislative Commission: The Dutch Translations of 1769 and 1794', in Waegemans (ed.), *Russia and the Low Countries*, 245–56.
197. [Decembrist investigation], *Rapport de la Commission d'Enquête* (St Petersburg: Pluchart, 1826); [Decembrist investigation], *Bericht der, zur Ausmittelung*

übelgesinnter Gesellschaften, in Russland, niedergesetzten Untersuchungens-Commission, übersetzt auf Befehl Seiner Majestät des Kaisers (St Petersburg: Kriegs-Buchdruckerey des General-Stabes, 1826); [Decembrist investigation], *Report of the Commission of Inquiry*, translated from French by G. Elliott (St Petersburg: Department of Public Instruction, 1826).

198. James Heard, *A Practical Grammar of the Russian Language* (St Petersburg: printed for the Author; Sold by Sleunine and Boosey & Sons, London, 1827).
199. Fonkich, *Grecheskie rukopisi*, 43, citing I. S. Nekrasov, 'Permskie pis'mena v rukpisiakh XV veka', *Zapiski imp. Novorossiiskogo universiteta* 51 (Odessa, 1890), 249–54.
200. Alekseev, *U kormila rossiiskogo gosudarstva*, 300–15; D. A. Morozov, 'Uigurskie nadpisi moskovskikh d'iakov (dopolnenie k drevnerusskoi diplomatike)', in Iu. M. Eskin (ed.), *Pamiati Lukicheva. Sbornik statei po istorii i istochnikovedeniiu* (Moscow: Drevlekhranilishche, 2006), 173–99; Morozov, 'Drevnerusskaia nadpis' uigurskim pis'mom', *Drevniaia Rus'. Voprosy medievistiki*, 2016.1(63), 99–103.
201. See the cluster of articles on this helmet by Iu. F. Igina, S. N. Bogatyrev and A. V. Lavrent'ev in *Peterburgskie slavianskie i balkanskie issledovaniia*, 2014.2, 67–140, and the continuation of the discussion in *Peterburgskie slavianskie i balkanskie issledovaniia*, 2015.1, 67–89.
202. T. E. Samoilova (comp. and introd.), *Vera i vlast'. Epokha Ivana Groznogo* (Moscow: Gosudarstvennyi istoriko-kul'turnyi muzei-zapovednik 'Moskovskii Kreml'', 2007), no. 20 (pp. 72–3).
203. Uzdenikov, *Monety Rossii*, 332–5.
204. Abramishvili, 'Iz istorii gruzinskogo knigopechataniia za predelami Gruzii'.
205. Bykova and Gurevich, *Grazhd.*, Appendix I, no. 32 (pp. 497–8).
206. A. G. Karimullin, 'Iz istorii tatarskoi knigi XVIII–pervoi poloviny XIX v.', *Kniga. Issledovaniia i materialy*, 18 (1969), 132–3.
207. A. Iu. Samarin, 'Deiatel'nost' "aziatskoi tipografii" I. K. Shnora (1785–1797) v svete novoi arkhivnoi nakhodki ', in Samarin, *Tipografshchiki i knigochety. Ocherki po istorii knigi v Rossii vtoroi poloviny XVIII veka* (Moscow: Pashkov dom, 2013), 244–52.
208. A. G. Karimullin, *U istokov tatarskoi knigi. Ot nachala vozniknoveniia do 60-kh godov XIX veka*, 2nd, corrected edn (Kazan: Tatarskoe knizhnoe izdatel'stvo, 1992), 112–87.
209. *SK XVIII v.*, no. 4,399. See G. A. Fafurin, *K istorii akademicheskoi torgovli v Rossii v epokhu Ekateriny II: deiatel'nost' Ioganna Veitbrekhta v Sankt-Peterburge* (Peterburgskoe lingvisticheskoe obshchestvo, 2010), 148–9, 325.
210. See e.g. the bilingual grammar of Russian for Armenians: Avraam Bogdanov, *Kratkaia rossiiskaia grammatika v pol'zu armianskogo iunoshestva, tshchatel'no i iasno s armianskim perevodom raspolozhennaia*

(Moscow: Avgust Semen, 1827); a Russian–Georgian phrasebook printed in Tiflis (Tbilisi) under the Russian military governor: *Sobranie Rossiiskikh razgovorov, v obshchezhitii upotrebliaemykh, s priobshcheniem Gruzinskogo perevoda, v pol'zu Blagorodnogo Iunoshestva* (Tiflis: Voenno-pokhodnaia tipografiia, 1819). On the teaching of languages of empire in national schools in Siberia, see Janet Hartley, 'Education and the East: The Omsk Asiatic School', in Maria Di Salvo, Valerie A. Kivelson and Daniel H. Kaiser (eds.), *Word and Image in Russian History: Essays in Honor of Gary Marker* (Boston: Academic Studies Press, 2015), 253–68.

5 Places and Times of the Graphosphere

1. Charlotte Roueché, 'Written Display in the Late Antique and Byzantine City', in E. Jeffreys (ed.), *Proceedings of the 21st International Congress of Byzantine Studies. London, 21–26 August 2006. Vol. 1. Plenary Papers* (Aldershot: Ashgate, 2006), 235–53; Franklin, *Writing, Society and Culture*, 233–41.
2. M. A. Orlova, *Naruzhnye rospisi srednevekovykh khramov. Vizantiia. Balkany. Drevniaia Rus'*, 2nd edn (Moscow: Severnyi palomnik, 2002), esp. 193–250.
3. Armando Petrucci, *Public Lettering: Script, Power, and Culture*, transl. Linda Lappin (University of Chicago Press, 1993), esp. 16–51.
4. See Simon Franklin, 'Information in Plain Sight: The Formation of the Public Graphosphere', in Franklin and Bowers (eds.), *Information and Empire*, 341–67.
5. See above, pp. 81–2.
6. T. S. Tsarkova and S. I. Nikolaev, 'Epitafiia peterburgskogo nekropolia', in A. V. Kobak and Iu. M. Piriutko (eds.), *Istoricheskie kladbishcha Sankt-Peterburga. Spravochnik-putevoditel'* (St Petersburg: Izdatel'stvo Chernysheva, 1993), 111–29; S. O. Androsov, 'O pervykh figurativnykh nadgrobiiakh v Rossii', in Androsov, *Ot Petra I k Ekaterine II*, 240–52.
7. Drboglav, *Kamni rasskazyvaiut ...*, 12–16; D. A. Petrov, 'Monumental'nye nadpisi P'etro Antonio Solari v Moskve', *Voprosy epigrafiki*, 5 (2011), 322–34.
8. See O. A. Belobrova, 'Latinskaia nadpis' na Frolovskikh vorotakh Moskovskogo Kremlia i ee sud'ba v drevnerusskoi pis'mennosti', in *Gosudarstvennye Muzei Moskovskogo Kremlia. Materialy i issledovaniia. Novye atributsii. Vypusk V* (Moscow: Iskusstvo, 1987), 51–7.
9. A. V. Grashchenkov, 'Plita s latinskoi nadpis'iu so Spasskoi bashni i titul gosudaria vseia Rusi', *Voprosy epigrafiki*, 1 (2006), 16–25; A. G. Avdeev, 'Utrachennaia nadpis' 1530 g. o stroitel'stve kremlia v Kolomne. Opyt rekonstruktsii soderzhaniia', *Voprosy epigrafiki*, 2 (2008), 178–89; G. G. Donskoi, 'Proklamativnaia funktsiia nadpisi na kolokol'ne Novospasskogo

monastyria', *Voprosy epigrafiki*, 7 (2013), Part 2, 199–205; V. B. Girshberg, 'Nadpis' mastera Poviliki', *Sovetskaia arkheologiia*, 1959.2, 248–9; A. G. Avdeev, 'Khramozdannye nadpisi XVI–XVII vv. Kostromy i kraia', *Kostromskaia zemlia*, 5 (2002), 158–65.

10. Luppov, *Kniga v Rossii v XVII veke*, 45–76; M. A. Alekseeva, 'Torgovlia graviurami v Moskve i kontrol' za nei v kontse XVII–XVIII vv.', in I. E. Danilova (ed.), *Narodnaia graviura i fol'klor v Rossii XVII–XIX vv. (K 150-letiiu so dnia rozhdeniia D. A. Rovinskogo)* (Moscow: Sovetskii khudozhnik, 1976), 140–58.
11. A. V. Lavrent'ev, 'Stareishie grazhdanskie monumenty Moskvy 1682–1700 gg.', in Lavrent'ev, *Liudi i veshchi. Pamiatniki russkoi istorii i kul'tury XVI–XVIII vv., ikh sozdateli i vladel'tsy* (Moscow: Arkheograficheskii tsentr, 1997), 177–202.
12. Lavrent'ev, 'Stareishie grazhdanskie monumenty', 178.
13. For probably the earliest extant inscribed law code in Greek, perhaps from the first half of the fifth century BCE, see Ronald F. Willetts, *The Law Code of Gortyn* (Berlin: De Gruyter, 1967); see also Roueché, 'Written Display', 251–2.
14. Simon Franklin, 'Printing and Social Control in Russia 2: Decrees', *Russian History*, 38 (2011), esp. 473–6.
15. Cf. Petrucci, *Public Lettering*, 53–5, for a similar oxymoronic expression with respect to this genre in Western Europe.
16. For the list, see D. D. Zelov, *Ofitsial'nye svetskie prazdniki kak iavlenie russkoi kul'tury kontsa XVII–nachala XVIII veka. Istoriia triumfov i feierverkov ot Petra Velikogo do ego docheri Elizavety* (Moscow: Editorial URSS, 2002), 140. Texts can be found partly in Tiukhmeneva, *Iskusstvo triumfal'nykh vrat*, 154–275, and partly in V. P. Grebeniuk and O. A. Derzhavina (eds.), *Panegiricheskaia literatura petrovskogo vremeni* (Moscow: Nauka, 1979), 135–80.
17. Sergei Bartenev, *Moskovskii kreml' v starinu i teper'*, 2 vols. (Moscow: Izdanie Ministerstva Imperatorskogo Dvora, 1916; facsimile reprint, Moscow: Russkii impul's, 2011), vol. II, 183–93.
18. Yu. K. Begunov, '"Opisanie vrat chesti . . . ": A Seventeenth-Century Russian Translation on William of Orange and the "Glorious Revolution"', *Oxford Slavonic Papers. New Series*, 20 (1987), 60–93.
19. *Na gzemze: gzymz/gezimz* = 'cornice'; from German *Gesims*, perhaps via Polish *Gsyms*: one of many borrowed neologisms that would surely have added to the sense of estrangement.
20. Grebeniuk and Derzhavina (eds.), *Panegiricheskaia literatura*, 136.
21. Text in Tiukhmeneva, *Iskusstvo triumfal'nykh vrat*, 157–212.
22. Grebeniuk and Derzhavina (eds.), *Panegiricheskaia literatura*, 156.
23. Grebeniuk and Derzhavina (ed.), *Panegiricheskaia literatura*, 154. For these meanings of *politicheskii* and *politichnyi*, see *Slovar' russkogo iazyka XVIII veka. Vypusk 21* (St Petersburg: Nauka, 2015), 171–2.

24. See, especially, the illustrations to Tiukhmeneva, *Iskusstvo triumfal'nykh vrat*, between pp. 96 and 97; also Alekseeva, *Iz istorii russkoi graviury*, 142–51, 188–94.
25. Alekseeva, *Graviura petrovskogo vremeni*, illustrations *passim*.
26. The West European prototype was the frontispiece to Georg Andreas Böckler, *Arithmetica nova militaris* (Nuremberg, 1661).
27. L. I. Sazonova, *Literaturnaia kul'tura Rossii. Rannee Novoe vremia* (Moscow: Iazyki slavianskikh kul'tur, 2006), 320–31. For verse epitaphs of the period: A. G. Avdeev, 'Russkaia sillabicheskaia epitafiia poslednei chetverti XVII–nachala vtoroi treti XVIII v.', *Palaeoslavica*, 25.1 (2017), 55–177. See also below, pp. 273–4.
28. S. O. Androsov, 'Raguzinskii v Venetsii: priobretenie statui dlia Letnego sada', in Androsov, *Ot Petra I k Ekaterine II*, 44–78; Cracraft, *Imagery*, 220–31.
29. Paul Keenan, 'The Summer Gardens in the Social Life of St Petersburg, 1725–1761', *SEER*, 88 (2010), 134–55.
30. Andreas Schönle, 'Private Walks and Public Gazes: Enlightenment and the Use of Gardens in Eighteenth-Century Russia', in Andrew Kahn (ed.), *Representing Private Lives of the Enlightenment* (Oxford: Voltaire Foundation, 2010), 167–85.
31. J. Stählin, *Original Anecdotes of Peter the Great, Collected from the Conversation of Several Persons of Distinction at Petersburgh and Moscow* (London and Edinburgh: J. Murray, J. Sewell, W. Creech, 1788), 249–52 (anecdote no. 75).
32. D. S. Likhachev, *Poetika sadov. K semantike sadovo-parkovykh stilei. Sad kak tekst*, 2nd edn (St Petersburg: Nauka, 1991), 126–8. For an outsider's scathing assessment of the inscriptions, see Giacomo Casanova's *Memoirs*, at the start of Chapter 21: English translation by Arthur Machen, http://ebooks.adelaide.edu.au/c/casanova/c33m/index.html; also Riazantsev, *Skul'ptura v Rossii*, 412–18.
33. Texts in T. L. Nikitina, *Russkie tserkovnye stennye rospisi 1670–1680-kh godov* (Moscow: Indrik, 2015), 198–205.
34. G. M. Zelenskaia, 'Znachenie nadpisei XVII veka v sozdanii sakral'nogo prostranstva v Novom Ierusalime pod Moskvoi', in A. M. Lidov (ed.), *Prostranstvennye ikony. Performativnoe v Vizantii i Drevnei Rusi* (Moscow: Indrik, 2011), 563–95; full critical editions of the verse inscriptions in Avdeev, *Starorusskaia epigrafika i knizhnost'*, 120–207.
35. See also below p. 252.
36. This verse 'chronicle' went though two 'editions' in the 1690s: see Avdeev, *Starorusskaia epigrafika i knizhnost'*, 143–93.
37. Cited in Andreas Schönle, *The Ruler in the Garden: Politics and Landscape Design in Imperial Russia* (Oxford, Bern, Berlin etc.: Peter Lang, 2007), 185.

38. Schönle, *The Ruler in the Garden*, 185, 193–205.
39. Svetlana Eremeeva, *Pamiati pamiatnikov. Praktika monumental'noi kommemoratsii v Rossii XIX–nachala XX v.* (Moscow: RGGU, 2015), 22–69.
40. *PSZ,* no. 4,071.
41. *PSZ,* no. 7,881.
42. *PSZ,* nos. 8,909, 9,016, 9,031, 9,073, 9,092, all from 1744.
43. *PSZ,* nos. 9,016, 9,073.
44. *PSZ,* nos. 8,147, 9,348, 11,127.
45. *PSZ,* nos. 21,963 (article 4), 27,180 (articles 15–23, 32–3), 27,787 (articles 30–1). For the approved drawings of the respective types of milepost, see the supplement to *PSZ*: *Chertezhi i risunki k sobraniiu*, 50.
46. Pushkin, *Sobranie sochinenii v desiati tomakh*, vol. II, 159.
47. Cited in D. Iu. Sherikh, *Peterburg den' za dnem. Gorodskoi mesiatseslov* (St Petersburg: 'Peterburg – XXI vek', 1998), 117–18. See also Ia. N. Dlugolenskii, *Voenno-grazhdanskaia i politseiskaia vlast' Sankt-Peterburga, 1703–1917* (St Petersburg: Zhurnal 'Neva', 2001), 278; S. Lebedev, *Nomernye znaki domov Peterburga. Zametki i nabliudeniia* (St Petersburg, 2010), www.liveinternet.ru/users/zimnyi/post285701342/.
48. See above, pp. 81–2.
49. *PSZ,* no. 16,187, in an annotation to article 63.
50. Heinrich von Reimers, *St. Petersburg am Ende seines ersten Jahrhunderts. Mit Rückblicken auf Entstehung und Wachsthum dieser Residenz unter den verschiedenen Regierungen während dieses Zeitraums*, vol. II (St Petersburg: F. Dienemann u. Comp., 1805), 285–6.
51. David Garrioch, 'House Names, Shop Signs and Social Organization in West European Cities, c. 1500–1900', *Urban History*, 21 (1994), 37–8.
52. Heinrich von Reimers, *St.-Peterburgische Adress-Buch auf das Jahr 1809* (St Petersburg: A. Pluchart, [1809]); Reimers, *Dictionnaire d'adress de St.-Pétersbourg pour l'année 1809, avec un plan et guide des étrangers à St-Pétersbourg* (St Petersburg: [n.p.], [1809]); Reimers, *Sanktpeterburgskaia adresnaia kniga na 1809 god* (St Petersburg: Schnoor, [1809]), p. iii. Reimers had recognised the usefulness of the measure as early as 1805, for statistical tables of Petersburg buildings and inhabitants published in his history of the city: Reimers, *St. Petersburg am Ende seines ersten Jahrhunderts*, 318.
53. See A. G. Cross, *St Petersburg and the British: The City Through the Eyes of British Visitors and Residents* (London: Frances Lincoln Ltd, 2008), 146.
54. Aleksei Grech, *Ves' Peterburg v karmane: spravochnaia kniga dlia stolichnykh zhitelei i priezzhikh, s planami Sanktpeterburga i chetyrekh teatrov*, 2nd expanded and corrected edn (St Petersburg: N. Grech, 1851), 3–4. The first edition had been published in 1846.
55. See above, p. 72.

56. On legislation, and on Debucour's aquatints, see above, p. 100.
57. *PSZ,* no. 9,350.
58. G. V. Esipov, *Tiazhelaia pamiat' proshlogo. Rasskazy iz del Tainoi Kantseliarii i drugikh arkhivov* (St Petersburg: A. S. Suvorin, 1885), 307.
59. *PSZ,* no. 10,032. Earlier decrees restricted the location of trade but without mentioning signs: *PSZ,* no. 7,940 (9 November 1739) and no. 8,674, articles 3–5 (2 December 1742).
60. On comparable restrictions in Western Europe, see Garrioch, 'House Names, Shop Signs and Social Organization', 37.
61. *PSZ,* no. 13,421.
62. *PSZ,* nos. 15,451, 15,462, 28 June and 8 July 1782; on earlier decrees forbidding merchants to trade from their houses, see e.g. *PSZ,* no. 7,940, of 9 November 1739. On Catherine's policies on trade and merchants, see de Madariaga, *Russia in the Age of Catherine the Great,* 299–303, 470–7.
63. Alla Povelikhina and Yevgeny Kovtun, *Russian Painted Shop Signs and Avant-garde Artists* (Leningrad: Aurora Art Publishers, 1991), 11–26; Sally West, *I Shop in Moscow: Advertising and the Creation of Consumer Culture in Late Tsarist Russia* (DeKalb: Northern Illinois University Press, 2011), 21–5; Sazikov and Vinogradova, *Naruzhnaia reklama Moskvy,* 11–18.
64. On the panorama, see Katherine Bowers, 'Experiencing Information: An Early Nineteenth-Century Stroll Along Nevskii Prospekt', in Franklin and Bowers (eds.), *Information and Empire,* 369–407.
65. Grigory Kaganov, *Images of Space: St. Petersburg in the Verbal and Visual Arts,* transl. Sidney Monas (Stanford University Press, 1997), 82.
66. See e.g. N. N. Skorniakova, *Vidy Moskvy. Akvarel' i risunok XVIII–nachala XX veka iz sobraniia Istoricheskogo muzeia* (Moscow: Istoricheskii muzei, 2017), nos. 40, 49, 52; cf. the absence of signs in no. 28 from the 1800s.
67. 'Distributed in every place, / On every building, countless signs' (*Chto dom, to vyvesok bez schetu / Razmeshcheno po vsem mestam*): Petr Tatarinov, *Zametki peterburgskogo zevaki* (1851), cited in Tat'iana Rudenko, *Modnye magaziny i modistki Moskvy pervoi poloviny XIX stoletiia* (Moscow: ZAO Izdatel'stvo Tsentrpoligraf, 2015), 18.
68. Fedor Distribuendi, *Vzgliad na moskovskie vyveski* (Moscow: Tipografiia I. Smirnova, 1836).
69. Tsentral'nyi gosudarstvennyi arkhiv goroda Moskvy, f. 32, op. 5, d. 102. I am grateful to Abram Reitblat for pointing out this reference, and for the information that in the 1830s 'Ensign Brazhnikov' appears to have submitted at least three other works to the Censorship Committee, none of which was published.
70. Distribuendi, *Vzgliad na moskovskie vyveski,* 25.

71. Distribuendi, *Vzgliad na moskovskie vyveski*, 17.
72. Distribuendi, *Vzgliad na moskovskie vyveski*, 3–4, 4–5, and in several of the works cited below.
73. Distribuendi, *Vzgliad na moskovskie vyveski*, 61.
74. K. N. Batiushkov, 'Progulka po Moskve', in his *Sochineniia v dvukh tomakh*, vol. II (Moscow: Khudozhestvennaia literatura, 1989), 288.
75. Pushkin, *Sobranie sochinenii v desiati tomakh*, vol. X, 135.
76. P. Vistengof, *Ocherki moskovskoi zhizni* (Moscow: Tipografiia S. Selivanovskogo, 1842), 134–5.
77. I. T. Kokorev, 'Publikatsii i vyveski', in Kokorev, *Moskva sorokovykh godov. Ocherki i povesti o Moskve XIX veka* (Moscow: Moskovskii rabochii, 1959), 73, 74; see also Alexander M. Martin, *Enlightened Metropolis: Constructing Imperial Moscow, 1762–1855* (Oxford University Press, 2013), 284–9.
78. E. I. Rastorguev, *Progulki po Nevskomy prospektu* (St Petersburg: Tipografiia Karla Kraiia, 1846), repr. in A. M. Konechnyi (ed.), *Chuvstvitel'nye progulki po Nevskomu prospektu* (St Petersburg: Petropolis, 2009), 121–210.
79. Rastorguev, *Progulki po Nevskomy prospektu*, 139–41.
80. In *Fiziologiia Peterburga*, 132.
81. E.g. *Fiziologiia Peterburga*, 120, 123–4.
82. 'Peterburgskie vyveski', *Illiustratsiia* 1848, no. 30 (28 Aug.), 81–2; text also at http://tiam-tula.ru/wp-content/uploads/2016/07/TIAM_public002.pdf.
83. E.g. the prominent inscription *BIRZHA 1810 GOD* above the portico of the St Petersburg custom house, as illustrated in the engraving by Ivan Cheskii, c. 1818: Ashmolean Museum, Talbot Collection, E-227.
84. V. N. Borzykh, *Kniga o znakakh strakhovaniia ot ognia (1827–1918)* (Moscow: Obshchestvo liubitelei strakhovykh drevnostei, 2016), esp. 9–19 on the history of the genre, which perhaps originated in late-seventeenth-century England.
85. A. S. Suvorin, *Rostopchinskie afishi 1812 goda. Bibliograficheskoe izdanie v 300 ekzempliarakh* (St Petersburg: Tipografiia A. S. Suvorina, 1889).
86. A. A. Zaitseva, 'Novye materialy o russkikh knizhnykh lavkakh v S.-Peterburge v kontse XVIII–nachale XIX veka', in S. P. Luppov et al. (eds.), *Knizhnoe delo v Rossii v XVI–XIX vekakh. Sbornik nauchnykh trudov* (Leningrad: BAN, 1980), 117–43; Marker, *Publishing*, 152–83; Iu. A. Gorshkov, *Ekonomicheskaia modernizatsiia knizhnogo dela v Rossii XVIII–pervoi poloviny XIX v.* (Moscow: Pashkov dom, 2009), esp. 163–225.
87. Gogol, *Polnoe sobranie sochinenii v 14 tomakh*, vol. VIII (1952), 179.
88. *Fiziologiia Peterburga*, 56.
89. S. I. Nikolaev, 'Imia na dereve (iz istorii idillicheskogo motiva)', *XVIII vek*, 22 (2002), 46–65. On the trope in English pastoral, see Leah Knight, 'Writing on Early Modern Trees', *English Literary Renaissance*, 41 (2011), 462–84.

90. Nikolaev, 'Imia na dereve', 62–4. On the importance of inscription in Karamzin's writings, see also T. V. Zvereva, 'Roman N. M. Karamzina *Pis'ma russkogo puteshestvennika* kak entsiklopediia nadpisei', *Ural'skii filologicheskii vestnik*, 2015.3, 41–50.
91. S. I. Nikolaev, 'Problemy izucheniia malykh stikhotvornykh form (Epitafiia)', *XVIII vek*, 16 (1989), 44–55; O. A. Prokopovich, 'Zhanr nadpisi v russkoi poezii XVIII–pervoi treti XIX v.' (Dissertatsiia na soiskanie uchenoi stepeni kandidata filologicheskikh nauk; Karagandinskii gosudarstvennyi universitet, 2000).
92. Fedor Polikarpov, *Kniga bukvar' slavenskimi, grecheskimi, rimskimi pismeny uchitisia khotiashchim* (Moscow: [n.p.], 1701), fol. 10v of the main (i.e. the second) foliation.
93. I. A. Bartenev and V. N. Batazhkova, *Russkii inter'er XVIII–XIX vekov* (Moscow: Svarog i K, 2000), 12.
94. For the early period there are monastic inventories. Particularly revealing from the late seventeenth century onwards are inventories drawn up in connection with property confiscations: see Iu. A. Tikhonov, *Mir veshchei v moskovskikh i peterburgskikh domakh sanovnogo dvorianstva (po novym istochnikam pervoi poloviny XVIII v.)* (Moscow: Kuchkovo pole, 2008).
95. Above, Chapters 2 and 3.
96. See e.g. E. A. Luk'ianov, *Inter'er v russkoi grafike XIX–nachala XX veka. Iz sobraniia Gosudarstvennogo istoricheskogo muzeiia* (Moscow: Istoricheskii muzei, 2016), with around forty pictures of interiors of the first half of the nineteenth century, where bare walls and surfaces appear to be the norm. Cf. the more cluttered interiors depicted towards mid century by Pavel Fedotov: Rosalind P. Blakesley, *The Russian Canvas: Painting in Imperial Russia, 1757–1881* (New Haven and London: Yale University Press, 2016), 207–17 (figs. 170–80).
97. On a collection of more than 100 Psalters for lending to monks at the Kirillo-Belozerskii monastery, see Dmitrieva and Sharomazov (eds.), *Opis' stroenii i imushchestva Kirillo-Belozerskogo monastyria 1601 goda*, 125 (ff. 219v–220 of the manuscript). On borrowings from the library of the same monastery nearly a century later, see Romanova, 'K istorii biblioteki Kirillo-Belozerskogo monastyria'. On the collection of a mid-seventeenth-century monk, see O. S. Sapozhnikova, *Russkii knizhnik XVII veka Sergii Shelonin* (Moscow and St Petersburg: Al'ians-Arkheo, 2010), 81–102.
98. M. I. Slukhovskii, *Russkaia biblioteka XVI–XVII vv* (Moscow: Kniga, 1973), 6. The modern word *biblioteka* was not in regular use before the eighteenth century.
99. Slukhovskii, *Russkaia biblioteka*, 8–17; Kukushkina, *Monastyrskie biblioteki russkogo severa*, 177–8.

100. *Opis' stroenii i imushchestva*, 121 (f. 207v).
101. Slukhovskii, *Russkaia biblioteka*, 17–19.
102. On the collections of, for example, Andrei Artamonovich Matveev, or of Feofilakt Lopatinskii, consisting mainly of non-Russian, non-Cyrillic books, see Kartashov and Polonskii (eds.), *Biblioteka A. A. Matveeva*; D. D. Gal'tsin and G. N. Pitul'ko, *Biblioteka Feofilakta Lopatinskogo (ok. 1680–1741). Katalog* (St Petersburg: Pushkinskii dom, 2016). On the second quarter of the eighteenth century, see esp. Luppov, *Kniga v Rossii v poslepetrovskoe vremia*.
103. E.g.: *Zhivopis' XVIII veka*, ed. L. I. Iovleva (Moscow: Krasnaia ploshchad', 1998), nos. 55, 80, 104, 180, 181 (portraits of Gavriil Derzhavin, Prince A. B. Kurakin and D. P. Troshchinskii, by Vladimir Lukich Borovikovskii (1757–1825); portraits of Prince A. M. Golitsyn and P. A. Demidov by Dmitrii Grigorevich Levitskii (1735–1822)).
104. *Zhivopis' XVIII veka*, nos. 176, 177; cf. also Lampi's portraits of Platon and Valerian Zubov in *Gosudarstvennyi Russkii muzei. Zhivopis'. XVIII vek. Katalog. Tom 1* (St Petersburg: Palace Editions, 1998), nos. 233, 234.
105. E.g. *Zhivopis' XVIII veka*, no. 66 (Borovikovskii's portrait of E. A. Dolgorukaia); in *Gosudarstvennyi Russkii muzei. Zhivopis'. XVIII vek*, no. 232 (Lampi's portrait of Grand Princess Maria Fedorovna as an artist); for the latter, see also Blakesley, *The Russian Canvas*, 274–7 and fig. 237.
106. D. V. Gusev, '"Obmanka" G. N. Teplova i neizvestnye fakty ego biografii', *Istoricheskii format*, 2016.1, 303–24; E. F. Petinova, *Russkie zhivopistsy XVIII veka. Biografii* (St Petersburg: Iskusstvo-SPB, 2002), fig. 2. See also the anonymous *trompe l'oeil* with documents from 1783 that illustrates the cover of the present volume. Images at *Zhivopis' XVIII veka*, no. 392; www.artcyclopedia.ru/teplov_grigorij_nikolaevich.htm; www.tretyakovgallerymagazine.com/articles/3–2012-36/objects-their-time.
107. L. V. Tydman, *Izba, dom, dvorets. Zhiloi inter'er Rossii s 1700 po 1840-e gody* (Moscow: Progress-Traditsiia, 2000), 42–3, 203.
108. T. M. Sokolova and K. A. Orlova, *Glazami sovremennikov. Russkii zhiloi inter'er pervoi treti XIX veka* (Leningrad: Khudozhnik RSFSR, 1982), 136–7.
109. I. A. Bartenev and V. N. Batazhkova, *Russkii inter'er XIX veka* (Leningrad: Khudozhnik RSFSR, 1984), figs. 97, 99, 100, 102, 104. For a description of a writer's study on a country estate, see e.g. the memoir of the study of Konstantin Aksakov at Abramtsevo, cited in V. P. Vikulova, 'Byt provintsial'noi usad'by i russkie pisateli pervoi poloviny XIX veka', www.domgogolya.ru/science/researches/202/.
110. The study was often also a bedroom: in a grand house the sleeping area might be set back in an alcove or behind a screen; in a more modest house or

apartment the study might have a couch against one wall: on the palatial version, see Tydman, *Izba, dom, dvorets*, 141–4.

111. E. g. Bartenev and Batazhkova, *Russkii inter'er XIX veka*, figs. 42, 43, 63.
112. For some reconstructed interiors of studies and 'study-boudoirs', with authentic furnishings, see A. M. Kuchumov, *Ubranstvo russkogo zhilogo inter'era XIX veka. Po materialam vystavki v Pavlovskom dvortse-muzee* (Leningrad: Khudozhnik RSFSR, 1977), esp. illustrations 16–26 (a study in the 1810s), 45–54 (a 'study-boudoir' in the 1820s) and 63–74 (a young man's study in the 1830s).
113. Pushkin, *Evgenii Onegin*, 2.III; 7.XIX, XXI (see also below, pp. 205–6); 8.XLVI; 8.V. For more on representations of the study in the literature of the early nineteenth century, see Sokolova and Orlova, *Glazami sovremennikov*, 131–54; also on ballrooms and reception rooms, 92–118.
114. S. A. Klepikov, 'Iz istorii russkogo khudozhestvennogo perepleta', *Kniga. Issledovaniia i materialy*, 1 (1959), 98–168.
115. For examples, see the illustrations in all three volumes of *Mosk. kirill. izd. RGADA.*
116. Klepikov, 'Iz istorii', 123 (fig. 16).
117. E. S. Kashutina and N. G. Saprykina, *Ekslibris v sobranii Nauchnoi biblioteki Moskovskogo gosudarstvennogo universiteta. Al'bom-katalog* (Izdatel'stvo MGU, 1985), nos. 1–13; P. A. Druzhinin, *Russkii geral'dicheskii superekslibris* (Moscow: Drevlekhranilishche, 2000); also E. A. Savel'eva, 'I.-D. Shumakher i pervyi ekslibris Biblioteki ego velichestva', in I. M. Beliaeva (ed.), *Kniga v Rossii. K istorii akademicheskoi biblioteki* (St Petersburg: Biblioteka RAN, 2014), 59.
118. On bookplates, see also below, p. 207.
119. I. M. Polonskaia, 'Russkaia izdatel'skaia oblozhka i pereplet XVIII v.', *Kniga. Issledovaniia i materialy*, 38 (1979), 152–61. Blank paper bindings are attested considerably earlier: see Slukhovskii, *Russkaia biblioteka*, 26.
120. Tikhonov, *Mir veshchei*, 68.
121. Michael Flier, 'K semioticheskomu analizu Zolotoi palaty Moskovskogo Kremlia', in *Drevnerusskoe iskusstvo. Russkoe iskusstvo pozdnego srednevekov'ia. XVI vek*, ed. A. L. Batalov et al. (St Petersburg: Dmitrii Bulanin, 2003), 178–87.
122. Texts in *Skazanie o kniaziakh vladimirskikh*, ed. R. P. Dmitrieva (Moscow and Leningrad: AN SSSR, 1955).
123. Bartenev, *Moskovskii kreml'*, vol. II, 183–93. Reconstruction in K. K. Lopialo, 'K primernoi rekonstruktsii Zolotoi palaty Kremlevskogo dvortsa i ee monumental'noi zhivopisi', in O. I. Podobedova, *Moskovskaia shkola zhivopisi pri Ivane IV. Raboty v Moskovskom kremle 40-kh–70-kh godov XVI v.* (Moscow: Nauka, 1972), 193–8.

124. O. A. Belobrova, 'O nekotorykh istochnikakh podpisei k siuzhetam rospisi Zolotoi palaty Moskovskogo Kremlia', *TODRL*, 53 (2003), 502–17.
125. See Daniel Rowland, 'Two Cultures, One Throne Room: Secular Courtiers and Orthodox Culture in the Golden Hall of the Moscow Kremlin', in Valerie A. Kivelson and Robert H. Greene (eds.), *Orthodox Russia: Belief and Practice Under the Tsars* (University Park: Pennsylvania State University Press, 2003), 33–57.
126. I. M. Sokolova, *Monomakhov tron. Tsarskoe mesto Uspenskogo sobora Moskovskogo kremlia* (Moscow: Indrik, 2001), 60–8, for an 'edition' of the inscriptions. See *Skazanie*, 53–5, on the relationship of this text to other versions of the *Tale*.
127. E.g. the ivory panels, probably by Italian and German masters, of a throne of Ivan III: see Bartenev, *Moskovskii kreml'*, vol. II, figs. 131–2 (between pp. 97 and 98).
128. E.g. in the Golitsyn residence, according to the 1689 inventory: Tikhonov, *Mir veshchei*, 60, 66.
129. *Domostroi*, ed. V. V. Kolesov and V. V. Rozhdestvenskaia (St Petersburg: Nauka, 1994), 18, 91 (chapter 11 or 8 of the text, depending on the version); English translation in *The Domostroi: Rules for Russian Households in the Time of Ivan the Terrible*, ed. and transl. Carolyn Johnston Pouncy (Ithaca and London: Cornell University Press, 1994), 73.
130. Paul of Aleppo, *The Travels of Macarius*, vol. I, 396.
131. Oleg Tarasov, *Icon and Devotion: Sacred Spaces in Imperial Russia*, transl. Robin Milner-Gulland (London: Reaktion Books, 2002), 52–6.
132. Iuliia Khod'ko, *Religioznyi lubok vtoroi poloviny XVIII–nachala XX veka iz sobraniia Russkogo muzeia* (St Petersburg: Palace Editions, 2012). See E. A. Mishina, *Ranniaia russkaia graviura. Vtoraia polovina XVII–nachala XVIII veka. Novye otkrytiia* (Leningrad: Gosudarstvennyi russkii muzei, 1979), 7 (n. 18).
133. Tikhonov, *Mir veshchei*, 60, again from the Golitsyn inventory of 1689.
134. Zabelin, *Domashnii byt russkikh tsarei v XVI i XVII stoletiiakh. Chast' I*, 230–3.
135. On *lubok* borrowings from Russian literature, see N. I. Rudakova, *Russkaia literatura v zerkale lubka. Narodnaia kartinka XVIII–nachala XX veka* (St Petersburg: RNB, 2015); on *lubok* versions of biblical texts, see A. A. Pletneva, *Lubochnaia Bibliia. Iazyk i tekst* (Moscow: Iazyki slavianskoi kul'tury, 2013).
136. T. A. Voronina, 'O bytovanii lubochnykh kartinok v russkoi narodnoi srede v XIX veke', in *Mir narodnoi kartinki. Materialy nauchnoi konferentsii 'Vipperovskie chteniia' – 1997. Vyp. XXX* (Moscow: Progress-Traditsiia, 1999), 192–212. See also Khod'ko, *Svetskii lubok*, 5, 25, 30.

137. E. I. Itkina, *Risovannyi lubok staroobriadtsev v sobranii Istoricheskogo muzeia* (Moscow: Istoricheskii muzei, 2017).
138. Victoria Avery, Melissa Calarescu and Mary Laven, *Treasured Possessions: From the Renaissance to the Enlightenment* (London: Philip Wilson, 2015).
139. In the Hermitage Museum, ERM-6482: see N. V. Kaliazina and G. N. Komelova, *Russkoe iskusstvo petrovskoi epokhi* (Leningrad: Khudozhnik RSFSR, 1990), no. 199.
140. See above, pp. 74–7.
141. Peter Davidson, 'The Inscribed House', in Michael Bath, Pedro F. Campa and Daniel S. Russell (eds.), *Emblem Studies in Honour of Peter M. Daly* (Baden-Baden: Valentin Koerner, 2002), 41–62; Andrew Morrall, 'Inscriptional Wisdom and the Domestic Arts in Early Modern Northern Europe', in Natalia Filatkina, Birgit Ulrike Münch and Ane Kleine-Engel, *Formelhaftigkeit in Text und Bild* (Wiesbaden: Reichert Verlag, 2012), 120–38.
142. On the lack of a tradition of textual samplers in Russia, see above, p. 91.
143. *Symbola et emblemata* (Amsterdam: Henricius Westenius, 1705). See Pedro F. Campa, 'Emblem Books in Russia', in Peter M. Daly (ed.), *Companion to Emblem Studies* (New York: AMS Press, 2008), 309–21.
144. Maslikh, *Russkoe izraztsovoe iskusstvo*, e.g. illustrations 213, 216–23 etc.
145. Gorbatova, *Khudozhestvennoe steklo XVI–XVIII vekov*, fig. 91.
146. Hermitage Museum: ERM-2721, 2776: Kaliazina and Komelova, *Russkoe iskusstvo petrovskoi epokhi*, no. 197.
147. Hermitage Museum: ERD-2479: Kaliazina and Komelova, *Russkoe iskusstvo petrovskoi epokhi*, no. 208.
148. In the Menshikov palace: museums.artyx.ru/books/item/f00/s00/z0000032/st014.shtml.
149. On these and several of the other objects mentioned in this paragraph, see above, Chapter 3.
150. Postnikova-Loseva, 'Zolotye i serebrianye izdeliia masterov Oruzheinoi palaty', 162–3.
151. Hermitage Museum: ERT-8878. See above, Fig. 3.9.
152. E. Grebenka, 'Peterburgskaia storona', in *Fiziologiia Peterburga*, 127.
153. Hermitage Museum: E-4006: Kaliazina and Komelova, *Russkoe iskusstvo petrovskoi epokhi*, no. 178.
154. Victoria and Albert Museum LOAN:GILBERT.342:1, 2–2008.
155. As in Borovikovskii's portrait of Nikolai Iakovlev: *Zhivopis' XVIII veka*, no. 80 (p. 75).
156. L. A. Petrova, 'Samovar-kukhnia iz sobraniia P. I. Shchukina. Voprosy atributsii i nekotorye aspekty izucheniia russkoi mednoi posudy XVIII

veka', in *Problemy atributsii pamiatnikov dekorativno-prikladnogo iskusstva XVI–XX vekov*, 167–8.
157. Zubets, 'Ob odnoi gruppe prianikov i prianichnykh dosok'.
158. Kalinichev, *Samovarnoe delo v Rossii*. Up to the early nineteenth century the manufacturers' names tended to be engraved in cursive-style lettering; subsequently the marks were stamped.
159. See Figs. 3.9, 3.10, 3.11 and 3.13.

6 Aspects of the Ecology of the Graphosphere

1. Cf. Barton, *Literacy: An Introduction to the Ecology of Written Language*.
2. E.g.: Crick and Walsham (eds.), *The Uses of Script and Print*; McKitterick, *Print, Manuscript, and the Search for Order*; Julia Boffey, *Manuscript and Print in London, c. 1475–1530* (London: British Library, 2012); Hanno Wijsman (ed.), *Books in Transition at the Time of Philip the Fair: Manuscripts and Printed Books in the Late Fifteenth and Early Sixteenth Century Low Countries* (Turnhout: Brepols, 2010); cf. P. F. Kornicki, 'Manuscript, Not Print: Scribal Culture in the Edo Period', *Journal of Japanese Studies*, 32.1 (2006), 23–52; Zsuzsa Barbarics-Hermanik, 'The Coexistence of Manuscript and Print: Handwritten Newsletters in the Second Century of Print, 1540–1640', in Walsby and Kemp (eds.), *The Book Triumphant*, 347–68.
3. For preliminary remarks on this approach, see Franklin, 'Mapping the Graphosphere'.
4. For analyses of eighteenth-century print production according to 'subject composition', see Marker, *Publishing*, statistical tables on pp. 25, 59, 60, 73, 84, 132, 141.
5. For contrasting approaches to the distribution of categories, see Kiselev, 'O moskovskom knigopechatanii XVII veka' (emphasising the ecclesiastical); and Pozdeeva, 'The Activity of the Moscow Printing House' (emphasising the instructional).
6. See above, pp. 125, 129–30.
7. Dmitrieva, Krushel'nitskaia and Mil'chik (eds.), *Opisi Solovetskogo monastyria XVI veka*, 109.
8. B. V. Sapunov, 'Izmenenie sootnoshenii rukopisnykh i pechatnykh knig v russkikh bibliotekakh XVI–XVII vv.', in Kniazevskaia et al. (eds.), *Rukopisnaia i pechatnaia kniga*, 42.
9. Kukushkina, *Monastyrskie biblioteki russkogo severa*, 169–76. On the early acquisition of printed books in more remote monasteries, see *Ot Viatki do Tobol'ska: tserkovno-monastyrskie biblioteki rossiiskoi provintsii XVI–XVIII vekov* (Ekaterinburg: Ural'skoe otdelenie RAN, 1994), esp. 10–19.

10. Sapunov, 'Izmenenie sootnoshenii', 42.
11. Cited in Sapunov, 'Izmenenie sootnoshenii', 48.
12. *PSZ*, no. 1,612, esp. articles 1, 3, 15.
13. See below, pp. 245–7.
14. E.g. Savel'eva, *Ocherk istorii formirovaniia pinezhskoi knizhno-rukopisnoi traditsii*; I. V. Pozdeeva (ed.), *Traditsionnaia kniga i kul'tura pozdnego russkogo srednevekov'ia. Chast' 2. Istoriia, knizhnost' i kul'tura russkogo staroobriadchestva* (Iaroslavl: Redmer, 2008); A. V. Pigin, *Pamiatniki knizhnoi stariny russkogo severa. Kollektsii rukopisei XV–XX vekov v gosudarstvennykh khranilishchakh Respubliki Kareliia* (St Petersburg: Dmitrii Bulanin, 2010).
15. See above, pp. 28–35.
16. See below, pp. 234–5.
17. On the production and text of the printed *Kormchaia kniga*, see E. V. Beliakova, L. V. Moshkova and T. A. Oparina, *Kormchaia kniga. Ot rukopisnoi traditsii k pervomu pechatnomu izdaniiu* (Moscow and St Petersburg: Institut rossiiskoi istorii RAN; RGADA; Tsentr gumanitarnykh initsiativ, 2017), 168–271.
18. Simon Franklin, 'K voprosu o malykh zhanrakh kirillicheskoi pechati', in D. N. Ramazanova (ed.), *450 let Apostolu Ivana Fedorova. Istoriia rannego knigopechataniia v Rossii (pamiatniki, istochniki, traditsii izucheniia)* (Moscow: Pashkov dom, 2016), 421–32.
19. Bykova and Gurevich, *Kirill.*, nos. 21, 31; cf. no. 24, perhaps from December 1702.
20. See below, p. 230.
21. E. L. Nemirovskii, *Azbuki Ivana Fedorova, ego uchenikov i posledovatelei*, ed. Iu. E. Shustova (Piatigorsk: SNEG, 2015), 22–149.
22. Nemirovskii, *Azbuki Ivana Fedorova*, 181.
23. For full lists of 'Cyrillic' primers and alphabet books, see Nemirovskii and Shustova, 'Kirillicheskie azbuki i bukvari XVI–XVIII vv.' On eighteenth-century civil-type primers: Zemtsova and Shitskova, 'Azbuki, bukvari, propisi grazhdanskoi pechati, izdannye v XVIII v.'. On the quantities of primers in the seventeenth century, see above, pp. 48–9. On the eighteenth-century circulation of printed primers and grammars in various languages, see Marker, *Publishing*, 191–7.
24. On translators in the early years of the Academy of Sciences press, see Marker, *Publishing*, 50–8.
25. *SK XVIII v.*, no. 1,289.
26. See Hughes, *Russia in the Age of Peter the Great*, 312–16; Mirko Grmek, 'The History of Medical Education in Russia', in C. D. O'Malley (ed.), *The History of Medical Education* (Berkeley, Los Angeles and London: University of California Press, 1970), 303–27; also Andreas Renner, *Russische Autokratie*

und europäische Medizin. Organizierte Wissenstransfer im 18. Jahrhundert (Stuttgart: Franz Steiner Verlag, 2010).

27. Bykova and Gurevich, *Grazhd.*, nos. 281, 353, 354, and *Dopoln.*, no. 83; text of the 1719 announcement in *PSZ*, no. 3,338.
28. S. M. Grombakh, *Russkaia meditsinskaia literatura XVIII veka* (Moscow: Akademiia meditsinskikh nauk, 1953), 24.
29. A. V. Sirenov, 'O rabote po "ispravleniiu" pechatnogo letopistsa v 1703 g.', in O. L. Novikova (ed.), *Letopisi i khroniki. Novye issledovaniia 2009–2010* (Moscow and St Petersburg: Al'ians-Arkheo, 2011), 355–67.
30. *Ukrainskie knigi kirillovskoi pechati XVI–XVIII vv.*, nos. 124, 133, 144, 145, 177; Bykova and Gurevich, *Kirill.*, nos. 10, 551; Bykova and Gurevich, *Grazhd.*, nos. 113, 299.
31. Cf. also a 'one-off' publication: *Kniga istoriografiia pochatiia imene, slavy i rasshireniia naroda slavianskogo* (St Petersburg, 1722), attributed on the title page to 'Mavrourbin'. This is a translation of a supplemented version of Mauro Orbini's *Il regno degli Slavi*, first printed in Pesaro in 1601. See *SK XVIII v.*, no. 8,177.
32. Wim Coudenis, 'Translation and the Emergence of History as an Academic Discipline in Eighteenth-Century Russia', *Kritika*, 17.4 (Fall 2016), 721–52.
33. The first three volumes in 1768–74, the fourth volume in 1784. The final volume was not printed until 1843.
34. Marker, *Publishing*, 201–11.
35. E.g. William Edward Brown, *A History of Seventeenth-Century Russian Literature* (Ann Arbor: Ardis, 1980); Sazonova, *Literaturnaia kul'tura Rossii*; R. B. Tarkovskii and L. R. Tarkovskaia, *Ezop na Rusi. Vek XVII. Issledovaniia. Teksty. Kommentarii* (St Petersburg: Dmitrii Bulanin, 2005).
36. See e.g. V. K. Bylinin and A. A. Iliushin (eds.), *Virshevaia poeziia (pervaia polovina XVII veka)* (Moscow: Sovetskaia Rossiia, 1989); *BLDR*, vol. 18 (2014).
37. O. I. Fedotov, *Osnovy russkogo stikhoslozheniia. Teoriia i istoriia russkogo stikha. Kniga 1. Metrika i ritmika* (Moscow: Flinta; Nauka, 2002), 139–85; A. P. Bogdanov, *Stikh torzhestva: rozhdenie russkoi ody, posledniaia chetvert' XVII–nachalo XVIII veka* (Moscow: Institut rossiiskoi istorii RAN, 2012).
38. On the variety of seventeenth-century verse, see esp. A. M. Panchenko, *Russkaia stikhotvornaia kul'tura XVII veka* (Leningrad: Nauka, 1973). On the verse components of the earliest surviving play, first performed in 1672, see *Artakserksovo deistvo. Pervaia p'esa russkogo teatra XVII v.*, ed. I. M. Kudriavtseva (Moscow and Leningrad: Izdatel'stvo AN SSSR, 1957), 75–6.
39. Panchenko, *Russkaia stikhotvornaia kul'tura*, 34–77.
40. Guseva, *Izd. kirill. XVI v.*, 1,265.

41. Iu. E. Shustova, 'Simvolika L'vovskogo stavropigiiskogo bratstva', *Gerboved"*, 2005.2(80), 94–104; also Shustova, 'Problema kompleksnogo istochnikovedcheskogo issledovaniia predislovii i posviashchenii izdanii l'vovskoi bratskoi tipografii kontsa XVI–XVII veka', in *Fedorovskie chteniia 2005* (Moscow: Nauka, 2005), 231–47.
42. *Ukrainskie knigi kirillovskoi pechati XVI–XVIII vv. Vypusk I*, nos. 15, 33, 37, 48, 51. See also L. I. Sazonova, 'Ukrainskie staropechatnye predisloviia kontsa XVI–pervoi poloviny XVII v. (osobennosti literaturnoi formy)', in Demin et al. (eds.), *Tematika i stilistika predislovii i posleslovii*, 153–87.
43. Bylinin and Iliushin (eds.), *Virshevaia poeziia*, 230–7, 321–2; but cf. the unpublished prefaces, ibid., 283–6, 293–320. See also a cycle of sixty-seven poems written for, but not printed in, the *Sobornik* of 1647: ibid., 325–63.
44. On inscribed verses at Nikon's New Jerusalem monastery, see above, pp. 154–5.
45. Franklin, 'Printing Moscow'.
46. A. A. Guseva, 'Oformlenie izdanii Simeona Polotskogo v Verkhnei tipografii (1679–1683 gg.)', *TODRL*, 38 (1985), 459.
47. A. S. Lavrov, 'Gravirovannyi list s virshami Sil'vestra Medvedeva', *TODRL*, 50 (1996), 519–25.
48. Above, p. 105; below, pp. 254–6.
49. However, these printed verses constitute a very small fragment of Karion Istomin's very extensive oeuvre of *un*published manuscript verses: Bogdanov, *Stikh torzhestva*, 381–621.
50. Bykova and Gurevich, *Kirill.*, no. 17 and fig. 5 (p. 72).
51. Complete texts in Ramazanova and Shustova, *Kirillicheskie bukvari*, 289–313.
52. Fedor Polikarpov, *Lexikon treiazychnyi / Lexikon triglotton / Dictionarium trilingue* (Moscow: [n.p.], 1704), fol. 1v.
53. Cf., however, another exception, because not produced in Moscow: Archbishop Ioann Maksimov's book of hagiographical verses, printed in 1705 at the Trinity monastery in Chernihiv in 1705: Bykova and Gurevich, *Kirill.*, no. 48.
54. Bykova and Gurevich, *Kirill.*, nos. 54 (and Polish text, Appendix II, p. 308), 71; see Feofan Prokopovich, *Sochineniia*, ed. I. P. Eremin (Moscow and Leningrad: AN SSSR, 1961), 209–14. This was the only one of Prokopovich's many verse compositions to be printed in his lifetime.
55. Bykova and Gurevich, *Grazhd.*, nos. 54a, 112, 653, 721, and *Dopoln.*, nos. 607, 609, 610, 620–623a–b. Cf. also a verse dialogue between Mercy and Truth attributed to Andrei Belobotskii and recorded as having been printed in 1712: Bykova and Gurevich, *Grazhd.*, no. 63 and *Dopoln.*, no. 13.
56. See the lists in the indexes to *SK XVIII v.*, vol. V, 133–4.
57. *SK XVIII v.*, no. 7,130.

58. A. S. Myl'nikov, 'Kul'turno-istoricheskoe znachenie rukopisnoi knigi v period stanovleniia knigopechataniia', *Kniga. Issledovaniia i materialy*, 9 (1964), 37–53 (esp. 41).
59. Marker, *Publishing*, 202.
60. See Marker, *Publishing*, 202–11.
61. Franklin, 'Mapping the Graphosphere', 551–4. On literary salons and circles, see M. Aronson and S. Reiser, *Literaturnye kruzhki i salony* (St Petersburg: Akademicheskii proekt, 2001 [1929]); Irina Murav'eva, *Salony pushkinskoi pory. Ocherki literaturnoi i svetskoi zhizni Sankt-Peterburga* (St Petersburg: Kriga, 2008); William Mills Todd III, *Fiction and Society in the Age of Pushkin: Ideology, Institutions, and Narrative* (Cambridge, MA: Harvard University Press, 1986), esp. 45–105.
62. *Statut der St. Peterburgischen Gesellschaft von Liebhabern der Wissenschaften, Litteratur und Künste* (St Petersburg: Marine-Buchdruckerei, 1805).
63. Mariia Maiofis, *Vozzvanie k Evrope: literaturnoe obshchestvo 'Arzamas' i rossiiskii modernizatsionnyi proekt 1815–1818 godov* (Moscow: Novoe literaturnoe obozrenie, 2008).
64. J. W. Saunders, 'The Stigma of Print: A Note on the Social Bases of Tudor Poetry', *Essays in Criticism*, 1 (1951), 139–64; cited in Alexandra Walsham, 'Preaching Without Speaking: Script, Print and Religious Dissent', in Crick and Walsham (eds.), *The Uses of Script and Print*, 228.
65. Katherine Bowers, 'Unpacking Viazemskii's *Khalat*: The Technologies of Dilettantism in Early Nineteenth-Century Russian Literary Culture', *Slavic Review*, 74.3 (Fall 2015), 529–52.
66. See http://emlo.bodleian.ox.ac.uk/home.
67. For a bibliographical survey, see O. V. Novokhvatko, 'Chastnaia perepiska XVII veka (k postanovke voprosa)', in *Palaeobureaucratica: Sbornik statei k 90-letiiu N. F. Demidovoi* (Moscow: Drevlekhranilishche, 2012), 246–63. See esp. the 528 letters in *Gramotki XVII–nachala XVIII veka*, ed. S. I. Kotkov, N. I. Tarasova and N. P. Pankratova (Moscow: Nauka, 1969). For a brief overview, see N. P. Pankratova, 'Iz istorii chastnoi perepiski na Rusi', in *Izuchenie russkogo iazyka i istochnikovedenie* (Moscow: Nauka, 1969), 127–55. See also the remarks of Daniel C. Waugh, 'What Was News and How Was It Communicated in Pre-Modern Russia?', in Franklin and Bowers (eds.), *Information and Empire*, 216–21.
68. D. M. Bulanin, 'Pis'movniki', in *SKKDR. Vyp. 2. Chast' 2*, 188–93.
69. William Mills Todd III, *The Familiar Letter as a Literary Genre in the Age of Pushkin* (Princeton University Press, 1976), 8–12.
70. See e.g. the practical advice offered in the essay on letter-writing by N. I. Grech, translated in Todd, *The Familiar Letter*, 204–8.

71. Precursors of the typewriter can be traced at least to the early eighteenth century, but standard production began only from the 1850s: Michael H. Adler, *The Writing Machine* (London: George Allen & Unwin, 1973). According to Olga E. Glagoleva, *Working with Russian Archival Documents: A Guide to Modern Handwriting, Document Forms, Language Patterns and Other Related Topics* (University of Toronto, 1998), 62, in Russia, typewritten documents appeared only after 1898.
72. See Simon Franklin, 'Three Types of Asymmetry in the Muscovite Engagement with Print', *CASS*, 51 (2017), 351–75.
73. See above, pp. 129–30.
74. D. V. Tiulichev, *Knigoizdatel'skaia deiatel'nost' peterburgskoi Akademii nauk i M. V. Lomonosov* (Leningrad: Nauka, 1988), 92–138; for an overview of the history of Russian printed newspapers, see Alison K. Smith, 'Information and Efficiency: Russian Newspapers, *ca.* 1700–1850', in Franklin and Bowers (eds.), *Information and Empire*, 185–211.
75. L. M. Kostiukhina, 'Novovizantiiskii ornament', in *Drevnerusskoe iskusstvo. Rukopisnaia kniga: sbornik vtoroi*, ed. O. I. Podobedova (Moscow: Nauka, 1974), 265–95.
76. Nemirovskii, *Istoriia slavianskogo kirillicheskogo knigopechataniia XV–nachala XVII veka, I*, 121–34; T. V. Dianova, 'Staropechatnyi ornament', in *Drevnerusskoe iskusstvo. Rukopisnaia kniga: sbornik vtoroi*, 296–335.
77. See E. I. Serebriakova, 'Ob ornamental'nom ubranstve rukopisei makarievskoi knigopisnoi masterskoi', in *Drevnerusskoe iskusstvo. Russkoe iskusstvo pozdnego srednevekov'ia. XVI vek*, ed. Batalov et al., 426–38.
78. E. V. Zatsepina, 'K voprosu o proiskhozhdenii staropechatnogo ornamenta', in Tikhomirov (ed.), *U istokov russkogo knigopechataniia*, 101–54; N. P. Kiselev, 'Proiskhozhdenie moskovskogo staropechatnogo ornamenta', *Kniga. Issledovaniia i materialy*, 11 (1965), 167–98.
79. E. L. Nemirovskii, 'Ornamentika pervykh moskovskikh pechatnykh knig', in *Trudy nauchno-issledovatel'skogo instituta poligraficheskogo mashinostroeniia, 21. Issledovatel'skie raboty po shriftam* (Moscow: Institut poligraficheskogo mashinostroeniia, 1962), 37–100.
80. E. S. Smirnova, 'Kontakty i protivostoianie russkoi i zapadno-evropeiskoi khudozhestvennoi kul'tury v XVI stoletii. Nekotorye nabliudeniia', *Aktual'nye problemy istorii i teorii iskusstva*, 6 (2016), 242–51; A. S. Preobrazhenskii, 'Zapadnye motivy i formy v postvizantiiskoi zhivopisi Moskovii. Predvaritel'nye razmyshleniia', ibid., 252–66.
81. E.g. N. V. Kvlividze, 'Zapadnoevropeiskie istochniki ikonografii "Chetyrekhchastnoi" ikony iz Blagoveshchenskogo sobora', in *Lazarevskie chteniia. Iskusstvo Vizantii, Drevnei Rusi, Zapadnoi Evropy* (Izdatel'stvo

MGU, 2008), 175–90; Ágnes Kriza, 'The Russian *Gnadenstuhl*', *Journal of the Warburg and Courtauld Institutes*, 79 (2016), 79–130; P. V. Maier, 'Zapadnoevropeiskie istochniki ikonografii "Plody stradanii Khristovykh": "Zhivoi Krest" i "Drevo Zhizni" v russkoi ikonopisi', *Vestnik PSTGU. Seriia V. Voprosy istorii i teorii khristianskogo iskusstva*, 2015.3(19), 52–80.

82. Belobrova, 'O nekotorykh istochnikakh podpisei'.
83. See www.runivers.ru/lib/book6958/.
84. Franklin, 'Three Types of Asymmetry', 359–69; also above, Fig 3.5.
85. I. V. Sosnovtseva, 'Ikony iz Oranienbauma v sobranii Russkogo muzei,' in *Stranitsy istorii otechestvennogo iskusstva. Vypusk XIX. Sbornik statei po materialam nauchnoi konferentsii* (St Petersburg: Palace Editions, 2011), 70–89.
86. E.g. the edition of Merian's engravings: *Icones biblicae* (Amsterdam: Danckert Danckertsz, 1659), where each illustration is printed together with verse quatrains in Latin, French, German, English and Dutch, as well as prose explanations in Dutch.
87. E.g. the three cycles in MS BAN, Arkh. D. 409, fols. 333–410v: see O. A. Belobrova, 'O drevnerusskikh podpisiakh k nekotorym niderlandskim tsel'nogravirovannym izdaniiam XVII v.', *TODRL*, 43 (1990), 70–8, and Belobrova, 'Bibliia Piskatora v sobranii Biblioteki Akademii nauk SSSR', in M. V. Kukushkina (ed.), *Materialy i soobshcheniia po fondam otdela rukopisnoi i redkoi knigi. 1985* (Leningrad: Nauka, 1987), 184–216.
88. O. A. Belobrova, 'Drevnerusskie virshi k graviuram Mattiasa Meriana', *TODRL*, 44 (1990), 443–79; Belobrova, 'Simeon Polotskii – avtor virsh k graviuram Biblii Mattiasa Meriana', *TODRL*, 49 (1996), 526–8. For the text in context, see Simeon Polockij [Polotskii], *Vertograd mnogocvetnyj*, 3 vols., ed. Anthony Hippisley and Lydia L. Sazonova, vol. III (Cologne, Weimar and Vienna: Böhlau Verlag, 2000), 452–510.
89. [Mardarii Khonykov], O. A. Belobrova, 'Virshi Mardariia Khonykova k graviuram Biblii Piskatora', *TODRL*, 46 (1993), 334–433 (text on pp. 345–433); extracts in *BLDR*, vol. 18 (2014), 269–92.
90. *BLDR*, vol. 18 (2014), 269–70.
91. Sirenov, 'O rabote po "ispravleniiu" pechatnogo letopistsa v 1703 g.', 363–4.
92. A. G. Avdeev, 'Epigraficheskie zametki', *Voprosy epigrafiki*, 8 (2015), 403–7.
93. A. G. Avdeev and D. A. Chernov, 'Stikhotvornye podpisi k knige Pesn' pesnei Solomona na freskakh XVII–XVIII vv. v Romanove-Borisoglebske i Kostrome', *Voprosy epigrafiki*, 5 (2011), 370–403.
94. Franklin, 'Three Types of Asymmetry', 372–4.
95. Above, pp. 40–2.
96. I. V. Dergacheva, *Drevnerusskii Sinodik: issledovaniia i teksty* (Moscow: 'Krug', 2011), esp. 9–19.
97. From a private collection (details available from the author).

98. D. A. Rovinskii, *Russkie narodnye kartinki*, 5 vols. (St Petersburg: Tipografiia AN, 1881), vol. III, 189–218.
99. See e.g. R. C. Alston, *Books with Manuscript: A Short Title Catalogue of Books with Manuscript Notes in the British Library* (London: British Library, 1994); H. J. Jackson, *Marginalia: Readers Writing in Books* (New Haven and London: Yale University Press, 2001); Boffey, *Manuscript and Print in London*, 76–80.
100. *Evgenii Onegin* 7.XXI–XXV; cf. the equivalent device in Emily Brontë's *Wuthering Heights*: cited in Jackson, *Marginalia*, 20–1.
101. L. I. Kiseleva, *Korpus zapisei na staropechatnykh knigakh. Vypusk 1. Zapisi na knigakh kirillicheskogo shrifta, napechatannykh v XVI–XVII vv.* (St Petersburg: BAN, 1992).
102. E.g. William H. Sherman, *Used Books: Marking Readers in Renaissance England* (Philadelphia: University of Pennsylvania Press, 2008); Stephen Orgel, *The Reader in the Book: A Study of Spaces and Traces* (Oxford University Press, 2015).
103. Small-scale exceptions tend to relate to 'traditional' books and manuscripts: e.g. O. V. Buraeva, 'Knizhnye marginalii zabaikal'skikh staroobriadtsev: proiskhozhdenie, forma, razmeshchenie', in *Staroobriadchestvo: istoriia i sovremennost', mestnye traditsii, russkie i zarubezhnye sviazi* (Ulan-Ude: Izdatel'stvo Buriatskogo gosudarstvennogo universiteta, 2015), 272–7.
104. See Rozov, 'Solovetskaia biblioteka i ee osnovatel' igumen Dosifei', 297; for the subsequent tradition, see Rozov, *Russkaia rukopisnaia kniga*, 46–9 (late sixteenth century); Sapozhnikova, *Russkii knizhnik XVII veka Sergii Shelonin*, fig. 6, between pp. 496 and 497 (mid seventeenth century).
105. Ia. N. Shchapov, 'K istorii russkogo knizhnogo znaka XV–XVII vv.', in Kniazevskaia et al. (eds.), *Rukopisnaia i pechatnaia kniga*, 85–93.
106. L. V. Belova, 'Gravirovannyi "ekslibris" ierodiakona Stefana Sakharova 1691 g. na staropechatnykh sluzhebnykh mineiiakh', in *Kniga v Rossii. Sbornik 1* (Moscow: Nauka, 2006), 260–71.
107. Savel'eva, *Katalog knig iz sobraniia Aptekarskogo prikaza*, 41, n. 33. On Erskine, see Robert Collis, *The Petrine Instauration: Religion, Esotericism and Science at the Court of Peter the Great, 1689–1725* (Leiden and Boston: Brill, 2012), 121–207. It is not clear whether Erskine's bookplate was produced in Russia. For illustrations of the bookplates of Erskine/Areskin and of Iakov Brius (both with Latin mottoes), see Kashutina and Saprykina, *Ekslibris v sobranii Nauchnoi biblioteki Moskovskogo gosudarstvennogo universiteta*, nos. 17, 18; T. V. Grebeniuk, *Vladel'cheskie knizhnye znaki v Otdele redkikh knig Rossiiskoi gosudarstvennoi biblioteki. Katalog* (Moscow: Pashkov dom, 2013), vol. III, 26–35.

108. See e.g. the marginal commentaries, mostly in Latin, of Stefan Iavorskii in a copy of the New Testament and Psalter printed in Kiev in 1692: Gal'tsin and Pitul'ko, *Biblioteka Feofilakta Lopatinskogo*, 597–627.
109. E. L. Nemirovskii, 'Illiuminirovannyi ekzempliar Ostrozhskoi Biblii 1581 g. s rukopisnymi dopolneniiami', *TODRL*, 38 (1985), 439–50.
110. M. A. Tsiavlovskii, *Stat'i o Pushkine* (Moscow: Izdatel'stvo AN SSSR, 1962), 218.
111. T. N. Protas'eva, 'Zapis' v khronografe XVII v.', in *Novoe o proshlom nashei strany. Pamiati akademika M. N. Tikhomirova* (Moscow: Nauka, 1967), 320–8.
112. A. G. Sakovich, 'Neizvestnyi ekzempliar Biblii Piskatora iz Predtecheva monastyria Krasnoi Slobody Temnikovskogo uezda Riazanskoi mitropolii', in *Pamiatniki kul'tury. Novye otkrytiia. Pis'mennost'. Iskusstvo. Arkheologiia. Ezhegodnik 1990* (Moscow: Krug, 1992), 18–27. On Iosif and his marginalia, see I. V. Pozdeeva, *Chelovek. Kniga. Istoriia. Moskovskaia pechat' XVII veka* (Moscow: Fantom-press, 2016), 269–91.
113. E.g., among many repetitions: '*V mirskie domy knigi davat' ne dlia chego . . . Se est' zloe knigam ubiistvo*', in Sakovich, 'Neizvestnyi ekzempliar', 20.
114. See e.g. Mary C. Erler, 'Pasted-In Embellishments in English Manuscripts and Printed Books, *c.* 1480–1533', *The Library*, 6th series, 14.3 (Sep. 1992), 185–206.
115. E. L Nemirovskii, 'Graviura na medi v russkoi rukopisnoi knige XVI–XVII vv.', in Kniazevskaia et al. (eds.), *Rukopisnaia i pechatnaia kniga*, 94–104; O. B. Vraskaia, 'Ob ornamentatsii rukopisnykh knig iz Kirillo-Belozerskogo monastyria', in *Drevnerusskoe iskusstvo. Rukopisnaia kniga. Sbornik tretii*, ed. O. I. Podobedova (Moscow: Nauka, 1983), 267–76; T. S. Borisova, 'Graviura na metalle v russkikh rukopisiakh XVI v.', in *Drevnerusskoe iskusstvo. Russkoe iskusstvo pozdnego srednevekov'ia. XVI vek*, ed. Batalov et al., 440–54; E. A. Mishina, 'Gravirovannaia zastavka raboty Feodosiia izografa (k voprosu o vremeni vozniknoveniia na Rusi gravirovaniia na metalle)', in *Kniga v prostranstve kul'tury* (Moscow: RGB, 2005), 64–6. On the career of Feodosii, son of Dionisii, see I. A. Kochetkov, *Slovar' russkikh ikonopistsev XI–XVII vekov* (Moscow: Indrik, 2003), 180–2.
116. O. R. Khromov, *Tsel'nogravirovannaia kniga i graviura v russkikh rukopisiakh XVI–XIX vekov. Katalog kollektsii Otdela pis'mennykh istochnikov Iaroslavskogo gosudarstvennogo istoriko-arkhitekturnogo i khudozhestvennogo muzeia-zapovednika* (Moscow: ART-RODNIK, 2013), 251–384.
117. O. A. Belobrova, 'O khronografe s graviurami Biblii Piskatora (RNB, Solovetskoe sobr., No. 1525/189)', *TODRL*, 55 (2004), 111–15.

118. Iu. A. Gribov, 'Rukopisnyi Sinodik s ksilograficheskimi illiustratsiiami – pamiatnik russkoi knizhnosti nachala XVIII v.', in *Zabelinskie nauchnye chteniia – 1999* (Moscow: Gosudarstvennyi istoricheskii muzei, 2000), 75–102.
119. I. V. Pozdeeva, 'Vnov' naidennyi sbornik Simeona Mokhovikova s graviurami G. P. Tepchegorskogo', in Danilova (ed.), *Narodnaia graviura i fol'klor*, 175–98.
120. Khromov, *Tsel'nogravirovannaia kniga i graviura*, nos. 73, 76, 98 (illustrations from Polikarpov), 103 (David).
121. Khromov, *Tsel'nogravirovannaia kniga i graviura*, nos. 73, 80, 84, 91, 105, 108. See also Khromov, 'Ob odnom listovom (letuchem) izdanii Moskovskogo pechatnogo dvora', in *Rumiantsevskie chteniia, 15. Materialy mezhdunarodnoi nauchnoi konferentsii (14–15 aprelia 2015)* (Moscow: Pashkov dom, 2015), Chast' 2, 207–20, on the earliest such woodcut blank attributable to the Moscow Print Yard, in a manuscript dated 1677.
122. O. R. Khromov, 'Russkaia rukopisnaia kniga s graviurami v kontekste obshcheevropeiskoi knizhnoi kul'tury XVII–XVIII vv. (spetsifika i obshchie tendentsii oformleniia zhanra)', in *Berkovskie chteniia 2011. Knizhnaia kul'tura v kontekste mezhdunarodnykh kontaktov* (Minsk: Tsentral'naia nauchnaia biblioteka NAN Belorusi; Moscow: Nauka, 2011), 375–9.
123. E. A. Mishina, 'Sviattsy Antonievo-Siiskogo monastyria i ikh predpolagaemyi avtor', in *Filevskie chteniia. Vyp. V. Materialy tret'ei nauchnoi konferentsii po problemam russkoi kul'tury vtoroi poloviny XVII–nachala XVIII vekov 8–11 iiulia 1993 goda* (Moscow: Tsentral'nyi muzei drevnerusskoi kul'tury i iskusstva imeni Andreiia Rubleva, 1994), 4–14.
124. Mishina, 'Sviattsy', 4–6. I have been able to inspect the two copies mentioned below, in the Russian State Library.
125. RGB MK H-345, described in S. A. Klepikov, 'Russkie gravirovannye knigi XVII–XVIII vekov', *Kniga. Issledovaniia i materialy*, 9 (1964), 141–77 (148–52).
126. RGB MK H-364.
127. E.g. the calendrical 'hands' in Khromov, *Tsel'nogravirovannaia kniga i graviura*, no. 94.
128. *SK XVIII v.*, vol. IV, nos. 264–523.
129. *SK XVIII v.*, vol. IV, no. 401.
130. *Mesiatsoslov na leto ot rozhdestva Khristova 1782, kotoroe est' prostoe, soderzhashchee v sebe 365 dnei* (St Petersburg: AN, [1781]).
131. *Almanach de la cour pour l'année 1786* (St Petersburg: AN, 1786), 2–49.
132. *Almanach de la cour pour l'année 1790* (St Petersburg: AN, 1790), 2nd pagination, 2–35.
133. E.g. A. V. Antonov, 'Iz istorii velikokniazheskoi kantselliarii: kormlennye gramoty XV–serediny XVI veka', in Antonov, *Istoriko-arkheograficheskie*

issledovaniia: Rossiia XV–nachala XVII veka (Moscow: Drevlekhranilishche, 2013), 7–108, esp. 74–105.

134. Eisemann, 'Fifty Thousand Veronicas', 80–92.
135. Andrew Pettegree, 'Broadsheets: Single-Sheet Publishing in the First Age of Print. Typology and Typography', in Pettegree (ed.), *Broadsheets*, 21.
136. Flavia Bruni, 'Early Modern Broadsheets Between Archives and Libraries: Towards a Possible Integration', in Pettegree (ed.), *Broadsheets*, 40.
137. For a preliminary description of the early phases ('phases 1–3' in the present survey), see Franklin, 'Printing and Social Control in Russia 3: Blank Forms'.
138. According to the archives of the Print Chancery: see *Mosk. Kirill. izd. 1651–1675*, 197, nos. 6–10.
139. See above, pp. 84–7.
140. A. A. Bulychev, 'Neskol'ko zamechanii o tak nazyvaemykh razreshitel'nykh gramotakh', *Russica romana*, 16 (2009), 9–36; Nikolaos A. Chrissidis, 'Between Forgiveness and Indulgence: Funerary Prayers of Absolution in Russia', in Nickolas Lupinin, Donald Ostrowski and Jennifer B. Spock (eds.), *The Tapestry of Russian Christianity: Studies in History and Culture* (Columbus: Ohio State University, 2016), 261–93.
141. Iu. E. Shustova, 'Geografiia izdanii razreshitel'nykh gramot vostochnykh patriarkhov v XVII v.', in *Istoricheskaia geografiia: prostranstvo cheloveka* vs *chelovek v prostranstve. Materialy XXIII Mezhdunarodnoi nauchnoi konferentsii. Moskva, 27–29 ianvaria 2011 g.* (Moscow: RGGU, 2011), 463–7.
142. *Mosk. Kirill. Izd. 1651–1675*, Appendix 1, 195–225, nos. 16, 54, 73, 74, 89, 90; note also no. 52, on the issue of *proshchennye gramoty* in March 1667. Extant documents are very scarce. See E. V. Ukhanova, 'K voprosu o razreshitel'nykh gramotakh vostochnykh patriarkhov v Rossii: novye ekzempliary v fondakh GIM', *Kapterevskie chteniia*, 8 (2010), 91–114.
143. *MPD – fakt i faktor russkoi kul'tury. 1652–1700 gody. Kniga 2*, 487. On the earlier tradition of such grants in manuscript, see N. A. Komochev, *Tsarskie zhalovannye gramoty svetskim litsam (1613–1696): istochnikovedcheskoe issledovanie* (Moscow: RGGU, 2016).
144. Note also the 1706 'one-off' issue of blank documents of safe passage (*oboronitel'nyi list*), for use in Ukraine and perhaps printed in Kiev: Bykova and Gurevich, *Kirill.*, no. 55.
145. RGADA, f. 104. I am grateful to Tatiana Lapteva for drawing this to my attention.
146. *Materialy dlia istorii Gangutskoi operatsii. Vypusk I, chast' II. Gramoty, ukazy i pis'ma Petra Velikogo* (Petrograd: Tipografiia Morskogo ministerstva, 1914), 119.
147. Franklin, 'Printing and Social Control in Russia 3', 124–5.

148. Franklin, 'Printing and Social Control in Russia 1'.
149. See a reference to 1,170 *podorozhnye pochtovye* printed at the Petersburg Printing House in 1716: Guseva, *Svod XVIII v.*, 548. A decree of the Senate of 23 January 1718 appears to require that all *podorozhnye* for travel between St Petersburg and Moscow must be printed, but the wording is open to interpretation: *PSZ*, no. 3,145.
150. I. A. Voznesenskaia, 'Patenty na chin v Rossii XVIII–XIX vv.', *CASS*, 50 (2016), 159–76.
151. Likhachev, *Katalog letuchikh izdanii*, 290, footnote.
152. Franklin, 'Printing and Social Control in Russia 3', 121–2.
153. E.g. the oaths of allegiance to the empress Anna Ioannovna in 1731: RGADA, f. 248, Senat. Kn. 8250. On ritual affirmation, see *PSZ*, no. 5,070, on the oath of allegiance to Peter II in May 1727. Other types of oath need further investigation: see e.g. a printed oath in German administered to Christopher Iohannes Richter, the Saxon owner of a St Petersburg tile factory, on his appointment to the rank of *kollezhskii sovetnik* in February 1755: http://rgada.info/opisi/248-opis_7/0259.jpg. I am grateful to Iuliia Shustova for this reference.
154. Likhachev, *Katalog letuchikh izdanii*, 137–41 (Section V, no. 1), citing a document of February 1725.
155. *PSZ*, no. 4,755.
156. Likhachev, *Katalog letuchikh izdanii*, 142 (Section V, no. 3).
157. Note also printed specimen blanks issued as guidance to scribes in their preparation of handwritten documents: see e.g. a printed instruction on the format for poll tax receipts in 1736: RGADA, f. 16, d. 366. I am grateful to Elena Korchmina for bringing this to my attention, and for her transcription.
158. *PSZ*, no. 5,410 (vol. VIII, pp. 147–97).
159. Ibid., p. 148.
160. Ibid., pp. 182–97.
161. SPb II RAN, coll. 238, op. 2, no. 191/1, p. 1.
162. *PSZ*, no. 10,777.
163. *Po ukazu Ee Imperatorskogo Velichestva dan sei pervyi veksel' v Sanktpeterburge ot solianoi kontory:* Iu. P. Bokarev et al., *Istoriia denezhnogo obrashcheniia Rossii. Den'gi Rossii s drevneishikh vremen do nashikh dnei. Al'bom-katalog denezhnykh znakov*, 2 vols. (Moscow: InterKrim-press, 2011), vol. I, 137; also A. E. Denisov, *Bumazhnye denezhnye znaki Rossii 1769–1917 godov. Chast' 1. Gosudarstvennye bumazhnye denezhnye znaki 1769–1843* (Moscow: Informelektro, 2002), 28.
164. *PSZ*, no. 11,016.

165. E.g. legislation of 19 December 1797, 13 March 1798 etc.: *PSZ*, nos. 18,284, 18,461. Cf. the sequence of some forty examples starting in 1798, in SPb II RAN, coll. 238, op. 2, ed. khr. 191/1.
166. See Denisov, *Bumazhnye denezhnye znaki*; Bokarev et al., *Istoriia denezhnogo obrashcheniia Rossii*, esp. 136–88.
167. *PSZ*, no. 13,219
168. See Denisov, *Bumazhnye denezhnye znaki*, 56–63.
169. *PSZ*, no. 13,219, articles 5, 24–6 (pp. 789–90).
170. Bokarev et al., *Istoriia denezhnogo obrashchenii*, vol. II, 307, n. 1. See also A. V. Bugrov, A. L. Vychugzhanin, F. F. Ivankin and S. V. Kalmykov, *Bumazhnyi rubl' v Rossii i v SSSR: 1843–1934. Vyborochnyi katalog podpisei i faksimile podpisei* (Moscow: InterKrim-press, 2012), 46, 59–60. This was in line with the tendency elsewhere: in England the first fully printed banknotes, without a cashier's signature, appeared in 1853.
171. 'Diplom vyrezan literami pochetnym chlenam na bol'shoi polulistovoi doske, odna doska': in B. V. Levshin (ed.), *Gravirovaľnaia palata Akademii nauk XVIII veka. Sbornik dokumentov* (Leningrad: Nauka, 1985), 98 (document no. 45).
172. SPF ARAN, f. 20, op. 2, d. 20: see http://db.ranar.spb.ru/lomonosov/work/work_8787.html.
173. SPb II RAN, coll. 238, op. 2, ed. khr. 205/1, no. 1, issued to the Commissioner for War (General-Krigskomisar) Aleksandr Ivanovich Glebov.
174. SPb II RAN, coll. 238, op. 2, ed. khr. 205/1, no. 3, issued on 7 November 1791 to Prince Sergei Ivanovich Viazemskii.
175. *Premudrost' Astrei. Pamiatniki masonstva XVIII–pervoi treti XIX veka v sobranii Ermitazha* (St Petersburg: Izdatel'stvo Gosudarstvennogo Ermitazha, 2013), e.g. nos. 232, 237, 238.
176. SPb II RAN, coll. 238, op. 2, ed. khr. 218, no. 14: *v povedenii prilichnom blagovospitannym i v priobretenii znanii, nauk, i rukodelii sootvetstvennykh ee polu.*
177. Eleonora Glinternik, *Reklama v Rossii XVIII–pervoi poloviny XX veka* (St Petersburg: Avrora, 2007), 17–18. Note, however, that a typeset ticket to a performance of Catherine II's comedy *O, Time!* (*O vremia*) at Peterhof on 22 July 1772 is not a blank; the date and day are part of the printed text: SPb II RAN, coll. 238, op. 2, ed. khr. 211/1, no. 8.
178. Glinternik, *Reklama v Rossii*, 17–18.
179. SPb II RAN, coll. 238, op. 2, ed. khr. 211/1, fol. 33.
180. SPF ARAN, f. 21, op. 7, ed. khr. 140, nos. 1–3.
181. Levshin (ed.), *Gravirovaľnaia palata*, 167 (document no. 107); see ibid., note 1, on earlier warnings (not conspicuously effective, it seems) against taking jobs on the side.

182. SPb II RAN, coll. 238, op. 2, ed. khr. 273/1, nos. 17, 30, dated 31 December 1798 and 17 January 1799, sent to the Vereiia District Court.
183. SPb II RAN, coll. 238, op. 2, ed. khr. 377/1, no. 23, dated 18 January 1805. Cf. the expansion of local use: *PSZ.2*, no. 10,304, dated 3 June 1837, on the use of printed and lithographed blanks in local administration, and even for printing the official part of *Gubernskie vedomosti* with spaces for annotation (art. 90, p. 461).
184. E.g. (from a private collection) passes issued by e.g. the military governor of St Petersburg (Miloradovich) in 1818, the military governor of Riga in 1823, the Russian consul-general in Hamburg in 1823, the governor of Courland at Mitau in 1824, and the Russian representative at Karlsbad in 1853.
185. From the same private collection as items in the previous note.
186. F. F. Ivankin, *Aktsionernoe i Vzaimnoe strakhovanie v Rossii 1827–1920. Katalog* (Moscow: Izdatel'skii dom Ruchen'kinykh, 2009), 144–6; Ivankin, *Strakhovye bumagi aktsionernykh obshchestv v Rossii (1827–1918 gg.)* (Moscow: [n.p.], 2005), 21.
187. SPb II RAN, coll. 238, op. 2, ed. khr. 211/1, no. 3.
188. SPb II RAN, coll. 238, op. 2, ed. khr. 211/1, no. 1.
189. SPb II RAN, coll. 238, op. 2, ed. khr. 211/3, is a collection of some fifty-four invitations to balls, dinners etc. mainly from the mid nineteenth century.
190. Bookplates, like banknotes, are very extensively catalogued. See e.g. Marguerite Studemeister, *Bookplates and Their Owners in Imperial Russia: An Illustrated Survey of Holdings at Stanford University* (Tenafly, NJ: Hermitage Publishers, 1991); cf. more than 18,000 bookplates listed in S. I. Bogomolov, *Rossiiskii knizhnyi znak 1700–1918*, 2nd edn (Moscow: Minuvshee, 2010). The first four volumes of Grebeniuk, *Vladel'cheskie knizhnye znaki* (2010–14), cover, in more than 2,000 pages, just the first three letters of the alphabet.
191. On specimens of tickets, see above, p. 134. On stagecoaches in Russia: Aleksandra Bekasova, 'Dilizhansy na dorogakh Rossii: ot zamysla – k praktike voploshcheniia', *Quaestio Rossica*, 5.1 (2017), 32–55.
192. See above, p. 60, on the fictional representation of this in Gogol's *Dead Souls*.
193. On the importance of blanks and job printing in the later nineteenth century, with examples mainly from the United States, see Gitelman, *Paper Knowledge*, 27–38.

7 Aspects of Authority and Status in the Graphosphere

1. See above, p. 100.
2. Kollmann, *Crime and Punishment in Early Modern Russia*, 254.
3. *PSZ.2*, nos. 39,504, 39,505.

4. See below, pp. 242–4.
5. Text in T. N. Protas'eva and M. V. Shchepkina, 'Skazaniia o nachale moskovskogo knigopechataniia. Teksty i perevody', in Tikhomirov (ed.), *U istokov russkogo knigopechataniia*, 210. On the date, see D. M. Bulanin, 'Skazanie izvestno o voobrazhenii knig pechatnogo dela', in *SKKDR. XVII v. Chast' 3*, 388–90.
6. [Simeon Polotskii], *Zhezl pravleniia* (Moscow: Pechatnyi dvor, 1667), *passim*.
7. *Pomorskie otvety*, available through Wikimedia Commons (https://commons.wikimedia.org/wiki/File:Pomorskie_otvety.djvu), Question 79, pp. 483–96. The phraseology was transferred to briefer, more 'popular' polemics of the time, such as Andrei Denisov's 'Homily on the New Wise Men' ('Slovo o novykh mudretsakh'), in Iukhimenko (ed.), *Literaturnoe nasledie Vygovskogo staroobriadcheskogo obshchezhitel'stva*, vol. I, 203–8 (esp. 206, on the authority of 'old-printed Muscovite and Belorussian books').
8. Richard Hellie (transl.), *The Muscovite Code of Law (Ulozhenie) of 1649. Part 1: Text and Translation* (Irvine, CA: Charles Schlacks Jr, 1988), 2.
9. The text in *PSZ*, no. 122, does not even mention printing.
10. Alekseeva, *Iz istorii russkoi graviury*, 10 (citing Nikol'skii, *Ob antiminsakh*, 41, 270).
11. *PSZ*, no. 1,612, articles 2, 3.
12. See above, pp. 71–2.
13. See Hughes, '"A Beard Is an Unnecessary Burden"'.
14. Tokens from 1698 are exceedingly rare, while the 1705 versions appear to have been in widespread use: see Rudenko, *Borodovye znaki 1698, 1705, 1724, 1725. Katalog*.
15. *PSZ*, no. 2,785.
16. Franklin, 'Printing and Social Control in Russia 2', 469–70, 483–5.
17. Annotated edition of the *plakat* of 1724 in *Rossiiskoe zakonodatel'stvo X–XX vekov*, vol. IV, ed. A. G. Man'kov (Moscow: Iuridicheskaia literatura, 1986), 208–10 (articles 12–16); Catherine's decree of 1726 in *PSZ*, no. 4,827. See Franklin, 'Printing and Social Control in Russia 1'.
18. See Hellie, *The Muscovite Law Code*, chapters 6, 18, 48 (pp. 10, 148, 150).
19. *PSZ*, nos. 3,334, 3,445.
20. E. V. Anisimov, *Podatnaia reforma Petra I* (Leningrad: Nauka, 1982), 227–35.
21. Anisimov, *Podatnaia reforma*, 253–5.
22. *PSZ*, no. 3,939.
23. E.g. the 47,500 sheets (probably amounting to around 180,000 blank passes) ordered from the printer Christopher Plantin for the Admiralty of Zeeland in 1632: see Pettegree, 'Broadsheets', 22.
24. See e.g. H. H., 'Die Entwicklung und Reform des deutschen Passwesens', *Deutsche Vierteljahrs-Schrift*, 29.1 (1866), 219–53 (224–5) on

analogous German legislation in 1710 and 1715; Maurice d'Hartoy, *Histoire du passeport français. Depuis l'antiquité jusqu' à nos jours* (Paris: Librairie ancienne Honoré Champion, 1937), 35, on French concern for the return of vagrants in 1724.

25. Vincent Denis, *Une histoire de l'identité. France, 1715–1815* (Seyssel: Champ Vallon, 2008), 69–83.
26. *PSZ*, no. 3,970. Also on the perils of copying see *PSZ*, no. 3,055.
27. *PSZ*, no. 3,223.
28. *PSZ*, no. 1,834.
29. Franklin, 'Printing and Social Control 2', 478–80.
30. *PSZ*, no. 4,827.
31. On forged passports, see Ol'ga Kosheleva, '"Bez pashportov i s vorovskimi pashporty" ili mozhno li obmanut' gosudarstvennyi kontrol'?', in O. I. Togoeva and Kosheleva (eds.), *Obman kak povsednevnaia praktika. Individual'nye i kollektivnye strategii povedeniia* (Moscow: Institut vseobshchei istorii RAN, 2016), 323–43; I. A. Voznesenskaia, 'O poddelke pasportov XVIII v.: na materiale sudebnykh del', in Iu. E. Shustova (ed.), *Vspomogatel'nye i spetsial'nye nauki istorii v XX–nachale XXI v.: prizvanie, tvorchestvo, obshchestvennoe sluzhenie istorika. Materialy XXVI Mezhdunarodnoi konferentsii* (Moscow: RGGU, 2014), 142–4. On concern about forgery before the requirement for print, see I. T. Pososhkov, *Kniga o skudosti i bogatstve i drugie sochineniia*, ed. and comm. B. B. Kafengauz (Moscow: AN SSSR, 1951), 111–12; English translation in Ivan Pososhkov, *The Book of Poverty and Wealth*, ed. and transl. A. P. Vlasto and L. R. Lewitter (London: Athlone Press, 1987), 244–5.
32. Klepikov, *Filigrani i shtempeli*, 28–30; S. A. Klepikov, *Filigrani na bumage russkogo proizvodstva XVIII–nachala XX veka* (Moscow: Nauka, 1978): e.g. nos. 627–9 (watermark *PASPORT*).
33. See e.g. Peter's decree of 1 March 1708, on propaganda documents purporting to have been printed in Moscow but issued by the Swedes using the types of the Dutch printer Jan Tessing, whom they detained on his way to Russia: *PSZ*, no. 2,188 (1 Mar. 1708); these documents 'are to be given no credence whatever'. Cf. also *PSZ*, no. 2,224 (3 Feb. 1709), and Bykova and Gurevich, *Kirill.*, Appendix I, no. 22.
34. Denis, *Une histoire de l'identité*, 26–7, 37–40.
35. Franklin, 'Printing and Social Control 1', 234–6.
36. *PSZ*, nos. 6,177, 8,889.
37. SPb II RAN, coll. 238, op. 2, ed. khr. 197.3.
38. Article 16 of Peter's *plakat: Rossiiskoe zakonodatel'stvo X–XX vekov*, vol. IV, 210.

39. Franklin, 'Printing and Social Control 3', 133–4; Franklin, 'Printing and Social Control 2', 487–8. On the notional system for the dissemination of printed decrees, and doubts concerning its efficacy, see Pososhkov, *Kniga o skudosti i bogatstve*, 153–4, 159; transl.: *The Book of Poverty and Wealth*, 295, 299.
40. *PSZ*, no. 4,924.
41. R. E. F. Smith and David Christian, *Bread and Salt: A Social and Economic History of Food and Drink in Russia* (Cambridge University Press, 1984), 181–2.
42. *PSZ*, no. 9,303.
43. *PSZ*, no. 18,600. See also V. G. Chernukha, *Pasport v Rossii 1719–1917* (St Petersburg: Liki Rossii, 2007), 50–4.
44. On forgery see also Christoph Schmidt, *Sozialkontrolle in Moskau. Justiz, Kriminalität und Leibeigenschaft 1649–1785* (Stuttgart: Franz Steiner Verlag, 1996), 289–91.
45. *PSZ*, no. 4,827.
46. *PSZ*, no. 8,509. The problem was not new, or unique to print as a medium of authentication. On 8 November 1701 Peter I forbade the sealing (i.e. official authentication) of *podorozhnye* without the name of the intended user and the purpose of the journey, since blank (*glukhie*) documents were open to abuse: *PSZ*, no. 1,877.
47. E.g. SPb II RAN, coll. 238, op. 2, ed. khr. 195–3, p. 04, printed in 1793 and signed and stamped on behalf of the governor of St Petersburg, but all details (the bearer, the journey, the number of teams etc.) are yet to be filled in.
48. Matvei Komarov, *Obstoiatel'noe i vernoe opisanie dobrykh i zlykh del rossiiskogo moshennika, vora, razboinika i byvshego moskovskogo syshchika Van'ki Kaina* (St Petersburg, 1779): critical edition in Ecatherina Rai-Gonneau (ed.), *Vie de Kain: bandit russe et mouchard de la tsarine* (Paris: Institut d'études slaves, 2008), 194; cf. also ibid., 168, for an account of how Kain apprehended a drunk who was found to possess several forged passports which he confessed to having stolen.
49. SPb II RAN, coll. 238, op. 2, ed. khr. 194, no. 3 (1–3).
50. Pushkin, *Sobranie sochinenii v desiati tomakh*, vol. V, 440.
51. Cf. an equivalent anecdote – also, as it happens, involving the procurement of horses – in Tomasi di Lampedusa, *The Leopard*, transl. Archibald Colquhoun (London: Vintage, 2007), 114: at post-stations on the road from Palermo 'all we had to say was "Urgent orders on His Majesty's Service" and horses appeared like magic; and we'd show them our orders, which were actually the bills of the Naples hotel wrapped up and sealed!'
52. Pushkin, *Sobranie sochinenii v desiati tomakh*, vol. V, 428.
53. *BLDR*, vol. 12 (2003), 524.
54. Text in Guseva, *Izd. kirill. XVI v.*, fig. 42.4–6. Tarasiev and Timofeev echo not only Fedorov's claim but also his vocabulary: in both colophons the

scribes are *nenauchenykh i neiskusnykh v razume*. On this theme in later sixteenth-century colophons, see also Demin, 'Russkie staropechatnye poslesoviia', 64–5.

55. *Stoglav*, ed. Emchenko, 255, 287–8.
56. *BLDR*, vol. 12 (2003), 534.
57. This echoes a phrase in the colophon of the 1568 Psalter (also, perhaps, partly the work of Nevezha), where it is stated that the tsar decided to found a press in order that his realm be 'filled with the word of God'. See Guseva, *Izd. kirill. XVI v.*, fig. 42.5.
58. Guseva, *Izd. kirill. XVI v.*, fig. 109.1–3. Note that Nevezha also uses the formula that his text has been 'written' by a 'corruptible' hand. Appropriately, Nevezha's spelling of 'corruptible' (*brenna*) is corrupt (*berna*): ibid., fig. 109.3.
59. Colophon in Guseva, *Izd. kirill. XVI v.*, fig. 115.1–4 (the claim to correction: 115.2 (fol. 246v. of the third foliation in the original)).
60. Guseva, *Izd. kirill. XVI v.*, fig. 128.2.
61. The *Apostol* of 1597, and two Menaia of June and August 1600: in Guseva, *Izd. kirill. XVI v.*, figs. 153.2–4, 167.1–5, 169.1–5.
62. On pre-Nikonian 'correction' of printed books, see A. V. Voznesenskii, 'Svedeniia i zametki o kirillicheskikh pechatnykh knigakh, 15. K istorii knizhnoi spravy na moskovskom Pechatnom dvore (o Triodi tsvetnoi 1604 g.)', *TODRL*, 58 (2007), 920–6; Voznesenskii, 'K istorii donikonovskoi i nikonovskoi knizhnoi spravy. Kavychnyi ekzempliar moskovskoi Psaltiri, izdannoi v dekabre 1645 g.', in E. M. Iukhimenko (ed.), *Patriarkh Nikon i ego vremia. Sbornik nauchnykh trudov* (Moscow: Gosudarstvennyi istoricheskii muzei, 2004), 143–61; E. N. Kazakova, 'Apostol 1644 g.: k probleme donikonovskoi knizhnoi spravy', ibid., 162–74 (note the colophon to the 1644 *Apostol* setting out in detail the principles of their editing).
63. See Frick, 'Sailing to Byzantium'.
64. See above, pp. 228–9.
65. E.g. N. N. Rozov, 'O kul'turno-istoricheskom znachenii rukopisnoi knigi posle vvedeniia knigopechataniia v Rossii', in Luppov (ed.), *Russkie knigi i biblioteki*, 13–22.
66. A. V. Voznesenskii, *Predvaritel'nyi spisok staroobriadcheskikh kirillicheskikh izdanii XVIII veka* (St Petersburg: Khronograf, 1994), nos. 1–12.
67. Voznesenskii, *Predvaritel'nyi spisok*, nos. 23–73. For summaries of the 'foreign' presses and their links with the Starodub region, see A. V. Voznesenskii, P. I. Mangilev and I. V. Pochinskaia, *Knigoizdatel'skaia deiatel'nost' staroobriadtsev (1701–1918). Materialy k slovariiu* (Ekaterinburg: Ural'skii gosudarstvennyi universitet, 1996), 8–24; also the map, p. 74, showing their geographical distribution. Note that several of the presses at Vilnius, Pochaiv and Suprasl were based at Uniate monasteries.

68. See Voznesenskii, *Predvaritel'nyi spisok*, nos. 61–2 (*Prolog* for Sep.–Nov. and Dec.–Feb.) and 63 (Gospel Homiliary). The latter is in Emel'ianova, *Staroobriadcheskie izdaniia*, no. 174.
69. E.g. Emel'ianova, *Staroobriadcheskie izdaniia*, nos. 25–55.
70. See the two volumes of a *Prolog*, which Emel'ianova dates to 'after 1788': Emel'ianova, *Staroobriadcheskie izdaniia*, nos. 165, 166.
71. For the fullest lists and publication details, see Emel'ianova, *Staroobriadcheskie izdaniia*.
72. Emel'ianova, *Staroobriadcheskie izdaniia*, 613–19.
73. Voznesenskii, *Predvaritel'nyi spisok*, 77–8.
74. A. V. Voznesenskii, 'Staroobriadtsy i ikh knigopechatnaia deiatel'nost': problemy izucheniia', *TODRL*, 64 (2016), 538–46.
75. Piksanov, 'Istoriia teksta "Goria ot uma"', 334–5. See also above, p. 35.
76. Panchenko, 'Simeon Polotskii'.
77. In Polotskii's *Rifmolofgion*: Simeon Polotskii, *Izbrannye sochineniia*, ed. Eremin, 159.
78. See e.g. the account of the foundation of a printing press in Nizhnii Novgorod in 1613, reproduced in Demin et al. (eds.), *Tematika i stilistika predislovii i posleslovii*: photographic inserts before p. 129.
79. Franklin, 'Printing Moscow'.
80. See above, p. 196.
81. Pushkin, *Polnoe sobranie sochineni v desiati tomakh*, vol. II, 30–5.
82. On the paradoxical aspirations to manuscript and print in the salon culture of the early nineteenth century, see also above, p. 197.
83. Above, pp. 74–84.
84. See above, pp. 175–6.
85. V. V. Filatov and Iu. B. Kamchatnova, *Naimenovaniia i nadpisi na ikonnykh izobrazheniiakh. Spravochnik dlia ikonopistsev. Izdanie 3-e, ispravlennoe* (Moscow: PRO-PRESS, 2010), 5–6.
86. Cited in Avdeev, *Starorusskaia epigrafika i knizhnost'*, 23.
87. For publication of sixteen such texts, from the 1670s and 1680s alone, from churches in Iaroslavl, Moscow, Pereiaslavl, Rostov, Sergiev Posad, Kostroma, Vologda and Suzdal, see Nikitina, *Russkie tserkovnye stennye rospisi*, 198–205.
88. See above, pp. 154–5.
89. Avdeev, *Starorusskaia epigrafika i knizhnost'*, 27–9.
90. Avdeev, *Starorusskaia epigrafika i knizhnost'*, 8. On the concept of the monastery under Nikon, see G. M. Zelenskaia, 'Novyi Ierusalim pod Moskvoi. Aspekty zamysla i novye otkrytiia', in A. M. Lidov (ed.), *Novye Ierusalimy. Ierotopiia i ikonografiia sakral'nykh prostranstv* (Moscow: Indrik, 2009), 745–73.

91. On edificatory public inscription, see above, Chapter 5.
92. Avdeev, *Starorusskaia epigrafika i knizhnost'*, 29–48.
93. O. A. Belobrova, 'Opisanie peterburgskogo Petropavlovskogo sobora v rukopisnykh sbornikakh XVIII v.', *TODRL*, 56 (2004), 623–34.
94. On the graphospheric imagination, see also above, pp. 167–8.
95. Above, p. 212.
96. A. A. Romanova, *Drevnerusskie kalendarno-khronologicheskie istochniki XV–XVII vv.* (St Petersburg: Dmitrii Bulanin, 2002), esp. the thirty-two illustrations between pp. 64 and 65.
97. Mykola Soroka, *Zorova poeziia v ukrains'kii literaturi kintsia XVI–XVIII st.* (Kyiv: Holovna spetsializovana redaktsiia literatury movamy natsional'nykh menshyn Ukrainy, 1997).
98. Facsimile edition: [Istomin], *Bukvar' sostavlen Karionom Istominym*; also above, pp. 105, 194.
99. In the wider context of European play alphabets, see Erika M. Boeckeler, *Playful Letters: A Study in Early Modern Alphabetics* (Iowa City: University of Iowa Press, 2017), 180–200. On Istomin's visual texts as subversive, see Gary Marker, 'A World of Visual Splendor: The Illustrated Texts of Karion Istomin', in Michael S. Flier, Valerie Kivelson, Erika Monahan and Daniel Rowland (eds.), *Seeing Muscovy Anew. Politics – Institutions – Culture: Essays in Honor of Nancy Shields Kollmann* (Bloomington, IN: Slavica, 2017), 173–88.
100. Facsimile of the presentation manuscript, plus transcription, analysis and commentary: Simeon Polotskii, *Orel rossiiskii*, ed. L. I. Sazonova (Moscow: Indrik, 2015).
101. Polotskii, *Orel rossiiskii*, fols. 2–54: fols. 1 and 55–7 are blank.
102. See Simeon Polotskii, *Izbrannye sochineniia*, ed. Eremin, 244–8.
103. Polotskii, *Orel rossiiskii*, fols. 18–28. Note that here Polotskii omits Melpomene but includes a Muse whom he calls Terpomene. Sazonova (commentary to *Orel rossiiskii*, 165–6) regards this as Polotskii's invention. However, the name Terpomene (in place of Terpsichore rather than Melpomene) appears in seventeenth-century lists in several languages, especially in popular works on mathematical games attributed to Jean Leurechon (first published 1624) and by Daniel Schwenter (first published 1636): e.g. [Jean Leurechon], *Récréation mathématique* (Pont-à-Mousson: Gaspar Bernard, 1629), 93–4; or Daniel Schwenter, *Deliciae physico-mathematicae* (Nuremberg: J. Dümler, 1661), 77.
104. Polotskii, *Orel rossiiskii*, fols. 29–45.
105. Many are listed in Sazonova's annotated word-list in *Orel rossiiskii*, 299–325.
106. Polotskii, *Orel rossiiskii*, fol. 45.

107. Polotskii, *Orel rossiiskii*, fol. 3–3v. On various definitions of this device, see C. L. Drage, *Russian Word-Play Poetry from Simeon Polotskii to Derzhavin* (London: School of Slavonic and East European Studies, 1993), 52–4.
108. Polotskii, *Orel rossiiskii*, fol. 48v–49v. On echo poetry in European literature, see Drage, *Russian Word-Play Poetry*, 25–31.
109. Polotskii, *Orel rossiiskii*, fol. 50.
110. Polotskii, *Orel rossiiskii*, fols. 50v–53.
111. E. P. Pod"iapol'skaia, 'Shifrovannaia perepiska v Rossii v pervoi chetverti XVIII veka', *Problemy istochnikovedeniia*, 8 (1959), 314–42. Cf., for the late seventeenth century, S. M. Shamin, 'Neizvestnaia tainopisnaia azbuka iz arkhiva prikaza tainykh del', *Drevniaia Rus'. Voprosy medievistiki*, 2010.2(40), 103–6.
112. Polotskii, *Orel rossiiskii*, fol. 17.
113. Ps. 18.5 in the Church Slavonic Bible (from the Greek Septuagint), equivalent (though with a slightly different text) to Ps. 19.4 in the Latin Bible and in most English versions.
114. Polotskii, *Orel rossiiskii*, fol. 46: Luke 6.45.
115. Note that Simeon Polotskii subsequently experimented with word-shapes in print, in books that he produced at the Upper Printing House: Guseva, 'Oformlenie izdanii Simeona Polotskogo'.
116. Sazonova in *Orel rossiiskii*, 327–32.
117. 'Mnenie preosviashchennykh mitropolitov Novgorodskogo Serafima i Kievskogo Evgeniia o Bibleiskom obshchestve', in *Sbornik istoricheskikh materialov, izvlechennykh iz arkhiva sobstvennoi Ego Imperatorskogo Velichestva kantseliarii*, ed. N. Dubrovin, vol. XII (St Petersburg: Gosudarstvennaia tipografiia, 1903), 376–8.
118. On the publications of the Russian Bible Society and the related controversies, see I. A. Chistovich, *Istoriia perevoda Biblii na russkii iazyk*, 2nd edn (St Petersburg: M. M. Stasulevich, 1899), 25–94; M. I. Rizhskii, *Istoriia perevodov Biblii v Rossii* (Novosibirsk: Nauka, 1976), 130–9; Stephen K. Batalden, *Russian Bible Wars: Modern Scriptural Translation and Cultural Authority* (Cambridge University Press, 2013), 41–88.
119. Batalden, *Russian Bible Wars*, 42–54.
120. George A. Kubler, *A New History of Stereotyping* (New York: J. J. Little & Ives Company, 1941), 23–71, on the chronology of the various techniques that have a claim to be called stereotyping; also the remarks of McKitterick, *Print, Manuscript and the Search for Order*, esp. 212–13, 219–20.
121. John Carter, 'William Ged and the Invention of Stereotype', *The Library*, 5th series, 15 (1960), 161–92.
122. Leslie Howsam, *Cheap Bibles: Nineteenth-Century Publishing and the British and Foreign Bible Society* (Cambridge University Press, 1991), 74–120.

123. See above, pp. 119, 142.
124. The tsar's authorisation was included in the prefatory matter of the first edition of the Russian New Testament: English translation in Batalden, *Russian Bible Wars*, 57.
125. *PSZ*, no. 26,598.
126. See, for example, stereotyped Church Slavonic editions among the lists of books available through the Moscow Society's shops: *O piatom general'nom sobranii moskovskogo otdeleniia Rossiiskogo bibleiskogo obshchestva v 1818 godu*, 33–4.
127. A partial annotated bibliography of the early editions is in Batalden, *Russian Bible Wars*, 210–18. This list does not claim to be complete.
128. *SK 1801–1825*, no. 624; not in Batalden's list.
129. Batalden, *Russian Bible Wars*, 124–62; for the sequence of Synodal publications that preceded the complete text, see the catalogue, ibid., 228–62.
130. Batalden, *Russian Bible Wars*, 53.
131. Shishkov's polemical pamphlets and letters: in *Sbornik istoricheskikh materialov*, 325–76.
132. See above, p. 115.
133. *Sbornik istoricheskikh materialov*, 368–71.
134. *Sbornik istoricheskikh materialov*, 336.
135. *Sbornik istoricheskikh materialov*, 353–5, 366–7.
136. *Sbornik istoricheskikh materialov*, 356–66.
137. *Sbornik istoricheskikh materialov*, 342–3.
138. *The Twenty-Ninth Report of the British and Foreign Bible Society* (London: J. Moyes, 1833), 47.
139. *The Twenty-Seventh Report of the British and Foreign Bible Society* (London: J. Moyes, 1831), 110–11.
140. A. G. Cross, 'George Borrow and Russia', *Modern Language Review*, 64 (1969), 363–71.
141. Barbara Skinner, 'Russia's Scriptural "Reformation" in the Late Eighteenth and Early Nineteenth Centuries', *Vivliofika*, 5 (2017), 73–102; also Ekaterina Mel'nikova, *'Voobrazhaemaia kniga': ocherki po istorii fol'klora o knigakh i chtenii v Rossii* (Evropeiskii universitet v Sankt-Peterburge, 2011), 117–46.

Bibliographies

There are two bibliographies. The first contains catalogues and editions; the second is labelled 'studies'. This is a device to make a very long list slightly less unwieldy than it might otherwise be. However, there is no absolutely consistent line between the two categories of publication. Several items could reasonably be included in either section, or in both. I hope that the general convenience of the subdivision outweighs the occasional irritation of having to check in two places.

1. Catalogues, Editions, Reference Works etc.

Abramova, N. E., *Serebro Anglii XVI–XX vekov* (Moscow: Gosudarstvennyi istoriko-kul'turnyi muzei-zapovednik 'Moskovskii Kreml'', 2014)

[Adodurov, V. E.] Uspenskii, B. A., *Pervaia russkaia grammatika na rodnom iazyke* (Moscow: Nauka, 1975)

[Adodurov, V. E.] Keipert, Helmut, with Andrea Huterer, *Compendium grammaticae Russicae (1731). Die erste Akademie-Grammatik der russischen Sprache* (Munich: Verlag der Bayerischen Akademie der Wissenschaften, 2002)

[Adodurov, V. E.] Filippov, K. A., and Volkov, S. S. (eds.), *Vasilii Evdokimovich Adodurov. 'Afangs-Gründe der Rußischen Sprache' ili 'Pervye osnovaniia rossiiskogo iazyka'* (St Petersburg: Nauka and Nestor-Istoriia, 2014)

Akty Solovetskogo monastyria 1479–1571 gg., ed. I. Z. Liberzon (Leningrad: Nauka, 1988)

Akty Solovetskogo monastyria 1572–1584 gg., ed. I. Z. Liberzon (Leningrad: Nauka, 1990)

Almanach de la cour pour l'année 1786 (St Petersburg: AN, 1786)

Almanach de la cour pour l'année 1790 (St Petersburg: AN, 1790)

Alston, R. C., *Books with Manuscript: A Short Title Catalogue of Books with Manuscript Notes in the British Library* (London: British Library, 1994)

Ankudinov, I. Iu. (ed.), *Pistsovye knigi Staroi Russy kontsa XV–XVII vv.* (Moscow: Rukopisnye pamiatniki Drevnei Rusi, 2009)

Artakserksovo deistvo. Pervaia p'esa russkogo teatra XVII v., ed. I. M. Kudriavtseva (Moscow and Leningrad: AN SSSR, 1957)

Avdeev, A. G., *Starorusskaia epigrafika i knizhnost'. Novo-Ierusalimskaia shkola epigraficheskoi poezii* (Moscow: PSTGU, 2006)

Azbuka Ivana Fedorova 1578 (Moscow: Kniga, 1983)

Baranova, S. I., *Moskovskii arkhitekturnyi izrazets XVII veka v sobranii Moskovskogo gosudarstvennogo ob"edinennogo muzeia-zapovednika Kolomenskoe-Izmailovo-Lefortovo-Liublino* (Moscow: MGOMZ, 2013)

Batiushkov, K. N., *Sochineniia v dvukh tomakh* (Moscow: Khudozhestvennaia literatura, 1989)

Begunov, Yu. [Iu.] K., '"Opisanie vrat chesti ... ": A Seventeenth-Century Russian Translation on William of Orange and the "Glorious Revolution"', *Oxford Slavonic Papers. New Series*, 20 (1987), 60–93

Beliaev, L. A., *Russkoe srednevekovoe nadgrobie. Belokamennye plity Moskvy i Severo-Vostochnoi Rusi XIII–XVII vv.* (Moscow: MODUS – GRAFFITI, 1996)

Beliaev, L. A. (ed.), *Russkoe srednevekovoe nadgrobie, XIII–XVII veka: materialy k svodu. Vypusk 1* (Moscow: Nauka, 2006)

Berkovich, V. A., and Egorov, K. A., *Moskovskoe belokamennoe nadgrobie. Katalog* (Moscow: TM Prodakshn, 2017)

[Betskoi, I. I.], *Ustav vospitaniia dvukhsot blagorodnykh devits* (St Petersburg: [Senate press], 1764)

Bibliia sirech' knigi vetkhago i novago zaveta po iazyku slovensku. Fototipicheskoe pereizdanie teksta s izdaniia 1581 goda (Moscow and Leningrad: Slovo – Art, 1988)

Biblioteka literatury Drevnei Rusi, 19 vols. (St Petersburg: Nauka, 1997–2015)

Bobrovnitskaia, I. A., *Russkaia raspisnaia emal' kontsa XVII–nachala XVIII veka. Katalog* (Moscow: Gosudarstvennyi istoriko-kul'turnyi muzei-zapovednik 'Moskovskii Kreml'', 2001)

Böckler, Georg Andreas, *Arithmetica nova militaris* (Nuremberg, 1661)

Bogdanov, Avraam, *Kratkaia rossiiskaia grammatika v pol'zu armianskogo iunoshestva, tshchatel'no i iasno s armianskim perevodom raspolozhennaia* (Moscow: Avgust Semen, 1827)

Bogomolov, S. I., *Rossiiskii knizhnyi znak 1700–1918*, 2nd edn (Moscow: Minuvshee, 2010)

Bokarev, Iu. P., et al., *Istoriia denezhnogo obrashcheniia Rossii. Den'gi Rossii s drevneishikh vremen do nashikh dnei. Al'bom-katalog denezhnykh znakov*, 2 vols. (Moscow: InterKrim-press, 2011)

Borzykh, V. N., *Kniga o znakakh strakhovaniia ot ognia (1827–1918)* (Moscow: Obshchestvo liubitelei strakhovykh drevnostei, 2016)

Brekke, Bernhard F., *The Copper Coins of Imperial Russia 1700–1917* (Malmö: Förlagshuset Norden AB, 1977)

Brekke, Bernhard F., and Bakken, Tom Willy, *The Copper Coinage of Imperial Russia 1700–1917. Supplement 1997. Includes: Errors, Overdates, Overstrikes and Fakes* (Oslo: Norsk Numismatik Vorlag A/S, 1997)

Bugrov, A. V., Vychugzhanin, A. L., Ivankin, F. F., and Kalmykov, S. V., *Bumazhnyi rubl' v Rossii i v SSSR: 1843–1934. Vyborochnyi katalog podpisei i faksimile podpisei* (Moscow: InterKrim-press, 2012)

Bylinin, V. K., and Iliushin, A. A. (eds.), *Virshevaia poeziia (pervaia polovina XVII veka)* (Moscow: Sovetskaia Rossiia, 1989)

[Catiforo, Antonio], *Zhitie Petra Velikogo Imperatora i Samoderzhtsa Vserossiiskogo i Ottsa Otechestva . . . na dialekte Italianskom, a potom na Grecheskom: s koego na Rossiiskii iazyk perevel statskii sovetnik Stefan Pisarev* (St Petersburg: pri Imp. AN, 1772)

[Charpentier, Jean-Baptiste], *Élémens de la langue russe ou Méthode courte et facile pour apprendre cette langue conformement à l'usage* . . . (St Petersburg: Imp. AN, 1768)

Chepurnov, N. I., *Nagradnye medali Gosudarstva Rossiiskogo. Entsiklopedicheskoe illiustrirovannoe izdanie* (Moscow: Russkii mir, 2000)

Cleminson, Ralph, Thomas, Christine, Radoslavova, Dilyana, and Voznesenskij, Andrej, *Cyrillic Books Printed Before 1700 in British and Irish Collections: A Union Catalogue* (London: British Library, 2000)

[Decembrist investigation], *Bericht der, zur Ausmittelung übelgesinnter Gesellschaften, in Russland, niedergesetzten Untersuchungens-Commission, übersetzt auf Befehl Seiner Majestät des Kaisers* (St Petersburg: Kriegs-Buchdruckerey des General-Stabes, 1826)

Rapport de la Commission d'Enquête (St Petersburg: Pluchart, 1826)

Report of the Commission of Inquiry, translated from French by G. Elliott (St Petersburg: Department of Public Instruction, 1826)

Denisov, A. E., *Bumazhnye denezhnye znaki Rossii 1769–1917 godov. Chast' 1. Gosudarstvennye bumazhnye denezhnye znaki 1769–1843* (Moscow: Informelektro, 2002)

Denisov, Andrei, 'Slovo o novykh mudretsakh', in Iukhimenko (ed.), *Literaturnoe nasledie Vygovskogo staroobriadcheskogo obshchezhitel'stva*, vol. I, 203–8

[Denisov, Andrei, et al.], *Pomorskie otvety*, available through Wikimedia Commons, https://commons.wikimedia.org/wiki/File:Pomorskie_otvety.djvu

Dergacheva, I. V., *Drevnerusskii Sinodik: issledovaniia i teksty* (Moscow: 'Krug', 2011)

D'iakov, M. E., *Medali rossiiskoi imperii*, 2 vols. (Moscow: ZAO Dukhovnaia niva, 2004–5)

Distribuendi, Fedor, *Vzgliad na moskovskie vyveski* (Moscow: Tipografiia I. Smirnova, 1836)

Dmitrieva, Olga, and Abramova, Natalya (eds.), *Britannia and Muscovy: English Silver at the Court of the Tsars* (New Haven and London: Yale University Press, 2006)

Dmitrieva, Z. V. (ed.), *Vytnye i opisnye knigi Kirillo-Belozerskogo monastyria XVI–XVII vv.* (St Petersburg: Dmitrii Bulanin, 2003)

Dmitrieva, Z. V., Krushel'nitskaia, E. V., and Mil'chik, M. I. (eds.), *Opisi Solovetskogo monastyria XVI veka* (St Petersburg: Dmitrii Bulanin, 2003)

Dmitrieva, Z. V., and Sharomazov, M. N. (eds.), *Opis' stroenii i imushchestva Kirillo-Belozerskogo monastyria 1601 goda: kommentirovannoe izdanie* (St Petersburg: Peterburgskoe vostokovedenie, 1998)

Dobin, Manfred A., *Pochtovye shtempelia Rossiiskoi Imperii: domarochnyi period* (St Petersburg: Standart Kollektsiia, 2009)

Domostroi, ed. V. V. Kolesov and V. V. Rozhdestvenskaia (St Petersburg: Nauka, 1994)

Domostroi: Rules for Russian Households in the Time of Ivan the Terrible, The, ed. and transl. Carolyn Johnston Pouncy (Ithaca and London: Cornell University Press, 1994)

[Dosifei], 'Slovo o sotvorenii zhitiia nachal'nik solovetskikh Zosimy i Savatiia', *BLDR*, vol. 13 (2005), 148–52

Drboglav, D. A., *Kamni rasskazyvaiut ... Epigraficheskie latinskie pamiatniki XV–pervaia polovina XVI v. (Moskva, Serpukhov, Astrakhan')* (Izdatel'stvo Moskovskogo universiteta, 1988)

Druzhinin, P. A., *Russkii geral'dicheskii superekslibris* (Moscow: Drevlekhranilishche, 2000)

Emel'ianova, E. A., *Staroobriadcheskie izdaniia kirillovskogo shrifta kontsa XVIII–nachala XIX veka* (Moscow: Pashkov dom, 2010)

Englishwoman in Russia; Impressions of the Society and Manners of the Russians at Home. By a Lady Ten Years Resident in that Country, The (New York: Charles Scribner, 1855)

Filatov, V. V., and Kamchatnova, Iu. B., *Naimenovaniia i nadpisi na ikonnykh izobrazheniiakh. Spravochnik dlia ikonopistsev. Izdanie 3-e, ispravlennoe* (Moscow: PRO-PRESS, 2010)

Fiziologiia Peterburga (Moscow: Sovetskaia Rossiia, 1984)

Fletcher, Giles, *Of the Russe Common Wealth* (London: T. D. for Thomas Charde, 1591)

Fokina, T. A., *Chasy masterov i predpriiatii Rossii XVIII–nachala XX vekov iz sobraniia Politekhnicheskogo muzeiia. Katalog* (Moscow: RQPF 'NIK', 2007)

Gal'tsin, D. D., and Pitul'ko, G. N., *Biblioteka Feofilakta Lopatinskogo (ok. 1680–1741). Katalog* (St Petersburg: Pushkinskii Dom, 2016)

Gavrilov, Matvei, *Neues deutsch-französisch-lateinisch-italianisch-russisches Wörterbuch. Novyi Leksikon na nemetskom, frantsuzskom, latinskom, italianskom i russkom iazykakh* (N. Novikov at Moscow University Press, 1781)

Glushetskii, A. A., *Rossii bronzovoe slovo: o chem govorit duzhnyi kolokol'chik* (Moscow: Tsentr delovoi informatsii ezhenedel'nika 'ekonomika i zhizn", 2007)

Kolokol'no-liteinoe delo v Rossii vo vtoroi polovine XVII–nachale XX veka. Entsiklopediia liteishchikov ([Moscow]: Ekonomicheskaia gazeta, 2010)

Gogol, N. V., *Polnoe sobranie sochinenii v 14 tomakh*, ed. N. F. Bel'chikov and B. V. Tomashevskii (Moscow and Leningrad: AN SSSR, 1937–52)

Gorbatova, I. V., *Khudozhestvennoe steklo XVI–XVIII vekov* (Moscow: Trilistnik, 2006)

Gosudarstvennyi Russkii muzei. Zhivopis'. XVIII vek. Katalog. Tom 1 (St Petersburg: Palace Editions, 1998)

Gramotki XVII–nachala XVIII veka, ed. S. I. Kotkov, N. I. Tarasova and N. P. Pankratova (Moscow: Nauka, 1969)

Grebeniuk, T. V., *Vladel'cheskie knizhnye znaki v Otdele redkikh knig Rossiiskoi gosudarstvennoi biblioteki. Katalog* (Moscow: Pashkov dom, 2010)

Grebeniuk, V. P., and Derzhavina, O. A. (eds.), *Panegiricheskaia literatura petrovskogo vremeni* (Moscow: Nauka, 1979)

Grebenka, E. P., 'Peterburgskaia storona', in *Fiziologiia Peterburga*, 107–31

Grech, Aleksei, *Ves' Peterburg v karmane: spravochnaia kniga dlia stolichnykh zhitelei i priezzhikh, s planami Sanktpeterburga i chetyrekh teatrov*, 2nd expanded and corrected edn (St Petersburg: N. Grech, 1851)

Grigorovich, D. V., 'Peterburgskie sharmanshchiki', in *Fiziologiia Peterburga*, 84–106

Groening, Michael, *Rossiiskaia grammatika. Thet är Grammatica russica, eller Grundelig handledning til ryska språket* (Stockholm: Pet. Momma, 1750)

Guseva, A. A., *Izdaniia kirillovskogo shrifta vtoroi poloviny XVI veka: svodnyi katalog*, 2 vols. (Moscow: Indrik, 2003)

Svod russkikh knig kirillovskoi pechati XVIII veka tipografii Moskvy i Sankt-Peterburga i universal'naia metodika ikh identifikatsii (Moscow: Indrik, 2010)

Harris, Robert P., *A Guidebook of Russian Coins 1725 to 1972*, 2nd edn (Amsterdam: Mevius & Hirschhorn Int., 1974)

Heard, James, *A Practical Grammar of the Russian Language* (St Petersburg: printed for the Author; Sold by Sleunine and Boosey & Sons, London, 1827)

Hellie, Richard (transl.), *The Muscovite Code of Law (Ulozhenie) of 1649. Part 1: Text and Translation* (Irvine, CA: Charles Schlacks Jr, 1988)

Iakovlev, Lukian, *Russkie starinnye znamena* (Moscow: Sinodal'naia tipografiia, 1865)

Iakovleva, P. N., *Podduzhnye, podsheinye kolokol'chiki, bubentsy i botala v sobranii Novgorodskogo muzeiia-zapovednika* (Novgorodskii muzei-zapovednik, 2010)

Icones biblicae (Amsterdam: Danckert Danckertsz, 1659)

Ioasafovskaia letopis' (Moscow: AN SSSR, 1957)

[Istomin, Karion], *Bukvar' sostavlen Karionom Istominym, gravirovan Leontiem Buninym, otpechatan v 1694 v Moskve* (Leningrad: Avrora, 1981)

Itkina, E. I., *Risovannyi lubok staroobriadtsev v sobranii Istoricheskogo muzeia* (Moscow: Istoricheskii muzei, 2017)

Iukhimenko, E. M. (ed.), *Literaturnoe nasledie Vygovskogo staroobriadcheskogo obshchezhitel'stva*, 2 vols. (Moscow: Iazyki slavianskikh kul'tur, 2008)

Ivankin, F. F., *Strakhovye bumagi aktsionernykh obshchestv v Rossii (1827–1918 gg.)* (Moscow: [n.p.], 2005)

Aktsionernoe i Vzaimnoe strakhovanie v Rossii 1827–1920. Katalog (Moscow: Izdatel'skii dom Ruchen'kinykh, 2009)

Ivanova, Elena, *Farfor v Rossii XVIII–XIX vekov. Zavod Gardnera* (St Petersburg: Palace Editions, 2003)

Ivanova, Elena, and Popova, Irina, *Farfor chastnykh zavodov Peterburga* (St Petersburg: Palace Editions, 2008)

Kagan, M. D., Ponyrko, N. V., and Rozhdestvenskaia, M. V., 'Opisanie sbornikov XV v. knigopistsa Efrosina', *TODRL*, 35 (1980), 3–300

Kaliazina, N. V., Komelova, G. N., Kostochkina, N. D., Kostiuk, O. G., and Orlova, K. A. (eds.), *Russkaia emal' XII–nachala XX veka iz sobraniia Gosudarstvennogo Ermitazha* (Leningrad: Khudozhnik RSFSR, 1987)

Kalinichev, S. P., *Samovarnoe delo v Rossii. Katalog-spravochnik* (Moscow: Khobbi Press, 2015)

Kartashov, N. S., and Polonskii, I. M. (eds.), *Biblioteka A. A. Matveeva (1666–1728). Katalog* (Moscow: GBL, 1986)

Kashutina, E. S., and Saprykina, N. G., *Ekslibris v sobranii Nauchnoi biblioteki Moskovskogo gosudarstvennogo universiteta. Al'bom-katalog* (Izdatel'stvo Moskovskogo universiteta, 1985)

Kaznakov, S. N., *Paketovye tabakerki Imperatorskogo farforovogo zavoda* (St Petersburg: [n.p.], 1913)

Kettering, Karen L., *Russian Glass at Hillwood* (Washington, DC: Hillwood Museum and Gardens, 2001)

Khod'ko, Iuliia, *Religioznyi lubok vtoroi poloviny XVII–nachala XX veka iz sobraniia Russkogo muzeia* (St Petersburg: Palace Editions, 2012)

Svetskii lubok. Konets XVIII–nachala XX veka (St Petersburg: Palace Editions, 2015)

[Khonykov, Mardarii] Belobrova, O. A., 'Virshi Mardariia Khonykova k graviuram Biblii Piskatora', *TODRL*, 46 (1993), 334–433

Khromov, O. R., *Tsel'nogravirovannaia kniga i graviura v russkikh rukopisiakh XVI–XIX vekov. Katalog kollektsii Otdela pis'mennykh istochnikov Iaroslavskogo gosudarstvennogo istoriko-arkhitekturnogo i khudozhestvennogo muzeia-zapovednika* (Moscow: ART-RODNIK, 2013)

King, John Glen, *The Rites and Ceremonies of the Greek Church in Russia* (London: W. Owen, J. Dodsley etc., 1772)

Kiseleva, L. I., *Korpus zapisei na staropechatnykh knigakh. Vypusk 1. Zapisi na knigakh kirillicheskogo shrifta, napechatannykh v XVI–XVII vv.* (St Petersburg: BAN, 1992)

Klepikov, S. A., *Filigrani i shtempeli na bumage russkogo i inostrannogo proizvodstva* (Moscow: Izdatel'stvo vsesoiuznoi knizhnoi palaty, 1959)

Filigrani na bumage russkogo proizvodstva XVIII–nachala XX veka (Moscow: Nauka, 1978)

Kochetkov, I. A., *Slovar' russkikh ikonopistsev XI–XVII vekov* (Moscow: Indrik, 2003)

Kokorev, I. T., *Moskva sorokovykh godov. Ocherki i povesti o Moskve XIX veka* (Moscow: Moskovskii rabochii, 1959)

[Komarov, Matvei], *Vie de Kain: bandit russe et mouchard de la tsarine*, ed. Ecatherina Rai-Gonneau (Paris: Institut d'études slaves, 2008)

Kostina, I. D., *Proizvedeniia moskovskikh serebrianikov pervoi poloviny XVIII veka. Katalog* (Moscow: Gosudarstvennyi istoriko-kul'turnyi muzei-zapovednik 'Moskovskii Kreml'', 2003)

Kolokola XIV–XIX vekov (Moscow: Gosudarstvennyi istoriko-kul'turnyi muzei-zapovednik 'Moskovskii Kreml'', 2015)

Kotoshikhin, G. K., *O Rossii v tsarstvovanie Alekseia Mikhailovicha*, ed. G. A. Leont'eva (Moscow: ROSSPEN, 2000)
Kovtun, L. S., *Azbukovniki XVI–XVII vv. Starshaia raznovidnost'* (Leningrad: Nauka, 1989)
Kratz, Gottfried, *Deutschsprachige Drucke Moskauer und Petersburger Verlage, 1731–1991. Aus den Beständen der Universitäts- und Landesbibliothek Münster: Ausstellungskatalog* (Lüneburg: Institut Nordostdeutsches Kulturwerk, 1995)
Kurbskii, Andrei, 'Predislovie k Novomu Margaritu', *BLDR*, vol. 9 (2001), 554–68
[Leurechon, Jean], *Récréation mathématique* (Pont-à-Mousson: Gaspar Bernard, 1629)
Levshin, B. V. (ed.), *Graviroval'naia palata Akademii nauk XVIII veka. Sbornik dokumentov* (Leningrad: Nauka, 1985)
Likhachev, N. P., *Katalog letuchikh izdanii i ikh perepechatok* (St Petersburg: Tip. V. S. Balasheva & Ko., 1895)
Likhacheva, L. D., *Drevnerusskoe shit'e XV–XVIII vekov v sobranii Gosudarstvennogo Russkogo muzeiia. Katalog vystavki* (Leningrad: Gosudarstvennyi Russkii muzei, 1980)
Litsevoi letopisnyi svod XVI veka. Russkaia letopisnaia istoriia. Kniga 17. 1483–1502 gg. (facsimile edition; Moscow: AKTEON, 2010)
Lomonosov, M. V., *Rossiiskaia grammatika* (St Petersburg: Imp. AN, 1755 [1757])
[Lomonosov, M. V.], *Russische Grammatik. Verfaßet von herrn Michael Lomonoßow . . . aus dem Rußischen übersetzt von Johann Lorenz Stavenhagen* (St Petersburg: Imp. AN, 1764)
Ludolf, Heinrich Wilhelm, *Grammatica russica* (Oxford: e theatro Sheldoniano, 1696)
Maiasova, N. A., *Drevnerusskoe shit'e. La broderie russe ancienne* (Moscow: Iskusstvo, 1971)
Drevnerusskoe litsevoe shit'e. Katalog (Moscow: Krasnaia ploshchad', 2004)
Maier, Ingrid (ed. and introd.), *Vesti-kuranty. 1656 g., 1660–1662 gg., 1664–1670 gg. Inostrannye originaly k russkim tekstam*, Pt 2 (Moscow: Iazyki slavianskikh kul'tur, 2008)
Maier, Ingrid, Shamin, S. M., Kuznetsova, A. V., et al., *Vesti-kuranty. 1671–1672 gg.* (Moscow: Azbukovnik, 2017)
Maksim Grek, 'Poslanie o fortune', *BLDR*, vol. 9 (2000), 306–12
Markelov, G. V., *Pisaniia vygovtsev. Katalog-intsipitarii. Teksty* (St Petersburg: Dmitrii Bulanin, 2004)
Markova, G. A., *Nemetskoe khudozhestvennoe serebro XVI–XVIII vekov v sobranii Gosudarstvennoi Oruzheinoi palaty* (Moscow: Iskusstvo, 1975)
Martynova, M. V., *Moskovskaia emal' XV–XVII vv. Katalog* (Moscow: Gosudarstvennyi istoriko-kul'turnyi muzei-zapovednik 'Moskovskii Kreml'', 2002)
Materialy dlia istorii Gangutskoi operatsii. Vypusk I, chast' II. Gramoty, ukazy i pis'ma Petra Velikogo (Petrograd: Tipografiia Morskogo ministerstva, 1914)

'Mavrourbin' [Mauro Orbini], *Kniga istoriografiia pochatiia imene, slavy i rasshireniia naroda slavianskogo* (St Petersburg, 1722)

Medvedev, Silvestr, *Izvestie istinnoe pravoslavnym i pokazanie svetloe o novopravlenii knizhnom i o prochem*, ed. and introd. Sergei Belokurov, in *ChOIDR*, 1885.4, 3rd pagination, 1–87

'Kniga o Manne khleba zhivotnogo': extracts in Aleksandr Prozorovskii, 'Sil'vestr Medvedev (Ego zhizn' i deiatel'nost'). Opyt tserkovno-istoricheskogo issledovaniia. Prilozheniia', *ChOIDR*, 1896.4, 452–538

Mesiatsoslov na leto ot rozhdestva Khristova 1782, kotoroe est' prostoe soderzhashchee v sebe 365 dnei (St Petersburg: AN, [1781])

Moiseenko, E. Iu., *Russkaia vyshivka XVII–nachala XX veka. Iz sobraniia Gosudarstvennogo Ermitazha* (Leningrad: Khudozhnik RSFSR, 1978)

Moiseenko, E. Iu., and Faleeva, V. A., *Biser i stekliarus v Rossii. XVIII–nachalo XX veka* (Leningrad: Khudozhnik RSFSR, 1990)

Moskovskie kirillovskie izdaniia XVI–XVII vv. v sobraniiakh RGADA. Katalog. Vypusk 1. 1556–1625 gg., ed. E. V. Luk'ianova and L. N. Gorbunova (Moscow: Arkheograficheskii tsentr, 1996); *Vypusk 2. 1626–1650*, ed. E. V. Luk'ianova (Moscow: Indrik, 2002); *Vypusk 3. 1651–1675*, ed. L. N. Gorbunova and E. V. Luk'ianova (Moscow: Indrik, 2003)

Nakaz ee Imperatorskago Velichestva Ekateriny Vtoryia samoderzhitsy vserossiiskiia dannyi Kommissii o sochinenii proekta novago Ulozheniia (St Petersburg: Imp. AN, 1770)

Nekrasov, N. A., 'Peterburgskie ugly', in *Fiziologiia Peterburga*, 132–52

Nemirovskii, E. L., *Gesamtkatalog der Frühdrucke in Kyrillischer Schrift, I: Inkunabeln* (Baden-Baden: Verlag Valentin Koerner, 1996)

Istoriia slavianskogo kirillicheskogo knigopechataniia XV–nachala XVII veka. I. Vozniknovenie slavianskogo knigopechataniia (Moscow: Nauka, 2003)

Knigi kirillovskoi pechati 1491–1550. Katalog (Moscow: Pashkov dom, 2009)

Slavianskie izdaniia kirillovskogo (tserkovnoslavianskogo) shrifta 1491–2000. Inventar' sokhranivshikhsia ekzempliarov i ukazatel' literatury. Tom II. Kniga 1, 1551–1592 (Moscow: Znak, 2011); *Tom II. Kniga 2, 1593–1600* (Moscow: Rukopisnye pamiatniki Drevnei Rusi, 2012)

Azbuki Ivana Fedorova, ego uchenikov i posledovatelei, ed. Iu. E. Shustova (Piatigorsk: SNEG, 2015)

Nemirovskii, E. L., and Shustova, Iu. E., 'Kirillicheskie azbuki i bukvari XVI–XVIII vv.: bibliograficheskii svod izdanii', in Tendriakova and Bezrogova (eds.), '*V Rossii nado zhit' po knige*', 185–338

Neuhäuser, Rudolf, *The Romantic Age in Russian Literature: Poetic and Aesthetic Norms (An Anthology of Original Texts 1800–1850)* (Slavistische Beiträge, 90, Munich: Otto Sagner, 1975)

Nikolaeva, S. G., *Kollektsiia gravirovannykh antiminsov v sobranii Gosudarstvennogo muzeiia istorii religii* (Trudy Gosudarstvennogo muzeiia istorii religii, 3; St Petersburg: Aktsioner i Ko., 2003)

Nikolaeva, T. V., *Proizvedeniia russkogo prikladnogo iskusstva s nadpisiami XV–pervoi chetverti XVI v.* (Moscow: Nauka, 1971) (Arkheologiia SSSR. Svod arkheologicheskikh istochnikov, E1-49)

Novgorodskie gramoty na bereste, tom X (Iz raskopok 1990–1996 gg.), ed. V. L. Ianin and A. A. Zalizniak (Moscow: Russkie slovari, 2000)

O piatom general'nom sobranii moskovskogo otdeleniia Rossiiskogo bibleiskogo obshchestva v 1818 godu (Moscow: Universitetskaia tipografiia, 1818)

Odom, Anne, *Russian Enamels: Kievan Rus to Fabergé* (London: Philip Wilson Publishers, 1996)

Russian Imperial Porcelain at Hillwood (Washington, DC: Hillwood Museum and Gardens, 1999)

[Olearius, Adam], *The Travels of Olearius in Seventeenth-Century Russia*, transl. and ed. Samuel H. Baron (Stanford University Press, 1967)

Paul of Aleppo, *The Travels of Macarius, Patriarch of Antioch*, transl. F. C. Balfour, vol. I (London: Oriental Translation Fund of Great Britain and Ireland, 1836)

Perepiska Ivana Groznogo s Andreem Kurbskim, ed. Ia. S. Lur'e and Iu. D. Rykov (Leningrad: Nauka, 1979)

Peters, D. I., *Nagradnye medali Rossii vtoroi poloviny XVIII stoletiia* (Moscow: Arkheograficheskii tsentr, 1999)

Pigin, A. V., *Pamiatniki knizhnoi stariny russkogo severa. Kollektsii rukopisei XV–XX vekov v gosudarstvennykh khranilishchakh Respubliki Kareliia* (St Petersburg: Dmitrii Bulanin, 2010)

Pis'ma i bumagi Petra Velikogo, vol. II (St Petersburg: Gosudarstvennaia tipografiia, 1889)

Pod tsarskim venzelem: proizvedeniia Imperatorskogo farforovogo zavoda iz sobraniia Gosudarstvennogo Ermitazha; katalog vystavki v gosudarstvennom komplekse muzeev Moskovskogo Kremlia, 17 oktiabria 2007–13 ianvaria 2008 (St Petersburg: Izdatel'stvo Gosudarstvennogo Ermitazha, 2007

[Poletika, G. A.], *Slovar' na shesti iazykakh: rossiiskom, grecheskom, latinskom, frantsuzskom, nemetskom i angliiskom, izdannyi v pol'zu uchashchagosia rossiiskogo iunoshestva* (St Petersburg: Imp. AN, 1763)

Polikarpov, Fedor, *Kniga bukvar' slavenskimi, grecheskimi, rimskimi pismeny uchitisia khotiashchim* (Moscow: [n.p.], 1701)

Lexikon treiazychnyi / Lexikon triglotton / Dictionarium trilingue (Moscow: [n. p.], 1704)

Polnoe sobranie zakonov Rossiiskoi imperii, 45 vols. (St Petersburg: II Otdelenie sobstvennoi Ego Imperatorskogo Velichestva kantseliarii, 1830), www.nlr.ru/e-res/law_r/search.php

Polnoe sobranie zakonov Rossiiskoi imperii. Sobranie vtoroe. S 12 Dekabria 1825 goda, 55 vols. (St Petersburg, 1830–84)

Polotskii, Simeon, *Zhezl pravleniia* (Moscow: Pechatnyi dvor, 1667)

Izbrannye sochineniia, ed. I. P. Eremin (Moscow and Leningrad: AN SSSR, 1953)

[Polotskii], *Vertograd mnogocvetnyj*, 3 vols., ed. Anthony Hippisley and Lydia I. Sazonova (Bausteine zur slavischen Philologie und Kulturgeschichte. Reihe B: Editionen. Neue Folge, Band 10; Cologne, Weimar and Vienna: Böhlau Verlag, 1996–2000)

Orel rossiiskii, ed. L. I. Sazonova (Moscow: Indrik, 2015)

'Poslesloviia k izdaniiam Ivana Fedorova', *BLDR*, vol. 12 (2003), 524–34

Pososhkov, Ivan T., *Kniga o skudosti i bogatstve i drugie sochineniia*, ed. and comm. B. B. Kafengauz (Moscow: AN SSSR, 1951)

The Book of Poverty and Wealth, ed. and transl. A. P. Vlasto and L. R. Lewitter (London: Athlone Press, 1987)

Premudrost' Astrei. Pamiatniki masonstva XVIII–pervoi treti XIX veka v sobranii Ermitazha (St Petersburg: Izdatel'stvo Gosudarstvennogo Ermitazha, 2013)

Prokhorov, G. M. (ed.), *Entsiklopediia russkogo igumena XIV–XV vv. Sbornik Prepodobnogo Kirilla Belozerskogo. Rossiiskaia Natsional'naia Biblioteka, Kirillo-Belozerskoe sobranie, no. XII* (St Petersburg: Izdatel'stvo Olega Abyshko, 2003)

Prokopovich, Feofan, *Sochineniia*, ed. I. P. Eremin (Moscow and Leningrad: AN SSSR, 1961)

Protas'eva, T. N., and Shchepkina, M. V., 'Skazaniia o nachale moskovskogo knigopechataniia. Teksty i perevody', in Tikhomirov (ed.), *U istokov russkogo knigopechataniia*, 198–214

Pushkin, A. S., *Sobranie sochinenii v desiati tomakh*, ed. D. D. Blagoi et al. (Moscow: Gosudarstvennoe izdatel'stvo khudozhestvennoi literatury, 1959–62)

Ramazanova, D. N., and Shustova, Iu. E., *Kirillicheskie bukvari iz sobraniia Nauchno-issledovatel'skogo otdela redkikh knig Rossiiskoi gosudarstvennoi biblioteki: opisanie izdanii i ekzempliarov* (Moscow: Pashkov dom, 2018)

Rastorguev, E. I., *Progulki po Nevskomy prospektu* (St Petersburg: Tipografiia Karla Kraiia, 1846), repr. in A. M. Konechnyi (ed.), *Chuvstvitel'nye progulki po Nevskomu prospektu* (St Petersburg: Petropolis, 2009), 121–210

Reimers, Heinrich von, *St. Petersburg am Ende seines ersten Jahrhunderts. Mit Rückblicken auf Entstehung und Wachsthum dieser Residenz unter den verschiedenen Regierungen während dieses Zeitraums*, vol. II (St Petersburg: F. Dienemann u. Comp., 1805)

St.-Peterburgische Adress-Buch auf das Jahr 1809 (St Petersburg: A. Pluchart, [1809])

Dictionnaire d'adress de St.-Pétersbourg pour l'année 1809, avec un plan et guide des étrangers à St-Pétersbourg (St Petersburg: [n.p.], [1809])

Sanktpeterburgskaia adresnaia kniga na 1809 god (St Petersburg: Schnoor, [1809])

Rossiiskoe zakonodatel'stvo X–XX vekov, vol. IV, ed. A. G. Man'kov (Moscow: Iuridicheskaia literatura, 1986)

Rovinskii, D. A., *Russkie narodnye kartinki*, 5 vols. (St Petersburg: Tipografiia AN, 1881)

Rudakova, N. I., *Russkaia literatura v zerkale lubka. Narodnaia kartinka XVIII–nachala XX veka* (St Petersburg: RNB, 2015)

Rudenko, I. V., *Pamiatnye zhetony Imperatorskoi Rossii (1721–1917 gg.)* (Rostov-on-Don: Omega Publisher, 2007)
Borodovye znaki 1698, 1705, 1724, 1725. Katalog (Rostov-on-Don: Omega Publisher, 2013)
Samoilova, T. E. (comp. and introd.), *Vera i vlast'. Epokha Ivana Groznogo* (Moscow: Gosudarstvennyi istoriko-kul'turnyi muzei-zapovednik 'Moskovskii Kreml'', 2007)
Sankt-Peterburg v akvareliakh, graviurakh i litografiiakh XVIII–XIX vekov: iz sobraniia Gosudarstvennogo Ermitazha, compiled by G. A. Miroliubova, G. A. Printseva and V. O. Looga (St Petersburg: Arka, 2009)
Savel'eva, E. A., *Katalog knig iz sobraniia Aptekarskogo prikaza* (St Petersburg: Alfaret, 2006)
Savel'eva, N. V., *Ocherki istorii formirovaniia pinezhskoi knizhno-rukopisnoi traditsii: opisanie rukopisnykh istochnikov* (Pinezhskaia knizhno-rukopisnaia traditsiia XVI–nachala XX vv., vol. I; St Petersburg: Dmitrii Bulanin, 2003)
Sbornik istoricheskikh materialov, izvlechennykh iz arkhiva sobstvennoi Ego Imperatorskogo Velichestva kantseliarii, ed. N. Dubrovin, vol. XII (St Petersburg: Gosudarstvennaia tipografiia, 1903)
Schwenter, Daniel, *Deliciae physico-mathematicae* (Nuremberg: J. Dümler, 1661)
Semenov, V. E., *Poddelki rossiiskikh monet* (St Petersburg: Konros-Inform, 2012)
Severin, G. M., *Monety Rossiiskoi imperii. Platinovye, zolotye, serebrianye. 1682–1917* (Moscow: Profizdat, 2006)
Shafirov, P. P., *A Discourse Concerning the Just Causes of the War Between the Swedes and Russia: 1700–1721*, introd. William E. Butler (Dobbs Ferry, NY: Oceana Publications, 1973)
Shchukina, E. S., *Monogrammy i podpisi na russkikh medaliakh XVIII–nachala XX vekov* (Kiev: Iunona-moneta, 2002)
Silkin, A. V., *Stroganovskoe litsevoe shit'e* (Moscow: Progress-Traditsiia, 2002)
Skazanie o kniaziakh vladimirskikh, ed. R. P. Dmitrieva (Moscow and Leningrad: AN SSSR, 1955)
Skorniakova, N. N., *Vidy Moskvy. Akvarel' i risunok XVIII–nachala XX veka iz sobraniia Istoricheskogo muzeia* (Moscow: Istoricheskii muzei, 2017)
Slovar' russkogo iazyka XVIII veka (Leningrad–St Petersburg, 1984–)
Sobranie Rossiiskikh razgovorov, v obshchezhitii upotrebliaemykh, s priobshcheniem Gruzinskogo perevoda, v pol'zu Blagorodnogo Iunoshestva (Tiflis: Voenno-pokhodnaia tipografiia, 1819)
Sokolov, S. P., *Svodnyi katalog russkikh medalei. 1462–1762* (Kiev: Kupola, 2005)
Sots, I. V., *Nouveau dictionnaire françois, italien, allemand, latin et russe*, 2 vols. (Moscow University Press, 1784, 1787)
Spasskii, I. G., *Talery v russkom denezhnom obrashchenii 1654–1659 godov. Svodnyi katalog efimkov* (Leningrad: Izdatel'stvo Gosudarsvennogo Ermitazha, 1960)
Russkie efimki. Issledovanie i katalog (Novosibirsk: Nauka, Sibirskoe otdelenie, 1988)

Stählin, J., *Original Anecdotes of Peter the Great, Collected from the Conversation of Several Persons of Distinction at Petersburgh and Moscow* (London and Edinburgh: J. Murray, J. Sewell, W. Creech, 1788)

Statut der St. Peterburgischen Gesellschaft von Liebhabern der Wissenschaften, Litteratur und Künste (St Petersburg: Marine-Buchdruckerei, 1805)

Stoglav. Issledovanie i tekst, ed. E. B. Emchenko (Moscow: Indrik, 2000)

Strukov, D., and Popov, I., *Risunki k izdaniiu 'Russkie starinnye znamena' Lukiana Iakovleva* (Moscow: Khromolitografiia V. Bakhman, 1865)

Studemeister, Marguerite, *Bookplates and Their Owners in Imperial Russia: An Illustrated Survey of Holdings at Stanford University* (Tenafly, NJ: Hermitage Publishers, 1991)

Suvorin, A. S., *Rostopchinskie afishi 1812 goda. Bibliograficheskoe izdanie v 300 ekzempliarakh* (St Petersburg: Tipografiia A. S. Suvorina, 1889)

Svod russkikh nadpisei / Corpus of Russian Inscriptions, http://cir.rssda.su/

Svodnyi katalog knig na inostrannykh iazykakh, izdannykh v Rossii v XVIII veke, 1701–1800, ed. E. A. Savel'eva and T. N. Shcherbakova, vols. I–III (Leningrad: Nauka, 1984–6)

Svodnyi katalog russkoi knigi grazhdanskoi pechati XVIII veka, 1725–1800, ed. I. P. Kondakov et al., 5 vols. (Moscow: Kniga, 1963–7)

Symbola et emblemata (Amsterdam: Henricius Westenius, 1705)

'T', 'Peterburgskie vyveski', *Illiustratsiia* 1848, no. 30 (28 Aug.), 81–2, http://tiamtula.ru/wp-content/uploads/2016/07/TIAM_public002.pdf

Tambovskie izvestiia, ed. and comm. V. V. Kanishchev, Iu. V. Meshcheriakov and Iu. A. Mizis (Tambovskii gosudarstvennyi universitet, 2012)

Tarkovskii, R. B., and Tarkovskaia, L. R., *Ezop na Rusi. Vek XVII. Issledovaniia. Teksty. Kommentarii* (St Petersburg: Dmitrii Bulanin, 2005)

Timofeev, V. N., Poretskina, E. N., and Efremova, N. N., *Memorial'nye doski Sankt-Peterburga. Spravochnik* (St Petersburg: Art-biuro, 1999)

Tomelleri, V. S. (ed.), *Der russische Donat: vom lateinischen Lehrbuch zur russischen Grammatik* (Bausteine zur slavischen Philologie. Neue Folge, Reihe B, 18; Cologne: Böhlau Verlag, 2002)

Trediakovskii, V. K., 'Razgovor mezhdu chuzhestrannym chelovekom i rossiiskim ob ortografii starinnoi i novoi i o vsem, chto prinadlezhit k sei materii', in Trediakovskii, *Sochineniia*, vol. III (St Petersburg: A. Smirdin, v tipografii AN, 1849), 1–316

[Turoboiskii, Iosif], *Politikolepnaia apotheosis dostokhvalnyia khrabrosti vserossiiskago Gerkulesa . . . Petra Aleksievicha*, in Tiukhmeneva, *Iskusstvo triumfal'nykh vrat*, 157–212

Twenty-Seventh Report of the British and Foreign Bible Society, The (London: J. Moyes, 1831)

Twenty-Ninth Report of the British and Foreign Bible Society, The (London: J. Moyes, 1833)

Ukrainskie knigi kirillovskoi pechati XVI–XVIII vv. Katalog izdanii, khraniashchikhsia v Gosudarstvennoi biblioteke SSSR imeni V. I. Lenina. Vypusk I.

1574 g.–I polovina XVII v., ed. T. N. Kameneva and A. A. Guseva (Moscow: GBL, 1976)
Uzdenikov, V. V., *Monety Rossii 1700–1917*, 4th edn (Moscow: IP Media, 2011)
Vilinbakhov, G. V., *Geral'dika na russkom farfore: katalog vystavki* (St Petersburg: Gosudarstvennyi Ermitazh, 2008)
Vistengof, P., *Ocherki moskovskoi zhizni* (Moscow: Tipografiia S. Selivanovskogo, 1842)
Voznesenskii, A. V., *Predvaritel'nyi spisok staroobriadcheskikh kirillicheskikh izdanii XVIII veka* (St Petersburg: Khronograf, 1994)
Willetts, Ronald F., *The Law Code of Gortyn* (Berlin: De Gruyter, 1967)
Zaglavnoe pis'mo drevnerusskikh rukopisnykh knig XIV–XV vv. Al'bom zarisovok M. G. Gal'chenko (Moscow: Tsentral'nyi muzei drevnerusskoi kul'tury i iskusstva imeni Andreiia Rubleva, 2004)
Zapas'ko, Iakym, and Isaevych, Iaroslav, *Pam'iatky knyzhkovoho mystetstva. Kataloh starodrukiv, vydannykh na Ukraini, kn. 1, 1574–1700* (Lviv: Vysha shkola, 1981)
Zemtsova, N. A., and Shitskova, A. B., 'Azbuki, bukvari, propisi grazhdanskoi pechati, izdannye v XVIII v. (bibliograficheskii ukazatel')', in Tendriakova and Bezrogova (eds.), '*V Rossii nado zhit' po knige*', 339–50
Zernova, A. S., *Knigi kirillovskoi pechati, izdannye v Moskve v XVI–XVII vekakh. Svodnyi katalog* (Moscow: GBL, 1958)
Zernova, A. S., and Kameneva, T. N., *Svodnyi katalog russkoi knigi kirillovskoi pechati XVIII veka* (Moscow: GBL, 1968)
Zhivopis' XVIII veka (Gosudarstvennaia Tret'iakovskaia galereia. Katalog sobraniia. Seriia Zhivopis' XVIII–XX vekov, vol. II), ed. L. I. Iovleva (Moscow: Krasnaia ploshchad', 1998)
'Zvuchat lish' pis'mena . . . ' k 150-letiiu so dnia rozhdeniia akademika Nikolaia Petrovicha Likhacheva. Katalog vystavki, ed. A. O. Bol'shakov and E. V. Stepanova (St Petersburg: Izdatel'stvo Gosudarstvennogo Ermitazha, 2012)

2. Studies

Abramishvili, A. Z., 'Iz istorii gruzinskogo knigopechataniia za predelami Gruzii (Rim, 1629–1800 gg. Moskva, 1705–1917)', *Kniga. Issledovaniia i materialy*, 3 (1960), 251–99
Adler, Michael H., *The Writing Machine* (London: George Allen & Unwin, 1973)
Afanas'eva, T. A., 'Izdaniia azbuk i bukvarei kirillovskoi pechati v XVIII veke', in *Iz istorii rukopisnykh i staropechatnykh sobranii* (Leningrad: GPB, 1979), 33–60
'Izdaniia kirillicheskoi pechati XVIII veka svetskogo soderzhaniia', in *Problemy istochnikovedcheskogo izucheniia rukopisnykh i staropechatnykh fondov* (Leningrad: GPB, 1979), 183–99

'Izdaniia zakonodatel'nogo kharaktera kirillicheskoi pechati v XVIII v.', in *Istochniki po istorii otechestvennoi kul'tury v sobraniiakh i arkhivakh Otdela rukopisei i redkikh knig* (Leningrad: GPB, 1983), 96–114

Agarkova, G. D., Astrakhantseva, T. L., and Petrova, N. S., *Russkii farfor* (Moscow: Planeta, 1993)

Akelev, Evgeny, 'When Did Peter the Great Order Beards Shaved?', *Quaestio Rossica*, 5.4 (2017), 1107–30

Alef, Gustav, 'The Political Significance of the Inscriptions on Muscovite Coinage in the Reign of Vasili II', *Speculum*, 34 (1950), 1–19

Alekseev, A. A., *Tekstologiia slavianskoi Biblii* (St Petersburg: Dmitrii Bulanin, 1999)

Alekseev, Iu. G., *U kormila rossiiskogo gosudarstva. Ocherk razvitiia apparata upravleniia XIV–XV vv.* (Izdatel'stvo Sankt-Peterburgskogo universiteta, 1998)

Alekseev, M. P., *Slovari inostrannykh slov v russkom azbukovnike XVII veka* (Leningrad: Nauka, 1968)

Alekseeva, M. A., 'Torgovlia graviurami v Moskve i kontrol' za nei v kontse XVII–XVIII vv.', in I. E. Danilova (ed.), *Narodnaia graviura i fol'klor v Rossii XVII–XIX vv. (K 150-letiiu so dnia rozhdeniia D. A. Rovinskogo)* (Moscow: Sovetskii khudozhnik, 1976), 140–58

'Maloizvestnye proizvedeniia russkogo iskusstva XVII–pervoi poloviny XVIII veka – gravirovannye antiminsy', in *Pamiatniki kul'tury. Novye otkrytiia. Ezhegodnik 1982* (Leningrad: Nauka, 1984), 430–51

Graviura petrovskogo vremeni (Leningrad: Iskusstvo, 1990)

Iz istorii russkoi graviury XVII–nachala XIX v. (Moscow and St Petersburg: Al'ians-Arkheo, 2013)

Androsov, S. O., *Ital'ianskaia skul'ptura v sobranii Petra Velikogo* (St Petersburg: Dmitrii Bulanin, 1999)

Ot Petra I k Ekaterine II. Liudi, statui, kartiny (St Petersburg: Dmitrii Bulanin, 2013)

Androsov, S. O., Bertash, A. V., and Talalai, M. G., *Antichnye i bibleiskie siuzhety v kamne i bronze. Peterburgskoe gorodskoe ubranstvo* (St Petersburg: Informatsionno-izdatel'skoe agentstvo 'LIK', 2006)

Angermann, Norbert., 'Neues über Nicolaus Bulow und sein Wirken in Moskauer Russland', *JGO*, 17 (1969), 408–19

'Deutsche Übersetzer und Dolmetscher im vorpetrinischen Russland', in Eckhard Hübner et al. (eds.), *Zwischen Christianisierung und Europäisierung: Beiträge zur Geschichte Osteuropas in Mittelalter und früher Neuzeit. Festschrift für Peter Nitsche zum 65. Geburtstag* (Stuttgart: Franz Steiner Verlag, 1998), 221–49

Anisimov, E. V., *Podatnaia reforma Petra I* (Leningrad: Nauka, 1982)

Petr Pervyi: blago ili zlo dlia Rossii? (Moscow: Novoe literaturnoe obozrenie, 2017)

Antonov, A. V., 'Iz istorii velikokniazheskoi kantselliarii: kormlennye gramoty XV–serediny XVI veka', in Antonov, *Istoriko-arkheograficheskie issledovaniia: Rossiia XV–nachala XVII veka* (Moscow: Drevlekhranilishche, 2013), 7–108

Aronson, M., and Reiser, S., *Literaturnye kruzhki i salony* (St Petersburg: Akademicheskii proekt, 2001 [1929])

Asharina, N. A., 'Russkie zavody khudozhestvennogo stekla XVII–XVIII vv.', in Asharina (ed.), *Iz istorii russkoi keramiki i stekla XVII–XIX vekov. Sbornik trudov* (Moscow: Gosudarstvennyi ordena Lenina Istoricheskii muzei, 1986), 3–16

Asharina, Nina, Malinina, Tamara, and Kazakova, Liudmila, *Russian Glass of the Seventeenth–Twentieth Centuries* (Corning, NY: Corning Museum of Glass, 1990)

Avdeev, A. G., 'Khramozdannye nadpisi XVI–XVII vv. Kostromy i kraia', *Kostromskaia zemlia*, 5 (2002), 158–65

'Utrachennaia nadpis' 1530 g. o stroitel'stve kremlia v Kolomne. Opyt rekonstruktsii soderzhaniia', *Voprosy epigrafiki*, 2 (2008), 178–89

'Epigraficheskie zametki', *Voprosy epigrafiki*, 8 (2015), 398–415

'Russkaia sillabicheskaia epitafiia poslednei chetverti XVII–nachala vtoroi treti XVIII v.', *Palaeoslavica*, 25.1 (2017), 55–177

'O nadpisi na kreste d'iaka Stefana Borodatogo', in G. E. Zakharov and A. Posternak (eds.), *Prikosnovenie k vechnosti. Sbornik statei* (Moscow: PSTGU, 2017), 162–9

Avdeev, A. G., and Chernov, D. A., 'Stikhotvornye podpisi k knige Pesn' pesnei Solomona na freskakh XVII–XVIII vv. v Romanove-Borisoglebske i Kostrome', *Voprosy epigrafiki*, 5 (2011), 370–403

Avdeev, A. G., and Pirogov, V. Iu., 'Kladbishche inozemtsev v Mar'inoi Roshche', *Voprosy epigrafiki*, 1 (2006), 36–48

Avdeev, A. G., and Vinogradov, A. Iu., 'Rekonstruktsiia grecheskoi stroitel'noi nadpisi 1634/35 g. iz Moskvy', *Voprosy epigrafiki*, 6 (2012), 43–9

Avery, Victoria, Calarescu, Melissa, and Laven, Mary, *Treasured Possessions: From the Renaissance to the Enlightenment* (London: Philip Wilson, 2015)

Avtokratov, V. N., 'K istorii zameny stolbovoi formy deloproizvodstva – tetradnoi k nachalu XVIII v.', *Problemy istochnikovedeniia*, 7 (1959), 274–86

Badurova, A. L., 'Razvitie chastnoi farforovoi promyshlennosti Peterburgskoi gubernii v kontsa XVIII–pervoi polovine XIX vv.', in N. A. Asharina (ed.), *Iz istorii russkoi keramiki i stekla XVII–XIX vekov. Sbornik trudov* (Moscow: Gosudarstvennyi ordena Lenina Istoricheskii muzei, 1986), 21–32

Balachenkova, A. P., 'Knizhnye inventari Kirillo-Belozerskogo monastyria XV–XVII vekov', *Ferapontovskii sbornik*, 5 (1999), 42–59

Barbarics-Hermanik, Zsuzsa, 'The Coexistence of Manuscript and Print: Handwritten Newsletters in the Second Century of Print, 1540–1640', in Walsby and Kemp (eds.), *The Book Triumphant*, 347–68

Bartenev, I. A., and Batazhkova, V. N., *Russkii inter'er XIX veka* (Leningrad: Khudozhnik RSFSR, 1984)

Russkii inter'er XVIII–XIX vekov (Moscow: Svarog i K, 2000)

Bartenev, Sergei, *Moskovskii kreml' v starinu i teper'*, 2 vols. (Moscow: Izdanie Ministerstva Imperatorskogo Dvora, 1916; facsimile reprint, Moscow: Russkii impul's, 2011)

Bartlett, Roger P., *Human Capital: The Settlement of Foreigners in Russia 1762–1804* (Cambridge University Press, 1979)

Bartlett, Roger, and Hughes, Lindsey (eds.), *Russian Society and Culture and the Long Eighteenth Century: Essays in Honour of Anthony G. Cross* (Münster: LIT Verlag, 2004)

Barton, David, *Literacy: An Introduction to the Ecology of Written Language*, 2nd edn (Oxford: Blackwell, 2007)

Batalden, Stephen K., *Russian Bible Wars: Modern Scriptural Translation and Cultural Authority* (Cambridge University Press, 2013)

Bazilevich, K. V., *Denezhnaia reforma Alekseia Mikhailovicha i vosstanie v Moskve v 1662 g.* (Moscow: AN SSSR, 1936)

Bekasova, Aleksandra, 'Dilizhansy na dorogakh Rossii: ot zamysla – k praktike voploshcheniia', *Quaestio Rossica*, 5.1 (2017), 32–55

Beliaev, L. A., and Iurasov, A. V. (eds.), *Ot Smuty k Imperii. Novye otkrytiia v oblasti arkheologii i istorii Rossii XVI–XVIII vv.* (Moscow and Vologda: Drevnosti Severa, 2016)

Beliakov, A. V., *Sluzhashchie Posol'skogo prikaza 1645–1682 gg.* (St Petersburg: Nestor-Istoriia, 2017)

Beliakova, E. V., Moshkova, L. V., and Oparina, T. A., *Kormchaia kniga. Ot rukopisnoi traditsii k pervomu pechatnomu izdaniiu* (Moscow and St Petersburg: Institut rossiiskoi istorii RAN; RGADA; Tsentr gumanitarnykh initsiativ, 2017)

Belobrova, O. A., 'Latinskaia nadpis' na Frolovskikh vorotakh Moskovskogo Kremlia i ee sud'ba v drevnerusskoi pis'mennosti', in *Gosudarstvennye Muzei Moskovskogo Kremlia. Materialy i issledovaniia. Novye atributsii. Vypusk V* (Moscow: Iskusstvo, 1987), 51–7

'Bibliia Piskatora v sobranii Biblioteki Akademii nauk SSSR', in M. V. Kukushkina (ed.), *Materialy i soobshcheniia po fondam otdela rukopisnoi i redkoi knigi. 1985* (Leningrad: Nauka, 1987), 184–216

'Drevnerusskie virshi k graviuram Mattiasa Meriana', *TODRL*, 44 (1990), 443–79

'O drevnerusskikh podpisiakh k nekotorym niderlandskim tsel'nogravirovannym izdaniiam XVII v.', *TODRL*, 43 (1990), 70–8

'Simeon Polotskii – avtor virsh k graviuram Biblii Mattiasa Meriana', *TODRL*, 49 (1996), 526–8

'O nekotorykh istochnikakh podpisei k siuzhetam rospisi Zolotoi palaty Moskovskogo Kremlia', *TODRL*, 53 (2003), 502–17

'O khronografe s graviurami Biblii Piskatora (RNB, Solovetskoe sobr., No. 1525/189)', *TODRL*, 55 (2004), 111–15

'Opisanie peterburgskogo Petropavlovskogo sobora v rukopisnykh sbornikakh XVIII v.', *TODRL*, 56 (2004), 623–34

Belova, L. V., 'Gravirovannyi "ekslibris" ierodiakona Stefana Sakharova 1691 g. na staropechatnykh sluzhebnykh mineiiakh', in *Kniga v Rossii. Sbornik 1* (Moscow: Nauka, 2006), 260–71

Beneva, I. V., *Istoriia Instrumental'noi palaty Peterburgskoi Akademii nauk (1724–1766)* (St Petersburg: Nauka, 1999)

Birzhakova, E. E., Voinova, L. A., and Kutina, L. L., *Ocherki po leksikologii russkogo iazyka XVIII veka. Iazykovye kontakty i zaimstvovaniia* (Leningrad: Nauka, 1972)

Blakesley, Rosalind P., 'Pride and the Politics of Nationality in Russia's Imperial Academy of Fine Arts, 1757–1807', *Art History*, 35.5 (Dec. 2010), 800–35

The Russian Canvas: Painting in Imperial Russia, 1757–1881 (New Haven and London: Yale University Press, 2016)

Bobrov, A. G., 'Knigopisnaia masterskaia Lisitskogo monastyria (Konets XIV–pervaia polovina XV v.)', in *Knizhnye tsentry Drevnei Rusi XI–XVI vv. Raznye aspekty issledovaniia* (St Petersburg: Nauka, 1991), 78–98

Bobrovnitskaia, I. A., 'Emalevaia chashka iz kollektsii Oruzheinoi palaty', *Muzei. Khudozhestvennye sobraniia SSSR*, 8 (1987), 111–21

Boeckeler, Erika M., *Playful Letters: A Study in Early Modern Alphabetics* (Iowa City: University of Iowa Press, 2017)

Boffey, Julia, *Manuscript and Print in London, c. 1475–1530* (London: British Library, 2012)

Bogatyrev, Sergei, 'The Heavenly Host and the Sword of Truth: Apocalyptic Imagery in Ivan IV's Moscow', in Valerie Kivelson, Karen Petrone, Nancy Shields Kollmann and Michael S. Flier (eds.), *The New Muscovite Cultural History: A Collection in Honor of Daniel B. Rowland* (Bloomington, IN: Slavica, 2009), 77–90

'Bronze Tsars: Ivan the Terrible and Fedor Ivanovich in the Décor of Early Modern Guns', *SEER*, 88.1–2 (Jan./Apr. 2010), 48–72

'The Patronage of Early Printing in Moscow', *CASS*, 51 (2017), 249–88

Bogdanov, A. P., *Stikh torzhestva: rozhdenie russkoi ody, posledniaia chetvert' XVII–nachalo XVIII veka* (Moscow: Institut rossiiskoi istorii RAN, 2012)

Bogdanov, V. P., and Karpiuk, G. V., *Ot azbuki Ivana Fedorova do sovremennogo bukvaria* (Moscow: Prosveshchenie, 1974)

Bogoiavlenskii, S. K., *Moskovskii prikaznyi apparat i deloproizvodstvo XVI–XVII vekov*, ed. and introd. S. O. Shmidt (Moscow: Iazyki slavianskoi kul'tury, 2006)

Bogoiavlenskii, S. K., and Novitskii, G. A. (eds.), *Gosudarstvennaia Oruzheinaia palata Moskovskogo Kremlia. Sbornik nauchnykh trudov po materialam Gosudarstvennoi Oruzheinoi palaty* (Moscow: Iskusstvo, 1954)

Bondarenko, A. F., *Istoriia kolokolov Rossii XI–XVII vv.* (Moscow: Russkaia panorama, 2012)

Iz istorii kolokolov Rossii. Izbrannye trudy po otechestvennoi kampanologii (Moscow: Russkaia panorama, 2014)

Kolokola v miniatiurakh Litsevogo letopisogo svoda XVI v. (Moscow: Russkaia panorama, 2014)

Borisova, T. S., 'Graviura na metalle v russkikh rukopisiakh XVI v.', in *Drevnerusskoe iskusstvo. Russkoe iskusstvo pozdnego srednevekov'ia. XVI vek*, ed. A. L. Batalov et al. (St Petersburg: Dmitrii Bulanin, 2003), 440–54

Bowers, Katherine, 'Unpacking Viazemskii's *Khalat*: The Technologies of Dilettantism in Early Nineteenth-Century Russian Literary Culture', *Slavic Review*, 74.3 (Fall 2015), 529–52

'Experiencing Information: An Early Nineteenth-Century Stroll Along Nevskii Prospekt', in Franklin and Bowers (eds.), *Information and Empire*, 369–407

Braat, J. et al. (eds.), *Russians and Dutchmen* (Baltic Studies, 2; Groningen: Institute for Northern and Eastern European Studies, 1993)

Brekle, Herbert E., 'Das typographische Prinzip. Versuch einer Begriffsklärung', *Gutenberg-Jahrbuch*, 72 (1997), 58–63

Brogi Bercoff, Giovanna, 'Plurilingualism in Russia and in the Ruthenian Lands in the Seventeenth and Eighteenth Centuries: The Case of Stefan Javors'kyj', in Ivanov and Verkholantsev (eds.), *Speculum Slaviae orientalis*, 9–20

Brown, Peter B., 'Muscovite Government Bureaus', *Russian History*, 10.3 (1983), 269–330

'How Muscovy Governed: Seventeenth-Century Russian Central Administration', *Russian History*, 36 (2009), 459–529

Brown, William Edward, *A History of Seventeenth-Century Russian Literature* (Ann Arbor: Ardis, 1980)

Bruni, Flavia, 'Early Modern Broadsheets Between Archives and Libraries: Towards a Possible Integration', in Pettegree (ed.), *Broadsheets*, 33–54

Budaragina, O. V., *Latinskie nadpisi v Peterburge* (St Petersburg: Kolo, 2016)

Buganov, V. I., *Razriadnye knigi poslednei chetverti XV–nachala XVII v.* (Moscow: AN SSSR, 1962)

Bulanin, D. M., *Perevody i poslaniia Maksima Greka* (Leningrad: Nauka, 1984)

'Pis'movniki', in *SKKDR. Vyp. 2. Chast' 2*, 188–93

'Skazanie izvestno o voobrazhenii knig pechatnogo dela', in *SKKDR. XVII v. Chast' 3*, 388–90

Bulychev, A. A., *Istoriia odnoi politicheskoi kampanii XVII veka* (Moscow: Iazyki slavianskoi kul'tury, 2004)

'Neskol'ko zamechanii o tak nazyvaemykh razreshitel'nykh gramotakh', *Russica romana*, 16 (2009), 9–36

Buraeva, O. V., 'Knizhnye marginalii zabaikal'skikh staroobriadtsev: proiskhozhdenie, forma, razmeshchenie', in *Staroobriadchestvo: istoriia i sovremennost', mestnye traditsii, russkie i zarubezhnye sviazi* (Ulan-Ude: Izdatel'stvo Buriatskogo gosudarstvennogo universiteta, 2015), 272–7

Bushkovitch, Paul, *Religion and Society in Russia: The Sixteenth and Seventeenth Centuries* (Oxford University Press, 1992)

Campa, Pedro F., 'Emblem Books in Russia', in Peter M. Daly (ed.), *Companion to Emblem Studies* (New York: AMS Press, 2008), 309–21

Carter, John, 'William Ged and the Invention of Stereotype', *The Library*, 5th series, 15 (1960), 161–92

Castells, Manuel, *The Information Age: Economy, Society and Culture*, 3 vols.; 2nd edn with new preface (Chichester: Wiley-Blackwell, 2010)

Certeau, Michel de, *The Practice of Everyday Life*, transl. Stephen Rendall (Berkeley: University of California Press, 1984)

Chekunova, A. E., *Russkoe kirillicheskoe pis'mo XI–XVIII vv. Uchebnoe posobie* (Moscow: RGGU, 2010)

Chentsova, V. G., 'Tsarskie sabli, saadak i pastyrskii posokh: k istorii veshchei iz Muzeev Moskovskogo Kremlia, privezennykh s Khristianskogo Vostoka v seredine XVII v.', *Kapterevskie chteniia*, 7 (2009), 234–49

Ikona Iverskoi Bogomateri (ocherki istorii otnoshenii grecheskoi tserkvi s Rossiei s serediny XVII v. po dokumentam RGADA) (Moscow: Indrik, 2010)

Chernaia, L. A., 'Verkhniaia tipografiia Simeona Polotskogo', in Robinson (ed.), *Simeon Polotskii i ego knigoizdatel'skaia deiatel'nost'*, 46–59

Chernov, V. A., *Russkii iazyk v XVII veke. Morfologiia* (Izdatel'stvo Krasnoiarskogo universiteta, 1984)

Cherepnin, L. V., *Russkaia paleografiia* (Moscow: Gosudarstvennoe izdatel'stvo politicheskoi literatury, 1956)

Chernukha, V. G., *Pasport v Rossii 1719–1917* (St Petersburg: Liki Rossii, 2007)

Chesnokova, N. P., 'Relikvii khristianskogo Vostoka v Rossii v seredine XVII veka (po materialam Posol'skogo prikaza)', *Vestnik tserkovnoi istorii*, 2.6 (2007), 91–128

'Dokumenty po istorii ital'ianskoi shkoly v Moskve (1697–1700 gg.): opyt sravnitel'nogo analiza', *Kapterevskie chteniia*, 9 (2011), 281–321

Chistovich, I. A., *Istoriia perevoda Biblii na russkii iazyk*, 2nd edn (St Petersburg: M. M. Stasulevich, 1899)

Choldin, Marianna Tax, *A Fence Around the Empire: Russian Censorship of Western Ideas Under the Tsars* (Durham: Duke University Press, 1985)

Chrissidis, Nikolaos A., *An Academy at the Court of the Tsars: Greek Scholars and Jesuit Education in Early Modern Russia* (DeKalb: Northern Illinois University Press, 2016)

'Between Forgiveness and Indulgence: Funerary Prayers of Absolution in Russia', in Nickolas Lupinin, Donald Ostrowski and Jennifer B. Spock (eds.), *The Tapestry of Russian Christianity: Studies in History and Culture* (Columbus: Ohio State University, 2016), 261–93

Collis, Robert, *The Petrine Instauration: Religion, Esotericism and Science at the Court of Peter the Great, 1689–1725* (Leiden and Boston: Brill, 2012)

Costas, Benito Rial (ed.), *Print Cultures and Peripheries in Early Modern Europe* (Leiden and Boston: Brill, 2013)

Coudenis, Wim, 'Translation and the Emergence of History as an Academic Discipline in Eighteenth-Century Russia', *Kritika*, 17.4 (Fall 2016), 721–52

Cracraft, James, *The Petrine Revolution in Russian Imagery* (University of Chicago Press, 1997)

The Petrine Revolution in Russian Culture (Cambridge, MA: Belknap Press of Harvard University Press, 2004)

Crick, Julia, and Walsham, Alexandra (eds.), *The Uses of Script and Print, 1300–1700* (Cambridge University Press, 2004)

Cross, Anthony G., 'George Borrow and Russia', *Modern Language Review*, 64 (1969), 363–71

By the Banks of the Neva: Chapters from the Lives and Careers of the British in Eighteenth-Century Russia (Cambridge University Press, 2007)

St Petersburg and the British: The City Through the Eyes of British Visitors and Residents (London: Frances Lincoln Ltd, 2008)

'English – A Serious Challenge to French in the Reign of Alexander I?', *Russian Review*, 74.1 (Jan. 2015), 57–68

Dadykin, A. V., 'Prikaz knigopechatnogo dela i sotrudniki Moskovskogo pechatnogo dvora vo vtoroi polovine XVII v.', in *MPD – fakt i faktor. 1652–1700. Kniga 1*, 129–70

Dahmen [formerly Koch], Kristine, 'The Use, Functions and Spread of German in Eighteenth-Century Russia', *Russian Review*, 74.1 (Jan. 2015), 20–40

Davidson, Peter, 'The Inscribed House', in Michael Bath, Pedro F. Campa and Daniel S. Russell (eds.), *Emblem Studies in Honour of Peter M. Daly* (Saecula spiritualia, 41; Baden-Baden: Valentin Koerner, 2002), 41–62

Debray, Régis, *Cours de médiologie générale* (Paris: Gallimard, 2001)

'Socialism: A Life-Cycle', *New Left Review*, 46 (Jul.–Aug. 2007), 5–28

Demidova, N. F., 'Biurokratizatsiia gosudarstvennogo apparata absoliutizma v XVII–XVIII vv.', in N. M. Druzhinin (ed.), *Absoliutizm v Rossii (XVII–XVIII vv.). Sbornik statei* (Moscow: Nauka, 1964), 206–42

Sluzhilaia biurokratiia v Rossii XVII v. i ee rol' v formirovanii absoliutizma (Moscow: Nauka, 1987)

Sluzhilaia biurokratiia v Rossii XVII veka (1625–1700). Biograficheskii spravochnik (Moscow: Pamiatniki istoricheskoi mysli, 2011)

Demin, A. S., 'Russkie staropechatnye posleslovia vtoroi poloviny XVI v. (otrazhenie nedoveriia chitatelei k pechatnoi knige)', in Demin et al. (eds.), *Tematika i stilistika predislovii i posleslovii*, 45–70

Demin, A. S., et al. (eds.), *Tematika i stilistika predislovii i posleslovii* (Moscow: Nauka, 1981)

Denis, Vincent, *Une histoire de l'identité. France, 1715–1815* (Seyssel: Champ Vallon, 2008)

Dianova, T. V., 'Staropechatnyi ornament', in *Drevnerusskoe iskusstvo. Rukopisnaia kniga: sbornik vtoroi*, ed. O. I. Podobedova (Moscow: Nauka, 1974), 296–335

Dittmar, Jeremiah E., 'Information Technology and Economic Change: The Impact of the Printing Press', *Quarterly Journal of Economics*, 126.3 (2011), 1133–72

Dixon, Simon, *The Modernisation of Russia 1676–1825* (Cambridge University Press, 1999)

Dlugolenskii, Ia. N., *Voenno-grazhdanskaia i politseiskaia vlast' Sankt-Peterburga, 1703–1917* (St Petersburg: Zhurnal 'Neva', 2001)

Dmitrieva, Nina, and Argent, Gesine, 'The Coexistence of Russian and French in the First Third of the Nineteenth Century: Bilingualism With or Without

Diglossia?', in Offord, Ryazanova-Clarke, Rjéoutski and Argent (eds.), *French and Russian in Imperial Russia*, vol. II, 228–42
Dmitrieva, R. P., 'Medovartsev, Mikhail', in *SKKDR. Vyp. 2, Chast' 2*, 109–13
Dmitrievskii, A. A., *Ispravlenie knig pri Patriarkhe Nikone i posleduiushchikh patriarkhakh*, [ed. A. G. Kravetskii] (Moscow: Iazyki slavianskoi kul'tury, 2004)
'Novye dannye po ispravleniiu bogosluzhebnykh knig v Moskve v XVII i XVIII vv.', [ed. Olga B. Strakhov], *Palaeoslavica*, 12.2 (2004), 71–197
Dolgova, S. R., 'O pervykh vladel'tsakh chastnykh tipografii v Rossii (I. M. Gartung i I. K. Shnor)', *Kniga. Issledovaniia i materialy*, 32 (1976), 178–80
Donskoi, G. G., 'Proklamativnaia funktsiia nadpisi na kolokol'ne Novospasskogo monastyria', *Voprosy epigrafiki*, 7.2 (2013), 199–205
Drage, C. L., *Russian Word-Play Poetry from Simeon Polotskii to Derzhavin* (London: School of Slavonic and East European Studies, 1993)
'Russian Model Conversations, c. 1630–1773', in Bartlett and Hughes (eds.), *Russian Society and Culture in the Long Eighteenth Century*, 149–66
Dumschatt, Sabine, *Ausländische Mediziner im Moskauer Rußland* (Quellen und Studien zur Geschichte des östlichen Europa, 67; Stuttgart: Franz Steiner Verlag, 2006)
Durov, V. A., *Ordena Rossii. Orders of Russia* (Moscow: Voskresen'e, 1993)
Edmonds, Mary Jaene, *Samplers and Sampler Makers: An American Schoolgirl Art 1700–1850* (Los Angeles and London: Charles Letts, 1991)
Edwards, Joan, *Sampler Making 1540–1940: The Fifth of Joan Edwards' Small Books on the History of Embroidery* (Dorking: Bayford Books, 1983)
Efimova: *see* Yefimova
Eisenstein, Elizabeth L., *The Printing Press as an Agent of Change*, 2 vols. (Cambridge University Press, 1979)
The Printing Revolution in Early Modern Europe, 2nd edn (Cambridge University Press, 2005)
Eisermann, Falk, 'Fifty Thousand Veronicas: Print Runs of Broadsheets in the Fifteenth and Early Sixteenth Centuries', in Pettegree (ed.), *Broadsheets*, 76–113
Emery, Jacob, 'Species of Legitimacy: The Rhetoric of Succession Around Russian Coins', *Slavic Review*, 75.1 (Spring 2016), 1–21
Eremeeva, Svetlana, *Pamiati pamiatnikov. Praktika monumental'noi kommemoratsii v Rossii XIX–nachala XX v.* (Moscow: RGGU, 2015)
Erler, Mary C., 'Pasted-In Embellishments in English Manuscripts and Printed Books, *c.* 1480–1533', *The Library*, 6th series, 14.3 (Sep. 1992), 185–206
Esipov, G. V., *Tiazhelaia pamiat' proshlogo. Rasskazy iz del Tainoi Kantseliarii i drugikh arkhivov* (St Petersburg: A. S. Suvorin, 1885)
Eskin, Iu. M., 'Pechati chlenov Boiarskoi Dumy v 1633 godu. K istorii russkoi "predgeral'diki"', *Russia mediaevalis*, 10.1 (2001), 205–23
Fafurin, G. A., *K istorii akademicheskoi torgovli v Rossii v epokhu Ekateriny II: deiatel'nost' Ioganna Veitbrekhta v Sankt-Peterburge* (Peterburgskoe lingvisticheskoe obshchestvo, 2010)

Febvre, Lucien, and Martin, Henri-Jean, *The Coming of the Book*, transl. David Gerard (London: Verso, 1997)

Fedorov-Davydov, G. A., *Monety Moskovskoi Rusi (Moskva v bor'be za nezavisimoe i tsentralizovannoe gosudarstvo)* (Izd. Moskovskogo universiteta, 1981)

Fedotov, O. I., *Osnovy russkogo stikhoslozheniia. Teoriia i istoriia russkogo stikha. Kniga 1. Metrika i ritmika* (Moscow: Flinta; Nauka, 2002)

Filyushkin, Alexander, 'Why Did Muscovy Not Participate in the "Communication Revolution" in the Sixteenth Century? Causes and Effects', *CASS*, 51.2–3 (2017), 339–50

Finkelstein, David, and McCleery, Alistair, *An Introduction to Book History* (New York and London: Routledge, 2005)

Flier, Michael, 'K semioticheskomu analizu Zolotoi palaty Moskovskogo Kremlia', in *Drevnerusskoe iskusstvo. Russkoe iskusstvo pozdnego srednevekov'ia. XVI vek*, ed. A. L. Batalov et al. (St Petersburg: Dmitrii Bulanin, 2003), 178–87

Florovskii, A. V., 'Frantsisk Skorina v Moskve', *TODRL*, 24 (1969), 155–8

Fonkich, B. L., *Grecheskie rukopisi i dokumenty v Rossii v XIV–nachale XVIII v.* (Moscow: Indrik, 2003)

Greko-slavianskie shkoly v Moskve v XVII veke (Moscow: Iazyki slavianskikh kul'tur, 2009)

Franklin, Simon, *Writing, Society and Culture in Early Rus, c. 950–1300* (Cambridge University Press, 2002)

'Printing Moscow: Significances of the Frontispiece to the 1663 Bible', *SEER*, 88 (2010), 73–95

'Mapping the Graphosphere: Cultures of Writing in Early Nineteenth-Century Russia (and Before)', *Kritika*, 12.3 (Summer 2011), 531–60

'Printing and Social Control in Russia 1: Passports', *Russian History*, 37 (2010), 208–37

'Printing and Social Control in Russia 2: Decrees', *Russian History*, 38 (2011), 467–92

'Printing and Social Control in Russia 3: Blank Forms', *Russian History*, 42 (2015), 114–35

'K voprosu o malykh zhanrakh kirillicheskoi pechati', in D. N. Ramazanova (ed.), *450 let Apostolu Ivana Fedorova. Istoriia rannego knigopechataniia v Rossii (pamiatniki, istochniki, traditsii izucheniia)* (Moscow: Pashkov dom, 2016), 421–32

'Three Types of Asymmetry in the Muscovite Engagement with Print', *CASS*, 51 (2017), 351–75

'Information in Plain Sight: The Formation of the Public Graphosphere', in Franklin and Bowers (eds.), *Information and Empire*, 341–67

Franklin, Simon, and Bowers, Katherine (eds.), *Information and Empire: Mechanisms of Communication in Russia 1600–1850* (Cambridge: Open Book Publishing, 2017)

Frick, David A., 'Sailing to Byzantium: Greek Texts and the Establishment of Authority in Early Modern Muscovy', *HUS*, 19 (1995; publ. 1997), 138–57

Gaidukov, P. G., and Grishin, I. V., 'Imennye den'gi velikogo kniazia Dmitriia Ivanovicha Donskogo (tipologiia i khronologiia)', in *Velikii Novgorod i srednevekovaia Rus'. Sbornik statei k 80-letiiu akademika V. L. Ianina* (Moscow: Pamiatniki istoricheskoi mysli, 2009), 323–64

Garrioch, David, 'House Names, Shop Signs and Social Organization in West European Cities, c. 1500–1900', *Urban History*, 21.1 (Apr. 1994), 20–48

Gavrilov, S. A., 'Borisoglebskii krest 1467 g.', *Sovetskaia arkheologiia*, 1985.2, 213–22

Gippius, A. A., 'Russkoe "neknizhnoe" zhitie Nikolaia Chudotvortsa v iazykovoi situatsii Litovskoi i Moskovskoi Rusi XV–XVII vv.', in Ivanov and Verkholantsev (eds.), *Speculum Slaviae orientalis*, 68–83

Girshberg, V. B., 'Nadpis' mastera Poviliki', *Sovetskaia arkheologiia*, 1959.2, 248–9

Gitelman, Lisa, *Paper Knowledge: Towards a Media History of Documents* (Durham and London: Duke University Press, 2014)

Glagoleva, Olga E., *Working with Russian Archival Documents: A Guide to Modern Handwriting, Document Forms, Language Patterns and Other Related Topics* (University of Toronto, 1998)

Glinternik, Eleonora, *Reklama v Rossii XVIII–pervoi poloviny XX veka* (St Petersburg: Avrora, 2007)

Gol'dberg, T. G., 'Iz posol'skikh darov XVI–XVII vekov. Angliiskoe serebro', in Bogoiavlenskii and Novitskii (eds.), *Gosudarstvennaia Oruzheinaia palata*, 435–506

Gol'dberg, T. G., Mishukov, F. Ia., Platonova, N. G., and Postnikova-Loseva, M. M., *Russkoe zolotoe i serebrianoe delo XV–XX vekov* (Moscow: Nauka, 1967)

Golubinskii, Aleksei, 'New Technology and the Mapping of Empire: The Adoption of the Astrolabe', in Franklin and Bowers (eds.), *Information and Empire*, 59–74

Goody, Jack, *The Domestication of the Savage Mind* (Cambridge University Press, 1977)

The Logic of Writing and the Organization of Society (Cambridge University Press, 1986)

Gorbatova, I. V., 'K voprosu o tak nazyvaemoi "aptekarskoi posude Petra Velikogo"', in A. K. Levykin (ed.), *Dekorativno-prikladnoe iskusstvo Zapadnoi Evropy* (Moscow: Moskovskii Kreml', 2006), 264–71

Gordeeva, M. Iu., 'Zarozhdenie chastnogo knigopechataniia v Rossii (po materialam senatskikh ukazov)', in V. P. Leonov (ed.), *Kniga v Rossii. Sbornik 1* (Moscow: Nauka, 2006), 147–56

Gorshkov, Iu. A., *Ekonomicheskaia modernizatsiia knizhnogo dela v Rossii XVIII–pervoi poloviny XIX v.* (Moscow: Pashkov dom, 2009)

Grafton, Anthony T., 'The Importance of Being Printed', *Journal of Interdisciplinary History*, 11.2 (Autumn 1980), 265–86

Grashchenkov, A. V., 'Plita s latinskoi nadpis'iu so Spasskoi bashni i titul gosudaria vseia Rusi', *Voprosy epigrafiki*, 1 (2006), 16–25

Grechanaia, E. P., *Kogda Rossiia govorila po-frantsuzski: russkaia literatura na frantsuzskom iazyke (XVIII–pervaia polovina XIX veka)* (Moscow: IMLI RAN, 2010)

Gribov, Iu. A., 'Rukopisnyi Sinodik s ksilograficheskimi illiustratsiiami – pamiatnik russkoi knizhnosti nachala XVIII v.', in *Zabelinskie nauchnye chteniia – 1999* (Trudy Gosudarstvennogo istoricheskogo muzeiia, 121; Moscow: Gosudarstvennyi istoricheskii muzei, 2000), 75–102

Griffin, Clare, 'The Production and Consumption of Medical Knowledge in Seventeenth-Century Russia: The Apothecary Chancery' (unpublished Ph.D. thesis, University College London, 2012)

Gritsevskaia, I. M., *Chtenie i chet'i sborniki v drevnerusskikh monastyriakh XV–XVII vv.* (St Petersburg: Dmitrii Bulanin, 2012)

Grmek, Mirko, 'The History of Medical Education in Russia', in C. D. O'Malley (ed.), *The History of Medical Education* (UCLA Forum in Medical Sciences, 12; Berkeley, Los Angeles and London: University of California Press, 1970), 303–27

Grombakh, S. M., *Russkaia meditsinskaia literatura XVIII veka* (Moscow: Akademiia meditsinskikh nauk, 1953)

Grove, Laurence, '"Pour faire tapisserie"?/Moveable Woodcuts: Print/Manuscript, Text/Image at the Birth of the Emblem', in David Graham (ed.), *The Emblematic Age in France: Essays in Honour of Daniel S. Russell* (Glasgow Emblem Studies, 2001), 95–119

Gusev, D. V., '"Obmanka" G. N. Teplova i neizvestnye fakty ego biografii', *Istoricheskii format*, 2016.1, 303–24

Guseva, A. A., 'Oformlenie izdanii Simeona Polotskogo v Verkhnei tipografii (1679–1683 gg.)', *TODRL*, 38 (1985), 457–75

Rabota s redkimi i tsennymi izdaniiami. Identifikatsiia ekzempliarov moskovskikh izdanii kirillovskogo shrifta 2-i poloviny XVI–XVII vv. Metodicheskie rekomendatsii (Moscow: GBL, 1990)

H. H., 'Die Entwicklung und Reform des deutschen Passwesens', *Deutsche Vierteljahrs-Schrift*, 29.1 (1866), 219–53

Hamburg, Gary M., *Russia's Path Toward Enlightenment: Faith, Politics, and Reason, 1500–1801* (New Haven: Yale University Press, 2016)

Harris, Michael, 'Printed Ephemera', in Michael F. Suarez and H. R. Woodhuysen (eds.), *The Book: A Global History* (Oxford University Press, 2013), 204–19

Hartley, Janet, 'Education and the East: The Omsk Asiatic School', in Maria Di Salvo, Valerie A. Kivelson and Daniel H. Kaiser (eds.), *Word and Image in Russian History: Essays in Honor of Gary Marker* (Boston: Academic Studies Press, 2015), 253–68

d'Hartoy, Maurice, *Histoire du passeport français. Depuis l'antiquité jusqu'à nos jours* (Paris: Librairie ancienne Honoré Champion, 1937)

Hennings, Jan, *Russia and Courtly Europe: Ritual and the Culture of Diplomacy, 1648–1725* (Cambridge University Press, 2016)

Higgs, Edward, *The Information State in England: The Central Collection of Information on Citizens Since 1500* (Basingstoke: Palgrave Macmillan, 2004)
'Personal Identification as Information Flows in England, 1500–2000', in Weller (ed.), *Information History in the Modern World*, 13–30
Hobart, Michael E., and Schiffman, Zachary S., *Information Ages: Literacy, Numeracy, and the Computer Revolution* (Baltimore and London: Johns Hopkins University Press, 1998)
Horstmeier, C., et al. (eds.), *Around Peter the Great: Three Centuries of Russian–Dutch Relations* (Baltic Studies, 4; Groningen: Institute for Northern and Eastern European Studies, 1997)
Howsam, Leslie, *Cheap Bibles: Nineteenth-Century Publishing and the British and Foreign Bible Society* (Cambridge University Press, 1991)
Hughes, Lindsey, *Russia and the West: The Life of a Seventeenth-Century Westernizer, Prince Vasily Vasil'evich Golitsyn (1643–1714)* (Newtonville, MA: Oriental Research Partners, 1984)
Russia in the Age of Peter the Great (New Haven and London: Yale University Press, 2000)
'"A Beard Is an Unnecessary Burden": Peter I's Laws on Shaving and Their Roots in Early Russia', in Bartlett and Hughes (eds.), *Russian Culture and Society in the Long Eighteenth Century*, 21–34
Humphrey, Carol, *Samplers* (Cambridge University Press, 1997)
Hussen, Arend H. Jnr, 'Catherine the Great's Instruction (Nakaz) to Her Legislative Commission: The Dutch Translations of 1769 and 1794', in Waegemans (ed.), *Russia and the Low Countries*, 245–56
Igoshev, V. V., *Iaroslavskoe serebro XVI–XVIII vv.* (Moscow: Modus graffiti, 1997)
Dragotsennaia tserkovnaia utvar' XVI–XVII vv. Velikii Novgorod. Iaroslavl'. Sol'vychegodsk (Moscow: Indrik, 2009)
Stroganovskoe khudozhestvennoe serebro XVI–XVIII vekov (Moscow: BuksMArt, 2018)
Imperatorskii farforovyi zavod 1744–1904 (St Petersburg: Sankt-Peterburg orkestr, 2003)
Isachenko, T. A., *Perevodnaia moskovskaia knizhnost' XV–XVII vv.* (Moscow: Pashkov dom, 2009)
Isaievych, Iaroslav, 'Greek Culture in the Ukraine: 1550–1650', *Modern Greek Studies Yearbook*, 6 (1990), 97–122
Iukht, A. I., *Russkie den'gi ot Petra Velikogo do Aleksandra I* (Moscow: Finansy i statistika, 1994)
Iurchyshyn, Oksana, 'Antyminsy Gravera Illi', *Rodovid*, 3.12 (1995), 20–8
Iurchyshyn: *see also* Yurchyshyn-Smith
Iurova, Elena, 'Vyshivka v inter'ere russkogo bidermeier', *Pinakoteka*, 4 (1998), 90–6
Ivanov, A. I., *Literaturnoe nasledie Maksima Greka* (Leningrad: Nauka, 1969)
Ivanov, V. I., *Bukhgalterskii uchet v Rossii XVI–XVII vv.: istoriko-istochnikovedcheskoe issledovanie monastyrskikh prikhodo-raskhodnykh knig* (St Petersburg: Dmitrii Bulanin, 2005)

Ivanov, Vyacheslav V., and Verkholantsev, Julia (eds.), *Speculum Slaviae orientalis: Muscovy, Ruthenia and Lithuania in the Late Middle Ages* (UCLA Slavic Studies. New Series, 4 (Moscow: Novoe izdatel'stvo, 2005)

Jackson, H. J., *Marginalia: Readers Writing in Books* (New Haven and London: Yale University Press, 2001)

Jekutch [Iekush], Ulrike, 'Nemetskoiazychnaia okkazional'naia literatura v Rossii XVIII veka', in P. Bukharkin, Jekutch and N. Kochetkova (eds.), *Okkazional'naia literatura v kontekste prazdnichnoi kul'tury Rossii XVIII veka* (St Petersburg: Filologicheskii fakul'tet SPbGU, 2010), 93–106

Jensen, Claudia, and Maier, Ingrid, 'Orpheus and Pickleherring in the Kremlin: The "Ballet" for the Tsar of February 1672', *Scando-Slavica*, 59.2 (2013), 145–84

'Pickleherring Returns to the Kremlin: More New Sources on the Pre-History of the Russian Court Theatre', *Scando-Slavica* 61.1 (2015), 7–56

Kachalkin, A. N., *Zhanry russkogo dokumenta dopetrovskoi epokhi* (Izdatel'stvo MGU, 1988)

'Nazvaniia dopetrovskikh delovykh tekstov', *Russkaia rech'*, 2.2 (2002), 73–80

Kachalov, N. N., *Steklo* (Moscow: AN SSSR, 1959)

Kaganov, Grigory, *Images of Space: St. Petersburg in the Verbal and Visual Arts*, transl. Sidney Monas (Stanford University Press, 1997)

Kaldor, Ivan L.,'The Genesis of the Russian "Grazhdanskii shrift" or Civil Type', *Journal of Typographic Research*, 3.4 (Oct. 1969), 315–44, and 4.2 (Spring 1970), 111–38

Kaliazina, N. V., and Komelova, G. N., *Russkoe iskusstvo petrovskoi epokhi* (Leningrad: Khudozhnik RSFSR, 1990)

Kameneva, T. N., 'Knigopechatanie v Chernigove (1646–1818)', *Problemy istochnikovedeniia*, 8 (1959), 267–313

Kamentseva, E. I., and Ustiugov, N. V., *Russkaia sfragistika i geral'dika* (Moscow: Vysshaia shkola, 1974)

Karimullin, A. G., 'Iz istorii tatarskoi knigi XVIII–pervoi poloviny XIX v.', *Kniga. Issledovaniia i materialy*, 18 (1969), 126–53

U istokov tatarskoi knigi. Ot nachala vozniknoveniia do 60-kh godov XIX veka, 2nd, corrected edn (Kazan: Tatarskoe knizhnoe izdatel'stvo, 1992)

Kashtanov, S. M., *Russkaia diplomatika* (Moscow: Vysshaia shkola, 1970)

'K istorii russko-grecheskikh kul'turnykh sviazei v XVI v.', in *Moskhovia I. Problemy vizantiiskoi i novogrecheskoi filologii. K 60-letiiu B. L. Fonkicha* (Moscow: Indrik, 2001), 209–17

Kazakova, E. N., 'Apostol 1644 g.: k probleme donikonovskoi knizhnoi spravy', in E. M. Iukhimenko (ed.), *Patriarkh Nikon i ego vremia. Sbornik nauchnykh trudov* (Moscow: Gosudarstvennyi istoricheskii muzei, 2004), 162–74

Keenan, Edward L., 'Ivan the Terrible and Book Culture: Fact, Fancy, and Fog. Remarks on Early Muscovite Printing', *Solanus*, 18 (2004), 28–50

Keenan, Paul, 'The Summer Gardens in the Social Life of St Petersburg, 1725–1761', *SEER*, 88 (2010), 134–55

Kharlamov, V. I., 'Metodicheskie i istochnikovedcheskie problemy sozdaniia spravochnykh posobii o rossiiskikh izdatel'stvakh XIX–XX vekov', in *Knizhnoe delo v Rossii v XIX–nachale XX veka. Vypusk 14. Sbornik nauchnykh trudov* (St Petersburg: RNB, 2008), 141–9

Khoteev, P. I., 'Frantsuzskaia kniga v biblioteke Peterburgskoi Akademii nauk (1714–1742 gg.)', in Luppov (ed.), *Frantsuzskaia kniga v Rossii*, 5–58

Nemetskaia kniga i russkii chitatel' v pervoi polovine XVIII veka (St Petersburg: Biblioteka RAN, 2008)

Khromov, O. R., 'Russkaia rukopisnaia kniga s graviurami v kontekste obshcheevropeiskoi knizhnoi kul'tury XVII–XVIII vv. (spetsifika i obshchie tendentsii oformleniia zhanra)', in *Berkovskie chteniia 2011. Knizhnaia kul'tura v kontekste mezhdunarodnykh kontaktov* (Minsk: Tsentral'naia nauchnaia biblioteka NAN Belorusi; Moscow: Nauka, 2011), 375–9

'Ob odnom listovom (letuchem) izdanii Moskovskogo pechatnogo dvora', in *Rumiantsevskie chteniia, 15. Materialy mezhdunarodnoi nauchnoi konferentsii (14–15 aprelia 2015)* (Moscow: Pashkov dom, 2015), Chast' 2, 207–20

Kiselev, I. A., *Datirovka kirpichnykh kladok XVI–XIX vv. Po vizual'nym kharakteristikam* (Moscow: Ministerstvo kul'tury RSFSR, 'Rosrestavratsiia', 1990)

Kiselev, N. P., 'O moskovskom knigopechatanii XVII veka', *Kniga. Issledovaniia i materialy*, 2 (1960), 123–86

'Grecheskaia pechat' na Ukraine v XVI veke. Ivan Fedorov i ego posledovateli', *Kniga. Issledovaniia i materialy*, 7 (1962), 171–98

'Proiskhozhdenie moskovskogo staropechatnogo ornamenta', *Kniga. Issledovaniia i materialy*, 11 (1965), 167–98

Kislova, E. I., 'Nemetskii iazyk v russkikh seminariiakh XVIII veka: iz istorii kul'turnykh kontaktov', *Vestnik PSTGU III: Filologiia*, 2015.1(41), 53–70

'"Latin" and "Slavonic" Education in the Primary Classes of Russian Seminaries in the Eighteenth Century', *Slověne*, 4.2 (2015), 72–91

Kivelson, Valerie, *Desperate Magic: The Moral Economy of Witchcraft in Seventeenth-Century Russia* (Ithaca and London: Cornell University Press, 2013)

Klepikov, S. A., 'Iz istorii russkogo khudozhestvennogo perepleta', *Kniga. Issledovaniia i materialy*, 1 (1959), 98–168

'Russkie gravirovannye knigi XVII–XVIII vekov', *Kniga. Issledovaniia i materialy*, 9 (1964), 141–77

Kloss, B. M., *O proiskhozhdenii nazvaniia 'Rossiia'* (Moscow: Rukopisnye pamiatniki Drevnei Rusi, 2012)

Kniazevskaia, T. B. et al. (eds.), *Rukopisnaia i pechatnaia kniga* (Moscow: Nauka, 1975)

Knight, Leah, 'Writing on Early Modern Trees', *English Literary Renaissance*, 41 (2011), 462–84

Koch, Kristine, *Deutsch als Fremdsprache im Russland des 18. Jahrhunderts* (Berlin and New York: Walter de Gruyter, 2002)

Koch: *see also* Dahmen

Kollmann, Nancy Shields, 'Marking the Body in Early Modern Judicial Punishment', *HUS*, 28 (2006), 557–65

Crime and Punishment in Early Modern Russia (Cambridge University Press, 2012)

The Russian Empire 1450–1801 (Oxford University Press, 2017)

Komochev, N. A., *Tsarskie zhalovannye gramoty svetskim litsam (1613–1696): istochnikovedcheskoe issledovanie* (Moscow: RGGU, 2016)

Kopanev, N. A., 'Rasprostranenie inostrannoi knigi v Peterburge v pervoi polovine XVIII v. (Po materialam akademicheskikh knizhnykh katalogov)', in Luppov (ed.), *Russkie knigi i biblioteki*, 38–53

'Rasprostranenie frantsuzskoi knigi v Moskve v seredine XVIII v.', in Luppov (ed.), *Frantsuzskaia kniga v Rossii*, 59–172

Kopreeva, T. N., 'Zapadnye istochniki v rabote novgorodskikh knizhnikov kontsa XV–nachala XVI v.', *Fedorovskie chteniia 1979* (Moscow: Nauka, 1982), 138–52

Kornicki, P. F., 'Manuscript, Not Print: Scribal Culture in the Edo Period', *Journal of Japanese Studies*, 32.1 (2006), 23–52

Korotkii, V. G., 'Meletii', in *SKKDR. XVII v. Chast 2*, 346–50

Kosheleva, Olga, '"Bez pashportov i s vorovskimi pashporty" ili mozhno li obmanut' gosudarstvennyi kontrol'?', in O. I. Togoeva and Kosheleva (eds.), *Obman kak povsednevnaia praktika. Individual'nye i kollektivnye strategii povedeniia* (Moscow: Institut vseobshchei istorii RAN, 2016), 323–43

Kostin, Andrei A., 'Acribiia i ameleiia, ili Gde *byt' dobroi zemle?* (grammatika Adodurova v kontekste i bez)', *Slověne*, 2006.1, 263–99

Kostiukhina, L. M., *Knizhnoe pis'mo v Rossii XVII v.* (Moscow: Gosudarstvennyi Istoricheskii muzei, 1974)

'Novovizantiiskii ornament', in *Drevnerusskoe iskusstvo. Rukopisnaia kniga: sbornik vtoroi*, ed. O. I. Podobedova (Moscow: Nauka, 1974), 265–95

Paleografiia russkikh rukopisnykh knig XV–XVII vv. Russkii poluustav (Trudy Gosudarstvennogo Istoricheskogo muzeiia, 108; Moscow: Gosudarstvennyi Istoricheskii muzei, 1999)

Kotilaine, Jarmo, and Poe, Marshall (eds.), *Modernizing Muscovy: Reform and Social Change in Seventeenth-Century Russia* (London: RoutledgeCurzon, 2004)

Kovrigina, V. A., *Nemetskaia sloboda Moskvy i ee zhiteli v kontse XVII–pervoi chetverti XVIII vv.* (Moscow: Arkheograficheskii tsentr, 1998)

Kozhin, A. N., *Literaturnyi iazyk Moskovskoi Rusi* (Moscow: Russkii iazyk, 1984)

Kraft, Ekkehard, *Moskaus griechisches Jahrhundert: russisch-griechische Beziehungen und metabyzantinischer Einfluss 1619–1694* (Quellen und Studien zur Geschichte des östlichen Europas, 43; Stuttgart: Franz Steiner Verlag, 1995)

Krasilin, Mikhail, 'Russkaia ikona XVIII–nachala XX vekov', in Liliia Evseeva et al., *Istoriia ikonopisi. Istoki, traditsii, sovremennost'* (Moscow: ART-BMB, 2002), 209–30

Kratts, G., 'Nemetskoiazychnye izdaniia v Moskve i Sanktpeterburge XVIII–XX vv.', in Slavgorodskaia (ed.), *Nemtsy v Rossii*, 179–91

Kriza, Ágnes, 'The Russian *Gnadenstuhl*', *Journal of the Warburg and Courtauld Institutes*, 79 (2016), 79–130

Kruglova, A. R., *Zolotoshveinoe rukodelie velikokniazheskikh i tsarskikh masterskikh XV–XVI vekov* (St Petersburg: Kolo, 2011)

Krutova, M. S., *Kniga glagolemaia. Semantika, struktura i var'irovanie nazvanii russkikh rukopisnykh knig XI–XIX vv.* (Moscow: Pashkov dom, 2010)

Kubler, George A., *A New History of Stereotyping* (New York: J. J. Little & Ives Company, 1941)

Kuchumov, A. M., *Ubranstvo russkogo zhilogo inter'era XIX veka. Po materialam vystavki v Pavlovskom dvortse-muzee* (Leningrad: Khudozhnik RSFSR, 1977)

Kudriavtseva, Tamara V., *Russian Imperial Porcelain* (St Petersburg: Slavia, 2003)

Kufaev, M. N., *Istoriia russkoi knigi v XIX veke* (Moscow: Pashkov dom, 2003 [1927])

Kukina, E. M., and Kozhevnikov, R. F., *Rukotvornaia pamiat' Moskvy* (Moscow: Moskovskii rabochii, 1997)

Kukushkina, M. V., *Monastyrskie biblioteki russkogo severa* (Leningrad: Nauka, 1977)

Kniga v Rossii v XVI veke (Peterburgskoe vostokovedenie, 1999)

Kvlividze, N. V., 'Zapadnoevropeiskie istochniki ikonografii "Chetyrekhchastnoi" ikony iz Blagoveshchenskogo sobora', in *Lazarevskie chteniia. Iskusstvo Vizantii, Drevnei Rusi, Zapadnoi Evropy* (Izdatel'stvo MGU, 2008), 175–90

Labutina, T. L., *Anglichane v dopetrovskoi Rossii* (St Petersburg: Aleteiia, 2011)

Lauryk, Iu. M., *Knigi i knigazbory kutseinskaga Bogaiaulenskaga manastyra u siaredzine XVII st.* (Minsk: Tekhnalogiia, 2012)

Lavrent'ev, A. V., *Liudi i veshchi. Pamiatniki russkoi istorii i kul'tury XVI–XVIII vv., ikh sozdateli i vladel'tsy* (Moscow: Arkheograficheskii tsentr, 1997)

Lavrov, A. S., 'Gravirovannyi list s virshami Sil'vestra Medvedeva', *TODRL*, 50 (1996), 519–25

Lebedev, S., *Nomernye znaki domov Peterburga. Zametki i nabliudeniia* (St Petersburg, 2010), www.liveinternet.ru/users/zimnyi/post285701342/

LeDonne, John P., 'Administrative Regionalization in the Russian Empire 1802–1826', *Cahiers du monde russe*, 43.1 (Jan.–Mar. 2002), 5–34

The Grand Strategy of the Russian Empire, 1650–1831 (Oxford University Press, 2004)

Leont'ev, A. K., *Obrazovanie prikaznoi sistemy upravleniia v russkom gosudarstve. Iz istorii sozdaniia tsentralizovannogo gosudarstvennogo apparata v kontse XV–pervoi polovine XVI v.* (Izdatel'stvo MGU, 1961)

Levin, V. D., *Ocherki stilistiki russkogo literaturnogo iazyka kontsa XVIII–nachala XIX v.: leksika* (Moscow: Nauka, 1964)

Levochkin, I. V., *Osnovy russkoi paleografii* (Moscow: Krug, 2003)

Liakisheva, S. I., 'Kul'tura russkogo usadebnogo rukodeliia', *Kul'tura: teoriia i praktika. Elektronnyi nauchnyi zhurnal*, 2015.1 (4) (MGU; 15 Feb. 2015), http://theoryofculture.ru/issues/36/753/

Liburkin, D. L., *Russkaia novolatinskaia poeziia: materialy k istorii. XVII–pervaia polovina XVIII veka* (Moscow: RGGU, 2000)

Likhachev, D. S., *Poetika sadov. K semantike sadovo-parkovykh stilei. Sad kak tekst*, 2nd edn (St Petersburg: Nauka, 1991)

Likhacheva, E. O., *Materialy dlia istorii zhenskogo obrazovaniia v Rossii*, 4 vols. (St Petersburg: Tipografiia M. M. Stasulevicha, 1890–1901)

Lincoln, W. Bruce, 'The Daily Life of St Petersburg Officials in the Mid-Nineteenth Century', *Oxford Slavonic Papers. New Series*, 8 (1975), 82–100

In the Vanguard of Reform: Russia's Enlightened Bureaucrats 1825–1861 (DeKalb: Northern Illinois University Press, 1982)

Liseitsev, D. V., Rogozhin, N. M., and Eskin, Iu. M., *Prikazy Moskovskogo gosudarstva XVI–XVII vv. Slovar'-spravochnik* (Moscow and St Petersburg: Tsentr gumanitarnykh initsiativ, 2015)

Litvinov, S. V., 'Anglomaniia v Rossii kak sotsio-kul'turnoe iavlenie (posledniaia tret' XVIII–seredina XIX vv.)' (Avtoref. diss. na soiskanie uchenoi stepeni kandidata kul'turologicheskikh nauk; MGU, 1998)

Lobachev, Sergey, 'Media and Message in Medieval Russia: Transition from Parchment to Paper', *CASS*, 47 (2013), 307–20

Longworth, Philip, *Alexis, Tsar of All the Russias* (London: Secker & Warburg, 1984)

Lopialo, K. K., 'K primernoi rekonstruktsii Zolotoi palaty Kremlevskogo dvortsa i ee monumental'noi zhivopisi', in O. I. Podobedova, *Moskovskaia shkola zhivopisi pri Ivane IV. Raboty v Moskovskom kremle 40-kh–70-kh godov XVI v.* (Moscow: Nauka, 1972), 193–8

Lotman, Iu. M., 'O semiosfere', *Trudy po znakovym sistemam*, 17 (1984), 5–23; transl. Wilma Clark, 'On the Semiosphere', *Sign System Studies*, 33 (2005), 205–29

Luk'ianov, E. A., *Inter'er v russkoi grafike XIX–nachala XX veka. Iz sobraniia Gosudarstvennogo istoricheskogo muzeiia* (Moscow: Istoricheskii muzei, 2016)

Luppov, S. P., *Kniga v Rossii v XVII veke* (Leningrad: Nauka, 1970)

Kniga v Rossii v poslepetrovskoe vremia 1725–1740 (Leningrad: Nauka, 1976)

(ed.), *Russkie knigi i biblioteki v XVI–pervoi polovine XIX veka* (Leningrad: BAN, 1983)

(ed.), *Frantsuzskaia kniga v Rossii v XVIII v.* (Leningrad: Nauka, 1986)

Lur'e, Ia. S., and Grigorenko, A. Iu., 'Kuritsyn Fedor Vasil'evich', in *SKKDR. Vtoraia polovina XIV–XVI v. Chast' 1*, 504–10

Madariaga, Isabel de, *Russia in the Age of Catherine the Great* (London: Weidenfeld & Nicolson, 1981)

Maier, Ingrid, and Mikhaylov [Mikhailov], Nikita, '"Korolevskii izvet ko vsem poddannym" (1648 g.) – pervyi russkii perevod angliiskogo pechatnogo teksta?', *Russian Linguistics*, 33.3 (Nov. 2009), 289–317

Maier, P. V., 'Zapadnoevropeiskie istochniki ikonografii "Plody stradanii Khristovykh": "Zhivoi Krest" i "Drevo Zhizni" v russkoi ikonopisi', *Vestnik PSTGU. Seriia V. Voprosy istorii i teorii khristianskogo iskusstva*, 2015.3(4), 52–80

Maiofis, Mariia, *Vozzvanie k Evrope: literaturnoe obshchestvo 'Arzamas' i rossiiskii modernizatsionnyi proekt 1815–1818 godov* (Moscow: Novoe literaturnoe obozrenie, 2008)
Makarov, B. S., *Gollandskie sadovye mastera v Sankt-Peterburge. Pervaia polovina XVIII veka* (St Petersburg and Groningen: NRTs, 2013)
Makhov, A. E., *Emblematika. Makrokosm* (Moscow: Intrada, 2014)
Makolkin, Anna, *A History of Odessa, the Last Italian Black-Sea Colony* (Lewiston, NY: Edwin Mellen Press, 2004)
The Nineteenth Century in Odessa: One Hundred Years of Italian Culture on the Shores of the Black Sea (1794–1894) (Lewiston, NY: Edwin Mellen Press, 2007)
Marikhbein, L. A., 'Istoriia chastnykh kollektsii frantsuzskoi knigi v Rossii XVIII–XIX vekov i ikh rol' v razvitii russko-frantsuzskikh kul'turnykh sviazei' (Diss. na soiskanie uchenoi stepeni kandidata istoricheskikh nauk; Moscow: Rossiiskii gosudarstvennyi sotsial'nyi universitet, 2008)
Marker, Gary, 'Russia and the "Printing Revolution": Notes and Observations', *Slavic Review*, 41.2 (1982), 266–83
Publishing, Printing and the Origins of Intellectual Life in Russia, 1700–1800 (Princeton University Press, 1985)
'Literacy and Literacy Texts in Muscovy', *Slavic Review*, 49.1 (Spring 1990), 74–89
'Faith and Secularity in Eighteenth-Century Russian Literacy, 1700–1775', in Robert P. Hughes and Irina Paperno (eds.), *Christianity and the Eastern Slavs. Volume II. Russian Culture in Modern Times* (California Slavic Studies, 17; Berkeley, Los Angeles and London: University of California Press, 1994), 3–24
'A World of Visual Splendor: The Illustrated Texts of Karion Istomin', in Michael S. Flier, Valerie Kivelson, Erika Monahan and Daniel Rowland (eds.), *Seeing Muscovy Anew. Politics – Institutions – Culture: Essays in Honor of Nancy Shields Kollmann* (Bloomington, IN: Slavica, 2017), 173–88
Marks, Steven G., *The Information Nexus: Global Capitalism from the Renaissance to the Present* (Cambridge University Press, 2016)
Martin, Alexander M., *Enlightened Metropolis: Constructing Imperial Moscow, 1762–1855* (Oxford University Press, 2013)
Martin, Russell E., 'The Petrine Divide and the Periodization of Early Modern Russian History', *Slavic Review*, 69.2 (Summer 2010), 410–25
Maslikh, S. A., *Russkoe izraztsovoe iskusstvo XV–XIX vekov*, 2nd edn (Moscow: Izobrazitel'noe iskusstvo, 1983)
Maslova, G. S., *Ornament russkoi narodnoi vyshivki* (Moscow: Nauka, 1978)
Mathiesen, Robert, 'Cosmology and the Puzzle of Early Printing in Old Cyrillic', *Solanus*, 18 (2004), 5–27
Matveev, V. Iu., *Mekhanicheskie iskusstva i Imperatorskaia Akademiia khudozhestv* (St Petersburg: Ruda i metally, 2010)
McKitterick, David, *Print, Manuscript, and the Search for Order, 1450–1830* (Cambridge University Press, 2003)

Medyntseva, A. A., *Gramotnost' v Drevnei Rusi. Po pamiatnikam epigrafiki X–pervoi poloviny XIII veka* (Moscow: Nauka, 2000)

Mel'nikova, A. S., *Russkie monety ot Ivana Groznogo do Petra Pervogo. Istoriia russkoi denezhnoi sistemy s 1533 po 1682 god* (Moscow: 'Finansy i statistika', 1989)

Mel'nikova, A. S., Uzdenikov, V. V., and Shikanova, I. S., *Den'gi v Rossii. Istoriia russkogo denezhnogo khoziaistva s drevneishikh vremen do 1917 g.* (Moscow: Strelets, 2000)

Mel'nikova, E. A., *'Voobrazhaemaia kniga': ocherki po istorii fol'klora o knigakh i chtenii v Rossii* (Evropeiskii universitet v Sankt-Peterburge, 2011)

Mel'nikova, O. N., *Iz istorii chasov v Rossii XVII–nachalo XX veka* (Moscow: Istoricheskii muzei, 2016)

Mel'nikova, S. I., 'K istorii nemetskogo teatra v Sankt-Peterburge: izdanie podnevnogo repertoira za 1799 g.', in Dittmar Dahlmann and Galina Smagina (eds.), *Nemtsy v Rossii. Nemetskii mir Sankt-Peterburga* (St Petersburg: Rostok, 2013), 182–91

Meshcherskii, N. A., *Istoriia russkogo literaturnogo iazyka* (Izdatel'stvo Leningradskogo universiteta, 1981)

Meyendorff, Paul, *Russia, Ritual and Reform: The Liturgical Reforms of Nikon in the Seventeenth Century* (Crestwood, NY: St Vladimir's Seminary Press, 1991)

Miller, David B., 'The Lübeckers Bartholomäus Ghotan and Nicolaus Bulow in Novgorod and Moscow and the Problem of Early Western Influences on Russian Culture', *Viator*, 9 (1978), 395–412

Mishina, E. A., *Ranniaia russkaia graviura. Vtoraia polovina XVII–nachala XVIII veka. Novye otkrytiia* (Leningrad: Gosudarstvennyi russkii muzei, 1979)

'Gravirovannye marki russkikh bumazhnykh fabrik v XVIII veke', in *Russkaia grafika XVIII–pervoi poloviny XIX veka. Novye materialy* (Leningrad: Iskusstvo, 1984), 12–25

'Sviattsy Antonievo-Siiskogo monastyria i ikh predpolagaemyi avtor', in *Filevskie chteniia. Vyp. V. Materialy tret'ei nauchnoi konferentsii po problemam russkoi kul'tury vtoroi poloviny XVII–nachala XVIII vekov 8–11 iiulia 1993 goda* (Moscow: Tsentral'nyi muzei drevnerusskoi kul'tury i iskusstva imeni Andreiia Rubleva, 1994), 4–14

'Gravirovannaia zastavka raboty Feodosiia izografa (k voprosu o vremeni vozniknoveniia na Rusi gravirovaniia na metalle)', in *Kniga v prostranstve kul'tury* (Moscow: RGB, 2005), 64–6

Morozov, A. A., 'Emblematika barokko v literature i iskusstve petrovskogo vremeni', *XVIII vek*, 9 (1974), 184–226

Morozov, D. A., 'Uigurskie nadpisi moskovskikh d'iakov (dopolnenie k drevnerusskoi diplomatike)', in Iu. M. Eskin (ed.), *Pamiati Lukicheva. Sbornik statei po istorii i istochnikovedeniiu* (Moscow: Drevlekhranilishche, 2006), 173–99

'Drevnerusskaia nadpis' uigurskim pis'mom', *Drevniaia Rus'. Voprosy medievistiki*, 2016.1(63), 99–103

Morrall, Andrew, 'Inscriptional Wisdom and the Domestic Arts in Early Modern Northern Europe', in Natalia Filatkina, Birgit Ulrike Münch and Ane

Kleine-Engel (eds.), *Formelhaftigheit in Text und Bild* (Wiesbaden: Reichert Verlag, 2012), 120–38

Moskovskii pechatnyi dvor – fakt i faktor russkoi kul'tury, 1618–1652 gg., ed. I. V. Pozdeeva, V. P. Pushkov and A. V. Dadykin (Moscow: Mosgosarkhiv, 2001)

Moskovskii pechatnyi dvor – fakt i faktor russkoi kul'tury, 1652–1700 gody. Knigi 1–2, ed. I. V. Pozdeeva, A. V. Dadykin and V. P. Pushkov (Moscow: Nauka, 2007)

Murav'eva, Irina, *Salony pushkinskoi pory. Ocherki literaturnoi i svetskoi zhizni Sankt-Peterburga* (St Petersburg: Kriga, 2008)

Murav'eva, Tat'iana, *Ivan Fedorov* (Moscow: Molodaia gvardiia, 2011)

Myl'nikov, A. S., 'Kul'turno-istoricheskoe znachenie rukopisnoi knigi v period stanovleniia knigopechataniia', *Kniga. Issledovaniia i materialy*, 9 (1964), 37–53

Nebolsin, A. G., *Zakonodatel'stvo o fabrichnykh i torgovykh kleimakh v Rossii i zagranitseiu* (St Petersburg: Tipografiia V. F. Kirshbauma, 1886)

Neliubov, Sergei, 'Ratniki na srednevekovykh russkikh perstniakh', *Tseikhgaus*, 15 (2001), 2–5

'Simvolika srednevekovykh russkikh perstnei', *Tseikhgaus*, 17 (2002), 4–8

Nemirovskii, E. L., 'Ornamentika pervykh moskovskikh pechatnykh knig', in *Trudy nauchno-issledovatel'skogo instituta poligraficheskogo mashinostroeniia, 21. Issledovatel'skie raboty po shriftam* (Moscow: Institut poligraficheskogo mashinostroeniia, 1962), 37–100

Vozniknovenie knigopechataniia v Moskve. Ivan Fedorov (Moscow: Kniga, 1964)

'Graviura na medi v russkoi rukopisnoi knige XVI–XVII vv.', in Kniazevskaia et al. (eds.), *Rukopisnaia i pechatnaia kniga*, 94–104

Andrei Chokhov (okolo 1545–1629) (Moscow: Nauka, 1982)

'Illiuminirovannyi ekzempliar Ostrozhskoi Biblii 1581 g. s rukopisnymi dopolneniiami', *TODRL*, 38 (1985), 439–50

Ivan Fedorov, okolo 1510–1583 (Moscow: Nauka, 1985)

'Pervaia moskovskaia tipografiia v svete novykh issledovanii. K 450-letiiu so dnia osnovaniia', in *Fedorovskie chteniia. 2003* (Moscow: Nauka, 2003), 11–52

'Sosushchestvovanie kirillovskogo tserkovnoslavianskogo i grazhdanskogo shriftov v XVIII v.', in *Tri stoletiia russkogo grazhdanskogo shrifta (1708–2008)* (Moscow: Pashkov dom, 2008), 156–9

Nikitina, T. L., *Russkie tserkovnye stennye rospisi 1670–1680-kh godov* (Moscow: Indrik, 2015)

Nikolaev, S. I., *Pol'skaia poezia v russkikh perevodakh. Vtoraia polovina XVII–pervaia tret' XVIII veka* (Leningrad: Nauka, 1989)

'Problemy izucheniia malykh stikhotvornykh form (Epitafiia)', *XVIII vek*, 16 (1989), 44–55

'Imia na dereve (iz istorii idillicheskogo motiva)', *XVIII vek*, 22 (2002), 46–65

Pol'sko-russkie literaturnye sviazi XVI–XVIII vv. Bibliograficheskie materialy (St Petersburg: Nestor-Istoriia, 2008)

'O kul'turnom statuse pol'skogo iazyka v Rossii vo vtoroi polovine XVII–nachale XVIII veka', *Russkaia literatura*, 2015.2, 132–8

Nikol'skii, Konstantin, *Ob antiminsakh pravoslavnoi russkoi tserkvi* (St Petersburg: Tipografiia Iakova Greia, 1872)

Nimchuk, V. V., *Movoznavstvo na Ukraini v XIV–XVII st.* (Kiev: Naukova dumka, 1985)

Novikova, O. L., and Sirenov, A. V., 'Sdelano v Chudove', *TODRL*, 55 (2004), 441–50

Novokhvatko, O. V., 'Chastnaia perepiska XVII veka (k postanovke voprosa)', in *Palaeobureaucratica: Sbornik statei k 90-letiiu N. F. Demidovoi* (Moscow: Drevlekhranilishche, 2012), 246–63

Obolensky, Dimitri, *Six Byzantine Portraits* (Oxford: Clarendon Press, 1988)

Offord, Derek, Ryazanova-Clarke, Lara, Rjéoutski, Vladislav, and Argent, Gesine (eds.), *French and Russian in Imperial Russia*, 2 vols. (Edinburgh University Press, 2015)

Offord, Derek, Rjéoutski, Vladislav, and Argent, Gesine, *The French Language in Russia: A Social, Political, Cultural, and Literary History* (Amsterdam University Press, 2018)

Okenfuss, Max, *The Discovery of Childhood in Russia: The Evidence of the Slavic Primer* (Newtonville, MA: Oriental Research Partners, 1980)

'Inauspicious Beginnings: Jan Thessing, Amsterdam, and the Origins of Petrine Printing', in Waegemans (ed.), *Russia and the Low Countries*, 15–24

Olmsted, Hugh M., 'Maksim Grek's "David and Goliath" and the Skaryna Bible', *HUS*, 19 (1995 [publ. 1997]), 451–75

O'Loughlin, Elissa, 'Wafers and Wafer Seals: History, Manufacture, and Conservation', *Paper Conservator*, 20 (1996), 8–15

Oman, Charles, *The English Silver at the Kremlin 1557–1663* (London: Methuen, 1961)

Oparina, T. A., *Inozemtsy v Rossii XVI–XVII vv.* (Moscow: Progress-Traditsiia, 2007)

Orgel, Stephen, *The Reader in the Book: A Study of Spaces and Traces* (Oxford University Press, 2015)

Orlenko, S. P., *Vykhodtsy iz Zapadnoi Evropy v Rossii XVII veka: pravovoi status i real'noe polozhenie* (Moscow: Drevlekhranilishche, 2004)

Orlova, M. A., *Naruzhnye rospisi srednevekovykh khramov. Vizantiia. Balkany. Drevniaia Rus'*, 2nd edn (Moscow: Severnyi palomnik, 2002)

Oshurkevich, L. A., 'Ukrainskie antiminsnye graviury XVII–pervoi poloviny XVIII veka', in M. A. Alekseeva and E. A. Mishina (eds.), *Narodnaia kartinka XVII–XIX vekov* (St Petersburg: Dmitrii Bulanin, 1996), 53–70

Ostrowski, Donald, 'The End of Muscovy: The Case for circa 1800', *Slavic Review*, 69.2 (Summer 2010), 426–38

Ot Viatki do Tobol'ska: tserkovno-monastyrskie biblioteki rossiiskoi provintsii XVI–XVIII vekov (Ekaterinburg: Ural'skoe otdelenie RAN, 1994)

Panchenko, A. M., *Russkaia stikhotvornaia kul'tura XVII veka* (Leningrad: Nauka, 1973)

'Simeon Polotskii', in *SKKDR. XVII vek. Chast' 3*, 362–79

Pankratova, N. P., 'Iz istorii chastnoi perepiski na Rusi', in *Izuchenie russkogo iazyka i istochnikovedenie* (Moscow: Nauka, 1969), 127–55

Parry, Roger, *The Ascent of Media: From Gilgamesh to Google via Gutenberg* (London and Boston: Nicholas Brealey, 2011)

Perrie, Maureen, '"Royal Marks": Reading the Bodies of Russian Pretenders, Seventeenth–Nineteenth Centuries', *Kritika*, 11.3 (Summer 2010), 535–61

Petinova, E. F., *Russkie zhivopistsy XVIII veka. Biografii* (St Petersburg: Iskusstvo-SPB, 2002)

Petrov, A. S., 'Drevnerusskoe shit'e: podvesnye naprestol'nye peleny. Opyt atributsii', in *Lazarevskie chteniia. Iskusstvo Vizantii, Drevnei Rusi, Zapadnoi Evropy. Materialy nauchnoi konferentsii 2009* (Izdatel'stvo MGU, 2009), 212–30

'Shityi obraz pod ikonoi. Izobrazheniia na podvesnykh pelenakh', in E. S. Smirnova (ed.), *Tserkovnoe shit'e v Drevnei Rusi: sbornik statei* (Moscow: Galart, 2010), 69–81

'"Znamia Ermaka" iz sobraniia Oruzheinoi palaty: legenda i fakty', *Quaestio Rossica*, 4.1 (2016), 157–69

Petrov, D. A., 'Monumental'nye nadpisi P'etro Antonio Solari v Moskve', *Voprosy epigrafiki*, 5 (2011), 322–34

Petrova, E. V., *Chelovek v informatsionnom prostranstve: sotsiokul'turnyi aspekt* (Moscow: Institut filosofii RAN, 2014)

Petrova, L. A., 'Samovar-kukhnia iz sobraniia P. I. Shchukina. Voprosy atributsii i nekotorye aspekty izucheniia russkoi mednoi posudy XVIII veka', in *Problemy atributsii pamiatnikov dekorativno-prikladnogo iskusstva XVI–XX vekov* (Trudy GIM, 202; Moscow: Istoricheskii muzei, 2015), 159–79

Petrucci, Armando, *Public Lettering: Script, Power, and Culture*, transl. Linda Lappin (University of Chicago Press, 1993)

Pettegree, Andrew (ed.), *Broadsheets: Single-Sheet Publishing in the First Age of Print* (Leiden and Boston: Brill, 2017)

'Broadsheets: Single-Sheet Publishing in the First Age of Print. Typology and Typography', in Pettegree (ed.), *Broadsheets*, 3–32

Piksanov, N. K., 'Istoriia teksta "Gore ot uma" i printsipy nastoiashchego izdaniia', in A. S. Griboedov, *Gore ot uma*, ed. N. K. Piksanov (Moscow: Nauka, 1969), 325–65

Pintner, Walter M., 'The Evolution of Civic Officialdom, 1755–1855', in Pintner and Rowney (eds.), *Russian Officialdom*, 190–226

Pintner, W. M., and Rowney, D. K. (eds.), *Russian Officialdom: The Bureaucratization of Russian Society from the Seventeenth to the Twentieth Century* (Chapel Hill: University of North Carolina Press, 1980)

Plavsic, Borivoj, 'Seventeenth-Century Chanceries and Their Staffs', in Pintner and Rowney (eds.), *Russian Officialdom*, 19–45

Pleshanova, I. I., 'Pskovskie arkhitekturnye keramicheskie poiasa', *Sovetskaia arkheologiia*, 1963.2, 212–16

Pletneva, A. A., *Lubochnaia Bibliia. Iazyk i tekst* (Moscow: Iazyki slavianskoi kul'tury, 2013)

Plotnikova, Iu. V., 'Miniatiurnye vyshivki kontsa XVIII–pervoi chetverti XIX veka iz sobraniia Otdela istorii russkoi kul'tury', *Soobshcheniia Gosudarstvennogo Ermitazha*, 60 (2003), 40–5

Pod"iapol'skaia, E. P., 'Shifrovannaia perepiska v Rossii v pervoi chetverti XVIII veka', *Problemy istochnikovedeniia*, 8 (1959), 314–42

Poe, Marshall, 'Elite Service Registry in Muscovy, 1500–1700', *Russian History*, 21.3 (1994), 251–88

'Muscovite Personnel Records, 1475–1550: New Light on the Early Evolution of Russian Bureaucracy', *Russian History*, 45.3 (1997), 361–77

Polonskaia, I. M., 'Russkaia izdatel'skaia oblozhka i pereplet XVIII v.', *Kniga. Issledovaniia i materialy*, 38 (1979), 152–61

Popov, G. V., 'Belokamennyi krest 1462/1467 goda iz Borisoglebskogo monastyria v Dmitrove', in *ΣΟΦΙΑ. Sbornik statei po iskusstvu Vizantii i Drevnei Rusi v chest' A. I. Komecha* (Moscow: Severnyi palomnik, 2006), 325–46

Postnikova-Loseva, M. M., 'Zolotye i serebrianye izdeliia masterov Oruzheinoi palaty XVI–XVII vekov', in Bogoiavlenskii and Novitskii (eds.), *Gosudarstvennaia Oruzheinaia palata*, 137–216

'Mastera-serebrianiki gorodov Povolzh'ia XVII veka. Iaroslavl', Nizhnii Novgorod, Kostroma', in *Drevnerusskoe iskusstvo. XVII vek*, ed. V. N. Lazarev, O. I. Podobedova and V. V. Kostochkin (Moscow: Nauka, 1964), 272–315

'Serebrianoe delo Pskova XVI–XVII vekov', in *Drevnerusskoe iskusstvo. Khudozhestvennaia kul'tura Pskova*, ed. V. N. Lazarev, O. I. Podobedova and V. V. Kostochkin (Moscow: Nauka, 1968), 157–73

'Serebrianoe delo v Novgorode XVI i XVII vekov', in *Drevnerusskoe iskusstvo. Khudozhestvennaia kul'tura Novgoroda*, ed. V. N. Lazarev, O. I. Podobedova and V. V. Kostochkin (Moscow: Nauka, 1968), 307–34

Povelikhina, Alla, and Kovtun, Yevgeny, *Russian Painted Shop Signs and Avant-garde Artists* (Leningrad: Aurora Art Publishers, 1991)

Pozdeeva, I. V., 'Vnov' naidennyi sbornik Simeona Mokhovikova s graviurami G. P. Tepchegorskogo', in I. E. Danilova (ed.), *Narodnaia graviura i fol'klor v Rossii XVII–XIX vv. (k 150-letiiu so dnia rozhdeniia D. A. Rovinskogo)* (Moscow: Sovetskii khudozhnik, 1976), 175–98

'The Activity of the Moscow Printing House in the First Half of the Seventeenth Century', *Solanus*, 6 (1992), 27–55

'Istoriko-kul'turnoe znachenie deiatel'nosti Moskovskogo pechatnogo dvora v pervoi polovine XVII veka', in *MPD – fakt i faktor. 1618–1652*, 9–49

'Mezhdu srednevekov'em i novym vremenem: novoe v deiatel'nosti Moskovskogo pechatnogo dvora vtoroi poloviny XVII v.', in *MPD – fakt i faktor. 1652–1700. Kniga 1*, 60–128

Chelovek. Kniga. Istoriia. Moskovskaia pechat' XVII veka (Moscow: Fantom-press, 2016)

(ed.), *Traditsionnaia kniga i kul'tura pozdnego russkogo srednevekov'ia. Chast' 2. Istoriia, knizhnost' i kul'tura russkogo staroobriadchestva* (Iaroslavl: Redmer, 2008)

Pozdeeva, I. V., and Turilov, A. A., '"TETRATI . . ., PECHATANY V KAZANE" (k istorii i predistorii kazanskoi tipografii XVI v.)', *Drevniaia Rus'. Voprosy medievistiki*, 2001.2(4), 37–49; 2001.4(6), 13–28
Preobrazhenskii, A. S., 'Zapadnye motivy i formy v postvizantiiskoi zhivopisi Moskovii. Predvaritel'nye razmyshleniia', *Aktual'nye problemy istorii i teorii iskusstva*, 6 (2016), 252–66
Prokopovich, O. A., 'Zhanr nadpisi v russkoi poezii XVIII–pervoi treti XIX v.' (Dissertatsiia na soiskanie uchenoi stepeni kandidata filologicheskikh nauk; Karagandinskii gosudarstvennyi universitet, 2000)
Protas'eva, T. N., 'Zapis' v khronografe XVII v.', in *Novoe o proshlom nashei strany. Pamiati akademika M. N. Tikhomirova* (Moscow: Nauka, 1967), 320–8
Pukhov, Evgenii, *Moneta 'efimok s priznakom'* (St Petersburg: PremiumPress, 2014)
Raab, H., 'Zu einigen niederdeutschen Quellen des altrussischen Schrifttums', *Zeitschrift für Slawistik*, 3 (1958), 323–35
Ramazanova, D. N., 'Bytovanie pervoi Greko-slavianskoi grammatiki (L'vov, 1591) v slavianskikh zemliakh v XVII–XVIII vv.', in *Fedorovskie chteniia 2003* (Moscow: Nauka, 2003), 277–84
'Knigi grecheskoi pechati tipografii Moskovskogo universiteta vo vtoroi polovine XVIII v.', in D. N. Bakun and A. Iu. Samarin (eds.), *Knizhnaia kul'tura. Opyt proshlogo i problemy sovremennosti. K 250-letiiu vuzovskogo knigoizdaniia v Rossii* (Moscow: Nauka, 2006), 243–8
'Grecheskie pechatnye knigi iz biblioteki Tipografskoi shkoly (novye materialy)', *Kniga. Issledovaniia i materialy*, 86 (2007), 104–17
'Istochniki dlia izucheniia ital'ianskoi shkoly Ioannikiia i Sofroniia Likhudov (chelobitnye uchenikov i uchitelei)', *Ocherki feodal'noi Rossii*, 13 (2009), 293–313
'Rukopisnaia i pechatnaia kniga v uchebnoi praktike Slaviano-greko-latinskoi akademii v kontse XVII veka', in Tendriakova and Bezrogova (eds.), '*V Rossii nado zhit' po knige*', 42–52
Reiser, S. A., *Russkaia paleografiia novogo vremeni. Neografiia* (Moscow: Vysshaia shkola, 1982)
Remneva, M. E., *Puti razvitiia russkogo literaturnogo iazyka XI–XVII vv.* (Izdatel'stvo MGU, 2003)
Renner, Andreas, *Russische Autokratie und europäische Medizin. Organizierte Wissenstransfer im 18. Jahrhundert* (Stuttgart: Franz Steiner Verlag, 2010)
Riazantsev, I. V., *Skul'ptura v Rossii XVIII–nachala XIX veka* (Moscow: Zhiraf, 2003)
Rickards, Maurice, *The Encyclopedia of Ephemera: A Guide to the Fragmentary Documents of Everyday Life for the Collector, Curator, and Historian*, completed and ed. Michael Twyman, with S. du Boscq de Beaumont and A. Tanner (London and New York: Routledge and The British Library, 2000)
Ritzarev, Marina, *Eighteenth-Century Russian Music* (Aldershot: Ashgate, 2006)
Rizhskii, M. I., *Istoriia perevodov Biblii v Rossii* (Novosibirsk: Nauka, 1976)

[Rjéoutski] Rzheutskii, Vladislav, 'O latyni v Rossii, i ne tol'ko', *Vivliofika*, 5 (2017), 143–8

Rjéoutski, Vladislav, and Speranskaia, Natalia, 'The Francophone Press in Russia: A Cultural Bridge and an Instrument of Propaganda', in Offord, Ryazanova-Clarke, Rjéoutski and Argent (eds.), *French and Russian*, vol. I, 84–102

Rjéoutski, Vladislav, Argent, Gesine, and Offord, Derek (eds.), *European Francophonie: The Social, Political and Cultural History of an International Prestige Language* (Oxford, Bern, Berlin etc.: Peter Lang, 2014)

Robinson, A. N. (ed.), *Simeon Polotskii i ego knigoizdatel'skaia deiatel'nost'* (Moscow: Nauka, 1982)

Rogozhin, N. M., *Posol'skii prikaz. Kolybel' rossiiskoi diplomatii* (Moscow: Mezhdunarodnye otnosheniia, 2003)

Romanchuk, Robert, *Byzantine Hermeneutics and Pedagogy in the Russian North: Monks and Masters at the Kirillo-Belozerskii Monastery, 1397–1501* (University of Toronto Press, 2007)

Romanova, A. A., *Drevnerusskie kalendarno-khronologicheskie istochniki XV–XVII vv.* (St Petersburg: Dmitrii Bulanin, 2002)

'K istorii biblioteki Kirillo-Belozerskogo monastyria: "knigi rozdatochnye" 1690–1694 gg.', in *Knizhnye tsentry Drevnei Rusi. Knizhniki i rukopisi Kirillo-Belozerskogo monastyria*, ed. N. V. Ponyrko and S. A. Semiachko (St Petersburg: Pushkinskii dom, 2014), 354–94

Romodanovskaia, V. A., 'O tseliakh sozdaniia gennadievskoi Biblii kak pervogo polnogo russkogo bibleiskogo kodeksa', in *Knizhnye tsentry Drevnei Rusi. Severnorusskie monastyri*, ed. S. A. Semiachko (St Petersburg: Dmitrii Bulanin, 2001), 278–305

'Sochineniia Laktantiia v perevode russkikh knizhnikov XV–XVI vv.', *TODRL*, 54 (2003), 407–34

Roueché, Charlotte, 'Written Display in the Late Antique and Byzantine City', in E. Jeffreys (ed.), *Proceedings of the 21st International Congress of Byzantine Studies. London, 21–26 August 2006. Vol. 1. Plenary Papers* (Aldershot: Ashgate, 2006), 235–53

Rowland, Daniel, 'Two Cultures, One Throne Room: Secular Courtiers and Orthodox Culture in the Golden Hall of the Moscow Kremlin', in Valerie A. Kivelson and Robert H. Greene (eds.), *Orthodox Russia: Belief and Practice Under the Tsars* (University Park: Pennsylvania State University Press, 2003), 33–57

Rozov, N. N., 'Solovetskaia biblioteka i ee osnovatel' igumen Dosifei', *TODRL*, 18 (1962), 294–304

Russkaia rukopisnaia kniga. Etiudy i kharakteristiki (Leningrad: Nauka, 1971)

'O kul'turno-istoricheskom znachenii rukopisnoi knigi posle vvedeniia knigopechataniia v Rossii', in Luppov (ed.), *Russkie knigi i biblioteki*, 13–22

Rudenko, Tat'iana, *Modnye magaziny i modistki Moskvy pervoi poloviny XIX stoletiia* (Moscow: ZAO Izdatel'stvo Tsentrpoligraf, 2015)

Rybina, E. A., *Inozemnye dvory v Novgorode XII–XVII vv.* (Izdatel'stvo MGU, 1986)

Rytikova, V. V., 'Nemetskie familii v stareishem nekropole Sankt-Peterburga', in G. I. Smagina (ed.), *Nemtsy Sankt-Peterburga. Nauka, kul'tura, obrazovanie* (St Petersburg: Rostok, 2005), 521–32

Sakovich, A. G., 'Neizvestnyi ekzempliar Biblii Piskatora iz Predtecheva monastyria Krasnoi Slobody Temnikovskogo uezda Riazanskoi mitropolii', in *Pamiatniki kul'tury. Novye otkrytiia. Pis'mennost'. Iskusstvo. Arkheologiia. Ezhegodnik 1990* (Moscow: Krug, 1992), 18–27

Samarin, A. Iu., 'Novye dokumenty o pervom vladel'tse chastnoi tipografii v Rossii I. M. Gartunge', in *Fedorovskie chteniia 2005* (Moscow: Nauka, 2005), 517–28

Tipografshchiki i knigochety. Ocherki po istorii knigi v Rossii vtoroi poloviny XVIII veka (Moscow: Pashkov dom, 2013)

Sapozhnikova, O. S., *Russkii knizhnik XVII veka Sergii Shelonin* (Moscow and St Petersburg: Al'ians-Arkheo, 2010)

Sapunov, B. V., 'Izmenenie sootnoshenii rukopisnykh i pechatnykh knig v russkikh bibliotekakh XVI–XVII vv.', in Kniazevskaia et al. (eds.), *Rukopisnaia i pechatnaia kniga*, 37–50

'Nemetskie knigi i gazety v Moskve v XVII stoletii', in *Nemtsy v Rossii: russko-nemetskie nauchnye i kul'turnye sviazi* (St Petersburg: Dmitrii Bulanin, 2000), 91–6

Saunders, J. W., 'The Stigma of Print: A Note on the Social Bases of Tudor Poetry', *Essays in Criticism*, 1 (1951), 139–64

Savel'eva, E. A., 'I.-D. Shumakher i pervyi ekslibris Biblioteki ego velichestva', in I. M. Beliaeva (ed.), *Kniga v Rossii. K istorii akademicheskoi biblioteki* (St Petersburg: Biblioteka RAN, 2014), 48–62

Sazikov, A. V., and Vinogradova, T. B., *Naruzhnaia reklama Moskvy. Istoriia, tipologiia, dokumenty* (Moscow: Russkii mir, 2013)

Sazonova, L. I., 'Ukrainskie staropechatnye predisloviia kontsa XVI–pervoi poloviny XVII v. (osobennosti literaturnoi formy)', in Demin et al. (eds.), *Tematika i stilistika predislovii i posleslovii*, 153–87

Literaturnaia kul'tura Rossii. Rannee Novoe vremia (Moscow: Iazyki slavianskikh kul'tur, 2006)

Sazonova, L. I., and Guseva, A. A. 'Burtsov Vasilii Fedorov', in *SKKDR. XVII v. Chast' 1*, 148–53

Schaeken, Jos, *Stemmen op berkenbast. Berichten uit middeleeuws Rusland: dagelijks leven en communikatie* (Leiden University Press, 2012)

Schippan, Michael, *Die Einrichtung der Kollegien in Russland zur Zeit Peters I.* (Forschungen zur osteuropäischen Geschichte, 51; Wiesbaden: Harrassowitz Verlag, 1996)

Schlüter, Wolfgang, *Die Nowgoroder Schra in sieben Fassungen vom 13. bis 17. Jahrhundert* (Dorpat: C. Mattiesen, 1911)

Schmidt, Christoff, *Sozialkontrolle in Moskau. Justiz, Kriminalität und Leibeigenschaft 1649–1785* (Quellen und Studien zur Geschichte des östlichen Europa, 44; Stuttgart: Franz Steiner Verlag, 1996)

Schönle, Andreas, *The Ruler in the Garden: Politics and Landscape Design in Imperial Russia* (Oxford, Bern, Berlin etc.: Peter Lang, 2007)

'Private Walks and Public Gazes: Enlightenment and the Use of Gardens in Eighteenth-Century Russia', in Andrew Kahn (ed.), *Representing Private Lives of the Enlightenment* (Oxford: Voltaire Foundation, 2010), 167–85

Ševčenko, Igor, and Strakhov, Olga B., 'Stikhi Manuila Fila v perevode Evfimiia Chudovskogo: u istokov russkogo vizantinovedeniia', *Palaeoslavica*, 18.1 (2010), 69–92

Semenov, V. E., *Monetnoe delo Rossiiskoi imperii* (St Petersburg: Konros-Inform, 2010)

Serebriakova, E. I., 'Ob ornamental'nom ubranstve rukopisei makarievskoi knigopisnoi masterskoi', in *Drevnerusskoe iskusstvo. Russkoe iskusstvo pozdnego srednevekov'ia. XVI vek*, ed. A. L. Batalov et al. (St Petersburg: Dmitrii Bulanin, 2003), 426–38

Serman, I. Z., '*Psaltyr' rifmotvornaia* Simeona Polotskogo i russkaia poeziia XVIII v.', *TODRL*, 18 (1962), 214–32

Shamin, S. M., 'Neizvestnaia tainopisnaia azbuka iz arkhiva prikaza tainykh del', *Drevniaia Rus'. Voprosy medievistiki*, 2010.2(40), 103–6

Kuranty XVII stoletiia. Evropeiskaia pressa v Rossii i vozniknovenie russkoi periodicheskoi pechati (Moscow and St Petersburg: Al'ians-Arkheo, 2011)

Shchapov, Ia. N., 'K istorii russkogo knizhnogo znaka XV–XVII vv.', in Kniazevskaia et al. (eds.), *Rukopisnaia i pechatnaia kniga*, 85–93

Shchukina, E. S., *Dva veka russkoi medali. Medal'ernoe iskusstvo v Rossii 1700–1917 gg.* (Moscow: TERRA, 2000)

Sherikh, D. Iu., *Peterburg den' za dnem. Gorodskoi mesiatseslov* (St Petersburg: 'Peterburg – XXI vek', 1998)

Sherman, William H., *Used Books: Marking Readers in Renaissance England* (Philadelphia: University of Pennsylvania Press, 2008)

Shevtsov, Vyacheslav V., 'The Introduction of Playing Cards in Russia', *CASS*, 50 (2016), 355–76

Shibaev, M. A., 'Predvaritel'nyi spisok avtografov Kirillo-Belozerskogo knizhnika Efrosina', in *Knizhnye tsentry Drevnei Rusi. Knizhniki i rukopisi Kirillo-Belozerskogo monastyria*, ed. N. V. Ponyrko and S. A. Semiachko (St Petersburg: izd. 'Pushkinskii dom', 2014), 81–102

Shitsgal, A. G., *Grazhdanskii shrift 1708–1958* (Moscow: Iskusstvo, 1959)

Russkii tipografskii shrift. Voprosy istorii i praktika primeneniia (Moscow: Kniga, 1985)

Shmidt, S. O., *Rossiiskoe gosudarstvo v seredine XVI stoletiia. Tsarskii arkhiv i litsevye letopisi vremeni Ivana Groznogo* (Moscow: Nauka, 1984)

Shmidt, S. O., and Kniaz'kov, S. E., *Dokumenty deloproizvodstva pravitel'stvennykh uchrezhdenii Rossii XVI–XVII vv. Uchebnoe posobie* (Moskovskii gosudarstvennyi istoriko-arkhivnyi institut, 1985)

Shohamy, Elana, and Gorter, Durk (eds.), *Linguistic Landscape: Expanding the Scenery* (New York and London: Routledge, 2009)

Shustova, Iu. E., 'Simvolika L'vovskogo stavropigiiskogo bratstva', *Gerboved"*, 2005.2(80), 94–104
'Problema kompleksnogo istochnikovedcheskogo issledovaniia predislovii i posviashchenii izdanii l'vovskoi bratskoi tipografii kontsa XVI–XVII veka', in *Fedorovskie chteniia 2005* (Moscow: Nauka, 2005), 231–47
'Azbuka v rossiiskikh izdaniiakh bukvarei XVII–pervoi chetverti XVIII v.', in *Tri stoletiia russkogo grazhdanskogo shrifta (1708–2008). Materialy nauchnoi konferentsii* (Moscow: Pashkov dom, 2008), 106–28
'Azbuka v pechatnykh kirillicheskikh bukvariakh iuzhnoslavianskoi i vostochnoslavianskoi traditsii v XVI–nachale XVIII v.', *Ocherki feodal'noi Rossii*, 14 (2010), 402–94
'Geografiia izdanii razreshitel'nykh gramot vostochnykh patriarkhov v XVII v.', in *Istoricheskaia geografiia: prostranstvo cheloveka* vs *chelovek v prostranstve. Materialy XXIII Mezhdunarodnoi nauchnoi konferentsii. Moskva, 27–29 ianvaria 2011 g.* (Moscow: RGGU, 2011), 463–7
Sidorov, A. A., 'Rukopisnost' – pechatnost' – knizhnost'', in Kniazevskaia et al. (eds.), *Rukopisnaia i pechatnaia kniga*, 227–45
Sinitsyna, N. V., 'Knizhnyi master Mikhail Medovartsev', in *Drevnerusskoe iskusstvo. Rukopisnaia kniga*, ed. O. I. Podobedova and G. V. Popov (Moscow: Nauka, 1972), 286–317
Maksim Grek (Moscow: Molodaia gvardiia, 2008)
Sipovskaia, Nataliia, 'Ordenskie servizy', *Pinakoteka*, 5 (1998), 16–23
Sirenov, A. V., 'O rabote po "ispravleniiu" pechatnogo letopistsa v 1703 g.', in O. L. Novikova (ed.), *Letopisi i khroniki. Novye issledovaniia 2009–2010* (Moscow and St Petersburg: Al'ians-Arkheo, 2011), 355–67
Skinner, Barbara, 'Russia's Scriptural "Reformation" in the Late Eighteenth and Early Nineteenth Centuries', *Vivliofika*, 5 (2017), 73–102
Slavgorodskaia, L. V. (ed.), *Nemtsy v Rossii. Problemy kul'turnogo vzaimodeistviia* (St Petersburg: Dmitrii Bulanin, 1998)
Slukhovskii, M. I., *Russkaia biblioteka XVI–XVII vv* (Moscow: Kniga, 1973)
Smirnova, E. S., 'Kontakty i protivostoianie russkoi i zapadno-evropeiskoi khudozhestvennoi kul'tury v XVI stoletii. Nekotorye nabliudeniia', *Aktual'nye problemy istorii i teorii iskusstva*, 6 (2016), 242–51
Smith, Alison K., 'Information and Efficiency: Russian Newspapers, ca. 1700–1850', in Franklin and Bowers (eds.), *Information and Empire*, 185–211
Smith, May, *The Influence of French on Eighteenth-Century Literary Russian: Semantic and Phraseological Calques* (Oxford and New York: Peter Lang, 2006)
Smith, R. E. F., and Christian, David, *Bread and Salt: A Social and Economic History of Food and Drink in Russia* (Cambridge University Press, 1984)
Soboleva, N. A., *Rossiiskaia gosudarstvennaia simvolika. Istoriia i sovremennost'* (Moscow: Gumanitarnyi izdatel'skii tsentr VLADOS, 2003)
Sokolova, I. M., *Monomakhov tron. Tsarskoe mesto Uspenskogo sobora Moskovskogo kremlia* (Moscow: Indrik, 2001)

Sokolova, T. M., and Orlova, K. A., *Glazami sovremennikov. Russkii zhiloi inter'er pervoi treti XIX veka* (Leningrad: Khudozhnik RSFSR, 1982)

Soll, Jacob, *The Information Master: Jean-Baptiste Colbert's Secret State Intelligence System* (Ann Arbor: University of Michigan Press, 2009)

Solodkoff, Alexander von, *Russian Gold and Silverwork: Seventeenth–Nineteenth Century* (New York: Rizzoli, 1981)

Soroka, Mykola, *Zorova poeziia v ukrains'kii literaturi kintsia XVI– XVIII st.* (Kiev: Holovna spetsializovana redaktsiia literatury movamy natsional'nykh menshyn Ukrainy, 1997)

Sosnovtseva, I. V., 'Ikony iz Oranienbauma v sobranii Russkogo muzei,' in *Stranitsy istorii otechestvennogo iskusstva. Vypusk XIX. Sbornik statei po materialam nauchnoi konferentsii* (St Petersburg: Palace Editions, 2011), 70–89

Spasskii, I. G., '"Zolotye" – voinskie nagrady dopetrovskoi Rusi', *Trudy Gosudarstvennogo Ermitazha IV. Numizmatika 2* (Leningrad: Izd. Gosudarstvennogo Ermitazha, 1961), 92–134

'Monetnoe i monetovidnoe zoloto v Moskovskom gosudarstve i pervye zolotye Ivana III', *Vspomogatel'nye istoricheskie distsipliny*, 8 (1976), 110–31

Speranskii, M. N., *Tainopis' v iugoslavianskikh i russkikh pamiatnikakh pis'ma* (Leningrad: AN SSSR, 1929; repr. Moscow: LIBROKOM, 2011)

Standage, Tom, *Writing on the Wall: Social Media, the First 2,000 Years* (London, New Delhi, New York and Sydney: Bloomsbury, 2013)

Stoliarova, L. V., and Kashtanov, S. M., *Kniga v Drevnei Rusi (XI–XVI vv.)* (Moscow: Universitet Dmitriia Pozharskogo, 2010)

Strakhov, Olga B., 'Attitudes to Greek Language and Culture in Seventeenth-Century Muscovy', *Modern Greek Studies Yearbook*, 6 (1990), 123–55

The Byzantine Culture in Muscovite Rus': The Case of Evfimii Chudovskii (1620–1725) (Cologne, Weimar and Vienna: Böhlau Verlag, 1998)

'"Russkii Goar" A. A. Dmitrievskii i ego stat'ia ob ispravlenii Sluzhebnika v Moskve v XVII i XVIII vv.', *Palaeoslavica*, 12.2 (2004), 47–70

'Jepyfanij Slavynec'kyj's Greek-Slavic-Latin Lexicon: The History, Contents, and Principles Underlying the Composition of Its Greek Portion (Preliminary Remarks)', *HUS*, 28 (2006 [publ. 2009]), 269–85

Sviatoslavskii, A. V., and Troshin, A. A., *Krest v russkoi kul'ture. Ocherk russkoi monumental'noi stavrografii* (Moscow: Drevlekhranilishche, 2000)

Tarasov, Oleg, *Icon and Devotion: Sacred Spaces in Imperial Russia*, transl. Robin Milner-Gulland (London: Reaktion Books, 2002)

Taruskin, Richard, *Defining Russia Musically: Historical and Hermeneutical Essays* (Princeton University Press, 1997)

Tendriakova, M. V., and Bezrogova, V. G. (eds.), *'V Rossii nado zhit' po knige'. Nachal'noe obuchenie chteniiu i pis'ma. Stanovlenie uchebnoi knigi v XVI–XIX vv.* (Moscow: Pamiatniki istoricheskoi mysli, 2015)

Thomson, Francis J., 'The Corpus of Slavonic Translations Available in Muscovy: The Cause of Old Russia's Intellectual Silence and a Contributory Factor to Muscovite Cultural Autarky', in B. Gasparov and O. Rayevsky-Hughes (eds.), *Christianity and the Eastern Slavs I: Slavic Cultures in the Middle Ages*

(California Slavic Studies, 16; Berkeley, Los Angeles and Oxford: University of California Press, 1993), 179–214

'The Slavonic Translation of the Old Testament', in Jože Krašovec (ed.), *The Interpretation of the Bible* (Journal for the Study of the Old Testament. Supplement Series, 289; Ljubljana and Sheffield: Sheffield University Press, 1998), 605–920

Thyrêt, Isolde, *Between God and Tsar: Religious Symbolism and the Royal Women of Muscovite Russia* (DeKalb: Northern Illinois University Press, 2001)

Tikhomirov, M. N., 'Nachalo knigopechataniia v Rossii', in Tikhomirov et al. (eds.), *U istokov russkogo knigopechataniia*, 9–40

'Prikaznoe deloproizvodstvo v XVII veke', in Tikhomirov, *Rossiiskoe gosudarstvo XV–XVII vekov* (Moscow: Nauka, 1973), 348–83

Tikhomirov, M. N., Sidorov, A. A., and Nazarov, I. N. (eds.), *U istokov russkogo knigopechataniia* (Moscow: AN SSSR, 1959)

Tikhonov, Iu. A., *Mir veshchei v moskovskikh i peterburgskikh domakh sanovnogo dvorianstva (po novym istochnikam pervoi poloviny XVIII v.)* (Moscow: Kuchkovo pole, 2008)

Timoshina, L. A., '"Greko-slavianskie shkoly" i russkaia zhizn' XVII v.', *Ocherki feodal'noi Rossii*, 14 (2010), 558–699

Tiukhmeneva, E. A., *Iskusstvo triumfal'nykh vrat v Rossii pervoi poloviny XVIII veka* (Moscow: Progress-Traditsiia, 2005)

Tiulichev, D. V., *Knigoizdatel'skaia deiatel'nost' peterburgskoi Akademii nauk i M. V. Lomonosov* (Leningrad: Nauka, 1988)

Todd, William Mills, *The Familiar Letter as a Literary Genre in the Age of Pushkin* (Princeton University Press, 1976)

Fiction and Society in the Age of Pushkin: Ideology, Institutions, and Narrative (Cambridge, MA: Harvard University Press, 1986)

Tolmachoff, Eugenia, *Ancient Russian Ecclesiastical Embroideries* (The Bulletin of the Needle and Bobbin Club, 31, 1947)

Torke, Hans-Joachim, 'Gab es im Moskauer Reich des 17. Jahrhunderts eine Bürokratie?', *FOG*, 38 (1986), 276–98

Troepol'skaia, N. G., 'Paleograficheskii analiz nadpisei na serebrianoi zhalovannoi posude XVII–XVIII vv.', in *Voprosy slaviano-russkoi paleografii, kodikologii, epigrafiki. Trudy Gosudarstvennogo ordena Lenina Istoricheskogo muzeia. Vypusk 63* (Moscow: Gosudarstvennyi Istoricheskii muzei, 1987), 62–70

Troitskii, S. M., *Russkii absoliutizm i dvorianstvo v XVIII v.: formirovanie biurokratii* (Moscow: Nauka, 1974)

Tsarkova, T. S., and Nikolaev, S. I., 'Epitafiia peterburgskogo nekropolia', in A. V. Kobak and Iu. M. Piriutko (eds.), *Istoricheskie kladbishcha Sankt-Peterburga. Spravochnik-putevoditel'* (St Petersburg: Izdatel'stvo Chernysheva, 1993), 111–29

Tsiavlovskii, M. A., *Stat'i o Pushkine* (Moscow: Izdatel'stvo AN SSSR, 1962)

Tsyganova, L. A., *Ital'ianskie mastera v Rossii XVIII veka: zhizn' i tvorchestvo* (Moscow: Principium, 2013)

Tydman, L. V., 'Pechi v inter'ere domov-dvortsov Moskvy XVIII v.', in V. P. Vygolov (ed.), *Pamiatniki russkoi arkhitektury i monumental'nogo iskusstva. Stolitsa i provintsiia* (Moscow: Nauka, 1994), 69–93

Izba, dom, dvorets. Zhiloi inter'er Rossii s 1700 po 1840-e gody (Moscow: Progress-Traditsiia, 2000)

Uchastkina, Z. V., *The History of Russian Hand Paper-Mills and Their Watermarks*, ed. and adapted J. S. G. Simmons (Hilversum: Paper Publication Society, 1962)

Razvitie bumazhnogo proizvodstva v Rossii (Moscow: Lesnaia promyshlennost', 1972)

Ukhanova, E. V., 'K voprosu o razreshitel'nykh gramotakh vostochnykh patriarkhov v Rossii: novye ekzempliary v fondakh GIM', *Kapterevskie chteniia*, 8 (2010), 91–114

Unkovskaya, Maria V., *Brief Lives: A Handbook of Medical Practitioners in Muscovy, 1620–1701* (London: Wellcome Trust, 1999)

Usachev, A. S., 'O kolichestve sokhranivshikhsia slaviano-russkikh rukopisnykh knig XVI v.', *Rumiantsevskie chteniia 2010. Ch. 2. Materialy mezhdunarodnoi nauchnoi konferentsii (20–22 aprelia 2010)* (Moscow: Pashkov dom, 2010), 186–9

'O geografii napisaniia russkikh rukopisnykh knig v XVI v. (materialy k istorii knigi v Rossii)', *Peterburgskie slavianskie i balkanskie issledovaniia* (*Studia slavica et balcanica petropolitana*), 2015.1, 141–68

'O vozmozhnykh prichinakh nachala knigopechataniia v Rossii. Predvaritel'nye zamechaniia', *CASS*, 51 (2017), 229–47

Knigopisanie v Rossii XVI veka: po materialam datirovannykh vykhodnykh zapisei, 2 vols. (Moscow and St Petersburg: Al'ians-Arkheo, 2018)

Uspenskii, B. A., *Iz istorii russkogo literaturnogo iazyka. XVIII–nachala XIX veka* (Izdatel'stvo MGU, 1985)

Kratkii ocherk istorii russkogo literaturnogo iazyka (XI–XIX vv.) (Moscow: Gnosis, 1994)

Istoriia russkogo literaturnogo iazyka (XI–XVII vv.), 3rd edn (Moscow: Aspekt Press, 2002)

Vokrug Trediakovskogo. Trudy po istorii russkogo iazyka i russkoi kul'tury (Moscow: Indrik, 2008)

Verkholantsev, Julia, *Ruthenica Bohemica: Ruthenian Translations from Czech in the Grand Duchy of Lithuania and Poland* (Slavische Sprachgeschichte, 3; Berlin, Münster, Vienna, Zurich and London: Lit Verlag, 2008)

Veselovskii, S. B., *D'iaki i pod'iachie XV–XVII vv.* (Moscow: Nauka, 1975)

Vikulova, V. P., 'Byt provintsial'noi usad'by i russkie pisateli pervoi poloviny XIX veka', www.domgogolya.ru/science/researches/202/

Vilinbakhov, G. V., *Simvoly Rossii. Ocherki po istorii russkoi geral'diki* (St Petersburg: Fakul'tet filologii i iskusstv Sankt-Peterburgskogo gosudarstvennogo universiteta, 2009)

Vishniakova, Iu. I., *Russkie pischebumazhnye fabriki v pervoi treti XIX veka. Spravochnik* (Moscow: Pashkov dom, 2018)

Vodarskii, Ia. E., and Istomina, E. G., *Pravoslavnye monastyri Rossii i ikh rol' v razvitii kul'tury (XI–nachalo XX v.)* (Moscow: Institut rossiiskoi istorii RAN; Tula: Grif i K., 2009)

Volodikhin, D. M., *Knizhnost' i prosveshchenie v Moskovskom gosudarstve XVII v.* (Izdatel'stvo Moskovskogo gorodskogo ob"edineniia arkhivov, 1993)

Vorob'ev, Iu. K., *Latinskii iazyk v russkoi kul'ture XVII–XVIII vekov* (Saransk: Izdatel'stvo Mordovskogo universiteta, 1999)

Latinskii iazyk v Rossii XVI–pervoi treti XIX veka (kul'turologicheskii aspekt) (Saransk: Izdatel'stvo Mordovskogo universiteta, 2015)

Voronina, T. A., 'O bytovanii lubochnykh kartinok v russkoi narodnoi srede v XIX veke', in *Mir narodnoi kartinki. Materialy nauchnoi konferentsii 'Vipperovskie chteniia' – 1997. Vyp. XXX* (Moscow: Progress-Traditsiia, 1999), 192–212

Voznesenskaia, I. A., 'Rukopisnye uchebniki brat'ev Likhudov nachala XVIII v. v peterburgskikh khranilishchakh', *TODRL*, 59 (2008), 369–75

'Lichnye pechati v Rossiiskoi imperii XVIII–XIX vv. (ottiski na deloproizvodstvennykh dokumentakh)', *Vestnik RGGU*, 12(74)/11 (2011), 234–44

'O poddelke pasportov XVIII v.: na materiale sudebnykh del', in Iu. E. Shustova (ed.), *Vspomogatel'nye i spetsial'nye nauki istorii v XX–nachale XXI v.: prizvanie, tvorchestvo, obshchestvennoe sluzhenie istorika. Materialy XXVI Mezhdunarodnoi konferentsii* (Moscow: RGGU, 2014), 142–4

'Patenty na chin v Rossii XVIII–XIX vv.', *CASS*, 50 (2016), 159–76

Voznesenskii, A. V., 'K istorii donikonovskoi i nikonovskoi knizhnoi spravy. Kavychnyi ekzempliar moskovskoi Psaltiri, izdannoi v dekabre 1645 g.', in E. M. Iukhimenko (ed.), *Patriarkh Nikon i ego vremia. Sbornik nauchnykh trudov* (Moscow: Gosudarstvennyi istoricheskii muzei, 2004), 143–61

'Svedeniia i zametki o kirillicheskikh pechatnykh knigakh 15. K istorii knizhnoi spravy na moskovskom Pechatnom dvore (o Triodi tsvetnoi 1604 g.)', *TODRL*, 58 (2007), 920–6

K istorii slavianskoi pechatnoi Psaltiri. Moskovskaia traditsiia XVI–XVII vekov. Prostaia Psaltir' (Moscow and St Petersburg: Al'ians-Arkheo, 2010)

'Staroobriadtsy i ikh knigopechatnaia deiatel'nost': problemy izucheniia', *TODRL*, 64 (2016), 538–46

Voznesenskii, A. V., Mangilev, P. I., and Pochinskaia, I. V., *Knigoizdatel'skaia deiatel'nost' staroobriadtsev (1701–1918). Materialy k slovariiu* (Ekaterinburg: Ural'skii gosudarstvennyi universitet, 1996), 8–24

Vraskaia, O. B., 'Ob ornamentatsii rukopisnykh knig iz Kirillo-Belozerskogo monastyria', in *Drevnerusskoe iskusstvo. Rukopisnaia kniga. Sbornik tretii*, ed. O. I. Podobedova (Moscow: Nauka, 1983), 267–76

Waegemans, E. (ed.), *Russia and the Low Countries in the Eighteenth Century* (Baltic Studies, 5; Groningen: Institute for Northern and Eastern European Studies, 1998)

Walsby, Malcolm, and Kemp, Graeme (eds.), *The Book Triumphant: Print in Transition in the Sixteenth and Seventeenth Centuries* (Leiden and Boston: Brill, 2011)

Walsham, Alexandra, 'Preaching Without Speaking: Script, Print and Religious Dissent', in Crick and Walsham (eds.), *The Uses of Script and Print*, 211–34

Waugh, Daniel C., 'What Was News and How Was It Communicated in Pre-Modern Russia?', in Franklin and Bowers (eds.), *Information and Empire*, 213–52

Waugh, Daniel C., and Maier, Ingrid, 'Muscovy and the European Information Revolution: Creating the Mechanisms for Obtaining Foreign News', in Franklin and Bowers (eds.), *Information and Empire*, 77–112

Weber, Johannes, 'Strassburg, 1605: The Origins of the Newspaper in Europe', *German History*, 24.3 (2006), 387–412

Weller, Toni, *Information History – An Introduction: Exploring an Emergent Field* (Oxford: Chandos Publishing, 2008)

(ed.), *Information History in the Modern World: Histories of the Information Age* (Basingstoke: Palgrave Macmillan, 2011)

West, Sally, *I Shop in Moscow: Advertising and the Creation of Consumer Culture in Late Tsarist Russia* (DeKalb: Northern Illinois University Press, 2011)

Wijsman, Hanno (ed.), *Books in Transition at the Time of Philip the Fair: Manuscripts and Printed Books in the Late Fifteenth and Early Sixteenth Century Low Countries* (Turnhout: Brepols, 2010)

Wilkinson, Alexander, 'The Printed Book on the Iberian Peninsula, 1500–1540', in Walsby and Kemp (eds.), *The Book Triumphant*, 78–96

Wimmer, E., 'Zu den katholischen Quellen der Gennadij-Bibel', in *Forschung und Lehre. Abschiedschrift zu Joh. Schröpfers* (Hamburg, 1975), 444–58

Yefimova, L., and Belgorodskaya, R., [L. V. Efimova and R. M. Belgorodskaia], *Russian Embroidery and Lace*, transl. Alexandra Ilf (London: Thames & Hudson, 1987)

Yurchyshyn-Smith, Oksana, 'Development of Byzantine Iconographic Tradition in Ukrainian Antimensia of the XVIIth Century', *Byzantinoslavica*, 59 (1998), 320–4

'The Antimension (1620) of Theophanes, Patriarch of Jerusalem', *Oriens christianus*, 88 (2004), 93–110

Yurchyshyn-Smith: *see also* Iurchyshyn

Zabelin, Ivan, *Domashnii byt russkikh tsarei v XVI i XVII stoletiiakh. Chast' I*, 4th edn (Moscow, 1918; repr. Moscow: Iazyki russkoi kul'tury, 2000)

Zaitseva, A. A., 'Novye materialy o russkikh knizhnykh lavkakh v S.-Peterburge v kontse XVIII–nachale XIX veka', in S. P. Luppov et al. (eds.), *Knizhnoe delo v Rossii v XVI–XIX vekakh. Sbornik nauchnykh trudov* (Leningrad: BAN, 1980), 117–43

Zatsepina, E. V., 'K voprosu o proiskhozhdenii staropechatnogo ornamenta', in Tikhomirov (ed.), *U istokov russkogo knigopechataniia*, 101–54

Zelenskaia, G. M., 'Novyi Ierusalim pod Moskvoi. Aspekty zamysla i novye otkrytiia', in A. M. Lidov (ed.), *Novye Ierusalimy. Ierotopiia i ikonografiia sakral'nykh prostranstv* (Moscow: Indrik, 2009), 745–73

'Znachenie nadpisei XVII veka v sozdanii sakral'nogo prostranstva v Novom Ierusalime pod Moskvoi', in A. M. Lidov (ed.), *Prostranstvennye ikony. Performativnoe v Vizantii i Drevnei Rusi* (Moscow: Indrik, 2011), 563–95
Zelov, D. D., *Ofitsial'nye svetskie prazdniki kak iavlenie russkoi kul'tury kontsa XVII–nachala XVIII veka. Istoriia triumfov i feierverkov ot Petra Velikogo do ego docheri Elizavety* (Moscow: Editorial URSS, 2002)
Zhirkov, G. V., *Istoriia tsenzury v Rossii XIX–XX vv.* (Moscow: Aspekt Press, 2001)
Zhivov, V. M., 'Azbuchnaia reforma Petra I kak semioticheskoe preobrazovanie', *Trudy po znakovym sistemam*, 19 (1986), 54–67
Iazyk i kul'tura v Rossii XVIII veka (Moscow: Shkola 'Iazyki russkoi kul'tury', 1996)
Istoriia iazyka russkoi pis'mennosti, 2 vols. (Moscow: Russkii fond sodeistviia obrazovaniiu i nauke, 2017)
Zvereva, T. V., 'Roman N. M. Karamzina *Pis'ma russkogo puteshestvennika* kak entsiklopediia nadpisei', *Ural'skii filologicheskii vestnik*, 2015.3, 41–50
Zubets, I. Z., 'Ob odnoi gruppe prianikov i prianichnykh dosok iz kollektsii Gosudarstvennogo muzeiia-zapovednika "Rostovskii kreml"', in *Problemy atributsii pamiatnikov dekorativno-prikladnogo iskusstva XVI–XX vekov* (Trudy GIM, 202; Moscow: Istoricheskii muzei, 2015), 300–11

Index